Lecture Notes of the Institute for Computer Sciences, Social Informatics and Telecommunications Engineering 279

More information about this series at http://www.springer.com/series/8197

Shuai Liu · Gelan Yang (Eds.)

Advanced Hybrid Information Processing

Second EAI International Conference, ADHIP 2018
Yiyang, China, October 5–6, 2018
Proceedings

 Springer

Editors
Shuai Liu (iD)
Hunan Normal University
Changsha, China

Gelan Yang
Hunan City University
Yiyang, China

ISSN 1867-8211   ISSN 1867-822X (electronic)
Lecture Notes of the Institute for Computer Sciences, Social Informatics
and Telecommunications Engineering
ISBN 978-3-030-19085-9   ISBN 978-3-030-19086-6 (eBook)
https://doi.org/10.1007/978-3-030-19086-6

This Springer imprint is published by the registered company Springer Nature Switzerland AG
The registered company address is: Gewerbestrasse 11, 6330 Cham, Switzerland

Preface

We are delighted to introduce the proceedings of the second edition of the 2018 European Alliance for Innovation (EAI) International Conference on Advanced Hybrid Information processing (ADHIP 2018). This conference brought together researchers, developers, and practitioners from around the world who are leveraging and developing hybrid information processing technology for smarter and more effective research and application. The theme of ADHIP 2018 was "Hybrid Big Data Processing."

The technical program of ADHIP 2018 consisted of 64 full papers, with an acceptance ratio of about 28.1%. Aside from the high-quality technical paper presentations, the technical program also featured two keynote speeches. The two keynote speeches were delivered by: (a) Dr. Guangjie Han from the Department of Information and Communication System at Hohai University, P. R. China, who has served as a co-chair for more than 50 international conferences/workshops and as a Technical Program Committee member of more than 150 conferences, as well as serving on the Editorial Boards of up to 20 international journals, including the IEEE *Network, IEEE Systems, IEEE ACCESS, Telecommunication Systems*, among others, and has guest edited a number of special issues of IEEE journals and magazines including the *IEEE Communications, IEEE Wireless Communications, IEEE Transactions on Industrial Informatics, Computer Networks*; and (b) Dr. Guan Gui from Focus Lab at Nanjing University of Posts and Telecommunications (NUPT), P. R. China, who is an IEEE Senior Member, and has been an editor of *Security and Communication Networks* (2012–2016), *IEEE Transactions on Vehicular Technology* (2017~), and *KSII Transactions on Internet and Information Systems* (2017~), as well as editor-in-Chief of *EAI Transactions on Artificial Intelligence* (2018~).

Coordination with the steering chairs, Imrich Chlamtac, Guanglu Sun, and Yun Lin, was essential for the success of the conference. We sincerely appreciate their constant support and guidance. It was also a great pleasure to work with an excellent Organizing Committee, and we thank them for their hard work in organizing and supporting the conference. In particular, we thank the Technical Program Committee, led by our TPC chair, Dr. Shuai Liu, who completed the peer-review process of technical papers and compiled a high-quality technical program. We are also grateful to the conference manager, Andrea Pieková, for her support and to all the authors who submitted their papers to the ADHIP 2018 conference and workshops.

We strongly believe that the ADHIP conference provides a good forum for all researchers, developers, and practitioners to discuss all scientific and technological aspects relevant to hybrid information processing. We also expect that future ADHIP conferences will be as successful and stimulating as indicated by the contributions presented in this volume.

April 2019

Shuai Liu
Gelan Yang

Organization

Steering Committee

Imrich Chlamtac	University of Trento, Italy
Yun Lin	Harbin Engineering University, China
Guanglu Sun	Harbin University of Science and Technology, China

Organizing Committee

General Chair
Shuai Liu   Hunan Normal University, China

General Co-chair
Gelan Yang   Hunan City University, China

TPC Chair
Shuai Liu   Hunan Normal University, China

Sponsorship and Exhibit Chair
Houbing Song   Embry-Riddle Aeronautical University, USA

Local Chair
Gelan Yang   Hunan City University, China

Workshops Chair
Yang Liu   Hunan City University, China

Publicity and Social Media Chair
Bing Jia   Inner Mongolia University, China

Publications Chair
Huiyu Zhou   University of Leicester, UK

Web Chair
Xiaochun Cheng   Middlesex University, UK

Posters and PhD Track Chair
Bing Jia   Inner Mongolia University, China

Panels Chair

Xiaojun Deng   Hunan University of Technology, China

Demos Chair

Bing Jia   Inner Mongolia University, China

Tutorials Chair

Qingxiang Wu   Yiyang Vocational and Technical College, China

Technical Program Committee

Hari M. Srivastava	University of Victoria, Canada
Guangjie Han	Dalian University of Science and Technology, China
Amjad Mehmood	University of Valencia, Spain
Guanglu Sun	Harbin University of Science and Technology, China
Gautam Srivastava	Brandon University, Canada
Guan Gui	Nanjing University of Posts and Telecommunications, China
Yun Lin	Harbin Engineering University, China
Arun K. Sangaiah	Vellore Institute of Technology, India
Gelan Yang	Hunan City University, China
Carlo Cattani	University of Tuscia, Italy
Bing Jia	Inner Mongolia University, China
Houbing Song	Embry-Riddle Aeronautical University, USA
Qingxiang Wu	Yiyang Vocational and Technical College, China
Xiaojun Deng	Hunan University of Technology, China
Zhaojun Li	Western New England University, USA
Tieying Liu	Inner Mongolia University, China
Han Zou	University of California, USA
Weina Fu	Inner Mongolia Agricultural University, China
Xiaochun Cheng	Middlesex University, UK
Wuyungerile Li	Inner Mongolia University, China
Huiyu Zhou	University of Leicester, UK
Weidong Liu	Inner Mongolia University, China
Juan Augusto	Middlesex University, UK
Jianfeng Cui	Xiamen University of Technology, China
Xuanyue Tong	Nanyang Institute of Technology, Singapore
Qiu Jing	Harbin University of Science and Technology, China
Zheng Pan	Inner Mongolia University, China
Gaocheng Liu	Inner Mongolia University, China
Meng Ye Lu	Inner Mongolia University, China
Chunli Guo	Inner Mongolia University, China
Tana	Inner Mongolia University, China
Dongye Liu	Inner Mongolia University, China
Weiling Bai	Inner Mongolia University, China

Contents

ℓ_p-ADMM Algorithm for Sparse Image Recovery Under Impulsive Noise

Dongbin Hao, Chunjie Zhang$^{(\boxtimes)}$, and Yingjun Hao

College of Information and Communication Engineering,
Harbin Engineering University, Harbin 150001, Heilongjiang, China
{dongbin_hao,zhangchunjie,443567277}@hrbeu.edu.cn

Abstract. The existing compressive sensing recovery algorithm has the problems of poor robustness, low peak signal-to-noise ratio (PSNR) and low applicability in images inpainting polluted by impulsive noise. In this paper, we proposed a robust algorithm for image recovery in the background of impulsive noise, called ℓ_p-ADMM algorithm. The proposed algorithm uses ℓ_1-norm substitute ℓ_2-norm residual term of cost function model to gain more image inpainting capability corrupted by impulsive noise and uses generalized non-convex penalty terms to ensure sparsity. The residual term of ℓ_1-norm is less sensitive to outliers in the observations than ℓ_1-norm. And using the non-convex penalty function can solve the offset problem of the ℓ_1-norm (not differential at zero point), so more accurate recovery can be obtained. The augmented Lagrange method is used to transform the constrained objective function model into an unconstrained model. Meanwhile, the alternating direction method can effectively improve the efficiently of ℓ_p-ADMM algorithm. Through numerical simulation results show that the proposed algorithm has better image inpainting performance in impulse noise environment by comparing with some state-of-the-art robust algorithms. Meanwhile, the proposed algorithm has flexible scalability for large-scale problem, which has better advantages for image progressing.

Keywords: Alternative direction method of multipliers ·
Augmented Lagrangian methods · Compressive sensing ·
Impulsive noise · Inpainting images

1 Introduction

Compressive Sensing (CS) illuminates that if signal is sparse or compressible, the measurement value of the target signal can be obtained by a non-adaptive linear mapping method far below the sampling frequency required by Shannon-Nyquist sampling theorem and recovering the signal from these measurement,

Supported by the National Natural Science Foundation of China under Grant 61671168, the Natural Science Foundation of Heilongjiang Province under Grant QC2016085 and the Fundamental Research Funds for the Central Universities (HEUCF160807).

S. Liu and G. Yang (Eds.): ADHIP 2018, LNICST 279, pp. 1–9, 2019.
https://doi.org/10.1007/978-3-030-19086-6_1

which has been a hot research topic in recent years [1,2]. Sparse representation of signals $\mathbf{x} \in \mathbb{R}^N$ the basic premise of CS theory application, but in real environment, many natural signals are not sparse in time domain. So it is necessary to transform the signal into other domains to make it sparse. The observation matrix $\mathbf{A} \in \mathbb{R}^{M \times N}$ "senses" the signal $\mathbf{x}$ to obtain the observation signal value $\mathbf{y} = \mathbf{Ax} \in \mathbb{R}^M$, which is obtained by inner product of the row vector of the observation matrix and the signal. During the observation, it will be interfered by Gaussian white noise, and its measured value is

$$\mathbf{y} = \mathbf{Ax} + \mathbf{n} \tag{1}$$

where $\mathbf{n} \in \mathbb{R}^M$ is additive gauss white noise. The recovery process of Compressed Sensing is the mapping process from low-dimensional data space to high-dimensional data space. The best cost function model for this process is

$$\min_{\mathbf{x}} \|\mathbf{x}\|_0 \qquad \text{s.t} : \mathbf{y} = \mathbf{Ax} \tag{2}$$

$\|\mathbf{x}\|_0 = |\text{supp}(\mathbf{x})| = \#\{i : x(i) \neq 0\}$. $\text{supp}(\mathbf{x})$ represents the support range of $\mathbf{x}$, $|\text{supp}(\mathbf{x})|$ represents "cardinality", that is to say, the number of non-zero elements in the statistical vector $\mathbf{x}$, but Solving sparse solution of formula (2) will be NP-hard problem [3,4] with the increase of signal dimension. In order to reduce computational complexity, Candes and Donoho prove that the ℓ_0 norm model can be replaced by ℓ_1 norm under the condition that Restricted Isometry Property (RIP) criterion is met, and the obtained solution is very similar to that under ℓ_0 norm model. Many researchers have proposed the solution of formula (2), such as basis-pursuit denoising (BPDN) [5] or LASSO [6], which minimizes the ℓ_0-norm relaxes to the ℓ_1-norm.

$$\min_{\mathbf{x}} \|\mathbf{x}\|_1 \qquad \text{s.t} : \|\mathbf{Ax} - \mathbf{y}\|_2 \leq \epsilon, \tag{3}$$

For formula (3), the constrained optimization problem of formula (3) can be converted into an unconstrained form by using Lagrange function

$$\widehat{\mathbf{x}} = \arg \min_{\mathbf{x} \in \mathbb{R}^{N \times 1}} \left\{ \|\mathbf{Ax} - \mathbf{y}\|_2^2 + \lambda \|\mathbf{x}\|_1 \right\} \tag{4}$$

where $\lambda > 0$ is a regularization parameter, which balances the twin cost of minimizing both error and sparsity. From a cost function model point of view, it plays a trade-off role.

Although the use of ℓ_1-regularization in the cost function model has good properties. The performance of the ℓ_1-regularization has two aspects drawbacks. First, ℓ_1 norm is non-differentiable at zero. Second, it would lead to biased estimation of large coefficients.

To address the above drawbacks, many improved methods have been proposed, such as the ℓ_q quasi-norm is used as the sparse term of the objective function, and its formula is modified to

$$\widehat{\mathbf{x}} = \arg \min_{\mathbf{x} \in \mathbb{R}^{N \times 1}} \left\{ \frac{1}{\lambda} \|\mathbf{Ax} - \mathbf{y}\|_2^2 + \|\mathbf{x}\|_q^q \right\}, \tag{5}$$

where $0 \le q < 1$, $\|\cdot\|_q^q$ is the ℓ_q quasi-norm defined as $\|\mathbf{x}\|_q^q = \sum_{i=0}^{N} |x_i|^q$.

At present, estimation methods based on CS sparse recovery mainly focus on robust denoising model under the Gaussian noise background. However, in practical applications, the measurement values are not only affected by Gauss noise, but also by non-gauss white noise. Impulse noise is discontinuous and the characteristics of short duration and large amplitude irregular pulses. Impulsive interfere may come from a sudden change in one bit of data during measurements process [7], and many image & video processing works [8,9]. It is well-known that ℓ_2-norm data-fitting is based on the least square method, so it is very sensitive to outliers in observed values. Moreover, the data-fitting efficiency using ℓ_2 norm is very low.

In recent years, various robust image processing methods have been proposed to suppress the interference of outliers in measurement. In [10], the Lorentzian-norm and Huber penalty function are used as residual terms of the objective function, and the objective function is optimized to recover sparse signals. In [11] the ℓ_1-norm is used as the residual term in the objective function and also as the sparse term, and is called ℓ_1-LA with the formula:

$$\widehat{\mathbf{x}} = \underset{\mathbf{x} \in \mathbb{R}^{N \times 1}}{\arg\min} \left\{ \|\mathbf{A}\mathbf{x} - \mathbf{y}\|_1 + \lambda\|\mathbf{x}\|_1 \right\}. \tag{6}$$

It has been shown in [11] that the ℓ_1-norm cost function has better suppression ability to impulse noise than ℓ_2-norm.

In this paper, using the ℓ_p quasi-norm $(0 \le p \le 1)$, as sparsity regular term of the objective function, the Eq. (6) can be rewritten as:

$$\widehat{\mathbf{x}} = \underset{\mathbf{x} \in \mathbb{R}^{N \times 1}}{\arg\min} \left\{ \|\mathbf{A}\mathbf{x} - \mathbf{y}\|_1 + \lambda\|\mathbf{x}\|_p^p \right\}. \tag{7}$$

In order to reduce the operation time of solving the objective function model and improve the processing ability of high-dimensional data, the objective function of formula (7) is solved by efficient alternating direction methods, called ℓ_p-ADMM. For more details about ℓ_p-ADMM algorithm, seen 4.1

2   Symmetric α-Stable $(S\alpha S)$ Distribution Model

α stable distribution does not have a unified and closed probability density function (PDF) expression, but its characteristic function (CF) can be expressed as [12]

$$\varphi(t) = \left\{ \exp\left(jat - \gamma^\alpha |t|^\alpha\right)[1 + j\beta \mathrm{sign}(t)\,\omega(t,\alpha)] \right\}. \tag{8}$$

where sign(t) is sign function, $0 < \alpha \le 2$ is the characteristic exponent, a is the location parameter, $\gamma > 0$ is the scale parameter, and $\omega(t,\alpha)$ formulation is expressed as

$$\omega(t,\alpha) = \begin{cases} \tan(\alpha\pi/2), & \alpha \ne 1 \\ (2/\pi)\log|t|, & \alpha = 1. \end{cases} \tag{9}$$

In this paper, we just need to consider Symmetric α-Stable ($S\alpha S$) distribution model when $\beta = 0$ in (8). There α-Stable distribution has two special cases. When $\alpha = 2$ and $\beta = 0$ is Gauss distribution; $\alpha = 1$ and $\beta = 0$ is Cauchy distribution.

3   Proximity Operator for ℓ_p-Norm Function

Consider the proximity operator of a function $g(\mathbf{x}) : \mathbf{x} \in \mathbb{R}^N$ with penalty η [13]

$$\text{prox}_{g,\eta}(\mathbf{t}) = \arg \min_{\mathbf{x}} \left\{ a \|\mathbf{x}\|_p^p + \frac{\eta}{2} \|\mathbf{x} - \mathbf{t}\|_2^2 \right\} \tag{10}$$

where $0 \leq p \leq 1$ and $a > 0$.

Case 1: $p = 0$. The expression of proximity operator of formula (10) is:

$$\text{prox}_{g,\eta}(\mathbf{t})_i = \begin{cases} 0, & |t_i| \leq \sqrt{2a/\eta} \\ t_i, & \text{others} \end{cases}, \quad i = 1, 2, \cdots, N \tag{11}$$

where t_i is the i-th element of the vector $\mathbf{t}$, and is well-known hard-thresholding operator.

Case 2: $0 < p < 1$. The proximity operator of formula (10) can be evaluated as [15]

$$\text{prox}_{g,\eta}(\mathbf{t})_i = \begin{cases} 0, & |t_i| < \tau \\ \{0, \text{sign}(\mathrm{t}_i)\,\beta\}, & |t_i| = \tau, \quad i = 1, \cdots, N \\ \text{sign}(\mathrm{t}_i)\, z_i, & |t_i| > \tau \end{cases} \tag{12}$$

where $\beta = [2a(1-p)/\eta]^{1/(2-p)}$, $\tau = \beta + (ap\beta^{p-1})/\eta$, z_i is the solution of $h_1(z) = paz^{p-1} + \eta z - \eta |t_i| = 0$, $z \geq 0$ [14].

Case 3: $p = 1$. This is the well-known soft-thresholding operator, which the proximity operator can be written as:

$$\text{prox}_{g,\eta}(\mathbf{t})_i = S_{a/\eta}(\mathbf{t})_i = \text{sign}(t_i) \max \{|t_i| - a/\eta, 0\} \tag{13}$$

4   Proposed ℓ_p-ADMM Algorithm

ADMM is parallel distributed algorithm, which is generally based on a convex optimization model with separable variables and is suitable for large-scale problems in cloud computing and image processing [16]. ADMM takes the form of a decomposition-coordination procedure, in which the solutions to small local subproblems are coordinated to find a global solution. ADMM mainly blend the benefits of dual decomposition and augmented Lagrangian methods for constrained optimization.

In the ADMM framework, the ℓ_1 loss term and the nonsmooth ℓ_p-regularization term are naturally separated. Using an auxiliary variable $\mathbf{v} \in \mathbb{R}^M$, the formulation (7) can be rewritten as

$$\min_{\mathbf{x}, \mathbf{v}} \left\{ \frac{1}{\lambda} \|\mathbf{v}\|_1 + \|\mathbf{x}\|_p^p \right\} \quad s.t.\ \mathbf{Ax} - \mathbf{y} = \mathbf{v}. \tag{14}$$

The augmented Lagrangian function of formula (14) can be written as

$$\mathcal{L}_\rho(\mathbf{v}, \mathbf{x}, \mathbf{w}) = \frac{1}{\lambda}\|\mathbf{v}\|_1 + \|\mathbf{x}\|_p^p - \langle \mathbf{w}, \mathbf{Ax} - \mathbf{y} - \mathbf{v}\rangle + \frac{\rho}{2}\|\mathbf{Ax} - \mathbf{y} - \mathbf{v}\|_2^2 \quad (15)$$

where $\mathbf{w}$ is a the dual variable, $\rho > 0$ is a penalty parameter. Then, ADMM is mainly consists of the following iterative steps:

$$\mathbf{v}^{k+1} := \arg\min_{\mathbf{v}} \left(\frac{1}{\lambda}\|\mathbf{v}\|_1 + \frac{\rho}{2}\left\|\mathbf{Ax}^k - \mathbf{y} - \mathbf{v} - \frac{\mathbf{w}^k}{\rho}\right\|_2^2\right) \quad (16)$$

$$\mathbf{x}^{k+1} := \arg\min_{\mathbf{x}} \left(\|\mathbf{x}\|_p^p + \frac{\rho}{2}\left\|\mathbf{Ax} - \mathbf{y} - \mathbf{v}^{k+1} - \frac{\mathbf{w}^k}{\rho}\right\|_2^2\right) \quad (17)$$

$$\mathbf{w}^{k+1} := \mathbf{w}^k - \rho\left(\mathbf{Ax}^{k+1} - \mathbf{y} - \mathbf{v}^{k+1}\right) \quad (18)$$

The $\mathbf{x}$-subproblem update step (17) actually resolved a penalized ℓ_1-ℓ_p problem. We use a basic method to speed up ADMM and approximate this subproblem. Let $\mathbf{u}^k = \mathbf{y} + \mathbf{v}^{k+1} + \mathbf{w}^k/\rho$, we can approximate the subproblem by linearizing the quadratic term of its cost function at point $\mathbf{x}^k$, which is expanded as follows:

$$\begin{aligned} \frac{1}{2}\left\|\mathbf{Ax} - \mathbf{u}^k\right\|_2^2 &\approx \frac{1}{2}\left\|\mathbf{Ax}^k - \mathbf{u}^k\right\|_2^2 \\ &+ \left\langle \mathbf{x} - \mathbf{x}^k, d\left(\mathbf{x}^k\right)\right\rangle + \frac{L_1}{2}\left\|\mathbf{x} - \mathbf{x}^k\right\|_2^2 \end{aligned} \quad (19)$$

where $d\left(\mathbf{x}^k\right) = \mathbf{A}^T\left(\mathbf{Ax}^k - \mathbf{u}^k\right)$ is the gradient of the quadratic term, $L_1 > 0$ is a proximal parameter.

Based on the (19) approximation, the $\mathbf{x}$-subproblem (17) becomes easy to solve by proximity operator (10), which can be efficiently solved as

$$\mathbf{x}^{k+1} = \operatorname{prox}_{\|\mathbf{x}\|_p^p, \rho}\left(\mathbf{b}^k\right) = \begin{cases} solved\ as\ (10), & p = 0 \\ solved\ as\ (11), & 0 < p < 1 \\ solved\ as\ (12), & p = 1 \end{cases} \quad (20)$$

with $\mathbf{b}^k = \mathbf{x}^k - (1/L_1)\mathbf{A}^T\left(\mathbf{Ax}^k - \mathbf{u}^k\right)$

Table 1. PSNR of the recovery image under the $S\alpha S$ noise environment.

Algorithm	L1LS-FISTA	LqLS-ADMM (q = 0.5)	YALL1	ℓ_p-ADMM (p = 0.2)	ℓ_p-ADMM (p = 0.5)	ℓ_p-ADMM (p = 0.7)
Shepp-Logan	13.04 (dB)	12.94 (dB)	29.44 (dB)	**41.29 (dB)**	41.02 (dB)	39.83 (dB)
MRI	15.51 (dB)	15.47 (dB)	25.27 (dB)	26.71 (dB)	27.23 (dB)	**27.39 (dB)**

The $\mathbf{v}$-update step (16) is a form of the proximity operator (13)

$$\mathbf{v}^{k+1} = S_{1/(\rho\lambda)}\left(\mathbf{Ax}^k - \mathbf{y} - \frac{\mathbf{w}^k}{\rho}\right) \quad (21)$$

For convex cases, the convergence property of the ADMM has been well solved. Recently, there are few explanations on the convergence of non-convex case [17].

5   Recovery of Images in the Impulsive Noise Environment

We evaluate recovery performance of the proposed algorithm in comparison with L1LS-FISTA [18], YALL1 [11] and LqLS-ADMM [19]. L1LS-FISTA solves the ℓ_1-Least Square formulation. YALL1 solves the ℓ_1-LA formulation (6). We mainly conduct reconstruction on the simulated images.

This experiment evaluates the performance of ℓ_p-ADMM algorithm on the image recovery under $S\alpha S$ impulsive noise environment. The test images are mainly "Shepp-Logan" and MRI images. The size of each image is 265×256, and this two-dimensional image is converted into one-dimensional image at the same time, which are set to $N = 65536$ and $M = round(0.4N)$. As shown in Fig. 1. Sensing matrix $\mathbf{A}$ is composed of discrete cosine transformation matrix as the measurement matrix and Haar wavelets as the basis functions. We only consider $S\alpha S$ the case of impulsive noise, whose parameters are set to $\alpha = 1$ and $\gamma = 10^{-4}$. PSNR is used to evaluate the recovery performance of the improved algorithm on images.

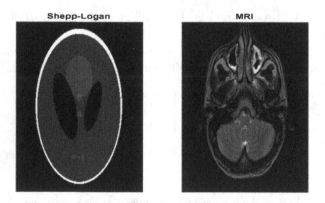

Fig. 1. Using two 256×256 images as test images.

The simulation results are shown in Table 1. It can be seen that the output PSNR of YALL1 algorithm for Logan and MRI images under $S\alpha S$ noise is higher than that of L1LS-FISTA and LqLs-ADMM algorithms. This is because the residual terms of L1LS-FISTA and LqLS-ADMM algorithms both adopt ℓ_2 norm, while ℓ_2 norm only has good suppression effect on Gaussian white noise and is very sensitive to noise. Therefore, L1LS-FISTA and LqLS-ADMM algorithms have poor recovery performance on images affected by impulse noise. However

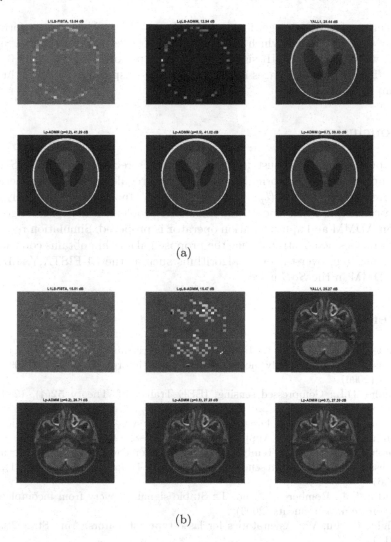

Fig. 2. Recovery images performance of the compared algorithms in $S\alpha S$ noise; (a): Averaged PSNR of Shepp-Logan for different algorithm; (b): Averaged PSNR of MRI for different algorithm.

Lp-ADMM algorithm using ℓ_p quasi-norm in sparse terms is better than that of YALL1, because ℓ_p quasi-norm can solve the deficiency of ℓ_1 norm.

It can be seen from Fig. 2 that the improved algorithm proposed in this paper has better recovery performance than other comparison algorithms under the $S\alpha S$ noise environment. It can be seen that L1LS-FISTA and LqLS-ADMM based on ℓ_2 norm as residual term have failed, while the ℓ_1-loss based algorithm, YALL1 and ℓ_p-ADMM have work well. ℓ_p-ADMM algorithm performance advantage over other algorithms. Furthermore, the simulation results show that in recovering the MRI image, for ℓ_p-ADMM, $p = 0.7$ yield better performance than $p = 0.2$ and $p = 0.5$, which is different from the results of recovery "Shepp-Logan", where $p = 0.2$ PSNR significantly better performance than $p = 0.5$ and $p = 0.7$. This is because images in real-life are not as sparse as synthetic images, but compressible.

6 Conclusion

This paper presents a robust formula for images recovery in the $S\alpha S$ noise, which improves the ℓ_1-LA formula by replacing ℓ_1-regularization with generalized non-convex regularization (ℓ_p-norm, $0 < p < 1$). In order to effectively solve the non-convex and non-smooth minimization problem, a first-order algorithm based on ADMM and approximation operator is proposed. Simulation results on recovery images demonstrated that the proposed algorithm obtains considerable performance gain over the other algorithms such as the L1-FISTA,YALL1 and LqLS-ADMM in the $S\alpha S$ noise.

References

1. Candès, E.J., Romberg, J., Tao, T.: Robust uncertainty principles: exact signal reconstruction from highly incomplete frequency information, pp. 489–509. IEEE Press (2006)
2. Donoho, D.L.: Compressed sensing. IEEE Trans. Inf. Theory 52(4), 1289–1306 (2006)
3. Donoho, D.L.: For most large underdetermined systems of linear equations the minimal. Commun. Pure Appl. Math. 59(6), 797–829 (2006)
4. Donoho, D.L., Elad, M., Temlyakov, V.N.: Stable recovery of sparse overcomplete representations in the presence of noise. IEEE Trans. Inf. Theory 52(1), 6–18 (2006)
5. Candès, E.J., Romberg, J., Tao, T.: Stable signal recovery from incomplete and inaccurate measurements (2006)
6. Knight, K., Fu, W.: Asymptotics for lasso-type estimators. Ann. Stat. 28, 1356 (2011)
7. Candès, E.J., Randall, P.A.: Highly robust error correction by convex programming. IEEE Trans. Inf. Theory 54(7), 2829–2840 (2008)
8. Bar, L., Brook, A., Sochen, N., Kiryati, N.: Deblurring of color images corrupted by impulsive noise. IEEE Trans. Image Process. 16(4), 1101–1111 (2007)
9. Civicioglu, P.: Using uncorrupted neighborhoods of the pixels for impulsive noise suppression with ANFIS. IEEE Trans. Image Process. 16(3), 759–773 (2007)
10. Carrillo, R.E., Barner, K.E.: Lorentzian iterative hard thresholding: robust compressed sensing with prior information. IEEE Trans. Signal Process. 61(19), 4822–4833 (2013)
11. Yang, J., Zhang, Y.: Alternating direction algorithms for l_1-problems in compressive sensing. SIAM J. Sci. Comput. 33, 250–278 (2011). Society for Industrial and Applied Mathematics
12. Nolan, J.: Stable distributions: models for heavy-tailed data (2005). http://Academic2.american.edu/jpnolan

13. Combettes, P.L., Pesquet, J.C.: Proximal splitting methods in signal processing. In: Bauschke, H., Burachik, R., Combettes, P., Elser, V., Luke, D., Wolkowicz, H. (eds.) Fixed-Point Algorithms for Inverse Problems in Science and Engineering. SOIA, vol. 49, pp. 185–212. Springer, New York (2011). https://doi.org/10.1007/978-1-4419-9569-8_10

14. Wen, F., Liu, P., Liu, Y., et al.: Robust sparse recovery in impulsive noise via ℓ_p-ℓ_1 optimization. IEEE Trans. Signal Process. **65**(1), 105–18 (2017)

15. Marjanovic, G., Solo, V.: On l_q optimization and matrix completion. IEEE Trans. Signal Process. **60**(11), 5714–5724 (2012)

16. Boyd, S., Parikh, N., Chu, E., Peleato, B., Eckstein, J.: Distributed optimization and statistical learning via the alternating direction method of multipliers. Found. Trends Mach. Learn. **3**(1), 1–122 (2011)

17. Hong, M., Luo, Z., Razaviyayn, M.: Convergence analysis of alternating direction method of multipliers for a family of nonconvex problems. SIAM J. Optim. **26**(1), 337–364 (2016)

18. Beck, A., Teboulle, M.: A fast iterative shrinkage-thresholding algorithm for linear inverse problems. SIAM J. Imaging Sci. **2**(1), 183–202 (2009)

19. Li, G., Pong, T.K.: Global convergence of splitting methods for nonconvex composite optimization. SIAM J. Optim. **25**(4), 2434–2460 (2014)

Research on the New Mode of Undergraduates' Innovation and Entrepreneurship Education Under the Background of 'Internet Plus'

Liyan Tu, Lan Wu$^{(\boxtimes)}$, and Xiaoqiang Wu

Inner Mongolia University for the Nationalities, Tongliao 028000, China
tlyimun@163.com, wlimun@163.com

Abstract. With the rapid development of network information technology and the popularity of mobile intelligent terminals, Internet industry has experienced rapid growth. As the main force for building socialism, college students have demonstrated unprecedented passion for innovation and entrepreneurship. In the 'Internet plus' background, under the innovation and entrepreneurship service platform for college students, resource scheduling is the key to the entire system, affecting the performance of the system. For this reason, this paper proposes a resource scheduling algorithm for college students' innovation and entrepreneurship service platform based on load balancing, and constructs a dynamic project resource allocation scheme, which improves the utilization of resources. Experimental results verify the effectiveness of the proposed resource scheduling algorithm, the match rate between the project and the university graduates has increased by 30%.

Keywords: Internet plus · College student entrepreneurship ·
Resource scheduling · Load balancing

1 Introduction

With the continuous development of Internet technology, human society has entered a new era of information-based social development, the Internet economy era. As a new force for innovation and entrepreneurship, college students rely on the 'Internet plus' to carry out innovation and entrepreneurship with broad prospects for development, and provide opportunities for college students to realize the success of innovation and entrepreneurship [1, 2]. 'Internet plus' is characterized by its rapid technological innovation, wide application range, and many business models as its basic characteristics, and has become an important driving force in the process of promoting China's economic and social development. Under the 'Internet plus' action plan, the Internet and traditional industries can be optimized and upgraded. In the process, more job opportunities that are consistent with the development of the times and the characteristics of college students can be derived [3, 4].

College students' innovation and entrepreneurship refers to college students who have used their own innovation and entrepreneurial abilities and possessed resource platforms to develop their own careers during or after their graduation [5]. The group of

S. Liu and G. Yang (Eds.): ADHIP 2018, LNICST 279, pp. 10–19, 2019.
https://doi.org/10.1007/978-3-030-19086-6_2

college students has a comparative advantage in 'Internet plus' innovation and entrepreneurship. For today's college students, the Internet is a part of their daily lives. They can use the Internet platform more familiarly to obtain the required information, so that college students can more easily grasp 'Internet plus' era of innovation and entrepreneurship. From this point of view, 'Internet plus' innovation and venture has become one of the patterns that college students are more inclined to choose in their innovation and entrepreneurship project activities. The 'Internet plus' era has provided favorable conditions to college students' innovation and entrepreneurial activities.

Based on the 'Internet plus' background, this paper proposes a suitable resource scheduling algorithm based on the 'Internet Plus' background, and combines the resource scheduling algorithm with various aspects of college students to match the project resources, so as to build a dynamic project resource allocation and scheduling model. The utilization of resources has been greatly improved.

2 Basic Model

2.1 Load Balancing

Load balancing has two meanings. On the one hand, a single heavy load operation is shared and distributed to multiple node devices for parallel processing. After each node device is processed, the results are summarized and returned to the user. The system processing capability is greatly improved [6]. This is what we often call a cluster technology. On the other hand, a large amount of concurrent access or data traffic is distributed to multiple node devices for processing, reducing the waiting time for users to respond. This is mainly for web applications such as Web servers, FTP servers, and enterprise critical application servers.

In order to meet different application requirements, a variety of load balancing technologies have emerged. Typical load balancing technologies include the following.

(1) Global/local load balancing

Global load balancing refers to load balancing between servers with different network structures and computers located in different locations [7]. The purpose of global load balancing is to further improve the quality of access, provide the nearest service, solve network congestion, and improve the response speed of the server.

Local load balancing refers to load balancing between servers that have the same network structure and computers located in the same location. The purpose of local load balancing is to effectively solve the problem of heavy network load. It does not need to stop existing services, change the existing network structure, but simply add a new server to the service group.

(2) Software/hardware load balancing

Software load is achieved by installing software to achieve load balancing. The advantages are low cost, flexible use, and simple configuration [8]. Its inadequacy is that the operation of the software will inevitably cause indefinite resource consumption. In general, resource consumption is directly proportional to the size of the function.

Therefore, when there is a relatively large connection request, the software itself mainly determines the success or failure of the server. Problems with the operating system itself often cause related security issues. In addition, due to the limitations of the operating system, software scalability does not show up well.

The strategy of hardware load balancing is to install special equipment to achieve load balancing, and the overall performance is well improved. In addition, due to the intelligent flow management and diversification of load strategies, the load balancing requirements can be optimized.

(3) Network-level load balancing

Starting from different levels of the network, relevant network load balancing techniques are used to solve different bottlenecks for overloading.

2.2   Resource Scheduling

The purpose of resource scheduling is to meet the system resource requirements as much as possible and to achieve the highest scheduling efficiency and minimum resource usage. The precondition for achieving this goal is to clearly grasp the resource holdings, demand, progress and other information of each subproject. The specific method is to allocate system resources based on resource availability and system requirements, using a reasonable deployment system and scientific technology methods. Resource scheduling is a necessary task for the management of the entire platform, and it is also a core issue to be resolved by the platform. A project platform often includes a large number of various types of resources.

Currently, commonly used resource scheduling algorithms include genetic algorithms, user direct assignment algorithms, shortest path algorithms, and greedy algorithms.

(1) Genetic algorithm

The complexity of genetic algorithms is relatively high. The idea of algorithm originated from the biological 'survival of the fittest.' It evolved with some evolutionary phenomena [9]. The genetic algorithm consists of four parts: coding, fitness function, genetic factor, and operating parameters. It has a wide range of applications and is mainly used to solve problems in machine learning, production scheduling, industrial operation management and other fields.

(2) User Direct Assignment Algorithm

User direct assignment algorithm is less complex. Because this algorithm does not consider the length of execution time and load conditions, it is suitable for jobs that have specific needs for resources. The idea of the algorithm is that the resource node assigned by the job is assigned by the user. The resource itself only determines the execution efficiency and completion time of the job.

(3) The shortest path algorithm

The shortest path algorithm is similar to the RIP protocol algorithm in the IP routing protocol [10]. The purpose is to complete the corresponding job with the shortest routing distance.

(4) Greedy algorithm

The greedy algorithm is also called the shortest completion time algorithm. What it is most concerned with is to complete the task in the shortest possible time. It is to schedule the task to the resource node with the shortest completion time to complete the calculation.

2.3 Web Service

Web Service provides an application to the outside world with an API that can be invoked via the Web [11]. Figure 1 shows the working principle of Web Service.

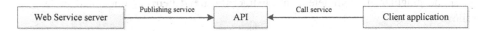

Fig. 1. Web Service working principle diagram

Web Service is a distributed, networked, modular component. It is used to perform certain specific tasks. The Web Service platform is a set of standards. In order to realize the goal of cross-platform and interoperability, Web Service is based solely on XML, XSD and other independent software vendors and platform-independent standards. It is a new platform for creating distributed applications and interoperability.

3 Load Balancing Based Resource Scheduling Algorithm

After a cluster system has been running for a period of time, the actual load on the node changes more or less compared to the amount of load recorded on the scheduler. Therefore, it is necessary to continuously query the load information and update the load information table. The purpose of the query is to make the actual load of the node match the load record. After the load query, you can see that the query data contains information that characterizes server features. However, detailed load information of a node is still difficult to characterize. Therefore, in order to obtain the load L_i of the server, information elements need to be integrated using the following formula

$$L_i = [k_1 \quad k_2 \quad k_3 \quad k_4 \quad k_5] \cdot \begin{bmatrix} a_i \\ b_i \\ c_i \\ d_i \\ e_i \end{bmatrix} \tag{1}$$

where a is the disk usage, b is the memory usage, c is the process share, d is the bandwidth share, and e is the CPU share. The factor k_j is used to emphasize the degree of influence of each part on this type of service. The bigger k, the factor has a significant impact on the service. The k-value is determined after much experimental verification. The coefficients that do not properly reflect the load capacity of the nodes should be constantly modified to ensure that the most appropriate set of coefficients can be found in the end.

3.1 Load Time Series Preprocessing

The preprocessing of system load data is mainly to pre-process the abstracted time series so that it meets the requirements of time series analysis model input. Pretreatment methods include time series analysis models of stationary, normality, and zero mean requirement.

(1) Extract trend items

First, it is judged whether $\{x_t\}$ is a non-stationary time series and contains a trend item. After the judgment is completed, first extract the trend items d_t contained in $\{x_t\}$ as follow

$$y_t = x_t - d_t \tag{2}$$

Calculated stationary time series $\{y_t\}$. Then, the time series $\{y_t\}$ is modeled. For trend item $\{d_t\}$, multiple regression can be used to estimate the time series $\{x_t\}$, and then combine y_t and d_t to calculate the final model.

(2) Zero processing

When the time series $\{x_t\}$ is a stationary time series and the mean is not equal to zero, the sequence $\{x_t\}$ mean $\hat{\mu}_x$ needs to be calculated. Then, perform zeroing according to the following formula

$$y_t = x_t - \hat{\mu}_t \tag{3}$$

After zero processing, a new sequence for modeling $\{y_t\}$ can be generated.

(3) Standardized processing

For a given observation sequence $\{x_t\}$, if the value is too large or too small, it will affect the accuracy of the model analysis. Therefore, in order to ensure the accuracy of calculations, $\{x_t\}$ is standardized.

Assuming that the observed time series is $\left\{x_t^{\{0\}}\right\}$, the data in $\left\{x_t^{\{0\}}\right\}$ is normalized as follows

$$x_t = \frac{x_t^{\{0\}} - \hat{\mu}_x}{\hat{\sigma}_x} \tag{4}$$

where $\hat{\mu}_x$ and $\hat{\sigma}_x$ are the estimated values of the mean and variance of $x_t^{\{0\}}$, respectively.

3.2 Model Parameter Estimation

Parameter estimation based on the characteristics of the ARMA model

$$x_t = \sum_{i=1}^{n} \varphi_i x_{t-i} - \sum_{j=1}^{m} \theta_j a_{t-j} + a_t \tag{5}$$

The idea of parameter estimation is to estimate the autoregressive parameter $\varphi_i (i = 1, 2, \cdots, m)$ using autocorrelation variance function R_k. First estimate φ_i, then estimate θ_i.

3.3 Load Sequence Prediction Algorithm

The overall flow of the system load time series prediction algorithm includes six stages: observation data preprocessing, autocorrelation coefficient calculation, partial correlation function calculation, AR(p) model ordering, data prediction, and standardized data restoration. The specific algorithm is as follows:

Algorithm input: System load time series $\{sp_t\}$

Algorithm output: System load forecast value at the next moment sp_{t+1}

Algorithm flow:

Step 1: Extract the trend items of the original data and eliminate the trend items in the system load time series. Zero-mean processing is implemented after eliminating trend entries.

Step 2: Estimates φ_i and θ_i.

Step 3: Based on the AIC criterion, the order of the model is tested for suitability. The model determines the order method is

$$\text{AIC}(p) = N \ln \sigma_a^2 + 2p \tag{6}$$

Among them, σ_a^2 is the residual variance, and AIC(p) is a function of the model order p.

Step 4: Predict the data value at the next moment and based on the differential intermediate data saved in the first step. Perform predictive data restores on data forecasts.

Step 5: Return the prediction result and the algorithm ends.

The algorithm flow chart is shown in Fig. 2.

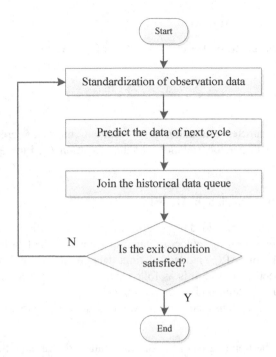

Fig. 2. Load prediction algorithm flow

4   Results and Analysis

In order to verify the accuracy and time efficiency of the scheduling algorithm, we have conducted multiple experimental studies on multiple to-do business nodes at multiple municipal offices on the youth entrepreneurship public service platform.

The analysis of college students' innovation and entrepreneurship patterns under the background of 'Internet Plus' shows that there is no adjustment to the algorithm when it comes to the allocation of projects. It takes a long time to go online and the workload of the system increases to a certain extent, which reduces the work enthusiasm for project distribution.

This section uses three servers and 70 clients as examples to verify the ARMA system load data prediction algorithm. The autocorrelation coefficient is calculated using 30 observations as a group. The initial autocorrelation coefficient curve is shown in Fig. 3. This group of coefficients tends to be stable near zero.

Figure 4 shows the prediction results of the ARMA model in this chapter. The blue curve is the observation data obtained from the acquisition system hardware resource usage. The red curve line is the ARMA predicted system load value. It can be seen from the figure that the ARMA model can accurately predict the load of the system.

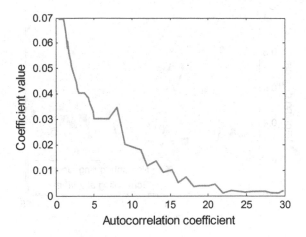

Fig. 3. Autocorrelation coefficient curve

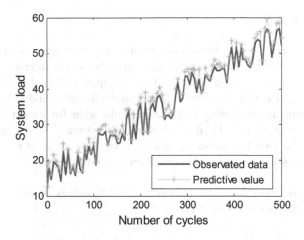

Fig. 4. Forecast result (Color figure online)

Figure 5 mainly compares the matching degree of the allocated items before and after the algorithm is used. It can be seen that before the algorithm was used, the match between the project and the youth was between 30% and 40%. That is to say, the tutors assigned by many projects did not know much about the other industries such as the entrepreneurial projects of the youth. This does not greatly help the project's growth and survival rate. However, after using the scheduling algorithm, the match between the project and youth is between 60% and 90%, and the matching degree has increased by more than 30%. Projects that are distributed in this way will have a positive effect on the growth of young people at the stages of pre-trial, actual ground-testing, and re-examination. As a result, the survival rate of entrepreneurial projects will be greatly increased.

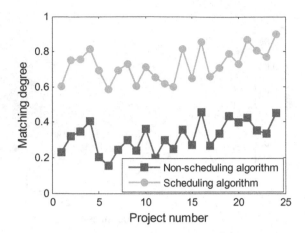

Fig. 5. Project matching degree analysis

5   Conclusion

The 'Internet plus' era is an era full of opportunities and challenges. As a fresh force for innovation and entrepreneurship, college students rely on the Internet for innovation and entrepreneurship with broad prospects for development. Based on the idea of load balancing, this paper constructs a dynamic resource allocation and scheduling model, and makes reasonable scheduling and resource allocation for each task, so that the utilization of resources can be dynamically and optimally distributed. With the development of the mobile Internet era and the popularity of smart phones, the youth entrepreneurship public service mobile platform needs further exploration.

Acknowledgements. Inner Mongolia University for Nationalities Ideological and Political Theory Teaching and Research Project (SZ2014009).

References

1. Xinchao, G.: Influence factors of the new internet technology on the development of physical education in colleges and universities. Agro Food Ind. Hi Tech **28**(1), 1508–1512 (2017)
2. Chunjiang, Y.: Development of a smart home control system based on mobile internet technology. Int. J. Smart Home **10**(3), 293–300 (2016)
3. Wu, H.: The "Internet Plus" action plan: opportunities and challenges. Frontiers **7**(1), 83–88 (2015)
4. Amadeo, M., et al.: Information-centric networking for the Internet of Things: challenges and opportunities. IEEE Netw. **30**(2), 92–100 (2016)
5. Dai, Z.C., et al.: Effects of leaf litter on inter-specific competitive ability of the invasive plant Wedelia trilobata. Ecol. Res. **31**(3), 367–374 (2016)
6. Ye, Q., et al.: User Association for Load Balancing in Heterogeneous Cellular Networks. IEEE Trans. Wireless Commun. **12**(6), 2706–2716 (2012)

7. Zhan, D., Qian, J., Cheng, Y.: Balancing global and local search in parallel efficient global optimization algorithms. J. Global Optim. **67**, 1–20 (2016)
8. Boardman, B., Harden, T., Martínez, S.: Limited range spatial load balancing in non-convex environments using sampling-based motion planners. Auton. Robots **3**, 1–18 (2018)
9. Rashid, M.A., et al.: An enhanced genetic algorithm for AB initio protein structure prediction. IEEE Trans. Evol. Comput. **20**(4), 627–644 (2016)
10. Cai, Y.D., et al.: Identification of genes associated with breast cancer metastasis to bone on a protein-protein interaction network with a shortest path algorithm. J. Proteome Res. **16**(2), 1027–1038 (2017)
11. Crasso, M., et al.: A survey of approaches to web service discovery in service-oriented architectures. J. Database Manage. **22**(1), 102–132 (2017)

Automatic Summarization Generation Technology of Network Document Based on Knowledge Graph

Yuezhong Wu[1,2], Rongrong Chen[3(✉)], Changyun Li[1,2],
Shuhong Chen[4,5], and Wenjun Zou[1]

[1] College of Artificial Intelligence,
Hunan University of Technology, Zhuzhou 412007, China
yuezhong.wu@163.com, lcy469@163.com, 1450793542@qq.com
[2] Intelligent Information Perception and Processing Technology Hunan Province
Key Laboratory, Zhuzhou 412007, China
[3] College of Business, Hunan University of Technology,
Zhuzhou 412007, China
415904214@qq.com
[4] School of Computer Science and Educational Software,
Guangzhou University, Guangzhou 510006, China
shuhongchen@gzhu.edu.cn
[5] School of Computer and Communication, Hunan Institute of Engineering,
Xiangtan 411104, China

Abstract. The Internet has become one of the important channels for users to access to information and knowledge. It is crucial that how to acquire key content accurately and effectively in the events from huge amount of network information. This paper proposes an algorithm for automatic generation of network document summaries based on knowledge graph and TextRank algorithm which can solve the problem of information overload and resource trek effectively. We run the system in the field of big data application in packaging engineering. The experimental results show that the proposed method KG-TextRank extracts network document summaries more accurately, and automatically generates more readable and coherent natural language text. Therefore, it can help people access information and knowledge more effectively.

Keywords: Knowledge graph · Automatic summarization ·
Automatic annotation · Network document

1 Introduction

In an open network environment, user need to rely on the network in the process of learning, work and life is also growing. The Internet has become an important platform for users to publish and obtain information in which network document resources are included. The information resources and the data generated by its application are growing in a geometric progression, making the "information overload" and "resource trek" problems more and more serious, which has seriously affected users efficiency in

S. Liu and G. Yang (Eds.): ADHIP 2018, LNICST 279, pp. 20–27, 2019.
https://doi.org/10.1007/978-3-030-19086-6_3

information acquisition [1]. Massive and excessive information are presented at the same time, making it impossible for users to easily obtain the resources they actually need. Automatic summarization is an effective mean to solve comprehensive and concise summarization from a large amount of text information. It has a great significance to improve the efficiency for user to obtain information.

However, the traditional extractive automatic summarization directly composes summarization by extracting key sentences in the original text, which, in turn, causes problems like incomplete coverage of the main content, lacking of contextual fluency, and duplication of synonymous information. The existing TextRank algorithm [2] is a graph-based sorting classical algorithm for text, which is mainly used in the fields of keyword extraction and automatic summarization. Knowledge graph [3] can better enrich and represent the semantics of resources and provide more comprehensive summary and more relevant information. Therefore, to deal with these problems, this paper improves the single document summary generation technology based on the extractive method, and proposes the improved extraction algorithm based on knowledge graph and TextRank to enhance the accuracy of summary generation, so that users can quickly and accurately find the network document resources they are interested in.

The remainder of the paper covers background and related work discussions (Sect. 2), the model of automatic summarization generation and detailed illustration (Sect. 3), the experiment and test results (Sect. 4), and the conclusions and future work (Sect. 5).

2 Related Research

Research on natural language generation enables computer to have the same function of expression and writing like human. That is, according to some key information and its expression in the machine, through a planning process, a high-quality natural language text is automatically generated. It is a branch of the field of natural language processing, involving multiple disciplines such as artificial intelligence, computer language processing, cognitive science and human-computer interaction. Currently, the general natural language generation system is a pipelined pipeline architecture, including 3 stages such as content planning, micro-planning and surface generation. In the field of current natural language generation systems, automatic summarization is a hot topic. According to the generation principle, it can be divided into extractive and abstractive; according to the number of input documents, it can be divided into single document summarization and multi-document summarization. Automatic summarization have variety of ways such as statistics-based, graph model-based, latent semantics-based, and integer programming-based currently. Gambhir et al. [4] gave a survey on recent automatic text summarization techniques. Lynn et al. [5] proposed an improved extractive text summarization method for documents by enhancing the conventional lexical chain method to produce better relevant information of the text using three distinct features or characteristics of keyword in a text. To alleviate incoherent summaries and same pronominal coreferences, Antunes et al. [6] proposed a method that solved unbound pronominal anaphoric expressions, automatically enabling the cohesiveness of the extractive summaries. Fang et al. [7] proposed a novel word-sentence co-ranking model named CoRank, which combined the word-sentence relationship with the graph-based unsupervised ranking model. CoRank is quite concise in the view of matrix operations, and its convergence can be theoretically guaranteed.

TextRank algorithm is widely used in automatic document summarization. Blanco et al. [8] constructs an unauthorised TextRank network map based on the co-occurrence information of terms in a certain window, which is applied to information retrieval. Combined with the structural features of Chinese text, Yu et al. [9] proposed an improved iTextRank algorithm, which introduced information such as title, paragraph, special sentence, sentence position and length into the construction of TextRank network graph, gave improved sentence similarity calculation method and weight adjustment factor, and applied to automatic summarization extraction of Chinese text.

The application of knowledge graph is coherently born to enrich and represent the semantics of resources. It was proposed by Google in 2012 to describe the various entities or concepts that exist in the real world and incidence relation between them. Knowledge graph is not a substitute for ontology. Ontology describes data schema of the knowledge graph, namely for knowledge graph building data schema equivalent to establishing its ontology. Knowledge graph basing on ontology enriches and expands, and the expansion is mainly embodied in the entity level. The knowledge graph is more accurate to describe the incidence of various relationships in the real world. The knowledge graph is a great promoter of the semantic annotation of digital resources, and promoting the efficient acquisition of knowledge and information. At present, Google, Sogou cubic, Baidu bosom, Microsoft Probase, etc. already preliminarily applied knowledge graph system in the industry. Most of them are general knowledge graph, which emphasizes the breadth of knowledge, and includes more entities. It is difficult to have complete and global ontology layer to unified management, and mainly used in the search business, and not high accuracy requirements. There are some industry knowledge graph, has high accuracy requirements, used for auxiliary complex decision support, the rich and the strict data patterns, etc. Liu, Xu et al. [10, 11] reviewed knowledge graph technology in academia. Hu [12] researched on the construction of knowledge graph based on the application. Li et al. [13] proposed an automatic knowledge graph establishment method and established a knowledge graph of packaging industry. In order to seek semantics support for searching, understanding, analyzing, and mining, Wu et al. [14] proposed a more convenient way which based on domain knowledge graph to annotate network document automatically. The method firstly adopts an upgraded TF-IDF model based on the contribution to quantify instances in knowledge graph, then analyzes the semantic similarity between unannotated documents and instances based on Jaccard distance and lexicographic tree distance comprehensively.

Aiming at the complex relationship of network documents, an automatic summarization extraction method based on knowledge graph is proposed. The entity relationship structure in knowledge graph can reflect the objective knowledge of event development. Applying its semantic characteristics to summarization generation technology can make the summarization more concise and comprehensive.

3 The Model of Automatic Summarization Generation

This paper proposes an automatic summarization generation technology based on knowledge graph and TextRank algorithm named KG-TextRank. Through the knowledge graph, the new meaning of the string is given, and the knowledge system related to the keyword is systematically made, so that the summarization generated by KG-TextRank is more consistent and comprehensive.

3.1 TextRank Algorithm

The classic TextRank algorithm is a graph sorting algorithm, which divides the text into several units, constructs a graph model for the nodes, and uses the voting mechanism to sort the important components in the text.

Let $G = (V, E)$ be a graph structure composed of text units, V is a fixed point set, and E is a edge set. $WS(V_i)$ is the score of the vertex V_i, and the iteration formula is:

$$WS(V_i) = (1 - d) + d * \sum_{V_j \in In(V_i)} \frac{w_{ji}}{\sum_{V_k \in Out(V_j)} w_{jk}} WS(V_j) \tag{1}$$

Where d is the damping coefficient, generally as 0.85; $In(V_i)$ is the set of all nodes pointing to node V_i; $Out(V_j)$ is the set of all nodes pointed to by node V_j; w_{ji} is the weight of the edge of node V_j to node V_i.

3.2 Industry Knowledge Graph Construction

The framework of industry knowledge graph construction method is shown in Fig. 1. It includes the lifecycle of domain knowledge graph, which mainly has five processes, namely, ontology definition, knowledge extraction, knowledge fusion, knowledge storage and knowledge application respectively. Each process has own methods and tasks. For example, D2RQ is used to transform the atomic entity table and the atomic relation table into RDF in knowledge extraction; defined the knowledge fusion rules to complete the knowledge fusion task while extracting knowledge with D2R and Wrappers, the tasks are such as entity merge, entity linking and attribute merge.

In this paper, based on the literature [13, 14], the authors obtain the semantic annotation knowledge graph. The semantic annotation helps the generation of sentence text and eliminates the ambiguity and ambiguity of natural language text. The entity in the knowledge graph can be used as a word segmentation dictionary. The semantics of entities, attributes and relationships provide synonymy, inclusion, etc., and remove ambiguity and ambiguity, thus provide standard, concise and comprehensive knowledge information.

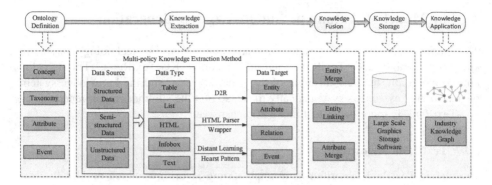

Fig. 1. The framework of industry knowledge graph construction method.

3.3   The Description of Implementation Algorithm

The authors improve the single document summary generation technology based on the extractive method named TextRank, and propose the improved extraction algorithm based on knowledge graph. The implementation flow chart of improved algorithm is as shown in Fig. 2.

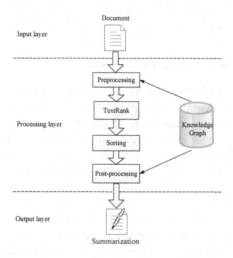

Fig. 2. The flow chart of implementation algorithm.

The computing process is as follows:

Firstly: Processing the input document and parsing into text T; then performing the word segmentation by entity dictionary of the industry knowledge graph and the general dictionary, and constructing the feature vector matrix of the text T; then extracting the keyword and computing the correlation degree of sentences.

Secondly: Constructing a TextRank network diagram and performing iterative calculation using TextRank algorithm.

Thirdly: Sorting and Selecting the top t sentences.

Finally: In the post-processing stage, simplifying and supplementing sentences based on industry knowledge graph, then outputting a concise and comprehensive summarization A_a according to the order of the original text.

4   Experiment and Evaluation

4.1   Constructing Packaging Knowledge Graph

We construct packaging knowledge graph, which is as shown in Fig. 3. For example, the knowledge graph includes the following basic concepts, namely, "packaging knowledge point", "Company", "Product", "Organization", "Patent", "Paper" and "Event". Major relations include "has product", "upstream", "downstream", "has patent", and "executive".

Fig. 3.   Packaging knowledge graph.

4.2   Algorithm Evaluation

In this paper, what is adopted is an evaluation method that using artificial abstract as a standard to calculate the precision rate and recall rate. Set up artificial abstract sentences sets as $A_m = \{S_{m1}, S_{m2}, \ldots, S_{mt}\}$, automatic summarization sentences sets as $A_a = \{S_{a1}, S_{a2}, \ldots, S_{at}\}$, where t is the sentence number of generating summarization.

The Precision Rate calculation formula is as follows:

$$P = \frac{|A_m \cap A_a|}{|A_a|} \tag{2}$$

The Recall Rate calculation formula is as follows:

$$R = \frac{|A_m \cap A_a|}{|A_m|} \tag{3}$$

The F-measure Value calculation formula is as follows:

$$F_1 = \frac{2 \times R \times P}{R + P} \tag{4}$$

Our experiment material are from own development system named China packaging industry large data knowledge graph system. We pick up a part of the academic papers from the system for the summarization generation, and choose number of each paper summarization within the four sentences, and process comparative analysis through computing precision rate (P), recall rate (R) and F- measure value. The Experimental Results are as shown in Table 1.

Table 1. Experimental results.

Algorithm	Precision rate	Recall rate	F_1 value
TextRank algorithm	0.467	0.333	0.389
KG-TextRank algorithm	0.554	0.448	0.495

From the results of Table 1, we can see that the improved KG-TextRank algorithm has higher precision rate, recall rate and F-measure value than the traditional TextRank algorithm, indicating that the use of domain knowledge graph helps to automatically generate summarization closer to manual summarization. At the same time, it was found that these values decreased with the increase of summarization sentences.

5 Conclusions

How to make sentences to extract more in line with the thinking of artificial screening in the field of automatic summarization research is research hot spot and focus. In this paper, based on the classic TextRank algorithm, the authors, by joining the industry knowledge graph, provide a technical implementation scheme for the automatic summarization. The experimental results show that the improved algorithm proposed in this paper improves the quality with a certain degree in the generated summarization.

The next step is to apply deep learning to learn and text eigenvector, researches on abstract summarization generation, experiments in packaging large-scale corpus, and constructs a complete packaging large data summarization system.

Acknowledgements. This work is supported in part by the National Natural Science Foundation of China under grant number 61502163, in part by the Hunan Provincial Natural Science Foundation of China under grant numbers 2016JJ5035, 2016JJ3051 and 2015JJ3046, in part by the Hunan Provincial Science and Technology Project under grant number 2015TP1003, in part by the Project of China Packaging Federation under Funding Support Numbers 2014GSZJWT 001KT010, 17ZBLWT001KT010, in part by the National Packaging Advertising Research Base and Hunan Packaging Advertising Creative Base under grant number 17JDXMA03, in part by the Intelligent Information Perception and Processing Technology Hunan Province Key Laboratory under grant number 2017KF07.

References

1. Wu, Y., Liu, Q., Li, C., Wang, G.: Research on cloud storage based network document sharing. J. Chin. Comput. Syst. **36**(1), 95–99 (2015)
2. Mihalcea, R., Tarau, P.: TextRank: bringing order into texts. In: Proceedings of EMNLP 2004, pp. 404–411. ACM, Barcelona (2004)
3. Amit, S.: Introducing the Knowledge Graph. Official Blog of Google, America (2012)
4. Gambhir, M., Gupta, V.: Recent automatic text summarization techniques: a survey. Artif. Intell. Rev. **47**(1), 1–66 (2016)
5. Lynn, H.M., Chang, C., Kim, P.: An improved method of automatic text summarization for web contents using lexical chain with semantic-related terms. Soft Comput. **22**(12), 4013–4023 (2018)
6. Antunes, J., Lins, R.D., Lima, R., Oliveira, H., Riss, M., Simske, S.J.: Automatic cohesive summarization with pronominal anaphora resolution. Comput. Speech Lang. (2018). https://doi.org/10.1016/j.csl.2018.05.004
7. Fang, C., Mu, D., Deng, Z., Wu, Z.: Word-sentence co-ranking for automatic extractive text summarization. Exp. Syst. Appl. Int. J. **72**(C), 189–195 (2017)
8. Blanco, R., Lioma, C.: Graph-based term weighting for information retrieval. Inf. Retrieval **15**(20), 54–92 (2012)
9. Yu, S., Su, J., Li, P.: Improved TextRank-based method for automatic summarization. Comput. Sci. **43**(6), 240–247 (2016)
10. Liu, Q., Li, Y., Duan, H., Liu, Y., Qin, Z.G.: Knowledge graph construction techniques. J. Comput. Res. Dev. **53**, 582–600 (2016)
11. Xu, Z.L., Sheng, Y.P., He, L.R., Wang, Y.F.: Review on knowledge graph techniques. J. Univ. Electron. Sci. Technol. China **45**, 589–606 (2016)
12. Hu, F.H.: Chinese knowledge graph construction method based on multiple data sources. East China University of Science and Technology, Shanghai (2014)
13. Li, C., Wu, Y., Hu, F.: Establishment of packaging knowledge graph based on multiple data sources. Revista de la Facultad de Ingeniería **32**(14), 231–236 (2017)
14. Wu, Y., Wang, Z., Chen, S., Wang, G., Li, C.: Automatically semantic annotation of network document based on domain knowledge graph. In: 2017 IEEE International Symposium on Parallel and Distributed Processing with Applications and 2017 IEEE International Conference on Ubiquitous Computing and Communications, pp. 715–721 (2017)

Research on Two-Dimensional Code Packaging Advertising and Anti-counterfeiting Based on Blockchain

Yuezhong Wu[1,2], Rongrong Chen[3(✉)], Yanxi Tan[4],
and Zongmiao Shao[1]

[1] College of Artificial Intelligence,
Hunan University of Technology, Zhuzhou 412007, China
yuezhong.wu@163.com, 2532023723@qq.com
[2] Intelligent Information Perception and Processing Technology,
Hunan Province Key Laboratory, Zhuzhou 412007, China
[3] College of Business, Hunan University of Technology,
Zhuzhou 412007, China
415904214@qq.com
[4] Department of Mechanical and Electrical Information Engineering,
Zhuzhou Industrial Secondary Specialized School, Zhuzhou 412008, China
tanyanxi@126.com

Abstract. With the rapid development of Internet technology and the national economy, the brand awareness of consumers and businesses is getting stronger and stronger. However, how to identify application solutions for counterfeit and shoddy goods is a serious challenge for commodity brand. This paper designs and implements a two-dimensional code packaging advertising and anti-counterfeiting model based blockchain. It is applied to process the commodity information in the packaging field, based on the decentralization, openness, autonomy, anonymity and non-tamper ability of blockchain, combined with two-dimensional code technology. The model is based on network transmission interaction, has the advantages of high unforgeability, low cost, easy implementation, fast access, etc. It has a good technical reference value for implementing packaging advertising, anti-counterfeiting and blockchain application.

Keywords: Blockchain · Two-dimensional code ·
Packaging Anti-counterfeiting · Advertising supervision

1 Introduction

With the rapid development of the market economy, in order to obtain high profits, some criminals have become increasingly rampant in the production of counterfeit and inferior products in the market. The fraudulent behaviors of food, non-staple food, medicine, health care products and other industries have not only caused huge losses to enterprises, but also threaten people's physical health and mental health; many high-quality imitations such as bags, jewelry and other valuables also damage the vital interests of consumers and affect the integrity of the market; the loss of confidence in

S. Liu and G. Yang (Eds.): ADHIP 2018, LNICST 279, pp. 28–36, 2019.
https://doi.org/10.1007/978-3-030-19086-6_4

the purchase and the loss of trust in the brand, have caused an incalculable impact on individuals and the market [1]. In order to increase consumers' credibility of products and safeguard the interests of businesses, anti-counterfeiting technology has begun to enter people's sights [2]. With the rapid development of the mobile Internet and the popularity of smart terminal devices, the application of two-dimensional code has been further promoted, especially in the application of packaging, which has been recognized and favored by many end users [3–6]. The two-dimensional code anti-counterfeiting technology encodes the corresponding information of each product into a two-dimensional code. The consumer can check the product information by scanning the two-dimensional code to check the authenticity of the product. However, the generation method of the two-dimensional code is convenient and simple. The copying cost is low, and the two-dimensional code of the counterfeit product is still the real product information released by the merchant, which makes the fake goods still rampant. So, it is urgent to need some safer and more reliable technical means to achieve the purpose of anti-counterfeiting. In 2009, the blockchain was first proposed by Nakamoto Satoshi [7] as a public ledger for recording bitcoin transactions that did not involve third parties. On the blockchain, each block contained some information, including the block hash value of the previous block, which forms the chain [8] from the creation block to the current block. This property of the blockchain guarantees the integrity and immutability of the data and can be used to verify the authenticity of the data [9]. With the development of technology, people realize that it is its true value by applying blockchain technology to the industry and promoting the economic development of the industry. Blockchain traceability anti-counterfeiting is considered to be one of the most promising blockchain landing areas, and it is also one of the primary areas where giants compete for blockchain application technology.

In order to solve the above problems, this paper combines two-dimensional code and blockchain technology to propose a packaging advertising and anti-counterfeiting model. The model is double-encrypted and more secure, and it also proposes a new model of advertising supervision. The main contributions of this paper are:

(1) Double encryption security anti-counterfeiting. Based on encryption with two-dimensional code and blockchain technology, it is double encrypted and integrities checking for the data. It guarantees the authenticity of the goods.
(2) New model of advertising supervision. Based on two-dimensional code and blockchain technology, brand safety is achieved through traceability, precision marketing and platform monitoring, providing a new mode of advertising supervision.

The remainder of this paper is organised as follows: Sect. 2 introduces the terminology and the related work. In Sect. 3, we also introduce the proposed packaging advertising and anti-counterfeiting model and algorithm design. In Sect. 4, we present the results and analysis for the experiment. Finally, we conclude in Sect. 5, and briefly touch on the future work.

2 Related Research

In order to increase consumers' credibility of products and protect the interests of businesses, anti-counterfeiting technology has begun to enter people's sights. At present, the anti-counterfeiting means in the packaging industry can be described as numerous, and are mainly classified into the following four categories according to their functional characteristics [2]. (1) Destructive anti-counterfeiting packaging: It is also called disposable anti-counterfeiting packaging. After the packaging function is once applied, it will not be restored once it is opened. Such forms of packaging are commonly found in packaging boxes, packaging bottles, packaging covers, and so on. (2) Laser holographic anti-counterfeiting mark: The laser holographic anti-counterfeiting mark uses an anti-counterfeiting means for laser-printing all information with anti-counterfeiting functions onto the substrate. It is not easy to be copied, but the cost is relatively high. (3) The telephone anti-counterfeiting system: it is to set a random string on each product and archive its records in the database. Consumers can use the telephone text message to check the authenticity of the product. (4) Printing anti-counterfeiting technology: it mainly refers to print on the packaging by using different printing processes and printing inks. This anti-counterfeiting technology is simple and easy, but once the process leaks, its anti-counterfeiting effect is completely lost. However, the above anti-counterfeiting technologies have the disadvantages of high anti-counterfeiting cost, easy copying, and difficulty in authenticity detection. Therefore, it is urgent to develop a simple and effective anti-counterfeiting technology instead.

As a new economic growth point, two-dimensional code has been the first development direction of the Internet of Things with its strong information capacity, high information density, high recognition rate, confidentiality, strong anti-counterfeiting function, wide coding range and low cost of use. The two-dimensional code anti-counterfeit packaging formed by the combination of traditional packaging technology and two-dimensional code will gradually lead the new trend [6]. As an important carrier for product integration transportation and distribution display, product packaging can transmit more abundant information by means of QR code, realize information integration of multi-level packaging, quality chasing backwards, anti-counterfeiting, business O2O Hutong, promotion advertisement push APP download and other functions. However, the current two-dimensional code generation method is simple, and the copying cost is low. Therefore, some safer and more reliable technical means are urgently needed to achieve the purpose of anti-counterfeiting.

Blockchain is an Internet database technology, which is characterized by decentralization, transparency and transparency, so that everyone can participate in database records. The blockchain is a unique way to store data in cryptocurrencies such as Bitcoin. The self-referencing data structure is used to store a large amount of transaction information. Each record is linked from the back to the front, and has the characteristics of openness, transparency, tampering and traceability [10–13]. Blockchains can generally be divided into three types: alliance chain, private chain and public chain. In the alliance chain, the blockchain's block and transaction validity are determined by a predetermined set of verifiers. This verification group forms an alliance. For example, to make a block in the alliance chain effective, an alliance is required. More than 50% of the members are signed, the new block is valid, the information on the blockchain can be public, or only visible to the members of the alliance; The private chain is a fully centralized blockchain, only the creation of the private chain. It is only possible to write information into the blockchain, which is a good choice for organizations that want to conduct internal audits; On the public chain, all data are publicly visible to anyone, all transaction information related to the address in the blockchain can be viewed by the public. However, many financial transactions do not want to be visible to everyone, so data privacy on the public chain is a relatively short issue.

3 The Model of Two-Dimensional Code Packaging Advertising and Anti-counterfeiting Based on Blockchain

3.1 System Architecture

The package advertisement and anti-counterfeiting model proposed in this paper is based on two-dimensional code technology and the blockchain network, aims to implement packaging anti-counterfeiting and advertising application scenarios. It has a three-tier system architecture, including: user, system service and blockchain, as shown in Fig. 1. In this architecture, the blockchain acts as the underlying platform, interacting mainly with system services, processing data, and providing data collaboration capabilities such as: decentralization, security and credibility, non-tamperable, smart contracts, collective maintenance, etc. A block contains Hash value, random number, block link, mining mechanism and Trading information; System service, supporting user and blockchain network interaction in the server, mainly includes two-dimensional code technology, packaging anti-counterfeiting technology, advertising supervision platform, system maintenance, etc.; The user includes three types of individual, enterprise user and supervisory platform user, and directly uses the application to perform system services such as two-dimensional code scanning, anti-counterfeiting, and advertisement supervision.

3.2 Model and Algorithm

The model proposed in this paper mainly completes the following functions: (1) packaging anti-counterfeiting technology; (2) advertising supervision platform. It quickly enters the functional module through the two-dimensional code, and obtains the corresponding result by the blockchain technology. The proposed model is as shown in Fig. 2.

Packaging Anti-Counterfeiting Technology. Double encryption, with two-dimensional code encryption and blockchain encryption, is more secure. At the consumer level, through opening the terminalized anti-counterfeiting two-dimensional code and transparent blockchain technology support, users can easily check the authenticity of the goods, cultivate the user's genuine awareness, and enhance the brand value.

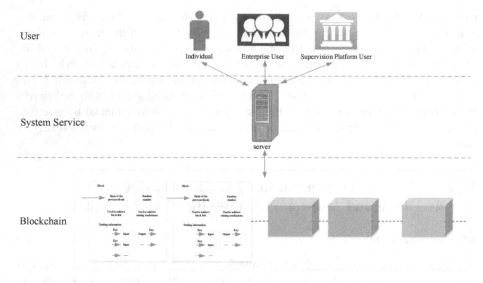

Fig. 1. System architecture.

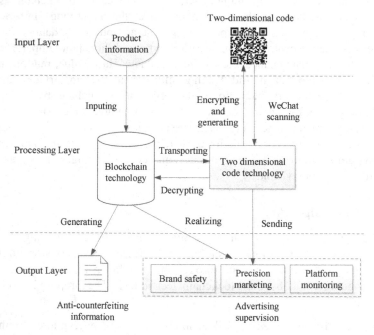

Fig. 2. Two-dimensional code packaging advertising and anti-counterfeiting model based on blockchain.

Step 1. Encrypt product data M to M′ through a blockchain;

Step 2. Encrypt M′ to M″ by two-dimensional code technology again;

Step 3. The user scans the two-dimensional code M″ by WeChat and obtain the anti-counterfeiting information.

Packaging Advertising Supervision Scheme. By implementing the functions of brand safety, precision marketing and platform monitoring to achieve comprehensive, accurate, scientific, digital and intelligent advertising supervision.

(1) Brand safety. Through the traceability function, the blockchain technology is used to integrate the information of all links from production to warehousing and write into the blockchain. Each piece of information has an independent special blockchain ID with digital signature of the product. And the time stamp, is to achieve a trace of the whole process of one thing and one code.

(2) Precision marketing. Through the intelligent contract of the blockchain, seen an advertisement each time and accepted by the user, the smart contract takes effect. Then the advertiser directly rewards the user and the traffic owner for improving the shopping experience of the consumer.

(3) Platform monitoring. It realizes the real-time advertising supervision, improves the efficiency of advertising supervision, guides users to timely discover and report illegal and illegal advertisements, and creates a good atmosphere for the integrity management of the advertising industry.

4   Experiment and Evaluation

In order to verifying the feasibility of the model and services designed in this paper, the authors build a blockchain environment and combine the two-dimensional code technology to simulate specific application examples.

4.1   Function Realization

Development Environment. The operating system we installed on the PC is Windows 10, the Python runtime environment is Python 3.6.4; the program development platform is PyCharm 2018.1.4 and Django web framework, and the database uses MySQL 5.5.

Packaging Anti-counterfeiting Technology. The function of packaging anti-counterfeiting is as show in Fig. 3. It includes anti-counterfeiting code, query number. It used to verify the authenticity of commodity.

Advertising Supervision Platform. The function of brand safety is as show in Fig. 4. It is the traceability function. Integrating the information from the production to the warehouse into the blockchain. Each piece of information has a unique and special blockchain ID, with the digital signature and time stamp of the product, providing users data support of a good bottom layer and quality control. It guarantees the quality of the company's own products.

Fig. 3. Anti-counterfeiting information.

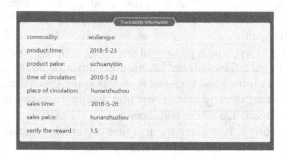

Fig. 4. Traceability information.

The function of precision marketing is as show in Fig. 5. It includes recommending users to view commodity advertising, signing smart contract, and rewarding the user. It improves the user's shopping experience.

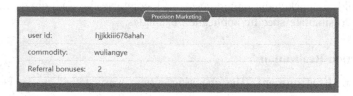

Fig. 5. Precision marketing information.

The function of platform monitoring is as show in Fig. 6. It includes verifying advertising delivery, counting the users, and Monitoring advertising traffic. It creates an atmosphere of integrity management in the advertising industry.

Fig. 6. Platform monitoring information.

4.2 Security Analysis

Firstly, blockchain technology makes distributed ledgers difficult to be hacked because it does not use a single database to store transaction records. Instead, it keeps multiple shared copies of the same database on the block, so hackers must tamper with the book information. Attacks against all replicas will be effective at the same time. This technology also has the ability to prevent unauthorized modifications or malicious tampering, as each transaction in the block becomes part of a permanent record and has a timestamp, participants can share the data and ensure that all copies of the account book are consistent with other copies at all times, and can be verified in real time using timestamps. If a ledger is tampered, it will be discovered immediately. But the reconciliation data can be tampered easily, when 51% of the members attack together.

Secondly, the information generated by the blockchain technology is encrypted by the two-dimensional code technology in the proposed model. The double encryption method makes the information and the system more secure.

5 Conclusions

By building in Blockchain environment, using two-dimensional code technology and web development technology, the authors realized a packaging advertising and anti-counterfeiting model. The experiments show that the proposed model in this paper achieves an efficient and secure for brand safety. We will improve packaging advertising and anti-counterfeiting algorithms to enhance security and achieve smart packaging in future.

Acknowledgements. This work is supported in part by the National Natural Science Foundation of China under Grants numbers 61502163, in part by the Hunan Provincial Natural Science Foundation of China under grant numbers 2016JJ5035, 2016JJ3051 and 2015JJ3046, in part by the Hunan Provincial Science and Technology Project under grant number 2015TP1003, in part by the Project of China Packaging Federation under grant numbers 2014GSZJWT001KT010, 17ZBLWT001KT010, in part by the National Packaging Advertising Research Base and Hunan Packaging Advertising Creative Base under grant number 17JDXMA03, in part by the Intelligent Information Perception and Processing Technology Hunan Province Key Laboratory under grant number 2017KF07.

References

1. Böhme, R., Christin, N., Edelman, B., et al.: Bitcoin: economics, technology, and governance. J. Econ. Perspect. **29**(2), 213–238 (2015)
2. Sriram, T., Rao, V.K.: Application of barcode technology systems. IECON Proc. **1**, 5–10 (1996)
3. Atzori, L., Iera, A., Morabito, G.: The internet of things a survey. Comput. Netw. **54**, 2787–2805 (2010)
4. Wang, Z.M.: Anti-counterfeiting of two dimensional code. China Brand Anti-counterfeiting **3**, 61 (2001)
5. Shu, C.: Application of two-dimensional code in advertising. Northeast Normal University (2015)
6. Gao, K., Zhang, Z.Q.: Application of QR code on anti-counterfeiting packaging. China Packag. Indus. **12**, 79–80 (2014)
7. Nakamoto, S.: Bitcoin: a peer-to-peer electronic cash system (2008)
8. Ethereum Homestead Documentation (2016). http://ethdocs.org/en/latest/
9. Blockchain Bitcoin Wiki (2017). https://en.bitcoin.it/wiki/Block_chain
10. An, R., He, D.B., Zhang, Y.R., Li, L.: The design of an anti-counterfeiting system based on blockchain. J. Cryptologic Res. **4**(2), 199–208 (2017)
11. Yuan, Y., Wang, F.-Y.: Blockchain: The State of the Art and future trends. Acta Automatica Sinica **42**(4), 481–494 (2016)
12. Han, Q., Wang, G.: A review of foreign research of BlockChain technology. Sci. Technol. Prog. Policy **35**(2), 154–160 (2018)
13. Wang, Y., Li, L., Hu, D.: A literature review of block Chain. J. China Univ. Min. Technol. (Soc. Sci.) **3**, 74–86 (2018)

An Improved Human Action Recognition Method Based on 3D Convolutional Neural Network

Jingmei Li, Zhenxin Xu$^{(\boxtimes)}$, Jianli Li, and Jiaxiang Wang

College of Computer Science and Technology, Harbin Engineering University,
Harbin 150001, China
18845898726@163.com

Abstract. Aiming at the problems such as complex feature extraction, low recognition rate and low robustness in the traditional human action recognition algorithms, an improved 3D convolutional neural network method for human action recognition is proposed. The network only uses grayscale images and the number of image frames as input. At the same time, two layers of nonlinear convolutional layers are added to the problem of less convolution and convolution kernels in the original network, which not only increases the number of convolution kernels in the network. Quantity, and make the network have better abstraction ability, at the same time in order to prevent the network from appearing the phenomenon of overfitting, the dropout technology was added in the network to regularize. Experiments were performed on the UCF101 data set, achieving an accuracy of 96%. Experimental results show that the improved 3D convolutional neural network model has a higher recognition accuracy in human action recognition.

Keywords: Human body motion recognition ·
3D convolutional neural network · Dropout

1 Introduction

As an important research direction in the field of computer vision, human action recognition has a wide range of application value and significant research significance in human-computer interaction, intelligent video surveillance, film animation, video retrieval, virtual reality and other fields. Although human action recognition is a research hotspot in the field of computer vision, there are still many challenges, such as the difference in the performance of the action, the complex background, and the differences in perspectives. At present, human action recognition can be divided into two categories: (1) traditional human action recognition methods; (2) human action recognition methods based on deep learning.

The traditional human action recognition mainly analyzes the video frame sequence, and it manually designs features to manually extract features to identify the action in the video. Bobick et al. [1] based on the assumption that the same actions have similar spatiotemporal data. They reconstruct the data by extracting the foreground parts of the video data, and then identify the actions by comparing the similarity

© ICST Institute for Computer Sciences, Social Informatics and Telecommunications Engineering 2019
Published by Springer Nature Switzerland AG 2019. All Rights Reserved
S. Liu and G. Yang (Eds.): ADHIP 2018, LNICST 279, pp. 37–46, 2019.
https://doi.org/10.1007/978-3-030-19086-6_5

of the foreground data in each video data. Sheikh et al. [2] used the motion trajectory of important human joints such as head, hand, and foot in the process of human motion to determine the similarity between motion samples based on similar invariance. Yamato et al. [3] proposed applying the Hidden Markov Model (HMM) to recognize human motion. Oliver et al. [4] generated a coupled hidden Markov model (CHMM) by applying multiple HMM to model the interactions between humans.

The introduction of deep learning brings new research directions to human motion recognition. The main goal is to construct an effective network recognition framework and to automatically learn features. It does not require manually designing and extracting features, so that the algorithm is not subject to artificial influence and thus has better robustness. Taylor et al. [5] proposed a model to learn the latent representation of image sequences from continuous images. The convolutional structure of the model can be extended to realistic image sizes by using a compact parametric quantization. The model extracts potential "flow file" that correspond to transitions between input frames, and it extracts low-level motion features in a multi-level framework of action recognition. It achieves competitive performance on both KTH and Hollywood2 datasets. Ji et al. [6] proposed a 3D convolutional neural network model for human action recognition. The hard link layer is used to extract pixel information such as grayscale values, horizontal gradients, vertical gradients, horizontal optical streams, and vertical optical streams in consecutive input video frames. And above information is alternately convolved and subsampled to combine information to get the final feature description. Experiments on the KTH and TRECVID 2008 datasets have shown more performance than some benchmarking methods. Experiments on KTH and TREC-VID2008 datasets show that it is more effective than some traditional methods.

2   Network Model Overall Design

Ji et al. [7] proposed a 3D convolutional neural network for video in 2013. They extended the convolutional neural network to three dimensions in order to extract spatial and temporal information in the video. It is proposed that the gray image of the continuous seven frames of the video combined with the horizontal gradient, the optical flow, the vertical gradient, and the optical flow feature map have a total of 5 channels as the input of the 3D CNN. Due to the very small size of the 3D CNN network at the time, some problems will arise. For example, in each layer of 3D CNN, the number of kernels is very small, which leads to fewer types of features learned at each layer, and weaker network expression capabilities. Its first convolution layer has 10 kernels and the second convolution layer has only 30 kernels. In order to solve the above problems, the paper uses the method of increasing the number of convolution layers to extend the convolutional layer to four layers. It including two linear convolution layers and two MLP (Multi-Layer Perceptron) convolutional layers, and then increase the number of network layers. It increases the abstraction capability of the network and use dropout to regularize the network to prevent over-fitting of the network.

2.1 Network Model Process Design

The network model process design is shown in Fig. 1. It mainly includes two parts: The first part mainly selects the parameters of the model. First, the data set is downloaded and pre-processed. And the pre-processed data is put into the model for training. Finally, the analysis of the output results to determine the impact of the input data on the performance and stability of the model. The second part is to load the trained model into the classification program. The classification algorithm used is the 3D CNN algorithm designed in this chapter.

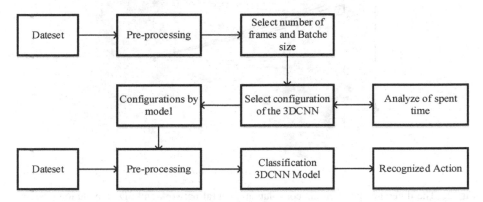

Fig. 1. Network model process design

2.2 3D Convolutional Neural Network

3D CNN can simultaneously compute two dimensional features in both time and space. It is achieved by convolving a 3D convolution kernel in a space consisting of several consecutive frames of image. Because of this structure, the feature map in the convolutional layer is connected to a plurality of frames in the next layer so as to capture motion information. The difference between 2D convolution and 3D convolution is clearly shown in Fig. 2. The 3D convolution formula is:

$$v_{ij}^{xyz} = \tanh\left(b_{ij} + \sum_{m}\sum_{p=0}^{P_i-1}\sum_{q=0}^{Q_i-1}\sum_{r=0}^{R_i-1} w_{ijm}^{pqr} v_{(i-1)m}^{(x+p)(y+q)(z+r)}\right) \tag{1}$$

In Formula 1, $\tanh(\cdot)$ is a hyperbolic tangent function, b_i is the offset of the feature map, R_i is the size of the three-dimensional convolution kernel in the time dimension and w_{ijm}^{pqr} is the value of the convolution kernel connected to the m feature maps in the previous layer at the point (p, q, r).

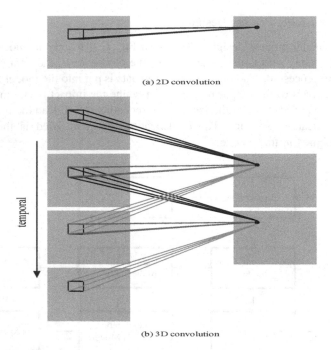

(a) 2D convolution

(b) 3D convolution

Fig. 2. The difference between 2D convolutional neural network and 3D convolutional neural network

2.3 NIN (Network in Network)

The forward neural network or multi-layer perceptron (MLP) is a non-linear model with strong abstraction ability. Therefore, adding MLP to the network will definitely increase the abstraction ability of the network. The linear convolutional layer and MLP convolution layer are shown in Fig. 3. The MLP convolutional layer uses a nonlinear activation function (ReLU in this paper) so that the feature map of the current layer is obtained. The MLP convolutional layer is calculated as shown in Formula 2:

$$f_{i,j,k_1}^1 = \max(w_{k_1}^{1^T} x_{i,j} + b_{k_1}, 0)$$
$$\cdots$$
$$f_{i,j,k_n}^n = \max(w_{k_n}^{n^T} f_{i,j}^{n-1} + b_{k_n}, 0)$$

$$(2)$$

In formula 2, (i,j) is the pixel index of the feature map, $x_{i,j}$ is the input at the center (i,j), k_n is the index of the feature map, n is the number of layers of the MLP. Because the ReLU activation function is used, the maximum value compared to 0 is used in all formulas.

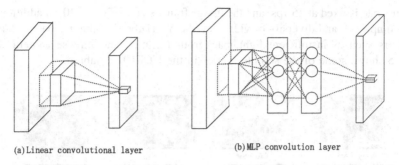

(a) Linear convolutional layer   (b) MLP convolution layer

Fig. 3. Linear convolutional layers and MLP convolutional layers

2.4   Network Architecture Design

The network architecture used in the experiment is shown in Fig. 4. It contains two hidden layers and four convolutional layers (two linear convolutions and two nonlinear convolutions). All convolutional layers use a $3 \times 3 \times 3$ convolution kernel size and set the number of MLP layers to 3. For the pooled layer, $2 \times 2 \times 2$ non-overlapping sliding windows are used. At each MLP layer and pooling layer, a Dropout regularization layer with a probability of 0.5 is used to prevent over-fitting of the network. Then there are a fully connected layer with 512 output neurons and a Dropout hidden layer with a probability of 0.25. Finally, there is a fully connected layer with 50 output neural units. The network has about 2.3 million parameters to be trained. This article chooses the Xavier method to initialize the network, and the activation function selects ReLU.

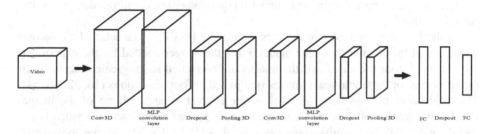

Fig. 4. Network architecture design

3   Experiment

3.1   Data Set Introduction

In 2012, scholars such as Soomro produced the UCF101 [8], the largest human action data set at that time, which included 101 types of actions and more than 1,300 video segments. And these actions can be roughly divided into five types, which are human and object interaction, human body movement, human-human interaction, playing musical instruments and sports. The video clips are all from the YouTube website, the frame rate is fixed at 25 fps, and the image frame size is 320×240. In addition, due to the complexity and diversity of videos on the YouTube site, the database is affected by factors such as insufficient light, background clutter, and intense camera shake. Figure 5 shows some of the sample frames in the UCF101 database.

Fig. 5. Partial sample video image frames in UCF101 database

3.2 Experimental Analysis and Design

According to the flow chart shown in Fig. 1, this experiment is divided into two parts. The first part: pre-processing the downloaded data set and parameter selection of the model; the second part: for the first part of the parameter selection, the data Set to the model for training.

In the first part, the first step is to preprocess the UCF101 data set, and the second step is to set the parameters of the model. First, the images needed for the experiment are extracted from the video and the images are converted to grayscale images. Then the resolution of these grayscale images is adjusted to four resolutions (16, 32, 48, 64). The adjustment process is to take values for every row and column of the image. Finally, the number of consecutive image frames required to represent the video is set, and the number of consecutive frames is defined as (5, 10, 15, 20, 25) five consecutive image frames. After setting this parameter value, use 60% of the sample for training, 20% for cross-validation, and 20% for model testing to train the model. After 10 trainings of this model, the performance indexes of these models are respectively counted: accuracy rate, precision rate, and recall rate. Finally, these models were analyzed to determine which configured model was able to achieve the highest degree of match and the shortest processing time.

In the second part, the data is preprocessed using the same preprocessing method as in the first part, and then the model already defined is used, in accordance with the Leave-One-Group-Out (LOGO) proposed by Reddy and Shah [9] in 2013. The protocol trains the model. The model was trained 30 times, and then the test set was tested using the model, and the test results were compared with the test results obtained by other methods. Finally, according to the data partitioning criteria in the first section, the datasets were again randomly divided by the same segmentation ratio and the models were tested. The model's observations have the following three parts: accuracy, accuracy, and recall.

3.3   Analysis of Results

Different resolutions are used as input to the model to evaluate the effect of different resolutions on the model. The results are shown in Fig. 6. In terms of image resolution, we can see from Fig. 6 that when the resolution of the input image is between 48 * 48 and 64 * 64, the model's accuracy index achieves better results. All values in this range are Must be higher than 94.9%. Especially when the resolution of the image is 64 * 64, the average accuracy of the model is 95.6%. In addition, another result can be obtained from Fig. 6: When the input image resolution is increased, the accuracy of the model is also improved. However, due to the limitations of the computer's memory, it is not possible to use the 25-frame resolution 64 * 64 image to train the model. In the input continuous image frame, it can be seen from Fig. 6 that when the input continuous image frame is 5 or 10, the model can obtain better accuracy. Despite this, the accuracy of the model and the average recall rate were 74.0% and 74%, respectively.

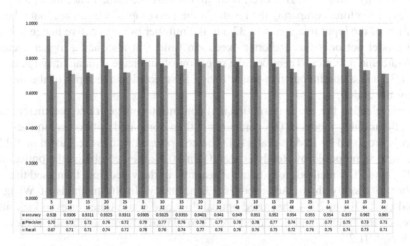

	5 16	10 16	15 16	20 16	25 16	5 32	10 32	15 32	20 32	25 32	5 48	10 48	15 48	20 48	25 48	5 64	10 64	15 64	20 64
accuracy	0.928	0.9306	0.9311	0.9325	0.9311	0.9305	0.9325	0.9355	0.9401	0.941	0.949	0.951	0.952	0.954	0.955	0.954	0.957	0.962	0.965
Precision	0.70	0.73	0.72	0.76	0.72	0.79	0.77	0.76	0.78	0.77	0.78	0.78	0.77	0.74	0.77	0.77	0.75	0.73	0.71
Recall	0.67	0.71	0.71	0.74	0.72	0.78	0.76	0.74	0.77	0.76	0.76	0.76	0.75	0.72	0.76	0.75	0.74	0.73	0.71

Fig. 6. Image resolution and the number of input frames

In addition to the image resolution and the number of consecutive frames, the execution time of the model is also considered. Figure 7 shows the time spent performing each model. From Fig. 7 the relationship between the input image resolution and the total number of images can be directly obtained. For example, when 16 * 16 resolution is applied, the execution time of the model does not change substantially. However, when the resolution of the image is increased, the execution time of the model will increase substantially linearly.

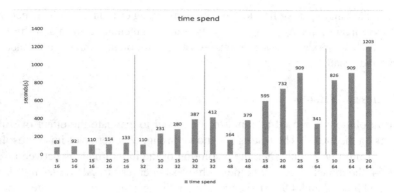

Fig. 7. Time spent running

A comprehensive comparison of each group of Figs. 6 and 7 is performed. When the input image resolution of the model is $64 * 64$ and it is a continuous 20-frame image, the execution time of the model is 1200 s. On the other hand, when the input image of the model is $32 * 32$ and is a continuous 5-frame image, the execution time of the model only takes 83 s. However, both are roughly the same in accuracy, recall and accuracy. Therefore, comparing the results in the two graphs, we can see that when the resolution of the input image is $32 * 32$ and the number of consecutive image frames is 5, the model not only has a shorter execution time, but also has a higher accuracy. Recall rate and accuracy. Therefore, the selection of an image with an image resolution of $32 * 32$ and a continuous five-frame image is selected as the input of the model to identify the action.

After selecting the image resolution and continuous image frame parameters of the model, the training model of this parameter is then compared with other similarly used protocols proposed by Reddy et al. [10]. The comparison results are shown in Table 1. In the method proposed by Reddy et al. [10] in 2013, they combined the optical flow, 3D-SIFT and PCA methods to extract the features in the video, and then used the SVM classifier to classify them. Achieved 76.9% accuracy. In the methods of Wang and Schmid et al. [10] in 2014, they used optical flow and dense trajectories to kick off the features of the frames, and then used SVMs to classify them, and finally achieved an accuracy of 91.2%.

Table 1. This method is compared with the above method

Method	Accuracy
Reddy and Shah	76.9%
Liu et al.	87.16%
Wang and Schmid	91.2%
Peng et al.	92.3%
Method of this article	96%

In the method proposed by Liu et al. [11] in 2015, they used visual word bags to extract features for use in motion recognition. Later, they used multi-perspective ideas for features by acquiring data similarities. Finally, they applied the extracted features to a linear SVM, which ultimately achieved an accuracy of 87.9%. In the method proposed by Peng et al. [12] in 2016, they used descriptors such as HOG, HOF, and MBH to extract features, combined these features into the output of descriptors in the bag of words, and then used SVM to perform human motion recognition. Finally, 92.3% accuracy was obtained on the UCF101 dataset. The method proposed in this paper obtains a 96% specific accuracy rate on the UCF data set. Compared with the previous method, the accuracy rate is increased by 3.7%.

4 Conclusion

This article first describes the 3D convolutional neural network and its application in human actions. Then, in order to address the deficiencies in its network, this paper makes targeted improvements: First, to address the problem of a small number of convolution kernels in the network, Two layers of MLP nonlinear convolutional layers are added in the network layer, which not only increases the number of convolution kernels in the network, but also improves the abstraction capability of the network model. Second, in order to prevent over-fitting phenomenon in the network, A layer of Dropout with a probability of 0.5 was added before each pooling layer, and a layer of Dropout with a probability of 0.25 was added before the last fully connected layer. Experiments on the data set UCF101 show that the accuracy of the proposed network model is improved by 3.7% compared with the method in Table 1. Therefore, the human motion recognition method proposed in this paper has certain research significance and practical value.

Acknowledge. This work was supported by the National Key Research and Development Plan of China under Grant No. 2016YFB0801004.

References

1. Bobick, A.F., Davis, J.W.: The recognition of human movement using temporal templates. IEEE Trans. Pattern Anal. Mach. Intell. **23**(3), 257–267 (2001)
2. Sheikh, Y., Sheikh, M., Shah, M.: Exploring the space of a human action. In: Tenth IEEE International Conference on Computer Vision, vol. 1, pp. 144–149. IEEE (2005)
3. Yamato, J., Ohya, J., Ishii, K.: Recognizing human action in time-sequential images using hidden Markov model. In: IEEE Computer Society Conference on Computer Vision and Pattern Recognition, pp. 379–385. IEEE Computer Society (1992)
4. Brand, M., Oliver, N., Pentland, A.: Coupled hidden Markov models for complex action recognition. In: Proceedings of the 1997 IEEE Computer Society Conference on Computer Vision and Pattern Recognition 1997, p. 994. IEEE (2002)
5. Taylor, G.W., Fergus, R., LeCun, Y., Bregler, C.: Convolutional learning of spatio-temporal features. In: Daniilidis, K., Maragos, P., Paragios, N. (eds.) ECCV 2010. LNCS, vol. 6316, pp. 140–153. Springer, Heidelberg (2010). https://doi.org/10.1007/978-3-642-15567-3_11

6. Ji, S., Xu, W., Yang, M., et al.: 3D Convolutional neural networks for human action recognition. IEEE Trans. Pattern Anal. Mach. Intell. **35**(1), 221–231 (2012)
7. Ji, S., Xu, W., Yang, M., et al.: 3D convolutional neural networks for automatic human action recognition. IEEE US8345984 (2013)
8. Soomro, K., Zamir, A.R., Shah, M.: UCF101: a dataset of 101 human actions classes from videos in the wild. Computer Science (2012)
9. Reddy, K.K., Shah, M.: Recognizing 50 human action categories of web videos. Mach. Vis. Appl. **24**(5), 971–981 (2013)
10. Wang, L., Qiao, Y., Tang, X.: Action recognition with trajectory-pooled deep-convolutional descriptors. In: Computer Vision and Pattern Recognition, pp. 4305–4314. IEEE (2015)
11. Liu, J., Huang, Y., Peng, X., et al.: Multi-view descriptor mining via codeword net for action recognition. In: IEEE International Conference on Image Processing, pp. 793–797. IEEE (2015)
12. Peng, X., Wang, L., Wang, X., et al.: Bag of visual words and fusion methods for action recognition. Comput. Vis. Image Underst. **150**(C), 109–125 (2016)

Multi-user ALE for Future HF Radio Communication by Leveraging Wideband Spectrum Sensing and Channel Prediction

Chujie Wu[(⊠)], Yunpeng Cheng, Yuping Gong, Yuming Zhang, Fei Huang, and Guoru Ding

College of Communications Engineering, Army Engineering University of PLA, Nanjing 210014, China
chujie128@163.com, chengyp2000@vip.sina.com, gyp78@sina.com, zhangym_2000@163.com, huangfeicjh@sina.com, dr.guoru.ding@ieee.org

Abstract. HF cognitive radio is considered to be one direction of fourth generation HF radios. In this paper, we investigate the problem of multi-user HF radio communication by leveraging the techniques of cognitive radio. In the presented system model, we consider the determination of optimal path between two points and propose a channel probing method based on coarse granularity wideband spectrum sensing as well as channel prediction. To cope with the problem of channel selection and link establishment, we adjust the channel selection strategy after every probing based on Stochastic Learning Automata (SLA) learning algorithm. The experimental results show that the channel selection based on SLA learning algorithm is better than random channel selection, and channel selection with predicted wideband spectrum sensing performs better in system performances than no-predicted narrowband spectrum sensing.

Keywords: HF radio communication · Multi-user · Channel probing · Channel selection strategy · SLA learning algorithm

1 Introduction

In the past 20 years, the telecommunication explosion has created an ever-expanding wireless communication applications and products, as well as spectrum congestion. With the burgeoning demand for communication services and capacity, more stringent requirements on the flexibility and adaptability are put forward on wireless communication equipment under the limited spectrum resources [1]. The High Frequency (HF) radio communication has been the earliest solution for wireless communication with the characteristics of long-distance transmission and wide coverage [2]. Limited by narrowband and unstable channel conditions, the development of HF communication has been restricted for a long time [3].

© ICST Institute for Computer Sciences, Social Informatics and Telecommunications Engineering 2019
Published by Springer Nature Switzerland AG 2019. All Rights Reserved
S. Liu and G. Yang (Eds.): ADHIP 2018, LNICST 279, pp. 47–56, 2019.
https://doi.org/10.1007/978-3-030-19086-6_6

Cognitive Radios (CR) have the potential to radically improve the performances, efficiency, and reliability of wireless networks and enable new applications such as dynamic spectrum access (DSA) to be developed [4]. In the past years, most of the researches in CR have been given to the frequency band above 30 MHz. Given the challenges in HF communication, scientists are taking the research of HF cognitive radios which can detect the frequency occupancy quickly [5]. Therefore, the goal of fourth generation HF communication system aims at selecting the optimal frequency adaptively and adjusting the waveform bandwidth automatically to realize fast Automatic Link Establishment (ALE) as well as high speed data transmission.

In order to extend functions in next generation HF radios, it's taking the exploration of adding some new elements to the ALE module such as propagation modeling, wideband spectrum sensing, available channel prediction. For example, the work in [6] use the ITS HF Propagation, an international mainstream HF link propagation model, to simulate the transmission path and power loss between two points. Shahid et al. [7] propose listen before transmit (LBT) in ALE based on cognitive radio sensing techniques to obtain ALE channels effectively. Haris et al. [8] introduce the Neural Network model to predict the likelihood of interference experienced by broadcast users and find the regularity in some channels.

This paper is a significant extension of previous works on HF channel selection of multi-transmitter to multi-receiver. The main contributions of this paper are summarized as follows.

- Present a HF wireless network model containing multiuser, and considering the determination of optimal path between transceiver.
- Propose a multi-user channel probing method combined coarse granularity wideband spectrum sensing and channel prediction.
- Develop a channel selection strategy based on SLA learning algorithm, and find the optimal channel for link establishment by the proposed strategy.

The reminder of the paper is organized as follows. The system model is presented in Sect. 2. In Sect. 3, a new channel probing method is proposed. In Sect. 4, we develop the channel selection strategy based on SLA learning algorithm. In Sect. 5, simulation results and discussion are presented, and we draw conclusions about this paper in Sect. 6.

2   System Model and Path Design

The system model is shown in Fig. 1, we consider the HF radio network consisting of N transmitting stations and n receiving stations $(n > N)$. Assuming there is no coordinator in the network to enable interactions among radios, and the radio stations take the asynchronous ALE to realize point-to-point communication. The channel quality is entirely unknown at the beginning, and the transmitting station cannot initiate channel probing until know the station number of receiver.

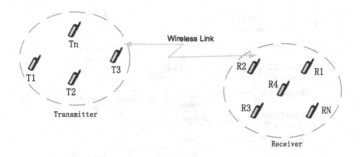

Fig. 1. System model.

ITS HF Propagation is a long-term frequency prediction software developed by National Telecommunications Bureau of the United State, the software can simulate transmission paths in ionosphere [9]. ICEPAC is one of the modules in the software usually used to predict the Maximum Usable Frequency (MUF), Circuit Reliability (REL), and Signal to Nosie Ratio (SNR) between two points [10]. To determine the path of transceiver station, we could analyze qualities of all possible links between two points to select the best path by ICEPAC. Details are described as follows.

Let φ define the set of $N \times n$ possible paths in the system model. We start by setting the system parameters including stations' locations, signal transmitting power, sunspot numbers, and a set of reference frequencies $I = \{f_1 \ f_2 \cdots \ f_i\}$. The MUF of each path as well as the SNR and REL of each reference frequency in the path can be obtained by simulation. Define the quality indicator of path h as:

$$\lambda_h = \omega_1 \times MUF_h + \omega_2 \times \overline{SNR}_{h(REL>0.9)}, \quad \forall h \in \varphi \tag{1}$$

where $\overline{SNR}_{h(REL>0.9)}$ represents the average SNR of all frequencies with REL over 90% in I, ω_1 and ω_2 is the corresponding weight ($\omega_1 > \omega_2$). We sort all paths by the values of λ and pick N paths with good indicators. Therefore, we identify N users in the HF radio network and each user contains a pair of transceiver. After assigning the transceiver station, we could start probing channel.

3   Channel Probing of Multi-user

The refraction of electromagnetic waves by the ionosphere causes the frequency-selective in HF, thus the range of usable frequencies varies with time, season, space, weather and other factors [11]. One of the solution is to find the available frequency supporting ALE through channel probing. Figure 2 shows the channel probing process in the standard of MIL-STD-188-141A [12], the transmitter sends a probing signal at each frequency to update the scores in the LQA matrix then selects an optimal frequency to call for link establishment. However, there is no coordination in the network, when optimal frequency probed is same for multiple users, signal collision would occur in the process of ALE. Moreover,

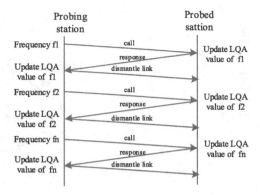

Fig. 2. Channel probing process in 2G-ALE.

the time spent on call and response of every frequency reduces the network throughput. To solve this problem, a new channel probing method of multiuser is proposed.

The method is based on coarse granularity wideband spectrum sensing and channel prediction. The narrowband spectrum sensing is opposite to wideband spectrum sensing using high spectral resolution to detect spectrum holes precisely at the cost of time delay, whereas the coarse granularity wideband spectrum sensing can find frequency band of low occupancy more quickly by reducing the sampling rate. Considering the time variability of HF, we can capture the trend in the variability of occupancy based on long-term wideband spectrum sensing results to predict relatively stable and idle channels at the time of link establishment. For example, we find the occupancy of certain frequency bands have 24-hour periodicity by weeks of spectrum sensing, which can predict the lowest occupancy bands when ALE. Moreover, combined the simulated MUF and predicted bands, we could determine the selectable channel set. The process of channel probing is shown in Fig. 3.

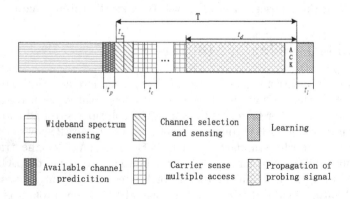

Fig. 3. Channel probing of multiuser.

Users have been in coarse granularity wideband spectrum sensing until ready to start establishing links. When preparing for ALE, the selectable channel set M_n of user n $(n \in N)$ is determined by sensed low occupancy band and predicted channels. Define the time slot of probing one channel as T, the transmitting station chooses one channel in M_n at the beginning, if chose channel sensed occupied, reselects until finding an idle one. There is a carrier sense multiple access (CSMA) mechanism before probing, if more than two users select same free channel and send frames at same time, collision would occur, in that case, trying to compete again after the time of t_c until one user accessing the selected channel successfully. Suppose the propagation of probing signal requires a minimum time t_{min}, once the signal is successfully transmitted, the receiver would send back an ACK to the transmitter, otherwise failure if ACK haven't received exceeding the time of t_{max}. At the end of each slot, every user will receive a payoff, and then apply a learning algorithm to update the channel selection strategy next slot.

For the convenience of analysis, it is assumed that spectrum sensing and channel prediction are perfect. The precondition of receiving ACK is $t_{min} < t_d < t_{max}$, and the channel probing time of user n is expressed as:

$$t_d^n = T - \alpha_n t_s - \beta_n t_c \tag{2}$$

where α_n and β_n respectively represent the number of sensed channels before finding an idle one and the number of competitions during the conflict.

We know from Fig. 3 that longer time spent on sensing and competition, shorter time for user's probing. However, in asynchronous mode, the receiver scans frequencies at a rate that allows the dwell on each frequency to be long enough to detect a signal [13], therefore more time on t_d^n is better.

4   Channel Selection and ALE

At present, there are many learning algorithms used for channel selection, such as no-regret learning algorithm [14], logarithmic linear learning algorithm [15], and spatial adaptive algorithm [16]. But these algorithms require coordination mechanism which is not feasible in the considered multiuser HF radio network. In this section, we develop a channel selection strategy based on SLA learning algorithm and illustrate how to establish link by the strategy.

Stochastic learning automata (SLA) based channel selection algorithm can adjust current channel selection strategy on the basis of historical action rewards [17], usually used in non-cooperative opportunity spectrum access of dynamic environment. Denote the reward value of user n in slot j as:

$$r_n(j) = \frac{S_{ACK}}{N \log_{T-t_{min}}^{(\alpha_n t_s + \beta_n t_c)}} \gamma_n ACK \tag{3}$$

where S_{ACK} represents received power of ACK, N is the local noise, γ_n indicates whether n successfully contends the selected channel or not, and ACK indicates whether the probed channel is idle or occupied in propagation.

Algorithm 1. SLA based channel selection algorithm

1: **Initialize:** Set $j = 0$ and initial channel selection probability vector $p_{nm}(j) = 1/M, \forall n \in N, m \in M$.
2: At the beginning of the jth slot, each user n selects a channel m according to its current channel selection probability vector $p_n(j)$.
3: In each slot, users perform channel probing. At the end of jth slot, each user n receives the reward $r_n(j)$ specified by (3).
4: All users update their channel slection probability vectors according to the following rule:

$$p_{nm}(j+1) = p_{nm}(j) + b\tilde{r}_n(j)(1 - p_{nm}(j)), \quad m \in M$$
$$p_{nl}(j+1) = p_{nl}(j) - b\tilde{r}_n(j)p_{nl}(j), \quad l \in M \,\&l \neq m \tag{4}$$

5: where $0 < b < 1$, $\tilde{r}_n(j)$ is the normalized reward defined as follows:

$$\tilde{r}_n(j) = r_n(j)/R_{\max} \tag{5}$$

6: If $\forall n \in N$, there exists a component of $p_n(j)$ which is approaching one, stop; Otherwise, go to step 2).

For users, the probability of selecting every channel is same at first slot, if user n selects channel m ($m \in M$) randomly and gets the $r_n(j)$ after probing, then the probability of selecting m next slot is updated as:

$$p_{nm}(j+1) = p_{nm}(j) + br_n(j)(1 - p_{nm}(j)) \tag{6}$$

and the probabilities of selecting other channels l ($l \in M \,\& l \neq m$) are updated as:

$$p_{nl}(j+1) = p_{nl}(j) - br_n(j)p_{nl}(j) \tag{7}$$

where b represents the iteration step. The detail of SLA learning algorithm is shown in Algorithm 1 [15].

At the end of each slot, every user would apply the SLA learning algorithm to update all channels' selection probabilities. After learning for many time slots, the probabilities eventually converged to nearly one or zero. The optimal channel corresponds to the probability approaching one, then the user can start calling and responding of asynchronous ALE in the optimal channel.

We assume the spectrum environment is stable in T_{sta} that the transmission rate of every channel remains constant. Define $T_{\cos}^n$ as the time from getting out of the wideband spectrum sensing to establish the link successfully, which is called ALE preparation time. So the system throughput is given by:

$$U = \sum_{n=1}^{N} \{(T_{sta} - T_{\cos}^n) \times R_n\}$$
$$T_{\cos}^n = jT + T_{shake} \tag{8}$$

where j is the number of time slots before reaching the convergence, T_{shake} is the time of "three-way handshake", R_n is the transmission rate of the probed channel by user n.

In contrast to 2G-ALE, the proposed ALE is carried out through the convergence of channel selection probability. The convergent speed of each user is different, the user with fast convergence can start link establishment firstly, decreasing the collision between users.

5   Simulation Results and Discussion

In the simulation, we set $T = 100$ ms, the time for narrowband spectrum sensing is $t_s = 5$ ms, and the waiting time when conflicts occur is $t_c = 5$ ms. Besides, $T_{sta} = 30$ s, $t_{min} = 20$ ms, $t_{max} = 80$ ms, $T_{shanke} = 780$ ms, and $b = 0.15$. In [18], the signal is detected as long as SNR reach at least 6 dB. We set the SNR of channels range from 6 dB to 10 dB, so every channel has different transmission rate. Moreover, the number of users $N = 8$, the total number of channels $F = 12$, and the number of available channels $S = 5$.

5.1   Algorithm Convergence Analysis

To show the evolution of channel selection probability of the SLA learning algorithm, Fig. 4 compare two channel selection methods based on SLA algorithm. The traditional SLA method refers to selecting channels one by one through narrowband spectrum sensing and having no prediction of available frequency band before probing, whereas the proposed SLA method is expressed in this paper, which reduces the selectable channels through wideband spectrum sensing and channel prediction.

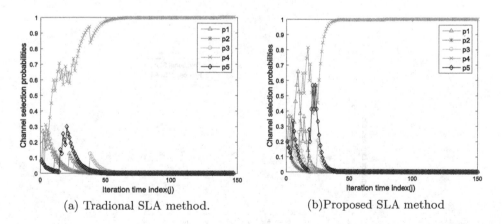

(a) Tradional SLA method.   (b)Proposed SLA method

Fig. 4. Evolution of the channel selection probability of arbitrary user.

The different lines in Fig. 4 represent the selection probability of arbitrary user on the available channels. It's seen that, the user finally chooses channel 4 for link establishment, which proves the convergent SLA algorithm is applicable to the system model. Meanwhile, the proposed SLA method has fewer iterations and faster convergence speed than traditional SLA method, because the method with no-predicted narrowband spectrum sensing costs more time in channel sensing and selecting.

5.2   System Performance Analysis

To analyze the impacts on system performances, the simulation scenario is in the same spectrum environment and each channel can only be accessed by one user.

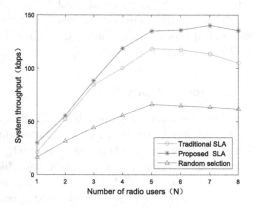

Fig. 5. System throughput with different number of users.

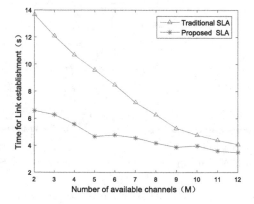

Fig. 6. Link establishment time with different available channels.

Figure 5 compare the system throughput of random channel selection, traditional SLA channel selection, proposed SLA channel selection with different number of users. We observe that, random channel selection would cause channels with low transmission rates selected by multiusers simultaneously, so performs worst in the throughput. In SLA learning algorithm, users tend to select channels with higher transmission rates, especially the proposed SLA channel selection method, faster convergence speed leaves more time for data transmission, thus the throughput is maximum. Besides, throughput increases with the number of users while $N < 5$, once the number of users exceed the number of available channels ($N > 5$) severe competition lead to slower convergence speed, which results in the throughput degradation.

A further comparison on link establishment time of two SLA channel selection method under different number of available channels is shown in Fig. 6. The results suggest the proposed SLA method is better while the available channels are few, and the differences between two methods become small as the number of available channels increase. As a result, channel selection with predicted wideband spectrum sensing performs better in system performances than no-predicted narrowband spectrum sensing.

6 Conclusion

In this paper, we propose a HF wireless network model containing multiuser, the optimal path between transceiver is determined by a long-term link propagation model in unknown channel statistics. Moreover, a new channel probing method for multiuser is presented which combines coarse granularity wideband spectrum sensing and channel prediction. To select optimal channel for ALE, we develop the channel selection strategy based on SLA algorithm. The simulation results prove that the channel selection based on SLA learning algorithm is better than random channel selection, and channel selection with predicted wideband spectrum sensing performs better in system performances than no-predicted narrowband spectrum sensing.

Acknowledgment. This work was supported in part by the National Natural Science Foundation of China under Grant 61871398, Grant 61501510, and Grant 61601192, in part by the Natural Science Foundation of Jiangsu Province under Grant BK20150717, in part by the China Postdoctoral Science Funded Project under Grant 2018T110426.

References

1. Koski, E., Furman, W.N.: Applying cognitive radio concepts to HF communications. In: The Institution of Engineering and Technology, International Conference on Ionospheric Radio Systems and Techniques (IET), pp. 1–6 (2009)
2. Prouvez, R., Baynat, B., Khalife, H., Conan, V., Lamy-Bergot, C.: Modeling automatic link establishment in HF networks. In: Proceedings IEEE Military Communications Conference, Tampa, FL, pp. 1630–1635 (2015)

3. Jorgenson, M.B., Cook, N.T.: Results from a wideband HF usability study. In: Proceedings IEEE Military Communications Conference, Tampa, FL, pp. 1454–1459 (2015)
4. Shukla, A.K., Jackson-Booth, N.K., Arthur, N.K.: "Cognitive radios" and their relevance to HF radio systems. In: Proceedings 12th IET International Conference on Ionospheric Radio Systems and Techniques (IRST 2012), York, pp. 1–6 (2012)
5. Vanninen, T., Linden, T., Raustia, M., Saarnisaari, H.: Cognitive HF - new perspectives to use the high frequency band. In: Proceedings 9th International Conference on Cognitive Radio Oriented Wireless Networks and Communications (CROWN-COM), Oulu, pp. 108–113 (2014)
6. Zhao, J., Zhao, N.: An overview of the international HF transmission link simulation model and its application analysis. China Radio 1, 47–49 (2017). (in Chinese)
7. Shahid, A., Ahmad, S., Akram, A., Khan, S.A.: Cognitive ALE for HF radios. In: Proceedings Second International Conference on Computer Engineering and Applications, Bali Island, pp. 28–33 (2010)
8. Haralambous, H., Papadopoulos, H.: 24-hour neural network congestion models for high-frequency broadcast users. IEEE Trans. Broadcast. 55(1), 145–154 (2009)
9. Tian, X., Lu, J.: Shortwave propagation over oceans and HF propagation prediction model. In: Proceedings IEEE International Conference on Computational Intelligence and Software Engineering, pp. 1–4 (2009)
10. Shang, H., An, J., Lu, J.: HF ground-wave over rough sea-surface and HF propagation prediction model ICEPAC. In: Proceedings IEEE Global Mobile Congress, pp. 1–4 (2009)
11. Johnson, E.E.: Staring link establishment for high-frequency radio. In: Proceedings IEEE Military Communications Conference, Tampa, FL, pp. 1433–1438 (2015)
12. Wang, J.: Research and Development of HF Digital Communications, pp. 1–4. Science Press, Beijing (2009). (in Chinese)
13. Xu, Y., Wang, J., Wu, Q., Anpalagan, A., Yao, Y.D.: Opportunistic spectrum access in unknown dynamic environment: a game-theoretic stochastic learning solution. IEEE Trans. Wireless Commun. 11(4), 1380–1391 (2012)
14. Hart, S., Mas-Colell, A.: A simple adaptive procedure leading to correlated equilibrium. Econometrica 68(5), 1127–1150 (2000)
15. Xu, Y., Wu, Q.: Opportunistic spectrum access using partially overlapping channels: graphical game and uncoupled learning. IEEE Trans. Commun. 61(9), 3906–3918 (2013)
16. Xu, Y., Wang, J., Wu, Q.: Opportunistic spectrum access in cognitive radio networks: global optimization using local interaction games. IEEE J. Sel. Top. Signal Process. 6(2), 180–194 (2012)
17. Bilal, A., Sun, G.: Automatic link establishment for HF radios. In: Proceedings 8th IEEE International Conference on Software Engineering and Service Science (ICSESS), Beijing, pp. 640–643 (2017)
18. Zhang, Y., Xue, W., Luo, W.: A signal detection method based on auto-correlation for the listen-before-transmit. In: Proceedings 3rd International Conference on Computer Science and Network Technology, Dalian, pp. 858–862 (2013)

SDN Dynamic Access Control Scheme Based on Prediction

Qian Cui, Shihui Zheng$^{(\boxtimes)}$, Bin Sun, and Yongmei Cai

[1] School of Computer Science and Engineering,
Xinjiang University of Finance and Economics, Urumqi 830000, China
shihuizh@bupt.edu.cn

Abstract. Through research on the access control of software defined network (SDN) northbound interfaces, we found that malicious OpenFlow applications (OF applications) abuse the northbound interfaces with ADD permissions, which can cause the controllers function failure and other serious harm or even crash directly. Most previous studies of this issue, such as those resulting in the ControllerDAC scheme, set static thresholds; and did not find effective solutions to those problems. This paper analyzes the characteristics of the input flows and proposes an SDN dynamic access control scheme based on prediction and dynamic adjustment of the load threshold. By examining the access characteristics of the OF application, we use a prediction algorithm to determine whether the application will disrupt the API with ADD permissions. This algorithm enables us to perform targeted dynamic access control for different types of applications. Experimental results show that compared with the aforementioned ControllerDAC scheme, our scheme effectively reduces the malicious flow table rate and limits the delivery of malicious flow tables, and the extra delay generated by our scheme is less than 10%.

Keywords: Software defined networking · OpenFlow application · Flow entry prediction · Network security

1 Introduction

Software defined networking (SDN) is an emerging software-based architecture and technology. SDN's most notable feature is that the control plane and data plane support a loosely coupled, centralized network state control, resulting in a transparent the upper-layer network infrastructure. An OF application can freely add and modify the flow table in the switches through the controller's open northbound interface. We find that the number of flow tables in the different controllers switch connections affects the controller's function; and what's worse it may cause the controller to crash. In paper [4] OpenvSwitch and Floodlight Controllers can store 140,000 flow rules, but once the malicious OF application inserts the flow table exceeds this limit, the new flow table will replace the original flow table or even the firewall flow table, thus destroying the security rules of the network itself. In our test when the RYU controller was connected to the OVS switch, that has more than 60,000 flow tables, the controller automatically deletes the previously stored flow tables damaging the network structure. When an

S. Liu and G. Yang (Eds.): ADHIP 2018, LNICST 279, pp. 57–67, 2019.
https://doi.org/10.1007/978-3-030-19086-6_7

ONOS controller [9] has more than 45,000 entries in the switch, there will be serious consequences of a direct controller crash. Most physical OF switches currently on the market typically have small flow table storages of approximately 8000 entries [12]. Protecting the controller from the malicious behavior of an OF application is a problem that needs to be solved.

[1–3, 6] the extension of security functions for controllers, such as Floodlight and NOX, enhance controller security by modifying controller's source code related functions. This method is affected by the controller's system architecture, programming language, etc. Building extensions is difficult and will increase the load on the controller. The idea [7, 8] of decoupling the security plane from the control plane is proposed. Such as controllerSEPA scheme, filter OF applications using security schemes. Repackaged and delivered to the controller through a secure northbound interface. This type of security scheme increases deployment flexibility and facilitates porting to any controller. Possible security issues with access controllers by analyzing OF applications, provides protection such as authentication, role-based authorization, etc. However, the paper [4] points out the defects in the above access control methods. In other words, the features of the interface that does not incorporate the controller provides more targeted protection. For example, an application with delete permission can still delete a flow table with a higher priority than him. Based on the functions of the northbound interface provided by the controller, this paper classifies the OF application access controller resources into four categories, that is, READ, ADD, UPDATE and REMOVE, and designs a corresponding security plan for each type of threat. This scheme uses a policy engine and static thresholds to set a more granular access policy for OF applications, effectively protecting the controller. However, static thresholds have limited protection for ADD permissions. For example, the ControllerDAC scheme sets the threshold for sending 50 flow rules in 60 s for DEFAULT classes of OF applications. For ONOS controller who only need twelve hours to make the flow OpenVswitch elevate to the upper limits. Therefore, when an attacker controls multiple applications, it requires only several hours to reach the switch's storage limit and cause the controller to crash. Table 1 summarizes the four APIs that we need to protect against abuse of ADD permissions.

Table 1. Controller needs to protect ADD permissions.

Controller	ADD permissions that need protection
OpenDaylight	/sal-flow:add-flow
ONOS	/flows/<deviceId> /link
Floodlight	/wm/staticflowpusher/json
RYU	/stats/flowentry/add /stats/groupentry/add

Our paper analyzes the input flows characteristics of OF applications [5] in relation to ADD permission problems. By using the Moving Average Algorithm, wen can predict the number of flow tables in time series. Determine whether the OF application is a malicious application, then we use the predicted number of flow tables as a basis to dynamically adjust the threshold. We decouple the security plane from the control plane, combining policy templates and dynamic thresholds to control the operation of the OF application's ADD access to the controller. Make the number of flow tables in the switch safe and reasonable. Our solution separates OF applications from controllers, did not modify the source code of the controller. Therefore, our solution is applicable to any controller.

This article is structured as follows: The first section describes the main problems existing in OF applications and our solutions. In section two, we propose a design and describe its prototype implementation. The third section simulates the abuse of ADD permissions by malicious OF applications, and make comparisons with the Controller DAC solution, and RYU controller solution to verify our proposed solution. The last section presents the study's conclusions.

2 SDN Dynamic Access Control Scheme Based on Prediction

The SDN dynamic access control scheme proposed by our paper, is composed of a dynamic access control module and a flow table threshold prediction algorithm module. Figure 1 depicts the scheme's architecture. Flow table threshold prediction algorithm modules use the number of flow tables delivered in each cycle, to estimate the number of arrivals for the next periodic flow table. After estimating the number of flow tables, an abnormal, determination causes an adjustment to the threshold of the OF applications. Dynamic access control module provides OF applications authentication and dynamic access control. If the OF application access count is less than the threshold, it allows the OF application normal access to the controller. If the number of accesses is greater than the threshold, the application is prevented from using the ADD permission to send the flow table, protect the controller from the abuse of ADD permissions.

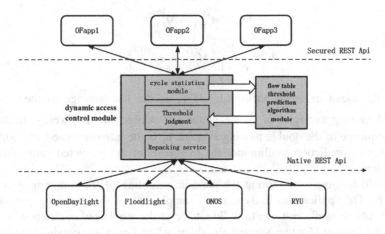

Fig. 1. SDN dynamic access control architecture based on prediction

2.1 Flow Table Threshold Prediction Algorithm

Flow table threshold prediction algorithms estimate the number of flow tables for the next period of the OF application through the Double Moving Average algorithm. The threshold is subsequently adjusted by a combination of trend changes and safety factors.

Data Analysis Based on Double Moving Average Algorithm
The flow table threshold prediction algorithm first enters the number of flow tables Y_t and spanning cycles n applied by the OF application through the ADD permission during the input period. Next, the Double Moving Average algorithm is used to analyze the historical data and, to outputs the predicted value at the next moment, the intercept a_t and the trend of change b_t. The specific algorithm process is as follows:

Let Y_t be the value of the flow table in the t th period, and the moving average $M_{t+1}^{(1)}$ of the $t+1$ period is:

$$M_{t+1}^{(1)} = \frac{Y_t + Y_{t+1} + \ldots + Y_{t-n+1}}{n} \tag{1}$$

n is the span of the moving average, and the larger n is, the better the smoothing effect is. To avoid systematic errors, a further moving average is based on the first average:

$$M_{t+1}^{(2)} = \frac{M_t^{(1)} + M_{t-1}^{(1)} + \ldots + M_{t-n+1}^{(1)}}{n} \tag{2}$$

Contained in the formula, $M_{t+1}^{(2)}$ is the double moving average of t th period, secondary motion correction eliminates the lag predictive value. The prediction model of the double moving average algorithm is:

$$M_{t+T} = a_t + b_t \cdot T \tag{3}$$

$$a_t = 2M_{t+1}^{(1)} - M_{t+1}^{(2)} \tag{4}$$

$$b_t = \frac{2}{n-1} \left(M_{t+1}^{(1)} - M_{t+1}^{(2)} \right) \tag{5}$$

T is the mean to move backwards, $M_{t+1}^{(1)}$ is the last average of the series of calculated moving averages. $M_{t+1}^{(2)}$ means the last double moving average in the calculated sequence of the double moving average. a_t is the intercept, used to modify the initial point of prediction to eliminate the hysteresis of the predicted value. b_t is the trend change.

It should be noted that during the periodic sampling of the outgoing flow table inserted by OF application, if there is no sample before the sampling period, and historical data is insufficient, the front flow table of the number of cycles is set to zero. Through the Double Moving Average algorithm, when $T = 1$, we obtained the forecast value of the flow tables for the next OF application.

Analysis of Threshold Dynamic Adjustment

Next, we enter the time predicted value M_{t+1}, the trend of change b_t and safety factor α to analyze the ADD operation of the application, and limit the operation of the OF application through the output threshold S_{t+1}, Specific analysis is as follows:

When the predictive value of the OF application is greater than the initial threshold set by the system, we can determine that the OF application abuses the ADD permission. To ensure the safety of the controller, it is necessary to reduce the threshold appropriately to militate against the threat generated by malicious OF applications.

This article proposes the concept of safety factor α. The fact adjusts according to the level of safety required in the controller's environment. Change trend b_t is used to indicate the degree about abuse of ADD permissions or abuse of OF applications, these factors act in unsion to adjust the threshold.

$$\begin{cases} S_{t+1} = S_t - (\alpha + |b_t|) \ M_{t+1} > S_{thr} \\ S_{t+1} = S_t + (\alpha + |b_t|) \ M_{t+1} < S_{thr} \end{cases} \tag{6}$$

S_t is the threshold at time t, S_{thr} is the initial threshold, M_t is the predicted value of flow table at time t, and $S_{thr} > S_t > 0$.

When the abuse of the control plane occurs, the flow table threshold prediction algorithm actively reduces the threshold to limit the delivery of malicious flow tables. When the abuse operation is released, the threshold prediction algorithm will actively increase the threshold (but will not exceed the application's default threshold) to ensure that the OF application normally accesses the controller.

2.2 Dynamic Access Control Module

The dynamic access control scheme filters the OF application using the authentication and authorization scheme. Combined with the threshold predicted by the threshold prediction algorithm, this limits the ADD permissions applied by the OF. The scheme consists of an OF application filtering module and periodic statistics module.

The OF application filter module applies an application name to each OF, and starts a thread to authenticate and authorize the accessed OF application.

We use the username and password to verify the validity of the OF application. Next, we use the role to distinguish between different OF applications. Every service request of the OF application, we requires verification of the application related information, such as: application name, permission, and access threshold. We refer to paper [10] to propose two roles:

ADMIN: The administrator authority has the highest security level. By default, the OF application with this authority can freely perform the ADD operation on the controller through the security extension without constraints.

DEFAULT: This authority is set to access for general applications. OF application of this type of role Prone to abuse ADD permission. In view of this situation, we will set a default threshold for this type of authority, and the default threshold will be changed according to the degree of abuse of the OF application.

Figure 2 shows the template for different OF application permissions and initial threshold settings. The template defines the application name OFapp2 of the OF application, the application role DEFAULT and the initial threshold set for this role, that is, this initial threshold settings allows OFapp2 to use ADD permissions 50 times every 60 s.

```
"apps":[
{
"appname":"ofapp1",
"api-roles":"admin",
"threshold seconds":"",
"times":"",
},
{
"appname":"ofapp2",
"api-roles":"default",
"threshold seconds":"60",
"times":"50",
}
]
```

Fig. 2. OF application access policy template

The OF application filter module first parses and counts OF application names, this module will only parse requests related to ADD operations, and we count the number of periodic visits of the OF application through the OF application name.

Periodic statistics modules will additionally enable a thread, This module will clear the record of the number of visits per period OF application, in order to ensure that the number of flow tables recorded in the next cycle will not be affected by the previous cycles. The application flow chart is as follows (see Fig. 3).

The overall scheme is described below: First, we filter all OF applications, OF application filtering modules will authenticate every request from OF app as well as checking the request's legality, and will record the total number of OF application accesses in the recording period through thread one. Next, we calculate the adjustment threshold through the flow table threshold prediction algorithm, then we clear the number of flow records recorded in the previous cycle to record the number of accesses for the next cycle. Adjust the threshold for the next cycle.

The second thread is the primary thread for dynamic access control. This thread will first record the number of accesses for each OF application, by judging with the thread's calculated threshold one. If the number of accesses is less than the threshold, it is allowed to go to the controller, otherwise it will prevent the delivery.

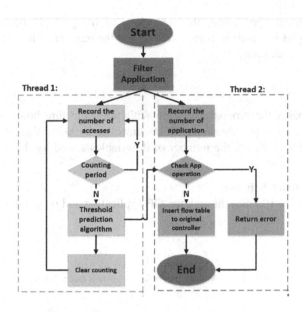

Fig. 3. Dynamic access control flow chart

3 Prototype and Experimental Validation

3.1 Experimental Environment and Parameters

To verify our solution, we first select the RYU controller, the switch selected is OpenvSwitch V2.0.2 used to store our repackaged ADD request. We chose the RYU controller and OVS switch as a direct connect solution.

This paper examines three different types of OF applications, shown in Table 2. We use ADD permissions to insert flow tables. Normal OF applications do not insert excessively many flow tables [11] within a certain period. Therefore, the methodology of constructing a flow table is: The normal application of the property we set the number of insert stream table is less than the default threshold, the flow table inserted by the abnormal applications will far exceed the default threshold.

Table 2. Three application under the flow table

OF application	Application properties	Authority	Threshold	Insert flow table
OFapp1	Normal	ADMIN	Null	20/cycle
OFapp2	Malicious	DEFAULT	50	Linear growth
OFapp3	Normal	DEFAULT	50	20/cycle

OFapp1 is the normal application with ADMIN authority. And use ADD permissions to insert the flow table at a frequency of 20 times/cycle. We do not set a threshold for this type of application. OFapp2 and OFapp3 have DEFAULT permissions.

OFapp2 is a normal application, the frequency of using ADD permission is 20 times/cycle. OFapp3 is a malicious application, and the number of inserted flow tables increases linearly with time.

3.2 Performance

This paper compares the proposed scheme with the static threshold scheme of the ControllerDAC and the non-threshold RYU controller by using three indicators: the delay of the security scheme, the number of flow tables stored by the switch and the malicious flow table rate.

Delay of the Security Scheme
We insert flow tables 10 times through the OF application and record the time delay of each access.

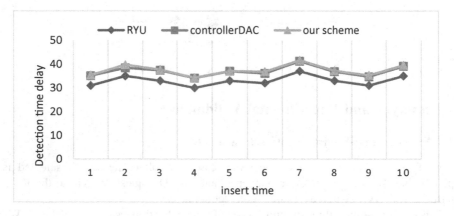

Fig. 4. Comparison of delays of the three schemes

It can be shown in Fig. 4, our scheme is compared to the ControllerDAC scheme, each access delay is within the range 1 ms. Compared to the original RYU controllers, our delay averages approximately 3–4 ms, and the average delay is approximately 10%, the delay is very small, and within the acceptable range. This property is observed because the main algorithm is calculated in another thread. The main thread only needs to obtain the threshold of the flow prediction algorithm to filter the application. Therefore, the impact of our scheme on the access efficiency of the OF applications is negligible.

Number of Flow Tables Stored by the Switch
We used the OF application of Table 2 to perform ADD access operations on the three schemes. We analyzed the number of flow tables existing in the switch, to verify whether our scheme can guarantee the flow of the switch within a safe range. The experimental results are shown in Fig. 5.

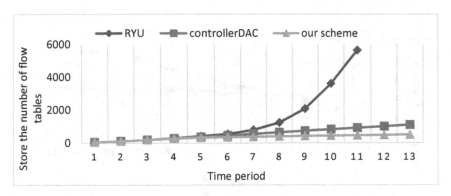

Fig. 5. Comparison of the number of flow entries stored in a switch

From the sixth observation period, our flow table threshold prediction algorithm detected an abnormal access by a malicious application. The number of RYU controller flow tables without any security protection after the next five cycles reached 7,000 and soon reached the limit of the flow table that the controller could tolerate. The DAC scheme has about 1000 flow lists after five cycles, compared with the RYU controller. The number of switches in the flow table is reduced, but it is still grows linearly, therefore over time, it reaches reached the upper limit of the controller. However, in the five cycles of the OF application abuse, the number of flow tables in our scheme has always kept a small amount, and tends to be stable. Therefore, our scheme was the best in protecting the controller when there is a malicious flow table.

The main reason is that in a source RYU controller without any protection, the controller is open to any OF application, so the malicious OF application can freely add the flow table without any control. In the ControllerDAC scheme, the setting for ADD permissions is static, this scheme does not identify malicious applications. All applications are issued according to the limit of 50 flow tables per period. Therefore, malicious flow tables will continue to increase over time and threaten the functionality of the controller. In our scheme, we detect a malicious OF application through the flow table threshold prediction algorithm. Dynamically reducing the threshold to zero prevents malicious flow table access, and effectively controls the number of flow tables in the switch, preventing controller crashes and other issues.

Malicious Flow Table Rate

The malicious flow table rate refers to the ratio of the number of flow tables generated by malicious applications to the total number of switch flows in the flow table stored in the switch. In general, malicious applications use switch resources and affect switch performance. Figure 6 compares the malicious flow table rates.

The formula for calculating the malicious flow rate is as follows:

$$FMFR = D_{af}/D_f \tag{7}$$

FMFR is the flow table match rate, D_{af} is the number of malicious flow tables in each cycle, and D_f is the total number of flows issued by all flow tables.

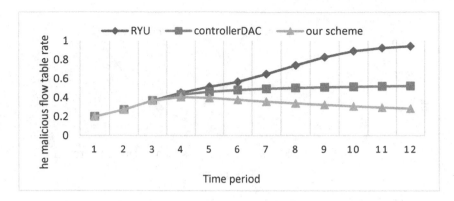

Fig. 6. Malicious flow table rate

It can be seen from Fig. 6 that the rate of malicious flow tables in the RYU controller remains at a notablely high level over time, and at the highest level, the percentage of malicious flow tables is close to 90%. The proportion of malicious flow tables for ControllerDAC reaches 40% to 50%, while the malicious flow table rate for our scheme remains below 40%.

In the RYU scheme, there is no restriction on Ofapp2, and the ControllerDAC scheme cannot distinguish the abnormal OF applications. Therefore, these abnormal flow tables enter the switch through the controller, occupy the switch resources, and threaten the security of the controller. In our scheme, the threshold is adjusted immediately after the abnormality of Ofapp2 is found and prevents insertion of malicious flow tables from being insert. At the same time for normal applications of ADMIN permissions OFapp1 we allow normal insertion of flow rules. Therefore, the malicious flow rate in the switch is effectively reduced.

4   Conclusions

This paper studies the northbound interface and determined that OF applications endanger the controller and network security by abuse ADD permissions. We designed a set of prediction-based dynamic access control schemes through analysis of security issues and comparing previous studies. The experimental results show that our solution evaluates the flow tables of malicious OF applications in a timely manner and implements targeted control based on the security authority. On the basis of guaranteeing efficiency, we can reduce the delivery of malicious flow tables. At the same time, our scheme separates the application layer from the control layer and can be flexibly deployed on most controllers. In the future, we plan to design a security plan for READ, UPDATE, and REMOVE permissions and develop a complete northbound interface security control scheme.

References

1. Scott-Hayward, S., Kane, C., Sezer, S.: Operationcheckpoint: SDN application control. In: Proceedings of the 2014 IEEE 22nd International Conference on Network Protocols, Ser., ICNP 2014, pp. 618–623 (2014)
2. Noh, J., Lee, S., Park, J., et al.: Vulnerabilities of network os and mitigation with state-based permission system. Secur. Commun. Netw. **9**(13): 1971–1982 (2016)
3. Porras, P., Shin, S., Yegneswaran, V., Fong, M., Tyson, M., Gu, G.: A security enforcement kernel for OpenFlow networks. In: Proceedings of the 1st Workshop on Hot Topics in Software Defined Networks, pp. 121–126. ACM, Helsinki (2012)
4. Tseng, Y., Pattaranantakul, M., He, R., Zhang, Z., Nait-Abdesselam, F.: Controller DAC: securing SDN controller with dynamic access control. In: IEEE ICC 2017 Communication and Information System Security Symposium (2107)
5. Alfred, R., Fun, T.S., Tahir, A., et al.: Concepts labeling of document clusters using a hierarchical agglomerative clustering (HAC) technique. In: Uden, L., Wang, L., Corchado Rodríguez, J., Yang, H.C., Ting, I.H. (eds.) The 8th International Conference on Knowledge Management in Organizations, pp. 263–272. Springer, Dordrecht (2013). https://doi.org/10.1007/978-94-007-7287-8_21
6. Porras, P., Cheung, S., Fong, M., Skinner, K., Yegneswaran, V.: Securing the software-defined network control layer. In: Proceedings of the 2105 Annual Network and Distributed System Security Symposium (NDSS 2015), pp. 1–15. Internet Society, San Diego (2015)
7. Banse, C., Rangarajan, S.: A secure northbound interface for SDN applications. In: Proceedings of the 2015 IEEE Trustcom/BigDataSE/ISPA (2015)
8. Tseng, Y., Zhang, Z., Nait-Abdesselam, F.: ControllerSEPA: a security-enhancing SDN controller plug-in for OpenFlow application. In: Proceedings of the 17th International Conference on Parallel and Distributed Computing, Applications and Technologies (2016)
9. ON.Lab: ONOS application permissions. https://wiki.onosproject.org/display/ONOS/ONOS+Application+Permissions
10. Porras, P., Cheung, S., Fong, M., Skinner, K.: Securing the software-defined network control layer. In: Proceedings of the 2015 Network and Distributed System Security Symposium (NDSS), February 2015
11. Benson, T., Akella, A., Maltz, D.A.: Network traffic characteristics of data centers in the wild. In: Proceeding of the 10th ACM SIGCOMM Conference on Internet Measurement, pp. 267–280. ACM (2010)
12. Kreutz, D., Ramos, F.M.V., Veríssimo, P., Rothenberg, C.E., Azodolmolky, S., Uhlig, S.: Software-defined networking: a comprehensive survey. CoRR, vol. abs/1406.0440 (2014). http://arxiv.org/abs/1406.0440

A Single Source Point Detection Algorithm for Underdetermined Blind Source Separation Problem

Yu Zhang[1], Zhaoyue Zhang[2], Hongxu Tao[1], and Yun Lin[1(✉)]

[1] College of Information and Communication Engineering,
Harbin Engineering University, Harbin 150001, China
linyun_phd@hrbeu.edu.cn
[2] College of Air Traffic Management, Civil Aviation University of China,
Tianjin 300300, China

Abstract. To overcome the traditional disadvantages of single source points detection methods in underdetermined blind source separation problem, this paper proposes a novel algorithm to detect single source points for the linear instantaneous mixed model. First, the algorithm utilizes a certain relationship between the time-frequency coefficients and the complex conjugate factors of the observation signal to realize single source points detection. Then, the algorithm finds more time-frequency points that meets the requirements automatically and cluster them by utilizing a clustering algorithm based on the improved potential function. Finally, the estimation of the mixed matrix is achieved by clustering the re-selected single source points. Simulation experiments on linear mixture model demonstrates the efficiency and feasibility for estimating the mixing matrix.

Keywords: Time-frequency domain · Mixing matrix estimation ·
Single source points detection

1 Introduction

Blind source separation (BSS) aims at recovering N source signals from P observation signals without any prior information. So far, research in this field has been widely applied to mechanical equipment fault diagnosis [8], speech signals [7], communication systems [9, 15, 16], etc. Our research is based on the underdetermined case, i.e. the number of source signals is greater than the number of observed signals ($N > P$).

At present, sparse component analysis (SCA) [12] is the most commonly used method to solve the problem of Underdetermined Blind Source Separation (UBSS). SCA usually adopts a two-step method that includes mixing matrix estimation and source signal recovery. The accuracy of the former directly affects the result of the latter, so research on the former is quite meaningful. In this paper, we aim at estimating the mixing matrix. The BSS algorithm based on single source points detection usually has high requirements on the sparsity of signals. In fact, signals have satisfactory sparsity in the time-frequency (TF) domain than in the time domain. Short-time Fourier transform (STFT) [11] is usually used to make signals get better sparsity.

S. Liu and G. Yang (Eds.): ADHIP 2018, LNICST 279, pp. 68–76, 2019.
https://doi.org/10.1007/978-3-030-19086-6_8

Only one source exists or plays a major role in TF domain are called single source points. If the source signal is sparse in the TF domain, then the observed signal will exhibit directional clustering property so that the mixed matrix can be estimated by utilizing the corresponding clustering algorithm. The direction corresponds to one column of the mixed matrix. In other words, the mixing matrix can be estimated if the direction of the single source points is estimated. Many scholars researched different approaches in this field. Some scholars [1, 3, 6, 14] made strategies to search for single source regions and then each element in the mixing matrix is estimated from the region. Some scholars [2–5, 10, 13] proposed various algorithm to realize the detection of single source points and finally the mixing matrix is estimated. This paper proposes a novel algorithm to estimate the mixing matrix based on single source points detection. The algorithm gets satisfactory performance than other algorithms.

This paper is organized as follows. In Sect. 2, we introduce the basic linear instantaneous mixed model and the basic theory of UBSS problem. Section 3 shows the process of our algorithm. We then give the simulation experiment results in Sect. 4 and draw conclusion in Sect. 5.

2   Problem Formulation

The linear instantaneous mixed model of BSS problems in the noiseless case can be expressed as

$$\mathbf{x}(t) = \mathbf{As}(t) = \sum_{m=1}^{M} \mathbf{a}_m s_m(t) \tag{1}$$

Where $M > N$, $\mathbf{x}(t) = [x_1(t), x_2(t), \ldots, x_N(t)]^T$ is the observation signal vector, $\mathbf{A} = [\mathbf{a}_1, \mathbf{a}_2, \ldots, \mathbf{a}_M] \in \mathbb{R}^{N \times M}$ is the mixed matrix, $\mathbf{s}(t) = [s_1(t), s_2(t), \ldots, S_M(t)]^T$ is the source signal vector, $\mathbf{a}_m$ is the mth column of the mixed matrix and $s_m(t)$ is the mth source signal. If only the mth source signal presents at t, Eq. (1) can be simplified as

$$\mathbf{x}(t) = \mathbf{a}_m s_m(t) \tag{2}$$

Under the condition of neglecting the amplitude, estimating the direction of the mixing signal vector also realizes the estimation of the first column vector of the mixed matrix. If the observation signal is sufficiently sparse, then all similar direction vectors can be obtained by clustering and the mixing matrix can be successfully estimated.

In the UBSS method, the necessary assumptions need to be satisfied. On one hand, the mixed matrix should be full column rank, On the other hand, there should be some single source points exists in the TF domain.

3 The Proposed Algorithm

We usually adopt STFT before estimating the mixing matrix to make signal sparser, we can obtain representations of the mixture signals

$$\mathbf{X}(t,f) = \mathbf{AS}(t,f) \tag{3}$$

Where $\mathbf{X}(t,f) = [X_1(t,f), X_2(t,f), \ldots, X_N(t,f)]^T$ and $\mathbf{S}(t,f) = [S_1(t,f), S_2(t,f), \ldots, S_M(t,f)]^T$ are the STFT coefficients of observation signals and source signals, respectively. The paper takes two observation signals and four source signals for example, so Eq. (3) can be written as

$$\begin{bmatrix} X_1(t,f) \\ X_2(t,f) \end{bmatrix} = \begin{bmatrix} a_{11} & a_{12} & \cdots & a_{1M} \\ a_{21} & a_{22} & \cdots & a_{2M} \end{bmatrix} \begin{bmatrix} S_1(t,f) \\ S_2(t,f) \\ \vdots \\ S_M(t,f) \end{bmatrix} \tag{4}$$

Assuming that there only source s_1 occurs at one TF point (t_p, f_p), we can obtain the following two formulas

$$X_1(t_p, f_p) = a_{11}S_1(t_p, f_p) = a_{11}[\text{Re}(S_1(t_p, f_p)) + j\text{Im}(S_1(t_p, f_p))] \tag{5}$$

$$X_2(t_p, f_p) = a_{21}S_1(t_p, f_p) = a_{21}[\text{Re}(S_1(t_p, f_p)) + j\text{Im}(S_1(t_p, f_p))] \tag{6}$$

Based on Eqs. (5) and (6), we have

$$X_1^*(t_p, f_p) = a_{11}\{\text{Re}[S_1(t_p, f_p)] - j\text{Im}[S_1(t_p, f_p)]\} \tag{7}$$

$$X_2^*(t_p, f_p) = a_{21}\{\text{Re}[S_1(t_p, f_p)] - j\text{Im}[S_1(t_p, f_p)]\} \tag{8}$$

where $X_1^*(t_p, f_p)$ and $X_2^*(t_p, f_p)$ are complex conjugates of $X_1(t_p, f_p)$ and $X_2(t_p, f_p)$, respectively. Based on Eqs. (5)–(8), we have

$$
\begin{aligned}
&\frac{X_1(t_p, f_p) X_2^*(t_p, f_p)}{X_2(t_p, f_p) X_1^*(t_p, f_p)} \\
&= \frac{a_{11}a_{21}\left[\text{Re}(S_1(t_p, f_p)) + j\text{Im}(S_1(t_p, f_p))\right]\left[\text{Re}(S_1(t_p, f_p)) - j\text{Im}(S_1(t_p, f_p))\right]}{a_{11}a_{21}\left[\text{Re}(S_1(t_p, f_p)) + j\text{Im}(S_1(t_p, f_p))\right]\left[\text{Re}(S_1(t_p, f_p)) - j\text{Im}(S_1(t_p, f_p))\right]} \\
&= 1
\end{aligned}
\tag{9}
$$

If two signals s_1 and s_2 are assumed to exist at some TF point (t_q, f_q), If we simplify $S_1(t_q, f_q)$ and $S_2(t_q, f_q)$ as S_1 and S_2, $X_1(t_q, f_q)$ and $X_2(t_q, f_q)$ can be simplified as X_1 and X_2

$$X_1 = [a_{11}\text{Re}(S_1) + a_{12}\text{Re}(S_2)] + j[a_{11}\text{Im}(S_1) + a_{12}\text{Im}(S_2)] \tag{10}$$

$$X_2 = [a_{21}\text{Re}(S_1) + a_{22}\text{Re}(S_2)] + j[a_{21}\text{Im}(S_1) + a_{22}\text{Im}(S_2)] \tag{11}$$

Similarly, $X_1^*(t_p, f_p)$ and $X_2^*(t_p, f_p)$ can be defined as

$$X_1^* = [a_{11}\mathrm{Re}(S_1) + a_{12}\mathrm{Re}(S_2)] - j[a_{11}\mathrm{Im}(S_1) + a_{12}\mathrm{Im}(S_2)] \tag{12}$$

$$X_2^* = [a_{21}\mathrm{Re}(S_1) + a_{22}\mathrm{Re}(S_2)] - j[a_{21}\mathrm{Im}(S_1) + a_{22}\mathrm{Im}(S_2)] \tag{13}$$

Based on Eqs. (10)–(13), we can obtain

$$\begin{aligned}
X_1 X_2^* = &[a_{11}\mathrm{Re}(S_1) + a_{12}\mathrm{Re}(S_2)][a_{21}\mathrm{Re}(S_1) + a_{22}\mathrm{Re}(S_2)] \\
&+ [a_{11}\mathrm{Im}(S_1) + a_{12}\mathrm{Im}(S_2)][a_{21}\mathrm{Im}(S_1) + a_{22}\mathrm{Im}(S_2)] \\
&+ j[a_{11}\mathrm{Im}(S_1) + a_{12}\mathrm{Im}(S_2)][a_{21}\mathrm{Re}(S_1) + a_{22}\mathrm{Re}(S_2)] \\
&- j[a_{11}\mathrm{Re}(S_1) + a_{12}\mathrm{Re}(S_2)][a_{21}\mathrm{Im}(S_1) + a_{22}\mathrm{Im}(S_2)]
\end{aligned} \tag{14}$$

$$\begin{aligned}
X_2 X_1^* = &[a_{11}\mathrm{Re}(S_1) + a_{12}\mathrm{Re}(S_2)][a_{21}\mathrm{Re}(S_1) + a_{22}\mathrm{Re}(S_2)] \\
&+ [a_{11}\mathrm{Im}(S_1) + a_{12}\mathrm{Im}(S_2)][a_{21}\mathrm{Im}(S_1) + a_{22}\mathrm{Im}(S_2)] \\
&- j[a_{11}\mathrm{Im}(S_1) + a_{12}\mathrm{Im}(S_2)][a_{21}\mathrm{Re}(S_1) + a_{22}\mathrm{Re}(S_2)] \\
&+ j[a_{11}\mathrm{Re}(S_1) + a_{12}\mathrm{Re}(S_2)][a_{21}\mathrm{Im}(S_1) + a_{22}\mathrm{Im}(S_2)]
\end{aligned} \tag{15}$$

The following two variables are assumed

$$\begin{aligned}
T_1 = &[a_{11}\mathrm{Re}(S_1) + a_{12}\mathrm{Re}(S_2)][a_{21}\mathrm{Re}(S_1) + a_{22}\mathrm{Re}(S_2)] \\
&+ [a_{11}\mathrm{Im}(S_1) + a_{12}\mathrm{Im}(S_2)][a_{21}\mathrm{Im}(S_1) + a_{22}\mathrm{Im}(S_2)]
\end{aligned} \tag{16}$$

$$\begin{aligned}
T_2 = &[a_{11}\mathrm{Re}(S_1) + a_{12}\mathrm{Re}(S_2)][a_{21}\mathrm{Re}(S_1) + a_{22}\mathrm{Re}(S_2)] \\
&- [a_{11}\mathrm{Im}(S_1) + a_{12}\mathrm{Im}(S_2)][a_{21}\mathrm{Im}(S_1) + a_{22}\mathrm{Im}(S_2)]
\end{aligned} \tag{17}$$

Equations (14) and (15) can be simplified as

$$X_1 X_2^* = T_1 + jT_2 \tag{18}$$

$$X_2 X_1^* = T_1 - jT_2 \tag{19}$$

Then, we can obtain

$$\frac{X_1 X_2^*}{X_2 X_1^*} = \frac{T_1 + jT_2}{T_1 - jT_2} = \frac{T_1^2 - T_2^2}{T_1^2 + T_2^2} + j\frac{2T_1 T_2}{T_1^2 + T_2^2} \tag{20}$$

If we want the Eq. (20) is equal to Eq. (9), we can get anyone of the following two conditions through setting T_2 as 0.

$$\frac{a_{11}}{a_{21}} = \frac{a_{12}}{a_{22}} \tag{21}$$

$$\frac{\mathrm{Re}(S_1)}{\mathrm{Re}(S_2)} = \frac{\mathrm{Im}(S_1)}{\mathrm{Im}(S_2)} \tag{22}$$

Given the assumption that the mixing matrix should be full column rank, we don't consider Eq. (21). Therefore, only when Eq. (22) is satisfied can Eq. (20) achieve the same consequence in Eq. (9). However, the probability of this situation is very low. Therefore, we set the following standard to detect single source points.

$$\frac{X_1(t,f)X_2^*(t,f)}{X_2(t,f)X_1^*(t,f)} = 1 \tag{23}$$

In practical applications, this condition is very demanding and difficult to achieve, so the relaxation condition is

$$\left| \mathrm{Re}\left(\frac{X_1(t,f)X_2^*(t,f)}{X_2(t,f)X_1^*(t,f)}\right) - 1 \right| < \varepsilon_1 \tag{24}$$

where ε_1 is a positive number that is close to 0.

After selecting the corresponding single source point, there are still some time-frequency points with low energy, which seriously affects the later estimation result. We set the following rule to remove low energy points to get better performance

$$\frac{\|\mathrm{Re}(\mathbf{X}(t,f))\|}{\max(\|\mathrm{Re}(\mathbf{X}(t,f))\|)} < \varepsilon_3 \tag{25}$$

where ε_3 is a number close to 1.

We cluster these selected points and get corresponding clustering centers through utilizing clustering algorithm. The number of the selected points is K and they are denoted as $(Y_k, Z_k) = (k = 1, 2, \ldots, K)$. Now we define the potential function as follows

$$J(\mathbf{b}_k) = \sum_{i=1}^{T} \{\exp[\beta \cos(\theta_{\mathbf{b}_k \mathbf{b}_i})]\}^\gamma \tag{26}$$

where $\mathbf{b}_k$ and $\mathbf{b}_i$ are single source points, and they are parameters that adjust the degree of attenuation of this function at non-extreme points. The potential function values at different points can be calculated by the above formula, and then a three-dimensional diagram about $\mathbf{b}_{k1}$, $\mathbf{b}_{k2}$ and $J(\mathbf{b}_k)$ is obtained. In this three-dimensional diagram, there are some significant peaks appearing, and the number of peaks is equal to the number of source signals. Assume that the amplitude of each point in the three-dimensional diagram is $P(k)(k = 1, 2, \ldots, K)$. In order to eliminate the interference term, we set the following smoothing function to

$$\hat{P}(k) = P(\mathrm{k})/\max(P(\mathrm{k})) \tag{27}$$

$$p_k = [\hat{P}(k-h) + 2\hat{P}(k-h+1) + \ldots + 2^{h-1}\hat{P}(k-1) + 2^h\hat{P}(k) \\ + 2^{h-1}\hat{P}(k+1) + \ldots + 2\hat{P}(k+h-1) + \hat{P}(k+h)]/(3 \cdot 2^h - 2) \tag{28}$$

where h is an integer that is >1, and p_k is the new peak amplitude. We set the following rule to get the correct peak position.

$$\begin{cases} p_{k-1} < p_k \ \text{and} \ p_{k+1} < p_k \\ p_{k-2} < p_k \ \text{and} \ p_{k+2} < p_k \end{cases} \tag{29}$$

Through this method, the subinterval position $\mathbf{b}_k$ corresponding to the peak and the initial clustering centers $(A_m, B_m) = (m = 1, 2, \ldots, M)$ can be obtained. Single source points close to the initial cluster center can be re-selected through following rules

$$\frac{A_m Y_k + B_m Z_k}{\sqrt{A_m^2 + B_m^2} \sqrt{Y_k^2 + Z_k^2}} > \varepsilon_4 \tag{30}$$

where ε_4 is a threshold between 0 and 1. The mixed matrix can be estimated through these re-selected single source points.

4 Simulation Results and Analysis

We consider four speech signals in [10] to test the practicality of the proposed algorithm. The sampling number is 160000, STFT size is 1024, Overlapping is 512, Weighting function is Hanning Window. $\varepsilon_1 = 0.999$, $\varepsilon_3 = 0.02$, $\varepsilon_4 = 0.997$. The mixed matrix $\mathbf{A}$ is defined as

$$A = \begin{bmatrix} 0.763 & 0.658 & 0.328 & 0.442 \\ 0.313 & 0.360 & 0.766 & 0.540 \end{bmatrix}$$

We consider the scatter plot of two time-domain observation signals under noiseless conditions. We reduce the number of points to reduce the amount of calculation. First, the descending order of the real parts at different frequency points after the time-frequency conversion of the first observation signal is performed in descending order. According to the order of the first observation signals, the order of the second observation signals is adjusted, and the time-frequency observation signals at the frequency points with large variances are selected. In this chapter, the corresponding observation signals at the first 50 points are selected before the single source point is detected. The scatter plot of two observation signals before detecting is shown in Fig. 1.

Figure 1 present obvious linear clustering characteristics, but some stray points affect this property. The existence of spurious points makes direct clustering will produce large estimation errors. At the same time, it can be found that a large number of scatter points are accumulated near the origin. However, the amplitudes of these scatter points are small, and the directions of the straight lines in the scatter plot are far less effective than the scatters far from the origin. We eliminate these points for better performance. The scatter plot of the two observation signals in the TF domain after detecting the single source point and removing the low energy point is shown in Fig. 2.

Figure 2 shows that the linear clustering characteristics of the two observation signals are more obvious. Finally, the mixing matrix is estimated.

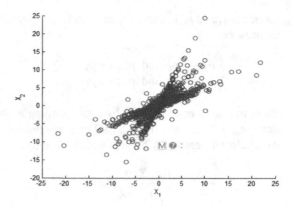

Fig. 1. The scatter plot of two observed signals in TF domain.

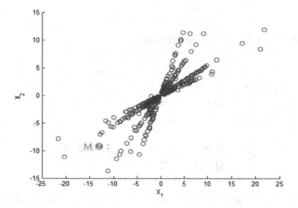

Fig. 2. The scatter plot of the two observation signals in the TF domain after detecting the single source point and removing the low energy point.

$$\hat{\mathbf{A}} = \begin{bmatrix} 0.7628 & 0.6568 & 0.3272 & 0.4407 \\ 0.3087 & 0.3611 & 0.7649 & 0.5405 \end{bmatrix}$$

We take the normalized mean square error (NMSE) to measure the performance of algorithms. It can be written as

$$\text{NMSE} = 10 \log \left[\frac{\sum_{i,j} (\tilde{a}_{i,j} - a_{i,j})^2}{\sum_{i,j} a_{i,j}^2} \right] \text{(dB)} \tag{31}$$

Where a_{ij} is the (i,j)th element of $\mathbf{A}$ and $\hat{a}_{ij}$ is the (i,j)th element of $\hat{\mathbf{A}}$. This parameter gets a lower value when the estimated mixed matrix is more similar to the real mixed matrix.

The result of the different algorithms are shown in Table 1.

Table 1. The NMSE comparison of different algorithms

The TIFROM algorithm	Dong's algorithm	Reju's algorithm	Our algorithm
−45.7654	−50.4102	−48.9157	−55.2361

From Table 1, we can find that our algorithm has lower NMSE, which means a better performance.

5 Conclusion

A novel algorithm is proposed to solve the problem of mixed matrix estimation in UBSS under linear instantaneous mixed model. First, a new method is proposed for detecting single source points. Then, the algorithm clusters them by utilizing a method based on the improved potential function. Finally, the mixing matrix is obtained. The detection algorithm is feasible and efficient, which lays the foundation for post-processing.

Acknowledgment. This work is supported by the National Natural Science Foundation of China (61771154) and the Fundamental Research Funds for the Central Universities (HEUCFG201830).

This paper is also funded by the International Exchange Program of Harbin Engineering University for Innovation-oriented Talents Cultivation.

Meantime, all the authors declare that there is no conflict of interests regarding the publication of this article.

We gratefully thank of very useful discussions of reviewers.

References

1. Abrard, F., Deville, Y.: A time-frequency blind signal separation method applicable to underdetermined mixtures of dependent sources. Sig. Process. **85**(7), 1389–1403 (2005)
2. Aissaelbey, A., et al.: Underdetermined blind separation of nondisjoint sources in the time-frequency domain. IEEE Trans. Sig. Process. **55**(3), 897–907 (2007)
3. Arberet, S., Gribonval, R., Bimbot, F.: A robust method to count and locate audio sources in a stereophonic linear instantaneous mixture. In: Rosca, J., Erdogmus, D., Príncipe, José C., Haykin, S. (eds.) ICA 2006. LNCS, vol. 3889, pp. 536–543. Springer, Heidelberg (2006). https://doi.org/10.1007/11679363_67
4. Dong, T., Lei, Y., Yang, J.: An algorithm for underdetermined mixing matrix estimation. Neurocomputing **104**, 26 (2013)

5. Kim, S.G., Chang, D.Y.: Blind separation of speech and sub-Gaussian signals in underdetermined case. In: INTERSPEECH 2004 - ICSLP, International Conference on Spoken Language Processing, Jeju Island, Korea, October 2004. DBLP (2004)
6. Xie, S., Yang, L., Yang, J.M., et al.: Time-frequency approach to underdetermined blind source separation. IEEE Trans. Neural Netw. Learn. Syst. **23**(2), 306–316 (2012)
7. Pedersen, M.S., Wang, D.L., Larsen, J., et al.: Two-microphone separation of speech mixtures. IEEE Trans. Neural Netw. **19**(3), 475–492 (2008)
8. Poncelet, F., Kerschen, G., Golinval, J.C., et al.: Output-only modal analysis using blind source separation techniques. Mech. Syst. Sig. Process. **21**(6), 2335–2358 (2007)
9. Zhou, J.T., Zhao, H., Peng, X., Fang, M., Qin, Z., Goh, R.S.M.: Transfer hashing: from shallow to deep. IEEE Trans. Neural Netw. Learn. Syst. https://doi.org/10.1109/tnnls.2018.2827036
10. Reju, V.G., Koh, S.N., Soon, I.Y.: An algorithm for mixing matrix estimation in instantaneous blind source separation. Sig. Process. **89**(9), 1762–1773 (2009)
11. Ming, X., Xie, S.L., Yu-Li, F.U.: Underdetermined blind delayed source separation based on single source intervals in frequency domain. Acta Electronica Sinica **35**(12), 2279–2283 (2007)
12. Yu, K., Yang, K., Bai, Y.: Estimation of modal parameters using the sparse component analysis based underdetermined blind source separation. Mech. Syst. Signal Process. **45**(2), 302–316 (2014)
13. Tu, Y., Lin, Y., Wang, J., et al.: Semi-supervised learning with generative adversarial networks on digital signal modulation classification. CMC Comput. Mater. Continua **55**(2), 243–254 (2018)
14. Li, Y., et al.: Underdetermined blind source separation based on sparse representation. IEEE Trans. Signal Process. **54**(2), 423–437 (2006)
15. Zheng, Z., Kumar Sangaiah, A., Wang, T.: Adaptive communication protocols in flying ad-hoc network. IEEE Commun. Mag. **56**(1), 136–142 (2018)
16. Zhao, N., Richard Yu, F., Sun, H., Li, M.: Adaptive power allocation schemes for spectrum sharing in interference-alignment-based cognitive radio networks. IEEE Trans. Veh. Technol. **65**(5), 3700–3714 (2016)

Identification and Elimination of Abnormal Information in Electromagnetic Spectrum Cognition

Haojun Zhao[1], Ruowu Wu[2], Hui Han[2], Xiang Chen[2], Yuyao Li[1], and Yun Lin[1(✉)]

[1] College of Information and Communication Engineering,
Harbin Engineering University, Harbin 150001, China
linyun_phd@hrbeu.edu.cn
[2] State Key Laboratory of Complex Electromagnetic
Environment Effects on Electronics and Information System (CEMEE),
Luoyang 471003, Henan, China

Abstract. The electromagnetic spectrum is an important national strategic resource. Spectrum sensing data falsification (SSDF) is an attack method that destroys cognitive networks and makes them ineffective. Malicious users capture sensory nodes and tamper with data through cyber attacks, and make the cognitive network biased or even completely reversed. In order to eliminate the negative impact caused by abnormal information in spectrum sensing and ensure the desired effect, this thesis starts with the improvement of the performance of cooperative spectrum sensing, and constructs a robust sensing user evaluation reference system. At the same time, considering the dynamic changes of user attributes, the sensory data is identified online. Finally, the attacker identification and elimination algorithm is improved based on the proposed reference system. In addition, this paper verifies the identification performance of the proposed reference system through simulation. The simulation results show that the proposed reference system still maintain a good defense effect even if the proportion of malicious users in the reference is greater than 50%.

Keywords: Cognitive radio · Cooperative spectrum sensing ·
Spectrum sensing data falsification (SSDF) · Bayesian learning

1 Introduction

Secondary users in cognitive radio jointly explore spectrum holes through cooperative spectrum sensing (CSS), thereby effectively utilizing the idle spectrum and reducing the impact on the primary users. This is an effective means to improve spectrum utilization and solve spectrum shortages. However, the emergence of malicious attacks, especially spectrum sensing data falsification, poses a serious threat to cooperative spectrum perception, causing the fusion center to make false perceptions and ultimately undermine the performance of the entire cognitive network [1].

Therefore, spectrum sensing data falsification has received widespread attention, and many researchers have proposed different identification and defense solutions from

© ICST Institute for Computer Sciences, Social Informatics and Telecommunications Engineering 2019
Published by Springer Nature Switzerland AG 2019. All Rights Reserved
S. Liu and G. Yang (Eds.): ADHIP 2018, LNICST 279, pp. 77–88, 2019.
https://doi.org/10.1007/978-3-030-19086-6_9

multiple perspectives. Literature [2] proposed a sensing user anomaly detection scheme based on data mining. The biggest advantage of this scheme is that the Fusion Center (FC) does not need to know the user's prior information in advance, and is closer to our actual life. Literature [3] analyzes the limit performance of cooperative spectrum sensing under Byzantine attack. This method identifies and removes the attacker before data fusion, which is easy to implement and can eliminate malicious users in a short time, but also leads to users. The analysis of dynamic interactions with the fusion center is missing. In order to ensure the stability of spectrum sensing, the literature [4] studied a scheme of trusted node help based on the user's reputation value. When the user's reputation value reaches the set threshold value and thus improves the perceived stability, the user's sentiment information will be uploaded to the Fusion Center for integration. In [5], the authors propose a distributed scheme using spatial correlation and anomaly detection, which is used to receive signal strength between adjacent SUs to detect malicious users in cooperative spectrum sensing. The authors in [6] studied the use of Bayesian methods to deal with methods for secondary user attacks to enhance the robustness of cooperative spectrum sensing. The method uses a statistical attack model, and each malicious node has a certain degree of attack probability.

Based on the methods mentioned in different literatures, this paper studied the robust perceptual user evaluation reference system based on reputation value, and then considering the dynamic change of user attribute, the online identification mechanism is introduced. Finally, the attacker identification and elimination algorithm is improved based on the proposed reference system, which eliminated the impact of abnormal data on the perceived performance under the combined effect.

2   System Model

2.1   Perceptual Process

In order to determine whether the licensed band is occupied by a Primary User (PU), each secondary user (SU) can use an energy detection scheme for sensing. For each secondary user, CSS can often be regard as a binary hypothesis test with the following formula [7]:

$$\begin{cases} H_0 : r(t) = n(t) \\ H_1 : r(t) = h(t)P_0(t) + n(t) \end{cases} \tag{1}$$

The working status of the licensed band can be divided into H_0 and H_1. H_0 indicates that the frequency band operates in an idle state, and H_1 indicates that the frequency band operates in a busy state. $r(t)$ is the received signal strength at time t, $n(t)$ is Gaussian white noise, $P_0(t)$ is the signal transmitted by the primary user, and $h(t)$ is the channel gain of the authorized user to the perceived user.

At the same time, two metrics are introduced, the detection probability P_d and the false alarm probability P_f, λ is the determine threshold.

$$\begin{cases} p_f = P(v_i = 1|H_0) = Q(\dfrac{\lambda - \mu_0}{\sigma_0}) \\[2mm] p_d = P(v_i = 1|H_1) = Q(\dfrac{\lambda - \mu_1}{\sigma_1}) \end{cases} \tag{2}$$

Among them, $\mu_0 = 2U, \sigma_0^2 = 4U, \mu_1 = 2U(\beta+1), \sigma_1^2 = 4U(2\beta+1), \beta$ is the signal to noise ratio received by the SU, $Q(z) = \frac{1}{\sqrt{2\pi}} \int_z^\infty e^{-\frac{x^2}{2}} dx$, which is the complementary cumulative distribution function of the standard normal distribution.

2.2 Perceptual Process

In cooperative spectrum sensing, the local decision result of each secondary user i is represented by the final FC global decision result. Considering the perceptual information of the upload error in the sensing process, the perceptual error probability Pc is introduced here, combined with the formula (2), there are:

$$\begin{cases} p_f' = p_f \cdot (1 - p_c) + (1 - p_f) \cdot p_c \\ p_d' = p_d \cdot (1 - p_c) + (1 - p_d) \cdot p_c \end{cases} \tag{3}$$

In order to better analyze the impact on the sensing network, the attack probability is also introduced into the spectrum falsifying frequency. When the authorized band sensing result is idle, the probability that the malicious user reports as busy is P_a, when the perceived frequency of the authorized band is busy, the probability that a malicious user reports as idle is P_b. The relevant perceptual performance formulas of malicious users after passing SSDF are:

$$\begin{cases} p_f^b = p_f \cdot (1 - p_b) + (1 - p_f) \cdot p_b \\ p_d^b = p_d \cdot (1 - p_a) + (1 - p_d) \cdot p_a \end{cases} \tag{4}$$

Considering the probability of transmission errors in the data reporting process, the false alarm probabilities of the honest and malicious users, and the detection probabilities are as follows.

For honest users, there are:

$$\begin{cases} p_f^H = p_f \cdot (1 - p_e) + (1 - p_f) \cdot p_e \\ p_d^H = p_d \cdot (1 - p_e) + (1 - p_d) \cdot p_e \end{cases} \tag{5}$$

For malicious users, there are:

$$\begin{cases} p_f^B = p_f^b \cdot (1 - p_e) + (1 - p_f^b) \cdot p_e \\ p_d^B = p_d^b \cdot (1 - p_e) + (1 - p_d^b) \cdot p_e \end{cases} \tag{6}$$

3   Robust Perceptual User Evaluation Reference System

3.1   Review of Existing Reference Systems

In order to eliminate the negative impact of abnormal information on the electro-magnetic spectrum, the existing defense reference system can be roughly divided into:

Global decisions as a reference (GDaR) [3, 8]. The final judgment is obtained by data fusion of the reported results of all the sensing nodes. Therefore, after the pro-portion of malicious users is greater than that of the honest users, the reference system will be invalid.

Trusted sensor's reports as a reference (TRaR) [4, 9]. The reference system assumes that some honest user sensors are known to the primary user, and the reported results are approximated by the true spectrum state and used to assess the reported values of other sensors.

3.2   The Proposed Reference System

Based on the limitations of the existing reference system performance, this paper discusses and proposes a robust cognitive user evaluation reference system.

The entire testing process consists mainly of the learning phase and the decision phase. The learning phase consists of a large segment of perceptual time slots in which the reference system will evaluate the perceptual users and update their reputation values cumulatively. Specifically, when the user is perceived as an attacker at a certain moment, the reputation value will be processed by +1. In the subsequent judgment stage, the obtained reputation value is compared with the credit threshold to judge the attribute of the current cognitive user.

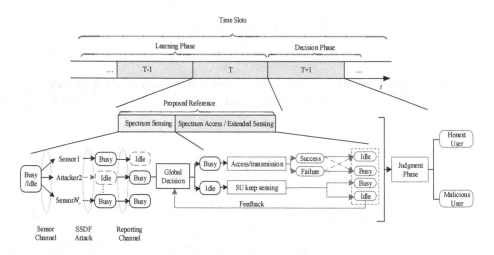

Fig. 1. The cognitive user evaluation reference system

As shown in Fig. 1, the sensing node reports the local sensing result, and the FC makes a decision on the band status according to the result of the fusion. However, due to the limitation of the decision mode, the result of the global decision alone is not reliable and cannot be given. Other perceptual users provide a reference. Therefore, the proposed reference combines the feedback information of the transmission result and the sensing mechanism of the full time slot. Specifically, when the frequency band working state of the global decision is busy, that is, when the global decision result $F = 1$, the SU or the FC continues to perceive, because the sensing performance of the SU itself may greatly increase with the sensing time slot. Increase, so a moderate expansion in time can improve its perceived performance. On the other hand, when the global decision result $F = 0$, that is, when the globally determined band operating state is idle, the SU will access the band to transmit data, and the following two situations often occur: the SU successfully accesses the licensed band, or the SU pair Access to the licensed band failed. In the case, if the SU successfully accesses the frequency band, then the result of the global decision F is correct. Otherwise, the result of the global decision F is wrong.

Obviously, after the SU access grant band transmission, there is an inferred error probability: $P(success|F = 0, H_1)$, that is, the probability of successful transmission when the band status is busy, and the probability $P(failure|F = 0, H_0)$ of failure transmission when the band status is idle.

4   Anomaly Identification Mechanism Based on Bayesian Learning

4.1   Bayesian Batch Learning Algorithm

To make the most of the historical data of spectrum sensing, this chapter first learns the known sample data D_T through the Bayesian batch learning algorithm, and combines the data $\mathbf{u}$ reported by the user in different time slots, realized the state judgment of the current authorized band H through secondary users.

In the cognitive wireless network, every i of the SU corresponds to an attribute w_i. Specifically, the attribute wi takes -1 or 1, 1 represents the user as an honest attribute, and -1 represents the user as a malicious attribute. Each SU has a corresponding weight k_i to measure the reputation. The weight ranged from 0 to 1. We can assume that the initial value of k_i is 0.5. Considering the independent features between samples, the joint probability $p(w)$ can be expressed as a multiplicative form:

$$p(\mathbf{w}) = \prod_i [k_i \delta(w_i - 1) + (1 - k_i)\delta(w_i + 1)] \qquad (7)$$

From the literature [10], the posterior probability of the working state of the predicted licensed band can be expressed as follows:

$$p(H|\mathbf{u}^{T+1}, D_T) = \int p(H|\mathbf{w}, \mathbf{u}^{T+1})p(\mathbf{w}|D_T)d\mathbf{w} \qquad (8)$$

The Bayesian predicted H is:

$$H^{Bayes}(\mathbf{u}^{T+1}, D_T) = \mathrm{U}\left(\int \mathrm{U}(\mathbf{w} \cdot \mathbf{u}^{T+1}) p(\mathbf{w}|D_T) d\mathbf{w}\right) \tag{9}$$

4.2   Bayesian Online Learning Algorithm

Consider a more general and practical way of attack. User attributes are no longer fixed, but exhibit time-varying. At this point, the perceived user's performance in the historical phase is quite different from the real-time spectrum sensing result. In response to this situation, this section proposes an online algorithm based on Bayesian principle (Fig. 2).

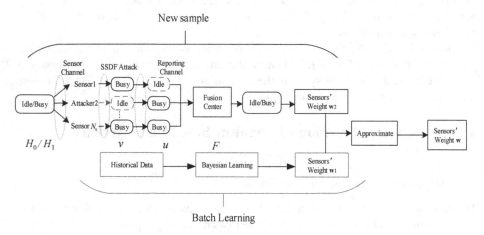

Fig. 2. Bayesian online learning identification mechanism

In general, the online learning model combines real-time learning of current perceptual data on the basis of a batch learning reference system based on Bayes theorem. In the batch learning phase, the Bayesian learning method is used to train the historical data of the cognitive users. Through the continuous iteration of the data to optimize the distribution $p(\mathbf{w})$ of the network parameters $\mathbf{w}$, the user can be found in the system. The weight value w_1. Then, for the current perceptual data, the user is assigned a weight value w_2 through the analysis processing of the system. The weight w_1 and the weight w_2 value are comprehensively processed, and finally the perceived weight of the user w is obtained.

The main idea of Bayesian online learning is to combine the results obtained from historical data with the results obtained from current data, and finally come to new conclusions. The advantage of such a process is that the historical data and the current data are taken into account first, so that the conclusions obtained are more reasonable; in addition, it is more in line with the actual situation, and the data is processed dynamically.

After observing the perceptual data $(F^{T+1}, \mathbf{u}^{T+1})$, the new observations are updated with the formula (8), and the online posterior probability after adding new data samples by the Bayesian criterion is [11]:

$$p(\mathbf{w}|D_T, (F^{T+1}, \mathbf{u}^{T+1})) \frac{p(F^{T+1}|\mathbf{w}, \mathbf{u}^{T+1})p(\mathbf{w}|D_T)}{\int p(\mathbf{w}|D_T)p(F^{T+1}|\mathbf{w}, \mathbf{u}^{T+1})d\mathbf{w}} \qquad (10)$$

5 Abnormal Data Elimination Based on Proposed Reference System

5.1 Identification of Abnormal Data

As can be seen from Fig. 3, the reference system will evaluate the sensing nodes in each time slot, and update their reputation values cumulatively, and distinguish between honest data and malicious data according to the last obtained reputation value. Each sensing node is assigned a measured reputation worth indicator, indicating the number of times the final decision A of the reference system in the T-slot is inconsistent with the reported result u of the node i. The reputation value n_i of the perceived node can be shown as:

$$n_i = \sum_{t=1}^{T} I_{(F[t] \neq u_0[t])} \qquad (11)$$

Where I is an indication function, it can be found that the higher the reputation value of the sensing node, the more likely the uploaded sensing data is not adopted by the fusion center. Comparing the reputation value of the node n_i with the set threshold η, finally we can identify the abnormal user or abnormal data:

$$\begin{cases} n_i > \eta, & \text{attacker} \\ n_i < \eta, & \text{honest sensor} \end{cases} \qquad (12)$$

5.2 Elimination of Abnormal Data

In order to measure the elimination of the anomaly data by the reference system, two indicators P_B^{iso} and P_H^{iso} are proposed here to measure the recognition and elimination of malicious users by the system. P_H^{iso} indicates the probability that an honest user is misjudged as a malicious user by the reference system after T time slots and is removed from the fusion center [3]:

$$P_H^{iso} = P(n_i > \eta) = \sum_{j=\eta+1}^{T} \binom{T}{j} P_H^j (1 - P_H)^{T-j} \qquad (13)$$

And P_B^{iso} represents the probability that the malicious user is identified and eliminated by the reference after T time slots:

$$P_B^{iso} = P(n_i > \eta) = \sum_{j=\eta+1}^{T} \binom{T}{j} P_B^j (1 - P_B)^{T-j} \tag{14}$$

P_B and P_H indicate the probability that the perceived data reported by the malicious user and the honest user are different from the FC decision results. In the eliminating process, the reputation value is used to identify the malicious attack user. By sensing the n_i comparison with the threshold η, and then the sensory node whose reputation value is greater than the threshold is judged as a malicious node, the reported data can be regarded as abnormal data. It is then removed from the cooperative spectrum perception.

5.3   Threshold and Efficient Purification Standards

For the threshold η in the proposed reference, the selection of η plays an important role in whether the system can efficiently complete data purification. If the threshold is low, some honest nodes will be mistakenly judged as malicious users, thus eliminating normal data. Conversely, if the threshold is set higher, it will make it difficult for a malicious user to be identified, and eventually the elimination of the abnormal information cannot be completed. Mathematically, optimization tries to satisfy the following effects:

$$\max_{\eta}(P_B^{iso} - P_H^{iso}) \tag{15}$$

For the above problems, the optimal threshold obtained after optimization are as follows:

$$\eta_{opt} = \left\lceil T \frac{\ln\left(\frac{1-P_H}{1-P_B}\right)}{\ln\left(\frac{P_B(1-P_H)}{P_H(1-P_B)}\right)} \right\rceil \tag{16}$$

Among them, this $\lceil \cdot \rceil$ represents the rounding function, and the threshold is rounded up. A detailed derivation of the formula can be found in [11–13].

6   Performance Analysis

6.1   Simulation Parameter Settings

In the simulation, 100 cognitive nodes are set to participate in the process of cooperative spectrum sensing. The probability that the authorized band works in the busy state is set to 0.2, $P_f^H = 0.2$, $P_d^H = 0.8$, $pb = P_{mal} = 1$. The simulation results took the average of 2000 trials. In order to reflect the superior performance of the proposed scheme, it is compared here with the Global decisions as a reference (GDaR) [14].

6.2   Analysis of Results

Figure 3 shows the change in the weight value and sensing node attributes with the time slot. It can be concluded that as the user attributes change, the proportion of users in data fusion changes accordingly. Since the properties of the sensing node oscillate between 1 and −1, the weights also increase or decrease dynamically. When the user presents a malicious attribute at a certain stage, the proportion of the data fusion is reduced. Conversely, if the user presents an honest attribute at the next moment, the proportion of the data fusion will increase. From the results, online learning has better adaptability to the situation when the user attribute changes dynamically. The changes presented by the perceived data can be processed in real time, and the system as a whole maintains excellent performance.

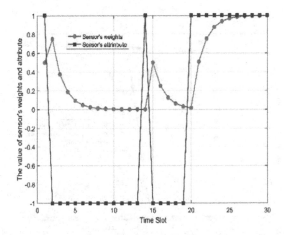

Fig. 3. The weight value and attribute of the sensory node change with the time slot

Figure 4 shows a comparison of false alarm probability and detection probability with Bayesian online learning and batch learning. Obviously, the performance of Bayesian online learning is further improved with the increase of time slots, and the overall performance of Bayesian batch learning is further reduced. From the perspective of false alarm probability, the performance of online learning algorithms is always better than the performance of batch learning. From the detection probability, with the increase of time slot, the performance of Bayesian batch learning algorithm decreases, and the performance of online learning seems better, and finally approaches 1 near. It can be seen that online learning has better adaptability to the situation when the user attribute changes dynamically, which reflects its reliability and feasibility.

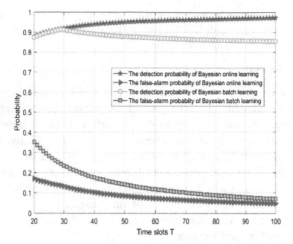

Fig. 4. Bayesian online learning and batch learning P_d and P_f changes with time slot T

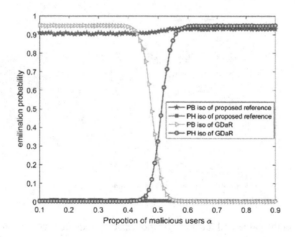

Fig. 5. Changes of P_B^{iso} and P_H^{iso} with attack users proportion α in two reference systems

Figure 5 shows the probability of a malicious user and an honest user being identified and eliminated in two references with the change of malicious users proportion α as follows. It can be found that the proportion α has little effect on the proposed reference system, and it always maintaining excellent performance. In contrast, with the increase of α, the performance of GDaR began to become unstable, especially when α is greater than 0.4, the GDaR reference system is reversed, and when it is greater than 0.5, the GDaR reference system is completely ineffective. This result shows the robustness of the proposed reference.

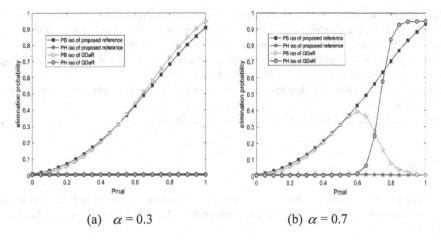

(a) $\alpha = 0.3$ (b) $\alpha = 0.7$

Fig. 6. Changes in two references and with the attack probability P_{mal}

Figure 6 shows the probability of malicious users and honest users being identified and eliminated under two references with the malicious attack probability P_{mal}. Figure 6(a) is a simulation when $\alpha = 0.3$. It can be seen that when the number of attackers is low, both reference systems maintain a relatively stable state. As the attack probability P_{mal} increases, the probability of the honest users elimination is close to 0, and the malicious user is identified and the probability of elimination is constantly rising. When $\alpha = 0.7$, it can be concluded from Fig. 6(b) that the elimination performance of the reference is basically the same as that at 0.3, which is stable and effective. However, the performance of GDaR increases with the probability of attack P_{mal}. The probability of elimination of honest users increases first and then increases. The probability of elimination of malicious users is the same as that of the reference system, and then gradually decreases to zero. In summary, the GDaR reference system exhibits similar performance to the proposed reference at $\alpha > 0.5$, with performance deteriorating at $\alpha > 0.5$, and the proposed reference is still stable.

7 Conclusion

This paper focuses on SSDF attacks in cooperative spectrum sensing, studied the robust perceptual user evaluation reference system based on reputation value, then introduced the online identification mechanism considering the dynamic change of user attribute. At last this paper improved the attacker identification and elimination algorithm based on the proposed reference. The simulation results verify the validity and robustness of the proposed reference system, and complete the online identification mechanism for dynamic users, which eliminates the influence of abnormal information on the reference system under the comprehensive effect.

Acknowledgment. This work is supported by the National Natural Science Foundation of China (61771154), the Fundamental Research Funds for the Central Universities (HEUCFG20 1830), and the funding of State Key Laboratory of CEMEE (CEMEE2018K0104A).

This paper is also funded by the International Exchange Program of Harbin Engineering University for Innovation-oriented Talents Cultivation.

Meantime, all the authors declare that there is no conflict of interests regarding the publication of this article.

We gratefully thank of very useful discussions of reviewers.

References

1. Benjamin, R.: Security considerations in communications systems and networks. In: Communications Speech & Vision IEEE Proceedings I, vol. 137, no. 2, pp. 61–72, April 1990
2. Li, H., Han, Z.: Catch me if you can: an abnormality detection approach for collaborative spectrum sensing in cognitive radio networks. IEEE Trans. Wirel. Commun. **9**(11), 3554–3565 (2010)
3. Rawat, S., Anand, P., Chen, H., et al.: Collaborative spectrum sensing in the presence of byzantine attacks in cognitive radio networks. IEEE Trans. Signal Process. **59**(2), 774–786 (2011)
4. Zeng, K., Paweczak, P., Cabri, D.: Reputation-based cooperative spectrum sensing with trusted nodes assistance. IEEE Commun. Lett. **14**(3), 226–228 (2010)
5. Chen, C., Song, M., Xin, C., et al.: A robust malicious user detection scheme in cooperative spectrum sensing. In: Proceedings of the IEEE Global Telecommunication Conference, pp. 4856–4861 (2012)
6. Penna, F., Sun, Y., Dolecek, L., et al.: Detecting and counteracting statistical attacks in cooperative spectrum sensing. IEEE Trans. Signal Process. **60**(4), 1806–1822 (2012)
7. Urkowitz, H.: Energy detection of unknown deterministic signals. Proc. IEEE **55**(4), 523–531 (1967)
8. Chen, R., Park, J.M., Bian, K.: Robust distributed spectrum sensing in cognitive radio networks. In: INFOCOM 2008, Phoenix, AZ, 13–18 April 2008
9. He, X., Dai, H., Ning, P.: A byzantine attack defender in cognitive radio networks: the conditional frequency check. IEEE Trans. Wirel. Commun. **12**(5), 2512–2523 (2013)
10. Solla, S.A., Winther, O.: Optimal perceptron learning: an on-line Bayesian approach. In: Saad, D. (ed.) On-Line Learning in Neural Networks, pp. 379–398. Cambridge University Press, Cambridge (1998)
11. Noh, G., Lim, S., Lee, S., et al.: Goodness-of-fit-based malicious user detection in cooperative spectrum sensing. In: Proceedings of the 76th IEEE Vehicular Technology Conference, pp. 1–5 (2012)
12. Althunibat, S., Denise, B.J., Granelli, F.: Identification and punishment policies for spectrum sensing data falsification attackers using delivery-based assessment. IEEE Trans. Veh. Technol. **65**(9), 7308–7321 (2016)
13. Zhao, Y., Song, M., Xin, C.: A weighted cooperative spectrum sensing framework for infrastructure-based cognitive radio networks. Comput. Commun. **2011**(34), 1510–1517 (2011)
14. Jo, M., Han, L., Kim, D.: Selfish attacks and detection in cognitive radio ad-hoc networks. IEEE Network **27**(3), 46–50 (2013)

Design and Implementation of Pedestrian Detection System

Hengfeng Fu[1], Zhaoyue Zhang[2], Yongfei Zhang[1], and Yun Lin[1(✉)]

[1] College of Information and Communication Engineering,
Harbin Engineering University, Harbin 150001, China
linyun_phd@hrbeu.edu.cn
[2] College of Air Traffic Management,
Civil Aviation University of China, Tianjin 300300, China

Abstract. With the popularization of self-driving cars and the rapid development of intelligent transportation, pedestrian detection shows more and more extensive application scenarios in daily life, which have higher and higher application values. It also raises more and more interest from academic community. Pedestrian detection is fundamental in many human-oriented tasks, including trajectory tracking of people, recognition of pedestrian gait, and autopilot recognition of pedestrians to take appropriate response measures. In this context, this paper studies the design and implementation of a pedestrian detection system. The pedestrian detection system of this article is mainly composed of two parts. The first part is a pedestrian detector based on deep learning, and the second part is a graphical interface that interacts with the user. The former part mainly uses the Faster R-RCNN learning model, which can use convolutional neural networks to learn features from the data and extract the features of the image. It can also search the image through RPN network for areas where the target is located and then classify them. In this paper, a complete pedestrian detection system is implemented on the basis of deep learning framework Caffe. Experiments show that the system has high recognition rate and fast recognition speed in real world.

Keywords: Pedestrian detection · Faster RCNN · Target detection · Deep learning

1 Introduction

In recent years, pedestrian detection has gradually become a research hotspot due to its wide application scenarios and its fundamental role in computer vision tasks. Pedestrians are ubiquitous in our images and videos, such as photos, entertainment videos, sports broadcasts, and video surveillance and authentication systems. Because of this, pedestrian recognition is the key step when automatically understanding media content.

The usage of pedestrian detection have great application value, and can play an auxiliary role in many human-oriented tasks, such as analysis of population flow, trajectory tracking of characters, and pedestrian gait recognition. In addition, the pedestrian detection system is also an important part of the safety system of autonomous vehicles. Therefore, the pedestrian detection system is also an integral part of

S. Liu and G. Yang (Eds.): ADHIP 2018, LNICST 279, pp. 89–98, 2019.
https://doi.org/10.1007/978-3-030-19086-6_10

many other human-related studies, and the improvement in pedestrian detection performance may greatly contribute to the improvement of other system performance. Although pedestrian testing has been extensively studied so far, recent research can still achieve significant improvements on the basis of the previous ones, indicating that the bottleneck of pedestrian detection has not been achieved, and the pedestrian detection system still has room for improvement.

In the process of recognizing pedestrians, the variety of postures is one of the main challenges of human recognition and other object recognition. The features of pedestrians that need to be classified will change with the change of posture. The appearance of the same object will change dramatically with different postures and perspectives, which is a big challenge to the identification.

There are many ways to solve pedestrian problems. These approaches often come down to the branch of machine learning, which uses machine learning to solve pedestrian detection problems. There are many ways to use manually selected features, such as HOG features [1]. But there are also low-level features that are randomly generated, such as the Haar feature [2]. These features are applied when training to determine whether it is a pedestrian's Feller model. There are also methods such as Adaboost [3] that combine to form a strong classifier by combining multiple simple classifiers. In addition to the above methods, an important processing method is to let the classifier learn the features. For example, CNN [4] used in this paper belongs to this classifier.

These factors make the design and implementation of pedestrian detection systems important. Finding the right method to construct a pedestrian detection system is the main content of this paper.

2   Related Works

At present, pedestrian testing has achieved a lot of research results. In 2012, Dollar et al. [5] reviewed pedestrian detection and compared the best pedestrian detection methods in recent years. In 2014, Benenson et al. [6] in the field of pedestrian detection, more than 40 methods were compared on the Caltech dataset; in 2015, Hosang et al. [7] studied the application of convolutional neural networks to pedestrian detection. In 2016, Zhang et al. [8] analyses the state-of-the-arts methods and address the localization errors and background/foreground discrimination.

HOG was presented by Dalal and Triggs at the 2005 CVPR meeting. HOG stands for Histogram of Oriented Gradient. In essence, HOG is a "feature descriptor." The feature descriptor has the following features. When the same type of object is observed under different conditions and different environments, for example, objects belonging to the pedestrian category, the obtained feature descriptors are also nearly the same. The HOG feature has several advantages over the previous feature for pedestrian detection: First, since the gradient direction histogram is operated on the local square cell of the image, it makes both the geometric and optical deformation of the image. And it can maintain good invariance, because these two deformations will only appear in the larger space of the same space; secondly, under the conditions of coarse spatial sampling, fine direction sampling and strong local optical normalization, As long as the pedestrian is generally able to maintain an upright posture, the pedestrian can be allowed to have some subtle body movements, and these subtle movements can be ignored without affecting the detection effect. Therefore, the gradient direction histogram is particularly suitable for human detection in images. Although a large number of pedestrian detection algorithms have been generated from the introduction of gradient histograms to the present, many algorithms have been improved based on gradient direction histograms.

At present, the mainstream deep-based learning target detection algorithms fall into two categories: one is the region-based target detection algorithm based on Faster RCNN [9], which generates candidate target regions, and classifies the regions for detection, such as: Faster RCNN, R-FCN [10] and so on. The advantage of this type of algorithm is that the detection accuracy is high, and the disadvantage is that the speed is slow. The other type is to convert the target detection into a regression problem solution represented by YOLO (You only look once), and input the original image to directly output the position and category of the object, such as: YOLO [11], SSD [12] and so on. The advantage of this type of method is that the detection speed is fast, and the detection of several tens of frames per second can be achieved, but the detection accuracy is low, and the detection for small targets is not sensitive.

This paper introduces the Faster R-CNN general target detection algorithm into the complex scene of pedestrian detection.

3 Pedestrian Detection System Design

3.1 Regional Proposal

In the Faster RCNN model, the regional proposal is completed by the RPN Regional Proposal Network. Specifically, RPN has two kinds of prediction tasks, namely binary classification and bounding box regression adjustment. In order to train in the practical application of the pedestrian detection system, the proposed anchor frame must be divided into two different categories. The first category is the anchor box with the bounding box IoU > 0.5 marked with a target, which can be seen as "foreground". Conversely, anchor frames that do not overlap with a bounding box or have an IoU value of less than 0.1 can be considered a "background." In order to maintain the normal foreground and background anchor frame ratio, the system samples the randomly generated anchor frame. Then, to measure the performance of the regional proposal, the RPN network will use the binary cross entropy to calculate the classification loss.

To avoid calculating meaningless backgrounds into regression losses, the system selects those anchor boxes that are marked as foreground. To calculate the regression loss. To calculate the target of the regression, we use the candidate region labeled as the foreground, and calculate the offset between the anchor box and the bounding box of the label compared to the bounding box of the label. The error L1 uses a smooth L1 loss function. The loss function is as follows:

$$smooth_{L_1}(x) = \begin{cases} 0.5x^2 & 3 \\ |x| - 0.5 & 2 \end{cases} \tag{1}$$

It's because the smooth L1 loss function decreases rapidly when the anchor frame and the bounding box are close, whereas the normal L1 loss function or the L2 loss function does not.

Due to many reasons such as the difference in image size and anchor frame size or aspect ratio, the number and position of anchor frames generated by RPN vary greatly during training. This has led to sometimes a relatively large change in the relative scale between the anchor frame of the background and the anchor frame considered to be foreground during training, and it is difficult to balance. In extreme cases, you may not even get any anchor frames that are considered foreground. In order to be able to learn at all times, a compromise method is adopted. This method sorts the anchor frames generated by the RPN according to the degree of coincidence with the bounding box of the label, and selects the box with the highest degree of coincidence as the foreground anchor box. Loss calculation. But this is not always possible.

3.2   IoU

The overlap ratio is defined by IoU (intersection over union). This indicator is used to calculate the coincidence of the border area of the label with the actual border area. It can be used to evaluate whether the bounding box matches the expectation. On a specific image, it can be used to measure the accuracy of the upper detection system. The calculation formula is as shown in the Eq. (2)

$$ \text{IoU} = \frac{S_I}{S_U} \tag{2} $$

The numerator is the area of the overlapping part in the bounding box of the two sides, and the denominator does not occupy the area shared by the two bounding boxes. From the perspective of the set theory, the former is the intersection of the set of pixels in the corresponding border, and the latter is the union. This is also the origin of the IoU name.

Predicting class labels are common in classic machine learning tasks, especially in categorical tasks. The result of the entire model operation is to output a two-category label, or a correct label that represents yes or no. The accuracy of the calculation of this type of two-category label is easy to understand. There are only two possibilities. When it comes to object detection tasks, the output is not that simple. In a real-world environment, the coordinates of the bounding box predicted by the detector may almost exactly match the pre-labeled coordinates representing the correct bounding box. The parameters of the detector model (image pyramid scale, sliding window size, feature extraction method, etc.) are different, and the perfect match between the predicted bounding box and the real bounding box is completely impractical. Because of this, to measure the accuracy of the bounding box, the definition of an evaluation metric is needed that rewards the bounding bounds of the predictions that overlap much with the bounding box of the label. This indicator is such that the predicted bounding box that is highly overlapping the labeled bounding box scores higher than the overlapping bounding bounding box, not the other way around. This is why IoU is an excellent indicator of the performance of a target detector. In summary, in pedestrian detection, the coordinates of the detector output are not required to match exactly with the label box, but should ensure that the bounding box predicted by the detector matches as much as possible.

3.3 Non-maximum Suppression

There are many detectors that have a three-step inspection process. The first is to search in the possible target area space based on the input image to generate a set of interest areas. The second step is to score the region of interest using a classifier or a regression. And the final step merges windows that may belong to the same object. This last step is often referred to as "non-maximum suppression". A common implementation of NMS is a simple selection of candidate boxes that are larger than a certain predefined IoU threshold, and because they may cover the same object, the candidate blocks with lower confidence levels are reduced. This algorithm is fast and simple and has significant advantages in removing redundancy.

Although the NMS process does not seem complicated, choosing a suitable IoU threshold is not straightforward for a variety of complex scenarios. When this threshold is too low, it is easy to erroneously discard many of the offer areas. The threshold of the key is set too high, and in the detection result, it is easy to obtain an offer that is too much for the same target detection area. The empirical value usually used is 0.6.

In some scenes where pedestrians are highly concentrated, such as crowded subways, mall exits, movie theater exits, etc., the threshold should be appropriately reduced. However, in the case where the target is too close, the NMS will definitely reduce the accuracy of the pedestrian detection system.

3.4 Training

It's a non-convex problem to optimizing the weight of neural networks. Therefore, in actual training, random gradient descent (SGD) or similar derivative methods such as momentum method and Nesterov's acceleration gradient (NAG) are generally used. In the gradient descent method, it is necessary to determine the learning parameters such as learning rate, weight decay and momentum. The learning rate determines the speed of weight update, and the high learning rate makes it easy for the search program to skip the optimal value. Too small will slow down the speed. Some adaptive methods are used because adjusting parameters manually requires constant modification of the learning rate.

Momentum is derived from Newton's law. The basic idea is to find the optimal "inertia" effect. When there is a flat region in the error surface, SGD can learn faster. For a certain weight, there is a formula like Eq. (3):

$$\omega_i \leftarrow \gamma \cdot \omega_i - \eta \frac{\partial E}{\partial \omega_i} \tag{3}$$

If the direction of last momentum is the same as the negative gradient direction of this time, then the magnitude of this decline will increase, so this can achieve the process of accelerating convergence.

Weight attenuation means that in practice, in order to avoid over-fitting of the network, some regular terms must be added to the cost function. For example, adding this regular term in SGD normalizes this cost function, and has a formula for a certain weight. As shown in Eq. (4):

$$\omega_i \leftarrow \omega_i - \eta \frac{\partial E}{\partial \omega_i} - \eta \lambda \omega_i \tag{4}$$

The purpose of this formula is to reduce the impact of unimportant parameters on the final result, and the useful weights in the network will not be affected by the weight decay. In machine learning or pattern recognition, over-fitting occurs, and when the network gradually over-fitting, the weight of the network gradually becomes larger. Therefore, in order to avoid over-fitting, a penalty term is added to the error function. The penalty term is the square of the weight of the property multiplied by the sum of the decay constants. It is used to punish large weights.

To perform training, we must determine the parameters for the solver of Caffe, Eq. (5) shows the weight update formula in this paper.

$$\begin{cases} v_{i+1} = 0.9v_i - 0.0005\epsilon\omega_i - \epsilon E \left[\frac{\partial L}{\partial \omega} |_{\omega_i} \right] \\ \omega_{i+1} = \omega_i + v_{i+1} \end{cases} \tag{5}$$

In the network implementation part, we chose the mainstream deep learning framework Caffe as an experimental platform. According to the current standard strategy based on the deep learning target detection method, the pre-trained model initialization training network is selected on the ImageNet classification task. The ZFNet convolutional neural network pre-trained by ImageNet classification is used to initialize the weight of the feature extraction network convolution layer. The entire network training process uses SGD back propagation to optimize the entire network model. The learning rate is 0.01, the momentum is 0.9, the weight decay is 0.0005, the learning rate is attenuated every 50,000 iterations, the attenuation factor is 0.1, and a total of 100,000 iterations are performed.

We train the network in this paper with data set comes from VOC2007, the entire data train set contains 5001 images. And we choose 200 pictures from internet as the test set, The image size is various and the pedestrians are in various scales.

The equipment used in the experiment was Ubuntu 16.04 operation system and GeForce GTX 765M graphic card.

4   Experiments

According to the parameter setting in the previous chapter, the learning rate is 0.01, the momentum is set to 0.9, and the weight decay is set to 0.005. The trained model is tested on the test set, and the detection in each picture is counted. And Table 1 show all the statistical data such as the number of pedestrians in the test set, the number of pedestrians detected, the number of pedestrians missed. And the accuracy, miss rate, and false alarm rate are calculated. The table is shown in Table 1.

Table 1. Pedestrian detection system detection result

Total	Detected	Undetected	Error-detected	Recall	Miss rate	False alarm rate
221	218	3	19	98.63%	1.36%	8.01%

As can be seen from Table 1, there are 221 pedestrians in the test set which includes 200 pictures. The pedestrian detection system detects 218 pedestrians among them, and 3 pedestrians are not detected, and the number of pedestrians detected incorrectly is 19. The calculated results show that the detection accuracy of the pedestrian detection system is 98.63%, the detection failure rate is 1.37%, and the false alarm rate is 8.01%.

4.1 Influence of Color on Pedestrian Detection System

In the pedestrian detection system, the device that collects the images may be able to acquire RGB image, but it can only acquire grayscale images too. In order to study the effect of color on the performance of the pedestrian detection system, the sample image is first converted into a grayscale image. Then, the number of pedestrians detected, the number of pedestrians detected, the number of pedestrians missed, and the relevant parameters are calculated. The results are shown in Table 2.

Table 2. Comparison of detection result on RGB image and grayscale image

Image	Total	Detected	Undetected	Error-detected	Recall	Miss rate	False alarm rate
RGB	221	218	3	19	98.63%	1.36%	8.01%
Grayscale	221	214	7	42	96.83%	3.17%	16.41%

Fig. 1. Detection result of the grayscale image

From the comparison of the RGB image and the grayscale image, it can be seen that after losing the color information, the detection accuracy is reduced, and the false alarm rate is increased. The reason can be inferred from the following figures, Figs. 1 and 2:

Fig. 2. Detection result of the RGB image (Color figure online)

As can be seen from Fig. 1, pedestrians walking on snowy days are grayed out because it is snowing. Therefore, the blue down jacket and pink skirt worn by pedestrians are very contrasting with the background. Comparing the Fig. 2, we can find that there is no color information in the grayscale image Fig. 1, and it can seen from the Fig. 1 that the gray color of the pedestrian lower body is similar to the gray background of the green belt, the upper body and the background of the trees, and the edge is blurred. The above reasons have led to a decline in the performance of pedestrian detection systems.

4.2   The Effect of Image Compression Quality on Pedestrian Detection System

In order to study the effect of image compression quality on the quality of pedestrian detection system, we re-compress the sample image by 80%, 60%, 40%, 20%, 10% quality parameters, and input the model for detection and statistics. The number of pedestrians present, the number of pedestrians detected, the number of pedestrians missed, and the relevant parameters were calculated. The results are shown in Table 3.

Table 3. Comparison of detection results of different compression quality downlink detection systems

JPEG quality factor	Total	Detected	Undetected	Error-detected	Recall	Miss rate	False alarm rate
100%	218	3	19	98.63%	1.38%	8.01%	8.01%
80%	218	3	19	98.63%	1.38%	8.01%	8.01%
60%	215	6	20	97.28%	2.71%	8.51%	8.51%
40%	215	6	20	97.28%	2.71%	8.51%	8.51%
20%	214	7	64	96.83%	3.17%	23.02%	23.02%
10%	210	11	142	95.02%	4.98%	40.34%	40.34%

It can be seen that although the image compression is very serious, the image detection accuracy remains high, showing the considerable stability of the detection algorithm. When the compression exceeds a certain threshold, it is 20% in this test set, and the detection false alarm rate will increase rapidly. This reminds us that the image quality should be kept at a reasonable level during pedestrian detection.

5 Conclusion

The pedestrian detection system in this paper has good stability for the pedestrians and achieve a detection rate of more than 95% and a false alarm rate and false alarm rate of less than 10%. At the same time, through experimental analysis, the system still has a good detection rate for grayscale images and low quality images, and has certain anti-interference ability, but the system still has room for improvement. Under the condition of using GPU acceleration, it takes 0.3 s–0.5 s per image for detecting in the detection process of the system. In the real world, the speed cannot meet the needs of real-time detection.

Acknowledgment. This paper is funded by the International Exchange Program of Harbin Engineering University for Innovation-oriented Talents Cultivation.

Meantime, all the authors declare that there is no conflict of interests regarding the publication of this article.

We gratefully thank of very useful discussions of reviewers.

References

1. Dalal, N., Triggs, B.: Histograms of oriented gradients for human detection. In: IEEE Computer Society Conference on Computer Vision and Pattern Recognition, CVPR 2005, vol. 1, pp. 886–893. IEEE (2005)
2. Viola, P., Jones, M.: Rapid object detection using a boosted cascade of simple features. In: Proceedings of the 2001 IEEE Computer Society Conference on Computer Vision and Pattern Recognition, CVPR 2001, vol. 1, p. I. IEEE (2001)
3. Hubel, D.H., Wiesel, T.N.: Receptive fields and functional architecture of monkey striate cortex. J. Physiol. **195**(1), 215–243 (1968)
4. Viola, P., Jones, M.J.: Robust real-time face detection. Int. J. Comput. Vis. **57**(2), 137–154 (2004)
5. Dollar, P., Wojek, C., Schiele, B., Perona, P.: Pedestrian detection: an evaluation of the state of the art. IEEE Trans. Pattern Anal. Mach. Intell. **34**(4), 743–761 (2012)
6. Benenson, R., Omran, M., Hosang, J., Schiele, B.: Ten years of pedestrian detection, what have we learned? In: Agapito, L., Bronstein, Michael M., Rother, C. (eds.) ECCV 2014, Part II. LNCS, vol. 8926, pp. 613–627. Springer, Cham (2015). https://doi.org/10.1007/978-3-319-16181-5_47
7. Hosang, J., Omran, M., Benenson, R., Schiele, B.: Taking a deeper look at pedestrians. In: Proceedings of the IEEE Conference on Computer Vision and Pattern Recognition, pp. 4073–4082. IEEE (2015)

8. Zhang, S., Benenson, R., Omran, M., Hosang, J., Schiele, B.: How far are we from solving pedestrian detection? In: Proceedings of the IEEE Conference on Computer Vision and Pattern Recognition, pp. 1259–1267. IEEE (2016)
9. Ren, S., et al.: Faster R-CNN: towards real-time object detection with region proposal networks. In: Advances in Neural Information Processing Systems, pp. 91–99 (2015)
10. Dai, J., Li, Y., He, K., Sun, J.: R-FCN: object detection via region-based fully convolutional networks. In: Advances in Neural Information Processing Systems, pp. 379–387 (2016)
11. Redmon, J., Divvala, S., Girshick, R., Farhadi, A.: You only look once: unified, real-time object detection. In: Proceedings of the IEEE Conference on Computer Vision and Pattern Recognition, pp. 779–788. IEEE (2016)
12. Liu, W., et al.: SSD: single shot MultiBox detector. In: Leibe, B., Matas, J., Sebe, N., Welling, M. (eds.) ECCV 2016, Part I. LNCS, vol. 9905, pp. 21–37. Springer, Cham (2016). https://doi.org/10.1007/978-3-319-46448-0_2

1090ES ADS-B Overlapped Signal Separation Research Based on Infomax Extension

Zhaoyue Zhang[1(✉)], Hongyan Guo[2], Yongfei Zhang[3], and Jicheng Dong[3]

[1] Civil Aviation University of China, Tianjin 300300, China
zy_zhang@cauc.edu.cn
[2] Binzhou University, Binzhou 256603, China
[3] Harbin Engineering University, Harbin 150001, China

Abstract. 1090ES ADS-B is a new technology in civil aviation, mainly used to monitor dynamic condition of aircrafts and share the flight information. However, the ADS-B signals are often interfered with other overlapped signals during the signal transmission, causing signal overlap and bringing difficulties to signal processing afterwards. This article applies Blind Source Separation (BSS) into the separation process of ADS-B overlapped signals and constructs the ADS-B overlapped signal separation model using Infomax algorithm, in order to separate ADS-B overlapped signals into single-way ADS-B signals and improve signal decoding rate.

Keywords: ADS-B · Blind Source Separation · Infomax extension

1 Introduction

Automatic Dependent Surveillance-Broadcast (ADS-B) obtains aircraft's location information via onboard GPS and sends its location information via onboard communication equipments. People on the earth could receive situation information sent from the aircraft and realize aircraft surveillance. ADS-B improves security and efficiency of the airspace and runway, decreases the cost and reduces the harmful influence on environment. However, ADS-B signals will overlap in the practical transmission, causing giant influence on ADS-B receiver's decoding, leading to aircraft location information default and abnormal aircraft monitoring. In the context of unknown source signals, BBS separates the mixed signals observed and restores the source signals. FastICA algorithm, Infomax algorithm and Maximum Likelihood Estimate algorithm are the most commonly used and efficient algorithms of BSS. This article sets forth the ADS-B based on Infomax extension algorithm and verifies the feasibility of using Infomax extension algorithm for ADS-B overlapped signal separation on the MATLAB simulation platform. In 1995, A.J. Bell and T.J. Sejnowski put forward BSS algorithm based on information-maximisation (Infomax for short) principle. T.W. Lee developed traditional Infomax algorithm and put forward an Infomax extension algorithm which could separate the sub-gaussian source and super-gaussian source. It can realize the kurtosis variance of ICA, select the appropriate nonlinear function, and realize signal synchronization separation [2].

© ICST Institute for Computer Sciences, Social Informatics and Telecommunications Engineering 2019
Published by Springer Nature Switzerland AG 2019. All Rights Reserved
S. Liu and G. Yang (Eds.): ADHIP 2018, LNICST 279, pp. 99–107, 2019.
https://doi.org/10.1007/978-3-030-19086-6_11

2   ADS-B Signal Model

1090ES ADS-B information includes 4 leading pulses and 112-bit message sequence. The information data block format adopts pulse position modulation (PPM) code (Fig. 1). ADS-B information includes 4 identification pulses, each lasting 0.5 ± 0.05 µs.

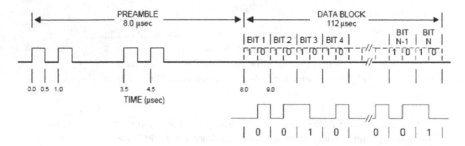

Fig. 1. ADS-B message transmission waveform

While several 1090ES ADS-B signals are transmitted in the mean time, there is the possibility that some parts of the pulse codes overlap. In Fig. 2, when signal 1(grey) and signal 2(white) are transmitted to the same ADS-B receiver, the signal power will overlap and wrong signal position will arise in PPM code, causing two-way or multipath signals can't be decoded correctly. When multipath signals overlap, it will cause that the position of one aircraft or several aircrafts can't be obtained and the messages will be lost. 1090ES ADS-B overlapped signal separation algorithm based on Infomax extension is to separate and restore ADS-B signals correctly with unknown 1090ES ADS-B source signals when 1090ES ADS-B signals overlap.

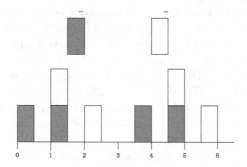

Fig. 2. ADS-B signal overlap model

3   BSS Principle

Supposing that we regard the multi-source data received from several 1090ES ADS-B base stations as observation signals, all the data received from each base station is the overlap of separated 1090ES ADS-B source signals. $s_1(t), s_2(t), s_3(t) \cdots s_n(t)$ is a observation signal vector from any N unit time, $x_1(t), x_2(t), x_3(t) \cdots x_m(t)$ show mixed vector signals received from m ADS-B base stations. In the mixture of ADS-B signals, we suppose that a_{ij} is an unknown constant matrix. The separation of ADS-B signals is how to separate the source signals $s_1(t), s_2(t), s_3(t) \cdots s_n(t)$ from the mixed observation signals received from the ADS-B receiver. So the ADS-B observation signals can be shown as:

$$X(t) = AS(t)$$

$X(t) = \{x_1(t), x_2(t) \cdots x_m(t)\}$ is the received observation signal from m dimension ADS-B base stations; $S(t) = \{s_1(t), s_2(t) \cdots s_n(t)\}$ is the n dimension vector formed by separated ADS-B source signals. In the mixed ADS-B model, a_{ij} is the separated component, and A is the mixture matrix formed by a_{ij}.

The algorithm model of ADS-B signal separation is to calculate the separated matrix W. Via the W, we can extract and restore ADS-B source signal $S(t)$ from the observation signal $X(t)$ mixed by ADS-B. Supposing that $Y(t)$ is the estimation signal of ADS-B source signal, so the separation system can be shown as:

$$Y(t) = WX(t)$$

3.1   The Principle of Infomax Extension Algorithm

The problem of blind signal separation is a process based on the maximum entropy of the separation system, using neural network or self-adaption algorithm and indirectly gaining high-order cumulants via nonlinear function. The framework of Infomax algorithm is shown as Fig. 3.

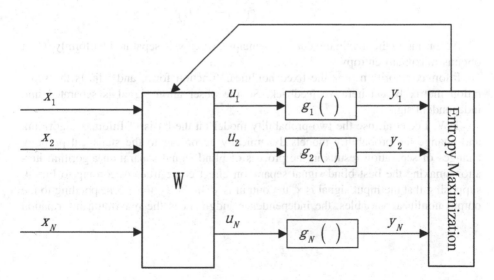

Fig. 3. Infomax algorithm

Among these, x is the multi-path ADS-B observation signal. It is mixed by N separated ADS-B source signals. The system output, $u = wx$, is the approach to true source s. $g_i()$ is a reversible monotone nonlinear function, and the nonlinear output is y_i. The maximum information transmission principle is used in the independence judgment of ADS-B signals, namely that making the interactive information $I(x,y)$ (or output entropy $H(y)$) between nonlinear output y and input x maximum, via adjustment on separation matrix W. According to the information above, the entropy $H(y)$ is defined as:

$$H(y) = H(y_1) + H(y_2) + \cdots + H(y_N) - I(y_1, y_2, \cdots y_N)$$

Among them, the interactive message $I(y_1, y_2, \ldots y_N)$ between nonlinear outputs is always non-negative. Only when nonlinear output y_i is separated from each other, there is $I(y_1, y_2, \ldots y_N) = 0$. At this time:

$$H(y) = H(y_1) + H(y_2) + \cdots + H(y_N)$$

So if $H(y)$ obtains the maximum, the nonlinear outputs need to be independent from each other, and at the same time the edge entropy $H(y_i)$ is required to obtain the maximum.

The selection of nonlinear function $g_i()$ is closely related to the value of edge entropy $H(y_i)$. In the Infomax algorithm, the nonlinear function always chooses *sigmoid* function.

$$y_i = g_i(u_i) = \frac{1}{1 + e^{-(au_i + b)}}$$

$$y_i' = g_i'(u_i) = \frac{a + e^{-(au_i + b)}}{\left(1 + e^{-(au_i + b)}\right)^2}$$

According to the maximum entropy principle, when y_i is separated uniformly, $H(y)$ obtains maximum entropy.

Infomax algorithm uses the fixed nonlinear function form, and adjusts the separation matrix W via iterative feedback. So the observation signal is separated into independent signals.

T.W. Lee et al. use the two-probability model on the basis of Infomax algorithm, and change the probability models dynamically according to the statistical property changes of separation results in the process of blind signal separation algorithm iteration, making the best blind signal separation effect come true. According to Fig. 4, supposing that the input signal is x, the output is y. In the system corresponding to the output nonlinear variables, the independence judgment is the maximum information

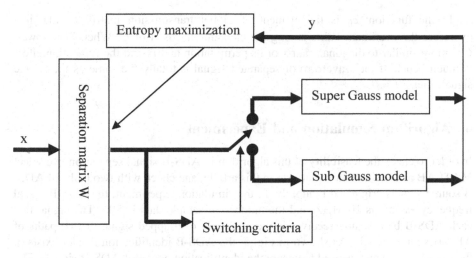

Fig. 4. Infomax extension algorithm model

transmission criterion. By adjusting the separation matrix W, the joint entropy $H(y)$ of nonlinear output y is maximized. Sub-Gaussian and Super-Gaussian probability density models are as followed:

$$p(u_i) = \frac{1}{2}\left(N\left(\mu, \sigma^2\right) + N\left(-\mu, \sigma^2\right)\right)$$

$$p(u_i) = p_G(u_i)\sec h^2(u_i)$$

Among them, $p_G(u_i) = N(0,1)$ is the Gaussian density function with zero mean value and unit variance.

So the adjustment function of W is:

$$\Delta W \propto \left[I - Ktanh(u)u^T - uu^T\right]W \begin{cases} k_{ii} = 1 : super - Gaussian \\ k_{ii} = -1 : sub - Gaussian \end{cases}$$

Among them, K is a N dimension diagonal matrix and a double probability model switching matrix. k_{ii} is the diagonal element.

3.2 Crosstalk Error

The ADS-B signal separation effect can be evaluated by crosstalk error, PI, which is defined as:

$$PI(C) = \frac{1}{M}\sum_{i=1}^{M}\left(\sum_{j=1}^{N}\frac{|c_{ij}|}{\max_j|c_{ij}|} - 1\right) + \frac{1}{N}\sum_{j=1}^{N}\left(\sum_{k=1}^{N}\frac{|c_{ij}|}{\max_j|c_{ij}|} - 1\right) - \frac{M-N}{N}$$

In the function: c_{ij} is the element of global transmission matrix C. $\max_j |c_{ij}|$ expresses the maximum value among the elements in row I of C. When PI is lower, C is more similar to diagonal matrix or its permutation matrix and the separation effect is much better. If the waveform of separated signal is totally the same as the source signal, then $PI = 0$.

4 Algorithm Simulation and Experiment

In order to check the feasibility of this algorithm in ADS-B signal separation, we select MATLAB as the simulation platform in this article, and check with two paths of ADS-B source signals originated randomly. In the simulation experiment, the ADS-B signal frequency sample is 10 MHz, and the number of sample data is 500. The signal that each ADS-B base station receives is the randomly overlapped signal of two paths of ADS-B source signals. As shown in Fig. 5, the ADS-B identification header exists in the front 80 us, which is used to ensure the identification power of ADS-B signals. The latter signal is the PPM coding signal, which uses the digital circuit coding.

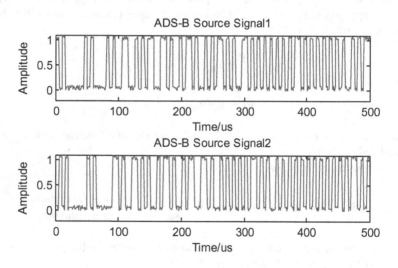

Fig. 5. ADS-B source signal

Using the digital matrix A originated randomly, we randomly mix and overlap the two paths of ADS-B source signals in Fig. 5 and we can obtain the mixed signals received in ADS-B base stations shown in Fig. 6. In the signals shown in Fig. 6, the identification of signal head couldn't be operated at all and it's hard to use normal ADS-B decoding algorithm to decode, causing the loss of two paths of ADS-B signals.

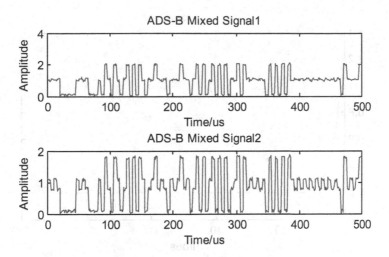

Fig. 6. Mixed ADS-B signals

We handle the signals via the Infomax extension algorithm, and separate the ADS-B mixed signals, gaining the separated ADS-B signals shown in Fig. 7. After comparing the ADS-B source signals shown in Fig. 5 and the separated ADS-B signals shown in Fig. 7, we can find that two paths of signals are substantially the same as each other, and the separated signals can be used to decode ADS-B signals. At the same time, in order to compare the error between source signals and separated signals, we output the signal crosstalk error in each iterative computation. As shown in Fig. 8, Infomax extension algorithm can separate ADS-B signals in a short time and has better astringency.

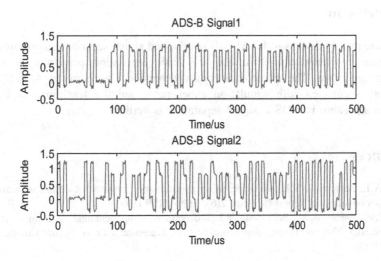

Fig. 7. ADS-B separated signals

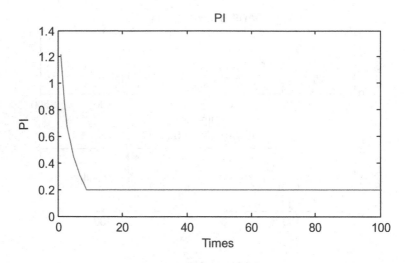

Fig. 8. Crosstalk error

5 Analysis of Simulation Results

Via the simulation analysis, it can be seen that the separated ADS-B signal waveform is substantially the same as the original signal, satisfying the ADS-B decoding algorithm's demands on ADS-B characteristic signals. From the PI curves, it can be seen that the error of separating noise signals via Infomax extension algorithm is little, which separates the ADS-B signals better. And ADS-B signal separation matrix can satisfy the demands of ADS-B separation more quickly. The value of PI in convergence is only 0.1957.

6 Conclusion

This article mainly discusses the ADS-B overlapped signal separation algorithm based on Infomax extension algorithm and the basic realization principle of Infomax extension algorithm. The effect of Infomax extension algorithm on ADS-B signal separation is checked with simulation experiment, and the feasibility of Infomax extension algorithm in ADS-B signal separation is verified.

References

1. Bell, A.J., Sejnowski, T.J.: An information maximization approach to blind separation and blind deconvolution. Neural Comput. **7**(6), 1129–1159 (1995)
2. Lee, T.W., Girolami, M., Sejnowski, T.J.: Independent component analysis using an extended infomax algorithm for mixed subgaussian and supergaussian sources. Neural Comput. **11**(2), 417 (1999)

3. Yan, H., Hua, H.: Noise removal in electroencephalogram signal via independent component analysis approach based on the extended information maximization. Chin. J. Tissue Eng. Res. (09) (2013)
4. Luo, Z., Zhou, W.: A modification to the blind source separation and its application on SEMG*. Chin. J. Sens. Actuators **22**(8) (2009)
5. Wu, X., Zhang, D.: The convergence property analysis of infomax algorithm. Comput. Eng. Appl. (7), 49–51, 59 (2003)
6. Guo, X., Wu, X., Zhang, D.: The application of Independent component analysis in the pattern extraction of mental EEG. Microcomput. Dev. (6), 36–39 (2002)

Real-Time Monitoring Technology of Potato Pests and Diseases in Northern Shaanxi Based on Hyperspectral Data

Yong-heng Zhang[✉] and Xiao-yan Ai

Yulin University, Yulin 719000, Shaanxi, China
haha6962@163.com

Abstract. When using traditional monitoring technology to monitor the disaster area of potato in Northern Shaanxi, there was a problem of insufficient monitoring accuracy. In view of the above problems, a real-time monitoring technology for potato pests and diseases based on hyperspectral data is put forward. Firstly, the geological environment of the monitoring area is briefly introduced. Hyper Spectral Remote Sensing is used to obtain the hyperspectral data of the damaged area of the potato in the study area, and pretreatment is performed to establish a regression model. Finally, the pre-processed hyperspectral data is obtained. Substituting data into the model, the area of potato pests and diseases in the research area is obtained. The results showed that the accuracy of the method was 20.29% higher than that of the traditional potato pest and disease monitoring technology, and the accurate monitoring of the disaster area was realized. It has practicality and superiority.

Keywords: Hyperspectral data · Potato · Diseases and insect pests · Affected area · Monitor

1 Introduction

The northern Shaanxi region is the old revolutionary area and is the central part of the Loess Plateau in China. It includes Yulin City and Yan'an City in Shaanxi Province. They are all in the northern part of Shaanxi, so they are called Northern Shaanxi. The terrain is high in the northwest and low in the southeast. The area is a continental monsoon climate. The annual average temperature is $9.4°$, the annual precipitation is 550 mm, and the frost-free period is 52 days. It is very suitable for the growth of crops, of which potato is one of the main crops in the area. It accounts for about 23% of the country's total crop output. However, pests and diseases are important factors that affect potato yield and quality. The common diseases and pests of potato in northern Shaanxi mainly include early blight, late blight, black shank, potato tuber moth, aphids, leafhoppers, golden needles, and ladybugs [1]. An early blight occurred in 2009, which resulted in a 10% reduction in the output of potato, a huge loss to the local agricultural economy, and a great impact on the agricultural production and ecological environment construction in China, which seriously restricted the sustainable development of agriculture in China. Therefore, people urgently need an effective method to monitor

S. Liu and G. Yang (Eds.): ADHIP 2018, LNICST 279, pp. 108–117, 2019.
https://doi.org/10.1007/978-3-030-19086-6_12

the occurrence and development of potato pests and diseases in time, control the area of damage and reduce the degree of harm.

The traditional real-time detection technology of crop diseases and insect pests based on GIS has obvious regional limitations, so it is impossible to predict crop diseases and insect pests in adjacent and similar planting areas. The real-time detection technology of crop diseases and insect pests based on Kinect is used to collect data in disaster-stricken areas. The result is unsatisfactory and the accuracy of detection is low, which can not provide effective technical support for pest detection. The use of Hyper Spectral Remote Sensing technology for real-time monitoring of potato diseases and insect pests has the advantages of large area, short period, and information obtained without interference. It has been paid more and more attention and has a broad prospect of development [2]. Taking the potato planting area of Yulin city in Northern Shaanxi Province as an example, the pests and diseases are monitored in real time. Firstly, the geological environment in the planting area was briefly introduced. Then Hyper Spectral Remote Sensing technology was used to obtain the hyperspectral data of the area affected by the potato in the study area, and pretreatment was carried out to establish a regression model. Finally, the pretreated high Spectral data were substituted into the model to obtain the area of potato pests and diseases in the study area. In order to verify the effectiveness of the real-time monitoring technology of potato pests and diseases in northern Shaanxi based on hyperspectral data, a comparative experiment was conducted together with the traditional pest and disease area monitoring technology. The results showed that comparing with the traditional monitoring technology of pests and diseases, the accuracy of the method was improved by 20.29%, and accurate real-time monitoring of potato pests and diseases was achieved.

2 Real-Time Monitoring Technology of Potato Pests and Diseases

Hyper Spectral Remote Sensing is the abbreviation of Hyperspectral Remote Sensing, it refers to the use of many very narrow (usually band width <10 nm) electromagnetic wave band to obtain relevant data from the target object, these data can form a complete and continuous spectral curve. Hyper Spectral Remote Sensing is one of the major technological breakthroughs made in the field of earth observation at the beginning of this century, and it is the leading edge technology of today's remote sensing [3]. Compared with the traditional remote sensing technology, Hyper Spectral Remote Sensing has the advantages of narrow band, many channels, and the combination of image and spectrum, and so on. It is imaging of the ground objects at the high spectral resolution and several hundred to hundreds of bands at the same time. Therefore, the spectral information of the ground objects is continuous and fine. This feature of Hyper Spectral Remote Sensing is very conducive to accurate real-time monitoring of the area affected by the feature [4]. The variation of spectral characteristics in the damaged potato area is the main basis for monitoring the area of potato pests and diseases by remote sensing. There are many diseases and insect pests of potato, such as early blight, late blight, black shank, potato tuber moth, aphid, leaf leafhopper, golden needle worm, ladybug and so on. The growth of potato is affected and appearance changes, such as leaf blight, falling or rhizome dead and so on. Therefore, according to the differences and structural anomalies of spectral reflectance obtained through remote sensing, especially the fine detection method with the help of Hyper Spectral Remote Sensing data, and under the support of geographic information system and expert system, the effective monitoring of the location and area of potato pests and diseases can be effectively realized.

2.1 Research Area

The study area is located in Yulin city of Northern Shaanxi, Yulin is located in the north of Shaanxi Province, Gansu, Ningxia, Inner Mongolia in the west, the Yellow River and Shanxi in the East, and Yanan in the south of Shaanxi. The geographical coordinates are: 36°57′–39°35′N, 107°28′–111°15′E. The sunshine time is long, and the average sunshine percentage is 59%–66%. In the continental monsoon climate, the temperature is evident throughout the four seasons. The pressure is high, the weather is clear, and there are many high clouds. Potatoes are the main grain crops in this area. The annual planting area is nearly 260 thousand hectares, accounting for about 30% of the grain crop area in the region. In recent years, because of the large amount of bacteria in the provinces and counties, the resistance to diseases and insect pests is not strong, and the outbreak of diseases and insect pests in the region is not strong, which leads to the serious reduction of wheat production in Yulin. In particular, early blight and ladybird pest were found in the potato field survey in 2009. The incidence time was the most serious in the past 20 years [5]. In addition, Yulin City Plant Protection Station randomly investigated 205 fields after the recurrence of potato pests and diseases, and found that 95 have been infected with pests and diseases, and the average disease and field rate reached 46.34%, which directly threatened potato planting safety.

2.2 Hyperspectral Data Acquisition and Preprocessing

On-site field observations were conducted on the study area on April 21, April 22, and April 25, 2009. A total of 34 sites were measured. In order to ensure the representativeness and validity of the spectral data, the selected observation sites covered the entire Yulin city, and the focus was on potato areas that were affected by pests and diseases. In all stations, potatoes in 26 site areas were affected by pests and diseases, and potatoes in the 8 station areas were not harmed. For the site where the potato was exposed to pests and diseases, spectral data of the four crop canopies were obtained at the same time, and two groups of data were collected from potato fields and neighboring normal potato areas under the pests and diseases. Ground field spectral observation instrument for ASD FieldSpec ProFR2500 spectrum radiometer, spectral range is 350–2500 nm, sampling interval in 350–1000 nm is 1.4 nm, in 1000–2500 nm is 2 nm. During observation, the probe is vertical downward, the height of the probe is 1.3 m, the angle of the field of view is 250, and the average value is repeated 30 times in the field of view, and the standard whiteboard is corrected before each spectrum measurement [6].

This study attempts to explore a commercial method for monitoring the disease and insect pests of Winter Wheat with wide band CCD images. The measured spectral reflectance of all winter wheat canopy is averaged according to the band width of satellite images: 520–600 nm (Green light wave band), 630–690 nm (light wave band), 760–900 nm (Near Infrared wave band), it matches ground measured spectrum data with remote sensing image data.

The pretreatment of the imaging spectrometer includes spectrometer calibration, spectral recovery, geometric correction, and atmospheric radiation correction. The complete pretreatment process for hyperspectral data of potato pests and diseases is shown in Fig. 1.

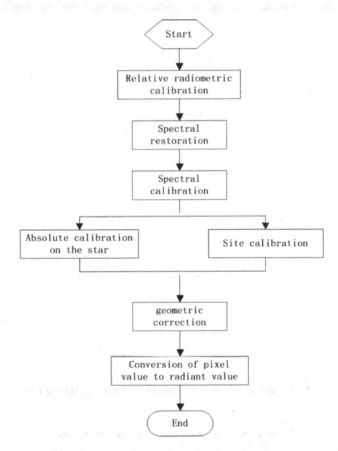

Fig. 1. Hyperspectral data preprocessing process

2.3   Potato Planting Range Information Extraction

In this study, the HJ-1A-CCD2 images obtained on January 22, 2008, were selected and supervised classification methods were used to extract potato planting areas in the study area. During the supervised classification process, the dispersion value of the transformation between the potato training sample and the other sample woods reached 2000, indicating that the separation between the potato and other land objects is very good for the selected sample and can be expected to be used. This training sample gets a better classification result [7].

Figure 2 shows the results of the classification, in which the green area is the extent of potato cultivation. The classification accuracy of the two ground objects of potato and non potato was taken into consideration, and 51 ground reference samples were selected to verify the accuracy. Table 1 shows the classification accuracy evaluation table. The overall accuracy of the classification is 94.12%, and the kappa coefficient is above 0.8. The planting area of potato in the classification results is 97 thousand and 930 ha, which is only 2.1% of the 100 thousand hectares recorded in Yulin plant protection station, which shows that the accuracy of the classification can meet the requirements.

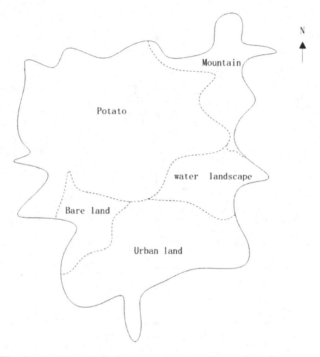

Fig. 2. Results of information extraction of potato planting range

Table 1. Classification accuracy evaluation table

Category	Reference data	Random sample number	Correct sample number	Producer's accuracy 5	User accuracy	Kappa coefficient
Non potato	35	36	35	95.44	98.14	0.9129
Potato	16	17	15	94.33	88.50	0.8329
Overall accuracy	94.14%					

2.4 Establishing a Logistic Regression Model

Above, we introduce hyperspectral data acquisition and pretreatment, and potato planting range information extraction. On this basis, the regression model should be established, and the data extracted before should be substituted into the model. The range of potato diseases and insect pests should be analyzed by AdaBoost algorithm in the model, and the area of potato diseases and insect pests in the study area should be obtained. Therefore, it is necessary to establish Logistic regression model.

The model takes the AdaBoost algorithm as the core and trains the different classifier (weak classifier) for the same training set. Then the classifier is set up to form a higher precision classifier (strong classifier). With the increase of the number of weak classifiers, the classification error rate decreases steadily. Moreover, the model can not be overfitted and the weak classifier can define itself, so it is suitable for application in various classification scenarios [8]. It is often used in the field of image processing, such as face detection, target detection, target tracking, etc. Considering the cost problem, the sampling amount is less. A limited number of training samples will lead to the limitation of classification accuracy. In this case, the AdaBoost algorithm is used to improve the accuracy rate.

AdaBoost constructs a strong classifier $A_m(x)(m = 1, 2, \cdots, M)$ by combining multiple weak classifiers linearly. The x here is the input vector. The AdaBoost algorithm is as follows:

Algorithm 1: AdaBoost algorithm

Sample data: $(x_1, y_1), \cdots, (x_m, y_m), y \in \{-1, 1\}$.

Step 1: Normalize each sample weight $D(i) = \dfrac{1}{N}$;

Step 2: For $m = 1, 2, \cdots, M$,

If you find the classifier $A_m(x)$, Make sample weight $D(i)$ distribution error B

minimum, $B = \sum D(i)$.

Calculate the trust rate by error rate C, $C = \dfrac{1}{2} \log B$

Update sample weight $D_1(i) = \dfrac{1}{N} A_m(x)$

The final strong classifier is:

$$A_m(x)' = D_1(i) \sum C \tag{1}$$

The principle of disease and pest monitoring is to use the spectral information obtained on the basis of the difference between the disease and the normal sample, the more significant the difference, indicating that the extracted spectral features are easier to separate the disease samples from the healthy samples. The barren coefficient is a measure of the similarity between the two statistical samples, which can be used to measure the correlation of the two groups of samples, and often measure the separability between the classes in the classification problem [9]. Therefore, the vegetation index is used as the feature vector, and the similarity measure of the feature vectors is defined by the Babbitt coefficient, and the similarity of the sample points to the normal samples and the disease samples is calculated respectively. Among them, F^H is the average value of the eigenvectors of all healthy samples, and F^D is the average value of the eigenvectors of all the disease samples. F^G represents the eigenvector of an arbitrary sample. According to the similarity between sample and disease sample and the difference between sample and healthy sample, a weak classifier is established, as shown in formula (2).

$$\Im\left(F^H, F^D, F^G\right) = \sum^{\delta} \sqrt{F^H F^D F^G} \tag{2}$$

Among them, δ is a domain value, and when the model is trained, it will be updated with the iteration of the AdaBoost algorithm to minimize the error rate on the training dataset.

2.5   Disaster Area Monitoring

The potato planting range information is substituted into the above established regression model, and the range of potato pest and disease is analyzed. When the probability is greater than 0.5, it is considered that the disease is endangered by pests and diseases, thus obtaining the area of potato infected by pests and diseases. Figure 3 is the area of potato and pest stress caused by the real-time monitoring technology of potato disease and insect pest area in Northern Shaanxi based on hyperspectral data. The red area is the potato under the stress of disease and insect, and the green potato growth area is in the picture. According to the statistical analysis, the proportion of Potato Planted by the method is 13.29% of the potato planting area in Yulin.

Fig. 3. Distribution of potato under disease and pest stress (Color figure online)

3   Contrast Experiment

To further analyze the monitoring accuracy of real-time monitoring techniques for potato pests and diseases in northern Shaanxi based on hyperspectral data, it matches the growth status of the potato on the site with the potato's disease-tolerance range, and analyze whether the results monitored by this method are consistent with the actual observations [10]. The potato growing area is divided into 34 site areas. The pests and diseases are monitored and the results are shown in Table 2.

Table 2. Comparison of monitoring accuracy of potato pests and diseases

Name	Number of insect pest stress stations	Point number of Health Station	Overall accuracy
Real time monitoring technology for potato diseases and insect pests in Northern Shaanxi Based on hyperspectral data	25	9	96.76%
Area monitoring technique of traditional diseases and insect pests	20	14	76.47%
Actual value	26	8	-

As can be seen from Table 2, there are a total of 34 measured sites, of which 26 wheat plants are under the threat of pests and diseases, and 8 sites are in a healthy growth condition. When using the method of this study to extract area information of pests and diseases, 25 sites of stress and 9 healthy sites are obtained, respectively, and the overall accuracy of monitoring is 96.76%. When using the traditional pest area monitoring technique, 20 diseases and insect pests and 14 healthy winter wheat sites are detected, and the overall precision reached 76.47%. In comparison, the real-time monitoring technology of potato disease and pest area based on hyperspectral data could meet the requirements of monitoring the disease and insect pests of the potato.

4   Conclusions

In this study, potato planting area in Yulin was taken as the research object. Using land acquisition data and hyperspectral remote sensing method, the hyperspectral data of potato affected area were collected and pretreated. The results were substituted into regression model to study the affected area of potato in planting area. The real-time monitoring of potato diseases and insect pests was realized, which provided technical support for the control of potato diseases and insect pests in planting area. But in practice, there are still some shortcomings. Because the geological conditions and environment in the disaster-stricken area of potato are not unified, the method in this paper is not satisfactory in the detection of the severity of the disaster. Therefore, this will become the focus of the next study, but also need to improve and update the real-time monitoring technology of potato pests and diseases, to achieve more accurate and comprehensive detection.

Fund Project. Agricultural Science Research Plan in Shaanxi Province of China: "Research on key technologies and application of Intelligent Prediction and Forecasting of Potato diseases and pests based on the Internet of Things" (NO. 2016NY141).

References

1. Guo, H.Y., Liu, G.H., Wu, L.G., et al.: Hyper-spectral imaging technology for nondestructive detection of potato ring rot. Food Sci. **37**(12), 203–207 (2016)
2. Bai, X.Q., Zhang, X.L., Zhang, N., et al.: Monitoring model of Dendrolimus tabulaeformis disaster using hyperspectral remote sensing technology. J. Beijing For. Univ. **38**(11), 16–22 (2016)
3. Xu, M.Z., Li, M., Bai, Z.P., et al.: Identification of early blight disease on potato leaves using hyperspectral imaging technique. J. Agric. Mechanization Res. **38**(6), 205–209 (2016)
4. Zhao, M.F., Liu, Z.D., Zou, X., et al.: Detection of defects on potatoes by hyperspectral imaging technology. Laser J. **37**(3), 20–24 (2016)
5. He, C., Zheng, S.L., Zhou, S.M., et al.: Estimation models of chlorophyll contents in potato leaves based on hyperspectral vegetation indices. J. South China Agric. Univ. **37**(5), 45–49 (2016)
6. Hu, Y.H., Ping, X.W., Xu, M.Z., et al.: Detection of late blight disease on potato leaves using hyperspectral imaging technique. Spectrosc. Spectr. Anal. **36**(2), 515–519 (2016)

7. Li, X.Y., Xu, S.M., Feng, Y.Z., et al.: Detection of potato slight bruise based on hyperspectral image and fruit fly optimization algorithm. Trans. Chinese Soc. Agric. Mach. **47**(1), 221–226 (2016)

8. Shi, F.F., Gao, X.H., Yang, L.Y., et al.: Identifying typical crop types from ground hyperspectral data: a case study in the Huangshui river basin, Qinghai province. Geogr. Geo Inf. Sci. **32**(2), 32–39 (2016)

9. Package seventy-three.: Spectral Image Analysis of Chinese Medicine Component Content Detection. Comput. Simul. **34**(07), 369–372 (2017)

10. Wang, G.B., Liu, W., Ming-Shan, L.I.: Green control technology of rice pests and diseases and integrated demonstration. J. Anhui Agric. Sci. **46**(09), 269–271 (2017)

Multi-mode Retrieval Method for Big Data of Economic Time Series Based on Machine Learning Theory

Hai-ying Chen[1] and Lan-fang Gong[2(✉)]

[1] Wuhan Institute of Design and Sciences, Wuhan 430205, China
chenhaiying3223@163.com
[2] Guangdong Polytechnic of Water Resources and Electric Engineering,
Guangzhou 510925, Guangdong, China
liuyoudan2018@163.com

Abstract. For traditional search methods affected by the index build time, resulting in poor search results, a multi-mode retrieval method for big data of economic time series based on machine learning theory is proposed. According to the good extensibility of big data, construct a retrieval model and use binary data conversion methods to match big data. The binary sequence is defined by the relationship between different data, the similarity of data features is calculated, and the candidate candidate sequence is filtered. Data with no similar features are filtered, and each sub-sequence set matching the pattern is given by similarity size. After the threshold is added, on the basis of slightly reducing the filtering amplitude, the calculation of the similarity matching in the big data retrieval process is greatly reduced, and combined with the fixed interval sampling matching method to determine the characteristics of big data, thereby realizing the machine learning theory. The multi-mode retrieval method for big data of economic time series based on machine learning theory retrieval. According to the experimental comparison results, the retrieval efficiency of the method can reach 95%, which provides effective help for large-scale retrieval of massive data.

Keywords: First machine learning · Second economic time series · Third big data · Forth retrieval

1 Introduction

As computer technology continues to innovate, data related to inter-industry trade can be collected and is growing at an unprecedented rate. Due to the booming and rapid spread of cloud computing, the Internet, and the Internet of Things, all kinds of information data are exploding, the big data era has come, The real-time analysis of big data is an important analytical tool that promotes in-depth research and discussion in the academia and industry. Econometrics is a discipline that studies the quantification of actual economic phenomena. Most economic data were time series and have a strong theoretical background [1]. Machine learning theory uses regular thinking to avoid overfitting the model. In linear regression, most of the performance was to add more

S. Liu and G. Yang (Eds.): ADHIP 2018, LNICST 279, pp. 118–125, 2019.
https://doi.org/10.1007/978-3-030-19086-6_13

and more independent variable parameters, which can easily lead to overfitting, therefore, in machine learning theory, it is necessary to add penalty items involving the complexity of the model to the parameter estimation objective optimization equation, predict and mine the interesting features in the data and describe them, according to a series of nonlinear data analysis methods, the economic time series of machine learning theory not only has a strong search effect on known data, but also has good prediction ability for unknown data [2].

2   Big Data Multi-pattern Retrieval Scheme Design

2.1   Search Model Construction

For the economic time series of machine learning theory, the design of multi-mode retrieval for big data is divided into six modules according to good scalability: data extraction conversion and loading access tools, data indexing/storage service, big data index Library, data repository, data retrieval service and Web query interface [3, 4]. The retrieval model design is shown in Fig. 1.

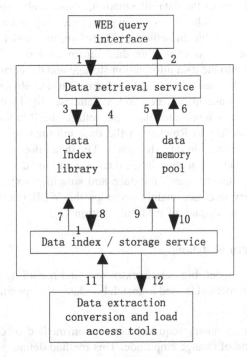

Fig. 1. Retrieval model

In Fig. 1, 1 indicates a sending request, 2 indicates a returned result, 3 indicates a search index library, 4 indicates a return, 5 indicates usage, 6 indicates return, 7 indicates index creation, 8 indicates return status, 9 indicates write storage, and 10 indicates return Status, 11 indicates write data, 12 indicates return status.

The data extraction transformation and loading access tool is mainly responsible for extracting the required raw data from the database. After conversion and cleaning, the data information including the data characteristics, applicable environment, retrieval process, and judgment flow is formed. Then the API interface provided by the index/storage service is called to load the data information into the data index database and data repository. Data extraction conversion and loading access tools currently support the following types of data sources: Kafka, Mongodb, Mysql, HBase, etc., by simply configuring the data source, data conversion XML, and data cleansing XML, the data extraction transformation and loading configuration of the access tool can be completed [5]. The data information index/storage service masks the data information index database and the data information repository externally by providing a unified call interface, thereby simplifying the access operation of external data information. In addition, in order to avoid the situation that the data information is only stored in the index storehouse and the storehouse when the index is not stored or only the index is not stored, the transaction control logic of the write operation is added.

The data information index database and the data information database are used to store the indexes and data of the data information, respectively. The advantage is that the full text retrieval function based on the inverted index is provided, and the obtained data performance is very stable and efficient. Therefore, the model separates the index and repository. In the process of writing data information into the model, the data information is written into the data information storage and the corresponding RowKey information is returned. Then use the data information and RowKey information to create an index in the case information index database [6]. In the query, firstly, it searches in the data information index database, returns the RowKey information, and then obtains data according to Rowkey in the data information index database, and returns it to the data information querying party. The data information retrieval service externally masks the data information index database and the data information storage library by providing a unified search interface and simplifies external retrieval operations. The WEB query interface mainly provides the WEB interface to the user to implement the query and display of data information [7].

2.2 Big Data Pattern Matching

In the above retrieval model, big data is extracted, and according to machine theory, binary data conversion method is used to match big data. The specific matching process is as follows:

(1) Data conversion: A binary sequence conversion method of character sequences based on the trend of change amplitude. This method defines the binary sequence by the relationship between the adjacent three points, thereby accurately reflecting whether the three points are convex growth (Decrease) or concave growth (Reduce) relationship;

(2) Data reduction: In order to facilitate the calculation of similarity between candidate sequences and patterns, a data reduction method based on trend proportions

is proposed. Both candidate sequences and patterns are reduced to the interval [0, 1], and the candidate after reduction is reduced. The minimum value of the sequence and pattern is 0, the maximum value is 1;

(3) Similarity calculation and filtering: In order to distinguish between the amplitudes of the convex growth (decrease) or the concave growth (decrease) of different change amplitudes, similarity is calculated for the reduced sequence, and the similarity degree is finally filtered. Give each set of sub-sequences that match the pattern [8].

For the matching of big data patterns, it can effectively solve the problem of data oscillation amplitude out of control, and solve the problem that the data sequence and pattern sequence segmentation rule are not similar as a whole, greatly improving the string matching efficiency, and simultaneously matching multiple candidate strings with other patterns. Sorting the similarity between them provides a basis for further accurate data retrieval [9].

2.3 The Implementation of Retrieval Scheme

Based on the above results of big data matching, an economic time series retrieval method based on machine learning theory was designed. The large data set A to be searched for uses the economic time series to perform similarity filter matching in the reference database $\{A_1, A_2, A_3, \ldots, A_n, \ldots\}$, as follows:

(1) If the total feature quantity of the intermediate data of the large data set A is greater than the total feature quantity of the intermediate data of the reference set, then it is directly determined that the second audio A is not similar;

(2) Set thresholds K_1 and K_2. In the process of data retention and match, if the average distance from the first n data economic time series is less than K_1, then it is directly determined that data n is a possible result;

(3) The threshold S is set. In the above process, the distance X of the previous m data economic time series is accumulated. If X is larger than the threshold S, the search is directly determined to be dissimilar;

(4) The threshold W is set. When the original data is used for matching, the first t feature feature similarity Y_t is compared first. Only when Y_t is greater than the threshold, the similarity degree Y_v of the overall data feature can be calculated; otherwise, it is directly determined that the search is not similar;

(5) The threshold η is set. In the above process, the original data feature retrieval error $R\varepsilon$ is accumulated for the first n times. If $R\varepsilon$ is greater than the threshold η, the retrieval is directly determined to be dissimilar;

(6) The threshold P is set. Because the adjacent economic time series have extremely high similarity, when the similarity between the data is lower than the threshold P, several times of data can be extracted appropriately, similarity matching is performed, and the big data retrieval is completed [10].

After the threshold is added, on the basis of slightly reducing the filtering amplitude, the similarity matching calculation amount in the big data retrieval process is greatly reduced, and the filtering speed and the retrieval speed can be effectively improved. In combination with the fixed-interval sampling matching method, the big data feature is rapidly implemented. Similarity judgments can achieve more efficient retrieval results, thereby realizing economic time series big data multi-model retrieval based on machine learning theory.

3 Experiments

In order to verify the effectiveness of the economic time series big data multi-mode retrieval method based on machine learning theory, the following experiment was conducted. The experimental reference database uses 2,000 randomly collected data from the network and repeatedly loads the above data 20 times to a database with a scale of 40,000. The experimental data are all randomly selected from the database.

3.1 Experimental Results and Analysis

The data is divided by the size of 32 MB, 64 MB, 128 MB, 256 MB, 512 MB and the different index creation time is shown in Fig. 2.

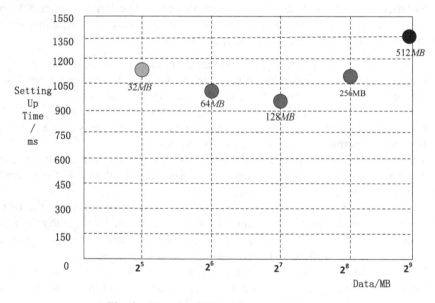

Fig. 2. Time for different index establishment

From Fig. 2 we can get the time for different index establishment. When the data is 32 MB, the index creation time is about 1100 ms. As the data grows larger, the index creation time is also reduced. Until the data size increases to 512 MB, the index creation time increases to 1350 ms. The index established using the traditional method is when the performance of 2 GB is the lowest, and it is lower than the normal time, this is because the set data size is the same, resulting in all the calculation results being processed, which greatly wastes the computing power of the server, thereby reducing the performance of data retrieval. On the other hand, the large-data multi-mode retrieval method of economic time series using machine learning theory is not affected by this point, and has a good search effect.

In order to verify whether the different index creation time has an effect on retrieval results, the traditional method is compared with the economic time series method of machine learning theory. The results are shown in Fig. 3.

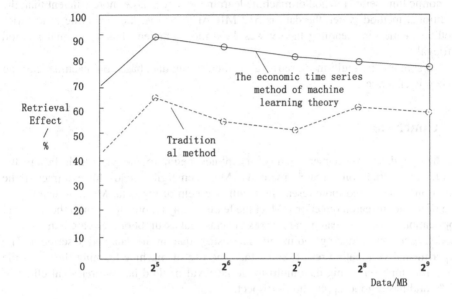

Fig. 3. Comparison of search results by different methods

From Fig. 3, we can see that the initial search effect of the traditional method can reach 78%, and the initial retrieval effect of the economic time series method of machine learning theory can reach 95%. As the amount of data increases, the retrieval efficiency gradually decreases. When the data is 32 MB, the retrieval effect by the traditional method is 65%, and the initial retrieval effect of the economic time series method of machine learning theory is 89%; When the data is 64 MB, the retrieval effect by the traditional method is 69%, and the initial retrieval effect of the economic time series method of machine learning theory is 85%; When the data is 128 MB, the retrieval effect is 55% using the traditional method, and the initial retrieval effect of the economic time series method of the machine learning theory is 82%; When the data is 512 MB, the retrieval effect is 59% using the traditional method, and the initial retrieval effect of the machine time learning method is 78%. It can be seen that using traditional methods will be affected by different index creation time, leading to poor retrieval results, while the economic time series method using machine learning theory will not be affected by different index setup time and have good retrieval results.

3.2   Experimental Conclusion

Based on the above experimental results, it can be concluded that when the data is 32 MB, the economic time series method of machine learning theory is 24% more efficient than the traditional method. When the data is 64 MB, the economic time series method of machine learning theory is 16% more efficient than the traditional method. When the data is 128 MB, the economic time series method of machine learning theory is 27% more efficient than the traditional method; when the data is 256 MB, the economic time series method of machine learning theory is 20% more efficient than the traditional method; when the data is 512 MB At that time, the economic time series method of machine learning theory was 19% more efficient than traditional method retrieval.

To sum up, the multi-mode retrieval method of big data based on machine learning theory is effective.

4   Conclusion

In the big data environment, many disciplines begin to merge, which brings the challenge of traditional search methods. Many emerging fields have attracted the attention of more and more researchers with the help of big data. Machine learning is one of the hot research directions. Machine learning pays more attention to the practical application value of research and relaxes the classical assumptions that are harsh on the model, focus on predicting and mining interesting data in the data and describe it. The experimental verification results show that, the use of machine learning theory in the economic time series big data multi-mode retrieval method has the retrieval effect of 95%, and has a good application prospect.

Fund Project. The 2018 annual scientific research project of Hubei Provincial Department of education. Based on modern statistical theory and machine learning theory, economic time series analysis is carried out (B2018371).

References

1. Su, T.F., Liu, Q.M., Su, X.C.: Research on crop remote sensing classification based on multiple vegetation index time series and machine learning. Jiangsu Agric. Sci. **45**(16), 219–224 (2017)
2. Dong, F., Liu, Y.F., Zhou, Y.: Abstracts based on LDA-SVM abstracts multi-classification emerging technologies prediction. J. Inf. **36**(7), 40–45 (2017)
3. Zhu, X., et al.: Research on network purchase behavior prediction based on machine learning fusion algorithm. Stat. Inf. Forum **25**(12), 94–100 (2017)
4. Sun, C.Y., Gong, L.T.: Research on interest rate pricing under the big data thinking: an empirical analysis based on machine learning. Fin. Theory Pract. **18**(7), 1–5 (2017)
5. Li, L., et al.: Parallel learning-a new theoretical framework of machine learning. Acta Automatica Sinica **43**(1), 1–8 (2017)

6. Jiao, J.Y., et al.: Review of typical machine learning platform under big data. J. Comput. Appl. **37**(11), 3039–3047 (2017)
7. Wu, Y.L., et al.: Construction and prediction of prospecting model based on big data intelligence. China Mining Mag. **26**(9), 79–84 (2017)
8. Xia, J.M., et al.: Physiological parameter monitoring system based on K-means and MTLS-SVM algorithm. Telecommun. Sci. **16**(10), 43–49 (2017)
9. Xing, X., et al.: Analysis of characteristics of multi-state traffic flow combined with viewable time series. Acta Physica Sinica **66**(23), 51–59 (2017)
10. Mei, Y.: Simulation of resource target information extraction in big data environment. Comput. Simul. **35**(03), 337–340 (2018)

Research on Parallel Forecasting Model of Short-Term Power Load Big Data

Xin-jia Li[1(✉)], Hong Sun[1], Cheng-liang Wang[1], Si-yu Tao[2], and Tao Lei[3]

[1] Jiangsu Fangtian Power Technology Co., Ltd., Nanjing 210096, China
rending0620@163.com
[2] Southeast University, Nanjing 210000, China
[3] South China Normal University, Guangzhou 510006, China

Abstract. The parallel prediction model of big data with traditional power load has a low prediction accuracy in different working conditions, so the parallel prediction model of big data for short-term power load is designed. The short-term power load forecasting theory is analyzed, and the short-term power load data are classified to select the short-term power load forecasting theory. The Map/Reduce framework is built on the basis of the theory, and the prediction process is designed through the Map/Reduce framework. The short-term power load data of the subnet and the big data of the short term power load are predicted respectively, and the construction of the parallel prediction model of the short-term power load big data is realized. The experimental results show that the proposed big data parallel prediction model is better than the traditional model, and can be switched under different working conditions, and the deviation between the forecasting curve and the actual load is small, the average deviation is 1.7, and the overall prediction effect is good.

Keywords: Short-Term load forecasting · Big data · Electrical load · Prediction algorithm

1 Introduction

With the rapid economic development, the power industry is facing increasing challenges. Among them, power system load forecasting is of great significance to the entire power industry. Power system load forecasting has become a hot topic in scientific research at present. It is to accurately grasp the future load trend, accurately grasp the overall layout of the power system, and maintain a safe and stable operating environment [1]. The tremendous changes in human life and the environment have made the impact of power loads increasingly complex. The existence of prediction error directly increases the additional cost of power system operation, which is not conducive to economic improvement. This paper proposes a parallel prediction model for short-term power load data. To study and analyze the power load forecasting, we propose a short-term power load forecasting scheme based on the Map/Reduce model theory, to establish a sub-network and global load forecasting model, and the parallel

S. Liu and G. Yang (Eds.): ADHIP 2018, LNICST 279, pp. 126–136, 2019.
https://doi.org/10.1007/978-3-030-19086-6_14

prediction model of the design is analyzed and tested. The test results show that the parallel prediction model proposed in this paper has a very high effectiveness.

2 Short-Term Power Load Forecasting Theory Analysis

2.1 Short-Term Power Load Big Data Classification Analysis

The power load forecasting is based on relevant historical data to restore load characteristics, and it estimates the time load in the future. The study of power load forecasting is of great significance and is not limited to estimating the load trend, the key point is that power load forecasting can be used as a basis for important work such as power grid planning and power dispatch, which effectively improving resource utilization and improving grid environment [2]. Before load forecasting, we must analyze the load characteristics, the load forecasting classification and the prediction steps, then make full preparations for further load forecasting.

The load forecasting content is complex and different divisions are obtained according to different criteria. According to the classification of electricity, it can be divided into agricultural power load, industrial power load and residential electricity load. According to the length of time, the power load forecast can be divided into long-term, medium-term, short-term and ultra-short-term power load forecasting [3]. Among the short-term power load forecasting, the forecasting object is the load at each moment of the day, the characteristic is that it has strong periodicity and is influenced by weather factors. Therefore, the forecasting model must consider the influence of weather factors, This prediction is usually used to assist in the determination of fuel supply for power generation, and to make an advance estimate of the operating power plant to ensure that the unit maintenance plan is properly scheduled. The main forecasting methods include periodic time series forecasting, neural network forecasting, and related predictions that take into account weather factors. Law et al. [4].

2.2 Selected Short-Term Power Load Big Data Prediction Theory

Usually, The main content of load forecasting research is to restore the load characteristic curve based on historical load. However, complex power system load characteristics are also affected by external factors. In the prediction and analysis of power load, it should be comprehensive and comprehensive. Under the joint action of internal and external factors, load forecasting has the characteristics of inaccuracy, condition, time, and method diversity [5].

Electric power load forecasting is of great significance to industry efficiency and even to social and economic development. The research process of load forecasting must be comprehensive and specific, and its implementation must be organized and orderly, and unnecessary error interference must be reduced. The specific forecasting process is mainly divided into the following steps: determining the target to collect data, sorting out the data, data preprocessing, establishing a prediction model, load forecasting, and result analysis [6]. The accurate implementation of each step of these steps will play a crucial role in ultimately obtaining effective prediction results, and each procedure must be strictly monitored. The specific process is shown in Fig. 1.

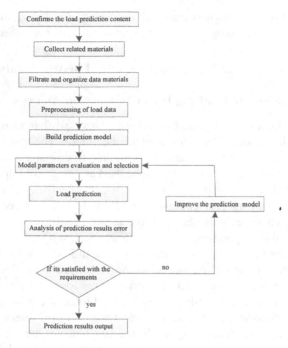

Fig. 1. Load forecasting flowchart

3 Model Design of Short-Term Power Load Big Data Parallel Prediction

3.1 Building a Map/Reduce Framework

Map/Reduce, first proposed by Goggle, is one of the most widely used frameworks for distributed processing of massive data (usually larger than 1TB) in recent years [7]. Map/Reduce is derived from the two core operations Map and Reduce of distributed processing. Map is responsible for distributing large tasks in parallel and distributed to multiple machines. Each machine only calculates the data stored in local memory. Reduce synthesizes the results of multiple machines in Map to get the final result. The entire running process takes the form of key-value pairs as input and output. The Map/Reduce workflow is shown in Fig. 2.

Data Locality (DL) is a feature of Map/Reduce. Map is responsible for breaking data, and Reduce is responsible for data aggregation [8]. The Reduce function is a summary of the results for intermediate operations. Although it does not have good parallel performance of the Map function, its calculation methods are mostly simple, so it is suitable for large-scale parallel operation. This simplified parallel computing programming model can shield the differences of the underlying physical structure, and only provide the available interfaces to the upper user. It stores data on compute nodes as much as possible, which can avoid the centralized upload of large amounts of raw data.

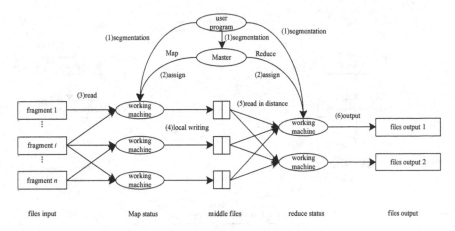

Fig. 2. The Map/Reduce workflow

Therefore, applying the Map/Reduce processing framework to big data processing in a smart grid not only reduces a large amount of communication overhead, but also can make full use of an idle device with a computing capability that is widely distributed in a power grid to exert a scale calculation capability.

3.2 Prediction Flow Design Based on Map/Reduce Framework

The grid load has statistically significant characteristics of periodicity and similarity. Based on the above-mentioned Map/Reduce functional program design to deal with the "divide and conquer" idea of big data, this paper proposes a short-term power load parallel prediction method based on big data, as shown in Fig. 3.

MapReduce is a programming model that can be used for data processing. It provides a universal, reliable and fault-tolerant distributed computing framework. MapReduce has some limitations on how to implement applications.

These restrictions are as follows:

All calculations are decomposed into map or reduce tasks

Tasks are defined mainly based on input data and output data.

Tasks depend on their input data and do not need to communicate with other tasks.

MapReduce uses the map and reduce functions to implement the application and execute these restrictions. These numbers are grouped into jobs and run as a whole: run mapper first and then reducer. Run as many tasks as possible. Because parallel tasks do not run on each other, they can be run in any order as long as the map tasks run before the reduce tasks.

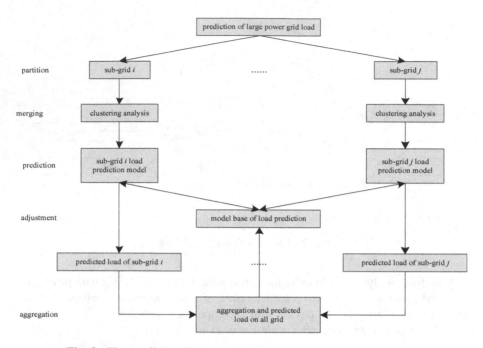

Fig. 3. The parallel prediction model of short-term power load big data

3.3   Realization of Short-Term Power Load Big Data Forecast

Based on the addition of meteorological monitoring devices at each substation of 110 kV and above, real-time meteorological data (temperature, humidity, rainfall, wind speed, etc.) and weather forecast data (predicted temperature, predicted humidity, predicted rainfall, forecasted wind speed) of each sub-network are collected. Data are quantified and interpolated, together with the load data to form the maximum data set available [9]. Based on the above studies, sub-networks and global load forecasting models were established.

3.3.1   Short-Term Power Load Forecast of the Entire Network

Without considering loss, the global load should be equal to the sum of all subnet loads, but in practice the global load is higher than the sum of all subnet loads. The degree of increase in each moment is different, and the relative stability is determined by factors such as the power consumption of the plant, network loss, and load. Set W_t as the proportional coefficient of the load of the global grid at the time of t and the sum of the n subnet loads at the corresponding time. k_t is the degree to which the global load is higher than the sum of the loads of the various subnets, and the fluctuation range is small. The relationship between the two is:

$$w_t = 1 + k_t \tag{1}$$

The load at each moment of the global power grid is the sum of all sub-network loads at the corresponding time multiplied by the proportional coefficient at the corresponding time. Set L_t to the global grid load at time t, where n is the number of subnets and $l_t(i)$ is the load of subnet i at time t. The formula is as follows:

$$L_t = w_t \times \sum_{i=1}^{n} l_t(i) \qquad (2)$$

Through the above two formulas, the global grid load value at a certain moment can be obtained.

3.3.2 Subnet Short-Term Power Load Big Data Forecast

Numerous studies have shown that meteorological factors are the dominant factors affecting short-term load; and among many meteorological factors, temperature has the most significant and regular effects on the power load in each region. In addition, due to the interaction between the urban heat island effect, temperature and humidity effects, and cumulative effects, the power load characteristics in summer become more complicated, especially for a large power grid that covers a large geographic area.

It sets a certain threshold, selects the influencing factor vector with higher similarity and the load at the corresponding time as the input of the sub-network prediction model, and performs the prediction one by one. According to the different load characteristics of each sub-network and the different influencing factors, the appropriate load forecasting model is selected to perform point-by-point load forecasting for each sub-network. The three-layer BP neural network load forecasting model has a better nonlinear system approximation capability in dealing with the stationary random time series of complex variables, and can easily account for factors such as temperature, rainfall, and relative humidity that have important influence on the power load. The role of [10]. Therefore, this paper selects three layers of BP neural network as the subnet load forecasting model in the load forecasting model library.

The BP network adopts a three-layer structure. The first layer is the input layer: the input variables are the variables related to the load to be predicted, including the daily type, THI, rainfall, and the historical load of the corresponding time; The second layer is the hidden layer. According to experience, the number of neurons in the hidden layer is 7–16, and the output of the hidden layer adopts the logsig function. The third layer is the output layer. It sets the load forecast value L at a certain time of the day to be predicted, adopts a linear transformation function, sets wi to be the connection weight of the hidden layer and the output layer neuron, and yi is the output of the hidden layer neuron. n is the number of hidden layer neurons. As shown in the equation:

$$L = \sum_{i=1}^{n} w_i y_i \qquad (3)$$

The adjustment of BP network connection weights and thresholds is the main component that affects the performance of BP network. In this paper, the "negative gradient descent" theory is adopted to adjust the connection weights and connection thresholds of input layer and hidden layer, hidden layer and output layer. The initial values of the connection weights and thresholds of the BP network are given randomly ($-1 < w < 1$), E is the sum of the error sum of the actual value and the network output; X is the learning rate; $w_{ij}(t)$ is the input layer. The connection weights of i-th neurons and j-th neurons of the hidden layer are calculated as follows:

$$w_{ij}(t) = -X\frac{E}{w_{ij}} + L \qquad (4)$$

In the same way, we can calculate the connection weight between the jth neuron in the hidden layer and the kth neuron in the output layer, i.e. $w_{jk}(t)$ is calculated as:

$$w_{jk}(t) = -X\frac{E}{w_{jk}} + L \qquad (5)$$

Y is the connection value between neurons. The meaning of the subscript is the same as the weight. Adjust the above two formulas to get:

$$Y_{ij}(t) = -X\frac{E}{Y_{ij}} + L \qquad (6)$$

$$Y_{jk}(t) = -X\frac{E}{Y_{jk}} + L \qquad (7)$$

Through the above several formulas, the load forecasting value at a certain moment can be obtained, and the connection weights and connection values between neurons can be obtained according to the difference between this value and a specific learning rate. According to the connection weight obtained, the system performance of the model can be directly judged. The three-layer BP neural network load forecasting model is shown in Fig. 4.

As a main model of artificial neural network, BP neural network is widely applied. It is a multi-layer forward network with one-way propagation. The input signal passes through the hidden layers from the input node to the output node. The output of each layer node only affects the input of the next layer node. It propagates back the error between the actual output and the expected output of the neural network. The whole training process is the process of the global error of the network tending to the minimum.

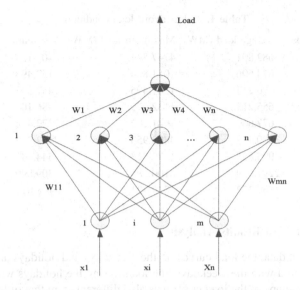

Fig. 4. Three-layer BP neural network load forecasting model

4 Test Analysis

In order to verify the validity and accuracy of the load forecasting method mentioned above, this paper uses the actual load data and meteorological data from a province in southern China as a basis for modeling and forecasting. A parallel short-term power load forecasting model based on big data was constructed for weekdays and body-building days, and compared with the load forecasting results of a centralized ARIMA model and other forecasting methods, and the forecasting effects and advantages of each method were analyzed. The study area is a province in southern China that covers a relatively large geographic area, it is with typical of a subtropical monsoon climate, where has high temperatures and rain in summer. July has the highest monthly average temperature in the year. During this period, due to the influence of high temperature, the accuracy of summer load forecasting is basically the lowest in the annual load forecasting work. Based on the 96-point real load monitoring data, real-time meteorological data and user data were collected and maintained throughout the province in summer, this paper applies the proposed method to carry out the short-term power load forecasting and error analysis in this region.

4.1 Selected Test Test Data

This article's simulation environment: HP Z220SFF sequence F4F06PA model workstation, Intel Xeon E3 quad-core processor, 3.2 GHz CPU frequency. In this paper, the area to be forecasted is divided into 9 sub-networks, and each sub-network is simulated by examples. Each subnet load data is shown in Table 1.

Table 1. Sub-network load conditions

Subnet number	Average load (MW)	Maximum load (MW)	Minimum load (MW)
1	3682.801	4747.841	2405.154
2	674.606	1051.854	157.493
3	876.213	1201.495	457.543
4	655.213	1132.079	286.105
5	677.669	941.172	322.466
6	3800.419	4803.953	2462.932
7	995.822	1279.813	544.847
8	2297.629	3100.285	1309.890
9	1362.372	1879.321	748.011

4.2   Prediction Test Results Analysis

For the daily load data, the load curves on the weekdays and holidays are significantly different. Compared with the weekdays, the load during the holidays was significantly reduced, and the shape of the load curve was also different from that of the normal day. In this section, the 96-point load of weekdays and body-wake days is selected to perform rolling forecasting and compared with the traditional load forecasting method to verify the validity and stability of the proposed load top-measurement method. The weekday forecast curve is shown in Fig. 5.

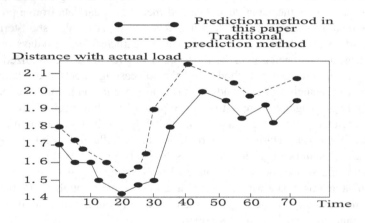

Fig. 5. The weekday forecast curve

As can be seen from the figure, for the weekday, the parallel forecasting model of short-term power load big data proposed in this paper has a better prediction result, and the deviation between the forecasting curve and the actual load is small, the average deviation is 1.7, and the overall prediction effect is good. However, the load forecasting value made by using other traditional forecasting methods has a large deviation from the actual value, especially in the load peaks and valleys, the load forecasting effect is not good, the average deviation is 1.9, which is 12% higher than this model.

The holiday forecast curve is shown in Fig. 6.

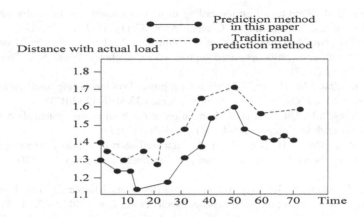

Fig. 6. Holiday forecast curve

As can be seen from the figure, the parallel forecasting model for the short-term power load big data proposed in this paper is also ideal. The deviation between the forecasting curve and the actual load is small, with an average deviation of 1.35, which has a good overall forecasting effect; However, the load forecasting value made by using other traditional forecasting methods has a large deviation from the actual value, especially in the load peak and valley periods, the load forecasting effect is not good, and the average deviation is 1.5, which is 11% higher compared to this model.

5 Conclusion

This paper proposes a parallel prediction model for short-term power load big data, analyzes the types and characteristics of different types of load forecasting, and proposes short-term power load forecasting steps. According to the forecasting steps and the Map/Reduce model theory, a short-term power load parallel prediction scheme is established to divide the sub-networks, and a short-term parallel load forecasting model based on sub-network and the whole network is established to achieve the research of this paper. The test data shows that the method designed in this paper has extremely high effectiveness. It is hoped that this paper can provide a theoretical basis for the study of short-term power load big data parallel prediction model.

Facing the large power load data in smart grid, in order to fully mine and analyze local and global information in the area to be predicted and avoid data anomalies and network congestion caused by uploading a large number of data sets, it is necessary to study and develop more effective short-term power load according to the characteristics of wide-area distribution of power grid sensing system. Big data prediction method.

References

1. Weekend, J.M.: Short-term load forecasting method combined with multi-algorithm multi-model and online second learning. Comput. Appl. **37**(11), 3317–3322 (2017)
2. Xiong, J.H., Niu, X., Zhang, C.G., et al.: Short-term load forecasting based on wavelet transform with Drosophila optimized support vector machines. Power Syst. Prot. Control **45**(13), 71–77 (2017)
3. Liu, D.D., Zhu, J.M., Huang, T.T.: Short-term power load forecasting based on time series and grey model. J. Qiqihar Univ. (Natural Science) **33**(3), 7–12 (2017)
4. Li, L., Yang, S.F., Qiu, J.P., et al.: Simulation research on power system short term load forecasting method. Comput. Simul. **34**(1), 104–108 (2017)
5. Wang, W.G., Dou, Z.H., Shen, J., et al.: Improved short-term load forecasting based on backstepping theory for fuzzy mean function. Hydroelectric Energy Sci. **14**(12), 208–211 (2017)
6. Zhi, L., Guoqiang, S., Zhinong, W., et al.: Short-term load forecasting based on variable selection and Gaussian process regression. Electr. Power Const. **38**(2), 122–128 (2017)
7. Song, R.J., Yu, T., Chen, Y.H., et al.: Similarity duplicate records detection algorithm for big data based on MapReduce model. J. Shanghai Jiaotong Univ. **52**(2), 214–221 (2018)
8. Xiao, W., Hu, J., Zhou, X.F.: Research review of parallel association rules mining algorithm based on MapReduce computing model. Res. Comput. Appl. **38**(1), 132–139 (2018)
9. Lei, J.S., Hao, X., Zhu, G.K.: Short-term power load forecasting based on "layered-pooling" model. Electric Power Constr. **38**(1), 68–75 (2017)
10. Su, X., Liu, T.Q., Cao, H.Q., et al.: Short-term load forecasting based on multi-distributed distributed BP neural network based on Hadoop architecture. Proc. CSEE **37**(17), 4966–4973 (2017)

Approximate Data Fusion Algorithm for Internet of Things Based on Probability Distribution

Xiao-qiang Wu$^{(\boxtimes)}$, Lan Wu, and Liyan Tu

College of Mechanical Engineering, Inner Mongolia University
for the Nationalities, Inner Mongolla, Tongliao 028043, China
wxqimun@163.com

Abstract. In the context of big data, data fusion in the perception layer of the Internet of Things is extremely necessary. Fusion data can reduce the amount of data traffic in the network, avoid wasting network resources and bring great convenience to users' observation and analysis. Aiming at the high computational complexity of the data fusion algorithm at the current, an approximate data fusion algorithm for the perception layer of the Internet of Things based on the probability distribution is proposed in this paper. Firstly, the data fusion model of the perception layer of the Internet of Things and the probability distribution model of the node data are analyzed. And then, disturbances are applied to the node data to achieve the purpose of concealing the collected data. Finally, the approximate fusion of data in the sensing layer is achieved by collecting the probability distribution of the data. The experimental results verify the effectiveness of the fusion algorithm and test the influence of the algorithm parameters on the fusion effect, which provides a reference for the engineering implementation of the algorithm.

Keywords: Big data · Internet of Things · Perception layer · Data fusion · Probability distribution

1 Introduction

Internet of Things technology is an extension of Internet technology. The Internet started from the end of the 20th century with the purpose of academic exchanges. It has gradually developed into a global information exchange platform [1, 2]. The Internet affects our society, economy and culture. Due to the pursuit of intelligence, people want to add various devices and articles to the Internet. In this context, people proposed the concept of the Internet of Things. The emergence of the Internet of Things has caused many problems, such as the problem of multi-sensor data fusion in sensor networks, information connectivity problems of multiple devices and items, data communication problems between sensors, and equipment monitoring and control problems.

A key issue that needs to be solved in the data fusion of the Internet of Things awareness layer is the contradiction between limited network resources and security requirements [3, 4]. To address this issue, scholars have proposed a variety of security data fusion schemes from different perspectives. The secure information aggregation

S. Liu and G. Yang (Eds.): ADHIP 2018, LNICST 279, pp. 137–144, 2019.
https://doi.org/10.1007/978-3-030-19086-6_15

protocol first presents the data fusion results of the data fusion node, and then uses efficient sampling and interaction verification to ensure that the fusion value is an approximation of the true value. However, this protocol requires high reliability data values and consumes high node resources [5]. The secure data aggregation and verification protocol uses a key sharing scheme to distribute keys to nodes in the cluster. At the same time, nodes in the cluster partially sign the average value of the calculated data in the cluster. This scheme can verify the integrity of the fused data, but the amount of calculation is large [6]. Luo proposed efficient and secure data aggregation, using fuzzy algorithms and model codes to eliminate redundant information sensed by sensor nodes and perform corresponding data fusion operations. This method helps to improve the confidentiality of data and the energy efficiency of sensor nodes [7]. Ganeriwal and Srivastava proposed a reputation based framework sensor networks trust model for wireless sensor networks when researching data fusion technology [8].

The above security scheme either increases the number of interactions between nodes or poses excessive challenges to the nodes' computation and storage resources. Therefore, an approximate data fusion algorithm for the perception layer of the Internet of Things based on the probability distribution is proposed. The chapters of the manuscript are arranged as follows. The first part is the introduction. The second part introduces the model of data fusion in the perception layer of the Internet of Things. The third part proposes the approximate fusion algorithm of sensory data. The fourth part analyzes the performance of the fusion algorithm. The fifth part is a simulation experiment. The last part is the conclusion.

2   Internet of Things Sensing Layer Data Fusion Model

The sensing layer is composed of various sensors or sensor networks and controllers. Its function is similar to that of human beings. It can acquire natural signals. It is mainly used to collect and process signals to a certain extent, form information or identify objects. The core technologies of this layer include sensor technology, computer control technology, and radio frequency technology. The core products involved include sensors, sensor networks, and controllers.

Multi-sensor data fusion is also called information fusion. For information fusion, it is difficult for researchers to give a consistent and comprehensive definition. The overall data produced by multiple sensors is denser than the information it has in its various components. The multi-sensor data fusion method relates to the quality and efficiency of information fusion, which is mainly reflected in the fusion algorithm. Therefore, the core problem in the research of information fusion technology is to study the fusion algorithm. Due to the diversity and complexity of information, information fusion methods must have certain parallel processing capabilities and robustness. In general, non-linear mathematical methods that are fault-tolerant, adaptable, memory-capable, and parallel-processing are all fusion algorithms. At present, the more common data fusion algorithms can be divided into two categories. They are data fusion method based on stochastic theory and artificial intelligence based data fusion method.

2.1 Network Models and Security Assumptions

Assume that the perception layer of the Internet of Things is large and the number of nodes is large. The node is fixed in position after it is deployed and will not be moved again. The network topology structure is a cluster tree hybrid structure whose model is shown in Fig. 1.

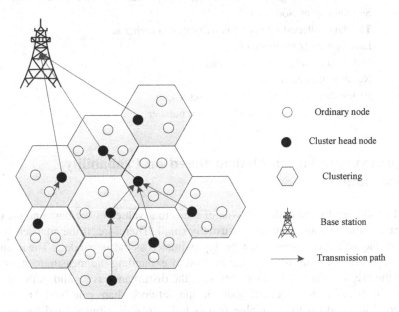

○   Ordinary node

●   Cluster head node

⬡   Clustering

🗼   Base station

⟶   Transmission path

Fig. 1. Network topology

The central node of the entire network is called a base station. The base station summarizes all the information. Each small area in the network forms a cluster. The nodes in the cluster responsible for data fusion aggregation are called cluster heads. A tree structure is formed between the cluster heads, and the result of the fusion is uploaded to the base station in a multi-hop manner.

2.2 System Parameter Design and Workflow

The data security fusion algorithm consists of two parts: data encryption and data fusion and ID compression fusion. Table 1 shows the meaning of symbols in the system.

Table 1. System parameters and meanings

Symbol	Representative meaning
S_i	The node numbered i
$Seed_i$	Shared secret random number seed shared by node i and base station
p_i	Data collected by node i
$f(x)$	The function that generates the session key, parameter x is a random number seed
key_i	Session key of Node i
$cipher_i$	The data collected by node i is encrypted in cipher text
Q	Large prime Q for modulus
Tab_i	List of child nodes of cluster head i
$Count$	Number of nodes in the cluster
$Length$	ID number compression coded packet length
$Number$	ID number compression coding group number

3 Approximate Fusion Method Based on Probability Distribution

The data collected by the nodes consists of the actual values of the data and measurement errors. The measurement error is usually small. Therefore, if the attacker directly intercepts the measured values, it can be approximated as the actual data. The main idea of the proposed algorithm is to use the method of expanding the measurement error to perturb the original data, so that the data after the disturbance is invalid to the attacker because the error is too large. All nodes in the network share rule bits: The original collected data is added to a variable that is uniformly distributed, and the result is transmitted to the cluster head. The cluster head receives the data of the nodes in the cluster and adds them directly. Because the intermediate process does not need to be decrypted, the algorithm satisfies the additive homomorphism feature, and the cluster head receives less data. If the attacker intercepts the fusion result of the cluster head and simply replaces the disturbance data superimposed by all the nodes with a uniformly distributed mathematical expectation, there is still a large error. Because the base station has data of the entire network, in the case of a large amount of data, more accurate results can be obtained by replacing the disturbance data with mathematical expectation.

The network consists of a base station and N clusters. The cluster heads are denoted by $A_1, A_2 \ldots, A_N$, respectively. Before the data transmission starts, the algorithm flow is described according to the node type.

3.1 Ordinary Leaf Node Fusion

Collect raw data, denoted as v_i. Generate random variable X_i, X_i is uniformly distributed $U(0, R)$, where R is the system given parameters. Calculate the fusion result according to the following formula

$$cp_i = v_i + X_i \tag{1}$$

The fusion result is passed to the cluster head.

3.2 Cluster Head Data Fusion

Let the cluster head receive data as $p_1, p_2, \ldots, p_i$. Calculate the sum of ciphertext received by cluster heads

$$sum_i = \sum_{j=1}^{n_i} p_i \tag{2}$$

The data received by each cluster head is

$$p_i = Enc(sum_i | num_i, key_i) \tag{3}$$

Each cluster head data is broadcast to the base station through multiple hops.

3.3 Base Station Data Fusion

According to the ID number and corresponding symmetric key, Data is decrypted based on the decryption function. The sum of the ciphertexts of all nodes is

$$sum = \sum_{i=1}^{N} sum_i \tag{4}$$

The sum of the original data collected by the node estimated by the base station is

$$total = sum - \sum_{i=1}^{k} num_i \tag{5}$$

Therefore, the actual average value of node data can be calculated by

$$average = total / N\_work \tag{6}$$

4 Performance Analysis

Approximate fusion method based on probability distribution uses ambiguous methods to encrypt data. For node S_i, the original data collected is v_i, the generated disturbance data is X_i, and the encrypted data is

$$p_i = v_i + X_i \tag{7}$$

The security of cryptographic algorithms lies in the degree of confusion between ciphertext and plaintext. When the number of nodes is large, the maximum value of the parameter R that the disturbance data obeys the uniform distribution is usually larger than the average value of the original collected data. Let

$$R = \mu + 3\sigma \tag{8}$$

At this time, data security is the highest. If the system security requirement is not very high, R can be appropriately reduced to reduce system errors.

5 Experiment Analysis

Assume that the network consists of N_group clusters. The number of child nodes in each cluster head is equal to C_Num and both are 100. The variables collected at different nodes in the same cluster are independent of each other and subject to the same normal distribution. The systematic error threshold is β, the perturbation data $X \sim U(0, R)$ added by each node in the network, the normal distribution image selects 0.025 points. Search for the appropriate R value based on the parameters. The goal of the search is that the base station can estimate the approximate value of the error threshold by statistical means. Through the way of controlling variables, study the influence of different parameters on the value of R. The experimental results are shown in Figs. 2, 3 and 4.

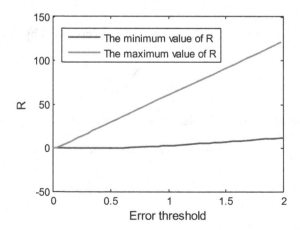

Fig. 2. Relationship between error threshold and R

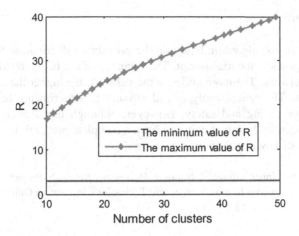

Fig. 3. Relationship between the number of clusters and R

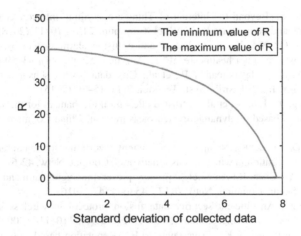

Fig. 4. Relationship between standard deviation and R

The parts between the two curves in Figs. 2, 3 and 4 are all the range of R that meets the requirements. On the basis of satisfying the requirements, increasing R increases the security of the system and decreases R to reduce the system error. Therefore, the R value needs to be set by the user according to the actual situation. As can be seen from Fig. 2, the maximum and minimum values of R increase as the error threshold increases. From Fig. 3, it can be seen that when the number of nodes in the cluster is fixed, the maximum value of R increases as the number of clusters increases, and the minimum value is independent of the number of clusters. As can be seen from Fig. 4, both the maximum and minimum values of R decrease as the standard deviation of the acquired data increases, and when the standard deviation is too large, the R value that meets the requirement may not be found.

6 Conclusion

An approximate fusion algorithm based on the probability distribution for the Internet of Things is proposes in the manuscript. The accuracy of the fusion results is related to the size of the network. The more nodes in the network, the higher the accuracy of the fusion results is. Theoretical analysis and simulation experiments have proved its feasibility, energy saving and safety. However, although this fusion algorithm can realize the data security fusion, it does not form a complete protocol. It still needs to be studied in terms of key distribution and key update.

Acknowledgements. Inner Mongolia National University Research Project (NMDYB1729). Inner Mongolia Autonomous Region Science and Technology Innovation Guide Project in 2018: KCBJ2018028.

References

1. Daza, L., Misra, S.: Beyond the Internet of Things: everything interconnected: technology, communications and computing. IEEE Wirel. Commun. **24**(6), 10–11 (2018)
2. Xiao, F., Miao, Q., Xie, X., et al.: Indoor anti-collision alarm system based on wearable Internet of Things for smart healthcare. IEEE Commun. Mag. **56**(4), 53–59 (2018)
3. Wang, M., Perera, C., Jayaraman, P.P., et al.: City data fusion: sensor data fusion in the Internet of Things. Int. J. Distrib. Syst. Technol. **7**(1), 15–36 (2015)
4. Gong, B., Wang, Y., Liu, X., et al.: A trusted attestation mechanism for the sensing nodes of Internet of Things based on dynamic trusted measurement. China Commun. **15**(2), 100–121 (2018)
5. Kalpakis, K., Dasgupta, K., Namjoshi, P.: Efficient algorithms for maximum lifetime data gathering and aggregation in wireless sensor networks. Comput. Netw. **42**(6), 697–716 (2003)
6. Wang, X., Mu, Y., Chen, R.: An efficient privacy-preserving aggregation and billing protocol for smart grid. Secur. Commun. Netw. **9**(17), 4536–4547 (2016)
7. Luo, W., Hu, X.: An efficient security data fusion protocol in wireless sensor network. J. Chongqing Univ. Posts Telecommun. Nat. Sci. Ed. **21**(1), 110–114 (2009)
8. Ganeriwal, S., Balzano, L.K., Srivastava, M.B.: Reputation-based framework for high integrity sensor networks. ACM Trans. Sens. Netw. **4**(3), 1–37 (2008)

An Adaptive Threshold VIRE Algorithm for Indoor Positioning

Boshen Liu and Jiaqi Zhen[✉]

College of Electronic Engineering, Heilongjiang University,
Harbin 150080, China
zhenjiaqi2011@163.com

Abstract. At present, global positioning system (GPS) is the most widely used positioning technology for outdoors, but when it is indoors, its positioning accuracy will become lower. The anti-jamming ability of radio frequency identification (RFID) is strong, and it can be carried out in bad environment. Because of its advantages of non-sight distance, non-contact, relatively low price and so on, the application of RFID can realize the requirement of high-precision positioning. By analyzing the existing indoor positioning system, an algorithm of selecting the adaptive threshold value in virtual reference elimination (VIRE) is proposed in this paper, it can find the appropriate threshold values for each target to accommodate complex changes in the indoor environment, simulation results manifest its effectiveness.

Keywords: Radio Frequency Identification · Adaptive threshold ·
Indoor positioning

1 Introduction

The most famous positioning technology is the Global Positioning system (GPS) in the United States. However, because of the shielding of satellite signals by buildings, GPS cannot provide an accurate indoor positioning. Radio Frequency Identification (RFID): a technology that uses radio frequency signals for contactless communication to identify and exchange information [1]. The data exchange is bidirectional and the RFID carries large information capacity, which can be used for identification. It can also be used for information exchange. Radio frequency can be divided into high frequency, microwave frequency, identification distance can reach tens of meters in microwave frequency band, the anti-interference ability of RFID without manual intervention is strong, and it can also be carried out in harsh environment [2]. It can be widely used in traffic scheduling, toll station, anti-counterfeiting, tracking, medical, library,

This work was supported by the National Natural Science Foundation of China under Grant 61501176, Natural Science Foundation of Heilongjiang Province F2018025, University Nursing Program for Young Scholars with Creative Talents in Heilongjiang Province UNPYSCT-2016017, the postdoctoral scientific research developmental fund of Heilongjiang Province in 2017 LBH-Q17149.

S. Liu and G. Yang (Eds.): ADHIP 2018, LNICST 279, pp. 145–150, 2019.
https://doi.org/10.1007/978-3-030-19086-6_16

production, logistics and other fields. It can meet the requirement of high precision positioning when it is used in positioning [3].

Based on the research of indoor positioning technology of the RFID, there are a variety of positioning methods, TOA, TDOA, AOA, RSSI method. TOA method relies on signal propagation time parameters, usually by using triangulation to achieve the positioning. TDOA method relies on signal propagation time difference as parameters, usually uses triangular positioning. AOA is mainly dependent on the signal propagation angle [4].

LANDMARC is a classical localization algorithm, which uses reference tags to achieve localization. In short, if the RSSI value of the target tag is consistent with that of the reference tag, the target tag is considered to be at the same location with the reference tag (the position of the reference tags are known at first). In the case of the same precision, this method uses the cheap reference tag to replace the expensive RFID reader, and the cost is greatly reduced [5]. But under the condition of high precision, a large number of RFID tags need to be arranged, which is not only expensive, but also prone to interference. The idea of VIRE is not to add additional reference tags, but to introduce grid virtual reference tags. The grid virtual reference tag is not an entity, but assumes that there is an existing reference tag at some coordinate point [6]. The power value of the virtual grid reference tag is not read from the reader, but is introduced by interpolation. When introduced, the grid virtual tag can be used as a reference value.

In this paper, an improved VIRE algorithm—IMP_VIRE is proposed. First, we analyze the existing LANDMARC and VIRE system, and propose a method of selecting the adaptive threshold value in VIRE. We use the method to find appropriate threshold values for each target tag to accommodate complex changes in the environment. The purpose is to enhance the accuracy of indoor localization.

2 Improvement of VIRE Algorithm

In LANDMARC, the RSSI values of virtual tags are not read by readers, they are calculated by linear interpolation. However, a large number of researches show that the signal attenuation basically accords with the log-distance path loss model, so the signal change is nonlinear, and the linear interpolation method does not accord with the signal attenuation law. So VIRE uses log-distance path loss model to interpolate.

In the proposed algorithm, we consider finding the appropriate threshold value for each target tag to adapt to the complex changes of the environment. We use $\omega_i = \omega_{1i} \times \omega_{2i}$ as a merge weight in VIRE, based on the theoretical analysis of clustering analysis of virtual reference tags selected by proximity map method is carried out. The adjacent virtual tags that are to be joined together are divided into a class. The weight value of each class is:

$$\omega_m = \frac{n_{cm}}{\sum\limits_{m=1}^{n_s} n_{cm}} \tag{1}$$

where n_{cm} represents the number of adjacent virtual tags adjacent to each other in class, n represents the total number of classes. $m \in (1, n_s)$, ω_m is a function related to the density of the selected virtual reference tag. The densest area has the largest ω_m. Using the following formula to represent the weights of each virtual reference tag in the same class:

$$\omega_q = \frac{1/E_q^2}{\sum\limits_{q=1}^{n} cm \ 1/E_q^2} \tag{2}$$

where $q \in (1, n_{cm})$ is the signal intensity Euclidean distance between virtual tag and target tag. In the same class, the greater the difference between the RSSI value of the virtual reference tag and the target tag, the bigger the E_q, the smaller the ω_q. Based on the weights ω_m and ω_q, it is determined that the location of the target tag is estimated as:

$$(x, y) = \sum\limits_{m=1}^{n_s} \omega_m \sum\limits_{q=1}^{n_{cm}} \frac{1/E_q^2}{\sum\limits_{q=1}^{n} cm \ 1/E_q^2} (x_q, y_q) \tag{3}$$

where (x_q, y_q) is the coordinate position of the adjacent virtual tag. And we call this algorithm IMP_VIRE.

VIRE not only provides the concept of virtual reference tag but also provides another concept: proximity maps. The entire region is divided into regions centered on each reference tag. When the target tag is compared with the RSSI value of a certain region, and when the difference is within a certain threshold, the area is marked as 1, on the contrary, the area is marked as 0. At this point, the map obtained is called the approximate map. After the approximate maps of each reader are obtained, the most likely region is found by using the intersection function. This process eliminates some areas where the location is not possible, thus improving the positioning accuracy.

The IMP_VIRE algorithm adaptively finds the appropriate threshold for each target tag using the following methods: First determine the target tag's range of adjacent tag.

$$R(A, V) = \left(1, \frac{\mu V}{A}\right) \tag{4}$$

where μ is the optimization parameter of the LANDMARC and A is the total number of actual reference tags. The initial threshold value th_0 is set according to the signal strength of the virtual tag, and the signal strength of the target tag and the signal intensity of the virtual tag are compared respectively. When the difference of the signal intensity between the target tag and the virtual tag is not greater than the initial threshold value of th_0, then select the virtual tag as the pseudo-adjacent virtual target tag. K readers select K groups of pseudo-adjacent virtual tags and select the same location's pseudo-adjacent virtual tags as the target tag's adjacent tag. Then judging the relationship between the number of adjacent tags m and the range of $R(A, V)$. Adjust the threshold with the following formula:

$$th_0 = th_0 - t_0 \times \frac{th_0}{V}, t > \left(\frac{\mu V}{A}\right) \tag{5}$$

$$th_0 = th_0 + \frac{th_0}{V}, t < 1 \tag{6}$$

So the process of IMP_VIRE can be describe as Fig. 1.

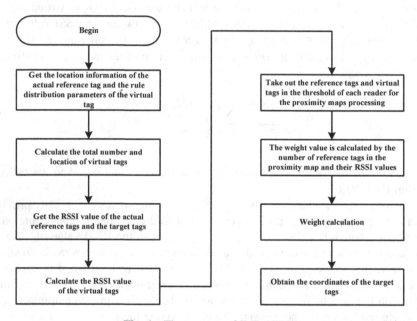

Fig. 1. The process of IMP_VIRE.

3   Experiment and Results

In order to verify that the improvement on the basis of VIRE does improve the positioning accuracy, the improved system simulation will be carried out in this chapter, and compared with the system before the improvement. The whole simulation was done in MATLAB 2014 environment. The entire area to be located is assumed to be located in a two-dimensional plane of 8 m × 8 m, while the reader is assumed to be placed on four angles of the plane, that is, the coordinates of the four readers are (0,0), (8,0), (0,8), (8,8) respectively. The simulation system will use the high frequency passive label as the reference tags and the target tags. The Experiment result is shown in Fig. 2, and the CDF curves in different regions can be clearly understood through Fig. 3.

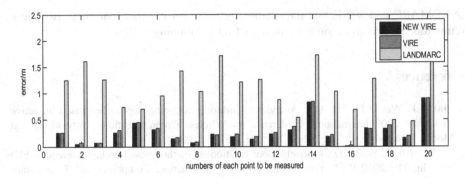

Fig. 2. Experiment result.

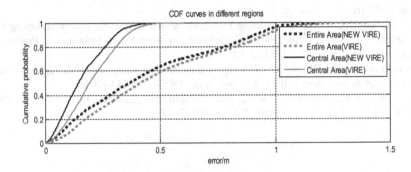

Fig. 3. CDF curves in different regions.

From these experiment results, it can be seen that the positioning error of each point is obviously decreased, and the positioning accuracy can be improved obviously by using NEW_VIRE. In the entire area, the positioning error of NEW_VIRE has more than 60% probability to lower than 0.5 m, and VIRE has less than 60% probability to lower than 0.5 m. The same argument to the comparison of the central area. It can be seen that compared with LANDMARC and VIRE, NEW_VIRE has higher localization accuracy.

4 Conclusion

In this paper, a new algorithm—IMP_VIRE is proposed. Considering the complexity of indoor environment, the single signal intensity threshold is no longer used. Instead, it adaptively finds the signal strength threshold for each tag to be positioned. In order to further improve the positioning accuracy, the new algorithm classifies the virtual reference tags selected by the proximity maps, and combining the weight value of Euclidean distance formula to estimate the location of the target tags. The effectiveness of IMP_VIRE is verified by simulation results, IMP_VIRE is the optimal algorithm in this paper. Its ability to adapt to the complex changes of the environment is better than

LANDMARC and VIRE, and the positioning accuracy is better than these two algorithms too. So it is more suitable for the RFID positioning system.

References

1. Zhu, F.J., Wei, Z.H., Hu, B.J.: Analysis of indoor positioning approaches based on active RFID. In: 2009 International Conference on Wireless Communications, Networking and Mobile Computing, Beijing, China, pp. 5182–5185 (2009)
2. Li, W., Wu, J., Wang, D.: A novel indoor positioning method based on key reference RFID tags. In: The 2010 IEEE Youth Conference on Information, Computing and Telecommunication, Shanghai, China, pp. 42–45 (2010)
3. Liu, X., Wen, M., Qin, G.: LANDMARC with improved k-nearest algorithm for RFID location system. In: 2010 IEEE International Conference on Computer and Communications, Chengdu, China, pp. 2569–2572 (2010)
4. Xu, Z., Zheng, H., Pang, M.: Utilizing high-level visual feature for indoor shopping mall localization. In: 2017 IEEE Global Conference on Signal and Information Processing, Montreal, Canada, pp. 1378–1382 (2017)
5. Grosinger, J., Pachler, W., Bosch, W.: Tag size matters: miniaturized RFID tags to connect smart objects to the internet. IEEE Microw. Mag. **19**(6), 101–111 (2018)
6. Hui, X., Kan, E.C.: Collaborative reader code division multiple access in the harmonic RFID system. IEEE J. Radio Freq. Identif. **2**(2), 86–92 (2018)

Two-Dimensional Super-Resolution Direction Finding Algorithm for Wideband Chirp Signals

Baoyu Guo and Jiaqi Zhen[✉]

College of Electronic Engineering,
Heilongjiang University, Harbin 150080, China
zhenjiaqi2011@163.com

Abstract. Conventional direction finding algorithms for wideband signal need to preliminarily estimate the Direction of Arrival (DOA) and power of the noise roughly, and it has large focusing error. In order to solve these problems, a super-resolution direction finding algorithm for two dimensional (2-D) wideband chirp signals is proposed, the Fractional Fourier Transform (FRFT) is applied to focus the energy of the signals in every frequency by the rotational characteristic of FRFT, then algorithm for narrowband signals is used to estimate the DOA, computer simulation results prove the effective of the algorithm.

Keywords: Wideband signals · Chirp signals · Direction of Arrival · Fractional Fourier Transform

1 Introduction

Spatial spectrum estimation algorithms are widely used in the fields of radar and mobile communication, but most of them are only adapt to the narrowband signals, that is the band of signal is far less than its center frequency, the signal envelope on every sensors is seem to be the same. But wideband signals are abounding in practical [1], it has been widely researched in recent years [2–5], one of them is Chirp signal. Generally speaking, algorithms of wideband signals are divided into two types: one is incoherent signal subspace method (ISM) [6], the other is coherent signal subspace method (CSM) [7, 8], the latter can deal with coherent signals, so it is obtained extensive research, its basic idea is to focus signal spaces of different frequencies to the reference frequency point, then we can get the covariance matrix of a single frequency, but it often needs to preliminarily estimate the DOA and power of the noise roughly, and it has a large focusing error. In this paper, focusing matrix is constructed by method of FRFT, then we estimate two-dimensional DOA of signals, wherever compare its performance with TCT algorithm.

This work was supported by the National Natural Science Foundation of China under Grant 61501176, Natural Science Foundation of Heilongjiang Province F2018025, University Nursing Program for Young Scholars with Creative Talents in Heilongjiang Province UNPYSCT-2016017, the postdoctoral scientific research developmental fund of Heilongjiang Province in 2017 LBH-Q17149.

S. Liu and G. Yang (Eds.): ADHIP 2018, LNICST 279, pp. 151–159, 2019.
https://doi.org/10.1007/978-3-030-19086-6_17

2   Signal Model

FRFT is a special formation of Fourier Transform, it is also related to rotation of the Wigner distribution of the given signal, it can be written

$$X_P(u) = \{F_P[x(t)]\} = \int_{-\infty}^{+\infty} x(t)K_P(t,u)\mathrm{d}t \tag{1}$$

where parameter p is called the fractional order of the transform, $F_P[\cdot]$ is kernel-based integral transformation of the form, the transform kernel $K_P(t,u)$ is

$$K_P(t,u) = \begin{cases} \sqrt{\frac{1-\mathrm{j}\cos\alpha}{2\pi}}\exp\left(\mathrm{j}\frac{t^2+u^2}{2}\mathrm{ctg}\alpha - \mathrm{j}ut\cos\alpha\right), \alpha \neq n\pi \\ \delta(t-u), \alpha = 2n\pi \\ \delta(t-u), \alpha = (2n\pm1)\pi \end{cases} \tag{2}$$

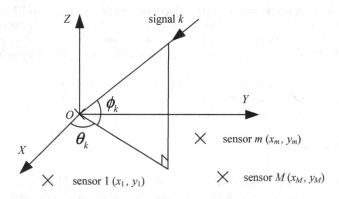

Fig. 1. Model of the signal.

As shown in Fig. 1, consider N chirp wideband signals emitted from the far field impinging on plane array of M sensors ($N < M$), arrange of the sensors is arbitrary, the phase reference point is the origin of coordinate, expression of chirp signals received by reference point is

$$s_0(t) = \exp\left[\mathrm{j}\pi\left(2f_0t^2 + kt\right)\right] \tag{3}$$

where f_0 is the initial frequency and k is the frequency modulation rate, we can obtain FRFT of the Eq. (2):

$$F_{\alpha s_0}(u) = \rho\,\exp\left[\mathrm{j}\frac{u^2(2k\cos\alpha - \sin\alpha) + 4\pi f_0 u - 4\pi^2 f_0^2 \sin\alpha}{2(2k\sin\alpha + \cos\alpha)}\right] \tag{4}$$

where $\rho = \sqrt{\frac{\cos \alpha + j \sin \alpha}{\cos \alpha + 2k \sin \alpha}}$, use FRFT on the chirp signals $x_m(t)$ received by mth sensor, that is

$$F_{\alpha x_m}(u) = F_{\alpha s_0}(u) \exp\left[j \frac{2k\tau_m^2 \cos \alpha - 4ku\tau_m - 4\pi f_0 \tau_m \cos \alpha}{2(\cos \alpha + 2k \sin \alpha)}\right] + F_{\alpha N}(u) \qquad (5)$$

where τ_m is the delay time to the reference sensor when the chirp signal arriving at the mth sensor, and $\tau_m = \frac{x_m \cos \varphi \cos \theta + y_m \sin \varphi \cos \theta}{c}$, φ, θ is separately the azimuth and elevation of the two-dimensional signal, c is speed of light, $F_{\alpha N}$ is FRFT of white Gaussian noise, the array manifold can be reduced from Eq. (4):

$$a(u, \alpha) = \left\{ \begin{array}{l} \exp\left[j \dfrac{2k\tau_1^2 \cos \alpha - 4ku\tau_1 - 4\pi f_0 \tau_1 \cos \alpha}{2(\cos \alpha + 2k \sin \alpha)}\right], \\ \cdots, \exp\left[j \dfrac{2k\tau_m^2 \cos \alpha - 4ku\tau_m - 4\pi f_0 \tau_m \cos \alpha}{2(\cos \alpha + 2k \sin \alpha)}\right] \end{array} \right\}^{\mathrm{T}} \qquad (6)$$

so it is affected by the parameters of the chirp signal, output of the array is defined as:

$$X(u, \alpha) = A(u, \alpha)S(u, \alpha) + N(u, \alpha) \qquad (7)$$

where

$$S(u, \alpha) = [s_1(u, \alpha), \cdots s_N(u, \alpha)]^{\mathrm{T}} \qquad (8)$$

it is the vector of the signal, and

$$N(u, \alpha) = [n_1(u, \alpha), \cdots, n_M(u, \alpha)]^{\mathrm{T}} \qquad (9)$$

it is the vector of the noise, then matrix of array manifold in FRFT domain can be expressed as:

$$A(u, \alpha) = [a(u, \alpha, \theta_1, \varphi_1), \cdots, a(u, \alpha, \theta_N, \varphi_N)] \qquad (10)$$

mathematical expectation of Eq. (4) can be written

$$E\left[F_{\alpha X_m}(u)F_{\alpha X_m}^{\mathrm{H}}(u)\right] = |F_{\alpha s_0}(u)|^2 + |F_{\alpha N}(u)|^2 \qquad (11)$$

where $E[.]$ denotes mathematical expectation, and

$$|F_{\alpha s_0}(u)|^2 = \left| \frac{1}{\cos \alpha + 2\pi k \sin \alpha} \right| \qquad (12)$$

so we can obtain the FRFT covariance matrix of X

$$R_X(u) = E\left[X(u)X^{\mathrm{H}}(u)\right] \qquad (13)$$

3 Focusing Energy of the Signals

In order to focus the energy of the signals, we need to estimate their frequencies, from Eq. (12), we have

$$\operatorname{ctg}\alpha = -k \tag{14}$$

where k is frequency modulation rate of chirp signal, combine Eqs. (6) and (14), we have

$$
\begin{aligned}
a(u, \alpha, \theta) = \{ &\exp[j(\operatorname{ctg}\alpha\tau_1 + 2ku \sec \alpha + 2\pi f_0)\tau_1], \cdots, \\
&\exp[j(\operatorname{ctg}\alpha\tau_m + 2ku \sec \alpha + 2\pi f_0)\tau_m]\}^{\mathrm{T}}
\end{aligned} \tag{15}
$$

steer vectors can be deduced from Eq. (15), it is easer than Eq. (5), computation is decreased obviously, then spatial spectrum can be obtained by the equation below:

$$P(\theta, \varphi) = \frac{1}{a^H(u, k, \theta, \varphi)\mathbf{R}^{-1}a(u, k, \theta, \varphi)} \tag{16}$$

When estimating the directions of one signals reflecting from multipath, we only need to know one modulation rate of them, as they are the same. The algorithm of the paper has two properties: (1) It does not need to preliminarily estimate DOA and the power of the noise roughly; (2) It focuses the energy of chirp signal by FRFT, so as to enhance the signal to noise ratio, the algorithm of the paper is summarized as follows:

Step 1: Determine frequency modulation rate k of chirp signal;
Step 2: Calculate the steer vectors matrix by FRFT;
Step 3: Collect data, form the correlation matrix $\mathbf{R}_X(u)$ by Eq. (13);
Step 4: Evaluate $P(\theta, \phi)$ versus θ, φ with (16).

4 Simulations

In order to verify the validity of the method in this paper and to compare the performance with other algorithms, some experiments with matlab are presented, in the experiment, without loss of generality, we consider an arbitrary plane array of 8 sensors, the coordinates are given by (0,0), (−0.16,0.12), (−0.049,0.086), (−0.22,0.055), (−0.079,−0.032), (0.065,0.13), (0.08,0.24), (0.037,−0.044), unit is meter. Some Chirp signals come from the same source, the frequency ranges from 4 GHz to 6 GHz, we separately use TCT algorithm and method in this paper to estimate DOA, FFT and FRFT is used in each snapshot to sample the frequency spectrum of the signals at 33 points, and take 100 times snapshots in every frequency.

Simulation 1 Spatial Spectrum
Consider two chirp signals arriving from directions (56°, 65°), (66°, 75°), (74°, 83°) respectively, SNR is 12 dB, Figs. 2 and 3 have shown the spatial spectrum of TCT-MVDR and algorithm of the paper. As seen from Figs. 2 and 3, by the course of

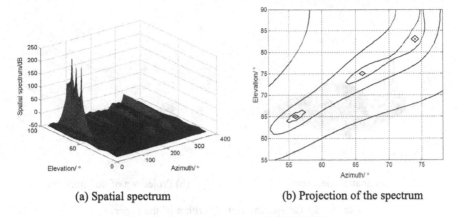

(a) Spatial spectrum   (b) Projection of the spectrum

Fig. 2. Spatial spectrum of TCT-MVDR.

focusing in FRFT domain, the spatial spectrum peak of algorithm of the paper is sharper than that of the TCT-MVDR.

Simulation 2 Precision of This Algorithm
Consider four far-field chirp signals arriving at the sensors from $(35°, 50°)$, $(45°, 60°)$, $(55°, 70°)$, $(65°, 80°)$ with same power, SNR varies from -5 dB to 15 dB, step size is 1 dB, 600 times Monte-Carlo trials have run for each SNR, the average of them is regarded as the measure result for this SNR. In order to describe the angle measurement accuracy, Root Mean Squared Error (RMSE) of two-dimensional angle measurement is defined as:

$$\text{RMSE} = \sum_{i=1}^{4} \sqrt{(\hat{\phi}_i - \phi_i)^2 + (\hat{\theta}_i - \theta_i)^2} \qquad (i = 1, 2, 3, 4) \qquad (17)$$

ϕ_i and $\theta_i (i = 1, 2, 3, 4)$ are respectively the true values of azimuth and elevation of the ith signal, $\hat{\phi}_i$ and $\hat{\theta}_i$ are separately the values estimated, Fig. 4 shows the RMSE of two algorithms versus SNR.

From Fig. 4 it is seen that RMSE of TCT-MVDR is larger than that of algorithm of the paper, when SNR is higher than 13 dB, RMSE of TCT-MVDR is zero, but that of algorithm of the paper is zero when SNR is 9 dB.

Simulation 3 Resolution Capability
Consider two signals respectively arriving from directions $(56°, 65°)$, $(56°, 70°)$, SNR is 6 dB, Figs. 5 and 6 have shown the spatial spectrum of TCT-MVDR and algorithm of the paper. From Figs. 5 and 6 we know when the signals are close, TCT-MVDR can not distinguish them, but algorithm of the paper can distinguish them at this moment.

Consider two chirp signals arriving at the sensors, in order to be convenient, the incident angle (ϕ, θ) is replaced by ϑ, resolving power boundary is generally defined that the peak of mean value of angles of two signals is equal to the mean peak value of two signals for spatial spectrum algorithm, that is

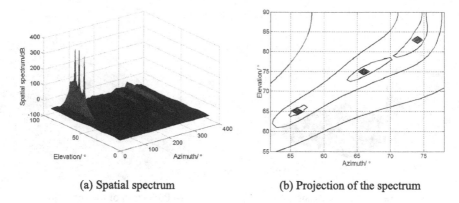

(a) Spatial spectrum   (b) Projection of the spectrum

Fig. 3. Spatial spectrum of algorithm of the paper.

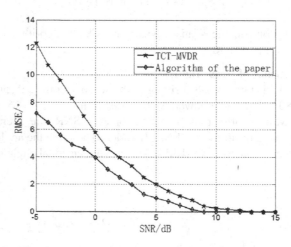

Fig. 4. The RMSE of three algorithms versus SNR.

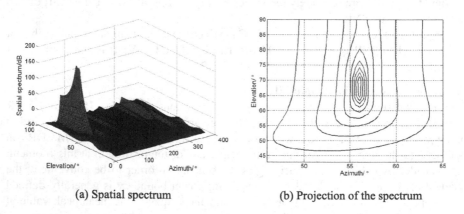

(a) Spatial spectrum   (b) Projection of the spectrum

Fig. 5. Resolution capability of TCT-MVDR.

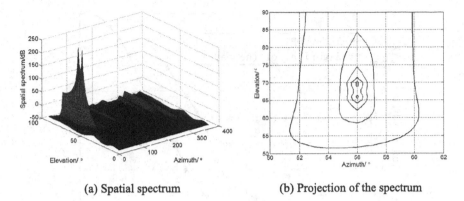

(a) Spatial spectrum   (b) Projection of the spectrum

Fig. 6. Resolution capability of algorithm of the paper.

$$P(\vartheta_m) = P_{\text{peak}} \tag{18}$$

where $\vartheta_m = (\vartheta_1 + \vartheta_2)/2$ is the mean value of two signals; $P(\vartheta_m)$ is the peak of that; P_{peak} is mean peak value of two signals, and the following equality is satisfied

$$P_{\text{peak}} = \frac{1}{2}[P(\vartheta_1) + P(\vartheta_2)] \tag{19}$$

In the course of searching spectrum peaks, if there is hollow between two spectrum functions of the signals, namely left of the Eq. (18) is less than the right, it is thought that the two signals can be resolved; if not, they can not be resolved. Resolution capability is defined as:

$$\gamma(\Delta) = 1 - \frac{2|F(\frac{\Delta}{2})|^2}{1 - |F(\Delta)|^2} \cdot \left\{ 1 - |F(\Delta)| \cos[\varphi_{F(\Delta)} - 2\varphi_{F(\Delta/2)}] \right\} \tag{20}$$

where

$$F(\Delta) = \frac{1}{M} \sum_{i=1}^{M} \exp\left\{ -j \frac{2\pi}{\lambda} (x_i \cos \phi + y_i \sin \phi) \times (\cos \theta_2 - \cos \theta_1) \right\} \tag{21}$$

We can know $\gamma(\Delta)$ can be defined as the measuring standard of resolution capability of two incident signals, the size of $\gamma(\Delta)$ is represented as degree of concavity between two spectrum peaks, the larger $\gamma(\Delta)$ is, the greater the degree of concavity is, the more power the resolution capability for two incident signal with space Δ is.

Consider two signals arriving at the sensors, their azimuths are both 45°, their elevations are taken 75° as point of symmetry, 600 times Monte-Carlo trials have run for each Δ, the average of them is regarded as the measure result for this Δ, here, we

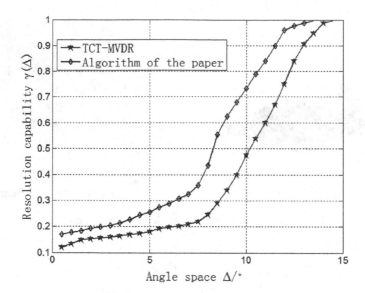

Fig. 7. Resolution capability of two algorithms with different angle spaces.

present the simulation result for resolution capability of two algorithms with different angle spaces, it is shown in Fig. 7.

From Fig. 7 it is seen the resolution capability of algorithm of the paper is better, as angle space increases, both of them are improving.

5   Conclusion

In this paper, we have used a kind of 2-D DOA estimation algorithm based on FRFT, it changes DOA estimation for wideband signals to that of narrowband signals, wherever, the energy of Chirp signal is more concentrative than in time-frequency, the performance of precision and resolution capability have been better.

References

1. Vinci, G., Barbon, F., Laemmle, B.: Wide-range, dual six-port based direction-of-arrival detector. In: 2012 Proceedings of Microwave Conference, Ilmenau, Germany, pp. 1–4 (2012)
2. Choliz, J., Angela, H.S., Valdovinos, A.: Evaluation of algorithms for UWB indoor tracking. In: 2011 Proceedings of Positioning Navigation and Communication, Dresden, Germany, pp. 143–148 (2011)
3. Bell, K.L., Zarnich, R.E., Wasyk, R.: MAP-PF wideband multitarget and colored noise tracking. In: 2010 Proceedings of Acoustics Speech and Signal Processing, Texas, USA, pp. 2710–2713 (2010)

4. Raines, B.D., Rojas, R.G.: Wideband tracking of characteristic modes. In: 2011 Proceedings of the 5th European Conference on Antennas and Propagation, Rome, Italy, pp. 1978–1981 (2011)
5. William, S., Salil, B., Adam, H.: System-level noise of an ultra-wideband tracking system. In: 2012 Proceedings of the 11th International Conference on Information Science, Signal Processing and their Applications, Montreal, Canada, pp. 634–639 (2012)
6. Shen, B., Yang, R., Ullah, S., Kwak, K.: Linear quadrature optimization-based non-coherent time of arrival estimation scheme for impulse radio ultra-wideband systems. IET Commun. 4(12), 1471–1483 (2010)
7. Wang, H., Kaveh, M.: Coherent signal-subspace processing for the detection and estimation of angles of arrival of multiple wide-band sources. IEEE Trans. Acoust. Speech Signal Process. 33(4), 823–831 (1985)
8. Acharyya, R.: Multiple classification without model order estimation. In: 2012 Proceedings of OCEANS, Yeosu, South Korea, pp. 1–6 (2012)

Research on Data Synchronism Method in Heterogeneous Database Based on Web Service

Yuze Li[1(✉)] and Hui Xuan[2,3]

[1] Department of Computer Engineering,
Beijing Institute of Automation Engineering, Beijing 100192, China
dahaiwuliangzs@163.com
[2] Tongfu Microelectronics Co., Ltd., Nantong 226000, China
[3] College of Computer Science and Communication Engineering,
Jiangsu University, Zhenjiang 212000, China

Abstract. As the synchronism effect of traditional methods is poor, the research on data synchronism method in heterogeneous database based on Web Service is proposed. Based on the structure of heterogeneous database, the synchronous execution flow is designed, and HTTP based SOAP transport protocols and XML standard are used to encode the data uniformly, the data source can be added or deleted at any moment. By decomposing the SQL statement in synchronous control module of heterogeneous database, the results data returned are converted into XML format with XML conversion function and are returned to uniform Web Service interface. The data synchronization in heterogeneous database based on Web Service is achieved through the local temporary table and its copy of source database. Through the comparative experiment, the following results can be concluded: the synchronism effect of data by data synchronism method in heterogeneous database based on Web Service reached 97%, which met the requirements for dealing with normal business in synchronism application system.

Keywords: Web Service · Heterogeneous database data · Synchronization

1 Introduction

With the development and expansion of modern enterprises, the integration, sharing of enterprise data and the integration of enterprise information have become increasingly important. In the process of information construction, many enterprise departments have established information application systems. However, due to the lack of unified information construction plan, the departments are independent of each other, the software system platform is inconsistent, the data standards are not uniform, and the interface is not perfect. Information between departments can not be shared and shared in time, thus forming information islands. Important enterprise information is generally stored and managed through different database systems, such as Sybase, DB2, Oracle, SQL Server, etc. Meanwhile, due to problems in interoperability, data islands are formed between data sources; the basic operating system of heterogeneous

S. Liu and G. Yang (Eds.): ADHIP 2018, LNICST 279, pp. 160–167, 2019.
https://doi.org/10.1007/978-3-030-19086-6_18

database can be UNIX, Windows XP, Linux; the heterogeneity of computer architecture, each participating database can be run on mainframes, minicomputers, workstations, PCs or embedded systems [1]. The heterogeneity of these heterogeneous database systems will adversely affect the information sharing of the system and hinder the resource sharing within and among enterprises. Therefore, how to effectively implement data sharing is one of the urgent problems in current development of information technology.

The traditional data synchronization method has strong autonomy, neither unified global mode nor local federation mode, which leads to poor transparency. Therefore, users must seek a new data language [2]. For the application environment with physical isolation gatekeeper, the reference [3] proposed a trigger-based SQL file-level heterogeneous database synchronization method, which is suitable for enterprise heterogeneous database synchronization. This paper will explain the working principle of heterogeneous database synchronization in the isolated gatekeeper environment, propose the overall framework of the synchronization system, and give the implementation details of the five steps of change capture, SQL file generation, file transfer, data update and fault handling. However, this method has a problem of poor synchronization. Reference [4] designed a new remote database synchronization mechanism, analyzed the process of application operation database, studied the method of capturing SQL from database connection driver, and proposed consistency check algorithm for data verification. But the synchronization effect of this method is not ideal. In view of the problem that data large-capacity communication often fails due to synchronization problems, the reference [5] analyzes the working principle of digital multiplex system, and explores the application of high-precision clock reference synchronization method at the transceiver end in clock correction, as well as bit synchronization and frame synchronization. The typical synchronization technique and verification of the data multiplexing process using FPGA simulation. However, this method takes a long time, but the final synchronization effect is poor.

Therefore, in order to realize the effect integration of information resources, the key is to realize the integration of heterogeneous databases. Through the analysis and research of Web Service, a data synchronization method in heterogeneous database based on Web Service is proposed, so that the data can be seamlessly communicated and shared in different heterogeneous databases, and the synchronization of data and structure changes can be ensured.

2 Structure Design of Heterogeneous Databases

For research on data synchronism method in heterogeneous database based on Web Service, the structure design of heterogeneous databases is conducted as Fig. 1.

As it's demonstrated in Fig. 1: the heterogeneous database architecture can be divided into three layers: user interface layer, integration processing layer, and database layer. The user interface layer is the interface between the system and the user. It is responsible for the registration of the integrated member database, the establishment of heterogeneous integration mode, receiving user input, and displaying query results. The integration processing layer is the core of the heterogeneous database system, including

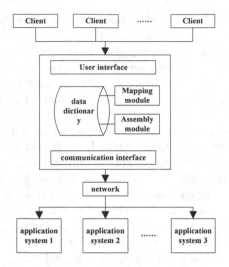

Fig. 1. Structure of heterogeneous databases

the central virtual database for user operations, data dictionary describing the data of each subsystem, data mapping module, data assembly module, and a communication interface. The integrated processing layer uses each function module and data dictionary to map the user's operation to the central virtual database as the operation to each subsystem. The distributed computing technology is used to return the results of each subsystem through the communication interface. The data assembly module is then assembled into the central virtual database, which is finally presented to the user. The member database of each application system is distributed in database layer, the physical operation of the database access is achieved to lay the foundation for data synchronization of heterogeneous databases.

3   Research on Data Synchronism Method Based on Web Service

According to the heterogeneous database structure designed above, the Web Service method is used to research the synchronization of heterogeneous database data. For different databases, access is required to use the data interface in the local system to connect to the database system, and to read data, and to establish corresponding Web Service for data integration calls. Because Web Services on different platforms or different database systems in different locations provide uniform data and consistent publishing methods to data integration in XML format, heterogeneous information of different database management systems can be shielded, so that data integration does not have to ignore the differences with databases. After obtaining the SOAP format information from heterogeneous data transmission centers, the heterogeneous databases are accessed to obtain the data from different database systems in XML format, and then these data are transmitted to heterogeneous transmission centers in the form of SOAP message.

3.1   Design of Synchronous Execution Flow

Synchronous execution flow is as follows:

① The underlying local data source firstly publishes the core database service, uses UDDI through the Web Service adapter to the heterogeneous data transmission center, which is registered in the intermediate database and is an initialization process;

② When the user has an operation request in the Web Service Unified Interface, the global SQL language is firstly transmitted to the control module through security mechanism, then optimized and converted into local SQL statement by the control module through its own SQL statement parser. The access to the intermediate database in the heterogeneous data transmission center in XML format through the XML converter is conducted;

③ If the database is not in the intermediate database, the structure synchronization process is performed. If there is an data change in the operation of the SQL statement, such as DML operation, the Web Service adapter call is used to update the relevant data in the database source, and performs the data synchronization process;

④ The operation result data is returned to the user in the form of XML by the XML converter in the control module.

This kind of loosely-coupled synchronous execution process based on Web Service can solve the problem of heterogeneous data integration across Internet better. In this architecture, the data is uniformly encoded using the HTTP-based SOAP transport protocol and the XML standard, so that heterogeneous information is shielded. At the same time, data sources can be deployed dynamically and data sources can be added or deleted at any time [6].

3.2   SQL Statement Decomposition

According to the synchronous execution flow, the structure of the heterogeneous database data synchronization control module is designed. Its function is to analyze the SQL statements transmitted from the unified interface of the Web Service, determine whether the format is correct or not, check the syntax decompose into sub-SQL statements, and obtain the results after processing [4]. Heterogeneous database data synchronization control module is shown in Fig. 2.

As it's demonstrated in Fig. 2: the control module is composed of SQL statement parser, data assembler, and data converter. SQL statement parser can parse and verify SQL statements, decompose global SQL statements into sub-SQL statements for each local database, get the connection information and table information of the specific connection to the local database, then send these information to the event manager, and finally perform sub-SQL statement operations; Data assembler can post-process data, but because there may be schema conflict and intersecting data between different data sources, it is necessary to post-process data according to user requirements; the data converter returns the forwarder as a result, and the result data returned by the database are converted into an XML format through XML conversion function and returned to the Web Service unified interface [7].

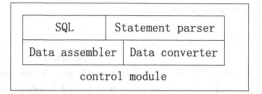

Fig. 2. Control module

3.3   Realization of Data Synchronism Method Based on Web Service

The SQL statement decomposed above is taken as method implementation statement to establish the local temporary table and copy of source database table [8]. The temporary table is generated based on the source database table information and the source table metadata in the base table, and the corresponding data is inserted into the intermediate database. When using by users, the data in the intermediate database is operated. After the data is used, the data in the intermediate database is compared with the copy. If there are changes, the remote database source should update the metadata through the event manager and Web Service adapter, which is shown in Fig. 3.

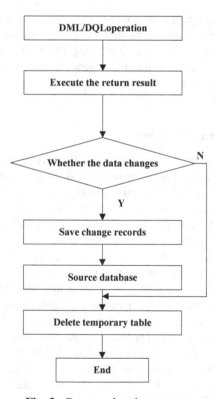

Fig. 3. Data synchronism process

When implementing server-side Web Service program, Delphi 7 Soap Server Application Wizard is used to create a Web Service-based application framework. The framework has implemented the mechanism for providing interfaces to clients, receiving and parsing remote Soap request messages, invoking corresponding processing functions and returning underlying functions such as Soap response messages. It is only necessary to define the custom interface for the client to call in this framework, and write the realization of data synchronization in heterogeneous database [9].

4 Experiment

In this paper, experiment is designed and analyzed for research on data synchronization method in heterogeneous database based on Web Service, and the effectiveness of the control method is verified through experiments, and then the efficient synchronization of heterogeneous database data is proved.

4.1 Experimental Analysis

Network Delay Impact Analysis
Under the influence of network delay, the data synchronization effects in heterogeneous databases by traditional method and Web Service method are compared. The results are shown in Fig. 4.

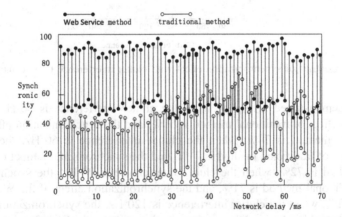

Fig. 4. Contrast of synchronization effect with network delay by two methods

As it's demonstrated in Fig. 4: When the network delay is 10 ms, the traditional method has a synchronization effect of 47%, and the Web Service method has a synchronization effect of 94%; when the network delay is 20 ms, the traditional method has a synchronization effect of 46%, and the Web Service method has a synchronization effect of 93%; when the network delay is 30 ms, the traditional method has a synchronization effect of 55%, and the Web Service method has a synchronization effect of 97%; when the network delay is 40 ms, the traditional method has a synchronization effect of 77%, and the Web Service method has a synchronization effect of 89%; when the network delay is 50 ms, the traditional method has a synchronization effect of 77%, and the Web Service method has a synchronization effect of 95%; when the network delay is 60 ms, the traditional method has a synchronization effect of 71%, and the Web Service method has a synchronization effect of 97%; when the network delay is 70 ms, the traditional method has a synchronization effect of 67%, and the Web Service method has a synchronization effect of 87%. Under the influence of network delay, the traditional method has poor synchronization effect, while the Web Service method has better synchronization effect.

Clutter Interference Analysis

Under the influence of clutter interference, the data synchronization effect in heterogeneous databases by traditional method and Web Service method are compared. The results are shown in Fig. 5.

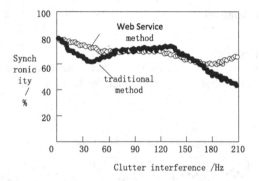

Fig. 5. Contrast of synchronization effect with clutter interference by two methods

As it's demonstrated in Fig. 5: when the clutter interference is 30 Hz, the synchronization effect of traditional method is 59%, and the synchronization effect of the Web Service method is 74%; when the clutter interference is 60 Hz, the synchronization effect of traditional method is 71%, and the synchronization effect of the Web Service method is 72%; when the clutter interference is 90 Hz, the synchronization effect of traditional method is 71%, and the synchronization effect of the Web Service method is 71%; when the clutter interference is 120 Hz, the synchronization effect of traditional method is 73%, and the synchronization effect of the Web Service method is 68%; when the clutter interference is 150 Hz, the synchronization effect of traditional method is 71%, and the synchronization effect of the Web Service method is 66%; when the clutter interference is 180 Hz, the synchronization effect of traditional method is 56%, and the synchronization effect of the Web Service method is 61%; when the clutter interference is 210 Hz, the synchronization effect of traditional method is 43%, and the synchronization effect of the Web Service method is 74%; when the clutter interference is 30 Hz, the synchronization effect of traditional method is 59%, and the synchronization effect of the Web Service method is 74%. It can be concluded that under the influence of clutter interference, the traditional method has poor synchronization effect, while the Web Service method has better synchronization effect.

4.2 Experimental Results

① Under the influence of network delay, the Web Service method has better synchronization effect for data in heterogeneous databases than the traditional method;

② Under the influence of clutter interference, the Web Service method has also better synchronization effect for data in heterogeneous databases than the traditional method. Therefore, the data synchronization method of heterogeneous database based on Web Service is feasible and effective.

5 Conclusion

In order to make the data synchronization method in heterogeneous database be applied and perfected in practice, many subsequent studies are needed. The future research work focuses on the construction of interregional federal systems. How to build a federal system on multiple data systems in multiple integrated regions is the focus of the next step. The model needs to be improved so that the model can handle a variety of complex business and enhance the practical application of the system.

References

1. Kuang, Y.C., Wang, F., Wei, L.H., et al.: Research on the bottom hole flow field analysis platform of PDC bit based on Web service. Chin. J. Eng. Des. **24**(4), 380–386 (2017)
2. Lai, Q.J., Xu, Z., Chen, D., et al.: Architecture of HVDC transmission design software based on WEB service. China Power **51**(2), 75–81 (2018)
3. Cui, H.X., Feng, J., Ma, W.J., et al.: Research and implementation of heterogeneous database synchronization based on netgap. Softw. Eng. **19**(2), 10–13 (2016)
4. Ding, J.L., Zhou, D.X., Wang, J., et al.: Remote database synchronization mechanism based on SQL capture from connection driver. Comput. Eng. **43**(9), 39–42 (2017)
5. He, S.T., Xue, L.S., Chen, X.H., et al.: Research on digital multiplex system with FPGA. Fire Control Command Control **41**(8), 37–40 (2016)
6. Pan, M.M., Li, D.D., Tang, Y., et al.: Design and implementation of accessing hybrid database systems based on middleware. Comput. Sci. **15**(5), 21–24 (2018)
7. Zhao, L.S., Li, G.Y., Wu, Z.Y., et al.: Historical data archiving technology based on hierarchical heterogeneous database system. Telecommun. Sci. **12**(s1), 21–22 (2018)
8. Liu, M., Li, Z.B., Xiong, T.: Simulation research of incomplete information optimization detection in heterogeneous database. Comput. Simul. **15**(11), 390–394 (2017)
9. Wu, L.H., Lu, Z.M., Gong, J.S., et al.: Integrating distributed heterogeneous food microorganism data by semantic web technology. China Biotechnol. **37**(3), 124–132 (2017)

Automatic Calibration System of English Lesson Plan Information Under Big Data Analysis

Huijun Liu[1(✉)], Liu Yong[2], and Ming-fei Qu[3]

[1] Faculty of Business and Foreign Studies, Hunan International Business
Vocational College, Changsha 410200, China
lhj6339@163.com
[2] Survey and Design Institute of Agricultural Seventh Division,
Kuitun 833200, Xinjiang, China
[3] Mechanical and Electronic Engineering School,
Beijing Polytechnic, Beijing 100176, China

Abstract. The traditional English course planning information automatic calibration system has poor precision, weak data analysis ability and low calibration accuracy. To solve this problem, the new English course plan information automatic calibration system is designed with big data analysis technology, and the hardware and software parts of the system are designed. Designed with high-precision ARM processor, TA64 embedded tracking chip and CS652 positioning chip, the hardware consists mainly of two types of power supply, calibrator and monitor in series and parallel. The software part is designed with five functional modules: teaching case information collection, information processing, information analysis, information correction and correction structure detection to complete software optimization. The effectiveness of the calibration system has been verified compared to traditional automatic calibration systems. The experimental results show that the system has strong data analysis capability, high precision after calibration, good calibration effect and large development space.

Keywords: Big data analysis · English teaching plan · English information ·
Automatic calibration

1 Introduction

With the improvement of the mode of education, English teaching has risen from the traditional primary teaching to the intermediate teaching, and the English teaching mode has become more and more diversified. Many colleges and universities want to abandon the rules of teaching, introduce high technology to improve the quality of teaching. The improvement of modern technology provides more opportunities for teaching methods, not only can improve teaching quality, but also can increase the use of modern technology. The introduction of multimedia teaching has greatly changed the English teaching mode and made the original empty English teaching more vivid and concrete. Multimedia teaching has been made up of many systems. This paper focuses on the automatic calibration system of English lesson plan information [1].

The calibration system is of great significance for the information determination of English teaching cases. A good calibration system can help teachers to determine the information taught better and improve the quality of the professors. In this paper, a new automatic calibration system for English lesson plan information is designed by using big data analysis technology. The hardware and software parts of the system have been designed, and the actual effect of the calibration system has been verified by experiments.

2 Hardware Design of Automatic Calibration System for English Lesson Plan Under Big Data Analysis

The automatic calibration system of English teaching case information is designed to refer to the globally recognized high precision processor ARM processor. The internal chip is a TA64 embedded tracking chip and a CS652 positioning chip [2]. The power design part is divided into two forms in parallel and series. The storage and storage device is used to store the program and parameters in the form of FLASH. The touchscreen is LCD touch screen, and the whole indoor positioning system hardware is connected by Ethernet.

The overall hardware structure of the English teaching plan information automatic calibration system is shown in Fig. 1 below.

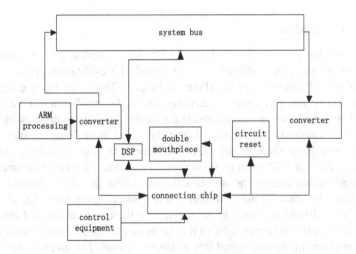

Fig. 1. Hardware architecture of automatic calibration system for English lesson plans

It can be seen from Fig. 1 that two transformers are connected to the system bus, which are an input transformer and an output transformer, and both transformers are connected to the connection chip. A DSP is also connected to the system bus, which is also connected to the connection chip. The amount of data processed by the ARM is transmitted to the output transformer, which in turn is transferred to the system bus. The connection chip plays a central role and is controlled by the control device and circuit reset in addition to the hardware device. This constitutes the hardware structure of the English class planning automatic calibration system.

2.1 Design of Power Supply

In the calibration system hardware, the power supply occupies an important position and provides power for the system. There are two types of power supply: centralized power supply and distributed power supply. The centralized power supply structure is composed of a module, which can not be segmented again in the process of use, resulting in high efficiency, but poor flexibility. The distributed power supply type is made up of several modules, which can be assembled freely and split flexibly while using, but the working efficiency is low [3]. The calibration system in this paper takes into consideration the advantages and disadvantages of centralized and distributed power supply. The two structures are combined together to build the power hardware [4]. The connection mode of the power circuit is connected in series and in parallel, which is connected in series with the active device and the load end of the adjusting unit, and the connection between the transformer and the control end is made. Join to ensure that the working mode is always in the linear mode. The collector voltage is between 15 V–25 V, and the power generated is between 100 W–500 W. The power supply circuit allows multiple types of voltages to pass through, and the reset chip inside generates a reset signal to provide maximum power.

2.2 Calibrator Design

The calibrator consists of two parts: signal conditioning board and DSP motherboard. In addition to receiving the calibration target signal, the calibration process can also receive the X light diffraction signal and the filter signal. These interference signals will greatly affect the accuracy of the calibration results, so the interference signals must be removed before the signals are stored inside the calibrator. The main work of the DSP motherboard is to collect and process filtered data, and the calibration data is transmitted to the computer through the USB interface. The signal tracking mode is a hardware filter, and the DSP main board is used to trace the signal by software filtering [5]. This combination makes the anti-interference effect greatly improved, and the acquisition rate can reach 10 m/s. Calibrator schematic diagram (see Fig. 2).

Because the calibration is easy to be affected by the environment and interference equipment, the signal will be unstable, so it is necessary to enlarge the process of signal acquisition and turn the voltage signal into a standard signal. The amplification mode is magnified by layer by layer and the number of the amplification layer is four layers: the first layer is the operation amplifier circuit to prevent the signal from drifting; the second layer circuit is added. The filter chip selects the interference signal; the third layer circuit introduces photoelectric isolation; the fourth level circuit inputs the voltage to the calibrator, amplifying the analysis and tracking signal [6].

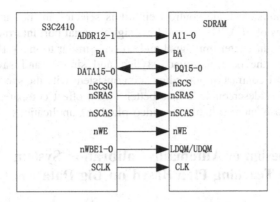

Fig. 2. Calibrator schematic diagram

2.3 Display Design

Using the most advanced liquid crystal material to make the display, we should pay more attention to the actual needs of the users, let the users make the main selection and match their own products, more modularized and liberalized, and more operable. The main parameters of the display are summarized in Table 1 as follows:

Table 1. Display parameters

Project	Parameter
Screen size	27 in.
Screen ratio	16:9
Panel material	IPS
Screen best resolution	2560 × 1980
Video interface	HDMI
USB interface	Two
Body color	Black/white/red/blue/green/purple
Screen ratio	16:9 (Widescreen)
High definition standard	1080p (Quan Gaoqing)
Panel type	MVA
Backlight	LED backlight
Dynamic contrast	100万:1
Static contrast	1000:1
Gray scale response time	5 ms

The DM64 developed by TI is a high-performance 32 bit fixed-point DSP for multimedia applications. The main frequency of the DSP is up to 720 MHz, and 8 parallel computing units can handle 5760MIPS, using the two level cache structure, 64 bit external memory interface [7]. It also integrates 3 configurable video ports, 10/100 Mbit/s Ethernet MAC and other peripherals. With DM642 as the core, the real-time acquisition, compression, playback and transmission function of the video signal is completed.

CPLD (programmable logic control) circuit is selected in the circuit, and it can realize the functions of FLASH, page address signal, serial port interrupt, clock signal, I/O control, reset signal, interrupt signal and so on. Similar to the WB9D of MEG in appearance design, the base is round, stylish and simple, and saves space. The brightness and 500:1 contrast of 300 cd/m^2 are consistent with the specifications of the mainstream LCD. Widescreen LCD has better visual effect compared with ordinary LCD products, and is more suitable for video playback applications.

3   Software Design of Automatic Calibration System for English Teaching Plan Based on Big Data Analysis

The software is programmed according to the hardware part of the calibration system, and the software flow chart is shown in Fig. 3.

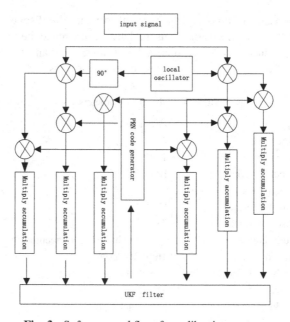

Fig. 3. Software workflow for calibration system

Calibration system software work is a complex process, which is divided into six steps. Introduce it to it:

(1) Collect the external information by the collector. The acquisition process is often aimed at multi-target, and the amount of information acquisition is very large, and there are some interference signals and weak signals. The collector eliminates the interference signal through the screening system, amplifies the weak signals with the amplifier, and selects useful signals to transmit to the processor [8].

(2) Processing calibration information. The 8 processing channels start work at the same time [9]. The collected information is classified according to the target, and the information of different targets is entered into different channels. There is a gap between channels and channels to avoid interference between information. The processed information is fed back to the computer system host and the mobile terminal respectively.

(3) Central system analysis. The results can not be displayed in the liquid crystal display immediately. To compare with the data of the internal database of the Internet of things, if there is a large deviation, the calibration result is inaccurate, and the last unit should be returned and relocated. If there is little difference between the internal data and the database, then the calibration result is more accurate.

(4) Determine the calibration information. The information of teaching plan is determined by different calibration nodes and recorded in the central system.

(5) The results were traced. After the calibration result is determined, the monitoring device is carried out in all directions to ensure the locking target and prevent the target from breaking the regulatory scope of the system.

(6) Show the results. When the target can be completely controlled by the calibration system, the IOT operation center [10] can display the result on the LCD LCD screen.

4 Experimental Research

In order to verify the actual working effect of the automatic calibration system of English teaching plan proposed in this paper, a contrast experiment is set up comparing with the traditional calibration system. The experimental environment was built using Matlab software to implement the proposed method and runs on an Intel Pentium Ml.6 GHz CPU.

4.1 Experimental Parameters

The experimental parameters are Table 2 as follows.

Table 2. Experimental parameters

Project	Parameter
Converter	A/D conversion
Working mode	SUA
Calibration time	20 min
Working frequency	300 Hz–1000 Hz
Calibration requirements	Accurate and fast
Calibration network	Internet

4.2 Experiment Process

According to the parameters set above, the traditional information automatic calibration system and the calibration system studied in this paper are used to calibrate an English teaching case at the same time to record the ability and accuracy of large data processing.

4.3 Experimental Results and Analysis

The results obtained are as follows (see Fig. 4).

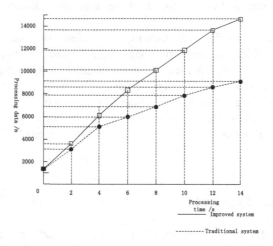

Fig. 4. Experimental results of large data processing capability

Figure 4 shows that when the processing time is 4 s, the data processed by the traditional correction system is 3600, and the data processed by the improved correction system is 3800; when the processing time is 8 s, the data processed by the traditional correction system is 6,900, and the correction system is improved. The processed data is 10,500; when the processing time is 12 s, the conventional correction system processes 8600 data, and the improved correction system processes 13800 data (Fig. 5).

When the data volume is 10000 MB, the accuracy of the traditional calibration system is 22%, and the accuracy of the improved calibration system is 43%. When the data volume is 20000 MB, the accuracy of the traditional calibration system is 32%, and the accuracy of the correction system is corrected. 61%; when the data volume is 30,000 MB, the accuracy of the traditional calibration system is 34%, the accuracy of the improved calibration system is 64%; when the data volume is 40,000 MB, the accuracy of the traditional calibration system is 41%, the correction is improved. The accuracy of the system is 82%.

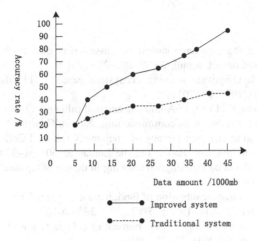

Fig. 5. Accuracy test results

4.4 Experimental Conclusions

According to the above experimental results, the experimental conclusions are as follows: the improved design of the automatic calibration system and the traditional automatic calibration system can calibrate the English teaching case information, but the improved calibration system processes the data in a larger amount of time per unit time and can Finding large amounts of data in a short period of time is more accurate than traditional calibration systems.

5 Concluding Remarks

Our country pays more and more attention to English education. The traditional oral instruction can not meet the current teaching plan. In order to improve the teaching efficiency, scientists continue to study effective educational means and high-tech technology. With the development of large data analysis technology, more and more high-tech cites large data analysis technology. In this paper, large data analysis is integrated into the automatic calibration system of English teaching case information, and the actual work effect of the system is verified by comparing with the traditional calibration system. The research shows that the system has a strong ability of data analysis, can quickly screen out a lot of information in a short time, compare with the information in the database, find out the wrong information and calibrate it, the calibration effect is good, and the ability is strong, it is the inevitable development direction in the future.

References

1. Zheng, H., Cai, Y.: Big data environment risk assessment of optimization model for the simulation analysis. Comput. Simul. **33**(9), 292–295 (2016)
2. Zhang, H.: English ubiquitous learning ecosystem based on big data analysis. Teach. Adimistration **13**(3), 107–109 (2017)
3. Zibin, N., Zmeureanu, R., Love, J.: Automatic assisted calibration tool for coupling building automation system trend data with commissioning. Autom. Constr. **61**, 124–133 (2016)
4. Ye, M.: A survey on information literacy of Zhejiang Vocational College English teachers under the big data environment. Jiaoyu Jiaoxue Luntan **33**(50), 31–32 (2017)
5. You, H.: A new model of college English teaching in the era of big data. Chin. J. ICT Educ. **45**(15), 80–82 (2016)
6. Zhong, R., et al.: Automatic calibration of fundamental diagram for first-order macroscopic freeway traffic models. J. Adv. Transp. **50**(3), 363–385 (2016)
7. Zhou, Y.: Analysis of the ecological environment of college English teaching in the era of big data. Heilongjiang Sci. **8**(3), 31–32 (2018)
8. Wang, Y.: Reflection on reconstructing the ecological system of college English teaching in the era of big data. J. Heilongjiang Coll. Educ. **36**(9), 128–130 (2017)
9. Wen, X.: Revelation of theme and rheme on college English writing: analysis of big data based on millions of English writing with the same theme. Heihe Xueyuan Xuebao **36**(7), 117–118 (2016)
10. Ye, S., Zhang, C., Wang, Y., et al.: Design and implementation of automatic orthorectification system based on GF-1 big data. Trans. Chin. Soc. Agric. Eng. **33**(s1), 266–273 (2017)

Design of Intelligent Driving System for Variable Speed Vehicle Based on Big Data Analysis

Nai-rong Zhang[1(✉)] and Wen Li[2]

[1] College of Electronics and Information Engineering, Sichuan University,
Chengdu 610065, China
zhangnairong123@sina.com
[2] Business School, Suzhou University of Science and Technology,
Suzhou 215009, China

Abstract. The traditional intelligent drive system of variable speed vehicle has the problem of low precision of driving target, so the intelligent drive system of variable speed vehicle based on big data analysis is designed. The hardware structure of intelligent driving system of variable speed vehicle is designed, and the hardware framework of the system is derived on the basis of the hardware structure, so as to complete the hardware design of intelligent driving system of variable speed vehicle. Respectively for automated driving simulation component library, automotive autopilot system protection module, the automatic speed control driving system design, complete the autopilot system software design, through software and hardware design to realize variable speed motor intelligent automatic driving system design. Experimental contrast can be seen that is based on the analysis of the large data variable speed auto intelligent automatic driving system compared with the traditional automatic driving method, driving the target precision increased by 15%, and has high effectiveness.

Keywords: Big data · Variable speed vehicle · Automatic driving · Intelligence

1 Introduction

With the development of Internet technology, the influx of massive data has made achievements in machine learning, data mining and other related fields. The big data era has rounded the door of artificial intelligence for years of silence, combined with statistical methodology, information theory, probability theory and other disciplines, a new Internet era is coming. In recent years, both enterprises, universities and scientific research institutions have invested a lot of manpower and material resources in the field of artificial intelligence to do forward-looking research. This also confirms that a wave of artificial intelligence sweeping the world with big data technology is coming to the face [1]. Auto driving (ATO) technology plays an important role in the modern urban traffic control system. It can control the speed of vehicle driving in two destinations, and its control effect has a direct impact on various performance indicators. Different

© ICST Institute for Computer Sciences, Social Informatics and Telecommunications Engineering 2019
Published by Springer Nature Switzerland AG 2019. All Rights Reserved
S. Liu and G. Yang (Eds.): ADHIP 2018, LNICST 279, pp. 177–186, 2019.
https://doi.org/10.1007/978-3-030-19086-6_20

control algorithms are applied to the automatic driving of automobiles, and their control effects are different. Therefore, both now and in the future, it is necessary to study the effective algorithm of automatic driving control, so as to maximize the operation of the vehicle. The traditional research on auto autopilot algorithm is based on off-line simulation based on Simulink. The simulation of pure software is not carried out in real time simulation environment. It can not realize real-time data generation, exchange and processing, and is detached from real car and vehicle equipment, and is helpful to the development of actual ATO products small [2]. A more real simulation environment is needed to study the ATO algorithm, and the control algorithm is placed in the real time system environment. The simulation data is generated and interactive in real time. It can also be connected to the real physical interface with the vehicle or other vehicle equipment. It has a more real and visual inspection control effect and the development of ATO products great help.

2 Design of Intelligent Driving System for Variable Speed Vehicle Based on Big Data Analysis

2.1 Hardware Structure Design of Automatic Driving System for Variable Speed Vehicle

The vehicle operation control system (ATC) consists of three parts: automobile overspeed protection system (ATP) auto driving system (ATO) and auto monitoring system (ATS). ATP completes the safety control of the car operation. Under the supervision of the ATP, ATO instead of the driver makes the car run efficiently and energy saving. ATS is responsible for monitoring the car system, so that the car describes the working process of the ATO system according to the scheduled time table transport 1 (Fig. 1):

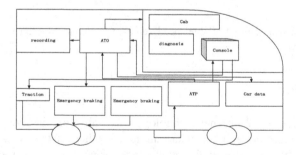

Fig. 1. Principle of intelligent automatic driving system for variable speed vehicle

ATO gets the command from ATS to run the vehicle, which is sent by the ground and transmitted through ATP. ATP passes useful information after processing to ATO, displays relevant information, and constantly monitors the work of ATO. ATO uses useful information to calculate the speed of the operation, obtain the control quantity, and execute the control command. At the same time, the driver can input the car information from the console and send the transmission equipment from the vehicle to the ground after the arrival of the control information and the control information to the station. The driver is transmitted to the ATS from the ground loop line [3]. ATS based on this car information, after determining the car's new task, once again through the ground transmission equipment to the ATO in the interval run, each to the track signal exchange, ATO receives new ground information, so that the speed adjustment such as ATO failure, then cut off the ATO person Working, ATP and ATS work [4].

2.2 Hardware Framework of Intelligent Automatic Driving System for Transmission Vehicles

In order to ensure the extensibility of the designed system, the system is based on the idea of model base, and adopts the object-oriented simulation method. In order to make the system independent of the specific column control system, the processing of the actual system component module is like the data processing of the database, and the system is separated into an independent model unit. The components of model units and model libraries constitute the structure of the intelligent driving system of the whole system, as shown in Fig. 2:

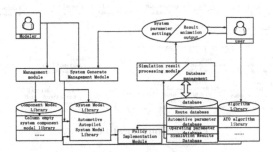

Fig. 2. Intelligent automatic driving system framework for transmission vehicles

The system framework is mainly divided into user interface layer, management layer and database. The component database contains the model of the component of the column control system. It can be said that the component database is the orderly management of the object library that consists of the column control system. The rationality of the decomposition of the system object directly affects the extensibility and the modifiable system database of the system in the future, and contains various columns connected by the component. Control system model, users can choose the required column control system model for simulation database to provide all kinds of data required for the simulation process of the column control system, and include a simulation result database.

3 Software Design of Intelligent Automatic Driving System for Variable Speed Vehicle

3.1 Design of Autopilot Simulation Component Library

The model library in the simulator uses hierarchical design. The component model library is composed of subsystems which are controlled by the car. Each subsystem is a component package, such as auto driving package containing several components that constitute a subsystem, each component has a hierarchical structure, may be a class or contain it. All kinds of classes, from simple to complex, macro to micro, from components to component packages are only an organization method of objects or classes in a system. It is a part of components that make up a variety of systems that can be connected to the required system from the required components from the different component packages to the required system [5]. The structure design of the automatic driving simulation component library is shown in Fig. 3.

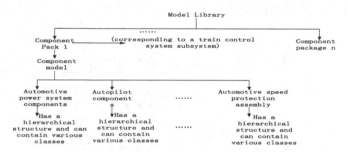

Fig. 3. Component library

3.2 Design of Auto Driving System Protection Module

Taking into account the safety of the automatic driving system, the ATO system should be operated under the security protection of the ATP system. It is mainly reflected in the generation of the ATO target velocity curve based on the ATP protection curve, and the speed generation is reduced according to the characteristics of vehicle and line conditions. Then first, there is a ATP protection curve. The ATP protection curve mainly includes ATP emergency braking curve and ATP emergency braking trigger curve [6]. The ATP emergency braking curve is a curve that the vehicle can never exceed. If the speed of the vehicle exceeds the speed of the ATP emergency braking curve, there will be danger. ATP emergency braking triggering curve is to ensure that the car does not touch the ATP emergency braking curve. When the speed of the vehicle exceeds the speed of the ATP emergency brake trigger curve, the vehicle immediately implements the emergency brake, which is a process of triggering tight braking. The emergency braking triggering curve should consider the braking characteristics of the vehicle itself, such as the time of traction and cut-off, the delay of braking establishment, and the current speed of the vehicle. We should also consider the slope value [7] of the line conditions of the vehicle. Because of the safety protection, the worst case should be considered. The current speed of the car is the maximum speed that the car can reach when the curve is designed, and the line slope is the maximum slope on the line. Each point on the ATP emergency braking trigger curve reaches the ATP emergency braking curve through the traction and cut-off stage and the braking establishment stage. In addition, in the low speed limit zone to the high speed limit area, we must ensure that the tail speed limit is low and the trigger speed will jump. Figure 4 is the schematic diagram of the protection module of the autopilot system:

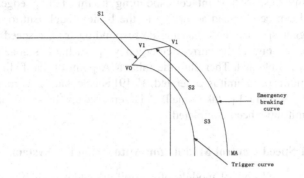

Fig. 4. Principle of auto driving system protection module

Figure 4 shows the ATP emergency braking curve and trigger curve at MA. ATP emergency braking curve generation method is: according to the fixed braking rate B, line speed limit V, according to:

$$v^2 = 2 * b * s \tag{1}$$

The location of the deceleration point should be calculated, and the curve of the deceleration part will be generated, which is combined with the static speed limit curve of the line to generate the ATP emergency braking curve. The method of generating ATP emergency brake trigger curve is: S_1 is the distance that the car walks in the time delay of traction and cut off, and S_2 is the distance [8] for the vehicle braking time delay. S_3 is the distance from the V_2 point to the MA point on the emergency braking curve. According to the basic physical formula, S_1, S_2 and S_3 are respectively expressed:

$$s_1 + s_2 + s_3 = s \tag{2}$$

S is the distance from the MA point to the current distance, $F(V0) = S$, S has known. There is only one V_0 for the unknown quantity, V_0 can be solved by one element two times equation. The formula for calculating the trigger speed of the constant speed part of the circuit is:

$$V_0 = V_{Lim} - A_1 * T_1 - A_2 * T_2 \tag{3}$$

V_{Lim} is the emergency braking speed for the current point. A_1 is the maximum traction acceleration of the vehicle, T_1 is the traction cut off time of the vehicle, and A_2 is the acceleration of the vehicle in braking delay time. T_2 sets up a delay for the brake of the car. V_0 is the trigger speed for the current point. Then it is judged whether the emergency speed limit of the current point is generated by the falling edge or by the static speed limit. If the current emergency speed limit is generated by the falling edge, it is possible to calculate the corresponding speed of the falling edge at a fixed braking rate of 0. As the false MA point corresponding to this falling edge. The current triggering speed can be obtained according to the basic model. But to make a judgement, if the trigger speed is less than the corresponding trigger speed of the falling edge. Then take the big. If the current emergency speed limit is generated by static speed limits, V_0 is obtained. Then find the false MA point on the falling edge above which the minimum speed limit is generated. V_1 [9] is calculated according to the basic model. Compare V_0 and V_1, take small. ATP emergency braking speed limit and trigger speed limit have been completed.

3.3   Design of Speed Control Module for Auto Autopilot System

The principle of speed control module of autopilot system is mainly that the target speed curve of ATO should be generated under the restriction of ATP emergency braking triggering curve. First, in the speed monitoring phase of the ceiling, the target speed curve of ATO is minus 5 km/h of the ATP emergency braking trigger curve. In the stage of vehicle speed reduction from high speed limit zone to low speed limit zone, the ATO target speed curve should be decelerated at a suitable deceleration rate and slowed down to a low speed limit area in advance. And in the parking phase, according to the target deceleration, there are two ways of parking. The first is that when the absolute value of the deceleration is large, the distance between the brake and the stop is smaller. The car must first reduce the speed to the limit speed of the station, and go into the station, and stop at the distance to the distance from the stop point calculated according to the speed and speed. The second situation is that when the absolute value of the speed reduction is not large, the parking distance is longer, the car will stop at the station, that is, the car will stop at the station and stop [10]. To sum up, we should design the target speed curve of ATO according to different situations. When the target velocity curve of ATO is generated, an appropriate controller can be designed to track the target speed curve and control the operation of the vehicle. ATO control car operation, there is a set of evaluation system to evaluate the performance of ATO. This evaluation system can evaluate the performance indexes of ATO respectively. Finally, the performance of ATO is evaluated by assigning weight coefficient to each performance index. The speed control module of the autopilot system is mainly concerned with three aspects: its safety, vehicle energy consumption and parking accuracy. First, in security, security is the speed limit that requires the car to not exceed the line. It can record the number of emergency braking times in the whole car as a standard for evaluating safety. Security is very important. If the whole process triggers emergency braking, it shows that ATO's algorithm still has a lot of shortcomings and needs improvement. If the emergency brake is not triggered throughout the whole process, the safety is 1 and the emergency braking is triggered, and the safety is 0. Set NEB to trigger the number of emergency braking. The evaluation function of security is:

$$s_1 = \left\{ \begin{array}{ll} 1 & neb = 0 \\ 0 & neb >\,= 1 \end{array} \right\} \tag{4}$$

In terms of energy consumption, the main indicator records the whole process of energy consumption. The formula for calculating energy consumption at each time is $P = F * v$, and because $F = M * a$, a can get $P = M * a * v$ according to gear and current speed. The total energy consumption of the whole process is P accumulation at every moment. A P and K can be set up to evaluate the performance index function of energy consumption. That is:

$$s_2 = \left\{ \begin{array}{ll} 1 & \sum p<\,= p0 * t \\ 1 - (\sum p - p0 * t) * \frac{k}{t} & p0 * t < \sum p<\,= \left(\frac{1}{k} + p0\right) * t \\ 0 & \sum p > \left(\frac{1}{k} + p0\right) * t \end{array} \right\} \tag{5}$$

In which P_0 and K are undetermined, and t is the time for the car to run. It can also directly record the whole energy consumption P and the evaluation criteria as a function of energy consumption. But this cumulative value is related to time. When comparing the energy consumption of different ATO algorithms, the running time should be consistent. According to the experience value, P_0 is $4M$, $K = 1/(16M * t)$.

Parking accuracy can record parking time specific location points and the specified parking points error to record parking accuracy. The parking accuracy is within 30 cm, which needs to be improved beyond 30 cm. When parking error is s, the evaluation index of parking accuracy is:

$$s_5 = \left\{ \begin{array}{ll} 1 & \Delta s < 10 \\ -0.05 * \Delta s + 1.5 & 10 <\,= -\Delta s <\,= 30 \\ 0 & \Delta s >\,= 30 \end{array} \right\} \tag{6}$$

The range of the results of the above function is 0–1. The greater the value, the better the performance of ATO.

The evaluation function of each performance index is S_1, the weight is A_1, the evaluation function of energy consumption is S_2, the weight is A_2, the evaluation function of the degree of precision is S_3, the weight is A_3, the evaluation function of the comfort degree is S_4, the weight is A_1, the evaluation function of the parking precision is S_5, and the weight is A_5, A_1, A_2. The actual line needs different values for different requirements. The evaluation function of the ATO algorithm is:

$$s = a_1 * s_1 + a_2 * s_2 + a_3 * s_3 + a_4 * s_4 + a_5 * s_5 \tag{7}$$

In general, A_1, A_2, A_3, A_4 and A_5 can be set to 0.2. After the completion of the hardware and software design, the intelligent driving system of variable speed vehicle is designed.

4   Experimental Analysis

4.1   Experimental Process

In order to verify the effectiveness of the intelligent driving system of the variable speed vehicle, the following comparative experiments are designed. Taking the same driving route of the same car as the experiment object, it is divided into two groups, of which the intelligent automatic driving system of the variable speed vehicle is the experimental group and the traditional method is used as the control group. On the premise of controlling the single variable, the change data of two groups of automobile driving changes are recorded, the difference between the line of the car and the target route is recorded, and the difference between the vehicle route and the target route is recorded, and the difference between the vehicle route and the target route is recorded. The difference of vehicle target difference. The corresponding conditions were set for the two sets of experimental data. In order to ensure the fairness of the experiment, the parameters of the experimental group and the control group were always consistent. In order to verify the difference between the intelligent automatic driving system and the traditional method of the transmission, the experimental group will operate the intelligent automatic driving system of the transmission vehicle according to the demand, while the traditional data detection is mainly handled manually.

4.2   Comparison of Difference Between Vehicle Route and Target Route

At the same time, the experimental group and the control group recorded the same traffic route and the target road change data, and compared the accuracy of the record. After recording 0–40 s, the difference between the change data of the route and the target route and the actual route data was also recorded. In order to avoid interference caused by sudden events, the experimental group and the control group have the same processing parameters. The concrete results are as follows (Fig. 5):

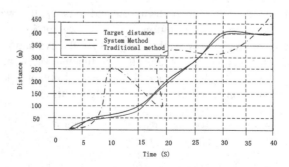

Fig. 5. Comparison of the difference between the route and the target route

With the increase of time, the experimental group has been in a relatively stable state, and the accuracy rate of data records is high, and the rate of data difference of the experimental group is about 4%. The overall efficiency of the control group was unstable, while the control group had a difference of 20%. Therefore, it can be proved that compared with the traditional method, the automatic driving system of variable speed vehicle can get a 19% increase in accuracy.

4.3   Comparison of Difference Between Parking Targets

The same data were processed in the experimental group and the control group at the same time, and the difference of parking target was recorded after 150 times. In order to avoid interference caused by sudden events, the experimental group and the control group have the same processing parameters. The concrete results are as follows (Fig. 6):

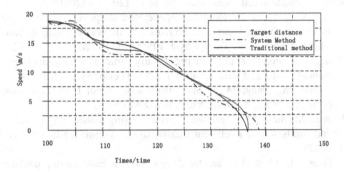

Fig. 6. Comparison of the difference between parking targets

Compared to the above picture, in the process of the difference of the parking target data, with the increase of the number of parking, the difference of the parking target of the intelligent automatic driving system of the transmission car is less than 5%. In the control group, with the increasing number of parking, the difference of parking targets was large, and the difference of parking targets was about 10%. Therefore, it can be proved that the automatic driving system of variable speed vehicle can effectively reduce the difference of parking targets.

5   Concluding Remarks

With the development of Internet technology, scientific research institutions have invested a lot of manpower and material resources in the field of artificial intelligence to do prospective research. Auto driving (ATO) technology plays an important role in the modern urban traffic control system. It can control the speed of car driving in two destinations and its control effect. Fruit has a direct impact on various performance indicators. Different control algorithms are applied to the automatic driving of automobiles, and their control effects are different. Therefore, both now and in the future, it is necessary to study the effective algorithm of automatic driving control, so as to maximize the operation of the vehicle. In the design process, the system framework is designed based on the working principle of the intelligent driving system of the variable speed vehicle. In the software design part, based on the design of the auto driving simulation component library, the auto driving protection module and the speed control module are designed to complete the design of the intelligent automatic driving system of the transmission vehicle based on the large data analysis.

References

1. Bingler, A., Mohseni, K.: Dual radio autopilot system for lightweight, swarming micro/miniature aerial vehicles. J. Aerosp. Inf. Syst. **14**(5), 1–13 (2017)
2. Li, W.Z., Chen, C.P., Mao, Y.Q., et al.: Dynamic analysis of coupled vehicle-bridge system with uniformly variable speed. Nonlinear Eng. **5**(3), 129–134 (2016)
3. Li, Y., Xu, C., Xing, L., et al.: Integrated cooperative adaptive cruise and variable speed limit controls for reducing rear-end collision risks near freeway bottlenecks based on micro-simulations. IEEE Trans. Intell. Transp. Syst. **PP**(99), 1–11 (2017)
4. Wen, J., Jiang, Z., Zhang, S., et al.: New periodically variable speed limits rule for highways with mathematical model and simulation. IET Intel. Transp. Syst. **12**(3), 227–235 (2018)
5. Oktay, T., Konar, M., Onay, M., et al.: Simultaneous small UAV and autopilot system design. Aircr. Eng. Aerosp. Technol. **88**(6), 818–834 (2016)
6. Al-Dweik, A.J., Mayhew, M., Muresan, R., et al.: Using technology to make roads safer: adaptive speed limits for an intelligent transportation system. IEEE Veh. Technol. Mag. **PP**(99), 1 (2017)
7. Deng, Y., Duan, H.: Control parameter design for automatic carrier landing system via pigeon-inspired optimization. Nonlinear Dyn. **85**(1), 1–10 (2016)
8. Bagheri, N.: Development of a high-resolution aerial remote-sensing system for precision agriculture. Int. J. Remote Sens. **38**(8–10), 2053–2065 (2017)
9. Chen, G., Zhang, W.: Neural network–based speed control method and experimental verification for electromagnetic direct drive vehicle robot driver. Adv. Mech. Eng. **9**, 12 (2017). (2017-12-01), 2017, 9(12):168781401774823
10. Lu, S., Liu, M., Cui, H., et al.: The application of variable integral gain double closed-loop control for vehicle inverters. Int. J. Control Autom. **9**(8), 323–338 (2016)

Research on Trend Analysis Model of Movement Features Based on Big Data

Hai Zou[1(✉)] and Xiaofeng Xu[2]

[1] Continuing Education Center, Zaozhuang Vocational College
of Science and Technology, Tengzhou 277599, China
hoiae251@sina.com
[2] Department of Physical Education,
Baoji Vocational and Technical College, Baoji 721006, China

Abstract. The motion feature data capture can well preserve the details of the motion and truly record the trajectory of the motion. It has been widely used in many fields such as virtual reality, three-dimensional games, film and television effects, and so on. With the widespread application of motion feature capture, how to analyze the trend data of sports features has become a hot topic. The main purpose of the trend analysis of the research motion characteristics is to better understand and describe the motion process of the objects so as to manage and reuse the motion capture data in the motion capture database. For the existing motion feature capture data in the motion capture database, the motion feature data behavior is precisely segmented, the motion template is extracted and calculated more quickly and efficiently, the motion behavior is identified, and the motion behavior in the motion sequence segment is automatically identified.

Keywords: Big data · Motion feature · Human motion information

1 Introduction

With the development of sports science research, the use of computer motion features for modeling and simulation and sports diagnosis has become an inevitable trend. In order to better analyze the trend of movement characteristics, the human movement characteristics are taken as an example. With the help of knowledge of sports biomechanics, the movement characteristics of athletes are simulated and tested. This method has a high theoretical and practical value, many scholars at home and abroad have carried out in-depth and meticulous research work [1]. The traditional athlete modeling method is based on Newton's law of motion. By simplifying the human body structure, writing the equation of motion, setting the initial conditions, and solving the equation, the simulation results are finally obtained. This method uses a simplified model, inevitably there will be a larger calculation error, and the model is difficult to modify. In order to solve these problems, based on the analysis of the human motion modeling and simulation research methods, a new idea of the trend information fusion modeling based on big data is proposed [2]. Starting from the acquisition and analysis of the motion information, it focuses on the feature extraction and classification of the

S. Liu and G. Yang (Eds.): ADHIP 2018, LNICST 279, pp. 187–194, 2019.
https://doi.org/10.1007/978-3-030-19086-6_21

ground reaction force information in the human body movement process, the surface electromyographic information of the human body, and the relevant parameters of the motion image analysis, and adopts a multi-source information fusion method to realize the motion. Automatic decomposition and identification of feature extraction process, and establish a trend analysis model of movement characteristics, in order to improve the accuracy of movement feature trend modeling and simulation, and lay the foundation for the construction of movement feature trend analysis system.

2 Motion Feature Parameter Calculation Method

The gesture of the movement can be represented by the global coordinates of each joint, or it can be expressed by the translation of the root joint and the rotation of the remaining joints [4]. The translation in three-dimensional space can be simply represented by the translation matrix, so the motion feature trend is analyzed using the calculation method of the human body joint global coordinates [3]. In the process of motion, the motion characteristic matrix can be regarded as a vector. When multiplied by the matrix, only the feature parameter information will affect the direction of the vector but will not change the size of the vector matrix. When you rotate a certain angle around the coordinate axis, you must first determine the positive direction [5]. It is specified that in the right-hand coordinate system, the counterclockwise rotation direction is positive when viewed from the positive end of the coordinate axis. In the same way, in the left-handed coordinate system, the clockwise rotation direction is positive when viewed from the positive end of the coordinate axis. This definition ensures that the same rotation matrix is used in either the right-handed or left-handed coordinate system. In the right-handed Cartesian coordinate system, the rotation matrix that rotates the α angle about the X axis is:

$$U_x(\alpha) = \begin{bmatrix} 1 & 0 & 1 \\ 0 & \cos\alpha & -\sin\alpha \\ 0 & \sin\alpha & \cos\alpha \end{bmatrix} \tag{1}$$

The rotation matrix that rotates by α degrees around the Y axis is:

$$U_y(\alpha) = \begin{bmatrix} \cos\alpha & 0 & \sin\alpha \\ 0 & 1 & 0 \\ -\sin\alpha & 0 & \cos\alpha \end{bmatrix} \tag{2}$$

The rotation matrix rotated by α degrees around the Z axis is:

$$U_z(\alpha) = \begin{bmatrix} \cos\alpha & -\sin\alpha & 0 \\ 0 & 1 & 0 \\ -\sin\alpha & 0 & \cos\alpha \end{bmatrix} \tag{3}$$

For an arbitrary rotation axis n that circumvents the origin, when rotating the e-angle, the vector n can be decomposed into three directions of x, y, z, and then obtained by cascading a simple rotation matrix of three components nX, ny, n. The final rotation matrix is:

$$U_i(\alpha) = \begin{bmatrix} i_x^2(1-\cos\alpha)+\cos\alpha & i_x i_y(1-\cos\alpha)-i_x\sin\alpha & i_x i_z(1-\cos\alpha)-i_y\sin\alpha \\ i_x i_y(1-\cos\alpha)+i_z\sin\alpha & i_y^2(1-\cos\alpha)+\sin\alpha & i_y i_z(1-\cos\alpha)-i_x\sin\alpha \\ i_x i_z(1-\cos\alpha)-i_y\sin\alpha & i_z i_y(1-\cos\alpha)+i_x\sin\alpha & i_z^2(1-\cos\alpha)+\sin\alpha \end{bmatrix} \quad (4)$$

In combination with the above algorithm, the data features of any rotation axis in the human body motion are extracted. If the movement is selected and moved around a rotation axis n, the movement feature data is expressed in the form of: The formula rotating around the n-axis is rotated, and finally the rotary axis is translated to the original position [6]. The value of the human motion gesture is captured and recorded, and the Euler angle representation method is used to calculate the motion feature relationship. Finally, the Euler angle's motion gesture feature calculation result is converted into a corresponding three-dimensional space coordinate system display diagram, as shown below (Fig. 1).

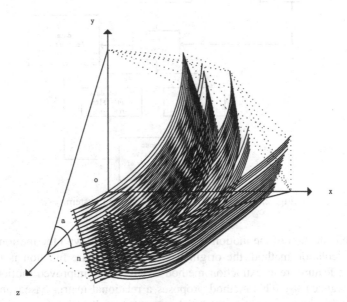

Fig. 1. Graphical display of human movement gesture features

3 Motion Characteristics Trend Analysis Model Design

The hardware part of the motion feature information acquisition system consists of PIR sensor, Fresnel lens, signal conditioning circuit, and digital-analog conversion device. The software part is programmed by Lab-VIEW software [7]. The design principle is as follows: When the walking human body passes through the PIR sensor, the PIR sensor receives the infrared radiation emitted by the human body, the Fresnel lens is added on the front end to increase the detection distance, and the electrical signal output by the sensor is processed through the amplifying and filtering circuit, and the data acquisition card is used. Perform A/D conversion and then access the computer for data analysis (Fig. 2).

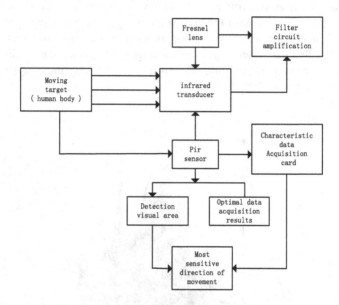

Fig. 2. Motion data feature acquisition system

After the collection of the motion feature data, combined with the motion template extraction calculation method, the original relationship feature function is improved, and a motion feature trend extraction method based on the improved motion relation template is realized [8]. This method proposes a relational matrix based on the relationship between human joints and spatial geometry to describe the spatial position relationships of the various joints of the human body. The relationship feature matrix of the same category of motion behaviors is aligned with the time axis by the method of dynamic time rounding. And record the time deformation process of the DTW, the aligned matrix is averaged and inverse transformed according to the recorded time deformation process, and finally quantized to obtain the category of motion behavior, so as to correspond to the movement trend template [9]. In the aspect of motion behavior recognition, a motion analysis feature trend analysis model based on motion templates is proposed to automatically identify the motion segments obtained by behavioral segmentation of the original motion data sequence [10]. The method divides the motion of the root node in the human skeleton model corresponding to the motion sequences to be identified into two types: root node motion and root node motionless. Based on the DTW method, the motion sequences to be identified are sequentially performed with motion templates of different motion behaviors. The similarity matching calculation achieves the automatic recognition of the motion behavior in the motion sequence segment. The trend analysis model of sports features is as follows (Fig. 3).

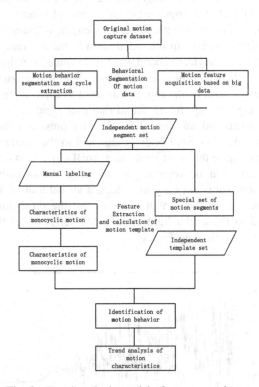

Fig. 3. Trend analysis model of movement features

As shown in the figure, the model can automatically perform behavior segmentation, cycle extraction, and motion behavior recognition on the original motion data sequence containing basic motion behaviors, and realize an important role in effective analysis and management of motion feature trends.

4 Experimental Results and Analysis

In order to verify the operational effect of the trend feature analysis model proposed in this chapter, the model was run in the software environment of Matlab2011. In the experiment, let the feature parameter be a value that can make the average number of neighbors per point account for 1% of the total points. Thirty-four motion sequences containing different behaviors were selected from the CMU database. Each motion sequence contained different behavior and complexity, including walking, running, jumping, boxing, and stretching. These sequences were segmented using the previous method. One volunteer who was healthy and had no abnormal gait was randomly selected as the study subject. Anthropometric parameters of volunteers were measured, including height, weight, forearm length, upper arm length, and hand length; The length of the forearm was the distance from the radial stem to the epicondyle, the upper arm was the shoulder to the epicondyle, the hand was the distance from the radial stem to the middle fingertip, and the length of the arm was the shoulder to the radius styloid process.

The motion capture system of the model was used to capture the movement of the upper extremities during walking. It was found that each rigid body was composed of at least three Marker points and was consolidated on the outside of the forearm and the upper arm by a gauze, Another rigid body is attached to the sternum to calculate the upper arm swing angle. Since the wrist joint has a small movement during walking, the handle and the forearm can be regarded as the same rigid body. For each key anatomical feature point that is not easy to collect, a virtual tool of the motion feature capture system is used to set the virtual Marker, and the three-dimensional motion feature track attached to the active light emitter Marker point of the test subject is obtained as shown in the following Fig. 4.

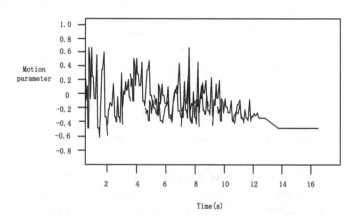

Fig. 4. Three-dimensional movement characteristics

Deltoid around the shoulder joint, the clavicle of the pectoralis major muscle, the biceps brachii, the latissimus dorsi, the major round muscle, and the posterior deltoid muscle during the swing arm are performed synchronous measurement and exercised on the main EMG signals of the anterior, also, their trends are analyzed. First, the test subjects were measured for ergonomic parameters, and then adhered in sequence according to the Marker points and the electromyography plan formulated above. Adjust the speed of the treadmill to 2 m/s before the start of the capture test. Each tester will perform at least several adaptive exercises to suit the laboratory's light, temperature, treadmill and other equipment. The testers are required to walk in a naturally relaxed state and then begin to capture measurements; each tester also performs multiple cycles of the same action. The test data is as follows (Fig. 5):

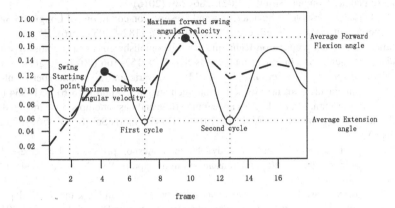

Fig. 5. Trend analysis of sports features

As can be seen from the figure, the method of folding and cross-validation is used to classify and recognize the motion feature data samples under slow, medium, and fast conditions, and it is found that the experimenter's motion features are accurately acquired and calculated. The tendency of the trend data of sports features confirms the effectiveness of the model. In summary, the trend analysis model based on big data can be effectively applied to the human motion trend classification and identification system.

5 Conclusion

Although there are certain regularities in the movement process, the complexity of the movement characteristics is still relatively high. The information describing the freedom of the movement model and the structure of the kinematic chain is too complex, resulting in the traditional movement modeling method in the structure of the human lower limb movement model. Due to the high complexity, it is impossible to accurately model the motion of human lower limbs. Therefore, a method for modeling human lower limbs kinematic chain motion combining human body dynamics is proposed. The problem of the motion curve simulation of the human kinematic chain is converted into the basic variable set. The variables include the zero-point moment of the human lower limbs, the gravity point and the posture relationship of the movement. The accurate analysis of human lower limb movement characteristics trends is achieved through the constraints of the human lower limb movement dynamics model. It is best to show through experiments that using the improved algorithm to analyze the trend model of the movement characteristics, which has a better running effect.

References

1. Liu, E., Huang, R.: Image segmentation simulation of lower limb movement characteristics of obese people. Comput. Simul. **33**(02), 286–289 (2016)
2. Liu, S., Jansa, L.: Reservoir characteristics and preservation conditions of Longmaxi Shale in the Upper Yangtze Block, South China. J. Geol. **90**(6), 2182–2205 (2016). English Version
3. Frimmel, K.: Mental preparation techniques and accomplishment of race goals by Ironman Triathletes: a qualitative investigation. Sports Sci. **7**(3), 157–166 (2017). English Version
4. Santolaria, P., Soler, C., Recreo, P., et al.: Morphometric and kinematic sperm subpopulations in split ejaculates of normozoospermic men. Asian J. Androl. **18**(6), 831–834 (2016)
5. Saito, K., Yoshimura, M., et al.: Pass appearance time and pass attempts by teams qualifying for the second stage of FIFA World Cup 2014 in Brazil. Sports Sci. **14**(3), 156–162 (2016). English Version
6. Tashiro, Y., Hasegawa, S., et al.: Body characteristics of professional Japanese Keirin cyclists: flexibility, pelvic tilt, and muscle strength. Sports Sci. **13**(6), 341–345 (2016). English Version
7. Cox, C., Ross-Stewart, L., et al.: Investigating the prevalence and risk factors of depression symptoms among NCAA division I collegiate athletes. Sports Sci. **25**(1), 14–28 (2017)
8. Koley, S., Aanchal: Correlations of handgrip strength with selected anthropometric variables and flexibility measure in Indian Inter-University Handball players. Sports Sci. **4**(2), 70–74 (2016). English Version
9. Hagiwara, G., Bryant, L., et al.: A cross-cultural comparison of the providing-receiving social supports in sports teams–Japanese and American student's athletes. Sports Sci. **25**(4), 210–218 (2016). English Version
10. Hua, J., Filaire, E., et al.: Predicting a failure of public speaking performance using multidimensional assessment. Sports Sci. **4**(4), 197–209 (2016). English Version

Research and Analysis on Comparison Scheme of IoT Encrypted Data in Cloud Computing Environment

Rong Xu[1(✉)] and Fu-yong Bian[2]

[1] School of Information Engineering,
Anhui Radio and TV University, Hefei 230022, China
xurong528528@163.com
[2] Chuxiong Medical College, Chuxiong 675005, China

Abstract. Conventional cloud computing iot encrypted data comparative analysis method to simple encryption scheme comparison, the accuracy of the scheme comparison is not high, for more complex data encryption scheme comparison, comparative stability lower deficiencies, therefore put forward under the cloud computing environment, the Internet of things encrypted data comparison analysis research. Introducing the sliding window technology, build the Internet of things to encrypt data security evaluation mechanism, determine the iot encrypted data comparison analysis algorithm, constructing iot encrypted data comparison analysis model is presented. Run the analysis model, analyze the iot encrypted data comparison scheme, and implement the iot encrypted data comparison scheme analysis. The experimental data show that the proposed scheme is more routine than the conventional scheme analysis, and the stability of the method is maintained at 70%–90%, which is suitable for the comparison scheme analysis of the network encryption data with different difficulty coefficients. The proposed method for comparative analysis of IoT encrypted data is highly effective.

Keywords: Cloud computing environment · The Internet of Things · Encrypt data · Comparative analysis

1 Introduction

The conventional cloud computing IoT encrypted data comparison analysis method can compare simply encrypted data schemes. When comparing with more complex encrypted data schemes, due to analysis technology limitations, there is a relatively low stability [1]. Thus, the research and analysis on comparison scheme of IoT encrypted data in cloud computing environment is proposed. The sliding window comparison technology is introduced, the security evaluation mechanism for IoT encrypted data is built, the analysis algorithm of IoT encrypted data comparison scheme is determined, and the analysis model of IoT encrypted data comparison scheme is constructed; using IoT encrypted data comparison scheme analysis model algorithm for parameter generation Gen, data partition Par, label generation Der, ciphertext generation Enc, and ciphertext comparison cmp calculations to determine the relationship between num,

S. Liu and G. Yang (Eds.): ADHIP 2018, LNICST 279, pp. 195–203, 2019.
https://doi.org/10.1007/978-3-030-19086-6_22

num*, to achieve the IoT encrypted data comparison scheme analysis. Thus, the research and analysis on comparison scheme of IoT encrypted data in cloud computing environment is completed. To ensure the effectiveness of designed IoT encrypted data comparison and analysis method, the IoT encrypted data test environment is simulated, by using two different methods of comparative analysis of IoT encrypted data, comparative stability simulation test is performed, the experimental results show that the proposed method for comparative analysis of IoT encrypted data is highly effective.

2 System Objective and Analysis

Research and analysis on comparison scheme of IoT encrypted data in cloud computing environment mainly includes:

(1) Solve the problems existing in the comparative analysis methods of conventional cloud computing IoT encrypted data, optimize the model building process, scientifically and reasonably combine modern computer technologies to build a security evaluation mechanism for IoT encrypted data.
(2) Optimize IoT encrypted data comparison scheme analysis algorithm design, analyze IoT encrypted data variable parameters.
(3) Optimize parameter generation Gen, data partition Par, label generation Der, ciphertext generation Enc, and ciphertext comparison cmp calculations to determine the relationship between num, num*, to achieve the IoT encrypted data comparison scheme analysis.

3 Construction of IoT Encrypted Data Comparison Scheme Analysis Model

3.1 Introduction of Sliding Window Comparison Technology

The sliding window comparison method is generally applied to power exponent operations. In general, the integer e is divided into fixed-length blocks, and then multiplication of non-zero block times is performed [2]. If the used block lengths are different, non-zero blocks can be reduced to reduce the total number of multiplications. This method of segmentation is called sliding window comparison. In practical applications, the sliding window comparison method will be optimized because in the binary representation of numbers, both zero and non-zero bits are significant. Therefore, no distinction is made between zero-window comparison and non-zero window comparison. Instead, the binary form of numbers is uniformly windowed so that each window is equal in size. This technique of improving efficiency by reducing the amount of calculation has attracted wide attention from various industries [3].

3.2   Construction of the Security Evaluation Mechanism of IoT Encrypted Data

Firstly, the weak distinguishable is defined. Data can be divided into strong data types and weak data types. Strongly typed languages is a language that always compels type definitions. Java and Python are strongly defined. If there is an integer, you can't treat it as a string if you don't convert it. Weakly typed definition language, a type of language that can be ignored, contrary to strongly typed definitions. VBScript is weakly defined [4]. In VBScript, the string '12' can be concatenated with the integer 3 to get the string '123', then it can be taken as an integer 123 without the need to display the conversion. Weakly typed data is called weak distinguishability. Then the security evaluation program under the weak characteristics of the IoT encrypted data scheme in cloud computing environment is introduced. This part is to prove that the IoT encrypted data security evaluation plan satisfies the weak distinguishability under the standard model [5].

It's assuming that challenger C and opponent A ask for weakly distinguishable competition. Firstly, Challenger C receives the security parameter $k \in N$ and the range parameter $n \in N$. The parameter generation algorithm Gen is then executed, i.e., Gen(k, n) = (param,mkey), and the generated public parameter param is returned to the opponent A. Opponent A inquiries Challenger C. During this process, Challenger C responds to the inquiry as follows:

First of all, Challenger C receives any inquiry number $0 < num < 2$, then executes the label generation algorithm Der and returns the generated label token = Der(param, mkey,num) [6].

Then, Challenger C receives any inquiry number $0 < num < 2n$, and then executes the encryption algorithm Enc and returns the ciphertext ciph = Enc(param,mkey,num).

Finally, Challenger C receives a set of numbers $0 < num * 0 < num * 1 < 2n$ that need to be interrogated. The challenger randomly selects $b \in \{0, 1\}$ and a ciphertext ciph* = Enc(param,mkey,numb) is generated [7]. In this process, Opponent A does not allow the following questions:

$$num = \sum_{i=0}^{n-1} \alpha_i 2^i; num_0^* = \sum_{i=0}^{n-1} \beta_i 2^i; num_0^* = \sum_{i=0}^{n-1} \gamma_i 2^i, \alpha_i, \beta_i, \gamma_i \in \{0, 1\} \tag{1}$$

In the formula: n is the number of times of inquiry and α_i is the probability that the enemy A can inquire the probability; and β_i is the probability that the enemy B can inquire, γ_i is the probability that the enemy C can inquire about.

On the end of process, the results that Opponent A send $b' \in \{0,1\}$ to C is $Exp_{C,A}^k = \begin{cases} 1, & b = b' \\ 0, & b \neq b' \end{cases}$, defined as in any polynomial time, after Opponent A asks, $Adv_{C,A}^k := \left| \Pr(Exp_{C,A}^k = 0) - \Pr(Exp_{C,A}^k = 1) \right|$ is ignorable for k in weak distinguishability, thus, the establishment of security evaluation mechanism for IoT encrypted data is performed.

3.3 Design of IoT Encrypted Data Comparison Scheme Analysis Algorithm

There are five steps for IoT encrypted data comparison scheme analysis algorithm, which are respectively parameter generation Gen, data partition Par, label generation Der, ciphertext generation Enc, and ciphertext comparison cmp.

Generation Gen needs to give the security parameter $k \in N$ and the range parameter $n \in N$. The algorithm outputs the public parameter param and the master key mkey, i.e., Gen(k,n) = (param,mkey). The data partition Par: num = $(b0, b1, \ldots, bn-1)$; $bi \in \{0, 1\}$ is the binary representation of the given number, the output value is num = $(B_0, B_1, \ldots, B_{m-1})$; $\frac{n}{m} = t$. Label generation Der needs to give public parameter param, master key mkey, and number num. Algorithm output label token, namely, token = Der(param,mkey,num). Ciphertext generation Enc needs to give public parameter param, master key mkey, and number num [8]. Algorithm output ciphertext ciph, namely, ciph = Enc(param,mkey,num). Ciphertext comparison cmp needs to give public parameter param, ciphertext ciph, ciph* and the corresponding label token of one ciphertext. Algorithm output result is $Cmp = \begin{cases} -1, & num > num^* \\ 0 & num = num^* \\ 1 & num < num^* \end{cases}$.

Figure 1 shows the schematic diagram of analysis model of the IoT encrypted data comparison solution. The system model includes three entities, namely data owners, cloud tenants, and cloud servers. The data owner needs to encrypt the shared data before uploading it to the cloud server [9]; the semi-trusted cloud server is responsible for data storage and retrieval operations; the cloud tenant is responsible for submitting query requests to get the size relationship of the data. Based on the sliding window comparison technology, the security evaluation mechanism for IoT encrypted data and design of IoT encrypted data comparison program analysis algorithm is used to achieve the construction of IoT encrypted data comparison program analysis model.

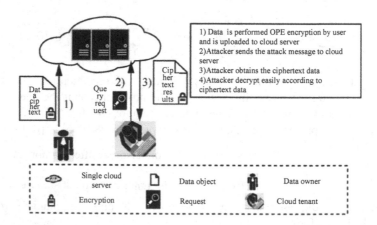

Fig. 1. IoT encrypted data comparison program analysis model

4   Analysis of IoT Encrypted Data Comparison Program

4.1   Operation Process of IoT Encrypted Data Comparison Program Analysis Model

It's assuming that the binary length of the number is nbit, each window contains tbit information, where n is a multiple of t. In fact, n can be of any length. If n cannot be divisible by t, it can be zero-padded until it is a multiple of t. For calculation convenience, the following representative meaning of formula is given: H_1 represents the function Hasla, H_2 represents the function Hash$_2$, H_3 represents the function Hash$_3$, H represents the hash function, mkey represents the master key, I represents the number Ls degree, n represents the number of hash function operations, m represents the number of windowing, and param represents the output parameter [10].

The parameter generation Gen, data partition Par, label generation Der, ciphertext generation Enc, and ciphertext comparison cmp calculation are performed by IoT encrypted data comparison scheme analysis model.

Generation Gen needs to give the security parameter $k \in N$ and the range parameter $n \in N$. H1, H2, H3 are randomly selected to satisfy the condition $\{0, 1\}^k \times \{0, 1\}^* \to \{0, 1\}^k$ algorithm outputs the public parameter param and the master key mkey. Among them, param $= (n, H_1, H_2, H_3)$.

Data partition Par needs to give the binary representation of the number num $= (b_0, b_1, \ldots, b_{n-1})$; $b_i \in \{0, 1\}$, the output of the algorithm is the packet data with windowing value t. After windowing, data is expressed as $num = (B_0, \ldots,$

$$B_{m-1}) = \sum_{i=0}^{m-1} B_i(2^t)^i; \frac{n}{m} = t, \text{ where } B_0 = (b_0, \ldots, b_{t-1}), \ldots, B_{m-1} = (b_{n-t}, \ldots, b_{n-1}).$$

Label generation Der needs to give the public parameter param, master key mkey, and number num after windowing. The above formula generates the label d_i. The label output by the Der algorithm is token $= (d_1, d_2 \ldots, d_m)$. Among them, there are $d_i = H_1(mkry, B_m, B_{m-1}, \ldots, B_i)$, $i = 1, 2, \ldots, m$.

Ciphertext generation En needs to give the public parameter param, master key mkey, and number num after windowing. The Enc algorithm randomly generates $I \in \{0, 1\}^k$ and label token $= (d_1, d_2 \ldots, d_m)$, generates fi, and outputs ciphertext ciph $= (I, (f_0, f_1 \ldots, f_m))$. In order to make the length of the ciphertext shorter, $(f_0, f_1 \ldots, f_{m-1})$ is

converted into an integer $F = \sum_{i=0}^{m-1} f_i(2^{t+1} - 1)^i$ to be stored, where $f_1 = H_1(d_{i+1}, I) + H_2(mkey, d_{i+1}) + B_i \bmod (2^{(t+1)} - 1)$.

Ciphertext comparison cmp calculation needs to give the public parameter param, ciphertext ciph $= (I, (f_0, f_1 \ldots, f_{m-1}))$, ciph$''$ $= (I', (f'_0, f'_1 \ldots, f'_{m-1}))$ and the corresponding label token of one ciphertext. The first different window $c_j = f_j - f'_j - H_3(d_{j+1}, I) \bmod (2^{(t+1)} - 1)$ is obtained by comparison, where $j = m - 1, \ldots, 1$. The output results of Cmp algorithm is

$$Cmp = \begin{cases} -1(num > num^*) & 1 \le c_j \le 2^t - 1 \\ 0(num = num^*) & c_j = 0 \\ 1(num < num^*) & 2^t \le c_j \le 2^{(t+1)} - 2 \end{cases} \quad (2)$$

The parameter generation algorithm is mainly used to generate the public parameter param and the master key mkey used in the following steps. The label generation algorithm is mainly used to generate label token related to the number num, and token* generated by the number num*. Similar to this process, the ciphertext generation algorithm is mainly used to generate the ciphertext ciph related to the number num, and the ciphertext ciph* generated by the number num*. The ciphertext comparison algorithm mainly uses the previously generated ciphertext data and the label associated with one of the numbers to perform a comparison operation, and ultimately determines the difference relationship between first different windows of a pair of ciphertexts ciph and ciph*.

4.2   Analysis of IoT Encrypted Data Comparison Program

Running the analysis model of the IoT encrypted data comparison program, it can be obtained that H_1, H_2, H_3 are pseudo-random functions, and then $|Adc^k_{C,A} - Adc^k_{C_B,A}| < \varepsilon$ and $Adc^k_{C_B,A} = 0$, the IoT encrypted data analysis program satisfies the weak distinguishability. It's assuming that a pair of ciphertexts ciph and ciph* that need to be compared are generated by number $num = \sum_{i=0}^{m-1} b_i 2^i = num = \sum_{i=0}^{m-1} B_i(2^t)^i$, $\frac{n}{m} = t$ and number $num = \sum_{i=0}^{m-1} \beta_i 2^i = num = \sum_{i=0}^{m-1} B'_i(2^t)^i$ known by Gen. Among them, t represents the window size of windowing, m represents the total number of windows.

It can be known by data partition Par that the label token generated by num and num* are expressed respectively token $= (d_1, d_2 \ldots, d_m)$ and token* $= (d'_0, d'_1 \ldots, d'_m)$. In addition, the ciphertext generated by num and num* are expressed respectively ciph $= (I, (f_0, f_1 \ldots, f_{m-1}))$ and ciph* $= (I', (f'_0, f'_1 \ldots, f'_{m-1}))$, to make the ciphertext shorter, $(f_0, f_1 \ldots, f_{m-1}), (f'_0, f'_1 \ldots, f'_{m-1})$ are converted respectively as $F = \sum_{i=0}^{m-1} f_i(2^{t+1} - 1)^i$ and $F = \sum_{i=0}^{m-1} f'_i(2^{t+1} - 1)^i$ to be stored.

From these relationships it can be seen that the components d and d' in the label token are only related to B_i, B_{i+1}, B'_i, B'_{i+1} and mkey. Assuming that l is the first different window of num and num*, then for i $= 1+1, \ldots, m - 1$, if $B_{i+1} = B'_{i+1}$, then $d_{i+1} = d'_{i+1}$.

If num = num*, $\forall i = 0, 1, \ldots, m - 1$, then Cmp output is 0. If num $\neq$ num*, for the first different window, the following formula is given by:

$$C_j = f_j - f'_j - F_3(d_{j+1}, I) \mod (2^{(t+1)} - 1) \quad (3)$$

Based on the analysis model of the IoT encrypted data comparison scheme analysis model, running the analysis model, and using the IoT encrypted data comparison scheme analysis model algorithm to perform parameter generation Gen, data partition

Par, label generation Der, ciphertext generation Enc, and ciphertext comparison cmp calculation, determine the relationship between num, num*, and to achieve the IoT encrypted data comparison program analysis.

5 Experimental Test and Analysis

To ensure the effectiveness of the analysis and comparison study of IoT encrypted data in cloud computing environment proposed in this paper, simulation experiments are conducted. In the test process, different IoT encrypted data were used as test objects to conduct comparative stability simulation tests. Different types of structures and difficulty coefficient of IoT encrypted data are simulated. In order to ensure the validity of the experiment, the conventional IoT encrypted data comparison and analysis method in cloud computing was used as a comparison object. The results of the two simulation experiments were compared and the test data was presented on the same data chart.

5.1 Preparation of Experimental Test

In order to ensure the accuracy of the simulation test process, the test parameters of the test are set. This article simulates the test process, uses different IoT encrypted data as the test object, uses two different methods of comparative analysis of IoT encrypted data, conducts a comparative stability simulation test, and analyzes the simulation test results. Because the analysis results obtained in different methods and the analysis methods are different, the test environment parameters must be consistent during the test. The test data set results in this paper are shown in Table 1.

Table 1. Test data set

Simulation experiment parameters	Implementation range/parameters	Observation
Difficulty coefficient of IoT encrypted data	DC0.1–DC1.6	DC unit of difficulty coefficient, maximum 2.0
IoT encrypted data	.DCD/.DGC, encryption of logic data, data volume 0–1 GB	Design analysis with two different methods
Simulation system	DJX-2016-3.5	Windows platform

5.2 Analysis of Experimental Test Results

During the testing process, two different methods of comparative analysis of IoT encrypted data were used to work in a simulated environment, and the changes in the comparative stability were analyzed. At the same time, due to the use of two different methods for comparative analysis of IoT encrypted data, the analysis results cannot be compared directly. For this purpose, third-party analysis and recording software is used to record and analyze the test process and results, and the results are displayed in the comparative curve of the test results. In the simulation test result curve, the third-party analysis and recording software function is used to eliminate the uncertainty caused by simulation laboratory personnel operation and computer simulation equipment, the comparative stability simulation test was conducted only for different IoT encrypted data, different methods for comparative analysis of IoT encrypted data. The test results are compared with the histogram shown in Fig. 2.

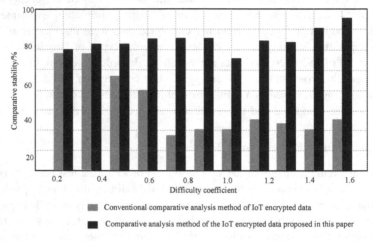

Fig. 2. Comparison of test results with histogram

Based on the results of the test histogram, using third-party analysis and recording software, the comparative stability of comparative analysis method of the IoT encrypted data proposed in this paper and the conventional comparative analysis method of IoT encrypted data in cloud computing are arithmetically weighted. The comparison and analysis method of the Internet of Things encryption data proposed in this paper is arithmetically weighted with the stability of the conventional cloud computing IoT encryption data comparison analysis method, and the comparison histogram is obtained. The stability of the method is maintained at 70%–90%, suitable for The analysis of networked encrypted data comparison schemes with different difficulty coefficients is more effective.

6   Conclusion

This paper presents the analysis and comparison of the IoT encrypted data in the cloud computing environment, based on the analysis model of the IoT encrypted data comparison program, the operation of analysis model and the analysis of IoT encrypted data comparison program is performed to achieve the study of this article. The experimental data shows that the method designed in this paper has extremely high effectiveness. It is hoped that the research in this paper will provide a theoretical basis for the comparative analysis of IoT encrypted data.

References

1. Meng, Q., Ma, J.F., Chen, K.F., et al.: IoT encrypted data comparison solution based on cloud computing platform. J. Commun. **1**(4), 34–37 (2018)
2. Cheng, Z.Q., Lian, H.P.: Research on encryption simulation of IoT communication characteristic data information. Comput. Simul. **33**(11), 324–327 (2016)
3. Cao, J.C.H., Li, C.: Study on IoT database storage system of maritime military mass data. Ship Sci. Technol. **33**(12), 175–177 (2016)
4. Ma, X.X., Yu, G.: Publicly accountable ciphertext-policy attribute-based encryption scheme. Comput. Sci. **44**(5), 160–165 (2017)
5. L, Y.: Realization of multi-card recognition in UHF radio frequency identification system in internet of things. Microelectron. Comput. **36**(11), 104–107 (2017)
6. Li, J.R., Li, X.Y., Gao, Y.L., et al.: Research on data forwarding model in internet of things. J. Softw. **22**(1), 196–224 (2018)
7. Qin, X.J.: Research on privacy protection encryption algorithms with smaller space in IoT environment. Bull. Sci. Technol. (2018)
8. Li, W., Ge, C.H.Y., Gu, D.W., et al.: Research on statistical fault analysis of LED lightweight password algorithm in internet of things environment. J. Comput. Res. Dev. **54** (10), 2205–2214 (2017)
9. Xu, J.G., Zhang, J.: IoT data parallel transmission path prediction simulation. Comput. Simul. **32**(1), 172–175 (2018)
10. Gu, W.J.: Research on data scheduling of shared resources in internet of things. Comput. Simul. **34**(1), 268–271 (2017)

DDoS Attack Detection
Based on RBFNN in SDN

Jingmei Li, Mengqi Zhang[(⊠)], and Jiaxiang Wang

Harbin Engineering University, 145, Nangtong, NJ, China
happy_zmq@163.com

Abstract. SDN is a new network architecture with centralized control. By analyzing the traffic characteristics of DDoS attack, and using the SDN controller to collect the traffic in the network, the important characteristics such as the IP address entropy ratio and the port entropy ratio related to the attack are extracted. According to the analysis of relevant eigenvalues, the RBFNN algorithm is used to classify the training samples to detect DDoS attacks. Finally, the SDN environment and DDoS attacks are simulated under Ubuntu, and the RBFNN algorithm detection model is deployed in the SDN controller. Compared with BPNN algorithm and Naive Bayes algorithm, it is proved that the algorithm performs DDoS attack detection with high recognition rate in a short time.

Keywords: DDoS · SDN · RBFNN

1 Introduction

The strategy of the Distributed Denial of Service (DDoS) attacks [1] is to send a large number of seemingly legitimate network packets to the target host through a number of "zombie hosts" (hosts that have been intruded or indirectly exploited by the attacker). Finally, the target host refuses service due to network congestion or server resource exhaustion. Therefore, detecting DDoS attacks quickly and accurately has become research hotspots in the field of Internet security. Software Defined Network (SDN) [2] is a new network architecture with centralized control, programmability and hardware versatility. Network administrators can monitor network traffic in real time [3]. Comparing with traditional networks using SDN to detect DDoS attacks has the advantage of real time the global network monitoring. At the same time, the centralized control characteristics of SDN also have network security problems. When the controller is attacked by DDoS, the control plane is decoupled from the data plane, causing the entire network to collapse. Therefore, detecting DDoS attacks in SDN has important research significance and use value.

At present, researchers have proposed some detection methods for DDoS attacks under the SDN network architecture. Wang et al. proposed a DDoS attack detection method based on BPNN in software defined network [4]. This method combines OpenFlow technology to analyze the eigenvalues in the switch flow table and uses the BPNN classification algorithm to detect DDoS attacks. Fu et al. proposed a DDoS attack detection method based on KNN classification algorithm [5]. This method

S. Liu and G. Yang (Eds.): ADHIP 2018, LNICST 279, pp. 204–213, 2019.
https://doi.org/10.1007/978-3-030-19086-6_23

extracts the key features of the flow table and uses the KNN algorithm to detect DDoS attacks. Shu et al. proposed a DDoS attack detection method based on conditional entropy [6]. The method extracts the TTL and the source IP address in the switch flow table, obtains the conditional entropy of the source IP address under the same TTL value, and further analyzes the entropy change by using the sliding window non-parametric CUSUM algorithm to detect the DDoS attack. Han et al. proposed a method for detecting DDoS attacks based on entropy values [7]. The method utilizes the characteristics of the centralized control of the controller to efficiently process the information of the data packet. The DDoS attack is detected by calculating the entropy value. Based on the research and analysis of the above methods, this paper proposes a DDoS attack detection method based on Radical Basis Function Neural Network in SDN.

2   Related Technologies

2.1   Software Defined Network

The SDN architecture is a new type of network architecture [8]. The SDN architecture is shown in Fig. 1, it is to separate the control plane of the network from the data forwarding plane. The control plane calculates the forwarding rules of the network packets by the controller. The main work of the data plane is that the network equipment (such as OpenFlow switch) processes networks packets according to the forwarding rules calculated by the controller [9]. The core technology of the SDN architecture is OpenFlow technology. The OpenFlow protocol implements the flow table query, add, delete and other operations between controller and switch [10].

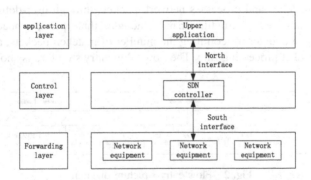

Fig. 1. SDN architecture diagram

2.2   DDoS Attacks in SDN

DDoS attacks take distributed attack, which occupies network resources through a large number of requests, causing the network paralysis and unable to provide services for legitimate users. There are controllers, switches and hosts in the SDN architecture.

According to the damage caused by DDoS attacks, DDoS attacks in SDN can be classified into three categories:

Switch denial of service. The information about the packets and the forwarding rules are stored in the flow table of the switch. When a DDoS attack occurs, a large number of false request messages are generated to occupy the flow table space of the switch. As a result, the switch can no longer allocate resources for legitimate requests.

Controller denial of service. When the information of the data packets do not match the forwarding information saved in the flow table, the controller is requested to calculate the forwarding rule of the data packets. When an attacker sends a large number of forged IP address packets, the switch will send a large number of requests to the controller, which occupies the computing and storage resources of the controller, and the controller cannot serve legitimate requests.

Host denial of service. The DDoS attacks use the defect in the host to send a large number of forged IP address requests to the target host. The computing resources, storage resources, and some other resources of the target host are occupied by the attack requests, so that the legitimate user request cannot be responded to.

3   RBFNN-Based DDoS Attack Detection

3.1   Attack Detection

RBFNN-based DDoS attack detection is divided into the following four steps:

Firstly analyze the characteristics of the DDoS attack in the SDN and the packet information in the switch flow table to determine the feature values. Using the eigenvalues of the DDoS attack dataset to train the RBFNN model to optimize the RBFNN model;

OpenFlow matches and processes network packets through user-defined or preset rules. The flow table entry structure mainly includes three parts, a header fields for packet matching, a counter for counting the number of matched packets, and an action for saving the packet processing rule. The flow table entry structure is shown in Fig. 2.

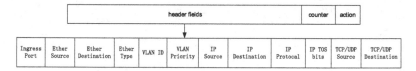

Fig. 2. Flow entry structure diagram

The DDoS attacks forge a large number of source IP addresses and sends request packets to the target host. When a DDoS attack occurs in SDN, a large number of data streams with certain regularity are generated. Because the source IP address is forged, the source IP address and source port in the data stream are scattered, and the destination IP address and destination port are concentrated. Therefore, applying IP address entropy ratio, port entropy ratio, match lookup ratio, average number of packets in per flow, and percentage of pair-flow are used as input parameters of the RBFNN.

IP address entropy ratio (EIP). When DDoS attacks occur, there are a large number of packets with forged IP addresses in the SDN. Therefore, the source IP address is more dispersed, and the destination IP address is more concentrated. The characteristics of the DDoS attack are described by calculating the entropy ratio of the source IP address to the destination IP address.

$$\text{EIP} = \frac{-\sum_{i=1}^{n} p\left(src_{p_i}\right) \log p\left(src_{p_i}\right)}{-\sum_{j=1}^{n} p\left(dest_{p_j}\right) \log p\left(dest_{p_j}\right)} \tag{1}$$

In the formula, src_{p_i} indicates the probability that the source IP address is p_i, and $dest_{p_i}$ indicates the probability that the destination IP address is p_j.

Port entropy ratio (Eport)

$$EPort = \frac{-\sum_{i=1}^{n} p(sport_i) \log(sport_i)}{-\sum_{j=1}^{n} p(dport_j) \log(dport_j)} \tag{2}$$

In the formula, $sport_i$ indicates the probability that the source port is i, $dport_j$ indicates the probability that the source port is j.

Match lookup ratio (MLR). When the switch receives data traffic, it will match flow entry. The source IP address of DDoS attacks stream is forged. Therefore, the matching rate of the switch will be drastically reduced.

$$MLR = \frac{Match}{Total} \tag{3}$$

In the formula, Math indicates the number of successful matching packets, Total indicates total number of packets.

Average number of packets in per flow (APF)

$$APF = \frac{\sum_{i=1}^{Ftotal} Pnum_i}{Ftotal} \tag{4}$$

In the formula, $Pnum_i$ indicates the number of packets in the data stream, $Ftotal$ indicates the number of all packets.

Percentage of pair-flow (PCF). When DDoS attacks occur, the data flow between the attacking host and the target host does not interact, so the interactive data flow will be drastically reduced.

$$PCF = \frac{2 * PFnum}{Flownum} \tag{5}$$

In the formula, *PFnum* indicates how many pairs of interactive streams, *Flownum* indicates total number of streams.

The controller periodically sends an instruction to the switch to collect the information in the flow table;

Set the controller period to 5 s, then controller sends the ofp_flow_stats_request packet to the switch to obtain the flow table information every 5 s.

Analyzing the data information in the collected flow table to extract feature values;

After obtaining the flow table information, the controller extracts the source IP address, the destination IP address, the port number, the pairs of the interaction stream in the flow table, and the size of the data packet. The extracted related information is calculated as the eigenvalues of the RBF neural network.

Using the RBFNN model for attack detection.

The calculated eigenvalues are used as input vectors of the RBF neural network, and the RBF neural network is used to identify normal traffic and attack traffic.

3.2   RBFNN Model Training

Through the above analysis of the characteristics of the DDoS attacks, the eigenvalues are IP address entropy ratio, port entropy ratio, match lookup ratio, average number of packets in per flow, and percentage of pair-flow. The eigenvalues is calculated by the source IP address, the destination IP address, the source port number and other informations, and is used as an input unit of the RBF neural network, and the RBF neural network trains and detects the DDoS attack through the input unit. The structural diagram of the RBF neural network is shown in Fig. 3.

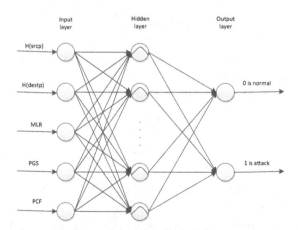

Fig. 3. RBF neural network structure diagram

RBF neural network is superior to BP neural network in terms of approximation ability, classification ability and learning speed. The training of the RBF neural network is divided into two phases:

Unsupervised learning of the hidden layer. The training of the hidden layer is to determine the parameters between the input layer and the hidden layer, and the parameters include the neuron center parameters and the corresponding width vector. The determination of the central parameters of the hidden layer neurons is a key issue in the RBF neural network. The common method for determining the central parameters is to select directly from a given training sample set according to a certain method, or to determine by clustering. In this paper, the K-means algorithm method is chosen to select the center of the hidden layer in the RBF neural network. The algorithm flow is shown in Fig. 4.

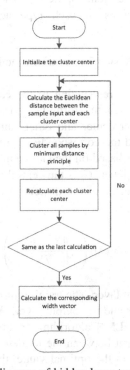

Fig. 4. Flow diagram of hidden layer training algorithm

The steps to calculate the center parameters using the K-means algorithm are as follows:

Set $c_{ji}(t)$ to be the central parameter of the j th hidden layer neuron for the i-th input neuron in the t-th iteration calculation, and the corresponding cluster domain is $w_{ji}(t)$.

Initialize the cluster center: Set $t = 1$, p is the total number of neurons in the hidden layer. Then the initial value of the central parameter is:

$$c_{ji}(t) = \min_i + \frac{\max_i - \min_i}{2p} + (j-1)\frac{\max_i - \min_i}{p} \tag{6}$$

In the formula, $\min_i$ is the minimum value of all input information of the i-th feature in the training set, and $\max_i$ is the maximum value of all input information of the i-th feature in the training set.

Calculate the Euclidean distance between the sample input and the cluster center $\|X_i - c_{ji}(t)\|$.

For the input samples X_i, cluster according to the principle of minimum distance: That is, if the Euclidean distance between X_i and $c_{ji}(t)$ is the smallest compared to the Euclidean distance of other cluster centers, then X_i belongs to $w_{ji}(t)$.

Recalculate the cluster centers of each type according to the classification $c_{ji}(t+1) = \frac{1}{N}\sum_{x\in w_{ji}(t)} x$.

If $c_{ji}(t+1) = c_{ji}(t)$, Return to step 2 to continue the iteration until the cluster center is unchanged.

Calculate the width vector corresponding to the central parameter of the hidden layer neuron, that is $D_{ji} = \sigma d_{ji}$, In the formula, σ is overlap coefficient, d_{ji} is the distance between the j th cluster center and other sample data centers. After determining the center parameter and the corresponding width vector, then calculating the output vector of the hidden layer based on the Gaussian function. z_j is the output value of the j-th neuron of the hidden layer, C_j is the central vector of the j th neuron in the hidden layer, D_j is the width vector of the th neuron in the hidden layer, X is input vector.

$$Z_j = \exp\left(-\left\|\frac{X - C_j}{D_j}\right\|^2\right) \tag{7}$$

Supervised learning of the output layer. The training of the output layer determines the weight between the hidden layer and the output layer. Weight training can be done by gradient descent algorithm and LMS algorithm. In this paper, the gradient descent method is used to train the weight between the hidden layer and the output layer. By adaptively adjusting the weight to the optimal value, the iterative calculation is as in Eq. 7:

$$W_{kj}(t) = w_{kj}(t-1) - \eta\frac{\partial E}{\partial w_{kj}(t-1)} + \alpha\left[w_{kj}(t-1) - w_{kj}(t-2)\right] \tag{8}$$

In the formula, $W_{kj}(t)$ represents the adjustment weight between the k th output neuron and the j th hidden layer neuron at the t-th iteration calculation. η is the learning factor and E is the evaluation function of the RBF neural network $E = \frac{1}{2}\sum_{l=1}^{N}\sum_{k=1}^{q}(Y_{lk} - O_{lk})^2$.

N is the number of hidden layer units, q is the number of output layer units, and Y_{lk} is the neural network output value of the k th output neuron at the l th input sample. O_{lk} is the expected output value of the k th output neuron at the l th input sample.

4   Experiment and Analysis

In order to verify the effectiveness of the RBFNN-based DDoS attack detection method, Under the ubuntu operating system, select Mininet to simulate the network environment, deploy the SDN with floodlight as the controller, and OpenVswitch as the switch. The network topology is shown in Fig. 5. The number 1 host is the target host, and the number 2 to number 6 host connected to the number 1 switch are normal traffic, mainly including TCP traffic, UDP traffic, and ICMP traffic. The number 6 to number 7 host connected to the number 3 switch are attacking hosts, and the TFN2K attack tool is used to generate DDoS attack traffic. The algorithm of the RBF neural network in the experiment is implemented with Python.

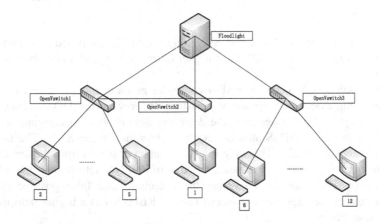

Fig. 5. Experimental network topology diagram

The controller collects the flow table information in the switch every other period, extracts the source IP address, the destination IP address and other information in the flow entry, and calculates the iput eigenvalue of the RBFNN according to the extracted information. The RBFNN algorithm classifies the traffic according to the calculated iput eigenvalue. If there is DDoS attack traffic, there is a DDoS attack in the SDN network. The results of this experiment were evaluated using two indicators: detection rate (DR) and false positive rate (FR). In the formula, TN represents the number of attack test samples that are correctly marked; FN represents the number of attack test samples that are incorrectly marked; TP represents the number of normal test samples that are correctly marked; and FP represents the number of normal test samples that are incorrectly marked.

$$DR = \frac{TN}{TN + FN} \tag{9}$$

$$FR = \frac{FP}{TP + FP} \tag{10}$$

By recording and analyzing the experimental results, the detection rate and false positive rate of the DDoS attack in this experiment are shown in Table 1, and BPNN and Naive Bayes method are used as the contrast:

Table 1. Test evaluation

Training number	Test number	Naive Bayes		BPNN		RBFNN	
Nomal/DDoS	Nomal/DDoS	DR	FR	DR	FR	DR	FR
2000/2000	1000/1000	91.44%	2.11%	92.13%	1.89%	97.56%	1.97%
3000/3000	1000/1000	92.58%	2.94%	93.4%	2.71%	98.20%	2.66%
4000/4000	1000/1000	93.47%	3.52%	94.5%	3.28%	99.73%	3.24%

Compared with Naïve Bayes and BPNN algorithm, the proposed algorithm based on RBF neural network under SDN has higher detection rate and relatively lower false positive rate.

When DDoS attacks occur, the SDN controller needs to quickly detect the DDoS attacks and implement corresponding measures to prevent the DDoS attacks from causing damage to SDN. Therefore, the detection time is also an important measurement parameter of the DDoS attacks detection algorithm in the SDN. The time line diagram of each algorithm is shown in Fig. 6. It can be observed from the line diagram that as the number of samples increases, the time of RBFNN detection is stable and the time is lower. Therefore, by analyzing the detection rate, false positive rate and detection time of the experimental record results, RBFNN has a higher detection rate and detection efficiency.

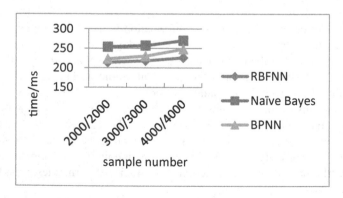

Fig. 6. The time line graph of each algorithm diagram

5   Conclusion

Through the traffic characteristics generated by the DDoS attacks and the flow table information in the switch, the five input key eigenvalues of the RBFNN are analyzed and calculated, and the RBFNN is optimally trained. The controller periodically collects flow table information, and analyzes the calculated eigenvalue IP address entropy ratio, port entropy ratio, match lookup ratio, average number of packets in per flow, and percentage of pair-flow as RBFNN inputs to detect DDoS attacks. Using the naive Bayes algorithm and BPNN algorithm as a comparison, it is proved that the RBFNN algorithm has higher detection rate and detection efficiency.

Acknowledgement. This work was supported by National Key Research and Development Plan of China (No 2016YFB0801004).

References

1. Santanna, J.J., van Rijswijk-Deij, R., Hofstede, R., et al.: Booters—an analysis of DDoS-as-a-service attacks. In: IFIP/IEEE International Symposium on Integrated Network Management, pp. 243–251. IEEE (2017)
2. Dixit, A., Hao, F., Mukherjee, S., et al.: ElastiCon; an elastic distributed SDN controller. Comput. Commun. Rev. **43**(4), 7–12 (2017)
3. Cohen, R., Lewin-Eytan, L., Naor, J.S., Raz, D.: On the effect of forwarding table size on SDN network utilization. In: Proceedings of the 33rd IEEE International Conference on Computer Communications, pp.1734–1742 (2014)
4. Wang, X., Zhuang, L., Hu, Y., et al.: DDoS attack detection based on BPNN in software defined networks. J. Comput. Appl. (2018)
5. Fu, X., Junqing, M., Xunsong, H., et al.: DDoS attack detection based on KNN in software defined networks. J. Nanjing Univ. Posts Telecommun. (Nat. Sci. Ed.) **35**(1), 84–88 (2015)
6. Shu, Y., Mei, M., Huang, W., et al.: Study on DDoS attack detection based on conditional entropy in SDN environment. Wirel. Internet Technol. **5**, 75–76 (2016)
7. Han, Z.: An entropy-based detection of DDoS attacks in SDN. Inf. Technol. **1**, 63–66 (2017)
8. Jia, W., Zhao, D., Ding, L.: An optimized RBF neural network algorithm based on partial least squares and genetic algorithm for classification of small sample. Appl. Soft Comput. **48**, 373–384 (2016)
9. Yan, Q., Yu, F.R., Gong, Q., et al.: Software-defined networking (SDN) and distributed denial of service (DDoS) attacks in cloud computing environments: a survey, some research issues, and challenges. IEEE Commun. Surv. Tutor. **18**(1), 602–622 (2016)
10. Sahi, A., Lai, D., Li, Y., et al.: An efficient DDoS TCP flood attack detection and prevention system in a cloud environment. IEEE Access **PP**(99), 1 (2017)

A Speed-up K-Nearest Neighbor Classification Algorithm for Trojan Detection

Tianshuang Li[1(✉)], Xiang Ji[2], and Jingmei Li[1]

[1] College of Computer Science and Technology,
Harbin Engineering University, Harbin 150001, China
447419029@qq.com
[2] The 73rd Institute of China Shipbuilding Industry Corporation,
Zhengzhou 450000, China

Abstract. Aiming at the problem that the traditional K-nearest neighbor algorithm has a long classification time when predicting Trojan sample categories, this paper proposes a speed-up K-nearest neighbor classification algorithm CBBFKNN for Trojan detection. This method adopts the idea of rectangular partitioning to reduce the dimensionality of the sample data. Combining the simulated annealing algorithm and the Kmeans algorithm, the sample set is compressed and the BBF algorithm is used to quickly classify the sample. The experimental results show that, the CBBFKNN classification algorithm can effectively reduce the classification time while the precision loss is small in IRIS dataset. In terms of Trojan detection, the CBBFKNN classification algorithm can guarantee higher accuracy and lower misjudgment rate and lower missed detection rate in shorter detection time.

Keywords: K-nearest neighbor algorithm · Kmeans algorithm ·
Trojan detection

1 Introduction

In recent years, with the progress of science and technology, there have been frequent threats to the global Internet network security, among which the Troy Trojan-horse has performed abnormally [1]. Research on Trojan detection technology cannot be delayed. Most of the communication data obtained by computers in the real world is characterized by large quantities and irregularities. How to quickly classify these communication data and determine whether it is a Trojan behavior will become the main content of the current study. The most basic classification methods are the K-nearest neighbor algorithm. The K-nearest neighbor algorithm was first proposed by Cover [2] and HART in 1967. The unclassified samples were assigned to the recent classification category according to the rules. This algorithm is a kind of supervised learning algorithm, and it has the advantages of low demand for data distribution, strong adaptability and high precision. However, it also has the disadvantages of slow convergence, poor processing of small sample and poor processing for high dimensional data. The improvement of K-nearest neighbor algorithm and its application in Trojan detection is a worthy research topic.

S. Liu and G. Yang (Eds.): ADHIP 2018, LNICST 279, pp. 214–224, 2019.
https://doi.org/10.1007/978-3-030-19086-6_24

At present, aiming at the problem of low classification efficiency of traditional K-nearest neighbor algorithm in large-scale training set, Ren [3] proposed a clustering-based accelerated K-nearest neighbor classification method. However, they neglected the similarity between the training sample and the unclassified samples. In the similarity calculation, the training samples were not weighted. The accuracy of the algorithm needs to be improved. Zuo [4] proposed an evaluation function based on improved simulated annealing Kmeans algorithm to accept poor solutions with the certain probability, but its classification effect on large-scale data was not good. Hu [5] proposed two improved K-nearest neighbors algorithms, which was an improved K-nearest neighbors algorithm based on hypersphere region partition and an improved K-nearest neighbors algorithms based on cuboid region partition. However, the improved K-nearest neighbor algorithm based on the hypersphere region partition was not suitable for datasets with large amounts of data and it had a long initial classifier construction time. The improved K-nearest neighbor algorithm based on the cuboid region partition had a short construction time but its accuracy was not high. Yao [6] proposed an improved Kmeans algorithm combed the simulated annealing clustering algorithm. The exchange mechanism of simulated annealing algorithm was used to replace the exchange mechanism of Kmeans center point to reduce the occurrence of local optimal solution. However, the mechanism of annealing was to accept disturbances with the certain probability, the probability was in the form of a random number. So it was difficult to control the results of the disturbance, and it needed to be improved.

Aiming at the problems of high time complexity [7–9] and low classification efficiency of the traditional K-nearest neighbor algorithm, this paper proposes a speed-up K-nearest neighbor classification method CBBFKNN (Clustering Best Bin First K-Nearest Neighbor) for Trojan detection. This method first uses the idea of rectangular partitioning to reduce the dimension of training samples and determine an optimal dimension. Then the Kmeans algorithm is used to cluster the samples in the training sample. In order to avoid the Kmeans algorithm from falling into the local optimal solution, the simulated annealing algorithm is used to obtain the optimal clustering set. Use the BBF (Best Bin First) algorithm to query the nearest K samples of the unclassified sample, and according to the principle of the minority obeying the majority to determine the category of the unclassified sample.

2 Speed-up K-Nearest Neighbor Classification Algorithm

The traditional K-nearest neighbor algorithm cannot efficiently calculate the similarity between the unclassified sample and a large number of training samples. This paper presents a speed-up K-nearest neighbor classification algorithm CBBFKNN.

The speed-up K-nearest neighbor classification algorithm CBBFKNN is performed as follows.

Step 1: Initialization. Assume that the labeled training sample set is $P_a = \{(x_i, y_i)\}_{i=1}^{N}$, $x_i \in X \subseteq R^h$ represents the eigenvector of the sample, R^h represents the h-dimensional space. N represents the number of training samples, x_i represents the training samples. The sample category for sample x_i is y_i, $y_i \in Y = \{c_i\}_{i=1}^{t}$, t represents the number of categories. The unclassified sample set is $P_b = \{(tx_j, ty_j)\}_{j=1}^{M}$, M represents the number of unclassified samples, tx_j represents the unclassified sample, ty_j represents the category of unclassified sample.

Step 2: Determine the division dimension. If we calculate each dimension, it will consume a lot of memories and time. So we first reduce the dimension of the samples. Assume that the initial samples dimension is h, the optimal dimension to be calculated is h'. The number of intervals to be divided in each dimension is d.

Step 2.1: Assume that the distribution of the samples is uniform, and the average number of samples in each interval in each dimension is $avg = P_a/d$. The initial value of the variable l is 1. The optimal dimension opt is initially 2.

Step 2.2: According to the sample distribution, count the actual number of training samples $q_1, q_2, \ldots, q_d$ in each interval.

Step 2.3: Calculate the distribution evaluation function W on each dimension, The W calculation formula is shown in formula (1).

$$W = \sum_{l=1}^{h} (q_l - avg)/d \tag{1}$$

Step 2.4: The calculation of α is used to determine the optimal dimension. The calculated value is stored in opt and the newly calculated α value is compared with opt. If it is bigger than opt, it is stored in opt, otherwise it is stored in opt with a probability of 0.5. The α calculation formula is shown in formula (2).

$$\alpha = \frac{1}{W^2} \tag{2}$$

Step 2.5: Set $l = l + 1$.

Step 2.6: If $l > h$, the algorithm skip to Step 2.7, otherwise the algorithm skip to Step 2.2.

Step 2.7: We output the optimal dimension opt.

Step 3: Combine the simulated annealing algorithm and the Kmeans algorithm to compress the training dataset.

Step 3.1: Select t training samples randomly as the category center of the initial t category, the initial category set is $S = \{s_c\}_{c=1}^{t}$.

Step 3.2: Calculate the distance of each training sample x_i from each category center s_c and assign the unclassified sample to the nearest category. The formula is shown in formula (3).

$$D(s_c) = \sum_{l=1}^{h'} \left(x_i^{(l)} - s_c^{(l)}\right)^2 \tag{3}$$

Step 3.3: Recalculate the center of each category. The formula is as shown in formula (4).

$$s_c^{(l)} = \frac{\sum_{i=1}^{r_c} x_i^{(l)}}{r_c} \qquad (4)$$

$s_c^{(l)}$ represents the l-dimensional attribute of the category c center, r_c represents the number of training samples in category c.

Step 3.4: Take the clustering result of Step 3.3 as the initial solution s_c of the simulated annealing algorithm. The variable i is initially 0. The number of iterations is t. The objective function F is defined as shown in formula (5). The initial temperature value T is set to 10.

$$F_s = \sum_{i=1}^{r_c} \left| x_i^{(l)} - s_c^{(l)} \right| \qquad (5)$$

Step 3.5: The perturbation method is to randomly change the category of a sample. The new objective function F_s' is calculated by formula (5).

Step 3.6: Calculate the value of ΔF by $\Delta F = F_s' - F_s$. Set $i = i+1$.

Step 3.7: If $\Delta F \leq 0$, the algorithm skip to Step 3.8, otherwise the algorithm skip to Step 3.9.

Step 3.8: Accept the new solution and assign s' to s. Assign F_s' to F_s.

Step 3.9: According to Metropolis guidelines, new solutions are accepted with probability p. The formula for the probability p is shown in formula (6).

$$p = \left(e^{-\frac{\Delta F}{2T}} \right) \qquad (6)$$

Step 3.10: If $i = t$, decrease the temperature T by $1°$ and the algorithm skip to Step 3.11, otherwise the algorithm skip to Step 3.5.

Step 3.11: It is determined whether the temperature value T is 0 or not. If T is 0, skip to Step 4. Otherwise set i to 0, skip to Step 3.5.

Step 4: Obtaining the optimal clustering result and the clustering result is $S = \{s_c\}_{c=1}^t$.

Step 5: In the set S, m samples are selected at random, and m samples are sorted using quick sort. Determine the median x_{avg}.

Step 6: Using the BBF algorithm to find the nearest k samples from the unclassified sample and determine the category of the unclassified sample. The median x_{avg} is the split plane of the BBF algorithm.

Step 6.1: The kd-tree is constructed with the median x_{avg} as the root node.

Step 6.2: Query the unclassified sample tx_j on the kd-tree. During the query, the distance d_i between the sample x_i and the median x_{avg} on the query path is calculated. Sort the calculated distance d_i.

Step 6.3: Backtracking checks the sample x_i with the highest priority. The priority is inversely proportional to d_i. Finally determine the k samples closest to the unclassified sample tx_j, and k samples make up the set $N_K(x)$.

According to the principle of the minority obeying the majority formula (7) is used to determine the category y_j of the unclassified sample tx_j.

$$ty_j = \arg \max_{c_j} \sum_{x_i \in N_k(x)} I(f(x_i) = c_j) \tag{7}$$

In the formula (7), I represent the indicator function, $y_i = f(x_i)$. I will be 1 when $y_i = c_j$, otherwise I will be 0.

Step 7: Repeat performs Step 6.1–Step 6.3 for each sample in the unclassified sample set P_b. The prediction category of each unclassified sample in the sample set P_b is compared with the real category of the unclassified sample, so as to test the performance of the classification algorithm.

Step 8: The algorithm ends.

3 Experimental Design and Analysis

The experiments in this paper are divided into two parts. The first part is the characteristic detection experiment of Iris based on IRIS dataset to verify the accuracy and efficiency of the proposed algorithm CBBFKNN. The second part is the detection experiment based on Trojan horse behavior sample. The algorithm CBBFKNN proposed in this paper is applied in Trojan detection aiming to verify the accuracy of the algorithm.

3.1 Characteristic Detection Experiment Based on IRIS DataSet

In order to verify the performance of the proposed speed-up K-nearest neighbor classification algorithm CBBFKNN, this paper classifies the characteristic of Iris by using CBBFKNN. The algorithm performance is compared with SVM, Naive Bayes and traditional K-nearest neighbor algorithm aiming to verify the feasibility of the classification algorithm which is proposed in this paper.

Experimental Environment. The experimental platform is Windows 10 64-bit operating system, pycharm software platform, Intel I5 CPU, 8G RAM.

This experiment uses the international standard dataset IRIS. Specific information is shown in Table 1.

Table 1. The information of IRIS dataset

Data sources	Data dimension	Number of samples	Number of categories
Iris characteristics	4	150	3

The IRIS dataset contains three species of Iris virginica, versicolor, and setosa. The four attributes of the flower are the sepal length, sepal width, petal length, and petal width.

In this experiment, the IRIS dataset was divided into two parts: the training set and the test set. Taken 70% of the IRIS dataset, 105 groups of data as the training set, and the other 45 groups of data are taken as the test set.

Experimental Parameter Configuration. The CBBFKNN classification algorithm proposed in this paper needs to determine the parameter k and the clustering parameter t. Take the clustering parameter t for 4 temporarily. Figure 1 shows the classification time curve of the classification algorithm when the clustering parameter t takes 4 and the parameter k takes different values. When the value of k is taken as 9, the classification time approaches the minimum value.

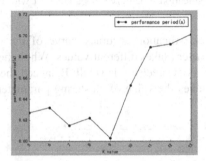

Fig. 1. The classification time curve of parameter k with different values

Figure 2 shows the classification accuracy curve of the classification algorithm when the clustering parameter t takes 4 and the parameter k takes different values. When the value of k is taken as 8, the classification time approaches the minimum value. Balanced the classification time and the accuracy, this paper takes the value of classification parameter k is 9.

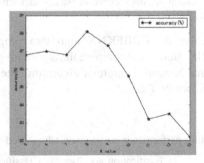

Fig. 2. The classification accuracy curve of parameter k with different values

The value of the classification parameter k is taken as 9, and the initial clustering parameters t are taken as 2, 3, 4, 5, and 6 respectively. Figure 3 shows the classification time curve of the classification algorithm when clustering parameter t takes different values. It shows that the classification time fluctuates little when the values of the parameters t are different.

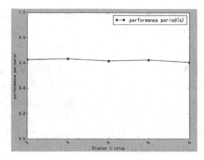

Fig. 3. The classification time curve of parameter t with different values

Figure 4 shows the classification accuracy curve of the classification algorithm when the clustering parameter t takes different values. When the value of the clustering parameter t takes 5, the loss of precision is small. Balanced the classification time and the accuracy, this paper takes the value of clustering parameter t is 5.

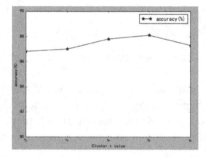

Fig. 4. The classification accuracy curve of parameter t with different values

Experimental Results. Use the CBBFKNN algorithm proposed in this paper to classify samples in the IRIS dataset and compare the algorithm performance with SVM, Naive Bayes and traditional K-nearest neighbor algorithm. The algorithm performance comparison results are shown in Table 2.

Table 2. Algorithm performance comparison table based on IRIS dataset

Algorithm	Classification accuracy/%	Classification time/s
SVM	91.8	0.932
Naive Bayes	92.5	0.853
K-nearest neighbor	93.9	0.884
CBBFKNN	93.6	0.842

It can be seen from Table 2 that the accuracy of the speed-up K-nearest neighbor classification algorithm CBBFKNN proposed in this paper is closest to that of the traditional K-nearest neighbor classification algorithm. CBBFKNN reduces the time for classification when the loss of accuracy is small.

3.2 Detection Experiment Based on Trojan Behavior Samples

In order to verify the effectiveness and practicability of the proposed speed-up K-nearest neighbor algorithm CBBFKNN in Trojan detection, this paper sets up the following experimental environment and tests the detection effect of the classification algorithm.

Experimental Environment. In order to ensure the authenticity of the data, the Trojan behavior sample in this paper is obtained in the following environment. The test environment consists of 18 hosts, of which 15 are operating normally on the Internet. Selecting 8 hosts that are surfing on the Internet to implant Trojans and extra choose one control terminal to generate Trojan corresponding traffic. Use common Trojans such as Glaciers, Broad Girls, Grey Pigeons, etc. for testing.

Sample Behavior Characteristics. Trojan communication and normal network communication have certain differences, so analyzing the Trojan's behavioral characteristics can effectively detect Trojans. The Trojan's communication process is divided into three phases: building connections, maintaining connections, and connecting interactions. (1) During the phases of building connections, Trojans will perform multiple DNS connection requests to the controller in a short period of time. (2) During the phases of maintaining connections, in order to maintain communication, the communication parties regularly send a large number of heartbeat packets. (3) During the phases of connecting interactions, a long connection is required. If the control terminal cannot communicate normally, the controlled terminal does not disconnect directly. They will send a large number of SYN packets to determine if the console is alive [10]. According to the above three phases of Trojan communication, this paper selects four characteristics to describe Trojan behavior. The characteristics are shown in Table 3.

Table 3. Behavioral characteristics table

Phases	Characteristic name
Building connections	Multiple DNS connection requests in a short time
Maintaining connections	The ratio of packets to total packets
Maintaining connections	Heartbeat packet time gap
Connecting interactions	The ratio of SYN packets to total packets

In the actual collection process, it is impossible to directly distinguish the phases of the characteristic generation, so the characteristic generation phase is not distinguished during the collection process.

Sample Collection Process

(1) We install VMWare Workstation 6.0 software for each computer in the lab. Select one computer as the controller and the virtual machine installs the Win7 operating system. Select 8 computers as the controlled machine, the virtual machine installs the WinXp operating system and installs multiple Trojans in the virtual machine. Use Wireshark software to intercept and capture the data messages generated by Trojan behavior. The control side performs the Trojan operation behavior, such as copies the files of the controlled machine, replacing the desktop wallpaper of the controlled machine. Use Wireshark software to intercept data generated by Trojan behavior.

(2) Preprocessing the collected data. The data messages generated by Trojan behavior get the category number 1, other behaviors get the category number 0.

(3) Taking the first 60% of the obtained data as the training set and the last 40% as the test set.

(4) Using the training set as the input of CBBFKNN classification algorithm, the clustering parameter t set as 50, the parameter k set as 7. And then classify the collected data.

(5) Using SVM, naive Bayes and traditional K-nearest neighbor algorithm to classify the collected data and compare the accuracy, misjudgment rate and missed rate with CBBFKNN. The evaluation criteria are defined as follows.
Accuracy = (The number of detected Trojan sessions − Misreported Trojans sessions)/Total number of sessions
Misjudgment rate = Misreported normal sessions/Total number of sessions
Missed rate = (Total number of sessions − The number of detected Trojan sessions − Misreported normal sessions)/Total number of sessions

Analysis of Results. In this experiment, the accuracy, misjudgment rate, and missed rate is used as the criteria for evaluating the performance of classification algorithms. The experimental data contains 2,805 samples of traffic characteristics, including 1,683 training samples and 1,122 test samples. Compare the algorithm CBBFKNN proposed in this paper with the SVM, Naive Bayes, and K-nearest Neighbor algorithm which is the supervised learning algorithm in the same data. Compare their classification accuracy, misjudgment, missed rate, and running time. The algorithm performance comparison results are shown in Table 4.

Table 4. Algorithm performance comparison table based on Trojan detection

Algorithm	Accuracy/%	Misjudgment rate/%	Missed rate/%	Running time/s
SVM	83.43	6.21	6.45	1357
Naive Bayes	83.68	5.42	5.98	1361
K-nearest neighbor	84.23	5.77	5.65	1285
CBBFKNN	84.33	5.65	5.60	1273

The accuracy of CBBFKNN classification algorithm proposed in this paper can reach 84.33%, the misjudgment rate is less than 6%, and the missed detection rate does not exceed 6%, which is improved compared with the traditional K-nearest neighbor algorithm. And its running time is lower than the traditional K-nearest neighbor algorithm, achieving a certain degree of speed-up. The classification method proposed in this paper has higher detection capability for some common Trojans, meanwhile the misjudgment rate and missed detection rate is controlled in a lower range, which indicates that the classification method has strong practical value.

Based on the above two experiments, the speed-up K-nearest neighbor classification algorithm CBBFKNN proposed in this paper can effectively improve the classification efficiency with a relatively high accuracy and has certain feasibility. In the detection of Trojans has a certain practical value.

4   Conclusion

Trojan detection technology has great significance in network security. How to reduce the detection time and improve the detection efficiency is an important issue at this stage. This paper presents a speed-up K-nearest neighbor classification algorithm CBBFKNN. The dimensionality reduction of training data is performed through the idea of rectangular partitioning. The Kmeans algorithm is used to compress the training sample set, and the BBF algorithm is used to quickly query the category of the sample to be measured. Experiments show that compared with the traditional classification algorithm, this algorithm can reduce the time for classification when the loss of accuracy is small in the IRIS dataset. In actual Trojan detection, CBBFKNN has improved performance in various aspects compared with traditional classification algorithms, which can ensure higher accuracy and lower misjudgment rate and lower missed rate. This algorithm has a certain practical value.

Acknowledge. This work was supported by National Key Research and Development Plan of China (No 2016YFB0801004).

References

1. Liu, H., et al.: Research on FAHP adjudgement algorithm based on the behavior of Trojan. Harbin Engineering University (2016)
2. Zhang, Q., Li, C., Li, X., et al.: Irregular partitioning method based K-Nearest neighbor query algorithm using map reduce. Comput. Syst. Appl. **9**, 186–190 (2015)
3. Ren, L.: Speeding K-NN classification method based on clustering. Comput. Appl. Softw. **10**, 298–301 (2015)
4. Zuo, N.: Application of improved K-means clustering method of simulated annealing algorithm in students' grades. Guangxi Educ. **31**, 149–152 (2017)
5. Hu, J.: Improved KNN classification algorithm based on region division. Qingdao University (2016)

6. Yao, L., Huang, H.: Rolling bearing fault diagnosis based on improved K-means simulated annealing clustering algorithm. Modul. Mach. Tool Autom. Manufact. Tech. **4**, 114–117 (2017)
7. Pan, L., Yang, B.: Study on KNN arithmetic based on cluster. Comput. Eng. Des. **30**(18), 4260–4262 (2009)
8. Lan, T., Guo, G.: Improved RSKNN algorithm for classification. Comput. Syst. Appl. **22**(12), 85–92 (2013)
9. Wang, C., Cheng, S., Yang, X.: K-nearest neighbor neural network classifier of samples reduction based on clustering. Inf. Sci. **10**, 1547–1549 (2010)
10. Li, W., Li, L., Li, J., Lin, S., et al.: Characteristics analysis of traffic behavior of remote access Trojan in three communication phases. Netinfo Secur. **5**, 10–15 (2015)

A Method of Estimating Number of Signal with Small Snapshots

Baoyu Guo and Jiaqi Zhen[✉]

College of Electronic Engineering,
Heilongjiang University, Harbin 150080, China
zhenjiaqi2011@163.com

Abstract. To determine the number of signals arriving on an array of sensors correctly is very important for most high resolution DOA (direction of arrival) estimation algorithms, the methods based on information theoretic criteria have good properties when there is a large snapshots, while it always leads to an error in the small snapshots field. A method based on the exact distribution of the eigenvalues of the sampling covariance matrix is proposed in the paper, it makes use of the model of information theoretic criteria at the same time, the new method has excellent performance when the snapshots is small, the computer simulation results prove the effective performance of the method.

Keywords: Determining number of signals · Direction of arrival · Information theoretic criteria · Small snapshots

1 Introduction

The super-resolution direction finding algorithms of spatial spectrum estimation are widely used in radar, sonar and mobile communication fields in recent years, especially algorithm of multiple emitter location and signal parameter estimation (MUSIC) [1] proposed by Schmidt, estimation of signal parameters via rotational invariance technique (ESPRIT) [2] and intelligent optimization algorithms [3–8], but the precondition of them is exactly knowing the number of signals. If the number estimated is not consistent with the truth, their performance will reduce greatly, even damage it, so it is the primary problem of every super resolution direction finding algorithm.

General methods for estimating number of signals are information theoretic criteria and Gerschgorin disk theoretic (GDE) [9], these methods respectively have their own merits and faults, one of the faults is that all of them need multiple snapshot, when the snapshot is small, they are not applicable.

This work was supported by the National Natural Science Foundation of China under Grant 61501176, Natural Science Foundation of Heilongjiang Province F2018025, University Nursing Program for Young Scholars with Creative Talents in Heilongjiang Province UNPYSCT-2016017, the postdoctoral scientific research developmental fund of Heilongjiang Province in 2017 LBH-Q17149.

S. Liu and G. Yang (Eds.): ADHIP 2018, LNICST 279, pp. 225–232, 2019.
https://doi.org/10.1007/978-3-030-19086-6_25

This paper proposed a new method based on the exact distribution of the eigen-values of the sampling covariance matrix on condition of small snapshots, first we make use of the matrices to construct a function, then combine the penalty function of information theoretic criteria to get a new criterion. The method has good performance when number of samples is small and is adapt to arbitrary array, wherever the computation is not complex at all.

2 Signal Model

As seen from Fig. 1, consider an array with M sensors in X-Y plane, the phase reference point of the array is defined as the origin, coordinate of the mth sensor is (x_m, y_m) $(m = 1, 2, \cdots, M)$. Assume there are N far-field narrowband signals arriving at the array, angles of arrival are separately (ϕ_i, θ_i) $(i = 1, 2, \cdots, N)$, ϕ_i and θ_i are separately defined as azimuth and elevation, so output of mth sensor can be written:

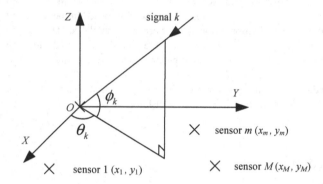

Fig. 1. Model of the signal.

$$x_m(t) = \sum_{i=1}^{N} s_i(t + \tau_{mi}) + n_m(t) \quad m = 1, 2, \cdots, M \tag{1}$$

where $\tau_{mi} = \frac{x_m \cos \phi_i \cos \theta_i + y_m \sin \phi_i \cos \theta_i}{c}$ is the propagation delay for the ith signal at the mth sensor with respect to the reference point of the array, $n_m(t)$ is corresponding the additive Gaussian white noise. The vector of array receiving data is

$$X(t) = A(\varphi, \theta)S(t) + N(t) \tag{2}$$

where $A(\varphi, \theta) = [a(\varphi_1, \theta_1), a(\varphi_2, \theta_2), \cdots, a(\varphi_N, \theta_N)]$ is the array manifold matrix, $S(t) = \left[S_1(t), S_2(t), \cdots, S_N(t)^T\right]$ is the signal vector, $N(t) = [N_1(t), N_2(t), \cdots, N_M(t)]^T$ is noise vector, suppose the signal $S_1(t), S_2(t), \cdots, S_N(t)$ is a stationary random process with zero mean, and they are not correlated with one other, covariance matrix of $X(t)$ is

$$R_X = E[X(t)X^H(t)] = AR_SA^H + \sigma^2 I \tag{3}$$

where $R_S = E[S(t)S^H(t)]$ is covariance matrix of the signal, decomposing R_X can acquire its M eigenvalues from larger to smaller as below:

$$\lambda_1 > \lambda_2 > \cdots > \lambda_N > \lambda_{N+1} = \cdots = \lambda_M = \sigma^2 \tag{4}$$

So if we can find the number n_E of the smaller eigenvalues of R_X, N would be calculated $N = M - n_E$. In fact, as affected by limited snapshot N and noise, covariance matrix R_X is estimated by limited observed data with

$$\hat{R} = \frac{1}{K}\sum_{i=1}^{K} x(t_i)x^H(t_i) \tag{5}$$

where K is the sampling times, the eigenvalues of $\hat{R}$ is not consistent with Eq. (4), wherever it satisfies

$$\lambda_1 > \lambda_2 > \cdots > \lambda_N > \lambda_{N+1} \geq \cdots \geq \lambda_M \tag{6}$$

That is, if decomposing $\hat{R}$, generally speaking, we can not get strictly n_E same smaller eigenvalues, so information theoretic criteria are needed.

3 Information Theoretic Criteria

Akaike information criterion (AIC) and minimum description length criterion (MDL) are proposed to solve the selection of model: suppose a group of observed data $X = [X_1, X_2, \cdots, X_K]$ and a serial of parameter probability model $f(x|\hat{\Theta})$, we need to choose the model which fits best. Akaike suggested choosing the model which makes value of AIC minimum, it can be expressed as

$$\text{AIC} = -2\log f(x|\hat{\Theta}) + 2p \tag{7}$$

where $\hat{\Theta}$ is the maximum likelihood estimation of parameter vector Θ, k is the free degree of parameter vector Θ, the first part of Eq. (7) is the log likelihood function term, the second part is penalty term. MDL criterion proposed by Rissanen J is defined as

$$\text{MDL} = -\log f(x|\hat{\Theta}) + \frac{1}{2}p\log K \tag{8}$$

It is seen the log likelihood function terms of two criteria are the same except a constant factor two, their penalty terms is a difference of $\frac{1}{4}\log K$ times. Information theoretic criteria need to a large sampling sizes, in practical, as the targets (for example plane, missile) usually move fast, we need to estimate their directions quickly, so the snapshot can not be too large, thereby it may leads to the failure calculation, so we must improve the criteria. Chiani proposed a lemma for MIMO networks based on exact eigenvalues distribution of sampling covariance matrix, it defined a function given by

$$f(l; \boldsymbol{\alpha}, \boldsymbol{\beta}) = C(\boldsymbol{\alpha}, \boldsymbol{\beta}) \det \boldsymbol{H}(l; \boldsymbol{\alpha}, \boldsymbol{\beta}) \prod_{i=1}^{n_{\min}} l_i^{K-n_{\min}} \tag{9}$$

where $n_{\min} = \min(M, K)$, and

$$C(\boldsymbol{\alpha}, \boldsymbol{\beta}) = \frac{(-1)^{K(M-n_{\min})}}{\Gamma_{(n_{\min})}(K) \prod_{i=1}^{L} \Gamma_{(m_i)}(m_i)} \times \frac{\prod_{i=1}^{L} \alpha_{(i)}^{m_i K}}{\prod_{i<j} (\alpha_{(i)} - \alpha_{(j)})^{m_i m_j}} \tag{10}$$

$\Gamma_{(m)}(a) \triangleq \prod_{i=1}^{m} (a-i)!$ and the vector $\boldsymbol{\alpha} = (\alpha_{(1)}, \alpha_{(2)}, \cdots, \alpha_{(L)})$ is the distinct order eigenvalues of $\boldsymbol{R}_X^{-1}$, $\boldsymbol{\beta} = (\beta_1, \beta_2, \cdots, \beta_L)$ is the corresponding multiplicities, det() denotes solving for the determinant. The matrix $\boldsymbol{H}(l; \boldsymbol{\alpha}, \boldsymbol{\beta})$ is $K \times K$ dimensional, elements of the matrix is

$$h_{i,j} = \begin{cases} (-l_j)^{d_i} e^{-\alpha_{(e_i)} l_j} & j = 1, 2, \cdots, n_{\min} \\ [M-j]_{d_i} \alpha_{(e_i)}^{M-j-d_i} & j = n_{\min}+1, \cdots, M \end{cases} \tag{11}$$

where $[a]_k = a(a-1) \cdots (a-k+1)$, $[a]_0 = 1$, e_i is the unique integer such as $\beta_1 + \cdots + \beta_{e_i-1} < i \leq \beta_1 + \cdots + \beta_{e_i}$ and $d_i = \sum_{k=1}^{e_i} \beta_k - i$.

We can extend the conclusions above to the estimation of number of signal, according to Eq. (9), distribution of the eigenvalues $\tilde{l} = (\tilde{l}_1, \tilde{l}_2, \cdots, \tilde{l}_{n_{\min}})$ of $\boldsymbol{W} = K\hat{\boldsymbol{R}}$ are decided by $f(\tilde{l}; \boldsymbol{\alpha}, \boldsymbol{\beta})$, where $\boldsymbol{\alpha}, \boldsymbol{\beta}$ are separately the eigenvalues and multiplicities of $\hat{\boldsymbol{R}}^{-1}$, and $\tilde{l}_i = Kl_i$, l_i are the eigenvalues of the estimated covariance matrix $\boldsymbol{W}$.

So we can get the new criteria as below

$$\begin{aligned} num &= \arg \min_{k \in \{0,1,\cdots,k_{\max}\}} \left\{ -\log f(\tilde{l}; \hat{\boldsymbol{\alpha}}^{(k)}, \boldsymbol{\beta}^{(k)}) + L(k, K) \right\} \\ &= \arg \min_{k \in \{0,1,\cdots,k_{\max}\}} \left\{ -\log \left| C(\hat{\boldsymbol{\alpha}}^{(k)}, \boldsymbol{\beta}^{(k)}) \times \det \boldsymbol{H}(\tilde{l}; \hat{\boldsymbol{\alpha}}^{(k)}, \boldsymbol{\beta}^{(k)}) \right| + L(k, K) \right\} \end{aligned} \tag{12}$$

where $\boldsymbol{\beta}^{(k)} = (M-k, 1, 1, \cdots, 1)$, the elements of $\hat{\boldsymbol{\alpha}}^{(k)} = (\hat{\alpha}_1^{(k)}, \cdots, \hat{\alpha}_{k+1}^{(k)})$ are the ML estimation of the $k+1$ distinct eigenvalues of $\hat{\boldsymbol{R}}^{-1}$ in the hypothesis of k signals, and $k_{\max} = n_{\min} - 1$, where $n_{\min} = \min(M, K)$.

The vector $\hat{\boldsymbol{\alpha}}^{(k)}$ can be calculated from the marginal distribution, we can obtain it from information theory criteria, giving

$$\hat{\alpha}_{(i)}^{(k)} = \begin{cases} \left(\frac{1}{(n_{\min}-k)} \sum_{j=k+1}^{n_{\min}} l_j \right)^{-1}, & i = 1 \\ \left(l_{k+2-i} \right)^{-1} & i = 2, \cdots, k+1 \end{cases} \tag{13}$$

The criterion above is reduced with the marginal distribution of the eigenvalues, the penalty function can be selected by the reference of AIC and MDL, we can get the improved criteria, we can call them improved AIC (IMAIC) and improved MDL (IMMDL) separately, in summary, the algorithm of the paper is summarized as follows

Step1: Make use of receiving data to evaluate $\hat{R}^{-1}$ and W;

Step2: Calculate the eigenvalues $\hat{\alpha}^{(k)}$, $\beta^{(k)}$ and $\tilde{l}$ with matrices $\hat{R}^{-1}$ and W;

Step3: Evaluate C with Eq. (10), and H with Eq. (11);

Step4: Construct penalty function according to the criteria of MDL or AIC;

Step5: Estimate number of signals with Eq. (12).

4 Simulation Analysis

In order to verify the validity of the method in this paper and to compare the performance with other algorithms, some experiments with matlab are presented, in the experiments, without loss of generality, we consider an arbitrary plane array of 6 sensors, the coordinates are given by: (0,0), (−0.16, 0.12), (−0.049, 0.086), (−0.22, 0.055), (−0.079, −0.032), (0.065, 0.13), unit is meter, the frequency of the signals are 4 GHz and corrupted by additive Gaussian noise, The signal-to-noise ratio(SNR) is defined as

$$SNR = 10 \log \left(\frac{\sigma_S^2}{\sigma_n^2} \right) \tag{14}$$

where σ_S^2 and σ_n^2 are respectively the power of signal and noise, we use criteria of MDL, AIC, IMAIC and IMMDL to estimate number of signals.

Experiment 1. The detection performance along with SNR.

Consider three far-field narrowband signals separately arriving from directions (56°, 65°), (66°, 75°), (80°, 85°), SNR varies from −5 dB to 15 dB, step size is 1 dB, snapshot times is 30, 500 times Monte-Carlo trials have run for each SNR, Fig. 2 shows the probability of success of the four criteria along with SNR.

It is seen from Fig. 2, the probability of success of criterion of IMMDL is up to 100% when SNR reaches 6 dB, that of MDL, IMAIC and AIC are up to 100% when SNR separately reaches 7 dB, 10 dB and 11 dB, probability of success of criterion of IMMDL is the highest, that of MDL is the second, IMAIC and AIC are separately the third and fourth in summary.

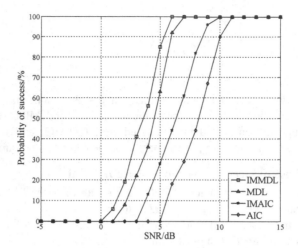

Fig. 2. Probability of success along with SNR.

Experiment 2. The detection performance along with snapshot.

We still consider three far-field narrowband signals separately arriving from directions (56°, 65°), (66°, 75°), (80°, 85°), snapshot times varies from 10 to 100, step size is 5, SNR is 10 dB, 500 times Monte-Carlo trials have run for each snapshot, Fig. 3 shows the probability of success of the four criteria along with the snapshot.

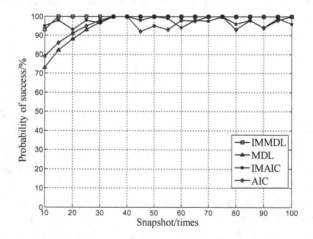

Fig. 3. Probability of success along with snapshot.

It is seen from Fig. 3, the probability of success of criterion of IMMDL is up to 100% when snapshot times reaches 15, that of MDL is up to 100% when snapshot times reaches 35, that of former is higher than that of the latter, that of IMAIC and AIC still have errors even if their snapshot times is large, they float constantly, so they are not consistent estimations, but when the snapshot is small, the probability of success of criteria of IMAIC and IMMDL are higher than MDL and AIC.

Experiment 3. The detection performance along with angular interval.

Consider two far-field narrowband signals separately arriving at the array, their azimuths are both 45°, their elevations are taken 60° as point of symmetry, angular interval is increasing gradually, it varies from 0° to 10°, step size is 0.5°, SNR is 12 dB, snapshot times is 30, here, we present the simulation result for the probability of success of the four criteria along with different angular intervals, it is shown in Fig. 4.

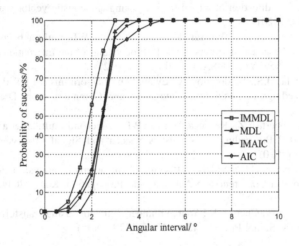

Fig. 4. Probability of success along with angular interval.

It is seen from Fig. 4, the probability of success of criterion of IMMDL is up to 100% when angular interval reaches 3°, that of MDL, IMAIC and AIC are up to 100% when angular interval separately reaches 3.5°, 4° and 5°.

5 Conclusion

As the traditional methods of estimating number of signals based on information theoretic criteria can not be performed well when there is small sampling times, in this paper, we use a kind of estimation method based on the exact distribution of the eigenvalues of Wishart matrices, it improved the estimation performance comparing with MDL, AIC criteria, the method can be adapt to arbitrary plane array and has low computation, computer simulations prove that the detection performance along with SNR, snapshot and angular interval are better than that of traditional information theoretic criteria.

References

1. Schmidt, R.O.: Multiple emitter location and signal parameter estimation. IEEE Trans. Antennas Propag. **34**(3), 276–280 (1986)
2. Roy, R., Kailath, T.: ESPRIT-estimation of signal parameters via rotational invariance techniques. IEEE Trans. Acoust. Speech Signal Process. **37**(7), 984–995 (1989)
3. Ferreira, T.N., Netto, S.L., Diniz, P.S.R.: Direction of arrival estimation using a low-complexity covariance-based approach. IEEE Trans. Aerosp. Electron. Syst. **48**(3), 1924–1934 (2012)
4. Zhong, X.H., Premkumar, A.B., Madhukumar, A.S.: Particle filtering and posterior Cramér-Rao bound for 2-D direction of arrival tracking using an acoustic vector sensor. IEEE Sens. J. **12**(2), 363–377 (2011)
5. Froehle, M., Meissner, P., Witrisal, K.: Tracking of UWB multipath components using probability hypothesis density filters. In: 2012 Proceedings of the International Conference on Ultra-Wideband, New York, USA, pp. 306–310 (2012)
6. Choliz, J., Angela, H.S., Valdovinos, A.: Evaluation of algorithms for UWB indoor tracking. In: 2011 Proceedings of Positioning Navigation and Communication, Dresden, Germany, pp. 143–148 (2011)
7. Kristine, L.B., Robert, E.Z., Rebecca, W.: MAP-PF wideband multitarget and colored noise tracking. In: 2010 Proceedings of Acoustics Speech and Signal Processing, Texas, USA, pp. 2710–2713 (2010)
8. Bryan, D.R., Roberto, G.R.: Wideband tracking of characteristic modes. In: 2011 Proceedings of the 5th European Conference on Antennas and Propagation, Rome, Italy, pp. 1978–1981 (2011)
9. Wu, H.T., Yang, J.F., Chen, F.K.: Source number estimators using transformed Gerschgorin radii. IEEE Trans. Signal Process. **43**(6), 1325–1333 (1995)

A Large-Scale Image Retrieval Method Based on Image Elimination Technology and Supervised Kernel Hash

Zhiming Yin$^{(\boxtimes)}$, Jianguo Sun, Xingjian Zhang, Liu Sun, and Hanqi Yin

College of Computer Science and Technology, Harbin Engineering University,
Harbin, China
{yinzhiming,sunjianguo,yinhanqi}@hrbeu.edu.cn
riosmail@126.com, sunliuhrbeu@163.com

Abstract. The Internet develops rapidly in the era of big data, which can be shown by the widespread uses of image processing software as well as digital images skills. However, there are a large number of redundant images in the network, which not only occupy the network storage but also slow down image search speed. At the same time, the image hash algorithm has received extensive attention due to its advantages of improving the image retrieval efficiency while reducing storage space. Therefore, this paper aims to propose a large-scale image retrieval method based on image redundancy and hash algorithm for large-scale image retrieval system with a large number of redundant images. I look upon the method into two phases: The first phase is eliminating the redundancy of repetitive images. As usual, image features need to be extracted from search results. Next, I use the K-way, Min-Max algorithm to cluster and sort the returned images and filter out the image classes in the end to improve the speed and accuracy of the image retrieval. Fuzzy logic reasoning comes to the last part. It can help to select the centroid image so as to achieve redundancy. The second phase is image matching. In this stage, the supervised kernel hashing is used to supervise the deep features of high-dimensional images and the high-dimensional features are mapped into low-dimensional Hamming space to generate compact hash codes. Finally, accomplish the efficient retrieval of large-scale image data in low-dimensional Hamming of the space. After texting three common dataset, the preliminary results show that the computational time can be reduced by the search image redundancy technology when filter out the invalid images. This greatly improves the efficiency of large-scale image retrieval and its image retrieval performance is better than the current mainstream method.

Keywords: Image retrieval · Image redundancy · Fast matching ·
Supervised kernel hashing · Fuzzy logic inference

This work is supported by the Fundamental Research Funds for the Central Universities (HEUCFG201827, HEUCFP201839).

S. Liu and G. Yang (Eds.): ADHIP 2018, LNICST 279, pp. 233–243, 2019.
https://doi.org/10.1007/978-3-030-19086-6_26

1   Introduction

In recent years, with the rapid development of technologies such as mobile Internet and social network media, hundreds of millions of pictures, video and other multimedia data are generated every day on the Internet. In the era of mobile Internet, people can take a variety of pictures and videos anytime and anywhere, and share them with friends on the Internet. These bring the explosion of digital pictures and videos through the Internet. Therefore, we should pay more extensive attention to the research of image retrieval technology.

The core of image retrieval technology was to find images that match the user's needs from the image database based on the information which provided by the user. The research of technology has been started since the 1970s and has been a research hotspot in the computer field. In the image search engine (Google, Baidu, Bing), it retrieved and query pictures in the massive Internet pictures through the image retrieval technology. In the application of e-commerce websites, it is necessary to find out the products that meet the requirements in a large number of products and use the mobile phone photographs to input the query pictures in order to realize shopping navigation. The map search technology is widely used in multiple major applications (Amazon shopping search, Baidu map, Taobao search).

At the same time, with the rapid development of the social networks such as Facebook, Flickr, and YouTube, the copying and dissemination of multimedia data such as images, videos, and audio is more convenient and fast. This make the Internet full of redundant data. For example, the literature [1] shows that up to 40% of the content on the Internet is duplicated. The literature [2] also pointed out that the video community YouTube's transmission traffic accounts for 20% of the entire Web traffic and 10% of the entire Internet traffic, of which more than 25% of the video is repeated or approximately repeated. The emergence of this situation not only causes a waste of a large amount of storage space but also makes the data retrieval take more time, which will seriously affecting the user experience.

In order to realize effective retrieval of the large-scale high-dimensional image data. The researchers proposed the Approximate Nearest Neighbor (ANN). Among them, the hash technique is the mainstream method to solve the problem of approximate nearest neighbor retrieval. The idea is to use the hash function family to map high-dimensional image features into low-dimensional space and map the closer distances of the original space to low-dimensional at the same time. The distance is still close in this space. Early hashing methods, such as position-sensitive hashing [3] (Locality SensitiveHashing, LSH) and its improved algorithm [4,5], use the random mapping to construct a hash function. In order to ensure a higher accuracy, it is necessary to generate a longer hash code. But as the hash code grows, the probability of the similar images' hash code mapping to go to the same hash bucket will gradually decrease and it will result in a lower recall rate. The hash functions constructed by LSH and its improved algorithm [4,5] are data-independent. In recent years, researchers have constructed some effective methods for how to combine data features. The compact hash functions proposes many algorithms. Weiss et al. [6] proposed a spectral hashing method (Spectral Hashing, SH), firstly analyzes the Laplacian matrix eigenvalues and eigenvectors of similar graphs, and then transforms the image feature vector coding problem into the dimension reduction problem of the Laplacian feature graph by relaxing the constraint conditions. Relying on the data to generate an index can achieves a higher accuracy than the random hash function method. The unsupervised method does not consider the semantic information of the image but the users tend to search the semantic information of the result. For this reason, Wang et al. [7] proposed the semi-supervised hash method by using the semantic similarity of the image as the supervised information (Semi-Supervised Hashing, SSH). On the basis of the semi-supervised, the researchers also proposed some full-supervised hash methods. The full-supervised hash method can achieve higher accuracy than the unsupervised method. Rate, but there are some problems such as complicated optimization process and low training efficiency, which seriously limit its application on large-scale data sets.

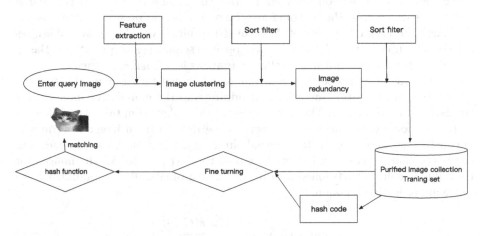

Fig. 1. Schematic diagram of image redundancy technology and large-scale image retrieval method for supervising kernel hashing

Therefore, in order to deal with the above challenges. This paper proposes a method based on large-scale image retrieval. The core idea is to reduce the computation time by filtering out invalid images through image redundancy technology, which greatly improves the efficiency of large-scale image retrieval. The whole method process is shown in Fig. 1. The method is divided into two phases: (1) The stage of eliminating the redundancy of repetitive images, at which the image feature will be performed on the retrieval result. Then use the K-way, Min-Max algorithm to cluster and sort the returned images and filter out the image classes in the end to improve the image retrieval speed and accuracy. Finally, use the fuzzy logic reasoning to simulate the human decision-making process. According to the image attribute information, an optimal solution that conforms to human perception is selected as the centroid image to achieve redundancy. (2) In the image matching stage: use the supervised kernel hash method to supervise the deep features of high-dimensional images, enhance the resolution of linear indivisible data, and use the equivalent relationship between hash code inner product and Hamming distance. A simple and effective objective function, combined with the similarity information of the training image, supervises the high-dimensional image features and generates a compact hash code. Finally, use the trained hash function to construct the image index to achieve efficient retrieval of large-scale image data.

2   Image Redundancy Based on the Clustering Algorithm and the Fuzzy Logic Inference

2.1   Clustering Strategy

Since there is a connection between most of the images returned by the search and the search terms, there should also be a connection between these images. Although the visual difference of the returned results is very large, we can always divide these images into classes with appropriate semantic interpretations. Based on this fact, we can confirm that cluster analysis is a feasible method.

The K-way min-max cut provides a more robust clustering by maximizing the cumulative intra-cluster similarity and minimizing the cumulative inter-cluster similarity simultaneously. The K-way min-max cut algorithm takes the following steps: (a) For a given image topic(query) C returned with n images, a graph G is constructed according to their visual similarity, where nodes are images and edges are characterized by the mixture-of-kernels $\kappa(\cdot, \cdot)$. (b) All the images for the topic C can be partitioned into K clusters automatically by minimizing the following objective function:

$$\min\{\psi(C, K, \hat{\beta}) = \sum_{i=1}^{K} \frac{s(G_i, \frac{G}{G_i})}{s(G_i, G_i)} \tag{1}$$

where $G = \{G_i | i = 1, \ldots, K\}$ is used to represent K images clusters, G/G_i describes the residual image clusters in G except G_i, and $\hat{\beta}$ is the set of optimal kernel weights. $s(G_i, G_i)$ and $s(G_i, \frac{G}{G_i})$ are respectively the similarity within the accumulative class and the similarity between the accumulative classes.

To solve this optimization problem by matrix form, we define $X = [X_1, \ldots, X_i, \ldots, X_K]$ where Xi is a binary indicator (0 and 1) used to indicate the appearance of images in the ith cluster G_i, i.e.:

$$x_i(u) = \begin{cases} 1, & u \in G_i \\ 0, & otherwise \end{cases} \tag{2}$$

and W is defined as a n × n symmetrical matrix with entry to be $W_{u,v} = \kappa(u, v)$. D is defined as a diagonal matrix and its diagonal components are $D_{u,v} =$

$\sum_{v=1}^{n} W_{u,v}$. Then an optimal partition of returned images can be achieved by:

$$\min\left\{\sum_{i=1}^{K}\frac{x_i^T(D-W)x_i}{X_i^TWX_i} = \sum_{i=1}^{K}\frac{x_i^TDXi}{X_i^TWX_i} - K\right\} \tag{3}$$

Then we can use $\tilde{W} = D^{-1/2}WD^{-1/2}$ and $\tilde{X}_i = \frac{D^{1/2}X_i}{\|D^{1/2}X_i\|}$ to get the objective function:

$$\min\left\{\sum_{i=1}^{K}\frac{1}{X_i^TWX_i} - K\right\} \tag{4}$$

Finally, the optimal solution for Eq. (1) can be achieved by solving the following eigen-problem: $.\tilde{W} \cdot \tilde{X}_i = \lambda_i \cdot \tilde{X}_i, i \in [1,\ldots,K]$.

2.2 Eliminate the Redundancy of Repetitive Images

Eliminating the redundancy of repetitive images means the image attribute should be consistent with human perception when select an optimal solution in the repeated image collection. Then delete other image copies and create a pointer to a centroid image, when necessary, it is transformed from the centroid image. The image has a lot of properties, different fields have different interest. There is currently no uniform standard. According to the purpose of redundancy and the visual perception characteristics of human beings, we give the image attribute definition at first.

Theorem 1. *Image attributes refer to the nature of the image. You can use a triple to represent P_i = (size, resolution, cLarity). In this triple, i represents the i-th image, P_i represents the image attribute of the user's attention with scalability, size represents the size of the image, resolution represents the image resolution, and clarity represents image clarity.*

According to the Theorem 1, we can see that the image attribute values can be easily obtained in practice and can be extended according to the situation. However, the values of these attributes represent different meanings and importance in different range. In practice, we need to select the appropriate centroid image according to experience. There is no specific quantitative standard yet, which can be the reference for the selection of centroid images. Therefore, this paper starts with the fuzzy logic reasoning. The empirical rules are used to simulate the human decision-making mode, and the quantitative information CQV (comprehensive quantitative values) which can represent the comprehensive information of the image is inferred from the image information of each dimension of the image. Select a centroid image based on CQV. The fuzzy logic reasoning process includes fuzzy, rule base, inference engine, and defuzzification. The specific process is shown in Fig. 2.

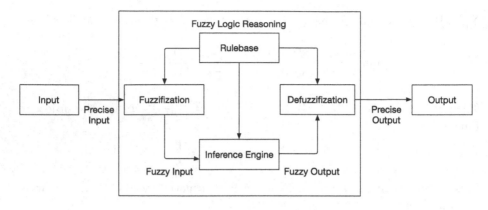

Fig. 2. Fuzzy logic reasoning

(1) Fuzzification: Converting explicit data from the outside world into appropriate linguistic ambiguous information. The ambiguous subset defined in this paper is L, ML, M, MB, B. The corresponding language variable is L = little, ML = medium little, M = medium, MB = medium big, B = big. Blurring process: First, the explicit data Pi is normalized and converted into corresponding linguistic variables. Then use the Gaussian membership function to assign a membership degree to each linguistic variable.

(2) Rule base: The rule base represents the whole thought system, it can be provided by experts or the test data sets which extracted by special training. The quality of the rule can directly affects the whole reasoning effect.

(3) Inference engine: Simulating the decision patterns of human thought by the approximate reasoning or the fuzzy reasoning. The core of the inference engine is to generate a fuzzy relation matrix according to the rules R. When the fuzzy relation matrix R is determined, the input fuzzy matrix A' can be outputted via R to B'.

(4) Unambiguous: The conclusion B' generated by fuzzy logic inference is a fuzzy output, and we need to convert it to a clear value. Here, the center of gravity method is used to deblur. As shown in Eq. (5), the end result is CQV.

$$CQV = \frac{\sum_{i=1}^{n} u_c(y_i) \times y_i}{\sum_{i=1}^{n} u_c(yi)} \tag{5}$$

3   Image Retrieval Based on Supervised Kernel Hash

To enhance the resolution of the hash function to the linearly inseparable high-dimensional data $X = \{x_1, \ldots, x_n\} \subset R^d$. We use the kernel function $k : R^d \cdot R^d \rightarrow R$ to construct the hash function $k : R^d \rightarrow \{1, -1\}$ and map the high-dimensional data to generate a hash code. The specific form of the hash function is:

$$f(x) = \sum_{j=1}^{m} k(x_{(j)}, x)a_j - b \tag{6}$$

$$h(f(x)) = sgn(f(x)) = \begin{cases} 1, & f(x) > 0 \\ -1, & f(x) \le 0 \end{cases} \tag{7}$$

among them, $a_i \in R, b \in R, x_{(1)}, \ldots, x_{(n)}$ is randomly selected samples from X and its total number is m. In order to implement the fast hash mapping, m is a constant much smaller than n. In addition to satisfying the similarity between the low-dimensional Hamming space and the original high-dimensional space, the hash function h(x) should also ensure that the generated hash code is balanced, that is, the hash function h(x) should be ensure that $\sum_{i=1}^{n} h(x_i) = 0$, then biased $b = \frac{1}{n} \sum_{i=1}^{n} \sum_{j=1}^{m} k(x_{(i)}, x) a_j$, substituting the value of b into the Eq. (6), we can know that:

$$f(x) = \sum_{j=1}^{m} \left(k(x_{(j)}, x) - \frac{1}{n} \sum_{i=1}^{n} k(x_{(j)}, x) a_j \right) = \mathbf{a}^T \overline{\mathbf{k}}(x) \tag{8}$$

In this equation, $\mathbf{a} = [a_1, \ldots, a_n]^T$, $\overline{\mathbf{k}} : R^d \to R^m$ is the mapping vector: $\overline{k} = \left[k(x_{(1)}, x) - \mu_1, \ldots, k(x_{(m)}, x) - \mu_m \right]^T$, $\mu_j = \frac{1}{n} \sum_{i=1}^{n} k(x_{(j)}, x_i)$, we can get the μ_j from beforehand calculate and the correlation information of training data is used for the supervised learning to get the vector $\mathbf{a}$.

If we ensure the dimension of the hash code is r, we need r vectors $\mathbf{a_1}, \ldots, \mathbf{a_r}$ to construct a hash function $\mathscr{H} = \{h_k(x) = sgn(\mathbf{a}^T \overline{\mathbf{k}}(x)) | k \in [1, r] \}$.

We can get the training image's tag information from the image's semantic relevance and spatial distance, $lable(x_i, x_j) = 1$ express that the image x_i and x_j is similar, $lable(x_i, x_j) = -1$ express that the image x_i and x_j has large difference. To describe the relationship between the image xi, xj in the label image set $\chi = x_1, \ldots, x_l$, we define the supervised matrix $\mathbf{S}$:

$$s_{ij} = \begin{cases} 1, & lable(x_i, x_j) = 1 \\ -1, & lable(x_i, x_j) = -1 \\ 0, & otherwise \end{cases} \tag{9}$$

among them, $lable(x_i, x_j) = 1, S_{ii} = 1, S_{ij} = 0$ represent that the similarity between image x_i and x_j is uncertainty. In order to enhance the distinguishing ability of hash codes and let the similarity between images can be judged efficiently in the bright space, the Hamming distance $D_h(x_i, x_j)$ of the images x_i, x_j should be made as much as possible meets:

$$D_h(x_i, x_j) = \begin{cases} 0, & S_{ij} = 1 \\ r, & S_{ij} = -1 \end{cases} \tag{10}$$

Due to the complex form of the Hamming distance calculation formula, it is difficult to directly optimizat, so this paper uses the vector inner product operation to calculate the distance between the hash code. Remember that the hash code for image x is code, $(x) = [h_1(x), \ldots, h_r(x)] \in \{1, -1\}^{1 \times r}$, the distance $D(x_i, x_j)$ of the image x_i, x_j is:

$$
\begin{aligned}
D(x_i, x_j) &= code_r(x_i) \cdot code_r(x_j) \\
&= |\{k|h_k(x_i) = h_k(x_j), 1 \le k \le r\}| \\
&\quad - |\{k|h_k(x_i) \ne h_k(x_j), 1 \le k \le r\}| \\
&= r - 2|\{k|h_k(x_i) \ne h_k(x_j), 1 \le k \le r\}| \\
&= r - 2D_h(x_i, x_j)
\end{aligned}
\tag{11}
$$

Equation (11) shows that the inner product of the hash code is consistent with the Hamming distance operation and $D(x_i, x_j) \in [-r, r]$. Normalized the $D(x_i, x_j)$ we can get that $S_{ij} = \frac{D(x_i, x_j)}{r} \in [-1, 1]$. In order to let the distance between the similarity matrix $S' = \frac{1}{r} H_l H_l^T$ supervising matrix S is the smallest, defining the objective function:

$$
min\Gamma = \left\| \frac{1}{r} H_l H_l^T - S \right\|_F^2
\tag{12}
$$

Of which, $\|\cdot\|_F^2$ represent to get the norm of the matrix Frobenius, $H_l = \begin{bmatrix} code_r(x_l) \\ \cdots \\ code_r(x_l) \end{bmatrix} \in \{1, -1\}^{l \times r}$ is the hash code matrix $\mathbf{x}_l$ of label image set. Extend $sgn(\cdot)$ to the matrix form. According to formula (8), H_l can be expressed as:

$$
H_l = \begin{bmatrix} h_l(x_l) & \cdots & h_r(x_l) \\ \cdots & \cdots & h_l(x_l) & \cdots & h_r(x_l) \end{bmatrix} = sgn(\bar{K}_l A)
\tag{13}
$$

Then sorting H_l into formula (12):

$$
min\Gamma(A) = \left\| \sum_{k=1}^{r} sgn(\bar{K}_l \alpha_k)(sgn(\bar{k}_l \alpha_k))^T - rS \right\|_F^2
\tag{14}
$$

Compared with the BRE, the objective function $\Gamma(A)$ calculates the similarity by the inner product, and the parameter A is more intuitive. Suppose that at the time of t = k, the vector $a_1^*, \ldots, a_{k-1}^*$ is known, and it is necessary to estimate a_k and define the matrix $R_{k-1} = rS - \sum_{i=l}^{k-1} sgn(\bar{k}_l a_l^*)(sgn(\bar{k}_l a_l^*))^T$, specialize $R_0 = rS$, the a_k can be estimated step by step through the greedy algorithm minimum (14):

$$
\begin{aligned}
&\|sgn(\bar{K}_l a_k)(sgn(\bar{K}_l a_k))^T - R_{k-1}\|_F^2 \\
&= ((sgn(\bar{K}_l a_k))^T sgn(\bar{K}_l a_k))^2 - 2(sgn(\bar{K}_l a_k))^T R_{k-1} sgn(\bar{K}_l a_k) + tr(R_{k-1}^2) \\
&= -2(sgn(\bar{K}_l a_k))^T R_{k-1} sgn(\bar{K}_l a_k) + l^2 + tr(R_{k-1}^2) \\
&= -2(sgn(\bar{K}_l a_k))^T R_{k-1} sgn(\bar{K}_l a_k) + const
\end{aligned}
\tag{15}
$$

By removing the constant term, we can get a more concise objective function:
$\vartheta(a_k) = -(sgn(\bar{K}_l a_k))^T R_{k-1} sgn(\bar{K}_l a_k)$

Due to the sgn(x) function in the objective function $\vartheta(a_k)$ is not continuous, and $\vartheta(a_k)$ is not a convex function, it is difficult to directly minimize the

$\vartheta(a_k)$. The literature [8] research show that when $|x| > 6$, the continuous function $\varphi(x) = 2/(1 + exp(-x)) - 1$ can have a good approximation to sgn(x). Therefore, this paper replaces sgn(x) to $\varphi(x)$ to get the approximate objective function $\vartheta(a_k)$: $\vartheta(a_k) = -(\varphi(\bar{K}_l a_k))^T T_{k-1} \varphi(\bar{K}_l a)k)$. We can minimize the $\vartheta(a_k)$ by gradient descent, and get the gradient of the $\vartheta(a_k)$ related a_k:

$$\nabla \vartheta(a_k) = -\bar{K}_l^T((R_{k-1}b) \odot (1 - b \odot b)) \tag{16}$$

$b = \varphi(\bar{k}_l, a_k) \in R^l$, $1 = [1, \ldots, 1]$ and $\odot$ represent the operation of inner product. The smoothed ϑ is not a convex function, and the global optimal solution cannot be obtained. In order to accelerate ϑ convergence, this paper uses the spectral analysis method in spectral hash [6] to generate the initial value of a_k^0, then use the method [9] to accelerate the gradient optimization process. After the vector coefficient a is obtained by supervised learning, the hash function $\mathcal{H}$ and the hash table H can be generated. Hash mapping the deep features of the query image can get the $code_r(x_q)$. Calculate the distance between $code_r(x_q)$ and the hash code in the hash table H, and put the return image with a closer distance as a result of the search.

4 Experiment and Analysis

4.1 Experimental Setup and Performance Evaluation

This article is based on the Image Net-1000 [10], and MNIST [11] to assess the methods in thus paper. The Image Net-1000 image set is a subset of the ImageNet and it is a evaluation data set of the Large Scale Visual Recognition Challenge (LSVRC). The evaluation dataset contains 1000 categories and a total of 1.2 million images. The dataset contains 70,000 sheets of 28×28 size handwritten digital grayscale pictures, numbers from 0 to 9, and in each category thousand pictures have 7 numbers.

The experimental hardware is configured as a 6G GPU which device is GTX Titan and Intel Xeon CPU, 16G server. The image retrieval performance indicators use Mean Average Precision (MAP), which is defined as follow:

$$MAP = \frac{Average\ precision\ of\ multiple\ image\ retrieval}{Number\ of\ searches} \times 100\% \tag{17}$$

4.2 Experimental Results and Analysis

In order to verify the performance of the Supervised Kernel Hash (KSH) search whether has an excellent performance. The more savvy, there are some current mainstream hashing methods in Image Net-1000. Experimental comparisons were made on the image set, including Locally Sensitive Hash Algorithm (LSH), Spectral hash algorithm (SH), Unsupervised iterative quantization hash algorithm (ITQ), The supervised hash algorithm that minimizes losses (MLH),

Table 1. Hamming sorting using different length hash codes on ImageNet-1000

	12bits	24bits	32bits	48bits
KSH	0.303	0.334	0.344	0.356
ITQ-CCA	0.259	0.278	0.281	0.286
MLH	0.168	0.189	0.204	0.208
BRE	0.151	0.180	0.193	0.195
SH	0.122	0.122	0.124	0.125
ITQ	0.160	0.164	0.170	0.173
LSH	0.120	0.122	0.117	0.117

Table 2. Hamming sorting using different length hash codes on MNIST

	12bits	24bits	32bits	48bits
KSH	0.857	0.877	0.884	0.892
ITQ-CCA	0.644	0.687	0.710	0.718
MLH	0.477	0.598	0.649	0.650
BRE	0.511	0.574	0.602	0.619
SH	0.270	0.274	0.275	0.277
ITQ	0.397	0.399	0.410	0.414
LSH	0.185	0.197	0.213	0.132

Binary Reconstruction Embedded Supervised Hash Algorithm (BRE), Supervised Iterative Quantization Hash Algorithm (ITQ-CCA) and other methods.

It can be seen from the Tables 1 and 2 that as the number of the bits of hash code r increased, the MAP value of each method increased. Comparing the image retrieval of each hash method MAP, the value shows that the search use this method (KSH) has a better performance than other mainstream methods. It is because that the unsupervised hash methods (such as LSH, SH, DSH, PCA-ITQ, etc.) and the supervised hash method BRE do not have a good use of the semantic information of the image to construct the hash function, and result a lower retrieval performance. But the KSH introduces the kernel function to construct hash, the function enhances the resolving power of linear indivisible data, and combines the similarity information of the image to train the hash function to generate a more compact hash code, this will improve the image retrieval performance.

5   Conclusion

In this paper, a large-scale image retrieval method based on image redundancy and hash algorithm is proposed for the large-scale image retrieval system with a large number of redundant images. The core idea of this method is to use the image redundancy technology to reduce the computation time by filtering out invalid images, and its image retrieval performance is better than the current mainstream methods. Beside, it has greatly improved the efficiency of large-scale image retrieval.

References

1. Yang, X., Zhu, Q., Cheng, K.T.: Near-duplicate detection for images and videos. In: ACM Workshop on Large-Scale Multimedia Retrieval and Mining, pp. 73–80. ACM (2009)
2. Pedro, J.S., Siersdorfer, S., Sanderson, M.: Content redundancy in YouTube and its application to video tagging. ACM Trans. Inf. Syst. **29**(3), 13–43 (2011)
3. Indyk, P., Levi, R., Rubinfeld, R.: Erratum for: approximating and testing k-histogram distributions in sub-linear time. In: ACM Symposium on Principles of Database Systems, pp. 343–343. ACM (2015)
4. Kulis, B., Grauman, K.: Kernelized locality-sensitive hashing. IEEE Comput. Soc. **34**(6), 1092–1104 (2012)
5. Datar, M., Immorlica, N., Indyk, P., et al.: Locality-sensitive hashing scheme based on p-stable distributions. In: Twentieth Symposium on Computational Geometry, pp. 253–262. ACM (2004)
6. Weiss, Y., Torralba, A., Fergus, R.: Spectral hashing. In: International Conference on Neural Information Processing Systems, pp. 1753–1760. Curran Associates Inc. (2008)
7. Wang, J., Kumar, S., Chang, S.F.: Semi-supervised hashing for large-scale search. IEEE Trans. Pattern Anal. Mach. Intell. **34**(12), 2393–2406 (2012)
8. Chang, S.F.: Supervised hashing with kernels. In: IEEE Conference on Computer Vision and Pattern Recognition, pp. 2074–2081. IEEE Computer Society (2012)
9. Nesterov, Y.: Introductory lectures on convex optimization. Appl. Optim. **87**(5), xviii, 236 (2004)
10. Deng, J., Dong, W., Socher, R., ImageNet: a large-scale hierarchical image database. In: IEEE Conference on Computer Vision and Pattern Recognition, CVPR 2009, pp. 248–255. IEEE (2009)
11. Li, F.F., Fergus, R., Perona, P.: Learning generative visual models from few training examples: an incremental bayesian approach tested on 101 object categories. In: Conference on Computer Vision and Pattern Recognition Workshop, p. 178. IEEE Computer Society (2004)

An Improved Eigenvalue-Based Channelized Sub-band Spectrum Detection Method

Chunjie Zhang, Shanshuang Li[(✉)], Zhian Deng, and Yingjun Hao

College of Information and Communication Engineering,
Harbin Engineering University, Harbin 150001, China
{zhangchunjie,lishanshuang,dengzhian,
443567277}@hrbeu.edu.cn

Abstract. Eigenvalue-based spectrum detection has become a research hot topic, which can make detection by catching correlation features in space and time domains. However, most existing methods only consider part of eigenvalues rather than all the eigenvalues. Motivated by this, this paper focuses on all the eigenvalues of sample covariance matrix in digital channelized system and proposes an improved sub-band spectrum detection method. Utilizing the distribution characteristics of the maximum eigenvalue of covariance matrix and the correlation of all the average eigenvalues, a better theoretical expression of detection threshold is obtained. The proposed method can not only overcome the affection of noise uncertainty, but also achieve high detection probability under low SNR environment. Simulations are performed to verify the effectiveness of the proposed method.

Keywords: Wideband digital receiver · Sub-band spectrum detection · Random matrix theory · Covariance matrix · Average eigenvalue

1 Introduction

Digital channelization technology is widely used in electronic warfare, wireless communications and other fields. Wideband digital channelized receiver [1] not only has the advantages of large dynamic range, wide instantaneous bandwidth and high sensitivity, but also has the ability to detect simultaneous arrival signals. Sub-band signal detection is a fundamental problem in digital channelized receiver research. Matched filter (MF) detection [2], energy detection (ED) [3], and cyclostationary detection (CSD) [4] are commonly used for sub-band signal detection method. However, the matched filtering method requires a priori information of the input signal. The energy detection is vulnerable to the noise uncertainty, and the detection threshold can not be accurately estimated under the condition of high noise power. The cyclostationary feature detection method has a high computational cost, which is hardly to achieve real-time signal processing. Each of methods above has different advantages and disadvantages.

To overcome these shortcomings, eigenvalue-based spectrum detection has been intensively studied recently, such as energy with minimum eigenvalue (EME) [5] and maximum-minimum eigenvalue detection (MME) [6] are proposed without any prior

S. Liu and G. Yang (Eds.): ADHIP 2018, LNICST 279, pp. 244–251, 2019.
https://doi.org/10.1007/978-3-030-19086-6_27

information and can achieve much better performance than ED. But these methods only consider part of eigenvalues, such as maximum, minimum, which does not make full use of correlation of all the eigenvalues. Motivated by this, arithmetic mean detection (ARMD) and arithmetic to geometric mean detection (AGM) are proposed in literature [7, 8] to detect the signal. However, the detection performance of these methods still needs to be improved under low SNR environment.

To address these issues, an improved eigenvalue-based digital channelized sub-band spectrum detection algorithm is proposed in this paper. we focus on digital channelized system and makes all the eigenvalues of covariance matrices for detection. Based on some latest random matrix theories, we use the ratio of the maximum eigenvalue to minimum average eigenvalues (MMAE) as the test statistic and derive a better theoretical expression of detection threshold. Simulations verify the effectiveness of the proposed algorithm.

2 System Model of Channelized Sub-band Spectrum Detection

As is shown in Fig. 1 is digital channelized sub-band spectrum detection structure, which consists of analysis filter bank and sub-band spectrum detection.

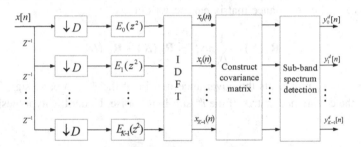

Fig. 1. Digital channelized sub-band spectrum detection structure

The signal $x(n)$ is decomposed into a plurality of sub-band signals by analysis filter bank. Here K represents the number of channels, D represents the decimation factor, and $E_{K-1}(z^2)$ represents the multiphase filter component of the uniform filter bank. Assume that the output signal of each sub-band is $x_i(n)$, and $x_i(n)$ consists of signal and noise.

$$x_i(n) = s_i(n) + w_i(n) \quad i = 0, 1, \ldots, K - 1 \tag{1}$$

Where $s_i(n)$ represents the real signal, $w_i(n)$ represents the noise. The detection of channelized sub-band signals can be equivalent to a binary hypothesis problem.

$$x_i(n) = \begin{cases} w_i(n), H_0 \\ s_i(n) + w_i(n), H_1 \end{cases} \tag{2}$$

Because of the eigenvalue-based sub-band spectrum detection algorithm operating on the sample covariance matrix, but the sub-band signal output from the analysis filter bank is a one-dimensional vector, we need to turn the sub-band signal into a matrix. The processing method in this paper is re-sample. We can get an $M \times N$ observed matrix through re-sampling sub-band signal.

$$\mathbf{x}_i = \begin{bmatrix} \mathbf{x}_i^1 \\ \mathbf{x}_i^2 \\ \cdots \\ \mathbf{x}_i^M \end{bmatrix} = \begin{bmatrix} x_i(0) & x_i(M) & \cdots & x_i(NM - M) \\ x_i(1) & x_i(M + 1) & \cdots & x_i(NM - M + 1) \\ \cdots & \cdots & & \cdots \\ x_i(M - 1) & x_i(2M - 1) & \cdots & x_i(NM - 1) \end{bmatrix} \tag{3}$$

Then the sample covariance matrix can be calculated as follows

$$\mathbf{R}_{x_i}(N) = \mathbf{x}_i \mathbf{x}_i^T / N \tag{4}$$

3   MEMAE Algorithm Detection Threshold Derivation

Assume that the received signal $s_i(n)$ and the noise $w_i(n)$ are uncorrelated. Under the hypothesis H_1, the covariance matrix can be written as

$$\mathbf{R}_{x_i}(N) = \frac{1}{N} \mathbf{x}_i \mathbf{x}_i^T = \mathbf{R}_{s_i}(N) + \mathbf{R}_{w_i}(N) \tag{5}$$

Where $\mathbf{R}_{s_i}(N)$ represents the covariance matrix of the ith sub-band signal, $\mathbf{R}_{w_i}(N)$ represents the covariance matrix of the ith sub-band noise. Under the hypothesis H_0, we have

$$\mathbf{R}_{x_i}(N) = \mathbf{R}_{w_i}(N) = \frac{1}{N} \mathbf{w}_i \mathbf{w}_i^T \tag{6}$$

$\mathbf{R}_{x_i}(N)$ is a special Wishart random matrix. Johnstone has found the distribution of the largest eigenvalue for real and complex matrix, respectively, as described in the following theorems [9].

Theorem 1. Assume that the noise is real. Let $A(N) = \frac{N}{\sigma^2} R_w(N)$, $\mu = (\sqrt{N-1} + \sqrt{M})^2$, $\upsilon = (\sqrt{N-1} + \sqrt{M})\left(\frac{1}{\sqrt{N-1}} + \frac{1}{\sqrt{M}}\right)^{1/3}$. Assume that $\lim\limits_{N \to \infty} \frac{M}{N} = c (0 < c < 1)$, then $\frac{\lambda_{\max}(A(N)) - \mu}{\upsilon}$ converges (with probability one) to the Tracy-Widom distribution of order 1.

Theorem 2. Assume that the noise is complex. Let $A(N) = \frac{N}{\sigma^2} R_w(N)$, $\mu = (\sqrt{N} + \sqrt{M})^2$, $\upsilon = (\sqrt{N-1} + \sqrt{M}) \left(\frac{1}{\sqrt{N-1}} + \frac{1}{\sqrt{M}} \right)^{1/3}$. Assume that $\lim\limits_{N\to\infty} \frac{M}{N} = c(0 < c < 1)$, then $\frac{\lambda_{\max}(A(N)) - \mu}{\upsilon}$ converges (with probability one) to the Tracy-Widom distribution of order 1.

Theorem 3. Assume that $\lim\limits_{N\to\infty} \frac{M}{N} = c(0 < c < 1)$, then $\lim\limits_{N\to\infty} \lambda_{\min} \approx \frac{\sigma^2}{N} (\sqrt{N} - \sqrt{M})^2$, $\lim\limits_{N\to\infty} \lambda_{\max} \approx \frac{\sigma^2}{N} (\sqrt{N} + \sqrt{M})^2$.

After constructing the sample covariance matrix of each sub-band signal, eigenvalue decomposition is performed on the sample covariance matrix of each sub-band signal. Under the hypothesis H_0, the noise variance can be approximately equal to

$$\sigma_n^2 \approx \frac{1}{M-1} \sum_{i=2}^{M} \lambda_i \tag{7}$$

Let $\lambda_1(\lambda_{\max}) > \lambda_2 > \cdots > \lambda_M (= \lambda_{\min})$ denote the eigenvalues, in the descending order, of the sample covariance matrix $\mathbf{R}_{x_i}(N)$ defined in (4). The average eigenvalue can be written as

$$\begin{aligned} \bar{\lambda} &= \frac{1}{M} \sum_{i=1}^{M} \lambda_i \\ &= \frac{\lambda_{\max}}{M} + \frac{1}{M} \sum_{i=2}^{M} \lambda_i \end{aligned} \tag{8}$$

According to Theorem 3 and Eq. (6), the Eq. (7) can be rewritten as

$$\bar{\lambda} = \frac{\sigma_n^2}{N} \left(\frac{(\sqrt{N} + \sqrt{M})^2}{M} + \frac{N(M-1)}{M} \right) \tag{9}$$

Since the output signal of the each sub-band is all derived from the same received signal, we have to take into account the average eigenvalues of all the sub-bands' sample covariance matrices rather than the average eigenvalue of the current sub-band's sample covariance matrix. Test statistic is defined as follows

$$\alpha^{MEMAE} = \frac{\max \lambda_i^j, j = 1, 2, \ldots, M}{\min \bar{\lambda}_i, i = 1, 2, \ldots, K} \tag{10}$$

Where $\max \lambda_i^j$ represents the maximum eigenvalue of the ith sub-band's sample covariance matrix, $\min \bar{\lambda}_i$ represents minimum value of the average eigenvalues of all the sub-band' sample covariance matrices.

Let γ_1 be threshold value, if $\alpha^{MMGAE} > \gamma_1$, signal exists, otherwise, signal does not exist. Because the improved algorithm only optimizes the selection of average eigenvalues, the algorithm actually uses the ratio of the maximum eigenvalue to the average eigenvalue as the test statistic.

The detection threshold γ_1 is calculated as follows

$$
\begin{aligned}
P_f &= p\left(\lambda_{\max}(\mathbf{R}_{x_i}(N)) > \gamma_1 \bar{\lambda}\right) \\
&= P\left(\frac{\sigma^2}{N}\lambda_{\max}(A(N)) > \gamma_1 \bar{\lambda}\right) \\
&\approx P\left(\frac{\lambda_{\max}(A(N) - \mu}{\upsilon} > \frac{\frac{N}{\sigma^2}\gamma_1\bar{\lambda} - \mu}{\upsilon}\right) \\
&= 1 - F_1\left(\frac{\frac{N}{\sigma^2}\gamma_1\bar{\lambda} - \mu}{\upsilon}\right)
\end{aligned}
\tag{11}
$$

By substituting μ, υ and Eq. (9) into Eq. (11), we finally obtain the decision threshold

$$
\gamma_1 = \frac{M(\sqrt{N} + \sqrt{M})^2\left(1 + \frac{(\sqrt{N} + \sqrt{M})^{-2/3}}{(NM)^{1/6}}F_1^{-1}(1 - P_f)\right)}{(\sqrt{N} + \sqrt{M})^2 + N(M - 1)}
\tag{12}
$$

Where $F_1^{-1}(\cdot)$ is the inverse function of the Tracy-Widom distribution of order 1. Note that the threshold γ_1 depends only on M, N and P_f, it does not change with the noise power.

4   Simulation Results

The simulation uses the digital channelized sub-band spectrum detection structure shown in Fig. 1. The sampling frequency is 960 MHz, $K = 32$, $D = 16$, and the filter bank adopts a fifty percent overlap structure. The bandwidth of each channel is 30 MHz, the processing bandwidth of each sub-band signal is 60 MHz. The pass-band cut-off frequency of prototype low-pass filter is set to 15 MHz, the stop-band frequency is set 30 MHz. The range of the input signal is 480–960 MHz. Let the input signal be LFM signal, the start frequency is 780 MHz, the bandwidth of LFM is 60 MHz, SNR = 13 dB. The amplitude-frequency response of the filter bank is shown in Fig. 2, the distribution of the signal spectrum can be clearly seen from this figure.

The baseband signal of each channel output is shown in Fig. 3. As we can see the output signal appears on channel 5, channels 6 and channels 7. Let the signal of channel 6 as a detected signal to verify the efficiency of the proposed algorithm. Figure 4 shows the comparison performance of different algorithms, including the proposed MMAE, MME and EME, in terms of the probability of detection (P_d) with respect to SNR is plotted.

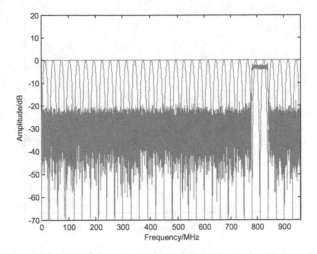

Fig. 2. Filter bank amplitude-frequency response

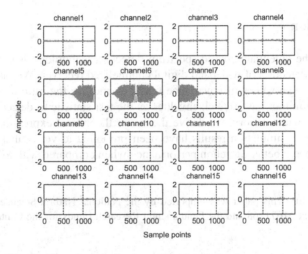

Fig. 3. Time domain features of each sub-band output signal

It can be seen from Fig. 4 that SNR has a great influence on the detection performance. Probability of detection (P_d) increases with SNR increases. The proposed eigenvalue-based MMAE method can achieve 90% detection probability at a SNR below −10 dB. However, to achieve the same probability of detection, the MME needs a SNR of about −9 dB, the EME needs a SNR of about −1 dB. Under low SNR environment, the detection performance of the MEMAE is always better than the MME and EME.

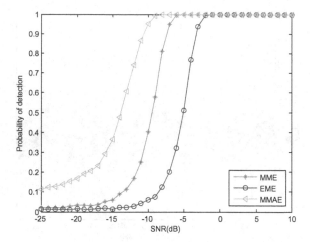

Fig. 4. Probability of detection: the number of samples for each sub-band signal is 1300, $M = 10$, $N = 130$, $P_f = 0.01$

5 Conclusion

In this paper, the eigenvalue-based spectrum detection technology is used to the sub-band spectrum detection of wideband digital channelized receiver. We make full use of all the average eigenvalues of covariance matrices and use the ratio of the maximum eigenvalue to minimum average eigenvalues as the test statistic to detect signal. Based on the random matrix theory, we derive the better theoretical expression of detection threshold. Finally, simulation results have been presented to verify that the proposed method can achieve better detection performance when compared with MME and EME method.

Acknowledgement. This paper was supported by the National Natural Science Foundation of China under Grant 61671168 and the Fundamental Research Funds for the Central Universities (HEUCF160807).

References

1. Zhang, W.X., Shi, F.M., Liu, T.: Model of non-leaking-alarms and non-aliasing channelized digital receiver. In: Sixth International Conference on Instrumentation and Measurement, Computer, Communication and Control, pp. 994–997. IEEE (2016)
2. Stoica, P., Li, J., Xie, Y.: On probing signal design for MIMO radar. IEEE Trans. Signal Process. **55**(8), 4151–4161 (2007)
3. Atapattu, S., Tellambura, C., Jiang, H.: Spectrum sensing via energy detector in low SNR. In: IEEE International Conference on Communications, pp. 1–5. IEEE (2011)
4. Xu, S., Zhao, Z., Shang, J.: Spectrum sensing based on cyclostationarity. In: The Workshop on Power Electronics & Intelligent Transportation System, pp. 171–174. IEEE Computer Society (2008)

5. Zeng, Y., Liang, Y.C.: Eigenvalue based spectrum sensing algorithms for cognitive radio. IEEE Trans. Commun. **57**(6), 1784–1793 (2009)
6. Liu, C, Jin, M.: Maximum-minimum spatial spectrum detection for cognitive radio using parasitic antenna arrays. In: IEEE/CIC International Conference on Communications in China, pp. 365–369. IEEE (2015)
7. Shakir, M.Z., Rao, A., Alouini, M.S.: Generalized mean detector for collaborative spectrum sensing. IEEE Trans. Commun. **61**(4), 1242–1253 (2013)
8. Wei, L., Tirkkonen, O.: Spectrum sensing in the presence of multiple primary users. IEEE Trans. Commun. **60**(5), 1268–1277 (2012)
9. Johnstone, I.M.: On the distribution of the largest eigenvalue in principal components analysis. Ann. Stat. **29**(2), 295–327 (2001)

Research on Secure Storage of Multimedia Data Based on Block Chaining Technology

Fei Gao[1,2(✉)] and Li Hui Zhen[3]

[1] School of Information Science and Technology,
Tibet University, Lhasa 850000, Tibet, China
h13467985201@163.com
[2] Science and Research Office, Tibet University, Lhasa 850000, Tibet, China
[3] Guangxi Teachers Education University, Nanning 530001, Guangxi, China
gongzuo0758@163.com

Abstract. When the traditional multimedia data security storage method is used to store the electronic commerce data, there are some problems such as insufficient security and slow encryption speed, which often lead to data leakage or loss. A secure storage method for multimedia data based on block chain technology is proposed. This method takes the study of multimedia data in the field of electronic commerce as an example. Firstly, the key technology of this method: block chain and multimedia data are introduced briefly, then the block chain of multimedia data is constructed. Finally, a multimedia data storage model of e-commerce is established on the basis of block chain structure. The model is divided into two parts: multimedia data addition Secret and multimedia data preservation. The protection of multimedia data is realized. The results show that compared with the traditional multimedia data security storage method, the security of this method is increased by 15% and the encryption speed is increased by 2 s. It is proved that this method can effectively protect the media data for many years and reduce the frequency of data leakage or loss.

Keywords: Block chain · Multimedia data · Secure storage · Four fork tree · Electronic commerce

1 Introduction

After the end of the third industrial revolution, computer network information technology was gradually promoted, and digital content based on networks was rapidly developing. So far, more and more data in the party, government, military, and enterprises have emerged in the form of multimedia. Data is no longer confined to written forms, but is preserved in a variety of forms, such as text, video, audio, images, etc. Multimedia data is more intuitive than traditional data, making it easier to query [1]. However, this form of data is also vulnerable to attacks by unauthorized people. Data leakage, data theft, data modification, data deletion, and other situations are not conducive to the safe preservation of data. Therefore, in order to deal with the above problems, there are an endless number of defense methods, such as firewalls and intrusion detection. However, these traditional security defense methods have been

© ICST Institute for Computer Sciences, Social Informatics and Telecommunications Engineering 2019
Published by Springer Nature Switzerland AG 2019. All Rights Reserved
S. Liu and G. Yang (Eds.): ADHIP 2018, LNICST 279, pp. 252–260, 2019.
https://doi.org/10.1007/978-3-030-19086-6_28

difficult to deal with the current threats as the means of illegal intrusion has increased. The existing technologies have obviously insufficient security and defense speed. In view of the above problems, using e-commerce multimedia data information as an example, a method of secure storage of multimedia data based on blockchain technology is proposed [2]. The key point of this method is to encrypt and process multimedia data, without the need of centralized verification, to achieve data security. Firstly, the blockchain technology and multimedia data involved in this method are briefly introduced. Then a blockchain structure of e-commerce data is constructed, and an e-commerce multimedia data storage model is established according to the structure. The model consists of two parts: one uses a quad-tree encoding encryption algorithm to encrypt multimedia data. After the encryption is completed, the encrypted data storage link is entered, and the storage of the encrypted data is implemented in the distributed storage mode to ensure the security of the multimedia data. In order to verify the performance of the multimedia data secure storage method based on blockchain technology, the method test was conducted. The results show that compared with the traditional safe storage method, this method improves the security by 15% and increases the encryption speed by 2 s. This method greatly guarantees the security of multimedia data and reduces the occurrence of data loss and confidentiality events.

2 Blockchain Method for Secure Storage of Multimedia Data

2.1 Blockchain Technology and Multimedia Data

Blockchain technology, also known as distributed ledger technology, abbreviated as BT, is a technology solution based on Bitcoin, which is a decentralized, high-trust way to collectively maintain a reliable database. Its characteristic is decentralization, openness, consensus mechanism, traceability, and high trust, and is a disruptive information applications following cloud computing, Internet of Things, and Big Data and has been applied in many areas [3]. Figure 1 below shows a typical blockchain.

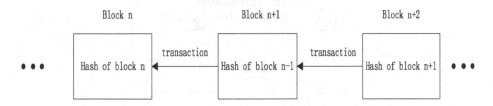

Fig. 1. Blockchain

Each block data in the blockchain contains a list of transactions and a hash of the previous block (with one exception, the first block of the blockchain does not contain this hash, called the Genesis Block). Any node in the network can access this ordered, backward-linked data block list, read network transaction data and calculate the status of all transactions in the network. In the blockchain network, all nodes form a peer-to-peer communication network. By copying each node to operate on the same blockchain, its working process is shown in Fig. 2 below.

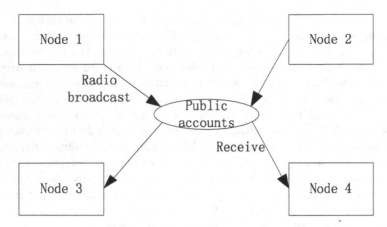

Fig. 2. Operation process of block

The above is an iterative process that repeats once every specified time interval. When each node in the network follows the above steps, the shared blockchains that they operate become a network activity record that is verified with time stamp [4].

2.2 Construction of Blockchain

The method of secure storage of multimedia data based on blockchain technology is to realize the storage and sharing of e-commerce data records on the basis of blockchain technology and cloud storage technology, and enhance the security and loss prevention of multimedia data. The structure is shown in Fig. 3.

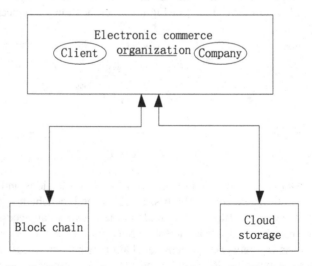

Fig. 3. Structure of e-commerce multimedia data blockchain

As it can be seen from Fig. 3, there are three main bodies in the blockchain structure, namely client, electronic commerce organization and company. The client cooperates with the company through the electronic commerce organization, understanding the business and processing through the company to generate multimedia data, data stored in the e-commerce database, the client has the right to use and process personal e-commerce data records, electronic commerce organization and company has the right to query, but can not handle privately. In this blockchain structure, information is shared and can be viewed by the three parties, but relatively private personal information does not appear in its public accounts, but is encrypted and stored in the cloud storage under the chain [5].

2.3 Construction of Multimedia Data Storage Model

According to the blockchain structure in Fig. 3, an e-commerce multimedia data storage model is established. The model is mainly composed of two parts: multimedia data encryption and multimedia data storage. The two parts are described in detail below.

Data Encryption. In order to ensure the security of multimedia data during transmission and storage, the most commonly used method is to encrypt the data before storing it. At present, there are three types of data encryption algorithms: direct encryption, selective encryption, combination of encryption and compression encoding [6]. In this secure data storage based on blockchain technology, a quad-tree encoding encryption algorithm in combination of encryption and compression encoding process is used to encrypt e-commerce multimedia data. Compared with the former two methods, it has the advantages of fast encrypted speed, high security, and not easy to crack.

Quad-tree encoding is one of the most effective data compression techniques so far. The basic idea is as follows: The multimedia data is recursively partitioned as four quadrants until the value of the sub-quadrant is monotonic, resulting in a reverse quad-tree. To scramble nodes in the same level of the quad-tree structure, the scrambling algorithm is given by:

$$K_H = \left[\prod_{h=1}^{H} \frac{(N_h + M_h)}{N_{h-1}} \right] \tag{1}$$

Where K_H is the quad-tree with a height of H, H is the height of quad-tree; N_h is the number of internal nodes; M_h is the number of external nodes.

When scrambling the data with Eq. (1), only after more than ten times of repeating scrambling, can the good effect be achieved. And it's obvious that the more the times of scrambling, the more time will be spent by scrambling, the slower the speed of scrambling, the scrambling times should be reduced to improve the scrambling speed, it can be given by Eq. (1):

$$\binom{N_{h+1}}{M_{h+1}} = K \binom{N_h}{M_h} (\mathrm{mod}\, M_h) \tag{2}$$

Therefore, there is matrix K(0), a scrambling is performed by using following Eq. (3), the scrambling effect is equal to that of multi scrambling with Eq. (1):

$$\begin{pmatrix} N_{h+1} \\ M_{h+1} \end{pmatrix} = K \begin{pmatrix} N_h \\ M_h \end{pmatrix} (\bmod K_0) \tag{3}$$

Multimedia Data Storage. After the multimedia data is encrypted, data storage begins. In this link, the database is the carrier of multimedia data information storage, so the design of the database is very important. There are many kinds of multimedia data and the number is huge. Therefore, the database must meet two functional requirements: classifying and storing file information; users can timely and accurately extract the required data information from the database [7]. The data performance needs to be flexible, efficient, safe, reliable, and less redundant. According to the above requirements, part of the database construction code is as follows:

```
<header>
    <div class="container d-flex clearfix">
        <div class="title-box">
            <h2 class="title-blog"> demand analysis
            <ahref="https://blog.csdn.net/huyr_123">HELL
            <p class="description"></p>conception framework design
        </div>
        <div class="opt-box d-flex justify-content-end">
            href="https://blog.csdn.net/huyr_/rss/list">
        </div>
    </div>
</header>
<body>
    <div class="article-info-box">Physical Database Design
        <div class="article-bar-top d-flex24772</span>
    <article>database implementation
        <div        id="article_content"        class="article_content        clearfix
csdn-tracking-statistics"    data-pid="blog"        data-mod=popu_307        data-dsm =
"post" >database operation and maintenance</div>
    </div>
</body>
end
```

After the database is established, the blockchain stores the multimedia data information in a distributed data storage mode. In each storage operation, the blockchain takes the previous encrypted data as the basis, and then integrates the data that needs to be stored in the current time to form a new multimedia data. Finally, the blockchain is again quad-tree encoded and encrypted to complete secure data storage. This fact that encryption is performed every time there is new data makes it difficult for the multimedia data in the blockchain to be modified and leaked [8]. In e-commerce data records, there are many image records, such as magnetic resonance imaging, CT, ultrasound, etc. Therefore, in this storage study, only image storage was studied.

After the image data is encrypted, the blocks can be classified according to their different characteristics, such as their colors, effects, and textures. And for fast storage, there must be appropriate index. Index is a structure that sorts the values of one or more columns in a database table. It can be used to quickly access specific information in a database table. In relational database, index is a table-related database structure that can make SQL statements that correspond to tables be executed faster. Table 1 is a typical e-commerce data index.

Table 1. E-commerce data index

Field name	Field type	Length	Explain
ID	Varchar	8	Data code
NAME	Varchar	6	Data name
SIZE	Bit	8	Data scale
Description	Varchar	5	Data description
Imgurl	Varchar	7	Data attachments
Abstract Start Date	Text	4	Data date
Abstract Title	Varchar	10	Data title

3 Method Test

In order to test the performance advantage of the multimedia data secure storage method based on blockchain technology designed this paper, a comparative experiment was conducted together with the traditional multimedia data storage method. The experiment is implemented in Matlab environment. The PC is configured as CPU Core i7 3.60 GHz. In the experiment, 90 storage nodes are set. The maximum storage capacity corresponding to each node is 2 TB, and the information data storage channel is 500 Mbit/s. Target information storage and reading information data is 5 TB.

3.1 Analysis of Security Test

The security of multimedia data storage is generally expressed by the aggressiveness of the method. Therefore, after using the blockchain technology-based multimedia data secure storage methods and traditional multimedia data secure storage methods to store data, typical operating system attack tools are used for testing. This test is performed mainly through three methods of DoS attacks, virtual machine attacks, and sharing memory attacks. Each attack was performed four times to determine whether the malicious attack was successful. The results are shown in Table 2.

Table 2. Comparative analysis results of security

Name	Secure storage method for multimedia data based on block chain technology	Traditional multimedia data security storage method
Dos attack 1	1	1
Dos attack 2	1	1
Dos attack 3	1	0
Dos attack 4	1	1
Virtual machine attack 1	1	1
Virtual machine attack 2	1	1
Virtual machine attack 3	1	0
Virtual machine attack 4	1	1
Shared memory attack 1	1	1
Shared memory attack 2	1	1

Note: 0 represents successful attack; 1 represents unsuccessful attack

From Table 2, it can be seen that for the 12 malicious attacks, the method of secure storage of multimedia data based on blockchain technology completely resisted several attacks, did not make illegal access successful, and the security reached 100%. While there are loopholes in traditional multimedia data secure storage methods. For 12 malicious attacks, one Dos attack and one virtual machine attack succeeded, breaking the security line, and the illegal personnel had access to multimedia data. The security was only 85%. Compared with the latter, the former is 15% higher than the latter, which proves that the method of secure storage of multimedia data based on blockchain technology is superior to traditional method of secure storage of multimedia data, which greatly ensures the security of multimedia data and is effective to reduce the occurrence of data loss or leakage events.

3.2 Encryption Processing Speed Test Analysis

In Matlab, the encryption speed of the data secure storage method designed in this paper is simulated and tested. Comparison of the encryption speed of two methods with different key lengths is performed to statistically analyze. Table 3 describes the comparison test results of encryption speed of different algorithms.

From Table 3, it can be seen that when the data is 200 bits, 400 bits, and 600 bits, the encryption speed of the two methods are roughly the same. After that, there is a huge gap. As the key length increases, the gap between the two increases. When the key length reaches 2000 bits, the encryption speed of the multimedia data secure storage method based on blockchain technology is 5 s, and the encryption speed of the traditional multimedia data secure storage method is 7 s, and the former is faster than the latter by 2 s.

Table 3. Comparison results of encryption speed of two methods

Key length(bit)	Secure storage method for multimedia data based on block chain technology (s)	Traditional multimedia data security storage method (s)
200	0.21	0.22
400	0.46	0.46
600	0.90	0.92
800	1.50	1.94
1000	2.65	3.74
1200	2.89	4.60
1400	3.30	5.40
1600	4.80	6.24
1800	4.96	6.53
2000	5	7

4 Conclusion

With the advancement of network information construction, multimedia data information has shown an explosive growth trend, among which confidential multimedia security issues have become increasingly prominent issues, especially e-commerce data, which is the privacy of customers. Related departments have come up with various data secure storage methods to prevent data leakage. Although these traditional methods for secure storage of multimedia data can effectively control the security of confidential multimedia information to a certain extent, as malicious attacks become more and more various, they are gradually becoming inadequate. In such case, the method of secure storage of multimedia data based on blockchain technology is proposed. Compared with the traditional multimedia data secure storage method, this method has improved the security and encryption speed, and basically achieved the purpose of this study.

References

1. Wen, L.: Spatial data and information fusion in multimedia sensor networks. Comput. Simul. **33**(10), 266–269 (2016)
2. Rui, Q., Shi, D.: Research on the security mechanism of dynamic data storage based on block chain technology. Comput. Sci. **45**(2), 57–62 (2018)
3. Zhenquan, W., Yuhui, L., Jiawen, K., et al.: Smart grid data secure storage and sharing system based on alliance block chain. Comput. Appl. **37**(10), 2742–2747 (2017)
4. Liehuang, Z., Feng, G., Meng, S., et al.: Summary of block chain privacy protection research. Comput. Res. Dev. **54**(10), 2170–2186 (2017)
5. Jiye, W., Lingchao, G., Aiqiang, D., et al.: Research on data security sharing network system based on block chaining. Comput. Res. Dev. **54**(4), 742–749 (2017)

6. Wang, X.: Research on double energy fuzzy controller of electric vehicle based on particle swarm optimization of multimedia big data. Int. J. Mobile Comput. Multimed. Commun. **8**(3), 32–43 (2017)
7. Qingyang, D., Xiuli, W., Jianming, Z., et al.: Information security protection framework based on block chain information physics fusion system. Comput. Sci. **45**(2), 32–39 (2018)
8. Yanxing, Y., Zhou, G.X.: Mass classification of educational multimedia data storage technology research. Modern Electron. Technol. **40**(8), 42–45 (2017)

Research on Accurate Extraction Algorithm for Fault Signal Characteristics of Mechanical Rolling Bearings

Yunsheng Chen[✉]

Mechatronics and Automatic Chemistry Department,
Guangzhou Huali Science and Technology Vocational College,
Zengcheng District, Guangzhou 511325, China
chen12yunsheng@sina.com

Abstract. Traditional fault signal feature extraction algorithms such as auto-correlation analysis algorithm, morphological gradient algorithm and other algorithms have the disadvantage of low accuracy. Therefore, a fault signal feature extraction algorithm based on wavelet frequency shift algorithm and minimum entropy algorithm is designed. Based on the noise removal algorithm of mechanical equipment based on wavelet frequency shift design and the mechanical fault identification algorithm based on minimum entropy algorithm, the two algorithms are integrated to generate the feature extraction algorithm of mechanical rolling bearing fault signal. In this way, the feature of fault signal is extracted, and an example is given. The experimental results of simulation and application environment design show that, compared with the traditional design, Compared with the fault signal feature extraction algorithm, the proposed algorithm can improve the accuracy of the analysis results by about 4% when using the same data.

Keywords: Keywords mechanical rolling bearing · Fault signal ·
Extracting signal feature · Accuracy

1 Introduction

In industrial machinery and equipment, the parts of the equipment that are most subject to wear are mechanical rolling bearings. When the rolling bearings are damaged, they often cause mechanical equipment to malfunction, in this regard, the fault signal characteristic of the rolling bearing needs to be extracted, and the fault point of the rolling bearing is determined according to the extraction result so as to be repaired in time. The traditional fault signal feature extraction algorithm has low accuracy. Therefore, this paper uses wavelet frequency shift algorithm to calculate the noise removal of the equipment, and uses the minimum entropy algorithm to identify the mechanical fault, Based on these two algorithms, the fault signal feature extraction algorithm is designed. Experimental results show that the algorithm designed in this paper is more suitable for the extraction of fault signal characteristics of mechanical rolling bearings than traditional algorithms.

© ICST Institute for Computer Sciences, Social Informatics and Telecommunications Engineering 2019
Published by Springer Nature Switzerland AG 2019. All Rights Reserved
S. Liu and G. Yang (Eds.): ADHIP 2018, LNICST 279, pp. 261–268, 2019.
https://doi.org/10.1007/978-3-030-19086-6_29

2   Design Fault Signal Feature Extraction Algorithm

This paper designs fault signal feature extraction algorithm based on wavelet frequency shift denoising algorithm and minimum entropy mechanical fault recognition algorithm.

2.1   Remove Mechanical Equipment Noise

In the process of collecting and transmitting the fault signal of the mechanical rolling bearing, it will be interfered and influenced from the outside and inside of the mechanical equipment, resulting in the use of an accurate extraction algorithm to extract fault signal characteristics, affected by the internal and external noise of the mechanical rolling bearing, the accuracy of the calculation result is reduced. Therefore, before the feature extraction of the fault signal of the mechanical rolling bearing, the wavelet algorithm is used to perform the noise removal calculation on the original signal of the mechanical device [1, 2].

The wavelet noise removal algorithm is to decompose the original signal of the mechanical equipment, use the high-pass filter and low-pass filter to perform frequency filtering on the original signal in turn, group the filtered signals, and conduct sampling at a ratio of 2:1, wavelet noise removal calculations were performed on the selected samples. When the wavelet noise removal calculation is performed, the selected sample signal is first subjected to wavelet frequency shift, so as to avoid the phenomena of mixed high and low frequency signal superposition when performing wavelet calculation [3].

The basic equation for frequency shift calculation is:

$$F[x(t)^{e0t}] = X(m - m_0) \tag{1}$$

Multiplying the signal $x(t)$ of the mechanical device with e^{0t}, the frequency of the signal can be decreased and the value $f_0 = m_0 \div 2\pi$ is decreased. Set the frequency of the original signal taken by the sample to be f_y. The frequency of the signal includes the frequencies of different sizes. The frequency of the largest value is denoted by $f_{max}.f_{max} = f_y \div 2$ In the noise removal calculation of mechanical equipment, the signal is sampled at each point. When the signal of the Jth layer is calculated by wavelet, the frequency of the sample signal is decreased to $f_y^J = 2 - {}^Jf_y$ and at the Jth layer, the maximum value of the signal frequency does not exceed the value of $f_y^J \div 2 = 2^{-J-1}f_y$, so when the high frequency signal is subjected to wavelet decomposition calculation, make sure that the wavelet shift value is $2^{-J-1}f_y$. That is, when high-frequency signal decomposition is performed on mechanical equipment signals, the frequency shift of the signal at layer J is $x_{2n+1}^J(t)$ times $e^{i\pi 2 - Jf}yt$, and t $= e^{i\pi t} = (-1)^t$, Then design a wavelet algorithm [3] to remove mechanical equipment noise, namely:

$$x_{2n}^{J+1}(t) = 1/2 \sum_m h(m - 2t)x_n^J(m) \tag{2}$$

$$x_{2n+1}^{J+1}(t) = 1/2(-1)^t \sum_m g(m - 2t)x_n^J(m) \tag{3}$$

$$x_m^J(t) = \sum_m h(t - 2m)x_{2n}^{J+1}(m) + \sum_m (-1)^t g(t - 2m)x_{2n+1}^{J+1}(m) \tag{4}$$

In the above equation, $x_n^J(m)$ represents the signal of the Jth layer; $x_{2n+1}^{J+1}(t)$ represents the high frequency shift signal of the Jth layer; $x_{2n}^{J+1}(t)$ represents the low frequency-shifted signal of layer J; $x_m^J(t)$ represents the fault signal of layer J of the mechanical device sample; h, g are independent variable parameters.

2.2   Identify Mechanical Failure Entropy

In order to improve the fault signal feature extraction accuracy of mechanical rolling bearing, this paper will design the minimum entropy algorithm to automatically identify the fault signal of mechanical equipment. The minimum entropy algorithm refers to highlighting the sharp pulse of the calculated data through the calculated deconvolution results when identifying a mechanical device failure. In the actual calculation process, the number of spikes will not be excessive, the minimum entropy deconvolution calculation is performed on the basis of the spike pulses, and iterative calculations are performed until the maximum kurtosis value appears. In the calculation process, the greater the calculated kurtosis value, the greater the proportion of impact components in the signal of the mechanical equipment. That is, this signal is the fault signal sent by the equipment; conversely, when the calculated kurtosis value is smaller, the proportion of the impact component in the signal of the mechanical equipment is smaller, that is, this signal is not a fault signal sent by the equipment [4–6].

When the mechanical rolling bearing fails, the fault signal of the mechanical device is set as s(n), and the calculation equation of s(n) is:

$$s(n) = h(n) \times x(n) + e(n) \tag{5}$$

In this equation, s(n) represents the fault vibration signal sent by the mechanical equipment; h(n) represents the calculated transfer function of the equation; x(n) represents the impact sequence of the mechanical rolling bearing; e(n) represents fault noise of mechanical equipment [7, 8].

In the actual calculation process, the value of x(n) will gradually decrease with the influence of the internal and external noise of the machine. When the value is the same as s(n), the fault signal characteristics of the mechanical equipment will disappear and the entropy value will gradually increase. A filter L(n) is set by the calculated deconvolution result, the value of s(n) is input into the equation, and the feature of x(n) is restored [9]. The equation is:

$$x(n) = L(n) \times s(n) = \sum L(n)s(n - 1) \tag{6}$$

By integrating Eqs. (3) and (4), a minimum entropy algorithm for identifying mechanical faults can be obtained, namely:

$$s(n) = h(n) \times \sum L(n)s(n-1) + e(n) \tag{7}$$

2.3   Implement Fault Signal Feature Extraction

The design mechanical equipment fault noise removal algorithm and 1.2 design mechanical fault identification minimum entropy algorithm are integrated to obtain the mechanical roller bearing fault signal feature extraction algorithm, namely:

$$x_{2n}^{J+1}(t) = 1/2 \sum_m h(m-2t)x_n^J(m) \tag{8}$$

$$x_{2n+1}^{J+1}(t) = 1/2(-1)^t \sum_m g(m-2t)x_n^J(m) \tag{9}$$

$$x_m^J(t) = \sum_m h(t-2m)x_{2n}^{J+1}(m) + \sum_m (-1)^t g(t-2m)x_{2n+1}^{J+1}(m) \tag{10}$$

$$s(n) = h(n) \times \sum L(n)s(n-1) + e(n) \tag{11}$$

The detailed fault data of the mechanical rolling bearing is brought into the fault signal feature extraction algorithm equation. First, Eqs. (8), (9) and (10) are used to separate the internal and external noise of the mechanical equipment and the sound information related to the equipment fault, the signal sent by the mechanical equipment is transformed by wavelet frequency shift to get the signal related to the fault signal characteristic calculation and the signal similar to the fault signal; then the calculated signal data is brought into Eq. (11), the minimum entropy calculation identifies the detailed signals of these signals that can reflect the characteristics of the mechanical rolling bearing fault signal, and uses the indicators of the time domain signal to calculate the fault signal frequency of the detail signal, according to the frequency of the fault signal, the characteristics of the fault signal are inferred, and then the fault signal characteristics of the mechanical rolling bearing are extracted.

3   Experimental Analysis

3.1   Experimental Data

The bearing rolling mill bearing fault data was used as experimental data. During the experiment, manual electric sparking was used inside the bearing of the SKF6502-5RS mechanical rolling bearing, a 0.012 inch diameter mechanical failure ring was created on the outside of the bearing and on the rolling elements. The motor was then used to perform data measurements and vibration signal frequency measurements on this faulty rolling bearing. The vibration signal acquisition frequency is 15000 Hz and the signal acquisition point frequency is 13000 Hz. The pre-calculated theoretical mechanical rolling bearing internal fault signal frequency is 750 Hz, the bearing external fault signal frequency is 872 Hz, and the bearing roller body fault signal frequency is 731 Hz.

3.2   Experimental Results and Analysis

After adopting the fault signal feature extraction algorithm and the traditional algorithm that are designed in this paper, the calculated results are plotted as a bending moment envelope. See Figs. 1, 2, and 3 for details.

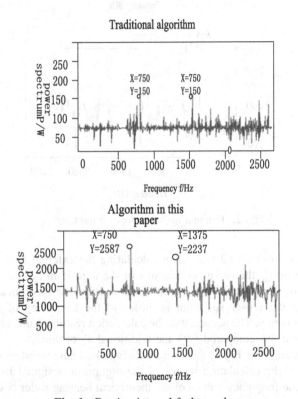

Fig. 1. Bearing internal fault envelope

As can be seen from Fig. 1, when calculating the characteristics of the bearing internal fault signal, the calculation results of the algorithm and the traditional algorithm designed in this paper are all the same as the frequency of the internal bearing fault signal of the theoretical bearing, which is 725 Hz. However, the power spectrum calculated by the algorithm at 725 Hz is obviously larger than that calculated by the traditional algorithm, and it is closer to the frequency of the theoretical internal fault frequency. The accuracy of the algorithm compared with the traditional algorithm is improved by about 4%.

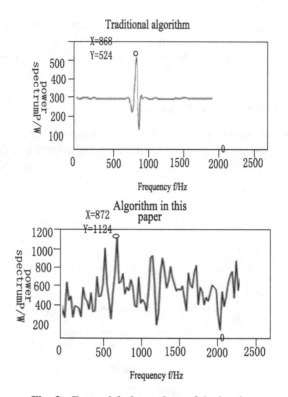

Fig. 2. External fault envelope of the bearing

It can be seen from Fig. 2 that when calculating the external fault signal characteristics of the bearing, the calculation results of the algorithm designed in this paper are the same as the frequency of the external fault signal of the theoretical bearing, both are 872 Hz, and the power spectrum is closer to the frequency of the theoretical external fault frequency. The accuracy of the calculation results of this algorithm is also improved by about 4% compared with the traditional algorithm.

As can be seen from Fig. 3, when calculating the characteristics of the bearing roller fault signal, the calculation results of the algorithm designed in this paper are more similar to the frequency values of the theoretical bearing roller body fault signal, compared with the calculation results of traditional algorithms. The calculation results of this algorithm are more accurate.

To sum up, when the fault signal characteristics of mechanical rolling bearing are accurately extracted, the algorithm designed in this paper is more accurate than the traditional algorithm, and the accuracy is improved by about 4%.

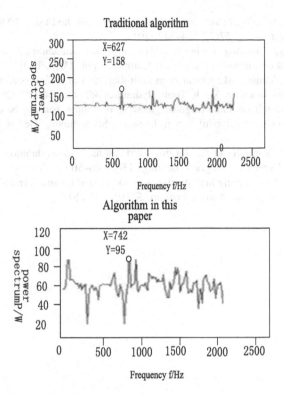

Fig. 3. Bearing roller fault envelope

4   Conclusion

This paper proposes a new fault signal feature extraction algorithm based on the wavelet frequency shift algorithm and the minimum entropy mechanical fault recognition algorithm, and improves the accuracy of the calculation results by removing noise and deconvolution calculations. The test data shows that the algorithm designed in this paper is about 4% more accurate than the traditional algorithm, and it has high effectiveness. It is hoped that the study in this paper can provide useful help for the accurate extraction of the fault signal characteristics of mechanical rolling bearings.

References

1. Saqirila: Fault feature extraction method of rolling bearing vibration signal based on MF-SVD. Autom. Petrochemical Ind. **53**(3), 31–36 (2017)
2. Guo, T., Deng, Z., Xu, M.: Application of improved EMD algorithm based on particle swarm optimization in bearing fault feature extraction. Vib. Shock **36**(16), 182–187 (2017)
3. Yuqing, M., Li, X., Zhai, Y.: Fault feature extraction method of bearing inner ring based on improved EMD and data binning. J. Shandong Univ. Eng. Ed. **47**(3), 89–95 (2017)

4. Jiang, Y., Li, R., Jiao, W., et al.: Fault feature extraction method using EMD and bispectrum analysis. Vib. Test Diagn. **37**(2), 338–342 (2017)
5. Chang, J., Wen, X.: Rolling bearing fault growth feature extraction and damage evaluation technology based on improved EMD. Res. Comput. Appl. **11**(5), 110–111 (2018)
6. Fu, D., Zhai, Y., Yuqing, M.: Research on fault diagnosis of rolling bearing based on EMD and support vector machine. Mach. Tools Hydraulics **45**(11), 184–187 (2017)
7. Guzhao, J.: Research on fault diagnosis method of rolling bearing based on correlation analysis and resonance demodulation technology. Shijiazhuang Tiedao University **12**(5), 220–222 (2017)
8. Liu, W., Liu, Y., Yang, S., et al.: An improved resonance demodulation method based on EMD and typical spectral histogram. Bearings **15**(2), 46–50 (2018)
9. Duan, J.: Research on bearing fault diagnosis method based on autocorrelation EMD and fast spectral kurtosis denoising. Autom. Instrum. **5**, 101–103 (2017)

Hybrid Manipulator Running Trajectory Prediction Algorithm Based on PLC Fuzzy Control

Yunsheng Chen[✉]

Guangzhou Huali Science and Technology Vocational College,
Zengcheng District, Guangzhou 511325, Guangdong, China
lalal2210@sina.com

Abstract. Aiming at the problem of multi-band motion and multi-joint inflection point of hybrid manipulator, the conventional trajectory prediction algorithm cannot satisfy the fast analysis and accurate control of motion trajectory. This paper proposes a hybrid manipulator running trajectory prediction algorithm based on PLC fuzzy control. Based on newton-andrews law, the dynamic model of hybrid manipulator was built, and the dynamics of hybrid manipulator was analyzed and the dynamic characteristics were determined. PLC fuzzy control unit is introduced, based on the kinematics characteristics of hybrid manipulator, the relevant input and output variables of PLC fuzzy control unit are determined, and the fuzzy strategy is implemented and analyzed. The construction of a hybrid manipulator based on fuzzy control is completed. The test data show that the proposed prediction algorithm is better than the conventional prediction algorithm, and the accuracy is improved by 57.42%, which is applicable to the prediction of the operation trajectory of the hybrid manipulator.

Keywords: PLC fuzzy control · Hybrid manipulator · Trajectory ·
Prediction algorithm

With the continuous development of equipment manufacturing industry, manipulator will replace people to complete repetitive or labor-intensive work. Due to the limitations of different tasks, hybrid manipulator has developed rapidly. However, the conventional trajectory prediction algorithm cannot satisfy the fast analysis and accurate control of motion trajectory of the hybrid manipulator [1]. Therefore, the hybrid manipulator running trajectory prediction algorithm based on PLC fuzzy control is proposed. Based on newton-andrews law, the dynamics of hybrid manipulator was analyzed and the dynamic model of hybrid manipulator was built, and the dynamic characteristics were determined according to the dynamic variation parameters. PLC fuzzy control unit is introduced, the relevant input and output variables of PLC fuzzy control unit are determined, and the fuzzy strategy is implemented and analyzed. The construction of the hybrid manipulator running trajectory prediction algorithm based on PLC fuzzy control is completed. To ensure the effectiveness of the designed manipulator trajectory prediction algorithm, it's necessary to simulate the manipulator testing environment, two kinds of manipulator trajectory prediction algorithms are used to

S. Liu and G. Yang (Eds.): ADHIP 2018, LNICST 279, pp. 269–277, 2019.
https://doi.org/10.1007/978-3-030-19086-6_30

perform the hybrid trajectory prediction analysis test. Test results show that the proposed manipulate trajectory prediction algorithm is highly effective.

1 System Object and Analysis

The objects of hybrid manipulator running trajectory prediction algorithm based on PLC fuzzy control mainly includes:

(1) Without relying on high-precision mathematical model analysis, relying on the PLC fuzzy control strategy, it is able to predict and judge the running trajectory of the hybrid manipulator and ensure high prediction accuracy.

(2) Through analysis of the motion of hybrid manipulator structure, the force state is fully understood, the dynamic characteristics are evaluated, and the PLC fuzzy control strategy is applied to determine the domain and parameters of the relevant input and output variables, and the motion trajectory prediction and analysis is performed.

(3) For the hybrid manipulator with multi-band motion and multi-joint inflection points, a general dynamics model is constructed to solve the problem that the conventional trajectory prediction algorithm cannot meet the requirements of rapid analysis and precise grasp of the trajectory.

2 Motion Analysis of Hybrid Manipulator Structure

2.1 Dynamic Model Construction of Hybrid Manipulator

To accurately analyze the trajectory of the hybrid manipulator, the dynamic model of the hybrid manipulator is firstly constructed. The dynamic model construction is based on the dynamic characteristics of the hybrid manipulator. The hybrid manipulator mainly includes three parts: manipulator, electric control and program control. The manipulator mainly completes the task of mechanical operation, which includes grasping unit, joint inflection point unit, kinetic energy providing mechanism, and other auxiliary mechanisms. Grasping unit is a work unit that completes the mechanical task, and the joint inflection point unit ensures that the task arrives safely from point A to point B, usually the traditional manipulator has one inflection point, while the hybrid manipulator can complete more complex work, generally has 2–3 key inflection points [2, 3], which results in great calculation difficulty to conventional trajectory prediction algorithm. Kinetic energy providing mechanism mainly includes the transmission mechanics mechanism such as motor, and provides kinetic energy for the mechanical part. Other auxiliary mechanisms mainly include mechanical lubrication unit, mechanical protection unit. Electric control exerts the control order of program to control the hybrid manipulator as well as to finish special task. Program control edits code according to different programs and control the manipulator according to design requirements.

Provided that the origin of hybrid manipulator with multi-band motion and multi-joint inflection point is O, the length of first-level hybrid manipulator is l_1, the length of second-level hybrid manipulator is l_2, and so on, the maximum head angle of first-level is θ_1, the mass of first-level manipulator is m_1, it's assuming that the mass of manipulator is uniform, with unit distance, the mass of manipulator m_1/l_1. The acceleration of mass center of first-level hybrid manipulator is v_{a1}, uniform motion speed is v_1, inertia tensor is I_1, effort torque is N_1, the acceleration of mass center, uniform motion speed, inertia tensor and effort torque of second-level hybrid manipulator are respectively v_{a2}, v_2, I_2, N_2, and so on. The structure of motion model of hybrid manipulator is shown as follows (Fig. 1).

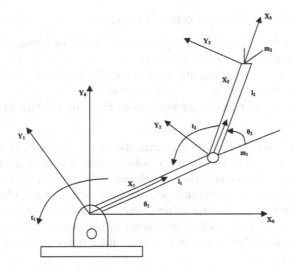

Fig. 1. Structure of motion model of hybrid manipulator

2.2 Dynamic Analysis of Hybrid Manipulator

Provided that the hybrid manipulator has i levels, the length of hybrid manipulator is l_i, the maximum head angle of is θ_i, the mass of manipulator is m_i, with unit distance, the mass of manipulator m_i/l_i. The acceleration of mass center of manipulator is v_{ai}, uniform motion speed is v_i, inertia tensor is I_i, effort torque is N_i. Based on newton-andrews law, the motion vectors of hybrid manipulator are analyzed. Based on Newton's first law of motion, the manipulator is stressed by downward gravity and upward braced force, with the influence of motor kinetic energy, the manipulator moves. It's assuming that motor kinetic energy provides E energy, and the mechanical connection consumes E_1 energy, the resistance to motion consumes E_2 energy, then $E_1+E_2 \ll E$, the mass that manipulator graspes is variable, there is certain uncertainty in path, provided that the grasping mass is m_x, the balance equation of dynamic vector is given by [4]:

$$m_i I_i N_i = \frac{\overset{i+.1}{i} \sin v_i \theta_i^2}{(E - E_1 - E_2) l_i} \qquad (1)$$

Provided that the variation period of mechanical motion vector is f, an upward moment of force is generated by the motion of manipulator form first-level to upper level, on the key joint, with the influence of inertia force I_i, when the manipulator graspes the object whose mass is m_x, the origin of hybrid manipulator keeps O, dynamic equilibrium is formed and meets the rules of following equation:

$$m_x I_i N_i = \cos v_i \theta_i^2 f / l_i (E - E_1 - E_2) \qquad (2)$$

From above equation, it can be concluded that:

If $E_S > E_R$, the hybrid manipulator presents the trend of upward motion, meanwhile, the inertia tensor value I_i is positive.
If $E_S < E_R$, the hybrid manipulator presents the trend of downward motion, meanwhile, the inertia tensor value I_i is negative.
If $E_S = E_R$, the hybrid manipulator keeps motionless, meanwhile, the inertia tensor value I_i is zero.

Where E_S represents the equilibrant of dynamic vector, E_R the dynamic equilibrium of hybrid manipulator. Based on newton-andrews law, the motion trend of hybrid manipulator is analyzed and conclusions are obtained. The conclusion of motion vector trend of hybrid manipulator is combined with the time control unit to obtain the motion vector status of hybrid manipulator in unit time. According to the status of motion vector, the motion direction is identified, based on variations of force, the dynamic motion mathematical prediction matrix of hybrid manipulator is built [5, 6], of which the equation is as follows:

$$D = |M(q)| = \begin{bmatrix} 0 \\ m_x f \\ 0 \\ I_i \end{bmatrix}, F = |G(q)| = \begin{bmatrix} E_S \\ 0 \\ E_R \\ I_i \end{bmatrix} \qquad (3)$$

Where D represents the control variable program of hybrid manipulator, F the dynamic variable control function of hybrid manipulator, E_S the equilibrant of dynamic vector, and E_R the dynamic equilibrium of hybrid manipulator.

2.3 Dynamic Characteristics of Hybrid Manipulator

Based on the dynamic analysis of hybrid manipulator, following dynamic characteristics can be confirmed:

1. With the increasement of key joint of manipulator, the calculation intensity increases, and geometric linear uncertainty increases.

2. The dynamic range of the dynamic model of the hybrid manipulator is wider, it can be simulated by the PLC fuzzy control unit, meanwhile, it can ensure high coupling and reduce the influence of random interference and uncertainty.
3. The dynamic inertia matrix of hybrid manipulator meets $q \in R^n$, $|M(q)| \leq d$, and d is a constant.
4. M(q)-2C is matrix inverse, and

$$m_x I_i N_i - \cos v_i \theta_i^2 f / l_i (E - E_1 - E_2) = 0 \quad \forall x \in R^n.$$

5. Gravity G(q) has threshold value for $q \in R^n$, where $|G(q)| \leq d \leq a$, the integration of threshold value is constant.

3 Structure Design of Trajectory Prediction Algorithm

3.1 Construction of PLC Fuzzy Control Unit

The construction of PLC fuzzy control unit is the basis of hybrid manipulator running trajectory prediction algorithm based on PLC fuzzy control, likewise, the motion analysis of hybrid manipulator structure is the basis of construction of PLC fuzzy control unit. Through the analysis data of hybrid manipulator motion, the influence of hybrid dynamic inertia and gravity is determined. The parameters value is assigned according to confirmed influence parameters, and fuzzy controller is introduced, which mainly includes calculation of control variables, fuzzification, quantification of fuzzy control, fuzzy inference, defuzzification and D/A transfer [7] (Fig. 2).

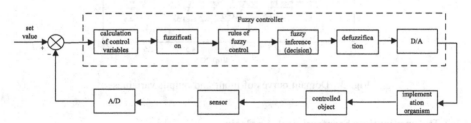

Fig. 2. Principle of fuzzy control

3.2 Confirme the Input and Output Variables of PLC Fuzzy Control Unit

The PLC fuzzy control unit is introduced according to the dynamic characteristics of hybrid manipulator, and kinematic analysis of the manipulator is performed. The control variable of PLC is the motion state of hybrid manipulator. When analyzing and predicting the fuzzy control, the control variable of PLC is converted from the motion state of hybrid manipulator to the definition threshold of fuzzy function, the input and output variable thresholds are compared and analyzed. The input variable thresholds include the inverse matrix constant of M(q)-2C, the motion compensation of the manipulator, and the dynamic inertia matrix of hybrid manipulator [8, 9]. Correspondingly, the output variable thresholds include the dynamic motion mathematical prediction matrix of hybrid manipulator and the variation period of mechanical motion vector.

3.3   Confirm the Parameters of PLC Fuzzy Control Unit

To confirme the parameters of PLC fuzzy control unit, it's necessary to confirme the input and output variable thresholds of fuzzy control unit, but dimension nonuniformity exists in inverse matrix constant of M(q)-2C and dynamic motion mathematical prediction matrix of hybrid manipulator, dimensionless processing for input and output variables is needed to confirme the domain and parameters of the input and output variables of PLC fuzzy control unit. With the calculation method of fuzzy control, the domain and parameters are determined rapidly by curve-parameter method, the domain curves of input and output variables are shown as follows [10] (Fig. 3).

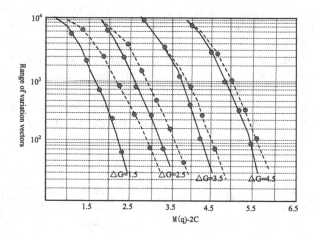

Fig. 3. Domain curves of input and output variables

3.4   Defuzzification Strategy and Analysis

The domain and parameters of the input and output variables are smaller than 2.5, the curve with lower ΔG value is selected to be substituted into fuzzy control unit, the trajectory prediction calculation is performed.

The domain and parameters of the input and output variables are smaller than 5.0 and larger than 2.5, the curve with higher ΔG value is selected to be substituted into fuzzy control unit, the trajectory prediction calculation is performed.

The domain and parameters of the input and output variables are larger than 5.0, the curve with mean ΔG value is selected to be substituted into fuzzy control unit, the trajectory prediction calculation is performed.

4 System Test and Analysis

To ensure the effectiveness of the proposed algorithm based on PLC fuzzy control for hybrid manipulators' trajectory prediction, system testing and analysis are carried out. In the testing process, different manipulators were used as test objects to perform the trajectory prediction analysis test of hybrid manipulators. Different key joints and structures of the manipulator are simulated. To ensure the validity of the test, the conventional manipulator trajectory prediction algorithm is used as a comparison object, and the results of the two simulation tests are compared. The test data was presented on the same data chart and the test conclusions are analyzed.

4.1 Preparation of System Test

To ensure the accuracy of the simulation test process, the test parameters are set. This paper simulates the test process, uses different manipulators as the test objects, uses two different manipulators' trajectory prediction algorithms, performs the hybrid manipulator's trajectory prediction analysis test, and analyzes the simulation test results. Because the analysis results and analysis methods obtained in different methods are different, therefore, the test environment parameters must be consistent during the testing process. The test data setting results in this paper are shown in Table 1.

Table 1. Test parameters

Item	Model	Range/parameters
Dynamic parameters of hybrid manipulator	Mitshubishi L5-14	300 kJ/h
Set the complexity of variable manipulator	∞ mechanical joint* mechanical freedom	0–80%
Analysis of error-tolerant rate of error	–	<0.05%

4.2 Test of Trajectory Prediction

During the test, two different manipulators' trajectory prediction algorithms were compared with the exact values of the simulation to analyze the changes in the manipulator's trajectory. At the same time, due to the use of two different manipulator trajectory prediction algorithms, the analysis results cannot be compared directly. For this purpose, third-party analysis and recording software is used to record and analyze the testing process and results, and the results are displayed in the comparison curve of results of this test. The test result comparison curve is shown in Fig. 4. Based on the third-party analysis and recording software, it can be concluded that the proposed prediction algorithm improves the accuracy of rapid analysis by 57.42% compared with the conventional prediction algorithm, and is suitable for the prediction of the trajectory of the hybrid manipulator.

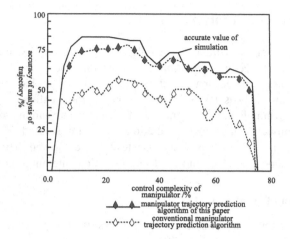

Fig. 4. Test result comparison curve

5   Conclusion

Hybrid manipulator running trajectory prediction algorithm based on PLC fuzzy control is proposed in this paper, based on motion analysis of hybrid manipulator structure, the dynamic model of hybrid manipulator is constructed to determine the dynamic characteristics of hybrid manipulator. Based on PLC fuzzy control unit, and the determination of domain and parameters of input and output variables, defuzzification strategy and analysis are performed. Test data show that the method designed in this paper is quite effective. The paper is written with the desire that the research will provide theoretical basis for trajectory prediction algorithm of manipulator.

References

1. Zhou, Y., Hu, D., Jin, R., Hu, J.: Application of fuzzy control based on PLC in ship rudder roll stabilization system. Mod. Electron. Tech. **39**(2), 140–142 (2016)
2. Wang, P., Hong, Y., Huang, H., et al.: Application of fuzzy PID controller based on PLC in hot air drying oven. Food Mach. **32**(12), 100–104 (2016)
3. Xu, Q., Yang, S., Yang, M.: Offline robot track intelligent optimization—based on improved differential evolution algorithm. Agric. Mech. Res. **39**(2), 191–195 (2017)
4. Huang, H., Zhang, G., Yang, Y.: Dynamic modeling and coordinate motion trajectory optimization for underwater vehicle and manipulator system. J. Shanghai Jiaotong Univ. **50**(9), 1437–1443 (2016)
5. Feng, D., Zhang, X., Zhang, X., et al.: RANSAC-based spatial circle fitting algorithm and it's application on motion range detection of a manipulator. Opt. Tech. **14**(2), 156–160 (2016)
6. Xu, J., Mei, J., Duan, X., et al.: A continuous trajectory planning transition algorithm for industrial robots. Chin. J. Eng. Des. **23**(6), 537–543 (2016)
7. Guo-zhen, B.A.I., Peng-xiang, J.I.N.G.: Trajectory planning of delta manipulators based on modified gravitational search algorithm. Control Eng. Chin. **24**(9), 1823–1828 (2017)

8. Zhang, L., Wei, P., Li, P., Wang, X., Liu, X.: Fabric grasp planning for multi-fingered dexterous hand based on neural network algorithm. J. Text. Res. **38**(1), 132–139 (2017)

9. Tong, Z., Guo, R., Li, L., Lin, Y.: Study on trajectory controlling of hydraulic sampling joint manipulator. Mach. Des. Manuf. **5**(11), 162–165 (2016)

10. Huang, Z., Xiang, Y., Li, Z., Lu, N.: Trajectory planning and design of control system for road cone automatic retractable manipulator. Chin. J. Constr. Mach. **15**(4), 283–290 (2017)

Construction of Design Characteristics Model of Manufacturing Structures for Complex Mechanical Parts

Yunsheng Chen$^{(\boxtimes)}$

Mechatronics and Automatic Chemistry Department,
Guangzhou Huali Science and Technology Vocational College,
Zengcheng District, Guangzhou 511325, China
chen12yunsheng@sina.com

Abstract. Traditional mechanical parts manufacturing structure design feature model can more complete mechanical parts structure design feature extracting, but for complex mechanical parts for structural design feature extraction, feature extraction error rates higher deficiencies, this proposed complex mechanical parts manufacturing characteristic model building structure design. Based on the ADO.NET structure, the design platform of complex mechanical parts manufacturing structure is built, the constraint equation of feature model is determined, and the framework of complex mechanical parts manufacturing structure design feature model is constructed. The feature model function of design structure design is designed, and the embedding of complex mechanical structure design software is realized by using XTF embedding technology, and the construction of complex mechanical parts manufacturing structure design feature model is completed. The experimental data show that the proposed complex feature model is 14.24% lower than the traditional model, and is suitable for the application of complex mechanical parts manufacturing structure design characteristics.

Keywords: Complex mechanical parts · Manufacturing structure design · Feature model construction · Data parameter import

1 Introduction

The traditional structural design feature model of mechanical parts can extract the design features of mechanical parts completely. However, when extracting the structural design features of complex mechanical parts, due to the limitations of the model basic frame, there is a deficiency in the extraction feature error rate [1]. To this end, the construction of a design feature model for the manufacturing of complex mechanical parts is proposed. Relying on the ADO.NET structure, the Data Reader object was introduced to perform read-only operations on the platform data flow, set up a structural design platform for manufacturing complex mechanical parts, calculate the random sample constraint state function, and substitute control model variables to obtain the design features of the complex mechanical part manufacturing structure. The constraint equation of the model completes the construction of a design model

S. Liu and G. Yang (Eds.): ADHIP 2018, LNICST 279, pp. 278–286, 2019.
https://doi.org/10.1007/978-3-030-19086-6_31

framework for the manufacturing structure of complex mechanical parts. In order to meet the performance requirements of the structural model design features of complex mechanical parts manufacturing, construct drawing function, data analysis function, intelligent AI mapping function, cloud computing function, use XTF embedded technology, optimize Design source, Mapping unit, and realize complex mechanical structure design software The embedding is completed and the proposed design model of the manufacturing structure of the complex mechanical parts is completed. In order to ensure the effectiveness of the designed mechanical design feature model of the mechanical parts, the test environment of the mechanical parts structure was simulated and designed. Two different mechanical parts were used to manufacture the structural design feature model, and the feature error rate simulation test was conducted. The test results showed that the proposed Mechanical parts manufacturing structure design feature model has extremely high effectiveness.

2 System Objectives and Analysis

The construction of complex mechanical parts manufacturing structure design feature model mainly includes:

(1) Solve the problems existing in the structural design feature model of traditional mechanical parts manufacturing, optimize the model building process flow, combine scientific and rational combination of modern computer technologies, and realize the construction of complex mechanical parts manufacturing structure design feature model.

(2) Optimize the structural design platform of traditional mechanical parts manufacturing, analyze the structural design variables of complex mechanical parts manufacturing structure, and determine the constraint equations of the manufacturing structural design feature model of complex mechanical parts.

(3) Manufacturing structural designs for complex mechanical parts, feature models for building drawing functions, data analysis functions, intelligent AI mapping functions, and cloud computing functions. Based on the embedding of complex mechanical structure design software, the construction of a design model for a complex mechanical part manufacturing structure is accomplished.

3 Construction of Complex Mechanical Parts Manufacturing Structure Design Feature Model Framework

3.1 Set up a Complex Mechanical Parts Manufacturing Structure Design Platform

The complex mechanical parts manufacturing structure design platform is an operating mechanism that carries the structural feature model of the manufacturing of complex mechanical parts. The operation design of the complex mechanical part manufacturing structure design platform directly affects the operation of the complex mechanical part manufacturing structural design feature model. For this reason, ADO.NET's structural platform is used as a structural design platform for manufacturing complex mechanical parts. ADO.NET structure platform mainly includes two core components of Data Set and .NET data provider, namely .NET Data Provider, and four core objects of Connection, Command, Data Reader and Data Adapter [2]. The Connection object mainly represents the connection of a specific complex mechanical data source, determines the correlation and specific relationship of the complex influence coefficient of the mechanical quantitative calculation, and traces back to the structural design database file, at the same time, in order to prevent repeated extraction, the data stream is marked, and the extracted data is marked with a specific character at the end of the string. The Command object is a data service platform, which analyzes the management authority for the mechanical design project. To ensure the security of the system operation, the project management staff assigns the user layer authority to use non-open source distribution, and this data has certain confidentiality. The Command object is to allow permission to extract data without destroying the object and encode the data to form a calculable character string. At this time, the generated data file is a numeric type. Because the data is continuously updated and does not maintain a certain value, the Data Reader object is introduced to perform read-only operations on the platform data stream and provide related technical information such as design project data and mechanical part data for the Command object. Its ADO.NET architecture diagram is shown in Fig. 1 [3].

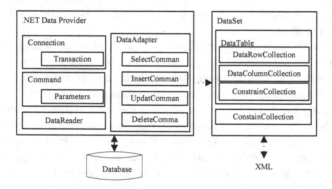

Fig. 1. ADO.NET architecture diagram

Where ADO.NET requires the hardware environment to use the TCP/IP network protocol. The CPU of the server is not less than 3.2 GHz, and the memory is not less than 8 GB of hot-swappable SAS hard drives and dual Gigabit Ethernet adapters. The software environment operating system adopts Windows 7 Ultimate Edition, database development tools select Visual Studio 2008 [4].

3.2 Determining Constraint Equations for Designing Feature Models of Manufacturing of Complex Mechanical Parts

In order to ensure the reliable operation of the manufacturing structural design platform for complex mechanical parts, the constraint equations for the design feature model of the manufacturing structure of complex mechanical parts are determined. Constrained complex mechanical parts manufacturing structure design feature variables are complex mechanical parts manufacturing structure design feature variables running on a controllable platform. Let's $f(x, \theta)$ be the overall characteristic model variable function, where $\theta \in \Theta$. A parameter vector consisting of one or more unknown parameters of the design variables, Θ for the parameter space, use $x_1, x_2, \ldots x_n$ to represent the characteristic model variables. Then the control model variable sample function $L(\theta; x_1, x_2, \ldots, x_n)$ can be expressed as [5]:

$$L(\theta) = (\theta; x_1, x_2, \ldots, x_n) = f(x_1, \theta)f(x_2, \theta) \ldots f(x_n, \theta) \qquad (1)$$

In the formula, $L(\theta)$ represents the characteristic model variable sample function, If a statistic $\hat{\theta} = \hat{\theta}(x_1, x_2, \ldots, x_n)$ satisfies the following conditions $L(\hat{\theta}) = \max_{\theta \in \Theta} L(\theta)$. Then say $\hat{\theta}$ is the condition constraint coefficient of θ, abbreviated as MLE. Let $x_1, x_2, \ldots, x_n$'s conditional coefficient $\theta \sim N(\mu, \sigma^2)$ have n random samples, the constraint state of the random sample can be expressed as:

$$L(\theta) = \prod_{i=1}^{n} f(x_i; \mu, \sigma^2) = \left(\frac{1}{\sqrt{2\pi}\sigma}\right)^n \exp\left\{-\frac{\sum_{i=1}^{n}(x_i - \mu)^2}{2\sigma^2}\right\} \qquad (2)$$

Take the logarithm of both sides of formula 2 and get $\ln L(\theta) = \frac{n}{2}\ln(2\pi\sigma^2)$ $-\frac{1}{2\sigma^2}\sum_{i=1}^{n}(x_i - \mu)^2$, substituting into formula 1 yields $\frac{\partial \ln L(\theta)}{\partial \sigma^2} = \frac{1}{\sigma^2}\sum_{i=1}^{n}(x_i - \mu)^2$, just do $\frac{\partial \ln L(\theta)}{\partial \sigma^2} = \frac{-n}{2\sigma^2} + \frac{1}{2\sigma^4}\sum_{i=1}^{n}(x_i - \mu)^2 = 0$. Substituting the constraint state of the random sample into the sample function of the control model variable yields the constraint equations for the manufacturing structural design feature model of the complex mechanical part as follows:

$$\begin{cases} \hat{\mu}_{MLE} = \frac{1}{n}\sum_{i=1}^{n} x_i = \overline{X} \\ \hat{\mu}_{MLE}^2 = \frac{1}{n}\sum_{i=1}^{n}(x_i - \overline{X}^2) = \frac{n-1}{n}s^2 \end{cases} \qquad (3)$$

Based on the complex mechanical parts manufacturing structure design platform, the hardware design of the structural model design framework of the complex mechanical parts manufacturing is realized, and the constraint equations of the structural design feature model are manufactured by using the complex mechanical parts. Completed the software construction of the structural design model framework for the manufacturing of complex mechanical parts, and realized the construction of a design model framework for the manufacturing of complex mechanical parts.

4 To Achieve the Construction of Complex Mechanical Parts Manufacturing Structure Design Feature Model

4.1 Complex Mechanical Parts Manufacturing Structural Design Feature Model Functional Architecture

The complex mechanical part manufacturing structure design feature model is a feature model used for the structural design of complex mechanical parts manufacturing. In order to meet the design requirements, the drawing function, data analysis function, intelligent AI mapping function, and cloud computing function are constructed.

Among them, the drawing function includes two-dimensional drawing function and three-dimensional drawing function. Including points, lines, surfaces, graphic editing, data conversion, 2D to 3D, 3D to 2D. The data analysis function, in the framework of the design feature model of complex mechanical parts manufacturing structure, based on the constraint equation of the complex mechanical parts manufacturing structure design feature model, using statistical data processing functions, data analysis of the manufacturing structural design features of complex mechanical parts [6]. The statistics of the data analysis results can also be used to predict the results. The intelligent AI mapping function can generate three-dimensional coordinates for simple mechanical part drawing, and data shunting for complex mechanical part drawing to prepare for data processing. The cloud computing function is to improve the computational convenience of the design feature model of the manufacturing structure of complex mechanical parts, and to ensure the accuracy of calculation. The data expansion calculation is based on the cloud computing function. The data extension interface is as follows (Fig. 2) [7].

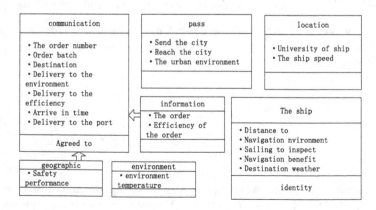

Fig. 2. Data extension interface

4.2 Complex Mechanical Design Software Embedded

The software embedded technology for the design of complex mechanical structures is the core technology for manufacturing structural design feature models for complex mechanical parts. Traditional mechanical parts manufacturing structure design feature model adopts conventional software embedded technology and is difficult to operate on high-performance platforms. Therefore, when extracting structural design features for complex mechanical parts, there is a disadvantage of high extraction feature error rate. For this reason, this article relies on regular JSF embedding technology to optimize Design source, Mapping unit, and incorporate XTF (Extended Triton Format) embedding technology for encoding processing. Using the strong compatibility of the XTF format [8], JSF files, DSE files, and MUT files are packaged into an XTF file program for modulation adjustment.

XTF embedding mainly includes three phases: data preparation phase, data processing phase, and data display phase. The data preparation phase provides data preparation for software designed for complex mechanical part structures. The data preparation stage works on the data preprocessing layer. The data preprocessing layer includes a file processing unit, a data packet processing unit, and a channel processing unit, and the data preparation of software data is based on Mapping unit processing [9]. The data processing stage is to process the prepared data, prepare to embed complex mechanical structure design software, start the embedded program, and finally use XTF's Embedded technology to realize the embedding of complex mechanical structure design software. The flowchart of the embedded mechanical design software is shown in the following Fig. 3 [10].

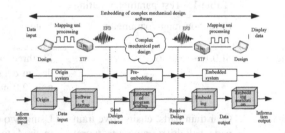

Fig. 3. Embedded software for complex mechanical design software

Based on the construction of complex mechanical parts manufacturing structure design feature model frame, the structure feature design model function of complex mechanical parts manufacturing structure is built, and the embedded design of complex mechanical structure design software is implemented using XTF embedded technology to complete the construction of the design feature model of the manufacturing structure of complex mechanical parts.

5 Test and Analysis

In order to ensure the validity of the design feature model construction of the manufacturing structure of complex mechanical parts proposed in this paper, the simulation test analysis was carried out. During the test process, different design and manufacture of mechanical part structures were used as test objects, and characteristic error rate simulation tests were conducted. Different types of mechanical structures for designing and manufacturing mechanical part structures, as well as extraction difficulty coefficients, are simulated. In order to ensure the validity of the test, traditional mechanical parts are used to manufacture the structural design feature model as a comparison object. The results of the two simulation simulation tests are compared and the test data are presented in the same data chart.

5.1 Test Preparation

In order to ensure the accuracy of the simulation test process, the test parameters of the test are set. This paper simulates the test process, uses different design and manufacture of mechanical parts as the test object, uses two different mechanical parts to manufacture the structural design feature model, carries out the characteristic error rate simulation test, and analyzes the simulation test results. Because the analysis results obtained in different methods are different from the analysis methods, the test environment parameters must be consistent during the test. The test data set results in this paper are shown in Table 1.

Table 1. Test parameter settings

Simulation test parameters	Execution range/parameter	Note
Design and manufacture of mechanical parts structure degree of difficulty	SL0.1 ~ SL1.6	SL three-dimensional design degree of difficulty unit, 2.0 maximum
Design and manufacture of mechanical parts	Gear train parts, chain drive train parts, belt drive train parts, worm drive train parts, screw drive train parts, coupling parts, clutch train parts, rolling bearing train parts, and sliding bearing train parts	Using two different design methods to conduct design analysis one by one
Simulation System	DJX-2016-3.5	Windows platform

5.2 Test Results Analysis

During the test, two different mechanical parts were used to fabricate the structural design feature model to work in a simulated environment, and the variation of the feature error rate was analyzed. At the same time, due to the use of two different mechanical parts to manufacture the structural design feature model, the analysis results cannot be compared directly. For this purpose, third-party analysis and recording software is used. The test process and results are recorded and analyzed, and the results are shown in the comparison results curve of this experiment. In the simulation test result curve, the third-party analysis and recording software function is used to eliminate the uncertainty caused by the simulation laboratory personnel operation and simulation of computer equipment factors. Only for different design and manufacture of mechanical parts structure, different mechanical parts manufacturing structure design feature model, the characteristic error rate simulation test. The comparison curve of the test results is shown in Fig. 4, where a is a structural design model of a traditional mechanical part, and b is a structural design model of a mechanical part. According to the results of the test curve, the third-party analysis and recording software was used to mathematically weight the feature error rate of the mechanical part manufacturing structure design feature model and the traditional mechanical part manufacturing structure design feature model. The proposed complex feature model is lower than the traditional model, and the extracted feature error rate is reduced by 14.24%, which is suitable for the application of complex mechanical part manufacturing structure design features.

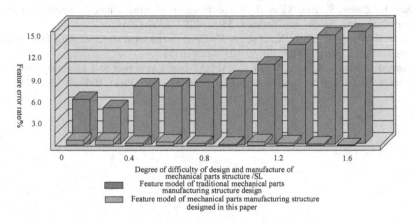

Fig. 4. Comparison of test results

6 Conclusion

This paper proposes the construction of a design feature model for the manufacturing of complex mechanical parts and the construction of a design feature model framework based on the manufacturing structure of complex mechanical parts. The use of complex mechanical parts manufacturing structure design feature model design, as well as the complex mechanical structure design software embedded technology, to achieve the study of this article. The experimental data shows that the method designed in this paper has extremely high effectiveness. It is hoped that the study of this paper can provide a theoretical basis for the manufacturing of structural design feature models for mechanical parts.

References

1. Peng, C., Fei, L., Junfeng, N.: Multi-objective monitoring integrated model of machining automatic production line and its application. Comput. Integr. Manuf. Syst. **23**(3), 473–481 (2017)
2. Weihui, W., Dongming, X., Xing, M.: Automatic ultra-light structural design and laser additive manufacturing of metal parts. Infrared Laser Eng. **009**(11), 124–131 (2016)
3. Wang, H., Riliang, L., Zhang, C.: Design and implementation of workshop reconfigurable automatic programming system based on processing features. Comput. Integr. Manuf. Syst. **22**(10), 2396–2407 (2016)
4. Zhou, L., Li, F., Li, J., et al.: Energy consumption correlation modeling of mechanical product manufacturing based on design features. Comput. Integr. Manuf. Syst. **22**(4), 1037–1045 (2016)
5. Huang, B., Zhou, L., An, L., et al.: Variant design method for machining and aero-engine parts driven by process model. J. Aeronaut. **38**(1), 290–304 (2017)
6. Song, S., Jian, B., Keqing, D.: Active remanufacturing design and timing control method of centrifugal compressor impeller. China Mech. Eng. **28**(15), 1862–1869 (2017)
7. Song, S., Wei, W., Keqing, D.: Active remanufacturing design based on structural function derived coefficients. J. Mech. Eng. **53**(11), 175–183 (2017)
8. Shao, L., Zhang, S., Bai, X., et al.: Three-dimensional process model construction method for milling parts. Mach. Sci. Technol. **35**(8), 1297–1301 (2016)
9. Zhang, K., Hang, C., Zhao, X., et al.: A 3D CAD model local structure retrieval method for design reuse. J. Agric. Mach. **48**(7), 405–412 (2017)
10. Wang, K., Zhang, S., He, W., et al.: SPEA2-based selection and assembly method for complex mechanical products. J. Shanghai Jiaotong Univ. **50**(7), 1047–1053 (2016)

UAV-Enabled Wireless Power Transfer for Mobile Users: Trajectory Optimization and Power Allocation

Fei Huang[1](✉), Jin Chen[1], Haichao Wang[1], Zhen Xue[1], Guoru Ding[1,2], and Xiaoqin Yang[1]

[1] College of Communications Engineering, Army Engineering University of PLA,
Nanjing 210014, China
huangfeicjh@sina.com, chenjin99@263.net, whcwl456@163.com,
xzalways@yeah.net, dr.guoru.ding@ieee.org, 15261856573@139.com
[2] National Mobile Communications Research Laboratory, Southeast University,
Nanjing 210096, China

Abstract. This paper studies an unmanned aerial vehicle (UAV)-enabled wireless power transfer system (WPTS) for mobile users, in which a UAV-installed energy transmitter (ET) is deployed to broadcast wireless energy for charging mobile users functioned as energy receivers (ERs) on the ground. Different from the most of the existing research on wireless energy transfer, a dual-dynamic scenario is proposed where a flying UAV transmits wireless power to charge multiple ground mobile users simultaneously. To explore the adjustable channel state influenced by the UAV's mobility, the UAV's power allocation and trajectory design are jointly optimized. For the sake of the fairness, we consider the maximum of the minimum of the energy harvested among the nodes on the ground during a finite charging period. The formulated problem above is a non-convex optimization on account of the UAV's power limit and speed constraint. An algorithm is proposed in the paper to jointly optimize power and trajectory. Simulation results indicate our design improves the efficiency and fairness of power transferred to the ground nodes over other benchmark schemes.

Keywords: Wireless power transfer · Unmanned aerial vehicle · Mobile users · Power allocation · Trajectory optimization

1 Introduction

Recently, unmanned aerial vehicles (UAVs) attract rapidly-increasing attention due to its promising technique in many fields, for example, typically in military and commercial domains. This is a trend that future facilities pursue increasingly automated and fast-deployed. A large number of applications spring up such as cargo transport, aerial surveillance and aerial photography owe to UAV's

S. Liu and G. Yang (Eds.): ADHIP 2018, LNICST 279, pp. 287–296, 2019.
https://doi.org/10.1007/978-3-030-19086-6_32

inherently flexibility and mobility [1,2]. Inspired by the advancement of UAVs-aided wireless communication [3], UAV-enabled wireless power transfer (WPT) has been presented as a emerging technique by utilizing UAVs as mobile energy transmitters (ETs).

In conventional WPT systems, energy transmitters (ETs) are deployed at fixed locations to charge distributed energy receivers (ERs) [4,5]. Under the conventional conditions, due to the severe propagation loss of long distance, such as shadowing and fading, the end-to-end WPT efficiency is generally low, particularly when the power transmission distance from the ETs to the ERs becomes relatively large. However, UAVs usually own better channel state to ground nodes because of higher chance of having line-of-sight (LOS) link between them. Thus, UAV-enabled wireless power transfer (WPT) gains the popularity lately due to its high channel gain. By exploiting its fully controllable mobility, the UAV can properly adjust locations over time (namely trajectory) to reduce the distance from target ground users to improve the efficiency of WPT. However, the fixed ground nodes mentioned previously cannot satisfy all of the applications, for instance, some creatures's active state needs to be measured in some oceans or lakes. In view of not destroying their original living environment, too many sensing nodes should not be deployed in it. But to cover the entire region, the sensing nodes must be mobile. In addition, their moving paths are arranged in advance. The sensing and movement of mobile sensing nodes both consume energy, so a UAV deployed is needed to charge them.

In this paper, we investigate the power allocation and trajectory design in UAV-enabled wireless power transfer system for mobile users where a UAV dispatched charges two mobile nodes on the ground at the same time. We formulate a non-convex optimization problem with the target to maximize the minimum of the energy harvested between the two nodes on the ground during a finite charging period, subject to the power limit and trajectory constraints. To deal with the formulated problem effectively, we present an efficient joint transmit power allocation and trajectory optimization algorithm [6]. Firstly two subproblems are investigated: Transmit power allocation with given trajectory and trajectory optimization with given transmit power. Furthermore, a lower bound of the non-convex function in trajectory optimization is obtained to handle this subproblem. Simulation results validate the proposed design outperforms other benchmark schemes in terms of higher min-energy transferred to mobile nodes on the ground.

2   System Model and Problem Formulation

We consider a scenario where a set of mobile nodes $\mathcal{K} = \{1, 2, ..., k, ...K\}$ are randomly dispersed on the ground and a UAV broadcasts energy to charge them. We assume that the UAV is deployed at a fixed altitude H. In practice, H will satisfy the minimum altitude that is required for terrain or building avoidance without frequent ascending or descending. Considering the efficiency of charging process, the UAV ought to accomplish transferring energy within a finite time duration. We focus on the particular flight period of the UAV, denoted by $\mathcal{T} \triangleq (0, T]$ with finite duration T in second (s). For ease of expression, the time horizon T is discretized into N equally spaced time slots. The elemental slot length is denoted as $\delta_t = {}^T/_N$ which is chosen to be sufficiently small in order that the location of the UAV can be assumed to approximately constant within each slot. Without loss of generality, we consider a three-dimensional Cartesian coordinate system, with all dimensions being measured in meters, where the initial and final locations of the UAV are given as $[x_0, y_0, H]$ and $[x_F, y_F, H]$ respectively, since the UAV's launching/landing locations are generally fixed for carrying out certain missions. Therefore, the UAV's trajectory can be expressed by $(x_U[n], y_U[n], H), n \in \mathcal{N} = \{1, ..., N\}$. The location of k-th mobile node on the ground at n-th slot is denoted by $(x_k[n], y_k[n], 0), \forall k \in \mathcal{K}, \forall n \in \mathcal{N}$. The number of discrete points reaches a balance between the computational complexity and the proper accuracy. Because the working area of nodes is spacious, there is no shielding and so on, so the wireless channel between the UAV and each ER is normally LOS-dominated. We adopt the free-space path loss model so the channel gain from the UAV to ER is modeled as

$$h_k[n] = \beta_0 d_k^{-\alpha}[n], \forall k \in \mathcal{K}, n \in \mathcal{N} \tag{1}$$

where

$$d_k[n] = \sqrt{(x_U[n] - x_k[n])^2 + (y_U[n] - y_k[n])^2 + H^2}, \tag{2}$$

β_0 is the channel power gain at the reference distance d_0 and α is environmental factor. Considering that the UAV's maximum flight speed is limited by $V_{\max}$, there should be constraints on the UAV's locations as follows:

$$(x_U[1] - x_0)^2 + (y_U[1] - y_0)^2 \leq (V_{\max}\delta_t)^2 \tag{3a}$$

$$(x_U[n] - x_U[n-1])^2 + (y_U[n] - y_U[n-1])^2 \leq (V_{\max}\delta_t)^2 \tag{3b}$$

$$(x_F - x_U[N-1])^2 + (y_F - y_U[N-1])^2 \leq (V_{\max}\delta_t)^2 \tag{3c}$$

The harvested power by k-th node at n-th slot is given by

$$E_k[n] = \eta\delta_t P_k[n] h_k[n], \tag{4}$$

From (1), (2) and (4), we can derive that

$$E_k[n] = \frac{\eta\beta_0\delta_t P_k[n]}{\left(\sqrt{(x_U[n] - x_k[n])^2 + (y_U[n] - y_k[n])^2 + H^2}\right)^\alpha}, \tag{5}$$

where $P_k[n]$ is the UAV's transmit power for k-th node at n-th slot and $0 \prec \eta \prec 1$ denotes the energy conversion efficiency of the rectifier at each ER. Assuming that the total amount of power transmitted to all ground nodes during the whole charging duration T is set as P_0. To ensure that all of the ground nodes have as equal charging chance as possible, maximizing the minimum power harvested by K nodes is considered via allocating the transmit power and optimizing the UAV's trajectory. To deal with the objective function and constraints more conveniently, we introduce auxiliary variables E, which denotes the minimum value of energy harvested by K nodes in charging duration T, denoted as $E = \min E_k, \forall k \in \mathcal{K}$. Mathematically, the investigated problem can be formulated as follows:

$$\max_{\{x_U[n], y_U[n], P_k[n]\}, E} E \tag{6a}$$

$$s.t. \sum_{n=1}^{N} \frac{\eta \beta_0 \delta_t P_k[n]}{\left(\sqrt{(x_U[n] - x_k[n])^2 + (y_U[n] - y_k[n])^2 + H^2}\right)^\alpha} \geq E, \forall k \in \mathcal{K} \tag{6b}$$

$$P_k[n] \geq 0, \forall k \in \mathcal{K}, n \in \mathcal{N} \tag{6c}$$

$$\sum_{n=1}^{N} P_k[n] \leq P_0, \forall k \in \mathcal{K} \tag{6d}$$

$$(x_U[1] - x_0)^2 + (y_U[1] - y_0)^2 \leq (V_{\max}\delta_t)^2 \tag{6e}$$

$$(x_U[n] - x_U[n-1])^2$$
$$+ (y_U[n] - y_U[n-1])^2 \leq (V_{\max}\delta_t)^2, n = 2, 3, ..., N-1 \tag{6f}$$

$$(x_F - x_U[N-1])^2 + (y_F - y_U[\dot{N}-1])^2 \leq (V_{\max}\delta_t)^2 \tag{6g}$$

From constraints above, we can see constraints (6c) (6d) represent the power budget and constraints (6e)–(6g) ensure UAV's location limited by its speed. This is a non-convex optimization problem due to involving the dual optimization of both transmit power and trajectory, which is difficult to be solved with standard convex optimization techniques.

3   Joint Transmit Power and Trajectory Optimization

Through observation, the optimization problem aforementioned is convex about the transmit power with given the UAV's trajectory, but non-convex about the UAV's trajectory with given transmit power. Moreover, a lower bound of $E_k[n]$ can be found with the given transmit power. Therefore, two subproblems are first investigated: Transmit power optimization with given trajectory and trajectory optimization with given transmit power. Afterwards, a joint transmit power allocation and trajectory optimization algorithm is designed.

3.1   Transmit Power Optimization with Given Trajectory

It applies to scenarios where the UAV takes on some prearranged missions or services, such as surveillance or cargo transportation along a fixed route. Thus, the trajectory is given in this case. With given trajectory, the transmit power allocation problem in which $\xi = \eta \beta_0 \delta_t$ is given as follows:

$$\max_{\{P_k[n]\}, E} E \tag{7a}$$

$$s.t.\xi \sum_{n=1}^{N} \frac{P_k\,[n]}{\left(\sqrt{\left(x_U\,[n] - x_k\,[n]\right)^2 + \left(y_U\,[n] - y_k\,[n]\right)^2 + H^2}\right)^{\alpha}} \geq E, \forall k \in \mathcal{K} \quad (7b)$$

$$P_k\,[n] \geq 0, \forall k \in \mathcal{K}, n \in \mathcal{N} \quad (7c)$$

$$\sum_{n=1}^{N} P_k\,[n] \leq P_0, \forall k \in \mathcal{K} \quad (7d)$$

Expression above is a standard convex optimization problem, so some existing algorithms can be used directly, such as the interior point method [7].

3.2 Trajectory Optimization with Given Transmit Power

Due to some certain UAVs' hardware limitations, the UAV's transmit power is divided equally during the whole charging duration, denoted by $\frac{P_0}{N}$ at each slot. With given transmit power $P_k\,[n]$, the trajectory optimization problem can be reformulated as follows:

$$\max_{\{X_U[n],\,Y_U[n]\},\,E} E \quad (8a)$$

$$s.t.\xi \frac{P_0}{N} \sum_{n=1}^{N} \frac{1}{\left(\sqrt{\left(x_U\,[n] - x_k\,[n]\right)^2 + \left(y_U\,[n] - y_k\,[n]\right)^2 + H^2}\right)^{\alpha}} \geq E, k \in \mathcal{K}$$
$$(8b)$$

$$(x_U\,[1] - x_0)^2 + (y_U\,[1] - y_0)^2 \leq (V_{\max}\delta_t)^2 \quad (8c)$$

$$(x_U\,[n] - x_U\,[n-1])^2 + (y_U\,[n] - y_U\,[n-1])^2 \leq (V_{\max}\delta_t)^2, n = 2,3,...,N-1$$
$$(8d)$$

$$(x_F - x_U\,[N-1])^2 + (y_F - y_U\,[N-1])^2 \leq (V_{\max}\delta_t)^2 \quad (8e)$$

Now, for the sake of analyzing the concavity and convexity of the problem, we denote the location of mobile nodes on the ground as $w_k\,[n] = (x_k\,[n], y_k\,[n])$. The trajectory of UAV projected onto the horizontal plane is $q\,[n] = (x_U\,[n], y_U\,[n])$. Then we assume that $\varphi = \|q\,[n] - w_k\,[n]\|^2$ and

$$f\,(\varphi) = \left(\varphi + H^2\right)^{-\frac{\alpha}{2}}, \quad (9)$$

so constraint (8b) is transformed into

$$\xi \sum_{n=1}^{N} \frac{P_0}{N} f\,(\varphi) \geq E. \quad (10)$$

The first-order derivative and second-class derivative of $f\,(\varphi)$ is $\nabla f\,(\varphi) = -\frac{\alpha}{2}\left(\varphi + H^2\right)^{-\frac{\alpha}{2}-1} \leq 0$ and $\nabla^2 f\,(\varphi) = \frac{\alpha}{2}\left(\frac{\alpha}{2} + 1\right)\left(\varphi + H^2\right)^{-\frac{\alpha}{2}-2} \geq 0$, respectively. Although $f\,(\varphi)$ is a convex function, but constraint (8b) is a non-convex set. By using the first-order Taylor expansion, we obtain the lower bound $f_{lb}(\varphi)$ for $f(\varphi)$, $f(\varphi) \geq f_{lb}(\varphi) = f(\varphi^{(i)}) + \nabla f(\varphi^{(i)})(\varphi - \varphi^{(i)})$. Last constraint (8b) is transformed into

$$\xi \frac{P_0}{N} \sum_{n=1}^{N} \left[f\left(\varphi^{(i)}\right) + \nabla f\left(\varphi^{(i)}\right)\left(\varphi - \varphi^{(i)}\right) \right] \geq E, \tag{11}$$

and it is a convex set. To this end, based on (8c)–(8e), an efficient algorithm is developed by iteratively optimizing the objective with the lower bound of constraint (8b). Denote $\{x_U{}^i[n], y_U^i[n]\}$ as the trajectory at i-th iteration, then the trajectory at $i+1$-th iteration is given by $\{x_U{}^{i+1}[n], y_U^{i+1}[n]\}$ with $x_U[n] = x_U^i[n] + \Delta_{x_U}^i[n]$ and $y_U[n] = y_U^i[n] + \Delta_{y_U}^i[n]$. $\Delta_{x_U}^i[n]$ and $\Delta_{y_U}^i[n]$ are the increments at i-th iteration. Thus,

$$r_{k,n}^{i+1} = \left((x_U[n] - x_k[n])^2 + (y_U[n] - y_k[n])^2 + H^2 \right)^{-\frac{\alpha}{2}}$$
$$= \left(d_{k,n}^i + f\left(\{\Delta_x^i[n], \Delta_y^i[n]\}\right) \right)^{-\frac{\alpha}{2}} \tag{12}$$

where

$$d_{k,n}^i = \left(x_U^i[n] - x_k[n] \right)^2 + \left(y_U^i[n] - y_k[n] \right)^2 + H^2,$$
$$f\left(\{\Delta_{x_U}^i[n], \Delta_{y_U}^i[n]\}\right)$$
$$= \left(\Delta_{x_U}^i[n] \right)^2 + \left(\Delta_{y_U}^i[n] \right)^2 + 2\left(x_U^i[n] - x_k[n] \right) \Delta_{x_U}^i[n]$$
$$+ 2\left(y_U^i[n] - y_k[n] \right) \Delta_{y_U}^i[n] \tag{13}$$

Since function $(a + x)^{-\alpha}$ is convex, there is

$$(a + x)^{-\frac{\alpha}{2}} \geq a^{-\frac{\alpha}{2}} - \frac{\alpha}{2} a^{-\frac{\alpha}{2}-1} x, \tag{14}$$

which results from the first order condition of convex functions. Based on the inequality (14), we have [8,9]

$$r_{k,n}^{i+1} \geq lbr_{k,n}^{i+1} = \left(d_{k,n}^i \right)^{-\frac{\alpha}{2}} - \frac{\alpha}{2} \left(d_{k,n}^i \right)^{-\frac{\alpha}{2}-1} f\left(\{\Delta_{x_U}^i[n], \Delta_{y_U}^i[n]\}\right) \tag{15}$$

Given the trajectory $\{x_U{}^i[n], y_U^i[n]\}$ at i-th iteration, the trajectory $\{x_U{}^{i+1}[n], y_U^{i+1}[n]\}$ at $i+1$-th iteration can be obtained by solving the following optimization problem.

$$\max_{\{\Delta_{x_U}^i[n], \Delta_{y_U}^i[n]\}, E} E \tag{16a}$$

$$s.t. \xi \frac{P_0}{K} \sum_{n=1}^{N} lbr_{k,n}^{i+1} \geq E, \, k \in \mathcal{K} \tag{16b}$$

$$\left(x_U^i[1] + \Delta_{x_U}^i[1] - x_0 \right)^2 + \left(y_U^i[1] + \Delta_{y_U}^i[1] - y_0 \right)^2 \leq (V_{\max}\delta_t)^2 \tag{16c}$$

Algorithm 1. Joint transmit power and trajectory optimization

1: Initialize the UAV's trajectory $\{x_U[n], y_U[n]\}^l$ and iteration number $l = 0$
2: **Repeat**
3:    Solve the problem (7a-7d) with given trajectory $\{x_U[n], y_U[n]\}^l$ by standard convex optimization techniques
4:    Update the transmit power $\{P_k[n]\}^{l+1}$ and minimum power harvested E^{l+1}
5:    **Repeat**
6:       Solve the problem (16a-16e) with given transmit power $\{P_k[n]\}^{l+1}$ and get the optimal solution $\{\Delta_{X_U}^i[n], \Delta_{Y_U}^i[n]\}$ at the i-th iteration
7:       Update the trajectory $x_U[n] = x_U^i[n] + \Delta_{x_U}^i[n]$ and $y_U[n] = y_U^i[n] + \Delta_{y_U}^i[n]$
8:    **Until** $E^{i+1} - E^i \leq \varepsilon$
9:    Update the trajectory $\{x_U[n], y_U[n]\}^{l+1} = \{x_U[n], y_U[n]\}^i$
10: **Until** $E^{l+1} - E^l \leq \varepsilon$
11: Return the trajectory $\{x_U{}^*[n], y_U{}^*[n]\}$ and transmit power $\{P_k^*[n]\}$

$$\left(x_U^i[n] + \Delta_{x_U}^i[n] - x_U^i[n-1] - \Delta_{y_U}^i[n-1]\right)^2$$
$$+\left(y_U^i[n] + y_U^i[n] - y_U^i[n-1] - y_U^i[n-1]\right)^2 \leq (V_{\max}\delta_t)^2, \; n = 2, ..., N-1 \tag{16d}$$

$$\left(x_F - x_U^i[N-1] - \Delta_{x_U}^i[N-1]\right)^2$$
$$+ \left(y_F - y_U^i[N-1] - \Delta_{y_U}^i[N-1]\right)^2 \leq (V_{\max}\delta_t)^2 \tag{16e}$$

which is a convex optimization problem and can be solved by using standard convex optimization techniques. Since the optimization variables are the increments at each iteration, a series of non-decreasing values can be obtained. On the other hand, these values must be upper bounded by the optimal solution to the problem.

3.3   Joint Transmit Power and Trajectory Optimization

Since the investigated joint trajectory optimization and power allocation problem is non-convex, finding the global optimal solution is extremely difficult [10]. Therefore, it is desirable to reach a suboptimal solution with an acceptable complexity. Based on the results in Sects. 3.1 and 3.2, an efficient algorithm that can gain suboptimal solution is designed. Since lower bounds are used to obtain a sequence of non-decreasing solutions, global optimality cannot be guaranteed for our proposed algorithm. As shown in Algorithm 1, the key idea of the proposed algorithm is to alternately optimize the transmit power and the trajectory. In each iteration, the main complexity of the proposed algorithm lies in the steps 3 and 6, which demands to solve a series of convex problems.

4   Simulations and Discussions

This paper studied a two-mobile-users UAV-enabled WPT system. We have investigated the maximization of the minimum power harvested by the nodes on the ground which subjects to limited energy budget and flying speed limit of the UAV. In this section, simulations are implemented to demonstrate the superiority of the proposed algorithm. We consider that $20 \times 20 \, \mathrm{m}^2$ area where a UAV broadcasts wireless energy for two mobile nodes on the ground. The two nodes have their own moving path, expressed by case I and case II respectively. Without loss of generality, the time slot length is chosen to be $\delta_t = 1\,\mathrm{s}$ and thus the number of discrete points is $N = 30$. The channel power gain at $d_0 = 1\,\mathrm{m}$ is $\beta_0 = 10^{-3}$. Other system parameters are as follows $H = 5\,\mathrm{m}$, $V_{\max} = 1\,\mathrm{m/s}$, $T = 30\,\mathrm{s}$, $P_0 = 5\,\mathrm{W}$, $\varepsilon = 0.01$. The initial locations and final locations of the UAV are both $(0, 10, 0)$ and $(20, 10, 0)$ respectively in two cases. For the benchmark, we consider the scenario that the UAV flies from the initial location to the final location along a straight line at a constant speed.

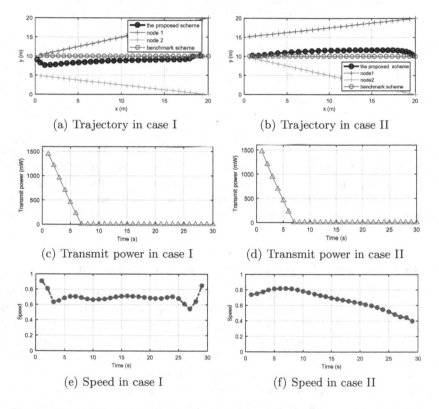

(a) Trajectory in case I

(b) Trajectory in case II

(c) Transmit power in case I

(d) Transmit power in case II

(e) Speed in case I

(f) Speed in case II

Fig. 1. The UAV's trajectory, transmit power and speed in considered scenes.

This trajectory is also used as the initial trajectory for the Algorithm 1. Figure 1 presents the UAV's trajectory, transmit power and speed in two cases. It can be observed from Fig. 1(a) and (b), the optimized trajectory approaches the more distant node in the beginning gradually in both cases. Under the circumstances, because the two nodes move without a break, so the UAV has to

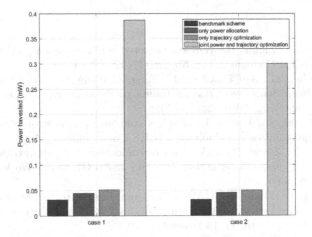

Fig. 2. Power harvested comparison in four conditions.

chase them ceaselessly, as shown in Fig. 1(e) and (f), which means the UAV will follow ground mobile nodes. Moreover, it can be observed from Fig. 1(c) and (d) that the transmit power is tightly related to the distance between the UAV and the nodes, which also signifies the necessity of joint transmit power allocation and trajectory optimization. The transmit power for the nodes in two cases is almost released at the beginning of the flight period. This is because the UAV is closer to the nodes in the beginning. The transmit power will be higher when the UAV approaches the nodes, which means better channel state. Conversely, when the UAV is away from the nodes, the corresponding transmit power becomes lower. To evaluate the performance of the proposed algorithm, four conditions are all investigated in two cases as shown in Fig. 2. It is observed that the proposed algorithm outperforms the benchmark, only power allocation and only trajectory optimization method. The main reason is that the optimized trajectory provides better channel quality and the proposed algorithm focuses most of the power on time slots with the best channel qualities.

5   Conclusion

In this paper, transmit power allocation and trajectory optimization problem for UAV-enabled mobile users WPTS was investigated, in which a UAV acting as a mobile energy transmitter (ET) transfers wireless energy for mobile nodes on the ground. The UAV's trajectory and transmit power are jointly optimized to achieve max-min power quantity. Simulation results validated the validity of the proposed algorithm. Furthermore, on the basis of the obtained results, we have found that the UAV tends to fly close to each node, and distribute power to the nodes with the best channel link at each time slot.

References

1. Bi, S., Ho, C.K., Zhang, R.: Wireless powered communication: opportunities and challenges. IEEE Commun. Mag. **53**(4), 117–125 (2015)
2. Wang, H., Ding, G., Gao, F., Chen, J., Wang, J., Wang, L.: Power control in UAV-supported ultra dense networks: communications, caching, and energy transfer. IEEE Commun. Mag. **56**(6), 28–34 (2018)
3. Zeng, Y., Zhang, R., Lim, T.J.: Wireless communications with unmanned aerial vehicles: opportunities and challenges. IEEE Commun. Mag. **54**(5), 36–42 (2016)
4. Xu, J., Zeng, Y., Zhang, R.: UAV-enabled wireless power transfer: trajectory design and energy region characterization. In: 2017 IEEE Globecom Workshops, Singapore, 4–8 December 2017
5. Xu, J., Zeng, Y., Zhang, R.: UAV-enabled multiuser wireless power transfer: trajectory design and energy optimization. In: 2017 23rd Asia-Pacific Conference on Communications, Perth, 11–13 December 2017
6. Wang, H., Ren, G., Chen, J., Ding, G., Yang, Y.: Unmanned aerial vehicle-aided communications: joint transmit power and trajectory optimization. IEEE Wirel. Commun. Lett. **7**(4), 522–525 (2018)
7. Wang, S., Huang, F., Zhou, Z.-H.: Fast power allocation algorithm for cognitive radio networks. IEEE Commun. Lett. **15**(8), 845–847 (2011)
8. Zeng, Y., Zhang, R., Lim, T.J.: Throughput maximization for UAV-enabled mobile relaying systems. IEEE Trans. Commun. **64**(12), 4983–4996 (2016)
9. Zeng, Y., Zhang, R.: Energy-efficient UAV communication with trajectory optimization. IEEE Trans. Wirel. Commun. **16**(6), 3747–3760 (2017)
10. Boyd, S., Vandenberghe, L.: Convex Optimization. Cambridge University Press, Cambridge (2004)

Manufacturing-Oriented Network Collaboration 3D Mechanical Components Rapid Design Technology

Yunsheng Chen[✉]

Mechatronics and Automatic Chemistry Department,
Guangzhou Huali Science and Technology Vocational College,
Zengcheng District, Guangzhou 511325, China
chenl2yunsheng@sina.com

Abstract. Traditional design method of 3 d mechanical parts to complete the design of mechanical parts, but lack of existing design cycle is long, not suitable for mechanical three-dimensional rapid design of the parts and components for manufacturing oriented network collaborative 3 d mechanical parts rapid design technology. Using three-dimensional mechanical parts the construction of the collaborative design platform, and the determination of network collaborative design principle based on the establishment of network collaborative design data transfer mode to complete network collaborative construction of three-dimensional mechanical model of rapid design components; Web-based collaborative design task decomposition, and the conflict of network collaborative design solutions, relying on the online conflict detection, access control, ORG connecting key technology to realize network collaborative 3 d mechanical parts rapid design. Experimental data show that the proposed rapid design technology compared with traditional design, shorten the design cycle by 84.41%, at the same time to ensure accuracy, good design is suitable for mechanical 3 d parts of rapid design.

Keywords: Network collaboration · 3d design · Mechanical parts ·
Rapid design technology

Traditional three-dimensional mechanical parts design methods can complete the design of mechanical parts, but there are deficiencies in the long design cycle, resulting in low design efficiency, difficult to apply high-efficiency enterprises, not suitable for the rapid design of mechanical three-dimensional parts [1], This proposes a manufacturing-oriented, network-based, collaborative 3D mechanical component rapid design technology. By using logical layer design, engine service layer design, and support layer design, a 3D mechanical parts collaborative design network platform is established to determine the principles of network collaborative design. Relying on the establishment of a network collaborative design data transfer mode, a network collaborative 3D mechanical component rapid design model is completed. Construction; based on the decomposition of network collaborative design tasks, and the solution to network collaborative design conflicts, relying on online conflict detection, access control, ORG connection key technologies, complete the proposed manufacturing-oriented network

S. Liu and G. Yang (Eds.): ADHIP 2018, LNICST 279, pp. 297–305, 2019.
https://doi.org/10.1007/978-3-030-19086-6_33

collaboration 3D mechanical parts rapid design technology. In order to ensure the effectiveness of the designed three-dimensional mechanical part design method, the mechanical design test environment was simulated to use two different three-dimensional mechanical parts design methods to carry out the design cycle simulation test. The experimental results show that the three-dimensional mechanical part design method is proposed High effectiveness.

1   System Objectives and Analysis

Manufacturing-oriented network collaboration 3D mechanical components rapid design technology mainly includes:

Using network coordination to replace the traditional design pattern of one person or several people, through the decomposition of the tasks of three-dimensional mechanical parts, relying on the collaborative network platform for design, the original workload of a dozen days was reduced to more than a dozen people a day's workload.

Constructing the principle of network collaborative design is to make designers design within the framework of collaborative design constraints, reduce design conflicts, and resolve the design conflicts through online detection.

Set up a network cooperation design data transmission mechanism to ensure the accuracy of data transmission for the collaborative design of 3D mechanical parts, and use online conflict detection, access control, and ORG connection key technologies to realize the rapid design of network collaborative 3D mechanical parts.

2   Constructing a Network Collaboration 3d Mechanical Component Quick Design Model

2.1   Build a Three-Dimensional Collaborative Design Network Platform for Mechanical Parts

The three-dimensional collaborative design of mechanical components network platform is an operating platform for rapid design models to ensure the smooth flow of collaborative information exchange. The establishment of a network collaborative design platform mainly includes three aspects: logical layer design, engine service layer design, and support layer design.

The logical layer design mainly consists of message system components, agent work components, resource cooperation components, event discussion components, and announcement release components. The use of system bus and engine service layer interconnection [2]. The engine service layer design mainly includes data flow engine, message flow engine, workflow engine, search engine, knowledge reasoning engine, sharing service, integration service, management service, and security service. Using integrated design, relying on the support layer of the operating system, database systems, network services, infrastructure platforms, transmission protocols to ensure the smooth flow of collaborative information exchange, successfully set up a network collaborative design platform.

2.2 Determining Principles of 3D Network Cooperative Design for Mechanical Parts

The three-dimensional network collaborative design of mechanical parts is to divide a whole three-dimensional mechanical parts into several units by means of decomposition. Different designers design the three-dimensional mechanical parts that are decomposed and finally assembled. Due to the fact that there is a large number of decompositions and it is easy to cause confusion in assembly, it is particularly critical to formulate principles for network collaborative design [3].

The principle of 3D network collaborative design of mechanical parts is based on the decomposition of the 3D network collaborative design task, naming the single 3D mechanical part unit that is decomposed, and using the key technology of network collaborative design to make the process principle of the 3D mechanical parts assembled quickly and automatically. The following takes T-shaped three-dimensional mechanical parts as an example to analyze the naming principles of 3D network collaborative design for mechanical parts. The naming principle is as follows:

Firstly, the origin of the three-dimensional coordinates of the T-shaped three-dimensional mechanical parts is constructed, the origin is set to O, and the origin is the graphic center of the designed three-dimensional mechanical parts. Then determine the three-dimensional coordinate orientation of the T-shaped three-dimensional mechanical part, and define the task of the collaborative design as the XY plane, and the positive direction is the Z-axis. Second, determine the unit distance of the three-dimensional coordinates of the T-shaped three-dimensional mechanical part, and finally encode the three-dimensional coordinate sequence according to the (O, X, Y, Z) display of the three-dimensional coordinates. The coding diagram of the T-shaped three-dimensional mechanical component unit is shown in Fig. 1(a). The assembly of the three-dimensional mechanical component unit code is shown in Fig. 1(b).

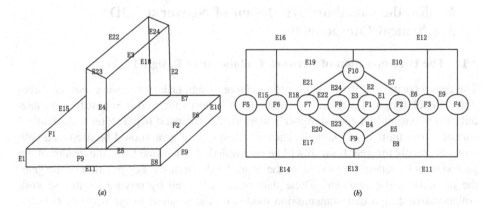

(a)   *(b)*

Fig. 1. Schematic diagram of assembly of T-shaped three-dimensional mechanical components

2.3   Establishing a Network Cooperative Design Data Delivery Model

The collaborative design data transfer of 3D mechanical parts is a conversation plat-form for ensuring technical exchanges between design and technical collaboration. The user side includes the session layer, message layer, and data layer for the extraction, compilation, and transmission of collaborative data. Transfer of data using STEP standards, based on XML converters, relying on TCP/IP protocol for data transfer [3]. Its network collaborative design data transfer mode process is shown in Fig. 2

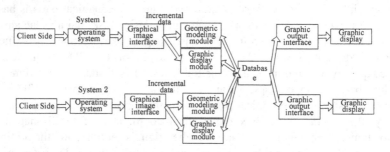

Fig. 2. Network cooperative design data transfer mode process

Relying on the establishment of a three-dimensional collaborative design network platform for mechanical parts, the principle of 3D network collaborative design for mechanical parts was determined, and a network collaborative design data transmission model was established to realize the construction of a network collaborative 3D mechanical parts rapid design model.

3   Realize the Collaborative Design of Networked 3D Mechanical Components

3.1   The Decomposition of Network Collaborative Design Tasks

The decomposition of the network collaborative design task is to ensure that the three-dimensional design of mechanical components is best split, and it is best to assemble, but also to ensure that each designer's workload is balanced [4]. Taking a mechanical part of a gear train as an example, each smallest unit of gear should be used as a split unit, and finally the gear train should be assembled. At the same time, the design of the gear system considers the module of the gear, the depth of the key position of the gear, the involute of the gear, etc. These data must be solved by relying on the network collaborative design data transmission mode and the solution to the network collabo-rative design conflict. Set a mechanical component as S, which is composed of n units of mechanical minimum units, i.e., do $S1$, $S2$, …, Sn, then build the decomposition function of the network collaborative design task as shown in Eq. 1.

$$k = \frac{\sum K_o + (R_k/S_{x,k})}{\sum (K_o + \Delta G_j)} \tag{1}$$

In the formula, K0 represents the design element, Rk represents the number of designers, Sx,k represents the organization capability, ΔGj represents the designed Bridgeman coefficient, its Bridgeman coefficient mainly depends on the design degree of difficulty, and the Bridgeman coefficient can be expressed by formula 2.

$$\Delta G_j = \sigma_o \gamma_i + \frac{\partial^2 q_k dx}{h_i} \tag{2}$$

In the formula, σ0 represents the minimum unit surface area of the three-dimensional mechanical design, qk represents the three-dimensional design degree of difficulty, and hi represents the three-dimensional design dynamic range.

3.2 Network Cooperative Design Conflict Resolution

The disadvantage of network co-design is the use of non-individual design solutions, but the use of multiple people to design solutions. When multiple people design at the same time, there may be a design conflict, resulting in the design of three-dimensional mechanical parts can not be assembled, there are many reasons for the design conflict. In order to solve the conflict of network collaborative design reasonably, the conflicts caused by different aspects are attributed to three types. The first type is the reason for the conflict parameters, the second round is the degree of conflict manifestation, and the third is the scope of conflict. Using three sets of conflict resolution process to resolve conflicts arising from the design parameters of many people [5].

The reasons for the first type of conflict parameters are mainly summarized in the following ten aspects: that is, different design goals, poor information flow, unreasonable resource allocation, and different evaluation criteria, different knowledge representation systems, unreasonable role assignments, different evaluation objectives, and interrelational constraints, as well as unreasonable resource allocation. Based on the above reasons, relying on the principle of collaborative design of three-dimensional networks of mechanical parts, the conflict parameter constraint equations are constructed so that the design objects, designers, and design software are within constraint equations, restricting the authority of the designer [6] and making reasonable design within the authority. Its conflict parameter constraint equation can be expressed by the following formula:

$$\begin{cases} D_a = \dfrac{\partial(q * w)dx + \partial(e)dx}{\|\partial(r+t) + \partial(y)\|dx} + \|\partial(u)dx\| \\[3mm] D_b = \dfrac{\partial(o * i)dx + \partial(u * y)dx}{\|\partial(t+r) + \partial(e)\|dx} + \|\partial(w)dx\| \end{cases} \tag{3}$$

In the formula, q represents different design goals, w represents poor information flow, e represents irrational resource allocation, r represents different evaluation criteria, t represents different knowledge representation systems, y represents unreasonable role assignment, u represents different evaluation goals, i represents mutual constraints, and o represents different resource allocations. If the design of three-dimensional mechanical components is $E1 \sim F12$, then according to the constraint equation D, the $E1 \sim F12$ constraint set $D = \{D_{E1}, D_{E2}..., D_{F12}\}$ is obtained. Its design objects, designers, and design software run in a constraint set D.

The degree of manifestation of the second type of conflict is mainly divided into the conflict of display and divergence, and is different from that of the first type of conflict, the extent of the appearance of the second type of conflict and the scope of the third type of conflict are technical conflicts. Therefore, technical solutions are adopted. Firstly, online conflict detection technology is used to check the cause of the conflict and adjust the conflict accordingly. Its online conflict detection technology is one of the key technologies for network collaborative design [7]. The degree of manifestation of the second type of conflict and the third type of conflict relied on online conflict detection technology to determine the elements involved in the conflict. Based on the design rules, the conflict was analyzed using the backtracking method, and parallelism and coupling were used to eliminate conflicts.

3.3   Network Cooperative Design Key Technologies

The key technologies of network collaborative design mainly include online conflict detection technology, access control technology, and ORG connection technology. The online conflict detection technology mainly discriminates between the second type and the third type of network collaborative design. Among them, online conflict detection technology mainly includes four kinds of detection technology based on Petri net, true value detection technology, constraint satisfaction-based detection technology, and heuristic-based detection technology. Due to the complexity of the causes of the conflict, four methods of joint detection are used for this purpose. Through the backtracking method to analyze the conflict, using the parallel and coupled way to eliminate the conflict [8].

Access control technology is a control technology that enables design agents, process agents, and management agents to communicate with each other through the Internet under the secure network cooperative operation. In order to ensure the security of the network collaborative design, the design agent, process agent, and management agent are subject to authentication management, certification management components, and authentication application components to complete the composition and supervision of the certification [9]. Password authentication component is used to supervise the design of Agent, process agent and management agent. The authentication management component mainly includes access rights handling for user groups, dynamic protocol processing, interaction description, and authorization processing. For the design of communication between departments, communication between management departments, and communication between process departments to provide network coordination communication security [10].

ORG connection technology is the core technology of network communication technology. Relying on HTTP protocol, ORB protocol performs data communication on web browsers of different objects, and synchronous system design tools for network co-design, asynchronous collaborative design tools, and message managers. ORG connection technology includes PDM database, ERP database, and call message database. Relying on J2EE server to achieve data communication, data communication structure shown in Fig. 3

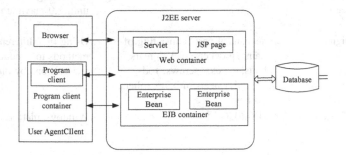

Fig. 3. Data communication structure

Based on the construction of network collaborative 3D mechanical components rapid design model, the use of network collaborative design task decomposition, reliance on network collaborative design conflict resolution methods, online conflict detection, access control, ORG connection key technologies, realize the rapid design of network collaboration 3D mechanical components.

4 Test and Analysis

In order to ensure the effectiveness of the manufacturing-oriented network collaborative 3D mechanical component rapid design technology proposed in this paper, simulation experiments were conducted. During the test process, different design mechanical components were used as test objects to conduct design cycle simulation tests. Different types of structures for designing mechanical components, as well as degree of difficulty, are simulated. In order to ensure the validity of the test, the traditional three-dimensional mechanical part design method was used as a comparison object. The results of the two simulation simulation experiments were compared and the test data was presented in the same data chart.

4.1 Test Preparation

In order to ensure the accuracy of the simulation test process, the test parameters of the test are set. This paper simulates the test process, uses different design mechanical parts as test objects, uses two different three-dimensional mechanical parts design methods, carries out the design cycle simulation test, and analyzes the simulation test results. Because the analysis results obtained in different methods are different from the analysis methods, the test environment parameters must be consistent during the test. The test data set results in this paper are shown in Table 1.

Table 1. Test parameter settings

Simulation test parameters	Execution range/parameter	Note
Three-dimensional mechanical parts design degree of difficulty	SL0.1～SL1.6	SL three-dimensional design degree of difficulty unit, 2.0 maximum
Analog Design Mechanical Components	Mechanical parts consisting of chain, sprockets, racks, gears, shafts, chucks, screws, rods, cams, flywheels, mixing rollers, and keys	Using two different design methods to conduct design analysis one by one
Simulation System	DJX-2016-3.5	Windows platform

4.2   Tests and Results Analysis

During the test process, two different three-dimensional mechanical parts design methods were used to work in a simulated environment and the changes in the design cycle were analyzed. At the same time, due to the use of two different three-dimensional mechanical parts design methods, the analysis results cannot be compared directly. For this purpose, third-party analysis and recording software is used to record and analyze the test process and results, the results are shown in the curve of the comparison results of this experiment. In the simulation test result curve, the third-party analysis and recording software function is used to eliminate the uncertainty caused by the simulation laboratory personnel operation and simulation of computer equipment factors, and only for different design mechanical parts and different three-dimensional mechanical parts design methods. Perform a design cycle simulation test. The comparison curve of the test results is shown in Fig. 4, where a is the traditional 3D mechanical part design method and b is the 3D mechanical part design method. According to the results of the test curve, the third-party analysis and recording software was used to arithmetically weight the design cycle of the proposed three-dimensional mechanical part design

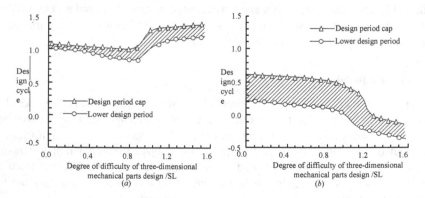

Fig. 4. Comparison of test results

method and the traditional three-dimensional mechanical part design method, and the proposed rapid design technology was compared with the traditional design, the design cycle is shortened by 84.41%. At the same time, it can guarantee a good design accuracy and is suitable for the rapid design of mechanical three-dimensional parts.

5 Conclusion

This paper proposes a manufacturing-oriented network collaboration 3D mechanical parts rapid design technology, based on the construction of a network collaborative 3D mechanical parts rapid design model, as well as the decomposition and conflict handling of network collaborative design tasks, using the key technologies of network collaborative design to achieve the research of this paper. The experimental data shows that the method designed in this paper has extremely high effectiveness. It is hoped that the study of this paper can provide a theoretical basis for the design method of three-dimensional mechanical parts.

References

1. Fan, Y., Liu, C., Wu, H., et al.: Full-scale 3D model-driven complex product intelligent manufacturing. Comput. Integr. Manuf. Syst. 23(6), 1176–1186 (2017)
2. Lai, X., Yang, Z., Xia, R., et al.: Research on remote two-way cooperative manufacturing system of mining machinery parts and components. Min. Res. Dev. 1, 109–112 (2018)
3. Huang, L., Zeng, H., Chen, P.: A three-dimensional point-to-point hierarchical scheduling algorithm for power collaborative simulation design. China Rural Water Hydropower 2016(3), 171–174 (2016)
4. Li, Z., Zhang, F., Wuming, S., et al.: 3D cooperative design of civil 3D and infraworks in general map specialty. Oil Gas Storage Transp. 35(6), 648–652 (2016)
5. Lvbei, S., Wang, Z., Yang, X., et al.: Research on control technology of integration maturity for aircraft design and manufacturing. Mech. Des. Manufact. 12, 262–264 (2017)
6. Wu, M., Zhu, J., Yang, K., et al.: A collaborative optimization design method for precise deformation of piezoelectric smart structures. 49(2), 380–389 (2017)
7. Ping, M., Liang, S., Hui, L., et al.: Cooperative behavior pattern mining method based on dynamic supply chain network. Comput. Integr. Manufact. Syst. 22(2), 324–329 (2016)
8. Yang, Y., Linfu, S., Hua, M.: Multi-tenant form customization technology for industrial chain collaborative cloud service platform. Comput. Integr. Manufact. Syst. 22(9), 2235–2244 (2016)
9. Zhao, T., Cao, Z., Qiu, M.: Familiar production forecasting method for semiconductor production line based on MAS fuzzy coordination. Comput. Integr. Manufact. Syst. 23(4), 852–859 (2017)
10. Zeng, H., Liang, H., Chen, P.: Power collaborative simulation design method based on mixed reality technology. China Rural Water Hydropower 36(1), 158–160 (2016)

Parallel Implementation and Optimization of a Hybrid Data Assimilation Algorithm

Jingmei Li and Weifei Wu[(✉)]

College of Computer Science and Technology,
Harbin Engineering University, Harbin 150001, China
{lijingmei,wuweifei}@hrbeu.edu.cn

Abstract. Data assimilation plays a very important role in numerical weather forecasting, and data assimilation algorithms are the core of data assimilation. The objective function of common data assimilation algorithms currently has a large amount of calculation, which takes more time to solve, thereby causing the time cost of the assimilation process to affect the timeliness of the numerical weather forecast. Aiming at an excellent hybrid data assimilation algorithm-dimension reduction projection four-dimensional variational algorithm that has appeared in recent years, the paper uses the MPI parallel programming model for parallel implementation and optimization of the algorithm, and effectively solves the problem of large computational complexity of the objective function. This effectively not only reduces the solution time of the algorithm's objective function, but also ensures the effect of assimilation. Experiments show that the speedup of the paralleled and optimized algorithm is about 17, 26, and 32 on 32, 64, and 128 processors, and the average speedup is about 26.

Keywords: Parallel · MPI · Data assimilation · Optimization

1 Introduction

Numerical weather forecasting is one of the important applications of high performance computing. It is a technique that solves a set of partial differential equations that describe the physical evolution of the atmosphere under the initial conditions that meet the conditions, so as to achieve a forecast for weather phenomena in the future [1]. As a forecasting problem, the quality of the initial value largely determines the accuracy of the numerical weather prediction. In numerical weather forecast, data assimilation technology is a technology that provides initial values for numerical weather prediction. It integrates observation information from various sources into the initial values of numerical weather prediction models. Based on strict mathematical theory, an optimal solution of the model is found between the model solution and the actual observation. This optimal solution can be used as the initial value of the numerical weather forecasting model which can be continuously recycled so that the result of the model solution continuously converges to the actual atmospheric state value.

The original version of this chapter was revised: The correction in author's name has been incorporated. The correction to this chapter is available at https://doi.org/10.1007/978-3-030-19086-6_65

© ICST Institute for Computer Sciences, Social Informatics and Telecommunications Engineering 2019
Published by Springer Nature Switzerland AG 2019. All Rights Reserved
S. Liu and G. Yang (Eds.): ADHIP 2018, LNICST 279, pp. 306–314, 2019.
https://doi.org/10.1007/978-3-030-19086-6_34

The data assimilation algorithm is the core of data assimilation technology is. The objective function of the algorithm is usually a high-dimensional linear equation and calculation of the linear equations will be very large, so the solution of the objective function requires high-performance computer and parallel computing technology. The common data assimilation algorithms include variational algorithms (3Dvar and 4DVar), set Kalman filter algorithm (EnKF), and hybrid ensemble variational data assimilation algorithms based on the them [2, 3]. The hybrid ensemble variational data assimilation algorithm has advantages of variational algorithm and EnKF. Nowadays, many hybrid assimilation methods have emerged. The hybrid idea has become the trend of the data assimilation method. The research work of the world's top forecast centers is ongoing in this area. Among them, Dimension-Reduced Projection 4DVar (DRP4DVar) is an excellent hybrid assimilation algorithm. Compared with the commonly used algorithms, the DRP4DVar has the advantages of easy parallel implementation and small storage space. Therefore, the efficient implementation of the algorithm has gradually been concerned by researchers.

In this paper, through the analysis of DRP4DVar, the algorithm is paralleled and optimized by using MPI on the parallel computing platform, and an efficient implementation method of the object function standard solution of DRP4DVar algorithm is obtained. The structure of this paper is as follows: The 2 Section analyzes the serial implementation of DRP4DVar algorithm in detail, and then carries out parallel and optimization. The experiments are designed and the experimental results are analyzed in 3 Section. The 4 Section summaries the all work of the paper.

2 Analysis, Parallel Implementation and Optimization of DRP4DVar

2.1 Analysis and Implementation of DRP4DVar

Dimension-Reduced Projection 4Dvar (DRP4Dvar) is derived from the EnKF algorithm and the 4DVar algorithm. The principle of the algorithm is to use a set of vectors generated by a set of perturbation sets, and to perform the projection operation on the basis vectors of the analysis increments of the model. After the projection is completed, the solution of the objective function is transformed into the solution of the coefficients of the set of basis vectors, which completes the projection of the model space to the base vector [4, 5]. Because the dimension of the sample space is small, it will generally not exceed 10^2, so the objective function dimension of the algorithm will not exceed 10^2. Therefore, theoretically the solution size of the algorithm will not exceed 10^2, and because of the inherent parallelism of the ensemble, the algorithm has good parallel efficiency. The improved objective function of DRP4DVar is formula (1).

$$\begin{cases} J(w) = \dfrac{1}{2}\{w^T w + \dfrac{1}{2}[Y' - r_b w]^T O^{-1}[Y' - r_b w]\} \\ Y^o = (y_0^o, y_1^o, \dots, y_N^o)^T \\ F(x) = (H_0 \circ M_{t0->t1}(x), H_1 \circ M_{t0->t2}(x), \dots, H_n \circ M_{t0->tn}(x))^T \end{cases} \tag{1}$$

In formula (1), the pattern space contains n samples, and n samples are represented as vector $x = [x_1, x_2, \ldots\ldots, x_n]$, averaging all values of n samples to get x_b as background field, also called initial value. Y^o is an observation vector containing an assimilation time, and also known as an observation space vector. $F(x)$ is the vector of $H_0 \circ M_{t0->t1}(x)$ at each moment, also known as the analog observation vectors. H_i is the observation operator at time t_i, $M_{t0->ti}$ is the model forecast operator from t_0 forecast to t_i. O is the observation error covariance matrix. $w = [w_1, w_2, w_3, \ldots, w_n]^T$ is an n-dimensional coefficient vector. $Y' = Y^o - F(x_b)$.

The sample ensemble vectors minus the background field vectors, which yield a perturbed ensemble vectors in the pattern spaces:

$$b = [x', x', \ldots\ldots, x'] = [x_1 - x_b, x_2 - x_b, \ldots\ldots, x_n - x_b] \tag{2}$$

The perturbation vector δx can be expressed as a linear combination of column vectors of b:

$$\delta x = x - x_b = w_1 x_1' + w_2 x_2' + \ldots + w_n x_n' = bw \tag{3}$$

The perturbation ensemble of the observation space is formula (4):

$$r_b = [F(x_1) - F(x_b), F(x_2) - F(x_b), \ldots, F(x_n) - F(x_b)] \tag{4}$$

Gradient of the cost function in formula (1):

$$\Delta J(w) = w + r_b^T O^{-1}(r_b w - Y') \tag{5}$$

Let formula (5) equal to 0:

$$(I + r_b^T O^{-1} r_b)w = r_b^T Y' \tag{6}$$

Solving the formula (6) can get the value of w, substituting the value of w into the formula (3), and adding the δx to the background field x_b to get the optimal analysis value:

$$x_a = x_b + \delta x \tag{7}$$

The dimension of Eq. (6) is n, where n is the number of samples and does not exceed 10^2 at most. Therefore, the formula (6) has a small dimension and the solution is easy. However, similar to EnKF, the lack of sample will also result in insufficient estimation of the background error covariance matrix, which will result in inaccurate results. In order to alleviate the impact of insufficient samples, localization technology is also needed [6, 7]. The coefficient matrix obtained by localization of the observation space is py, the dimension is $my \times mb$, mb is the localized modal number, my is the number of observation points. The coefficient matrix obtained by localization of the model space is px, and the dimension is $mx \times mb$, mb is also the localized modal number, mx is the number of grid points in the horizontal direction.

py and r_b do Shure product to get r'_b, px and b do Shure product to get b'. Using r'_b instead of r_b, b' instead of b, in formula (3) and (6), we can get the following formulas:

$$\delta x = b'w \tag{8}$$

$$(I + (r'_b)^T O^{-1}(r'_b))w = r'^T_b Y' \tag{9}$$

$$(I + (\frac{r_b}{\sqrt{o}})'^T (\frac{r_b}{\sqrt{o}})')w = (\frac{r_b}{\sqrt{o}})'^T Y' \tag{10}$$

Solve Eq. (10) using the modified conjugate gradient algorithm and solve it strictly according to the mathematical formula. The detailed solution processes are as follows:

1. Given an initial value w_0, $d_0 = r^0$, computing $r_0 = b - Aw_0$.
2. Compute $\alpha^k = \ <r^k, d^k> \ / <d^k, Ad^k>$.
3. Compute $w_{k+1} = w_k + \alpha^k d_k$.
4. Compute $r^{k+1} = b - Aw_{k+1}$.
5. Judge whether w_{k+1} meets the requirements, and if it does, stop the calculation, otherwise, continue the subsequent steps.
6. Compute $\beta^k = -<r^{k+1}, Ad^k> \ / <d^k, Ad^k>$
7. Compute $d^{k+1} = r^{k+1} + \beta^k d_k$, return step 1 and continue.

However, localization must be added to reduce the influence of the false correlation of the estimated background error covariance matrix on the analysis results due to the lack of sample size. After localization, the dimensionality of the cost function formula (10) is on the order of 10^{10}. At this point, matrix A requires approximately 190 GB of storage space, which has exceeded the memory size of the most processors. Therefore, formula (10) cannot be calculated directly.

In order to solve the problem of matrix A storage difficulty, in view of the relatively powerful computing power of the processor, computing is cheaper than storage, so a serial implementation strategy is designed by exchanging computing for storage. The core idea of this strategy is: When the matrix A is used in the algorithm, the intermediate results that interact with A are processed first. The matrix A is not stored directly, that is, only the form of the matrix A is retained, and the specific matrix A is not stored. The strategy uses the processor's powerful computing power in exchange for storage of matrix A.

The core functions of formula (10) include: the grd function for calculating the residual, the ax function for calculating Ad^k, the function ddot3 for the vector dot multiplication operation, and the pybo operation function for calculating the right end vector. The parallel implementation of the algorithm is: the above conjugate gradient algorithm is solved on the root processor, and then the result is sent to all processors by utilizing the MPI communication function to perform formula (7) and (8) calculation.

The storage space required for the above objective function implementation of the DRP4DVar algorithm is greatly reduced, but it is less optimistic in the consumption time of the calculation, especially when running a large-scale case, the consumption time is longer, the real-time measurement under the high-resolution case about two hours or more. In order to shorten the calculation time of the DRP4DVar algorithm, optimization work is also required.

2.2 Optimization of DRP4DVar Algorithm

Based on the DRP4DVar algorithm in Sect. 2.1, in order to improve the computational efficiency of the algorithm and shorten the running time, the algorithm is optimized. After many tests, the function pybo, grd, and ax calculations take the most time, so the optimization work is done for them.

After analyzing the three functions, the loop operations are similar, and the number of loops is about $nn \times jpx \times jpy \times jpz \times myb$, where nn is the number of samples, and the maximum is no more than 10^2, jpx, jpy, and jpz are the number of localization coefficients in three directions of horizontal and vertical, respectively. The number of coefficients does not exceed 10^2. The parameter myb indicates that the number of observations is on the order of 10^5. Therefore, the loop magnitude is about 10^{11}. At present, the most processors have a frequency of 10^9, so each of these three operations requires at least 100 s. Therefore, the purpose of optimization is to reduce the size of the loop, which in turn will reduce the time-consumption.

The parallel implementation strategy in Sect. 2.2 is improved as follows:

(1) Filter the observation data according to the corresponding relationship with the background field and remove the abnormal observation points.
(2) In the root processor, observation data and background field data are divided in all processors according to geographic location information.
 3) The root processor uses the MPI sending policy to distribute the divided data to all processors, so that each processor is allocated a reasonable amount of data, avoiding the load imbalance on some processors. The improvement strategy reduces the computational size on each processor, thereby reducing computational time-consuming and improving the overall computational efficiency.

Through optimization operations, the time consumed by the DRP4DVar algorithm is theoretically reduced by an order of magnitude compared to the pre-optimization. Therefore, when calculating large-scale calculations, the time-consumption can also be the ideal range.

3   Experimental Design and Analysis of Results

To evaluate the benefit of the optimized DRP4DVar, we design many experiments. The experimental platform is a Linux cluster, which includes one login node and 16 computing nodes. Each compute node contains 2 physical CPU cores, and each physical CPU has 6 physical cores. Therefore, the test platform can provide up to 192 cores of computing resources. The detailed parameters of the computing node are shown in Table 1.

Table 1. Node parameters

Name	Parameters
CPU	Intel(R) Xeon(R) X5650@ 2.67 GHz
RAM	46 GB
Operating System	Red Hat Enterprise Linux Server release 6.3 (Santiago)
System kernel	2.6.32–279.el6.x86_64
C compiler	icc version 15.0.2
Fortran compiler	ifort version 15.0.2
MPI version	Intel(R) MPI Library 5.0

3.1 Experimental Design

In order to test the effect of the optimized DRP4DVar algorithm, two kinds of examples are designed: low-resolution case and high-resolution case. High-resolution case contains more data, low-resolution case contains less data. The cases can test the calculation efficiency under different calculations.

Case 1 is a low-resolution case where the simulation area is 129 * 70 horizontal grid points and 50 vertical layers. Case 2 is a high-resolution case where the simulation area is a horizontal grid point is 409 * 369, 29 vertical layers. In Case 1, the number of observations used for assimilation is 15729 and 2225 observations are used in Case 2. The number of observations will affect the solution time of the core conjugate gradient algorithm in the algorithm implementation, and the resolution will affect the calculation time of the initial value increment of the model. Two different kinds of experiments were set up according to two cases: low-resolution experiment and high-resolution experiment. Low-resolution experiment uses the algorithm before and after optimization to simulate case 1 under three parallel degrees on 32, 64, and 128 processors. High-resolution experiment uses the number of processors in three parallel degrees 32, 64, and 128, simulating algorithm before and after optimization for case 2.

The following information can be obtained by analyzing the results of two groups of experiments: Under low-resolution examples, the pre-optimization and post-optimization algorithms achieve time-contrast information under the same degree of parallelism. Similarly, under the high-resolution case. Under the same degree of parallelism, the time-consumption and results by the simulating case 1 and the case 2 are compared between the pre-optimization and post-optimization algorithms.

3.2 Results Analysis

For the two kinds of experimental conditions designed in Sect. 3.1, the experimental results were analyzed. The analysis includes the following two parts: the comparison of the results between before and after optimization, the comparison of consumption time between before and after optimization Therefore, this section is divided into correctness analysis and performance analysis.

(1) Correctness analysis

Figures 1 and 2 are incremental graphs of the four assimilation variables T, U, V and Q, respectively, in the serial implementation of the algorithm and the parallel implementation. It can be seen that the size of the increments of the four assimilation variables in the two results is exactly the same, and the form of the field of each variable is also the same. Therefore, the result of the algorithm optimization is exactly the same as the result before the optimization, so the result after the optimization is correct.

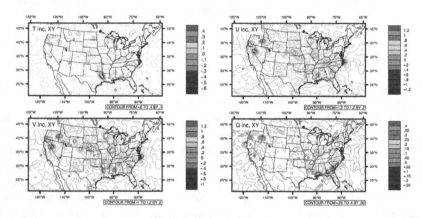

Fig. 1. Incremental graph of four assimilation variables by DRP4DVar serial implementation

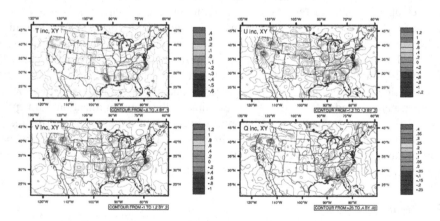

Fig. 2. Incremental graph of four assimilation variables by DRP4DVar parallel implementation

(2) Performance analysis

The first is a low-resolution case where 32, 64, and 128 processors are used to simulate case 1 respectively. Figure 3 is a comparison chart of the time consumed by running the calculation case 1 between pre-optimization and post-optimization of the algorithm.

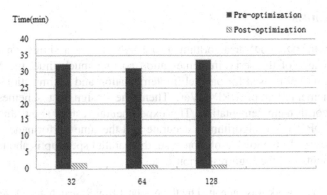

Fig. 3. Time-consumption of simulating case 1 between pre-optimization and post-optimization under three parallel degrees

From Fig. 3, it can be concluded that on the three processor numbers in case 1, the consumption time between pre-optimization and post-optimization has been significantly reduced.

On 32 processors, the time-consumption before optimization is about 18 times of post-optimization, on 64 processors the times is about 26 and on 128 processors the pre-optimization is about 33 times comparing with post-optimization.

Through analysis, it can be seen that the time of the optimized algorithm under the low-resolution case 1 is greatly reduced. Under the three types of processors, the optimized consumption time is about 1/26 of the time before the optimization, that is, the parallel speedup approximately reaches 26.

It can be concluded from Fig. 4 that in the case of the three processors, the consumption time before and after optimization is also significantly reduced. It can be seen from the analysis that the simulation time of the optimized algorithm in the high-resolution case 2 is reduced compared with the pre-optimization. Under the three processor numbers, the consumption time of post-optimization is about 1/4 of the pre-optimization. The speedup reaches about 4.

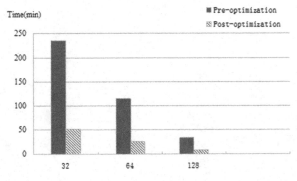

Fig. 4. Time-consumption of simulating case 2 between pre-optimization and post-optimization under three parallel degrees

4 Conclusions

In this paper, the DRP4DVar algorithm in the hybrid data assimilation algorithm is analyzed. Because of the serial implementation costing much time, the MPI parallel programming model is used for parallel implementation and optimization to obtain an efficient implementation of DRP4DVar. Then, the design test schemes verify the optimized algorithm implementation. The experimental results show that the implementation of DRP4DVar algorithm is accurate and the time performance of the algorithm is improved. In the low-resolution case, the parallel speedup is about 26, and the speedup is about 4 in the high-resolution case.

Acknowledge. This work was supported by the National Key Research and Development Plan of China under Grant No. 2016YFB0801004.

References

1. Miyoshi, T., Kondo, K., Terasaki, K.: Big ensemble data assimilation in numerical weather prediction. Computer **48**(11), 15–21 (2015)
2. Nerger, L., Hiller, W.: Software for ensemble-based data assimilation systems-Implementation strategies and scalability. Comput. Geosci. **55**(5), 110–118 (2013)
3. Ma, J., Qin, S.: The research status review of data assimilation algorithm. Adv. Earth Sci. **27**(7), 747–757 (2012)
4. Wang, B., Liu, J., Wang, S., Cheng, W., et al.: An economical approach to four-dimensional variational data assimilation. Adv. Atmos. Sci. **27**(4), 715–727 (2010)
5. Liu, J., Wang, B., Xiao, Q.: An evaluation study of the DRP-4-DVar approach with the Lorenz-96 model. Tellus Series A-Dyn. Meteorol. Oceanogr. **63**(2), 256–262 (2011)
6. Han, P., Shu, H., Xu, J.: A comparative study of background error covariance localization in EnKF data assimilation. Adv. Earth Sci. (2014)
7. Evensen, G.: The Ensemble Kalman Filter: theoretical formulation and practical implementation. Ocean Dyn. **53**, 343–367 (2003)

Research on Vectorization Method of Complex Linear Image Data

Jinbao Shan[1](✉) and Weiwei Jiang[2]

[1] College of Information Technology and Art Design,
Shandong Institute of Commerce and Technology,
Jinan 250103, Shandong, China
shanjb1980@sina.com
[2] College of Food and Drug, Shandong Institute of Commerce and Technology,
Jinan 250103, Shandong, China

Abstract. The traditional data extraction method of complex linear pixel image data can not cope with the vibration and noise of data in the process of data vectorization, which causes the problem of low accuracy of the extraction results. To solve this problem, a complex vector image extraction method is proposed. The MATLAB method is used to remove the noise of complex linear pixel images. In this way, the preprocessing of complex linear pixel image data is provided as the condition of segmentation. The two value algorithm is used to segment the complex linear pixel image data, and the minimum value of the target function is calculated. The data curves are drawn according to the calculation results. Vectorization of image data. The experimental results of the simulated application environment design show that the accuracy of the extraction result is about 45% compared with the traditional extraction method when the same image data is used.

Keywords: Complex line element image · Data vectorization extraction · Image preprocessing · Image segmentation

1 Introduction

Because the traditional extraction method of complex linear pixel image data extraction has the problem of low accuracy and poor integrity, this paper uses MATLAB to preprocess and calculate images, divide the images through two values algorithm, and designs a vector extraction method of complex heterotin image data based on these two algorithms. Experimental results show that the method designed in this paper is more suitable for image data extraction than traditional methods.

S. Liu and G. Yang (Eds.): ADHIP 2018, LNICST 279, pp. 315–321, 2019.
https://doi.org/10.1007/978-3-030-19086-6_35

2 Design of Vectorization Method for Complex Linear Image Data

2.1 Preprocessing of Complex Linear Pixel Image Data

In order to extract the vectorization data of complex linear pixel images, it is necessary to read the image first and preprocess it, and normalize the image information for subsequent processing. A complex linear pixel digital image can be expressed as a real matrix structure. Most complex linear images can be expressed as a two-dimensional matrix by using MATLAB software. The matrix expression of the image is as follows [1, 2]:

$$f(x,y) = \begin{bmatrix} f(0,0) & f(0,1) & \cdots & f(0,N-1) \\ f(1,0) & f(1,1) & \cdots & f(1,N-1) \\ \vdots & \vdots & \vdots & \vdots \\ f(M-1,0) & f(M-1,1) & \cdots & f(M-1,N-1) \end{bmatrix} \tag{1}$$

In this formula: $f(x,y)$ represents the image, M is the width of the image, N is the height of the image, x represents the row number, and y represents the number of columns. Each element in the matrix corresponds to a single pixel point in the image. There is a one-to-one correspondence between the coordinates of the corresponding pixels in the image and the index of the matrix, and the element values represent different luminance or gray [3]. In the spatial coordinates of the pixel points of the image, the pixels are regarded as discrete unit and represented by the corresponding coordinate pairs, which is similar to the plane right angle coordinate system, and that the Y coordinates are increasing from top to bottom. In MATLAB, the image can be read by calling the imread function. The specific information of the image or the element value of the pixel point corresponding to the digital matrix can be viewed through the imfinfo or imview function. The subsequent operation of the image is actually the operation of the digital matrix.

Image noise refers to the discrete-time pixel points which are deviating from the original image and interfering with the subsequent recognition process because of the influence of the acquisition or transmission of the image. It is the non source information in the image, such as the noise of the outer camera itself and the noise of the transmission circuit. Noise is often visually different from adjacent pixels. It can be regarded as a random variable and can be described by probability density function. The basic model used for image noise processing is as follows [4]:

$$y = Hx + \tau \tag{2}$$

In this formula: y is a complex linear image with noise τ, and H is known, unknown or only partially statistical information.

To sum up, when we are preprocessing a complex line image, it should be extracted and processed first, and the denoising process is carried out. The calculation equation of the image preprocessing is as follows:

$$f(x,y) = f(M-1, N-1, aC_1 + bC_2 + cC_3), \quad y = Hx + \tau \tag{3}$$

2.2 Complex Linear Pixel Image Data Segmentation

Image segmentation means the binarization of an image, which means that the pixels of an image are divided into two similar parts according to the gray level. The process is similar to the data according to the approximate attribute of the data, which is similar to [5–7].

A complex line element image is divided into two classes S_1 and S_2, m_1 and m_2 are two categories of gravity centers, and i represents the number of image segmentation. The two valued problem of the image is divided into S_1 and S_1, so that the following objective functions are minimum:

$$f(m_1, m_2) = \sum_{i=1}^{2} \sum_{l \in S_l} n_l (l - m_i)^2 \tag{4}$$

Threshold t can be obtained from the final division results S_1 and S_2.

Here, the function $f(m_1, m_2)$ is called a weighted error square sum function, and the l in the formula represents the gray level number of the image, and n_l represents the number of pixels with the gray level of l, that is, the weighting factor, and the center of gravity is calculated by the lower formula [8, 9]:

$$m_i = \frac{1}{d_i} \sum_{l \in S_l} n_l l, \quad i = 1, 2 \tag{5}$$

$$d_i = \sum_{l \in S_l} n_l, \quad i = 1, 2 \tag{6}$$

In this formula, d represents the dependent variable. For the following analysis, the square error of the weighted error of class S_i is as follows:

$$f_i = \sum_{i \in S_l} n_l (l - m_i)^2 \tag{7}$$

A new iterative algorithm is derived below, whose purpose is to find a partition that can make the objective function $f(m_1, m_2)$ minimum [10].

That is, suppose that a gray level k is in class S_i, and if it is moved to class S_j, then m_j becomes m_j^*.

$$m_j^* = m_j + \frac{(k-m_j)n_k}{d_j + n_k} \qquad (8)$$

In this formula, n_k represents the number of pixels with a gray level of K. At the same time, f_j increased to:

$$f_j^* = f_j + \frac{d_j n_k (k-m_j)^2}{d_j + n_k} \qquad (9)$$

When $d_i \neq n_k$, by similar deduction, we can get the formula of m_i and f_i, by similar deduction.

$$m_i^* = m_i - \frac{(k-m_j)^2}{d_j + n_k} \qquad (10)$$

$$f_i^* = f_i - \frac{d_i n_k (k-m_j)^2}{d_i - n_k} \qquad (11)$$

To sum up, the calculation formula of complex linear image segmentation is as follows:

$$f_{\min}(m_1, m_2) = (m_j - \frac{(k-m_j)n_k^2}{d_j + n_k})(f_i - \frac{d_i n_k (k-m_j)^2}{d_i + n_k}), \; \frac{d_i n_k (k-m_i)^2}{d_i - n_k} > \frac{d_j n_k (k-m_j)^2}{d_j - n_k} \qquad (12)$$

2.3   Vector Extraction of Image Data

The image preprocessing algorithm designed by 1.1 and the 1.2 design image segmentation algorithm (the image two value algorithm) are integrated, and then the algorithm model which can extract the data of the complex linear pixel image is summarized, namely:

$$f(x,y) = f(M-1, N-1, aC_1 + bC_2 + cC_3), \quad y = Hx + \tau \qquad (13)$$

$$f_{\min}(m_1, m_2) = (m_j - \frac{(k-m_j)n_k^2}{d_j + n_k})(f_i - \frac{d_i n_k (k-m_j)^2}{d_i + n_k}), \; \frac{d_i n_k (k-m_i)^2}{d_i - n_k} > \frac{d_j n_k (k-m_j)^2}{d_j - n_k} \qquad (14)$$

First, the complex linear pixel images which need to be extracted from the data are brought into the Eq. (13) to extract and denoise. In the process of processing, only the useful feature information in the image is processed. After the preprocessing, the image affected by the noise can be restored. Then, the reconstructed image data is brought into (14), and the image data is segmented and converted into a two value black-and-white map based on the image data. The calculated $f(m_1, m_2)$ values are the proportional factor of the coordinate axis, and all the features except the image are set to the background color, and then the pixels of the image are searched in the gray matrix. Coordinates, multiplied by the scale factor, can get the true coordinates of each point of the curve. For the pixels with multiple Y values, the mean value of the Y value is processed to get the coordinates of each point of the image. In order to draw the data graph with image data as the horizontal and vertical coordinates, the vectorization of image data is realized.

3 Experimental Analysis

3.1 Experimental Data

In order to verify the accuracy of the method, we extract the experimental image from the complex linear image with a function of $y = \sin x + 25 \cos(5x) + e^{x/2} + 200$, as shown in Fig. 1. The data extraction method designed in this paper is used to extract the JIN line data of the graph, and the horizontal and vertical coordinates of the image data curve are calculated, and the image data coordinates are drawn.

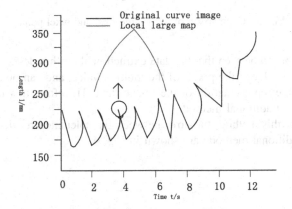

Fig. 1. Original curve image and local large map

3.2 Experimental Results and Analysis

The data is calculated by using the method and the traditional method respectively, and the graph of the image data is drawn according to the calculation results. See Fig. 2 for details.

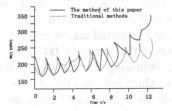

Fig. 2. Data graph

From Fig. 2, it can be seen that the curves drawn according to the results of this method are more consistent with the original ones, while the curves drawn according to the traditional algorithms are less similar to the original ones, that is to say, this algorithm is more accurate for the image data extraction than the traditional algorithm.

Image enlargement with a horizontal coordinate of 3.5 to 4 and a vertical coordinate of 210–235 in Fig. 2, observe the pixel coordinates and the curves obtained after calculation. See Fig. 3 for details.

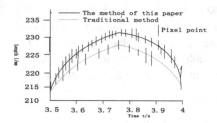

Fig. 3. Comparison of local large map and pixel points

From Fig. 3, it can be seen that the data extraction algorithm designed in this paper can take the mean value at the pixels of the multi Y value, and can obtain more pixels and more complete representation of the image data. Therefore, this method is more complete than the traditional method.

The results of this method, the error between the calculated results and the actual values of the traditional methods are shown in Fig. 4.

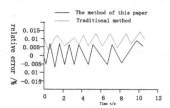

Fig. 4. Error contrast diagram

As can be seen from Fig. 4, the relative error of the calculation results in this method fluctuates in the range of −0.7%–+1.2%, and the mean of the relative error is 0.0018, indicating that the overall deviation is 0.18%; the standard deviation is 0.0084, indicating that the deviation of the overall data is very small. The relative error of the traditional algorithm fluctuates in the range of 0.005%–+1.5%, and the mean value of the relative error is 0.0068, indicating that the overall deviation is 0.68%, and the standard deviation is 0.0164, which indicates that the deviation of the overall data is larger. That is, compared with the traditional methods, the accuracy of the calculation results is higher and the extracted data are more complete.

Many experimental results show that the data extraction integrity and accuracy of this method are more than 45% of the traditional method, so this method is more suitable for the extraction of vectorization data of complex linear pixel images.

4 Concluding Remarks

In this paper, a new method of image data extraction is proposed. The method is based on the image preprocessing algorithm and image segmentation algorithm. By removing noise and image two value calculation, the accuracy of the calculation results is improved. The test data show that the accuracy of this method is improved by about 45% compared with the traditional method, and it has high effectiveness. It is hoped that this study can provide useful help for the vectorization of complex linear image data.

References

1. Chang, J., Liu, H., Zhang, Y.: An image feature extraction algorithm based on big data. Mob. Commun. **41**(4), 79–83 (2017)
2. Jiang, D.: A data extraction method based on image recognition technology and its mobile terminal: CN106372198A[P]. **1**(01), 10–11 (2017)
3. Yu, X., Chen, E., Ji, P., et al.: Data collection and clustering analysis of crowdsourcing images. Geospatial Inf. **15**(11), 16–17 (2017)
4. Tang, J.: Design of image acquisition and processing system. Sci. Consult **11**(44), 109–111 (2017)
5. Li, L.: Design of high-speed acquisition system for fuzzy image information data. Mod. Electron. Tech. **40**(8), 110–113 (2017)
6. Duan, S., Zhu, F., Yan, X.: Study of multi-window binarization algorithm for image processing. Comput. Eng. Appl. **53**(17), 212–217 (2017)
7. Cao, Y., Baojie, X.V., Xiaoli, X.V., et al.: Two value research of image based on improved Bernsen algorithm. Plant Maint. Eng. **14**(18), 26–28 (2017)
8. Zhou, L., Jiang, F.: A survey of image segmentation methods. Appl. Res. Comput. **34**(7), 1921–1928 (2017)
9. Liang, J., Liang, L.: Optimization of feature data extraction in large data environment. Comput. Simul. **11**(12), 345–348 (2017)
10. Liu, H., Yang, L., Hou, X., et al.: An improved fuzzy c-means algorithm for image segmentation. J. Zhengzhou Univ. (Nat. Sci. Ed.) **49**(2), 66–71 (2017)

Modeling Analysis of Intelligent Logistics Distribution Path of Agricultural Products Under Internet of Things Environment

Xiaoyan Ai[(⊠)] and Yongheng Zhang

Yulin University, Yulin 719000, China
zcmddnl111@163.com

Abstract. Aiming at the insufficiency of the logistics distribution model of traditional agricultural products, this paper puts forward the optimization modeling analysis of the intelligent logistics distribution route of agricultural products under the Internet of Things. According to the logistics distribution model of agricultural products under the Internet of Things environment, the intelligent logistics distribution path of agricultural products is optimized and modeled and analyzed. The objective function of the shortest path of the model is calculated, and constraint conditions are set, thereby completing the intelligent logistics distribution path optimization modeling of agricultural products. Experimental parameters are set and traditional methods with path optimization modeling analysis methods are compared. From the comparison results, When the time is 10:00, the difference between the accuracy of the traditional method and the accuracy of the intelligent logistics distribution route optimization model is the largest, with a difference of 80%. It can be seen that the use of intelligent logistics distribution route optimization modeling and analysis has higher accuracy. It can be seen that the path optimization modeling and analysis method has higher precision in the analysis of agricultural products intelligent logistics distribution route, and provides an effective solution to ensure freshness of agricultural products.

Keywords: Internet of Things · Agricultural products · Logistics distribution · Path optimization

1 Introduction

The Internet of Things is the convergence and integration of various perceptual technologies, modern communication technologies, artificial intelligence, and automation technologies to create an intelligent network that can sense the real world. In the future, with the advent of the 5G era, new applications for the Internet of Things will emerge in an endless stream, and 4G obviously cannot meet the requirements. 5G has obvious advantages in terms of bandwidth speed and energy efficiency, and the end-to-end delay will be reduced. These characteristics are particularly important for the application of the Internet of Things. At present, the application of the Internet of Things is limited to some independent small systems. When we talk about big blueprints such as

S. Liu and G. Yang (Eds.): ADHIP 2018, LNICST 279, pp. 322–329, 2019.
https://doi.org/10.1007/978-3-030-19086-6_36

"Smart City" and "Smart Earth", we need a unified framework that seamlessly connects, and 5G is just a good opportunity to provide a unified framework. According to data from the Internet Data Center, the global Internet of Things market will exceed US $3 trillion by 2020. Under the background of China's "Internet Plus" strategy, the scale of the Internet of Things industry has been met with unprecedented development conditions. It is now entering a stage of rapid development from the stage of overall distribution, and it is playing the role of "core productivity" to promote the rapid development of the world economy. Agricultural products are difficult to distribute because of their characteristics of perishability [1]. The combination of the Internet of Things and the circulation of agricultural products simply means the use of technologies such as RFID radio frequency identification. Through the information network, real-time monitoring and sharing of information on the state of agricultural products and the status of vehicle transportation in the distribution process are realized, and according to this, intelligent operations are carried out.

The problem of multi-objective path optimization research can be analyzed from two aspects. It can be generally divided into single-factor single-object path optimization and multi-factor multi-objective path optimization. Among them, the multi-objective path optimization problem is mainly based on the optimization study that considers the minimum cost, the highest customer satisfaction, or the shortest delivery distance, and is more comprehensive, scientific, and reasonable than the single-objective optimization problem. Literature [2] proposed that the agricultural Internet of Things is an emerging technology that exploits agricultural productivity, improves the level of precision of agricultural equipment, and realizes intelligent agricultural production. It integrates agricultural information perception, data transmission, and intelligent information processing technology, and is based on field planting. Significant demand for facilities in horticulture, livestock and poultry farming, aquaculture and agricultural product logistics, and planning of distribution routes, but the method is less accurate. Therefore, the main issue of the study is how to solve the problems of low efficiency and information lag in the distribution of agricultural products through the Internet of Things technology, to plan distribution routes scientifically and rationally, while improving distribution efficiency and ensuring the quality of agricultural products, improve customer satisfaction and reducing distribution costs. Thus, to achieve a balance between the economic efficiency of agricultural products enterprises and customer satisfaction.

2   Analysis of Logistics Distribution Model of Agricultural Products Under Internet of Things

Aiming at the insufficiency of the logistics distribution model of traditional agricultural products, combined with features of Internet of Things and agricultural products, the model of agricultural products distribution under the environment of Internet of Things was proposed. As shown in Fig. 1.

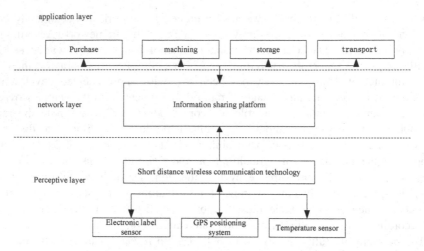

Fig. 1. Agricultural product logistics distribution model in the Internet of Things environment

Through Fig. 1, the intelligent operation of agricultural products such as procurement, distribution processing, transportation and warehousing, transportation, quality traceability, etc. It is implemented to promote the transition from agriculture to intensive production, and improve the utilization ratio of agricultural resources and the level of information. The pattern of agricultural product distribution under the Internet of Things environment can be divided into three basic levels: the perception layer, the network layer, and the application layer. The sensory layer transmits the collected information to the information sharing platform through various sensing technologies. The network layer allows various agricultural product information to be transmitted to the application layer through the underlying bearer network, supports the transmission, routing, and control of the agricultural product information of the sensing layer, and ensures the exchange of data in the network transmission; The application layer is the use of Internet of Things technology, through the unified management of various types of sensing data, to achieve a direct experience of agricultural products in the distribution process of intelligent [3].

3 The Construction of Intelligent Logistics Distribution Route Optimization Model

3.1 Problem Description

According to the logistics distribution model of agricultural products under the Internet of Things environment, the intelligent logistics distribution path of agricultural products is modeled and analyzed. The problem can be described as: There are n vehicles in m distribution centers, which provide i kinds of material distribution services for k locations. The load capacity of each vehicle is not the same, and some of the materials must be used together. The goal is to optimize the vehicle's driving path so as to shorten the distance traveled by the vehicle on the premise of meeting the freight requirements. At the same time, through the Internet of things technology to optimize the waiting time between different types of materials, in order to minimize the distribution costs of power supplies [4].

3.2 Model Basic Assumptions

(1) Consider only one logistics center, that is, the distribution center. According to the customer's order demand, the vehicle needs to start from the distribution center and return to the distribution center after completing the distribution service.
(2) Each customer's demand for agricultural products can not exceed the maximum carrying capacity of the delivery vehicle. Using a single vehicle distribution can make the vehicle load, speed, driving costs and other conditions are fixed;
(3) Each customer has one and only one vehicle for distribution, but each vehicle can provide distribution services to multiple customers;
(4) The customer's demand for agricultural products, expected delivery time period, tolerable delivery time period, distribution center and customer's specific geographic location are all known;
(5) The demand for agricultural products by customers within the delivery service time is constant [5].

3.3 Model Construction

Assuming that $S_1, S_2, \ldots, S_n$ species are needed, which are provided by p distribution centers $m_1, m_2, \ldots, m_n$, providing delivery services for $m_{p+1}, m_{p+2}, \ldots, m_{p+n}$ demand sites [6]. The demand for each of these materials is $q_1, q_2, \ldots, q_n$. $\{n_i | 1 \leq i \leq n\}$ represents a collection of parking lots; $m_1, m_2, \ldots, m_n$ represents the number of vehicles owned by the depot; $\{Z_i^m | 1 \leq m \leq m_i\}$ represents the load capacity of vehicles in each depot; $\{d_{ab} | 1 \leq a \leq i+n, 1 \leq b \leq i+n\}$ represents distances from each point [7]. The elements satisfy the following relationship:

(1) $d_{ab} = 0$ indicates the distance between the supply points themselves is 0;
(2) $d_{ab} = d_{ba}$ indicates that there is no direction between the two points;

λ_{ab}^n represents the stability factor of the path taken by vehicle n; t_{ab}^n indicates the safety factor of the time required for the vehicle n to travel; C_1^n represents the material loss cost of the path taken by the vehicle n; C_2^n represents the supply delay cost of the path taken by vehicle [8]. Among them, several coefficients of λ_{ab}^n and t_{ab}^n are obtained through the data collection of path information using RFID and GPS and other Internet of Things technologies in material distribution [9]. According to the fluctuations in the overall transportation process, find the mean and variance. If the variance is smaller, the higher the stability of the road, the lower the cost of material loss [10]. t_{ab}^n is determined by the real-time status and path information of all vehicles collected by the information system. Through information sharing, collaborative operations between suppliers and enterprises can be realized, delays in delivery or early arrival risks can be reduced, and waiting time between each other can be reduced, thereby saving a lot of time costs.

It can be assumed that the decision variables are as follows:

$$x_{in}^{ab} = \begin{cases} 1, & \text{vehicles passing by distribution center} \\ 0, & \text{other conditions} \end{cases}$$

$$y_{in}^{ab} = \begin{cases} 1, & \text{there is vehicles} \\ 0, & \text{other conditions} \end{cases} \tag{1}$$

Build the model shortest distance objective function:

$$\min A = \sum_{a=1}^{p+k} \sum_{b=1}^{p+k} \sum_{i=1}^{p+k} \sum_{n=1}^{p+k} x_{in}^{ab} y_{in}^{ab} \tag{2}$$

The model needs to meet the following constraints:

① The total demand for each vehicle's distribution cannot exceed its carrying capacity, that is:

$$\sum_{a=1}^{p+k} \cdot q_a \cdot \sum_{b=1}^{p+k} \cdot x_{in}^{ab} y_n^i \leq C_m^n \tag{3}$$

② The number of vehicles departing from each delivery is equal to the number of vehicles returning to the distribution center and does not exceed the number of vehicles it owns, that is:

$$\sum_{a=1}^{p+k} \sum_{a=p+1}^{p+k} \cdot x_{in}^{ab} y_n^i = \sum_{i=1}^{i} \sum_{a=p+1}^{p+k} \cdot x_{in}^{ab} y_n^i \leq m_a \tag{4}$$

This can obtain the optimal model of logistics distribution.

4   Verification Analysis

In order to verify the accuracy of modeling and analysis of intelligent logistics distribution routes for agricultural products under the Internet of Things environment, the following experimental verification analysis was conducted.

4.1   Experimental Parameter Settings

Assuming that there are M_1, M_2, and M_3 three material reserve centers in a certain place. There are four kinds of power supplies N_1, N_2, N_3, and N_4, including switch contactors, towers, cables, and transformers, which are required to be distributed. Materials are distributed to the four construction sites and are represented as Z_1, Z_2, Z_3, and Z_4, respectively. There are 30 vehicles in total, which are randomly distributed at the B_1, B_2, B_3 parking lots. The parking lot parameter information is shown in Table 1.

Table 1. Yard parameter information

Vehicle number	The parking lot	Vehicle load (t)	Vehicle speed (km/h)
1	B_2	50	40
2	B_1	80	45
3	B_3	60	43
4	B_1	30	42
5	B_3	60	39
6	B_2	20	41

According to the parameters of the yard parameters shown in Table 1, the experiment was analyzed.

4.2   Experimental Results and Analysis

Weather Influence
Under the influence of weather, the accuracy of traditional method and intelligent logistics distribution route optimization modeling analysis method was compared and analyzed. Through the different kinds of weather, we can fully verify the advantages of this method. The results are shown in Fig. 2.

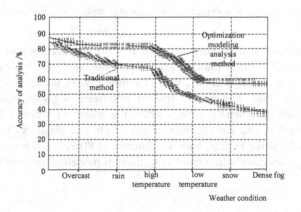

Fig. 2. Comparison of the accuracy of two methods under the influence of weather

From Fig. 2, we can see that when the weather is cloudy, the accuracy of traditional method analysis is 75%, and the accuracy of intelligent logistics distribution route optimization modeling is 81%; When the weather is raining, the accuracy of the traditional method analysis is 11% lower than the accuracy of the intelligent logistics distribution route optimization modeling analysis; When the weather is at a high temperature, the difference between the accuracy of the traditional method and the accuracy of the intelligent logistics distribution route optimization modeling model is the greatest; When the weather is heavy fog, the accuracy of the two methods has reached a minimum, the accuracy of the traditional method analysis is 38%, and the accuracy of the intelligent logistics distribution route optimization modeling analysis is 56%. It can be seen that, under the influence of the weather, the use of intelligent logistics distribution route optimization modeling has higher accuracy.

Road Traffic Impact
Under the influence of road traffic, the accuracy of traditional method and intelligent logistics distribution route optimization modeling analysis method was compared and analyzed. The results are shown in Fig. 3

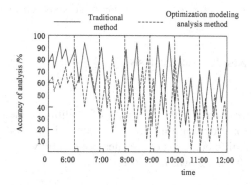

Fig. 3. Comparison of the accuracy of two methods under the influence of road traffic

In Fig. 3, we can see that when the time is 6:00, the accuracy of the traditional method analysis is 35% lower than the accuracy of the intelligent logistics distribution route optimization modeling analysis; When the time is 7:00, the accuracy of traditional method analysis is 60% lower than that of intelligent logistics distribution route optimization modeling; When the time is 10:00, the difference between the accuracy of the traditional method and the accuracy of the intelligent logistics distribution route optimization model is the largest, with a difference of 80%. It can be seen that the use of intelligent logistics distribution route optimization modeling and analysis has higher accuracy.

4.3 Experimental Conclusion

① Under the influence of the weather, the use of intelligent logistics distribution route optimization modeling has higher accuracy.
② Under the influence of road traffic, the use of intelligent logistics distribution route optimization modeling accuracy is high.

From this, we can see that the intelligent logistics distribution path optimization model analysis of agricultural products is accurate under the Internet of Things environment.

5 Conclusion

Agricultural information is the infiltration of modern information technology into every aspect of agricultural production and operation. It is an important hot issue in current social development and the only way for future agricultural development. The study of the distribution model of agricultural products under the Internet of Things environment is essentially how to reasonably use the Internet of Things technology to solve the problem of lagging agricultural product information, making agricultural products add value in the distribution process, making the consumer groups of agricultural products grow, and increasing the competition and overall benefits of the agricultural market. The future research direction is to continuously improve the accuracy of the logistics distribution route selection, and better provide a more convenient way for agricultural product distribution.

Fund Project. Agricultural Science Research Plan in Shaanxi Province of China: "Research on key technologies and applications of Smart agriculture planting and logistics distribution based on the Internet of Things" (NO. 2017NY132).

References

1. Zhu, Z.Y., Chen, Z.Q.: Petri net modeling and analysis of wisdom traceability service system in Internet of Things. J. Intell. Syst. **12**(4), 538–547 (2017)
2. Li, D.L., Yang, W.: Analysis and development trend of agricultural IoT technology. J. Agric. Res. **11**(1), 1–20 (2018)
3. Sun, M.M., Zhang, C.Y., Lin, G.L., et al.: Problem of cold chain logistics distribution and path optimization of fresh agricultural products. Jiangsu Agric. Sci. **45**(11), 282–285 (2017)
4. Fan, S.Q., Zhai, D., Sun, Y.: Research on the optimization of distribution routes for fresh agricultural products cold chain logistics. Freshness Process. **10**(6), 106–111 (2017)
5. Zhang, L.Y., Wang, Y., Fei, T., et al.: Chaotic perturbation simulated annealing ant colony algorithm for low carbon logistics path optimization. ComEngApp **53**(1), 63–68 (2017)
6. Feng, L., Liang, G.Q.: Design and simulation of vehicle distribution scheduling targeting in networking. Comput. Simul. **34**(4), 377–381 (2017)
7. Huang, X.X.: Optimization of cold chain distribution path for fresh agricultural products under carbon tax and carbon limit rules. J. Shanghai Marit. Univ. **39**(1), 74–79 (2018)
8. Jia, X.Z., Qi, H.L., Jia, Q.S., et al.: Optimization of distribution routes of fresh produce in the same city under real-time road conditions. Jiangsu Agric. Sci. **45**(17), 292–295 (2017)
9. Xiao, M.H., Li, Y.N., Li, W.: The analysis of the development of the logistics industry in the Internet of Things environment and its countermeasures: a case study of Jiangxi Province. Bus. Econ. **24**(4), 167–173 (2017)
10. Chen, Y., Liu, Y., Chen, X.R., Liu, R.: Simulation analysis method of pesticide residue pollution based on visual analysis. Comput. Simul. **34**(10), 347–351 (2017)

Intelligent Fusion Technology of Crop Growth Monitoring Data Under Wireless Sensor Networks

Yongheng Zhang$^{(\boxtimes)}$ and Xiaoyan Ai

Yulin University, Yulin 719000, Shaanxi, China
shujun55753@yahoo.com

Abstract. Using adaptive weighted data fusion technology, the relative error of crop growth monitoring data is relatively large, accuracy is not high, and its fusion is not effective. In view of the above problems, the intelligent fusion technology of crop growth monitoring data under wireless sensor network is proposed. The technology consists of three parts: Using LEACH (Low Energy Adaptive Clustering Hierarchy) protocol to realize rapid processing and transmission of monitoring data. Accurate fusion of monitoring data through BP (Back Propagation) neural network; the two models are combined to construct the data fusion algorithm BPDFA (Back-Propagation Data Fusion Algorithm) model, so as to achieve intelligent fusion of crop growth monitoring data. By using the unique information processing characteristics of BP neural network, multi-information processing and transmission at the same time, the efficiency of processing is improved, and the fusion of crop growth information is realized. The results show that the intelligent fusion technology and adaptive weighted data fusion technology proposed in this study, the relative error is reduced by 3.72 °C, the accuracy is higher, and the fusion effect is better.

Keywords: Wireless sensor network · Monitoring data · Data fusion · LEACH protocol · BP neural network

1 Introduction

Appropriate environment plays an important role in promoting the growth and high yield of crops. Therefore, real-time monitoring of crop growth environment has always been an important task for agricultural development. At present, research on agricultural monitoring technology at home and abroad attaches great importance and has achieved some results. In recent years, wireless sensor networks with low cost, small size, low power consumption and multiple functions have emerged [1]. Wireless sensor network is a data-centric network. Its basic function is to collect and return the monitoring data of the area where the sensor node is located. However, in the process of collecting information, each node transmits data to the convergence node separately, which not only wastes the extremely limited energy of the sensor node, but also reduces the efficiency of information collection. How to reduce data communication, reduce energy consumption of nodes, and extend the network lifetime have become a hot topic in wireless sensor networks [2]. Data fusion technology is one of the key

S. Liu and G. Yang (Eds.): ADHIP 2018, LNICST 279, pp. 330–339, 2019.
https://doi.org/10.1007/978-3-030-19086-6_37

technologies to solve the above problems. The research of data fusion technology mainly focuses on fusion algorithm and routing protocol. These two aspects play different roles in data fusion. The former uses neural networks to reduce the amount of data transmitted to sink nodes, reducing communication energy consumption, and prolonging the network lifetime. The latter uses LEACH protocol to select valuable information for the former to merge and transmit. Finally, the two are combined to build a data fusion algorithm BPDFA model to complete the integration of crop growth monitoring data. In recent years, many experts have done a lot of research and achieved some results. Documentation [3] a method of wireless sensor network and sensor fusion is proposed, which effectively improves the data acquisition efficiency, but does not realize the purpose of real-time acquisition. Documentation [4] an adaptive predictive weighted data fusion method based on wireless sensor network is proposed, which can improve the capacity consumption of sensor network nodes, but the processing time is too long. To verify the effectiveness of the fusion technique, comparative experiments were conducted. The results show that compared with the adaptive weighted data fusion technology, the relative average error of the data fusion method in this study is reduced by 3.72 °C, which shows the advantages of this technology.

2 Data Fusion in Wireless Sensor Networks

Data fusion technology is a very important technology in wireless sensor networks. This technology uses a number of algorithms to process a large amount of raw data collected by sensor nodes to perform in-network processing, remove the redundant information, and transfer only a small amount of meaningful processing results to the aggregation node [3, 4]. In other words, the data fusion technology in wireless sensor networks includes two aspects: one is the transmission of fused data to the sink node; the other is the fusion processing of monitoring data.

3 Transmission of Crop Growth Monitoring Data

In the study of this chapter, the crop growth monitoring data was transmitted based on the LEACH routing protocol.

3.1 Cluster Head Selection

LEACH protocol cluster head selection method: In the initial stage of each cluster, each node randomly generates a number between [0.1]. If this number is less than the set threshold S(n), the corresponding node will be selected as Cluster heads, thus broadcasting their episodes of becoming cluster heads. When passing through the cluster head, the threshold S(n) is set to zero. The threshold S(n) is expressed as:

$$S(n) = \begin{cases} 0 & n \notin \theta \\ \frac{\alpha}{1-\alpha^*[r \bmod(1/\alpha)]} & n \in \theta \end{cases} \qquad (1)$$

In the formula, α represents the percentage of the number of cluster head nodes in the number of all nodes of the wireless sensor network, r represents the number of "rounds" performed by the current cluster head election, θ represents a set, and elements in the set are The cluster head sensor nodes have not been selected in the $1/\alpha$ round.

3.2   Cluster Initialization

The initial stage of the cluster is also the establishment stage of the cluster, which is to prepare for the monitoring data transmission in the stable stage. This stage mainly includes the determination of the cluster head node and forms a cluster structure with its neighboring nodes; in each cluster structure, the cluster. The head node allocates TDMA (Time Division Multiple Access) time slices for other intra-cluster nodes.

3.3   Cluster Stability

After the establishment of the cluster is completed, the sensor node transmits the collected data to the cluster head node in the assigned time slot; the cluster head node first performs information fusion after receiving all the data packets from all the member nodes in the cluster, and the received data is received. The data packets of the packet and cluster head node are compressed into a packet of equal length. The fused data packet is then transmitted to the sink node using different CDMA (Code Division Multiple Access) codes to reduce the communication traffic. After the sink node receives the data of the cluster head node. The data is transmitted to the monitoring center for data processing. After a period of time, the network re-enters the cluster establishment phase and performs the next round of cluster reconstruction. Figure 1 is a visual data flow chart.

3.4   The Choice of the Optimal Number of Cluster Heads

In the LEACH protocol, the number of cluster heads can find the optimal value range. The idea is to minimize the total energy consumed by the network in each round, and the number of cluster heads in the corresponding network is optimal, that is, the number of cluster heads [5].

The total energy consumption Z of a cluster head node in a frame is:

$$Z = [LE\,(N/K - 1) + LF\,(N/K - 1)] \cdot M \tag{2}$$

In the formula, L is the number of bits of information for each data; E is the energy consumed for data fusion; N is the number of sensor nodes; K is the number of cluster head nodes; F is the distance from the cluster head node to the base station; M is each The average coverage area of clusters.

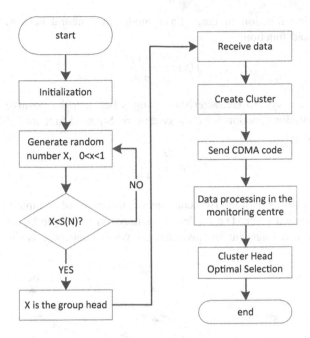

Fig. 1. Flow chart of visual data transmission

4   Fusion of Monitoring Data

Due to the limited energy of the wireless sensor network, in order to extend the life cycle of the WSN (Wireless Sensor Networks), the LEACH routing protocol was used in the previous chapter, and the optimal number of cluster heads was selected in conjunction with the efficient use of energy [6]. This chapter mainly introduces the data fusion technology in the cluster selection of the LEACH routing protocol in the previous chapter. That is, the BP neural network algorithm is used in each cluster structure to process the data collected by node crop growth monitoring so as to reduce the data transmitted to the sink node. Quantity, reduce communication energy consumption, reach the purpose of prolonging network life cycle [7].

BP network is a forward neural network using BP algorithm. It is based on multi-layer perceptrons and adds back propagation signals. It can better deal with non-linear data information and has good generalization ability. Applied to system model identification, prediction or control BP. BP neural network obtains learning guidelines, feedback data collected through learning criteria standards, extract sign information, and under the role of reasoning machines, matches the sign with knowledge in the knowledge base, and then obtains key information for Fusion. Complete the processing of data information. The combination of BP neural network and wireless sensor network can tell the state of real-time response data transmission.

The excitation function in the neuron model in a neural network is usually a nonlinear Sigmoid function:

$$f(x) = \frac{1}{1 + e^{-x}} \tag{3}$$

Only when the system characteristic changes between the positive and negative regions, the excitation function selects a symmetric Sigmoid function, also known as a hyperbolic function:

$$f(x) = \sin \frac{e^{-x}}{1 + e^{-x}} \tag{4}$$

The network structure of the BP neural network consists of an input layer, an output layer, and an implicit layer. The hidden layer may have multiple layers, but the most commonly used is a single hidden layer three-layer BP network, as shown in Fig. 2.

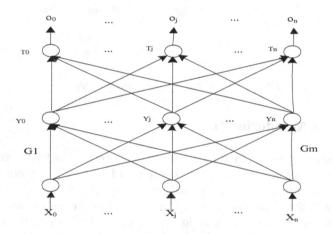

Fig. 2. Network structure of BP neural network

Each layer vector is X, Y, O, where the input vector is: X = (X0, ..., Xj, ..., Xn)T, and the hidden layer vector is: Y = (Y0, ..., Yj, ..., Ym). The output layer vector is: O = (O1, ..., Oj, ..., Ot). The connection weight matrix G = (G1, ..., Gj, ..., Gn) between the input layer and the hidden layer neurons. The connection weight matrix T = (T1, ..., Tk, ..., Th) between the hidden layer and the output layer neurons. The relationship between the input layer signal x_i and the hidden layer signal y_i is shown in Eqs. (5) and (6).

$$net_j = \sum_{j=1}^{n} G_{jn} x_j \quad j = 1, 2, 3, \cdots, n \tag{5}$$

$$y_j = f(net_j) \tag{6}$$

The relationship between the hidden layer signal and the output layer signal is shown in Eqs. (7) and (8).

$$net_k = \sum_{k=1}^{m} T_{kn} y_j \quad k = 1, 2, 3, \cdots, h \tag{7}$$

$$O_k = f(net_k) \tag{8}$$

The error function β is shown in formula (9).

$$\beta = \frac{\sum_{k=1}^{1}}{2} O_k^2 y_j^2 \tag{9}$$

It can be known from formula (9) that the error function is changed by the connection weight value Δ between layers, as shown in formula (10). μ represents the learning rate, which is generally a constant of $(0, 1)$.

$$\Delta = \mu \left(\sum_{k=1}^{1} O_k^2 y_j^2 \right) y_j (1 - y_j) x_n \tag{10}$$

Assuming that the weights of this and the next hidden layer and output layer are T_{kh} and G_{jn} respectively, there are formulae (11) and (12).

$$T_{kh} = T_{kn}^{n-1} + \Delta T_{kn}^{n} \tag{11}$$

$$G_{jn} = G_{jn}^{n-1} + \Delta G_{jn}^{n} \tag{12}$$

The BP neural network algorithm is trained through the above calculation cycle. Each training will re-adjust the weights and thresholds of each layer. The termination condition of the loop is that the overall error is less than the preset value or the number of network training reaches a preset number of times. The value and threshold are also determined [8]. After training through the network, the data to be fused are input. The neural network will perform fusion processing on the trained thresholds and weights to extract the eigenvalues of the data. When processing data, because wireless sensors apply the information conduction characteristics of BP neural networks and apply the excited mode of neuron transmission information, this dynamic process is carried out simultaneously with information processing and information transmission to reduce the transmission of data information. Effective control of time, increased efficiency.

5 Data Fusion Algorithm BPDFA Model

The data fusion technology is applied to the routing layer of the wireless sensor network. Based on the routing protocol, the BP neural network is introduced and a new data fusion algorithm (abbreviated as BPDFA) is proposed. The BPDFA data fusion algorithm selects the optimal cluster head through the LEACH routing protocol and forms a stable clustering structure. In each clustered structure, the cluster sensor nodes collect a large amount of raw monitoring data for preprocessing, and then transmit it to the cluster head node performs data processing again in the cluster head node and sends it to the sink node [9]. BPDFA data fusion algorithm is to use BP neural network algorithm to process data between cluster sensor node and cluster head node. The model of data fusion algorithm BPDFA is shown in Fig. 3.

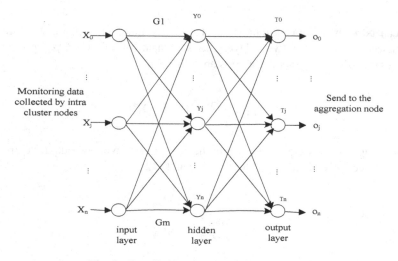

Fig. 3. Data fusion algorithm BPDFA model

According to the BPDFA algorithm model in Fig. 2, the data collected by the nodes in the wireless sensor network can be fused. In the wireless sensor network networking, the status of the nodes in the network and the position of the nodes are determined first. After the status of the network nodes is determined, the wireless sensor network starts to select the optimal cluster head. At this time, the cluster head obtains the information of all nodes in the cluster. After the clustering structure is stable, the cluster head node sends the relevant information of all cluster nodes to the aggregation node. The aggregation node constructs a BP neural network structure based on the obtained network information and collects a sample training neural network matching the node information in the cluster in the sample database, thereby obtaining related neural network parameters. The aggregation node sends the parameters of each layer of the neural network to the corresponding cluster node. The clustering structure of wireless sensor networks can use the trained BP neural network model to process the data fusion. Finally, the processed data is transmitted to the aggregation node in the shortest path, so the BPDFA algorithm completes the data fusion in the wireless sensor network deal with.

6 Comparative Experiment

To verify the effectiveness of the intelligent fusion technology of crop growth monitoring data under the wireless sensor network in this study, a monitoring area was selected in the laboratory, and 30 temperature sensor nodes and 3 sub-layer routing nodes constitute a wireless sensor network. Temperature sensor node number 1–30, each node collected 10 times a single test data, 10 tests at different temperatures, the baseline true values were 13.5 °C, 17.20 °C, 20.80 °C, 23.70 °C, 25.0 °C, 27.0 °C, 29.0 °C, 31.0 °C, 33.0 °C, 35.0 °C. The three sub-layer nodes are numbered 1–3. Each sub-layer node is connected to five ordinary nodes, which correspond to sensor nodes 1–10, 11–20, and 21–30 respectively.

Taking the 10 experimental data as an example, the experimental data are processed using the data fusion technology and the adaptive weighted data fusion technology respectively, and the experimental data fusion results are displayed. The results are shown in Table 1.

Table 1. Contrast of two kinds of technical data fusion values with true values

Number	1	2	3	4	5	6	7	8	9	10
True value (°C)	13.6	17	20	23	25	27	29	31	33	35
Data fusion technology in this paper (°C)	13.6	17.2	20.1	23	25.1	27	28.9	31	33	35.1
Adaptive weighted data fusion technology (°C)	13.2	16.5	20.3	22.8	25.5	27.4	28.5	30.7	32.5	34.6

In order to visually show the degree of approximation between the fusion value and the true value of the two calculation methods, the true value is normalized to 0, and the obtained relative value of the fusion value is shown in Fig. 4.

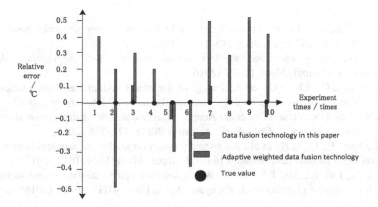

Fig. 4. Relative error of fusion value

In the experiment, the relative average error of the monitoring data fusion technique in this study was smaller than the relative average error of the adaptive weighted fusion technique. The relative average error of the former was only 0.06 °C and the latter was 3.8 °C. The relative error of the two was relatively different 3.74 °C. It can be shown that the monitoring data fusion technology of this study is superior to the adaptive weighted fusion method. It is more stable, mainly because the layered adaptive weighted fusion method does not remove gross errors at the beginning, resulting in large calculation bias.

7 Conclusion

With the constant intelligence of modern society, wireless sensor network technology has gradually attracted the attention of various industries, and data fusion technology can comprehensively process a large amount of information collected by multiple sensors and obtain final decision based on the fusion result. The BP neural network is combined with the LEACH routing protocol to handle the data fusion and transmission problems in wireless sensor networks. Compared with the past, the fusion has high accuracy, good stability, and is simple and easy to implement. While satisfying the real-time requirements of data fusion, the accuracy of the measurement data is improved. Although the calculation amount is increased, the amount of data transmission is reduced theoretically. It can save the energy of wireless sensor nodes, extend the life span of wireless sensor networks, lay a foundation for the development of crop growth data monitoring technology, and promote the sustainable development of China's agriculture.

Fund Project. Agricultural Science Research Plan in Shaanxi Province of China: "Research on key technologies and application of Intelligent Prediction and Forecasting of Potato diseases and pests based on the Internet of Things" (NO. 2016NY141).

References

1. Qiu, L.D., Liu, T.J., Fu, P.: Data aggregation in wireless sensor networks based on deep learning. Appl. Res. Comput. **3**(1), 185–188 (2016)
2. Li, L.: Ant colony optimized wireless sensor networks data aggregation algorithm. Microelectron. Comput. **33**(6), 68–72 (2016)
3. Jin, C., Cai, G.Q., Chen, G., et al.: Design of fire alarm system based on wireless sensor networks and sensor fusion technology. Instrum. Tech. Sens. **4**(6), 66–68 (2016)
4. Yu, X.W., Fan, F.S., Zhou, L.X., et al.: Adaptive forecast weighting data fusion algorithm for wireless sensor network. J. Chin. Sens. Actuators **30**(5), 772–776 (2017)
5. Fei, H., Xiao, F., Li, G.H., et al.: An anomaly detection method of wireless sensor network based on multi-modals data stream. Chin. J. Comput. **40**(8), 1829–1842 (2017)
6. Chen, C.L., Cui, L., Xu, T.Y., et al.: Wireless-sensor and multi-data fusion technological research of sunlight greenhouse. J. Shenyang Agric. Univ. **47**(1), 86–91 (2016)

7. Huang, T.H., Kai, K., Wang, Y.L., et al.: Firefly algorithm optimized neural network data fusion in wireless sensor network. Instrum. Tech. Sens. **5**(7), 103–107 (2016)

8. Xu, H.Y., Yang, Y.: Scheme of data aggregation based on data flow density for wireless sensor networks. Control Eng. Chin. **25**(1), 165–169 (2018)

9. Xiang, L.F.: Research on automatic monitoring of mobile data in sensor networks. Comput. Simul. **34**(11), 447–450 (2017)

A QA System Based on Bidirectional LSTM with Text Similarity Calculation Model

Wenhua Xu, Hao Huang, Hao Gu, Jie Zhang, and Guan Gui[(⊠)]

College of Telecommunication and Information Engineering,
Nanjing University of Posts and Telecommunications, Nanjing 210003, China
guiguan@njupt.edu.cn

Abstract. The development of deep learning in recent years has led to the development of natural language processing [1]. Question answering (QA) system is an important branch of natural language processing. It benefits from the application of neural networks and therefore its performance is constantly improving. The application of recurrent neural networks (RNN) and long short-term memory (LSTM) networks are more common in natural language processing. Inspired by the work of machine translation, this paper built an intelligent QA system based on the specific areas of the extension service. After analyzing the shortcomings of the RNN and the advantages of the LSTM network, we choose the bidirectional LSTM. In order to improve the performance, this paper add text similarity calculation in the QA system. At the end of the experiment, the convergence of the system and the accuracy of the answer to the question showed that the performance of the system is good.

Keywords: QA system · Deep learning · RNN · LSTM

1 Introduction

With the development of deep learning in recent years, the field of natural language processing has also developed rapidly [2]. QA system is a very popular research direction in the field of natural language processing. People can submit problems expressed in natural language to the QA system, and the system will return compact and accurate answers instead of just returning a collection of pages like a search engine. In other words, the QA system saves resources with maximum efficiency to find the answers most needed by users. The history of intelligent QA system can be traced back to the beginning of artificial intelligence (AI). Alan M. Turing, father of artificial intelligence, proposed an imitating game at the beginning of the book [3], which can be considered as the beginning of QA system. Turing test showed that a computer was intelligent if it can communicate in natural language like humans. Therefore, the field of natural language processing was popular in the world. This prompted a large number of researchers to explore language techniques by studying QA system.

In recent years, researchers have applied the sequence-to-sequence model in machine translation [4]. The model is further optimized in [5], and the authors used the LSTM model to obtain better performance than RNN model. Some scholars have used TFIDF to design a question and answer system [6].

S. Liu and G. Yang (Eds.): ADHIP 2018, LNICST 279, pp. 340–347, 2019.
https://doi.org/10.1007/978-3-030-19086-6_38

This paper proposed a QA system that combines the bidirectional LSTM model with a text similarity model. There are search systems and generative systems; this paper combines these two systems together. After training, the model's loss and the results of the test have achieved good performance.

The structure of the paper is as follows. Section 2 introduces some model structures and our model in the QA system. Section 3 shows the structure of the QA system. Section 4 reports our results include the system's convergence and partial results of question-answer testing compared with a single Bidirectional LSTM model.

2   Model Structure

2.1   Encoder-Decoder Model

In most cases, the encoder-decoder model is used to process natural language problems [4]. One of the most significant features of the encoder-decoder framework is that it is an end-to-end learning algorithm, which is a model for sequence-to-sequence problems. Briefly, it is just an input sequence $\mathbf{x} = [x_0, x_1 \cdots x_N]^T \in R^N$, to generate another output sequence $\mathbf{y} = [y_0, y_1 \cdots y_N]^T \in R^N$. Sequence-to-sequence model has many applications, such as translation, document harvesting, QA system, and so on [2] (Fig. 1).

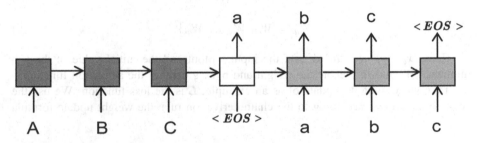

Fig. 1. An encoder-decoder model. This is the process of encoding the input and then decoding it. The encoder is to convert the input sequence into a vector of fixed length; decoder is to convert the previously generated fixed vector into an output sequence. The input is "A, B, C", and after encoding and decoding output "a, b, c".

2.2   RNN Encoder-Decoder Model

Because of the inconsistency of the input and output, it is difficult to separate these different sequences into separate samples for training, but RNN can deal with this problem. The input sequence is encoded using a recursive neural network (RNN) and a variable length sequence output is generated using another set of decoder RNN [7]. Then sent it to the network to training, this architecture has been proven perform better than the traditional phrase-based models (Fig. 2).

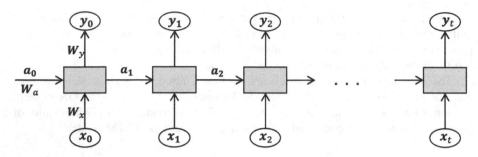

Fig. 2. A typical RNN model, where a_0 is an artificially fabricated activation value, usually a zero vector.

$$a_t = g\left[W_a(a_{t-1}, x_t)^T + b_a\right] \tag{1}$$

$$y_t = g\left(W_y a_t + b_y\right) \tag{2}$$

$$a_t = [a_{t0}, a_{t1}, \ldots a_{tk}]^T \tag{3}$$

$$W_y = [W_{y0}, W_{y1}, \ldots W_{yk}]^T \tag{4}$$

$$W_x = [W_{x0}, W_{x1}, \ldots W_{xk}]^T \tag{5}$$

$$W_a = [W_{a0}, W_{a1}, \ldots W_{ak}]^T \tag{6}$$

Here, 'x_t', 'y_t' and 'a_t' denote the input, output and the initial value in the t-th moment, 'W' and 'b' denote the weight and bias. g denotes the activation function.

Take the weight W_0 update of as an example. L is the loss function. We use the cross-loss entropy. According to the chain derivation rule, the weight update formula is:

$$\frac{\partial L}{\partial W_0} = \frac{\partial L}{\partial W_t} \cdot \frac{\partial W_t}{\partial W_{t-1}} \cdots \cdots \frac{\partial W_1}{\partial W_0} \tag{7}$$

It can be seen from the formula, that if the gradient is bigger than 1, the gradient will exponentially increase with the number of iterations; if the gradient value is smaller than 1, with the increase in the number of network layers, the gradient will gradually disappear, and the RNN's memory will fade slowly [8]. This is the problem of the disappearance of the RNN gradient.

2.3 Bidirectional LSTM Encoder-Decoder Model

Because of the gradient disappearance, the RNN cannot achieve the real memory characteristic when address long sequence [9]. If we make the gradient is equal to 1 at all the time that the gradient disappearance will be solved. Therefore, we should make a constraint to ensure that the gradient value is equal to 1 all the time. The LSTM model made improvements to RNN and solved the problems of gradient disappearance and gradient explosion [10].

In Fig. 3, 'f_t', 'i_t' and 'o_t' denote the output of forget gate, output of input gate and output of output gate. '$\widetilde{c(t)}$' denotes the intermediate variable in the t-th moment and σ denotes the sigmoid function. 'c_t' denotes the input in the t-th moment.

$$f_t = \sigma\left(W_f \cdot [y_{t-1}, x_t] + b_f\right) \tag{8}$$

$$i_t = \sigma(W_i \cdot [y_{t-1}, x_t] + b_i) \tag{9}$$

$$\widetilde{c(t)} = \tanh(W \cdot [y_{t-1}, x_t] + b_C) \tag{10}$$

$$o_t = \sigma(W_o \cdot [y_{t-1}, x_t] + b_o) \tag{11}$$

$$c_t = f_t \cdot c_{t-1} + i_t \cdot \widetilde{c(t)} \tag{12}$$

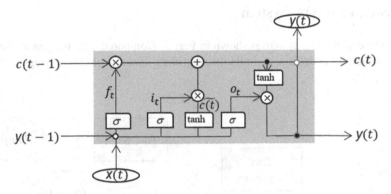

Fig. 3. LSTM encoder-decoder Model.

In order to make the system performance better, this paper used bidirectional LSTM network. Compared with unidirectional networks, bidirectional LSTM network can remember more information [12].

In Fig. 4, bidirectional LSTM is superimposed by traditional LSTM and performs better than traditional LSTM networks. The bidirectional LSTM consists of LSTM in both directions. The forward LSTM network can remember the information in the previous sequence, and the reverse can remember the information behind.

2.4 Text Similarity Calculation

A text similarity calculation is added to this QA system. TF-IDF is used to calculate the word frequency set of words in text, and combines them with vectors to calculate the similarity by comparing the cosine distances between different sets of vectors in linear space.

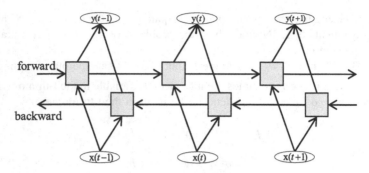

Fig. 4. A bidirectional LSTM network

This is mainly used to calculate the similarity between the input question and the question in the training set. If they are very similar, the answer to the input question is the answer to the stationery in the training set.

3 Structure of QA System

The structure of the QA system is shown in Fig. 5. Compared with the general seq2seq model, this model added a text similarity algorithm. The model can be roughly divided into two parts.

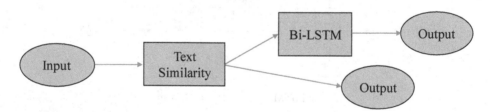

Fig. 5. The structure of the QA system

First, the input sentence is matched with the sentence in the training set by the text similarity algorithm. If the similarity with the corpus's question is extremely high, the corpus answer is output directly. If not very similar, it will enter the Bidirectional LSTM model for training to get the final output.

For the similarity evaluation, we set a threshold. The value of this threshold is set to 0.8 based on a large number of experiments. Only when the similarity between the input and the question in the corpus is higher than this threshold, the answer to the question in the corpus is output. If it is below this threshold, the final output will be obtained through the training results of Bidirectional LSTM.

4 Experiment and Discussions

4.1 Dataset

In order to complete this specific QA system, we created a new dataset which is closely related to our mission. By manual tagging, the questions and answers of the corpus are separated into two documents. The 12 categories questions and answers are mainly selected, each of which contains about 1000 answers and 1000 questions. The goal of training is to make reasonable and accurate answers to certain questions.

4.2 Simulation Results

Figure 6 displays the training process of the model, and it describes the continuous reduction of loss as the number of iterations increases. It can be obviously seen that loss shows a downward trend and eventually stabilizes. The moment loss tend to be stabilize when model tend to converge. The simulation result shows that after about 2000 iterations, model is convergent enough to 0.11. This showed that the bidirectional LSTM could be used to build the QA system.

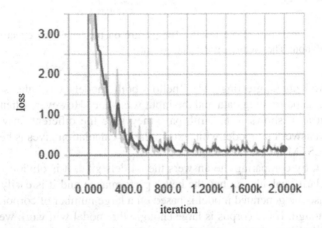

Fig. 6. Performance curve for Bidirectional LSTM model from tensor board.

4.3 Performance Comparison with Other Model

Figure 7 shows that under the same training set, both models can complete the task. It is obviously that both two models can give answers when asked. But after carefully comparing the results, we can find that the model with text similarity calculation gives the better answers which are more humanize. As far as the final display results are concerned, the effect of the model with text similarity calculation did exceed the single effect of using only the bidirectional LSTM network in some questions.

4.4   Performance Analysis

It can be seen from the Fig. 7 that adding text similarity calculation to the model can improve the performance of the QA system.

input sentence: 你好
output sentence: 您好南京首屏您考虑做百度推广吗

input sentence: 您是哪里
output sentence: 我们南京首屏主要是做百度推广的

input sentence: 怎么推广的
output sentence: 只要搜索关键词就能在百度找到您

input sentence: 有没有优惠活动
output sentence: 我们现在已经是最优惠的价格了

input sentence: 信息流是什么
output sentence: 信息流根据用户搜索习惯进行推荐

input sentence: 那好吧，不需要了
output sentence: 不好意思打扰您了

input sentence: 我不是负责人
output sentence: 您可以告诉我负责的联系方式吗

input sentence: 不方便告诉
output sentence: 不好意思打扰您了

input sentence: 再见
output sentence: 再见祝您生活愉快

input sentence: 你好
output sentence: 您好南京首屏您考虑做百度推广吗

input sentence: 你是哪里
output sentence: 不客气记下来了

input sentence: 怎么推广的
output sentence: 不好意思我们现在没有免费试用

input sentence: 有没有优惠活动
output sentence: 好的谢谢您我记下来了

input sentence: 信息流是什么
output sentence: 信息流根据用户搜索习惯进行推荐

input sentence: 那好吧，不需要了
output sentence: 不好意思打扰您了

input sentence: 我不是负责人
output sentence: 您可以告诉我负责的联系方式吗

input sentence: 不方便告诉
output sentence: 好的谢谢您我记下来了

input sentence: 再见
output sentence: 不客气

Fig. 7. This is a small part of the results. The picture on the left is the effect of adding text similarity calculation. The picture on the right is not.

When asked about greetings like 'hello', both models have the same answers because of the same training data and the input was short. However, when asked about other question as it shows in the fifth pair, they give the different answers and it is obviously the answer that model with text similarity calculation gives is better than that bidirectional LSTM gives.

As a result, by comparing the answers the models give, it is obviously that model with text similarity calculation has the better performance and it is easily accepted by people. Because the generated model is based on a large number of corpora, our corpus may not be enough. If the corpus is large enough, the model will work well. However, using text similarity model to make a QA system, as long as the input question can find a matching sentence in the corpus, it can output a relatively accurate answer. Conversely, for questions that are not in the corpus, they may not be handled well enough. In this case, we can use the generated model to get the answer. Combining the generated model with the text similarity model can find the most appropriate answer and build a relatively good performance QA system.

5   Conclusion

The work of this paper was mainly to obtain inspiration from machine translation and apply the model of machine translation to the QA system in the extension service field. After analyzing the memory defects of the RNN model from a mathematical view, we chose a bidirectional LSTM network and created a specific data set for this area. And this paper add a text similarity model in the QA system. According to the results of the final experiment, the QA system showed that model with text similarity calculation has the better performance. However, there is still much room for improvement in this QA system. Next, we may try to add attention mechanism to the model and looking for a better text similarity method.

References

1. LeCun, Y., Bengio, Y., Hinton, G.: Deep learning. Nature **521**(7553), 436 (2015)
2. Spyns, P.: Natural language processing in medicine: an overview. Methods Inf. Med. **35**(04), 285–301 (1996)
3. Turing, A.M.: Computing machinery and intelligence. In: Epstein, R., Roberts, G., Beber, G. (eds.) in Parsing the Turing Test, pp. 23–65. Springer, Dordrecht (2009). https://doi.org/10.1007/978-1-4020-6710-5_4
4. Van Merri, B.: Learning phrase representations using RNN encoder–decoder for statistical machine translation. In: Empirical Methods in Natural Language Processing, Doha, Qatar, 25–29 October 2014, pp. 1724–1734 (2014)
5. Sutskever, I., Vinyals, O., Le, Q.V.: Sequence to sequence learning with neural networks. In: Neural Information Processing Systems, Kuching, Malaysia, 3–6 November 2014, pp. 3104–3112 (2014)
6. Zhao, S.H., Li, J.-Y., Xu, B.-R., et al.: Improved TFIDF-based question similarity algorithm for the community interlocution systems. Trans. Beijing Inst. Technol. **37**(9), 982–985 (2017)
7. Bahdanau, D., Cho, K., Bengio, Y.: Neural machine translation by jointly learning to align and translate. In: International Conference on Learning Representations, San Diego, CA, USA, 7–9 May 2015, pp. 1–6 (2015)
8. Tran, K.M., Bisazza, A., Monz, C.: Recurrent memory networks for language modeling. In: North American Chapter of the Association for Computational Linguistics, San Diego, CA, USA, 12–17 June 2016, pp. 321–331 (2016)
9. Werbos, P.J.: Backpropagation through time: what it does and how to do it. Proc. IEEE **78** (10), 1550–1560 (1990)
10. Bengio, Y., Simard, P.Y., Frasconi, P.: Learning long-term dependencies with gradient descent is difficult. IEEE Trans. Neural Netw. **5**(2), 157–166 (1994)
11. Hochreiter, S., Schmidhuber, J.: Long short-term memory. Neural Comput. **9**(8), 1735–1780 (1997)
12. Greff, K., Srivastava, R.K., Koutnik, J., Steunebrink, B.R., Schmidhuber, J.: LSTM: A Search Space Odyssey. IEEE Trans. Neural Netw. Learn. Syst. **28**(10), 2222–2232 (2017)
13. Graves, A., Fernandez, S., Schmidhuber, J.: Bidirectional LSTM networks for improved phoneme classification and recognition. In: International Conference on Artificial Neural Networks, Warsaw, Poland, 11–15 September 2005, pp. 799–804 (2005)

Channel Estimation for mmWave Massive MIMO via Phase Retrieval

Zhuolei Xiao[1,2(✉)], Yunyi Li[1], and Guan Gui[3]

[1] College of Electronic and Optical Engineering and College
of Microelectronics, Nanjing University of Posts and Telecommunications,
Nanjing, China
sky_south@163.com
[2] School of Computer and Information Engineering,
Fuyang Normal University, Fuyang, China
[3] College of Telecommunication and Information Engineering,
Nanjing University of Posts and Telecommunications, Nanjing, China
guiguan@njupt.edu.cn

Abstract. The research on channel estimation technology is a core technology for mmWave massive MIMO in 5G wireless communications. This paper proposed a greedy iterative phase retrieval algorithm for channel estimation from received signal strength (RSS) feedback which is common in wireless communication systems and is used to compensate for temporal channels. We consider a Modified Gauss-Newton (MGN) algorithm to approximate the square term of the system model as a linear problem at each iteration and it is embedded in the 2-opt framework for iteration to get the optimal estimation. Our algorithm does not need to modify the system, but only need RSS feedback for channel estimation. The simulation results show that the algorithm performs better than the traditional conventional algorithm.

Keywords: Channel estimation · Received signal strength · Sparse channel · Phase retrieval

1 Introduction

As one of the core technology for 5G wireless communications, millimeter-wave Massive MIMO can effectively improve spectrum efficiency, energy efficiency and stability of the system [1]. Due to the use of a large number of base station transmit antennas to achieve highly selective spatial multiplexing in massive MIMO, it is partially important to obtain accurate channel state information (CSI) [1]. Therefore, the research on channel estimation technology is a core technology for massive MIMO, and many achievements have been achieved.

Several novel channel estimation schemes based on phase retrieval have recently been proposed for mm-Wave massive MIMO [2–4]. [2] proposed a new phase-less pilot scheme, phase-less pilot is needed at the receiver needs, which means only the magnitudes on the received pilot tones is used for channel estimation, and the phase of the pilot can be used to carry additional user data or to compensate for other signal

S. Liu and G. Yang (Eds.): ADHIP 2018, LNICST 279, pp. 348–355, 2019.
https://doi.org/10.1007/978-3-030-19086-6_39

characteristics. Based on the concept of time-varying beamforming, phase modulation and phase retrieval, [3] proposed a novel channel estimation and tracking framework based on Received Signal Strength (RSS)/Channel Quality Indicator (CQI) feedback, and proposed a generalized maximum likelihood estimator (GMLE) to estimate and track the downlink channel based on the auto-regressive channel evolution model. Wang et al. proposed in [4, 5] a multiuser magnitude-only (MO-)MIMO, and classified channel estimation and multi-user detection problems into quantized phase retrieval and solves the quantified PR problem in the framework of generalized approximate message delivery.

In order to improve the accuracy of signal estimation, this paper proposes a channel estimation scheme based on greedy iterative phase retrieval. Inspired by the novel channel estimation and tracking framework based on RSS/CQI feedback in [3], we know that MIMO channels can be estimated from RSS/CQI alone, using (pseudo) random transmit beamforming vectors, and channel coefficients recovered based on random measurements of phase retrieval. The proposed algorithm in this paper is under this feedback-based channel estimation framework, establishes the relevant channel system model, and obtains the optimal channel coefficients via the improved Gaussian Newton method. The simulation results show that the proposed channel estimation based on greedy iterative phase retrieval algorithm can obtain better performance than traditional estimation schemes.

The rest of this paper is organized as follows. We discuss the core ideas of phase retrieval and the problem of massive MIMO with downlink channel estimation in Sect. 2. Section 3 describes the proposed algorithm in details. Simulation results are presented in Sect. 4, and conclusions are drawn in Sect. 5.

2 Phase Retrieval and Massive MIMO

In this section, we firstly reviewed the core ideas of phase retrieval [6–9], which will help us to understand the proposed algorithm on channel estimation. Then, we considered a typical mm-Wave massive MIMO system with the downlink channel estimation problem.

2.1 Sparse Phase Retrieval

The recovery of a signal from the magnitude measurements of its Fourier transform is known as phase retrieval, which is motivated by applications like channel estimation [2], noncoherent optical communication [10] and underwater acoustic communication [11]. Due to the loss of Fourier phase information, this problem always be treated as an ill-posed problem. Therefore, the uniqueness of the signal and the minimization of the least-squares error in recovering the signal cannot be guaranteed.

In the phase retrieval problem, we are interested in estimating a signal $\mathbf{x} \in \mathbb{R}^N$ from the magnitude-squared of an M point DFT of this signal. i.e.

$$y_l = \left| \sum_{m=1}^n x_m e^{-\frac{2\pi j(m-1)(l-1)}{M}} \right|^2, l = 1, \cdots, M \tag{1}$$

Here $\mathbf{x}$ is sparse is k-sparse with k nonzero padding as the signal to be evaluated. This formulation is equivalent to the matrix-vector multiplication $y = |\mathbf{Fx}|^2$, where $\mathbf{F} \in \mathbb{C}^{M \times N}$ is the first N columns of the M-point DFT matrix with elements $\phi = e^{-\frac{2\pi j(m-1)(l-1)}{M}}$.

To recover the signal $\mathbf{x}$ which contains s nonzero elements at most. From the measurements y_i, we consider a minimizing the sum of squared errors cost as

$$\min_{\mathbf{x}} \sum_{i=1}^N \left(|\mathbf{F}_i \mathbf{x}|^2 - y_i \right)^2 \quad s.t. \ \|\mathbf{x}\|_0 \le s \tag{2}$$

And this problem will be combined with downlink channel estimation and solved in the following content.

2.2 System Model of Massive MIMO

In this paper, inspired by the novel channel estimation and tracking framework based on RSS/CQI feedback in [3], MIMO channels can be estimated from RSS/CQI alone, using (pseudo) random transmit beamforming vectors, and channel coefficients recovered based on random measurements of phase retrieval. Therefor we consider a downlink channel estimation problem of the typical mmWave massive MIMO system, and the system model can be given by

$$\mathbf{r} = \mathbf{w}^H \mathbf{h} \mathbf{x} + \mathbf{n} \tag{3}$$

where $\mathbf{r} \in \mathbb{C}^N$ is the received signal in the receiver, $\mathbf{w} \in \mathbb{C}^N$ is the beamforming vectors which can help transmitter send signal to the receiver, $\mathbf{h} \in \mathbb{C}^N$ is a complex valued vector at the transmitter using a special type of limited feedback information, and $\mathbf{n} \sim \mathcal{CN}(0, \sigma^2)$ is the additive white Gaussian noise. What we want to do in this paper is to estimate the channel coefficient $\mathbf{h}$ based on Received Signal Strength (RSS)/Channel Quality Indicator (CQI) feedback. And due to the characteristics of massive MIMO itself, we think its channels are sparse, i.e. $\|\mathbf{h}\|_0 \le s$.

At the receiver, RSS is sent to the transmitter through the channel in the form of digital or analog feedback, and the form of RSS is $|\mathbf{r}_i|^2$. Then we need to estimate the channel coefficient $\mathbf{h}$ from the given feedback signal magnitude information $|\mathbf{r}_i|^2$. Therefore, defining $y_i = |\mathbf{r}_i|^2$, the model of the system model is given by

$$\min_{\mathbf{h}} f(\mathbf{h}) \equiv \sum_{i=1}^N \left(y_i - |\mathbf{r}_i|^2 \right)^2 = \sum_{i=1}^N \left(y_i - |\mathbf{w}^H \mathbf{h}|^2 \right)^2 \quad s.t. \ \|\mathbf{h}\|_0 \le s \tag{4}$$

which is a phase retrieval problem. In this paper, the transmitter picks the beamforming vectors $\mathbf{w}$ to send signal to the receiver, and we consider $\mathbf{w}$ to be rows of a DFT matrix $\mathbf{W}$ as the M-point DFT matrix $\mathbf{F}$ with elements $\phi = e^{-\frac{2\pi j(m-1)(l-1)}{M}}$.

3 Greedy Iterative Phase Retrieval Based Downlink Channel Estimation

For the quadratic problem (4) we proposed a greedy iterative phase retrieval algorithm, which actually is a Gauss-Newton method with sparse prior information. In this section, we show how to optimally solve (4) in polynomial time. We embed a new Gauss-Newton method in the 2-opt algorithm framework to get the optimal estimation.

3.1 Support Information Using Auto-correlation

Before introducing the algorithm, we begin by presenting the above quadratic problem (4) in terms of the auto-correlation function. The mth entry of $\left|\mathbf{w}^H\mathbf{h}\right|^2$ is

$$
\begin{aligned}
\left|\mathbf{w}^H\mathbf{h}\right|^2 &= \sum_{n=0}^{N-1} \phi^{nm} h_n \sum_{v=0}^{N-1} \phi^{-vm} h_v^* \\
&= \sum_{k=1-N}^{N-1} \phi^{km} \sum_{n=\max(k,0)}^{\min(N-1+k,N-1)} h_n h_{n-k}^* \\
&= \sum_{k=1-N}^{N-1} \phi^{km} g_k
\end{aligned}
\tag{5}
$$

where

$$
g_k = \sum_{n=\max(k,0)}^{\min(N-1+k,N-1)} h_n h_{n-k}^*, \quad k = 1-N, \cdots, -1, 0, 1, \cdots, N-1.
\tag{6}
$$

denote the k-lag autocorrelation of $\mathbf{h}$. We usually think that in the massive MIMO environment, the channel is usually sparse. Therefore, the support of $\mathbf{h}$ is sparse, namely, there is no support cancelations occurring in g_k. Then, we can divide the support of $\mathbf{h}$ into two sets S_1 and S_2.

Denote the set of known indices in the support by S_1. Due to the relationship of the freedom degree and shift-invariance of $\mathbf{h}$, we can think that the index of the first and last non-zero elements of the autocorrelation sequence g_k is within S_1. Next, denote the set of unknown indices in the off-support by S_2, and the indices in S_2 are satisfied $g_{k-1} \neq 0$. Note that when the measurements are noisy, there are nonzero elements in the autocorrelation, which means there only the first element exist in S_1 and other elements are all in S_2.

3.2 An Efficient GNM Algorithm

To estimate the channel, we should solve the problem (4) optimally, which is a nonlinear least squares problem. Here we invoke a Modified Gauss-Newton (MGN) algorithm [12, 13] to approximate the square term in (4) as a linear problem at each iteration.

In order to avoid the latter algorithm being trapped into a local optimal solution when invoking the GN algorithm, we reward a weight parameter λ_i for $f(\mathbf{h})$, and the simulation results show that it effectively reduces the possibility of getting into a local optimal solution. The weight λ_i will randomly be 1 or 1.5. Finally we can write (4) as

$$\min_{\mathbf{h}} f(\mathbf{h}) \equiv \sum_{i=1}^{N} \left(y_i - |\mathbf{w}^H \mathbf{h}|^2 \right)^2 = \sum_{i=1}^{N} p_i^2(\mathbf{h}) \tag{7}$$

At each iteration, we expand and approximate the first order Taylor of $p_i(\mathbf{h})$ around $\mathbf{h}_k$ as

$$p_i \approx p_i(\mathbf{h}_k) + \nabla p_i(\mathbf{h}_k)^T (\mathbf{h} - \mathbf{h}_k) \tag{8}$$

which is a linear least squares problem. Via GN method we can get the solution of the problem (7)

$$\mathbf{h}_{k+1} = \mathbf{h}_k - \left(J(\mathbf{h}_k)^T J(\mathbf{h}_k) \right)^{-1} J(\mathbf{h}_k)^T \mathbf{h}_k \tag{9}$$

where the element of the Jacobian matrix $J(\mathbf{h}_k)$ is $J_{ij} = \partial p_i / \partial h_j$, the direction vector $\mathbf{d}_k = \mathbf{h}_k - \mathbf{h}_{k+1}$, and the choice of stepsize t_k is a backtracking procedure, i.e.

$$f(\mathbf{h}_k - t_k \mathbf{d}_k) < f(\mathbf{h}_k) - t_{k+1} \nabla f(\mathbf{h}_k)^T \mathbf{d}_k \tag{10}$$

where $t_k = \left(\frac{1}{2}\right)^n$, n is a nonnegative minimum integer.

Algorithm 1. MGN algorithm

Input: Combining matrix $\mathbf{W}$, and measurement y_i at the receiver, the given indices set S, the maximum number of iterations L, the stopping threshold ξ and the initial stepsize $t_0 = 0.5$.

Output: The optimal estimate of sparse channel $\mathbf{h}$ of (4)

1. Generate an initial vector $\mathbf{h}_0$ with the given support S.
2. **for** $k = 0, 1, \cdots, L$ **do**
3. $\mathbf{h}_{k+1} = \mathbf{h}_k - (J(\mathbf{h}_k)^T J(\mathbf{h}_k))^{-1} J(\mathbf{h}_k)^T \mathbf{h}_k$.
4. The direction of Gaussian Newton is $\mathbf{d}_k = \mathbf{h}_k - \mathbf{h}_{k+1}$, and the stepsize $t_k = \left(\frac{1}{2}\right)^n$ which should satisfy $f(\mathbf{h}_k - t_k \mathbf{d}_k) < f(\mathbf{h}_k) - t_{k+1} \nabla f(\mathbf{h}_k)^T \mathbf{d}_k$.
5. Advance $\mathbf{h}_{k+1} = \mathbf{h}_k - t_k \mathbf{d}_k$, if $\| \mathbf{h}_{k+1} - \mathbf{h}_k \| < \xi$, then stop the iteration, otherwise go to step 3.
6. **end for**

3.3 2-opt Method of the Support Information

2-opt is a local search algorithm, which change two elements at each iteration [14]. In this paper, we use it as the external framework of our algorithm. First, we have an initial random support set S of the channel coefficient $\mathbf{h}$, and S satisfy the support constraints $S_1 \subseteq S \subseteq S_2$. Then, the two indices i in S_1 and j in S_2 are exchanged at each iteration. The index i in S_1 is correspond to the current iterate value $\min_k |\mathbf{h}_k|$, and the index j in S_2 is correspond to $\max_k \nabla f(\mathbf{h}_k)$. After the exchange is completed, the MGN algorithm will be invoked for a new round of iterations. After the optimal value is output, it will be exchanged until the optimal solution is obtained.

Algorithm 2. 2-opt algorithm

Input: Combining matrix $\mathbf{W}$, the measurement y_i at the receiver, the stopping threshold τ and the maximum number of index exchanging T.

Output: The optimal estimate of sparse channel $\mathbf{h}$

1. Generate a random index set S_0, then $\mathbf{h}_0 = MGN[w_i, y_i, S_0, L]$
2. **for** $k = 0,1,\cdots$ **do**
3. $i = \min_k |\mathbf{h}_k|, j = \max_k \nabla f(\mathbf{h}_k)$, make an exchange between them to generate a new index set S_k
4. $\mathbf{h}_{k+1} = MGN[w_i, y_i, S_k, L]$
5. If $f(\mathbf{h}_{k+1}) < f(\mathbf{h}_k)$, then advanced k, otherwise continue to exchange up to T. Stop if $f(\mathbf{h}_{k+1}) < \tau$, and the output is $\mathbf{h}_{k+1}$.
6. **end for**

---

4 Simulation Results

In this section, we study the performance of the proposed phase restoration based massive MIMO channel estimation through simulation results. Here we are given some system parameters, the number of maximum indices in index set S is $n = 64$ and the number of the sampling measurement y_i is $N = 128$. In order to recover the channel estimation $\mathbf{h}$, we use $\tau = 10^{-10}$ and $T = 10000$.

Figure 1 shows the recovery probability under different channel sparse level. We observed that almost 100% successful recovery with SNR = 1001 which is treated as noiseless. And the recovery probability under SNR < 30 is also very high before the sparse level $k < 10$. The result presents that we can recover the channel estimation $\mathbf{h}$ accurately in the sparse channel.

Figure 2 compares the normalized mean square error (NMSE) performance against the signal-to-noise (SNR). Here we compare the proposed algorithm with the other two commonly used algorithms: OMP-based [15] algorithm and SD-based [16] algorithm. It is clear that in the vast majority of cases, the proposed algorithm performs much better than the other two algorithms, especially when SNR < 10 or SNR > 15, and the larger the SNR, the better the performance of the channel estimation based on greedy iterative phase retrieval algorithm.

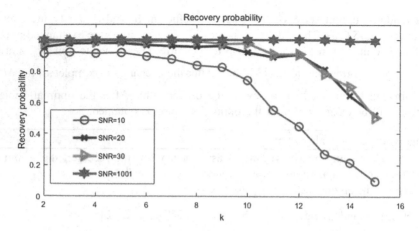

Fig. 1. Recovery probability under different sparse level of proposed algorithm

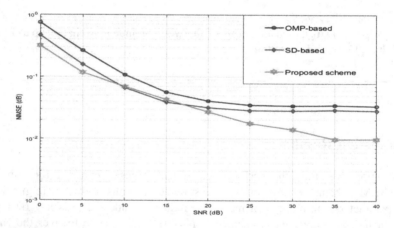

Fig. 2. NMSE performance comparison of different channel estimation schemes against SNR

5 Conclusions

In this paper, we have proposed a greedy iterative phase retrieval algorithm, which is a fast algorithm for estimating the channel estimation from the RSS feedback information at the receiver. Since the RSS feedback does not contain any phase information, we can use the phase retrieval method to perform channel estimation. Our core algorithm is a Gaussian Newton algorithm and it is embedded in the 2-opt framework for iteration. Simulations show that the algorithm performs well in recovering channel coefficients and is more robust to noise.

Acknowledgment. This work was supported by the Natural Science Foundation of Fuyang Normal University (2015KJ007) and the Horizontal project of Fuyang Normal University (XDHX201741).

References

1. Rappaport, T.S., et al.: Millimeter wave mobile communications for 5G cellular: it will work! IEEE Access **1**, 335–349 (2013)
2. Walk, P., Becker, H., Jung, P.: OFDM channel estimation via phase retrieval. In: Asilomar Conference on Signals Systems and Computers, pp. 1161–1168 (2015)
3. Qiu, T., Fu, X., Sidiropoulos, N.D., Palomar, D.P.: MISO channel estimation and tracking from received signal strength feedback. IEEE Trans. Signal Process. **66**(7), 1691–1704 (2018)
4. Wang, S., Zhang, L., Jing, X.: Phase retrieval motivated nonlinear MIMO communication with magnitude measurements. IEEE Trans. Wirel. Commun. **16**(8), 5452–5466 (2017)
5. Wang, S., Li, Y., Wang, J.: Multiuser detection in massive MIMO with quantized phase-only measurements. In: Proceedings of the IEEE International Conference on Communications, pp. 4576–4581, June 2015
6. Candès, E.J., Strohmer, T., Voroninski, V.: PhaseLift: exact and stable signal recovery from magnitude measurements via convex programming. Commun. Pure Appl. Math. **66**(8), 1241–1274 (2013)
7. Soltanolkotabi, M.: Algorithms and theory for clustering and nonconvex quadratic programming. Ph.D. thesis, Stanford University (2014)
8. Chen, Y., Candès, E.J.: Solving random quadratic systems of equations is nearly as easy as solving linear systems. Commun. Pure Appl. Math. **70**(5), 822–883 (2017)
9. Wang, G., Giannakis, G.B., Eldar, Y.C.: Solving systems of random quadratic equations via truncated amplitude flow. IEEE Trans. Inf. Theory **64**(2), 773–794 (2018)
10. Karp, R.M., Sherman, G.: Optical Communications. Wiley Interscience, New York (1976)
11. Stojanovic, M., Proakis, J.G., Catipovic, J.A.: Phase-coherent digital communications for underwater acoustic channels. IEEE J. Ocean. Eng. **19**(1), 100–111 (1994)
12. Bertsekas, D.P.: Nonlinear Programming. Athena Scientific, Nashua (1999)
13. Bjork, A.: Numerical Methods for Least Squares Problems. Society for Industrial Mathematics, Philadelphia (1996)
14. Papadimitriou, C.H., Steiglitz, K.: Combinatorial Optimization: Algorithms and Complexity. Dover, New York (1998)
15. Méndez-Rial, R., Rusu, C., Alkhateeb, A., González-Prelcic, N., Heath Jr., R.W.: Channel estimation and hybrid combining for mmWave: phase shifters or switches? In: Proceedings of Information Theory and Applications Workshop (ITA), pp. 90–97, February 2015
16. Gao, X., Dai, L., Han, S., Chih-Lin, I., Wang, X.: Reliable beamspace channel estimation for millimeter-wave massive MIMO systems with lens antenna array. IEEE Trans. Wirel. Commun. **16**(9), 6010–6021 (2017)

Interactive Design of Web User Interface Adaptive Display

HuiZhen Li[1(✉)] and Fei Gao[2,3]

[1] Guangxi Teachers Education University, Guangxi, Nanning 530001, China
gongzuo0758@163.com
[2] School of Information Science and Technology, Tibet University,
Lhasa, Tibet 850000, China
h13467985201@163.com
[3] Science and Research Office of Tibet University, Lhasa, Tibet 850000, China

Abstract. Aiming at the weakness of the human-computer interaction function in the current Web user display interface, long system feedback time and high error rate of data query, an interactive Web user interface display interactive design was proposed. Firstly, the requirements of user interface display are analyzed from the aspects of user role positioning, design availability analysis and interaction interface influence factors, and then the interactive scheme research of Web user interface is given. The overall interactive design scheme includes the operating program design, the usability design and the adaptive design of the interface color. From the above three points of view, the function of the design is expounded, and the convenience and friendliness of the interface are improved. Simulation results show that the proposed adaptive interaction design method can effectively shorten the feedback time of the system and reduce the error rate of data query. Adaptive display based on the advantages of human-machine interaction can better meet the needs of Web users.

Keywords: Web user · Display interface · Adaptive · Interactive design

1 Introduction

Web network is a global dynamic text and graphical information interaction system based on HTML and HTTP protocol [1, 2]. The Web user interface is derived from a digital model of the working environment, and provides the user with a full range of three-dimensional internet services by the way of the web site. Web net user interface has always been a visual expression method, and webpage as the carrier's new design. Web network organizes the content [3] of the site based on the user's interaction needs, and adaptively adjusts the contents and overall layout of the interaction display. With the evolution and upgrading of HTML technology, CSS technology has also evolved to the latest generation of. Literature [4] designed a control program based on the Physical Experiment and Industrial Control System (EPICS) architecture to realize remote monitoring of the RF ion source experiment and debugging process. The NBI RF ion source control program is integrated. The development interface (Control System Studio, CSS) interactive interface development module (Best OPI Yet, BOY)

S. Liu and G. Yang (Eds.): ADHIP 2018, LNICST 279, pp. 356–364, 2019.
https://doi.org/10.1007/978-3-030-19086-6_40

implements a friendly human-computer interaction interface, uses Jython to implement interface logic, and supports server/client and EPICS communication architectures. Literature [5] designed NBI RF ion source control program realizes friendly human-computer interaction interface through the integrated development platform (Control System Studio, CSS) interactive interface development module (Best OPI Yet, BOY), uses Jython to realize interface logic, supports server/client End and EPICS two communication architectures. The user interface of the web site is no longer only a display of the content of the Internet, it also carries the interaction link with the Web users, and whether the success of the business is also the standard for the design of the Web. Because of the particularity of the Internet, Web user interface design has become an interdisciplinary and cross domain knowledge complex. In order to provide better comprehensive services for the network users, it is necessary to use the Internet technology, human-computer interaction technology, computer graphics, programming and so on to provide more efficient network service [6–8].

2   Web User Interface Adaptive Display Design Requirements

2.1   User Role Positioning

In the overall Web user interface adaptive design, including the most important two design elements, namely human and interactive interface dialogue system. The first requirement of adaptive interface display design is for users of the network to perform roles in the following 5 aspects. (1) The purpose, that is, the use of Web users and the deep motivation of the interactive system, the human-computer interaction interface should meet the user's most basic requirements, so that the function of the system is more comprehensive and intelligent. (2) Behavior, that is, Web users' habit of using man-machine, can understand the user's usage behavior in detail, and be able to do the next work arrangement. (3) Attitude, that is, how Web users perceive their man-machine interaction system, can provide users with the most basic needs. (4) Ability, users have different preferences for network interaction system, each has their own strengths. We should choose the best and most university mode. (5) Skills, the various elements related to the user's needs, the user's personal information, and the use preference of the user, and more accurately grasp the user's use habits through the analysis of the skills.

2.2   Usability Analysis of Prototype Design

Through the analysis of the above role positioning, the key interactive design points are selected and accumulated, that is, user location and user needs, interactive interface design [9, 10] research requirements, as shown in Fig. 1:

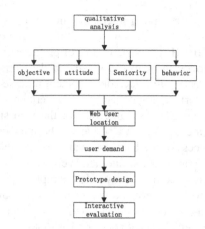

Fig. 1. Web user interface design requirements for adaptive interaction

2.3   Analysis of Factors of Adaptive User Interface Interaction Design

In the process of man-machine interaction between Web users and desktop, there are many factors that will affect the final interaction results. These factors mainly include the user's subjective factors, the user's knowledge reserve, professional background, interest and preference, and personal preference, while the objective factors include the current level of industry development, the hardware configuration used, the software system installed, and the completeness of the adaptable software. These factors affect the final interaction results.

3   Realization of Web User Interface Adaptive Display Interaction Design

Web user interface adaptive display interactive design, including the operating program design, interactive feasibility analysis method and the software interface color adjustment and other different components.

3.1   Operating Program Design

In the beginning of human-computer interaction, it is necessary to sort out the work program of the system first, start the human-computer interaction system and realize the different functions of the system according to the different purposes. Adjusting the various parameters of interface settings mainly includes different functions such as leveling, preheating, document filtering and program classification. The operation interface program design is an important step and key step before the prototype design. The specific execution procedure is shown in Fig. 2.

File filtering is one of the key steps in Web user interface adaptive display and interactive design, which is part of pseudo code designed for file filter program.

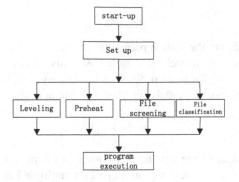

Fig. 2. The operation interface program design

DFJJINFRRS="""" **

USEdedeSDK=""""

&SQL （Var intern=document fofo

Var intern=session CAL

&SQL （.i Sussess　return 0***;

.iiiie return 1***

sjly Var inrin=startdate,zdh****

coce=1:f_endmrld

QQJ （insert into MRIP_dailydata）

.isussess　return****

WRLKPIname

Through the operation of the pseudo code, the Web user interface adaptive display interactive design can be realized, and the files can be filtered effectively. First, through the interface program flow, complete the initial adaptive display steps, then file filtering, input the pseudo code, to achieve the design of display interaction.

3.2   Usability Analysis

Based on 2.1 program setting and research analysis results, this paper uses a comprehensive heuristic result understanding scheme to analyze the feasibility of the adaptive interaction scheme. In the selection of the scheme and the feasibility evaluation, in order to select the best and high quality interactive scheme, this paper uses multiple linear regression to determine the feasibility of the interaction scheme. Assuming that the Web user interface adaptively displays interactive design, the multiple linear regression model is as follows:

$$y = \xi_0 + \xi_1 x + \tau \tag{1}$$

Among them, ξ_0 and ξ_1 are the system parameters of multiple linear regression models, and τ is the error of model selection. At this time, a set of constant $\{(x_i, y_i), i = 1, 2, 3, \ldots, n\}$ for basic program selection is given, based on least squares and multiple linear regression models for classification and digital prediction.

$$\hat{y} = \hat{\xi}_0 + \hat{\xi}_1 x \tag{2}$$

The parameters $\hat{\alpha}_0$ and $\hat{\alpha}_1$ of the new human-computer interaction system are the least squares estimation of the parameters ξ_0 and ξ_1 of the multiple linear regression model. The goodness of fit of the detection system is W^2, which describes the relationship between the explanatory variable and the explanatory variable, that is, it can determine the feasibility of the final human-computer interaction scheme with the explanatory variable.

$$W^2 = \frac{W_1^2}{W_2^2} = \frac{\sum_{i=1}^{n} (\hat{y}_i - \bar{y})^2}{\sum_{i=1}^{n} (y_i - \bar{y})^2} = 1 - \frac{\sum_{i=1}^{n} (\bar{y} - \hat{y}_i)^2}{\sum_{i=1}^{n} (\bar{y} - y_i)^2} \tag{3}$$

Among them, W_1^2 and W_2^2 are $\sum_{i=1}^{n} (\hat{y}_i - \bar{y})^2$ and $\sum_{i=1}^{n} (y_i - \bar{y})^2$ respectively, so the coefficient of determination of the model is η: the square of correlation coefficient.

$$\eta = \frac{\left[\sum_{i=1}^{n} (x_i - \bar{x})(y_i - \bar{y}) \right]^2}{\sum_{i=1}^{n} (x_i - \bar{x})^2 \sum_{i=1}^{n} (y_i - \bar{y})^2} \tag{4}$$

Evaluation and cognitive process browsing are two evaluation methods to analyze the usability of the design prototype, and the evaluation method of cognitive process browsing also requires a Web user to participate in it. The evaluation method also describes the whole operation process to improve the user's understanding and understanding of the human-computer interaction function of the Web interface.

3.3 Implementation of Software Interface Color Selection and Adaptive Interaction Design

Color design is also a key part of the whole Web user adaptive interface design. Color can give Web users the feeling of beauty. The color design of software interface represents the user's first impression and determines the operation efficiency of users in the whole environment. Different colors have different psychological hints, which bring different user experience to Web users. In the human-computer interaction process of network users, users need to obtain accurate human interaction information, more need to get a beautiful feeling and good interaction system. The color of the system UI interface will determine the loyalty of the user to a great extent. The main color matching of the interface and the color of the key prompt should not only express the information accurately, but also play an important role in accurately communicating the information. Adaptive interface display has powerful system function, which can provide a variety of options according to different user's Web user preferences. For example, some users prefer lively warm hue, some users like quiet cold hue, adaptive display scheme can provide users with multiple choices and bring more relaxed and good users. Good experience.

In this paper, an adaptive interactive mode is designed to design the specific operation program and color selection method. Based on the multiple linear regression method, the feasibility of the specific design scheme is determined to meet the network needs of different Web users.

4 Experimental Results and Analysis

4.1 Setting of Experimental Environment

The purpose of the simulation experiment is to verify the superiority and effectiveness of the adaptive display interface design compared with the traditional design. The simulation experiment environment is composed of multiple network servers and user's terminal interaction interface systems. The related network service level and network parameters are set, as shown in Tables 1 and 2, respectively.

Table 1. Service level and systematization initial value

Service distribution level	Upper limit value	Lower limit value
1 Lower	25	8
2 Intermediate	32	15
3 Senior	41	25

4.2 Experimental Results and Analysis

This paper first verifies the adaptive Web user interaction time, because the design has an adaptive advantage and can balance the load capacity of the system, so it has a significant advantage in the response time of human-computer interaction. The number of samples selected is 200. The average response time of this paper is about 0.2 s, and it is stable in the whole sample space, and there is no obvious fluctuation. And the interaction time of the traditional interactive mode not only exceeds the design scheme in each sample space range, but also is not good in the stability performance.

As shown in Fig. 3, comparing the system response time of the proposed method with the traditional method, the number of samples in 200 groups is selected. The response time of this method fluctuates greatly, while the response time of the traditional method is relatively stable. When the number of test samples is 100, the response time of this method is 0.52 s; the response time of the traditional method is 0.2 s, the biggest difference.

Table 2. Experimental parameter setting

	Web parameters	Set value
Human-computer interaction system	Equipment model	*RRITD* – 8.0
	RAM	8 G
	Bandwidth	100 M
	CPU	G850
	Highest primary frequency	2.8 GHz
	Development tool	VS 2013
	Operating system	Windows 10

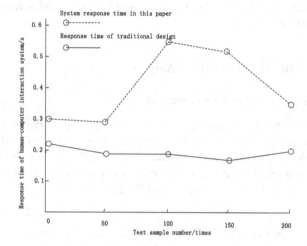

Fig. 3. System response time comparison

The design has obvious advantages in the error rate control of data query. As shown in Fig. 4, the error rate of data query in this paper can be controlled within 0.2%, which is better than the traditional human-computer interaction design.

The error rate of the traditional human-machine interaction system is close to 0.4%, and the fluctuation is large and the stability is not enough in the whole range of sample changes. The results of the data analysis prove that the adaptive display based on the advantages of human-machine interaction design in terms of functionality can better meet the needs of Web users.

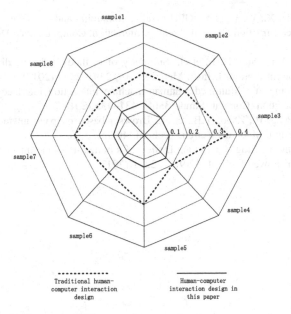

Fig. 4. Common SDN network user control error rate performance

5 Concluding Remarks

Whether the display interface of human-computer interaction is friendly and convenient will ultimately determine the number of access to Web users. This article has designed a Web user interaction mode under the adaptive mode for the shortcomings of the traditional human-computer interaction system. The article gives the concrete control and feasibility scheme demonstration, and the simulation experiment results also prove the article. The superiority and applicability of the design.

References

1. Liu, L., Zhang, Ch., Zhang, Q.X., et al.: Analysis and verification of a SkyDrive authentication protocol. Comput. Appl. **37**(S1), 317–320 (2017)
2. Weng, Z.H., Wang, P.: Heterogeneous multi network Http/2 energy cost control video stream transmission model. Comput. Eng. Des. (1), 5–10 (2018)
3. Gu, Y.R., Zhu, Z.Y.: Sorting algorithm for important nodes in complex networks based on LeaderRank and node similarity. J. Univ. Electron. Sci. Technol. Chin. **46**(2), 441–448 (2017)
4. Sun, J.N., Wang, X.C.H., et al.: A method for the preparation of K_2CsSb photocathode by using the theoretical model of reflectivity. Infrared Technol. **39**(12), 1087–1091 (2017)
5. Hu, C.H.D., Chen, G.Y., Xie, Y.H., et al.: NBI based RF ion source control program design based on CSS. Core Technol. **40**(11), 39–44 (2017)

6. Shao, X.Q., Nie, X., Wang, B.Y.: GPU parallel computing and accelerated real-time visual housing 3D reconstruction and virtual reality interaction. Comput. Aided Des. Graph. **29**(1), 52–61 (2017)
7. Lu, X., Chen, X.L., Sun, H.H., et al.: Summary of methods of haptic display for natural human-machine interaction. J. Instr. Meter **33**(10), 2391–2399 (2017)
8. Jing, G.D., Zhang, Y.: Multimedia human-machine interaction interface visual accuracy evaluation simulation. Comput. Simul. **35**(4), 431–435 (2018)
9. Hu, Z.H.M., Peng, B., Zhao, Y.B., et al.: Browser based on page interaction mechanism architecture design. Modern Electron. Technol. **40**(15), 59–63 (2017)
10. Wang, W., Song, J., Xing, J.Y., et al.: Design of a human-machine interactive photovoltaic array simulator. Power Technol. **17**(9), 1322–1 (2017)

Method for Quickly Obtaining User Browsing Behavior Data Under Cloud Computing

Jinbao Shan[✉] and Haitao Guo

College of Information Technology & Art Design,
Shandong Institute of Commerce and Technology, Jinan 250103, China
maojun1980@126.com

Abstract. Under cloud computing, traditional user browsing behavior data acquisition method cannot optimize data classification, which results in slow and low accuracy of data acquisition. For this reason, a fast method to obtain user browsing behavior data under cloud computing is proposed. Using node processing user browsing behavior data, complete the query the user browsing behavior data collection, provide the conditions for data classification optimization, the data to calculate the similar characteristics after multiple iterations data peak, peak according to complete the user browsing behavior data classification, the classification of output data integration, realize the cloud user browsing behavior fast data acquisition. Compared with the traditional data acquisition method, the data acquisition speed of the design method is increased by 20 min and the accuracy is increased by 45%. The experimental data show that the overall performance of the proposed method is better than the traditional method, and it has strong practicability and high reference value.

Keywords: Cloud computing · User browsing behavior data ·
Fast data acquisition · Acquisition speed

1 Introduction

In the era of big data, with the rapid development of the Internet, the rapid growth of the number of users browsing will generate a large amount of user browsing behavior data. The traditional method cannot achieve rapid acquisition of massive data. Therefore, the rapid acquisition of user browsing behavior data has become an urgent need to be solved [1].

Reference [2] proposed a mobile Internet big data user behavior analysis engine solution, designed the key modules of user behavior data acquisition system, big data warehousing and preprocessing components and big data user behavior analysis model. It is verified that this method can effectively collect user behavior information, but there is a defect that the collection efficiency is not high when faced with massive data. In the reference [3], an improved hierarchical clustering algorithm CURE is proposed. The algorithm uses the Map Meduce function to parallelize the way of sampling and processing data in the original algorithm. At the same time, combined with the concept of interval number, the mobile user data is represented by an interval, calculate the interval distance to adapt to the uncertainty of mobile user data, thereby improving the

S. Liu and G. Yang (Eds.): ADHIP 2018, LNICST 279, pp. 365–371, 2019.
https://doi.org/10.1007/978-3-030-19086-6_41

accuracy of clustering. Although the algorithm can guarantee the accuracy of clustering, the implementation process of the algorithm is more complicated and not simple enough.

Due to the fact that the traditional data acquisition method has a slower acquisition rate, lower acquisition accuracy, and lower acquisition accuracy. This article designed a user browsing behavior data query and data classification optimization algorithm, combine the two algorithms to generate a data acquisition algorithm, and enumerate examples. Because the traditional data acquisition method has the disadvantages of slow acquisition speed, low acquisition rate, and low acquisition accuracy, this article designs a user browsing behavior data query and data classification optimization algorithm that combines two algorithms to generate data acquisition. Experimental results show that the proposed method improves the data acquisition accuracy by 45%, which shows that the proposed method is more suitable for acquiring user browsing behavior data than the traditional method.

2   Cloud Computing User Browse Data Acquisition Method Design

2.1   Collect Query User Browsing Behavior Data

When querying the user's browsing behavior data, it is necessary to first determine the query node. When receiving a query request, each node needs to sense and simultaneously collect the data source of the area covered by the node, and perform operations such as calculation and processing on it. Get result sets that tend to request, the energy required to set the above stages is e_i. Each node then transmits data to the query node along its own path, in the process of transmission, each node conducts fusion processing on the received data.

When the node i Transfer information to j, node i energy required to transmit unit information $e_l(i)$ can be described as:

$$e_l(i) = (e_i + e_d r_{ij}^n)B \tag{1}$$

$$r_{ij} = \sqrt{(x_i - x_j)^2 + (y_i - y_j)^2} \tag{2}$$

In the formula, e_l used to describe the energy required to deliver each bit of information, unit is J/b; e_d used to describe the unit energy loss during mass data transmission in a distributed cloud computing environment, e_l and e_d Mainly depends on the query node itself; Parameter n Used to describe the channel loss index, mainly depends on distributed cloud computing network environment; The greater the noise, n the greater the value, usually take 2 and 4; r_{ij} used to describe the transmission distance; B is a fixed value. x and y denotes the data's independent variables [4].

Node j slave node i the energy required to receive the unit information $e_r(j)$ can be described as:

$$e_r(j) = e_r B \tag{3}$$

In the formula, e_r used to describe the energy required to receive each bit of information, unit is J/b.

Then the information of the K layer node needs to be transmitted through the $K - 1$ node, assume that the distance between the i layer node and the $i - 1$ layer is d_i, the energy consumption of a message transmission can be calculated by the following formula [5–7]:

$$e_k = \sum_{i=1}^{k} (e_l + e_d d_i^n) B$$
$$= (k e_l + e_d \sum_{i}^{k} d_i^n) B \tag{4}$$

However, not all node information on the M layer is passed to the root node, after the information on the M layer is sent to the $M - 1$ layer, data fusion processing is required, there is less information to reach the root node, therefore, e_k is the ultimate value of the quantity of information.

Assume that under a query request, the node i conducts m message sending and n message receiving, the remaining energy of the node i after the query can be described as:

$$E_{leave} = e - \sum_{a=1}^{m} e_l(i, j_a) - \sum_{b=1}^{n} e_r(i, j_b) - e_i \tag{5}$$
$$and \quad j_a, j_b \in N_i$$

In the formula, $\sum_{a=1}^{m} e_l(i, j_a)$ and $\sum_{b=1}^{n} e_r(i, j_b)$ are used to describe the energy consumption of m information transmission and n information reception respectively; e_i is used to describe the energy consumption required by node i to process data.

In summary, after calculating the energy consumption required for each node to process user browsing behavior data, the data can be queried according to the calculation result.

2.2 Data Optimization Classification

After successfully querying users for browsing behavior data, these data are classified and optimized. For databases that contain large amounts of data in a cloud computing environment. The data text is described by $p(t)$, the designed transmission operator is described by $h_i(t)$, complete the convolution operation, $n_{pi}(t)$ is used to describe classification interference, the genetic iterative classification spread can be described as [8, 9]:

$$p_n(t) = p(t) * h_i(t) + n_{pi}(t) \qquad (6)$$

Among them, $h_i(t)$ is used to describe how $p(t)$ performs mass data classification and optimization in a cloud computing environment, the classification response function between data is:

$$S_{ri}(t) = S(t) * h_i(t) + n_{ri}(t) \qquad (7)$$

Among them, $S_{ri}(t)$ is used to describe the corresponding function of classification between data; $h_i'(t)$ is used to describe the corresponding channel function of the massive data in the cloud computing environment in the $S(t)$ classification process, then there are:

$$\begin{aligned} r_i(t) &= S_n(t) * p_{ri}(-t) \\ &= S(t) * (-t) * h_i(t) * h_i(-t) + n_{1i}(t) \end{aligned} \qquad (8)$$

Among them, $n_{li}(t)$ is used to describe classification interference items of similar characteristic data when classifying, then:

$$\begin{aligned} r(t) &= \sum_{i=1}^{M} r_i(t) * p(t) \\ &= S(t) * p(t) * p(-t) * \sum_{i=1}^{M} h_i(t) * h_i(-t) + \sum_{i=1}^{M} n_i(t) \end{aligned} \qquad (9)$$

If the peak of the $p(t)$ autocorrelation amplitude is prominent, there are:

$$p(t) * p(-t) \cong \delta(t) \qquad (10)$$

In the formula, δ is the coefficient [10].

In this way, the formula for optimizing the mass data classification in the cloud computing environment is:

$$\begin{aligned} r(t) &\cong S(t) * \delta(t) * \sum_{i=1}^{M} \delta(t) + \sum_{i=1}^{M} n_i(t) \\ &= MS(t) + \sum_{i=1}^{M} n_i(t) \end{aligned} \qquad (11)$$

Because nodes that exceed the distribution area mainly use multi-hop to transmit information, it is assumed that there are M layers in the distributed cloud computing environment. Then, the information of the n_i layer node needs to be transmitted through the S layer, and is transmitted layer by layer to the source node. According to formula

(11), we can get the classification of massive data in the cloud computing environment. In the formula, $r(t)$ represents the result of massive data classification.

2.3 Realizing Fast Acquisition of User Data in Cloud Computing

Integrate 1.1 Designed User Browsing Behavior Data Query Algorithms and 1.2 Designed Data Optimized Classification Algorithms, get a quick calculation algorithm for cloud computing user browsing behavior data, namely:

Bring user browsing information into the data acquisition algorithm formula, first, use formula (4) and (5) to calculate the energy consumption required for each node to process user browsing behavior data, the calculated result is the user browsing data on each node; then the calculated query data is brought into formula (11), calculate the peak value of the similar feature data at the time of classification by genetically iterative classification calculations, this completes the optimization of data classification, output the same type of data directly, in this way, the user's browsing behavior data under cloud computing can be quickly obtained.

3 Experimental Analysis

3.1 Experimental Data

In order to verify the validity of the design method of this article, it will be tested. The experimental data comes from the browsing sequence of different types of users on a website. The site has 90 main navigation bars, there is a cross between the navigation bar contents, and the navigation bar nests up to four levels. The personnel involved in the experiment came from people of different age groups, different career backgrounds, and different educational backgrounds. By using the user behavior data to obtain the mathematical model on the client side, the user behavior data of the experimenter browsing the website is obtained, and the duration is 160 min.

3.2 Experimental Results and Analysis

The comparison between the data collected by this method and the traditional method in the same time is shown in Fig. 1.

As can be seen from Fig. 1, under the same operation time, the data scale obtained by the method in this paper is larger than that obtained by the traditional method, and with the increase of time. The larger the gap between the data acquisition scale of this method and the traditional method is, the faster the data acquisition speed and more data are obtained.

As can be seen from Fig. 2, when the data set increases gradually, the acquisition hit ratio of both the present method and the traditional method decreases to a certain extent. In the range of error tolerance, the acquisition hit ratio of this method is obviously higher than that of the traditional method, which proves the effectiveness of this method.

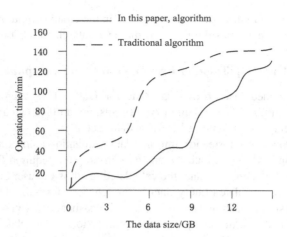

Fig. 1. Data collection

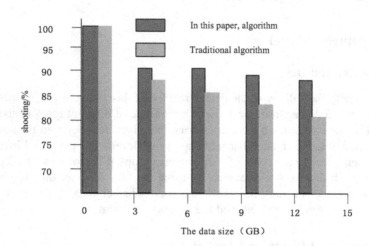

Fig. 2. Shows the hit ratio comparison

Table 1. Data acquisition error

	In this paper, algorithm	Traditional algorithm
Mean absolute error	0.342	4.161
Root mean square error	1.240	10.520

The data acquisition error of the algorithm and the traditional algorithm in this paper is shown in Table 1.

Several experimental results show that the design of data acquisition method compared with traditional methods, data acquisition speed faster, data capture ratio higher, obtain the result accuracy is higher, and speed, shooting and accuracy are increased by about 45%.

4 Conclusion

In this paper, the method of data acquisition of browsing behavior of cloud computing users is designed to improve the speed, hit rate and accuracy of data acquisition through data query and data optimization classification. The test data show that compared with the traditional methods, the method designed in this paper has improved the speed, the hit rate and the accuracy by about 45%. It is hoped that this study can provide useful help for users to obtain browsing behavior data.

References

1. Alharbi, S.: An empirical investigation on the impact of trust mediated determinants and moderating factors on the adoption of cloud computing. Int. J. Inf. Technol. Comput. Sci. 9(11), 12–22 (2017)
2. Gdaniec, N., Szwargulski, P., Knopp, T.: Fast multi-resolution data acquisition for magnetic particle imaging using adaptive feature detection. Med. Phys. 44(12), 6456 (2017)
3. Gao, C., Wang, H., Wang, J.: An improved CURE algorithm based on the uncertainty of mobile user data clustering. Comput. Eng. Sci. 38(4), 768–774 (2016)
4. Namasudra, S., Roy, P.: Time saving protocol for data accessing in cloud computing. IET Commun. 11(10), 1558–1565 (2017)
5. Zhe, D., Zhen, Q., Zheng, W.T., et al.: A recommendation model based on browsing behaviors of mobile users. J. Univ. Electron. Sci. Technol. China 46(6), 907–912 (2017)
6. Bo, Z., Jin, L.: Research on the acquisition and application of user data in publishing industry against the background of big data. Editors' Friend 12(8), 26–31 (2017)
7. Guohua, Y., Jingjing, K., Fang, L.: Data source description approach for deep web based on domain features and user query-based sampling. Libr. Inf. Serv. 1(15), 138–145 (2017)
8. Taieb, C.: A quick model method for obtaining real-height parameters from routine ionospheric data. Radio Sci. 2(10), 1263–1267 (2016)
9. Wang, Y.: Accurate detection of user characteristic data in large data network. Comput. Simul. 34(6), 415–418 (2017)
10. Yang, J., Shi, Z., Liu, Z.: Simulation research on fast acquisition of terminal user information based on big data analysis. Comput. Simul. 1(2), 110–111 (2018)

Precipitation Prediction Based on KPCA Support Vector Machine Optimization

Fangqiong Luo[1], Guodong Wang[2(✉)], and Yu Zhang[3]

[1] School of Mathematics and Computer Science,
Guangxi Science Technology Normal University, Laibin 546199, Guangxi, China
luofangqiong123@163.com
[2] Computer Science Department, Massachusetts College of Liberal Arts,
North Adams, MA 01247, USA
wgdaaa@gmail.com
[3] College of Information and Communication Engineering,
Harbin Engineering University, Harbin 150001, China

Abstract. In this paper, kernel principle component analysis (KPCA) is employed to extract the features of multiple precipitation factors. The extracted principle components are considered as the characteristic vector of support vector machine (SVM) to build the SVM precipitation forecast model. We calculate the SVM parameters using particle swarm optimization (PSO) algorithm, and build the cooperative model of KPCA and the SVM with PSO to predict the precipitation in Guangxi province. The simulation results show that the prediction outcome, resulting from the combination of KPCA and the SVM with PSO, is consistent with the actual precipitation. Comparisons with other models also demonstrate that our model has advantages in fitting and generalizing in comparison other models.

Keywords: Kernel principle component analysis (KPCA) ·
Particle swarm · Support vector machine (SVM) · Precipitationion

1 Introduction

The wide scope of drought, flood and other climatic disasters has been occurring frequently in China. It causes serious impacts on life safety and economic establishment. With the rapid development of economics, those disasters bring more severe economic losses than before, which increases the demand of more precise weather forecast. Accordingly, the prediction of drought and flood trends becomes an important issue for the atmosphere scientists. Climate changes are more and more remarkable, and precipitation becomes more important for predictions of drought and flood. Therefore, precipitation prediction has a guiding significance for the exploitation and optimal utilization of regional water

© ICST Institute for Computer Sciences, Social Informatics and Telecommunications Engineering 2019
Published by Springer Nature Switzerland AG 2019. All Rights Reserved
S. Liu and G. Yang (Eds.): ADHIP 2018, LNICST 279, pp. 372–381, 2019.
https://doi.org/10.1007/978-3-030-19086-6_42

resource. It has been also an important factor for the warning and solution of regional drought and flood [1].

During the past decades, many solutions and models have been proposed to address the precipitation prediction. Authors of [2] adopted five different methods to select appropriate values for SVM regression analysis. Authors of [3] predicted precipitation by using SVM. Authors of [4] predicted the drought and flood disasters of Zhejiang province in flood season using SVM regression. Yang et al. [5] adopted time sequence analysis and Monte Carlo for precipitation prediction. They found out that time sequence analysis is suitable to precise prediction and the Monte Carlo model can objectively demonstrate the overall characteristics of precipitation distribution. Authors of [6] employed the ARIMA time sequence model to predict monthly precipitation of Shandong province. Zhou et al. [7] used BP neural network for the drought prediction of Zhenzhou city. Tao et al. [8] adopted Markov chain model for the precipitation prediction of Yinchuan area. Liu et al. [9] established the monthly precipitation prediction model for the flood season of southwestern Henan by using the least squares SVM.

All of the above methods have achieved desirable accuracy of precipitation prediction for a longer time span, e.g., a month or several months. However, it is still a challenge to predict a shorter time span, e.g., daily precipitation prediction. In order to tackle this challenge, we proposed to combine the KPCA, PSO and SVM to establish a precipitation prediction model of higher accuracy. In particular, this model is able to achieve accurate daily precipitation prediction, which has been verified by simulation in Guangxi province.

2   Extraction of Precipitation Impact Factors Using KPCA

Scholkopf et al. extended PCA to non-linearity and proposed KPCA in 1999. KPCA is an extracting method for nonlinear features. It is able to map the original vector to a high-dimensional characteristic space through nonlinear kernel function: $F = \{\phi(x) : X \in R^n\}$. Then it carries out PCA algorithm on characteristic space F. Compared to PCA, KPCA can not only extract nonlinear features, but also has better recognition performance [10]. The nonlinear and low-dimensional characters of KPCA allow a better dimension-reduction extraction from numerous meteorological physical factors, which is very helpful for the feature dimension reduction of precipitation system.

The KPCA algorithm can be described as follows. Suppose there are n samples $x_1, x_2, \cdots, x_n$ in the input space R^d, and the n samples form a data matrix X, which maps the data samples from input space to high-dimensional characteristic space F through nonlinear mapping function. Assume that mapping has been centralized, that means the mean value of the mapping data is zero.

$$\sum_{i=1}^{n} \alpha_i \varphi(x_i) = 0 \tag{1}$$

Then the covariance matrix C in characteristic space F is

$$C^F = \frac{1}{n}\sum_{j=1}^{n}\varphi(x_j)\varphi(x_j)^T \tag{2}$$

Carry out characteristic value decomposition for covariance matrix C according to the following formula.

$$\lambda V = C^F V \tag{3}$$

In the formula, the nonzero characteristic value λ's corresponding characteristic vector locates in the subspace generated from $\varphi(x_1), \varphi(x_2), \cdots, \varphi(x_n)$, thus, the following equation is tenable.

$$\lambda(\varphi(x_k)V = (\varphi(x_k)C^F V), \quad k = 1, 2, \cdots, n \tag{4}$$

According to PCA theory, V can be described as the linear combination of $\varphi(x_i), i = 1, 2, \cdots, n$.

$$V = \sum_{i=1}^{n}\alpha_i\varphi(x_i) \tag{5}$$

Substitute (2) and (5) into (4) to get the following formula.

$$\lambda\sum_{i=1}^{n}\alpha_i(\varphi(x_k)\cdot\varphi(x_i)) = \frac{1}{n}\sum_{i=1}^{n}\alpha_i(\varphi(x_k)\cdot\sum_{j=1}^{n}\varphi(x_j))(\varphi(x_j).\varphi(x_i))$$

$$k = 1, 2, \cdots, n \tag{6}$$

Define matrix $k(x_i, x_j)_{n\times n}$ as

$$k(x_i, x_j) = (\varphi(x_i)\cdot\varphi(x_j)) \tag{7}$$

Then formula (6) can be describes as

$$n\lambda\alpha = k\alpha \tag{8}$$

In the above formula, $\alpha = (\alpha_1, \alpha_2, \cdots, \alpha_n)^T$. Suppose V_k is No. K characteristic vector of V. Carry out normalization progressing on it, namely $V_k V_k = 1$, then the mapping data $\varphi(x)$ of arbitrary vector X in original input space has the projection on characteristic vector V_k shown as follow.

$$(V^k\cdot\varphi(x)) = \sum_{i=1}^{n}\alpha_i^k(\varphi(x_i)\cdot\varphi(x)) \tag{9}$$

That is the requested principle component. In practice, the sample data does not always satisfy that the mean value of mapping data is zero. If so, the value K in formula (8) is

$$\overline{K} = K - IK - KI - IKI \tag{10}$$

In the above equation, I is $n\times n$ unit matrix of which the parameter is $\frac{1}{n}$. Under this circumstance the No. k dimension's nonlinear principle component is

$$t_k = \overline{V^F}\cdot\varphi(x) = \sum_{i=1}^{n}\overline{\alpha_i^k}(\varphi(\overline{x_i})\cdot\varphi(\overline{x})) = \alpha_i^k\sum_{i=1}^{n}\overline{\alpha_i^k \overline{K}}(x_i, x) \tag{11}$$

3   Principle of SVM Regression

SVM is an intelligent learning algorithm proposed by Vapnik based on the structure risk minimization theory in statistics. Utilizing kernel function, the SVM regression maps the nonlinear regression problem of low-dimensional space to high-dimensional characteristic space. The sample is linearly separable in high-dimensional space, so after nonlinear transformation, the linear regression problem is resolved. The principle of SVM regression algorithm is described as follows.

Suppose the training sample set is $\{(x_i, y_i), i = 1, 2, \cdots, n\}, x_i \in R^m, y_i \in R$. X_i is the input vector with m dimensions. y_i is the output value. R is all real numbers' set space. n is the number of samples. The nonlinear mapping $\varphi(x)$ will map the sample space from original space R^m to high-dimensional characteristic space R^h. So the optimal linear decision function can be established in the high-dimensional space.

$$f(x) = \omega \cdot \phi(x) + b \qquad (12)$$

In the above function, ω is a weight vector, $\omega \in R^h$, and b is offset. Here the non-sensitive loss function ϵ is introduced and the structure risk minimization theory is considered. Then the regression problem is converted into the following optimization problem.

$$min[\frac{1}{2} \parallel \omega \parallel^2 + C \sum_{i=1}^{n} (\xi_i + \xi_i^*)]$$

$$s.t. \begin{cases} y_i - \omega\phi(x_i) - b \leq \epsilon + \xi_i \\ -y_i + \omega\phi(x_i) + b \leq \epsilon + \xi_i^*, & i = 1, 2, \cdots, l \\ \xi_i \geq 0, \xi_i^* \geq 0 \end{cases} \qquad (13)$$

In the above formula, c is penalty factor. The bigger value of c means greater penalty on the samples whose training error is bigger than ϵ. ξ_i and ξ_i^* represent relaxation factors. ϵ defines the error bound of regression function, and the smaller value of ϵ means smaller error of regression function. According to Mercer condition, there exist mapping function ϕ and kernel function $K(.,.)$ which enable $K(x_{(k)}, x_{(l)} = \phi(x_k)^T \phi(x_l)$. By bringing in the Lagrangian Multiplier, the problem's dual optimization can be formulated as follows.

$$max[\frac{1}{2} \sum_{i,j=1}^{l} (a_i - a_i^*)(a_j - a_j^*)K(x_i, x_j) - \sum_{i=1}^{l}(a_i + a_i^*)\epsilon + \sum_{i=1}^{l}(a_i - a_i^*)y_i]$$

$$s.t. \begin{cases} \sum_{i=1}^{l}(a_i - a_i^*) = 0, & i = 1, 2, \cdots, l \\ 0 \leq a_i \leq c \\ 0 \leq a_i^* \leq c \end{cases} \qquad (14)$$

Use quadratic programming to solve formula (14), and get parameters a_i, a_i^*. Then figure out b with KKT condition, thus get the estimating expression of SVM regression equation as follow.

$$f(x) = \sum_{i=1}^{l}(a_i - a_i^*)K(x_i, x) + b \qquad (15)$$

In the equation,the sample (x_i, y_i) is support vector with the $(a_i - a_i^*)$ being nonzero sample. Common kernel functions mainly include linear kernel function, polynomial kernel function and radial basis function. The radial basis function is adopted in this paper.

$$K(x_i, x) = exp\left\{ -\frac{\parallel x_i - x \parallel^2}{2\sigma^2}\right\} \tag{16}$$

where σ is the width of the radial basis kernel function.

4   Establishment of Precipitation Prediction Model

4.1   Data Progressing and Extraction of Precipitation Prediction Factor

The data adopted to do prediction is referred from the documents of [11,12]. The numerical weather prediction products are 48-h forecast fields, including: (1) T213 figures from China Meteorological Administration, 17 conventional meteorological elements and physical elements field of its index bed (100–120°E, 15–30°N, 1°×1°, totally 336 lattice points). (2) Japanese refined net precipitation forecast field (100–120°E, 15–30°N, 1.25°×1.25°, totally 221 lattice points). A general investigation is carried out on the numerical forecast product field and forecast object field from 2003 to May of 2007 in Guangxi province. Prediction factor selection area is the lattice area with significance level remarkably higher than 0.75. In the area, the minimum mean value of 2 adjacent lattice points are candidate factors. The factors whose significance level reach or surpass 0.99 are prediction factors. The amount of candidate precipitation factors of May in area 1, area 2 and area 3 are 26, 19 and 30, respectively. In this paper, the prediction was taken from the data ranging from 2003 to May, 2008 in the area 1.

In the coupling, non-linearity and information redundancy existing among prediction factors will disturb the model's prediction strategy, and the prediction model does not lead to an ideal estimating result. In this paper, utilizing KPCA, dimension reduction is carried out for the 26 precipitation factors which are selected through cluster investigation. Then we select 8 main integrative factors as final precipitation prediction factors. Take the 8 main factors as the input variables for SVM net, and establish the daily precipitation prediction model, which continuously predicts the precipitation of area 1 from 2003 to May, 2008. Meanwhile, we select 6 main factors as the input variables for SVM net, and establish the monthly precipitation prediction model for the time period from 2001 to 2006.

4.2   Normalization Progressing of Data

The dimensions and orders of magnitude of extracted prediction factors are different form one another, so they are not suitable for PCA. Thus, normalization progressing is in demand for them. The normalization progressing on every dimension of extracted prediction factors can be carried out by using the following method.

$$S' = \frac{S - S_{min}}{S_{max} - S_{min}} \tag{17}$$

In the above formula, S' is the prediction factor value after the normalization progressing. S is the prediction factor value before the normalization progressing. S_{min} is the minimum value of prediction factor values. S_{max} is the maximum value of the prediction factor values. By using this way, the relative maximum response value, absolute maximum response value, mean value and the curve's data fitting parameter of every prediction factor are all in the range of [0, 1], which is in favor of later data progressing.

4.3   SVM Parameter Optimization Based on PSO

Because the kernel parameter and error penalty parameter may have a great impact on the prediction performance of SVM, optimization for the two parameters is of great importance. The PSO is a global optimization methods based on swarm intelligence. It is excellent in global optimization and particularly suitable for the selection and optimization of model parameters. Therefore, in this paper the PSO is adopted to optimize SVM parameter and to figure out the optimal kernel parameter and the error penalty factor. We select the minimum mean square error (MSE) as fitness function.

$$MSE = \frac{1}{n} \sum_{i=1}^{n} (y_i' - y_i)^2 \tag{18}$$

In the above formula, n is the number of prediction samples. y_i and y_i' are the measured value and the predicted value of No.i prediction sample, respectively.

During the progress of particle optimizing, every particle stands for a potential optimal solution for the extreme value optimization problem. The essential characteristics of particle are described by three indexes, including location, speed and fitness value. The speed decides the direction and distance of particle's movement. The fitness value is calculated through fitness function and it decides whether the particle is good or bad. In every circulation, the particle updates according to individual optimum and global optimum. The specific steps of PSO optimizing SVM parameter can be found in [13–15].

4.4   Establishment of Model

There are roughly four steps for the establishment of precipitation model. Step 1, use clustering analysis to handle the regional prediction and the prediction factors are extracted from fields general investigation. Step 2, extract the nonlinear characteristic factors from precipitation system by KPCA. Step 3, optimize the kernel parameter σ and error penalty factor c through PSO. Step 4, take the calculated optimization parameter value as SVM's optimal learning parameter to predict the samples. The establishment of model is shown in Fig. 1.

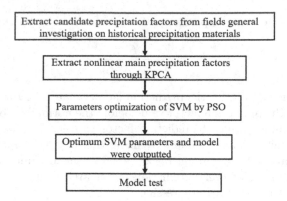

Fig. 1. Establishing progress of SVM precipitation model.

5   Analysis on Application Examples

5.1   Simulation of Precipitation in Guilin, Guangxi on a Daily Basis

Take the area 1 as an example. The data was collected through 148 days from 2003 to May of 2007 in Guilin, Guangxi are used as model training sample. The 31-day data of the May of 2008 works as testing sample. Figure 2 is a working sketch of the fitness of testing samples' data by improved RBF net model, KPCA-SVM model and KPCA-PSO-SVM model, respectively. As depicted in the figure, the testing result of KPCA-PSO-SVM model is generally in consistent with actual data, which indicates that among the three models, KPCA-PSO-SVM model has the best predicting performance, minimum total deviation and highest accuracy.

In order to analyze the predicting results more comprehensively, the following four evaluation indexes are introduced in this paper: mean absolute error (MAE1), maximum absolute error (MAE2), frequency of errors, which are greater than 25 mm (F1), and frequency of errors, which are smaller than 5 mm (F2). The error comparison between predicting results of the three models and T213 numerical prediction is listed in Table 1.

As demonstrated in Table 1, both MAE1 and MAE2 of KPCA-PSO-SVM model are smaller than those of the other four models, which proofs the high accuracy of KPCA-PSO-SVM model. Suppose that predictions with the errors being smaller than 5 mm are the reference value, and those with error being greater than 25 mm are unreliable prediction. Then we can find that the duration of the reference value using KPCA-PSO-SVM model and RBF net model is 17 days, which is longer than that of the other two models. However, the unreliable frequencies of KPCA-PSO-SVM model and RBF net model are 1 and 2, respectively, which means that KPCA-PSO-SVM model has better prediction performance.

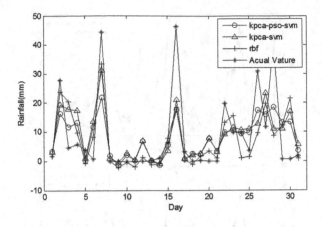

Fig. 2. Daily prediction rendering of area 1 during the 31 days in May.

Table 1. Analysis on comparison between the three prediction models and T213 numerical prediction.

Error statistics	RBF	KPCA-SVM	T213	KPCA-PSO-SVM
MAE1	32.7	29.8	36.1	28.7
MAE2	6.90	7055	7.92	6.81
F1	2	2	5	1
F2	17	13	15	17

5.2 Simulation of Precipitation in Guilin, Guangxi on a Monthly Basis

To verify the model's generalizing and stabilizing ability, the KPCA-PSO-SVM model proposed in this paper is applied in the monthly precipitation prediction of Guilin, Guangxi. It will be compared to the prediction of KPCA-SVM model and the improved RBF neural net model. Monthly precipitation data from 2001 to 2016 in Guilin, Guangxi is used in the simulation, including simulating data of the 156 months from 2001 to 2013 and testing data of the 36 months from 2014 to 2016.

Figure 3 lists the comparison between the monthly precipitation prediction results of the three models and the actual data, namely improved RBF net model, KPCA-SVM model and KPCA-PSO-SVM model. The simulating result shows that the testing simulation's data trends of these models are almost identical to the actual data tend. Among the three models, the KPCA-PSO-SVM model has the smallest deviation and better consistency, and it can be regarded an important reference for the protection against flood and drought.

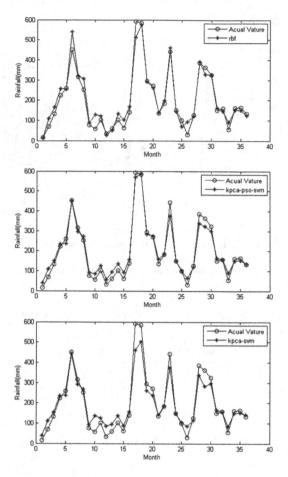

Fig. 3. The forecasting effect of three models between 2014–2016.

6   Conclusions

The accuracy of precipitation prediction is an important research topic for disaster reduction and prevention. With rapid development of economy and science technology, the requirement for high climatic prediction accuracy becomes increasingly higher. However, the combined influence of general atmospheric circulation and local circulation changes brings great difficulties in prediction. In this paper, based on the data from China Meteorological Administration and the Japanese refined net prediction, we adopted KPCA to extract the precipitation weather factors to optimize the SVM parameter through PSO to establish the daily precipitation prediction model in Guangxi. Meanwhile, it is applicable to the monthly precipitation prediction of Guilin, Guangxi. Simulation results show that in both aspects of maximum prediction error and mean prediction error, KPCA-PSO-SVM prediction achieves higher accuracy and shows better generalizing ability than other methods. It demonstrates desirable stability and can work as a good reference for practical precipitation prediction.

References

1. Toda, Y., Abe, F.: Prediction of precipitation sequences within grains in 18Cr-8Ni austenitic steel by using system free energy method. ISIJ Int. **49**(3), 439–445 (2009)
2. Ouyang, Q., Wenxi, L., Dong, H., et al.: Study on precipitation prediction based on SVM regression analysis. Water-Saving Irrig. **9**, 38–41 (2014)
3. Ni, Y.: Study on Donggang precipitation prediction model based on SVM. Water Conservancy **2**, 133–134 (2014)
4. Teng, W., Shanxian, Y., Bo, H., et al.: Application research of SVM regression in flood and drought prediction in flood season. J. Zhejiang Univ. (Science) **35**(3), 343–347 (2008)
5. Yang, L., Xiwen, L., Liu, P., et al.: Time sequence analysis and the application of Monte Carlo in precipitation prediction. Environ. Sci. Technol. **34**(5), 108–112 (2011)
6. Sun, M., Kong, X., Geng, W., et al.: Time sequence analysis on shandong monthly precipitation based on ARIMA model. J. Ludong Univ. (Natural Science) **29**(3), 244–249 (2013)
7. Zhou, Z., Xie, B.: Application of BP neural net in Zhenzhou drought prediction and strategies of disaster reduction and prevention. Chin. Rural Water Conservancy Hydroelectricity **12**, 97 (2011)
8. Tao, W., Hui, Q., Li, P., et al.: Application of weighting Markov chain in precipitation prediction of Yinchuan area. South-to-North Water Divers. Water Sci. Technol. **8**(1), 78–81 (2010)
9. Liu, D., Fu, W.: Prediction test of least squares SVM in precipitation of flood season. In: The 33rd Annual Meeting of Chinese Meteorological Society S1 Supervision, Analysis and Prediction of Disaster Whether. Publishing House, Xi'an, pp. 929–934 (2016)
10. Gao, X.: Kernel feature extraction method and its application research. Nanjing University of Aeronautics and Astronautics (2010)
11. Luo, F., Jiansheng, W., Jin, L.: Integrated precipitation prediction model based on least squares SVM. J. Tropic. Meteorol. **27**(3), 577–584 (2011)
12. Luo, F.: Optimize RBF neural net precipitation prediction model based on LLE. Comput. Digit. Eng. **41**(5), 749–752 (2013)
13. He, X., Wang, Y., Wen, B.: Quantitative research on special engineering costs based on PSO SVM. Electricity Grid Clean Energy **31**(12), 27–30 (2015)
14. Li, T., Zeng, X.: Simulation of flow and sediment of yanhe basin based on PSO SVM. J. Basis Sci. Eng. **23**(7), 79–87 (2015)
15. Meng, J.: Study on long-term precipitation prediction model for arid region based on PSO-LSSVM. J. Yangtze River Sci. Res. Inst. **10**, 36–40 (2016)

IP Network Traffic Analysis Based on Big Data

Hanqi Yin[1]([✉]), Jianguo Sun[1], Yiqi Shi[2], and Liu Sun[1]

[1] Department of Computer Science and Technology,
Harbin Engineering University, Harbin, China
{yinhanqi,sunjianguo}@hrbeu.edu.cn, sunliuhrbeu@163.com
[2] Harbin University of Commerce, Harbin 150028, China
740165656@qq.com

Abstract. Big data is a hot topic in the current academia and industry circles, which is influencing people's daily lifestyles, work habits and ways of thinking. Due to the complexity of data itself and the huge amount of data, big data faces many problems in the process of collection, storage and use. It requires a new processing model to have greater decision making, insight and process optimization capabilities to accommodate massive, high growth rates and diverse information. The strategic significance of big data is not to master huge data information, but to conduct specialized analysis and processing of these meaningful data. This paper focuses on the analysis of IP network traffic under big data, and studies the sources of existing network traffic, the purpose of traffic analysis, and the common analysis methods for big data traffic. The structure and usability of Hadoop-based traffic analysis framework are mainly studied, and a new prospect is proposed for the future development direction.

Keywords: Big data · Traffic analysis · Hadoop

1 Introduction

With the development of Internet application technology and the expansion of the Internet scale, a large number of mobile terminals access the network for resource sharing and information communication. The operating mechanism and complex behavioral characteristics of the Internet make it difficult to control the data or behavior in the Internet. Since network traffic can reflect the complex dynamic characteristics of the Internet, people can improve the performance of the Internet by controlling, scheduling, shaping the network traffic, helping people to understand the behavior of the network more deeply.

From the perspective of network architecture, network traffic is the foundation of all studies, so all research on the characteristics of network applications

This work is supported by the Fundamental Research Funds for the Central Universities (HEUCFG201827, HEUCFP201839).

and the behavior of the network itself can be obtained through research on network traffic. By analyzing the traffic characteristics carried on the network, it is possible to find an effective way to explore the internal operating mechanism of the network. Network traffic can directly reflect the performance of the network. In the network, if the traffic received by the network exceeds its actual carrying capacity, it will cause network performance degradation. Throughput is an important indicator of network performance. An ideal network should accept all traffic until its maximum throughput limit. However, in an actual network, if network traffic is poorly controlled or network congestion occurs, throughput will decrease and network performance will decrease. The relationship between network traffic and throughput is shown in Fig. 1. It can be seen from Fig. 1 that in order to further improve the network performance, it is necessary to study the network traffic, extract the parameters that can characterize the network traffic, and find the controllable performance parameters by modeling, simulating and analyzing the network traffic, to achieve effective control of traffic, improve and optimize network performance.

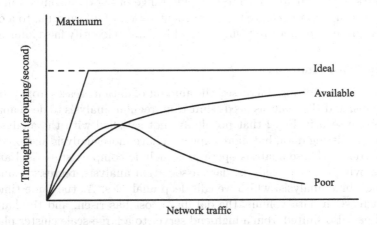

Fig. 1. The relationship between network traffic and throughput.

2   Big Data Analysis in the Network

2.1   The Goal of Big Data Analysis

At present, big data analysis is applied in various fields of science, medicine and commerce. Although its use is very wide, its main objectives are reflected in the following parts:

(1) *Acquire knowledge and predict trends*

People have been doing data analysis for a long time, and the primary and most important purpose is to acquire and utilize knowledge. Because big data contains a lot of original and real information, big data analysis can effectively abandon individual differences and help people grasp the law behind things more accurately. Based on the extracted knowledge, it is possible to predict natural or social phenomena more accurately.

(2) *Analyze personalized features*

Individual activities meet the characteristics of some groups, but also have distinct personality characteristics. Like the slender tail in "The Long Tail" theory, these features can vary wildly.

(3) *Identify the truth through analysis*

Error message is worse than no message. Because the dissemination of information in the network is very convenient, the harm caused by false information on the network is also greater. Due to the wide range of big data sources and their diversity, it can help to achieve the de-authentication of information to a certain extent. At present, people are trying to use big data to identify false information.

2.2 Big Data Analysis

As the data in the network increases, the amount of data increases from terabytes to petabytes, and the analysis needs shift from regular analysis to deep analytics [4]. It can be seen in Fig. 2 that people are not satisfied with the analysis and detection of existing data, but more expect to have more analysis and prediction of future trends. These analysis operations include complex statistical analysis such as moving average analysis, data association analysis, regression analysis, and market blue analysis, which we call deep analytics. At the same time, due to the increase in data volume, the database cost has risen, and the hardware platform has also shifted from a high-end server to a large-scale cluster platform composed of low-end and medium-end hardware.

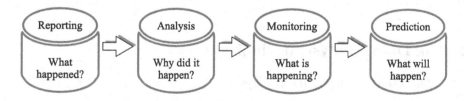

Fig. 2. Trands in data analysis.

Data analysis is the core process of big data applications. According to different levels, it can be roughly divided into three categories: computing architecture, query and index, and data analysis and processing.

In terms of computing architecture, MapReduce is currently a widely used big data set computing model and framework. In order to meet some analysis requirements of high task completion time, its performance was optimized in literature [12]. Literature [3] proposed a data flow analysis solution based on MapReduce architecture, MARISSA, which enables it to support real-time analysis tasks. Literature [2] also proposes a TiMR framework based on MapReduce for real-time stream processing for applications with high real-time requirements such as advertising push.

In terms of query and index, because big data contains a large amount of unstructured or semi-structured data, the query and indexing technology of traditional relational databases is limited, and NoSQL class database technology gets more attention.

In terms of data analysis and processing, the main technologies involved include semantic analysis and data mining. Due to the diversified nature of data in a big data environment, it is difficult to unify terms and then mine information when performing semantic analysis on data. Literature [7] studies the heterogeneity of semantic ontology in semantic analysis. Traditional data mining technology is mainly aimed at structured data, so it is urgent to study unstructured or semi-structured data mining technology. Literature [6] proposed a mining technology for image files, while literature [5] proposed a retrieval and mining technology for large-scale text files.

3 Traffic Analysis Based on Hadoop

3.1 Hadoop Architecture

Hadoop is a software framework based on JAVA for distributed intensive data processing and data analysis. It is largely based on MapReduce technology, but at the same time it is not just a distributed file system for storage, but a framework for executing distributed applications on large clusters of general purpose computing devices.

In Fig. 3 depicts the various layers of the ecosystem, in addition to the core Hadoop distributed file system (HDFS) and MapReduce programming framework, it also includes closely linked HBase database clusters and ZooKeeper clusters [1]. HDFS is a master/slave architecture that performs CRUD (Create, Read, Updata, and Delete) operations on files through directory paths, providing high-reliability underlying storage support for the entire ecosystem. MapReduce adopts the idea of "divide and conquer" to distribute the operation of large-scale data sets to the sub-nodes under the management of a master node, and then the final results are obtained by integrating the intermediate nodes of each sub-node, thus providing better computing power for the system. HBase is located in the structured storage layer, and the Zookeeper cluster provides stable services and failover mechanism for HBase.

Hadoop was originally used to deal with single applications such as search, but with the advent of the big data era, Hadoop should be able to adapt to more applications. For different types of applications, the MapReduce parallel

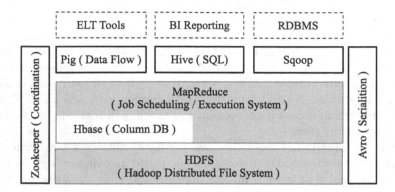

Fig. 3. Hadoop framework.

computing framework needs to optimize its deficiencies. For example, in order for MapReduce to process more tasks at the same time, the job scheduling algorithm needs to be optimized. HBase is an open source database based on Hadoop. It has problems such as slow response speed and single point of failure. It needs to optimize performance in order to provide high performance, high reliability and real-time literacy. As the bottom layer of Hadoop storage, HDFS needs to quickly access files of different sizes and enhance its security performance. Balancing performance, efficiency, and usability from a holistic perspective can further enhance Hadoop's capabilities.

3.2   Hadoop Analyzes the Feasibility of Mobile Traffic Data

With the development of technology, we can get more and more data, and all kinds of companies that can get data want to get more data, which brings data storage problems. There is no doubt that there is a lot of information in the data, and its research value and commercial value are endless. Therefore, how to analyze massive data efficiently and obtain the required information from the data becomes another problem. The collected data has various formats. With the growth of data volume, the traditional database storage method can no longer meet the storage requirements of data. Users gradually feel that the database is bulky, unable to analyze data flexibly, or even cannot store the data volume equal to the data collection volume achieved.

Hadoop can deal with these problems well. It consists of the underlying distributed file system and the upper layer MapReduce distributed computing framework. The distributed file system is highly scalable, can store a variety of data, and uses data redundancy to ensure data reliability and improve computational efficiency. In addition, it supports multiple computing frameworks and provides interfaces that allow users to flexibly extend their applications. And there are hundreds of configuration parameters to provide users with a variety of resource allocation options, all types of users can configure and manage Hadoop according to their actual needs.

Hadoop was originally designed to run on a cluster of inexpensive PCs, with hardware errors and machine failures as normal, so Hadoop doesn't need very expensive hardware devices to support it. Hadoop itself is an open source framework that can be freely modified, and an active public community brings together users and enthusiasts around the world to discover problems in the Hadoop and provide solutions. The existing versions of Hadoop are enough to give users a good experience, and it is very convenient to customize according to their own needs. It does not require a high level of developer skills, and has a lot of learning materials and low learning costs. In addition, although maintenance and management are very big problems for large clusters, because Hadoop is an open source system, maintenance costs are relatively low.

3.3 Hadoop Application in Traffic Analysis

In the field of traffic monitoring and analysis, literature [11] proposed a flow analysis algorithm based on MapReduce, which can analyze the target port of flow records statistically. In this paper, the computational efficiency of the algorithm is compared with "flow-tools", a mainstream flow data processing tool. The results show that the mapreduce-based flow analysis algorithm can save 72% of the computation time. It is also verified that Hadoop can cope well with single point of failure. On this basis, the Yeonhee Lee in order to solve the DDoS attack detection technology can tolerate response time facing the challenge of mass data processing flow, based on graphs is a HTTP GET flood attack detection algorithm, put forward a real-time framework, the use of distributed cluster power to detect DDoS attacks [9]. And puts forward an extensible framework based on Hadoop and transport processing, and designed a new binary input frame, set as high speed calculation and message solution, efficient storage framework includes a variety of graphs algorithm analysis of message, can analyze mass message [8]. In addition to this, and further puts forward a scalable traffic monitoring system based on Hadoop, can from IP, TCP, HTTP and NetFlow perspective TB level of Internet traffic, for different network layer, the system can use graphs of the distributed algorithm to efficiently deal with and analyze network traffic, experiments show that as the growth of the number of cluster nodes, the analysis of the system than CoralReef and TIPE's Pcap more efficient [10]. The main components of the whole system includes a can receive real-time trace binary format, Netflow, IP, TCP and HTTP analysis algorithm of graphs, and a simple query system based on the Hive. At the analysis and presentation layer of the system, the author integrated the previous studies and provided TCP re-traditional count, five-tuple flow statistics and DDoS analysis.

3.4 Inadequacies of the Hadoop Platform

Hadoop has some inherent flaws and problems with unsuitable environments due to its design goals, architecture, and distributed features:

(1) *Small document problem*

HDFS was originally developed for streaming large files. To ensure data redundancy and flexibility, when HDFS stores data, the file is divided into files by 64M per block by default. If you need to store a large number of files smaller than 64M, there will be many problems. Even if the file is smaller than 64M, HDFS will still treat it as a 64M block for storage, which will waste a lot of storage space. The NameNode will record the location of each file. A large number of small files will occupy a large amount of storage space of the NameNode, which is easy to cause a single point bottleneck. Processing many of these small files can also take more time and resources than processing large files.

(2) *Real-time processing access*

Hadoop is not suitable for online data processing that requires low latency data. For example, the update of the stock system requires everyone to know in time that there is no delay. Similarly, implementing a real-time/flow-based processing model is not a strength of Hadoop because it does not support data that continues to arrive at operations that require immediate processing.

(3) *Unable to modify the file at will*

Hadoop supports storage for multiple writes per write, and is very inefficient if you add or modify files.

(4) *Configuration and optimization issues*

Hadoop has more than 190 configuration parameters. How to configure it reasonably in different production environments, and make full use of resources to make the system run efficiently is a very important issue. Some mechanisms of Hadoop itself can not be applied to all environments, and some unreasonable mechanisms are improved, which is another optimization direction.

4   Hadoop Performance Optimization

4.1   Hadoop Job Scheduling Algorithm

In Fig. 4, the TaskScheduler is a component of the JobTracker, and the relationship between the function and the call is between them. The interaction between Client, JobTracker and TaskTracker is through network RPC. Then we will analyze the general principle of the scheduler:

① Client submits a job to JobTracker via submitJob() function.
② TJobTracker notifies TaskScheduler to call its internal function initJob() to initialize the job and create some internal data structures.
③ The TaskTracker reports its resources to the JobTracker via a heartbeat, such as how many free map slots and reduce slots.
④ If JobTracker finds that the first TaskTracker has free resources, the JobTracker will call TaskScheduler's assignTasks() function, returning some task list to the first TaskTracker. At this point, the TaskTracker will execute the task assigned by the scheduler.

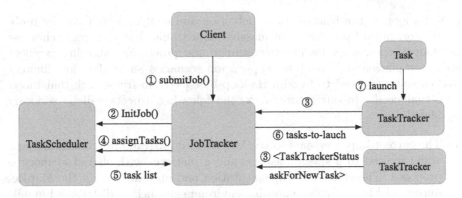

Fig. 4. Job scheduling algorithm.

4.2 HDFS Small File Processing Capability

In response to the handling of the small files mentioned above, Hadoop itself provides three solutions, namely archive file technology, serial file technology and merged file technology, all of which require users to write their own programs, and all of them are insufficient. Therefore, it has not been widely adopted (Fig. 5).

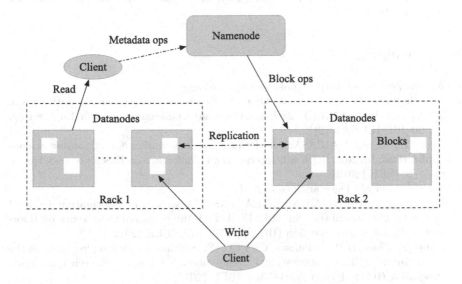

Fig. 5. HDFS architecture.

5 Conclusion

As an open source framework for cloud computing technology, Hadoop has helped many enterprises solve the problem of storage and processing of big data.

Using Hadoop in the field of traffic detection and analysis can solve the problem of storage and processing of massive data traffic. Existing researches use the Hadoop framework for message storage and processing, showing excellent processing efficiency. The above application scenarios show that for different environments, we need to build a Hadoop-based system framework that meets the actual needs. In our future work, the following aspects will be seriously considered.

(1) The current improvements to the MapReduce programming model are generally limited to a specific aspect, and a platform with shared memory is proposed. Therefore, the implementation and optimization of the MapReduce model for parallel computing environments such as distributed mobile platforms will also be an important research direction.
(2) Existing Hadoop plating algorithms are more about fairness, but real-world calculations often require higher efficiency. Combining the resources owned by the system with the current load state, it is still an important research direction to propose a more fair and efficient scheduling algorithm.
(3) Currently HDFS and HBase can support both structured and unstructured data, while fast-generated big data imposes higher real-time requirements on the underlying access platform. Therefore, it is necessary to design an access platform that supports high-efficiency, low-latency, and supports complex types of data.

References

1. Apache Zookeeper. http://zookeeper.apache.org/
2. Chandramouli, B., Goldstein, J., Duan, S.: Temporal analytics on big data for web advertising. In: 2012 IEEE 28th International Conference on Data Engineering, pp. 90–101. IEEE (2012)
3. Dede, E., et al.: MARISSA: MapReduce implementation for streaming science applications. In: 2012 IEEE 8th International Conference on E-Science (e-Science), pp. 1–8. IEEE (2012)
4. Falsafi, B., et al.: Deep analytics (2011)
5. Gubanov, M., Pyayt, A.: MEDREADFAST: a structural information retrieval engine for big clinical text. In: 2012 IEEE 13th International Conference on Information Reuse and Integration (IRI), pp. 371–376. IEEE (2012)
6. Kang, U., Chau, D.H., Faloutsos, C.: PEGASUS: mining billion-scale graphs in the cloud. In: 2012 IEEE International Conference on Acoustics, Speech and Signal Processing (ICASSP), pp. 5341–5344. IEEE (2012)
7. Ketata, I., Mokadem, R., Morvan, F.: Biomedical resource discovery considering semantic heterogeneity in data grid environments. In: Hruschka, E.R., Watada, J., do Carmo Nicoletti, M. (eds.) INTECH 2011. CCIS, vol. 165, pp. 12–24. Springer, Heidelberg (2011). https://doi.org/10.1007/978-3-642-22247-4_2
8. Lee, Y., Kang, W., Lee, Y.: A hadoop-based packet trace processing tool. In: Domingo-Pascual, J., Shavitt, Y., Uhlig, S. (eds.) TMA 2011. LNCS, vol. 6613, pp. 51–63. Springer, Heidelberg (2011). https://doi.org/10.1007/978-3-642-20305-3_5

9. Lee, Y., Lee, Y.: Detecting DDoS attacks with Hadoop. In: Proceedings of the ACM CoNEXT Student Workshop, p. 7. ACM (2011)
10. Lee, Y., Lee, Y.: Toward scalable internet traffic measurement and analysis with Hadoop. ACM SIGCOMM Comput. Commun. Rev. **43**(1), 5–13 (2013)
11. Lee, Y., Kang, W., Son, H.: An internet traffic analysis method with MapReduce. In: Network Operations and Management Symposium Workshops (NOMS Wksps), 2010 IEEE/IFIP, pp. 357–361. IEEE (2010)
12. Verma, A., Cherkasova, L., Kumar, V.S., Campbell, R.H.: Deadline-based workload management for MapReduce environments: pieces of the performance puzzle. In: 2012 IEEE Network Operations and Management Symposium (NOMS), pp. 900–905. IEEE (2012)

Seam Carve Detection Using Convolutional Neural Networks

Mehtab Iqbal[1], Lei Chen[1(✉)], Hengfeng Fu[2], and Yun Lin[2]

[1] College of Engineering and Computing, Georgia Southern University,
Statesboro, GA, USA
lchen@georgiasouthern.edu
[2] College of Information and Communication Engineering,
Harbin Engineering University, Harbin 150001, China

Abstract. Seam carving is a form of content-aware image modification. This modification can vary from resizing to clipping of content within an image. This can be easily used to alter images to achieve steganographic goals or the propagation of misleading information. Deep learning, particularly Convolutional Neural Networks have become prolific in today's image-based intelligent systems. However, it has been found that convolutional networks specialized for image classification tend to perform poorly for steganalysis—specifically seam carving. In this paper, we propose a convolutional neural network architecture which is able to learn the nuances of seam carved images.

Keywords: Steganalysis · Seam carving · Convolutional Neural Networks

1 Introduction

Steganography is a form of covert communication which relies on utilizing a data container to hide messages [1]. With social media and their prolific use, channels for hidden communications are abundant [2]. An image speaks a thousand words they say. With the pervasiveness of smartphones, using images and image-based social media is very common [2]. Most of these images are in the compressed JPEG format [2].

These JPEG images can easily be used as containers to hide information. They may also be and are often used as secret message carriers. This embedded information in an image is neither visible to the viewer, nor is it detected by firewalls. Furthermore, it is very difficult to detect if any alteration has been made to an image without the original image to compare with. As a result, alongside steganography, content-aware image re-targeting algorithm such as Seam Carving has gained a lot of popularity [3].

Seam Carving relies on minimizing the energy cost of a seam through dynamic programming [4] to alter an image. It is a very efficient algorithm for resizing an image by removing the low energy content of the image [5]. It is often used to remove objects from an image [6]. This removal of objects from images can have a serious impact on the semantic value of an image [6] by altering the overall semantic content of the whole image, which is even more troublesome given the nature of information sharing in today's world—highly image-based through use of social media and the internet. There have been many algorithms and models to detect seam carving, for example, Liu [7]

S. Liu and G. Yang (Eds.): ADHIP 2018, LNICST 279, pp. 392–407, 2019.
https://doi.org/10.1007/978-3-030-19086-6_44

have used re-compression techniques to detect seam carving, and Ke et al. [3] observed the seam patterns by seam carving the image again, in order to determine seam carved effects in an image.

Although many novel processes and algorithms to detect seam carving exits, deep learning has only recently started being used in steganalysis [8]. This is because steganalysis requires a detection of stego-noise, which is a very weak signal and visual processing networks are not geared towards detecting them [9]. With increasing research in deep learning based steganalysis, in particular, the use of modified convolutional neural networks, [8] and the advances in deep learning frameworks [10] it is becoming increasingly possible to train models for use in other applications. Some frameworks such as Caffe [11], Theano [12], Tensorflow [13], etc. have made available deep learning libraries that leverage the capabilities of mobile devices, allowing mobile applications to load trained models and utilize it towards classification problem without the cost of transferring a large amount of data back to the server for processing [10].

Using these advancements, whilst keeping in mind, the limitation of a portable device, we propose a Tensorflow based convolutional model that can be sufficiently trained so that the model can be loaded and made portable for use in various applications. To achieve this, we would look into local binary patterns as used by Yin et al. [6], and use the structural design proposed by Xu et al. [8] which utilizes a modified convolutional layer for feature extraction.

2 Literature Review

2.1 Steganography and JPEG Images

The mechanism of sending secret messages by hiding them in innocuous medium consequently making the communication invisible is known as Steganography [14, 15]. Steganography hides the very existence of secret messages and masks the presence of communication by making the true message not discernible to the observer [16, 17]. While steganographic methods strive for high security and capacity, usually these techniques are not concerned with robustness [18]. Several techniques of image steganography include spatial domain, transform domain-based methods and spread spectrum method [19, 20]. Images that have hidden messages or the carrier images in steganography are called the cover images [19].

Although cover images can have many formats, the most popular choice for steganographers are digital files, that can compress images with a small loss of perceptual quality [1]. In addition, the tools used for steganography encompasses bit-wise methods that can apply a least significant bit (LSB) insertion and noise manipulation [21]. Such tools are known as image domain tools [21]. JPEG is an image type that can ensure minimum data loss through direct manipulation and recovery by using the Discrete Cosine Transform (DCT) [21]. In JPEG images, information is hidden by modulating the rounding choices of the DCT coefficients thus making detection of such messaged difficult [14]. To combat these issues and the increasing popularity of steganographic methods, a new field of Steganalysis is established [20]. This technique relies on the changes in the statistical characteristics of an image to detect the embedded data [20].

2.2   Seam Carving

Seam carving is a technique used towards content-aware scaling, in other words, pixels on the least significant seams are removed or inserted, in order to alter the size of an image [4]. This is achieved by defining an energy function based on the gradient in order to identify the seams containing the lowest energy [22, 23]. For an image I of dimension n × m, the vertical seam is defined as

$$s^x = \{s_i^n\}_{i=1}^n = \{(x(i), i)\}_{i=1}^n = s.t \, \forall i, \, x(i-1)| \leq 1 \tag{1}$$

Where x maps pixels such that, $x : [1, \ldots, n] \to [1, \ldots, m]$ in other words, i denotes the row coordinate, and the corresponding column coordinate is given by $x(i)$. Similarly, the horizontal seam is given by the equation

$$s^y = \{s_j^n\}_{j=1}^n = \{(y(j), j)\}_{j=1}^n = s.t \, \forall j, \, x(j-1)| \leq 1 \tag{2}$$

Where y maps pixels $y : [1, \ldots, m] \to [1, \ldots, n]$. An image can be altered by modifying the seams containing the least energy seam. The energy function for a vertical seam is denoted by the energy function $E(s)$.

$$E(s) = \sum_{i=1}^n e((x(i), i)) \tag{3}$$

Where the energy function for each pixel is given by $e(I)$.

$$e(I) = \left| \frac{\partial}{\partial x} I \right| + \left| \frac{\partial}{\partial y} I \right| \tag{4}$$

Similarly, the parameters just need to be flipped and s^y used instead of s^x in order to calculate the least every horizontal seam. Finally, the lowest energy seam can be calculated by minimizing the energy function which can be achieved through dynamic programming [6] and a minimum energy matrix M can be build using the relationship below:

$$M(i,j) = e(i,j) + min(M(i-1, j-1), M(i-1, j), M(i-1, j+1)) \tag{5}$$

Figure 1 compares image resizing using Seam Carved technique versus reshaping. Furthermore, Fig. 2 shows how seam carving can be used to remove objects from images [24].

2.3   Steganalysis and Detection of Seam Carving

The technique for detecting and analyzing files that are potential carrier files and have hidden data using Steganography is called Steganalysis. The objectives of this measure can be three levels: detecting, extracting and disabling or destroying hidden messages.

Fig. 1. Seam carving vs regular resizing

Fig. 2. Seam carving to remove the object from the image

There are several ways of performing steganalysis on carrier files including the Raw Quick Pair (RQP) technique, Regular-Singular analysis (RS) technique, Histogram Characteristic Function (HCF) technique [19].

When there is a change to close color pairs on high-color images, it can indicate that the image has an embedded message. The raw quick pairs (RQP) technique is based on an observation and assumption. When there is an observed change in colors close to the pairs on high-color, it can indicate that the image has an embedded message. This technique also assumes that the total number of pixels is significantly larger than the number of unique colors in the cover image [25]. Although this technique shows the existence of a message, it cannot calculate the length of the messages. Its limitations include the cover image to have less than 30% unique colors of the total pixel [26] and neither can this technique be applied to grayscale images, as they have less than 256 colors and is not enough to reflect changes in an insertion operation.

The Regular Singular (RS) analysis technique is built on the observation that randomizing LSB of the images influences its smoothness [27], whereas the Histogram Characteristic Function (HCF) is based on investigating the characteristics of image histograms and the effect on histograms caused by embedding secret images. Regular Singular analysis technique both finds and calculates the length of the message hidden in an image. However, the complexity time of RS is O (n), where n is the number of pixels in an image.

Certain improvements were made to the HCF technique [28, 29]. The first improvement calibrates by down-sampling the images and the second technique combines two adjacent pixels as opposed to averaging four adjacent pixels and is known as alternative calibration. Adjacency histogram, another improvement made to this technique can detect grayscale images [28]. To make the grayscale histogram parser, the two-dimensional adjacency histogram is used [26]. This histogram uses the pixel intensity of two adjacent pixels as one data point. There is no one size fit all solution for steganalysis of any sort, this is especially true for seam carving. Research on seam carving forensics has been done since 2009 [3]. Sarkar et al. [5] theorized that if enough seam is changed within an image, then the inter-pixel correlation and co-occurrence matrix should undergo sufficient change. This change is expected to be reflected in the local block-based DCT coefficients of the JPEG image [30]. They utilized a Markov random process in order to develop a probability matrix to represent the process and trained an SVM using 50% of the data. They achieved about 80% accuracy for their work.

Additionally, Fillion and Sharma [31] proposed statistical features that include bias of energy distribution, the dispersal of seam behavior, and the affection of wavelet absolute moments. Their model managed to attain an accuracy of up to 91.3% for as low as 20% seam-carved images. Ryu et al. [32] trained their SVM model using average column energy, average row energy, average energy, max seam. Their model achieved accuracy between 71.52% and 93.5% but failed to detect object removal.

Towards the detection of content-aware alteration in JPEG images, Qingzhong Liu [33, 34], merged shift-recompression based features in the spatial domain, and neighboring joint density in DCT domain together. Wei et al. [35] divided images into 2×2 mini-squares with pairing 2×3 candidate patches to observe possible effects of seam carving. Then, taking into account the patch transition probability they extracted a 252 dimension feature set which they used to train an SVM classifier, resulting in up to 95.8% accuracy on 20% seam carved images. Yin et al. [6], extracted the local binary pattern, generally used for texture classification, and reached an accuracy of 97% in best cases at 21% seam carved images.

2.4   Convolutional Neural Networks and Steganalysis

Convolutional neural networks (CNN) have been used very widely in computer vision and has made many large achievements [8]. However, steganalysis and visual processing for artificial intelligence are very different tasks [9]. Qian et al. [9] have tested several visual processing CNNs towards steganalysis and the consensus is that they did perform up to the task. They also, in their 2015 paper [9] proposed a modification for the convolutional layer in a CNN to detect stego-content. They called this Gaussian-Neuron CNN (GNCNN), and it relied on a Gaussian function as the activation function.

$$f(x) = e^{-\frac{x^2}{\sigma^2}} \tag{6}$$

where, σ determines the width of the curve.

According to them, this function is supposed to generate a significant positive response when the input intervals are small [9]. Xu et al. [8] proposed a whole network architecture based on the GNCNN and introduced batch normalization prior to a $\tanh(x)$ activation function.

They also used a High Pass Filter (HPF) on the image before using it as an input in their neural network. After three stages of convolution, they activated the last convolutional layer with a linear rectifier (ReLu) function, followed by a fully connected layer and Softmax for classification. They tested their architecture on S-Uniward [36], and HILL [37] utilized steganography. They managed to achieve between 58.44% and 79.24% accuracy on HILL, and 57.33% and 80.24% on SUNIWARD.

Recently, Sedighi and Fridrich [38] introduced the use of histogram layer into a convolutional model in order to achieve remarkable learning again S-UNIWARD based stego images. In fact, it is convolutional network is increasingly being used to tackle steganalysis tasks.

3 Methodology

3.1 Data

We collected a dataset from Sam Houston State University's [39] image database, which contains a set of 1000 images. Five hundred of these are untouched JPEG images and the other five hundred were manipulated versions of the images using seam carving at the quality of 75. All original images are everyday pictures of dimensions 1234×1858, or 1858×1234. The seam carved images ranges from resizing in either horizontal, and/or vertical direction, removed content, or other forms of modifications. Figures 3 and 4 shows some samples of the images from the dataset. Figure 3 contains the original images, and Fig. 4 show the corresponding seam carved images. Some changes are obvious, but others contain subtle signal changes, not visually perceptible.

We excluded all images that were only resizing of the original image, or in other words, if there were dimensional alteration between the original and the seam carved image, we excluded it from the dataset. There were a total of 8 such images and that reduced our dataset size to 992 images. Our model constrained us to train on smaller resized versions of the image. Excluding resized images from our dataset eliminates ambiguity in labeling when we resize our images for uniformity. This is explained in more detail in the training section of this paper.

3.2 Feature Exploration

We considered a few random samples to compare and explore the differences within the image pair, to determine the feature differences. We started with the images shown in Fig. 5.

First, we generated histograms for the images and then compared the histograms of the two images to find subtle differences in the shape. Since we were interested in the luminance distribution of the images, we started by converting the image from the RGB color space to grayscale. Also, in order to capture all pixel values, we did not threshold but used 256 bins as seen in Fig. 6. Then, we decided to see if each color channel elucidated more information. We treated each channel similar to our grayscale image

Fig. 3. Original image preview

Fig. 4. Seam carve image preview

and superimposed all the resulting histogram data onto a single graph as seen in Fig. 7. Although subtle, we see a change in direction in the red and green channel near the center peak.

Next, we wanted to explore how each pair of color was distributed among each pixel. For each pairwise combination of channels, we used 32 bins to see the distribution. The outcome is depicted in Fig. 8, and this set of data was yet another set of feature used in the model.

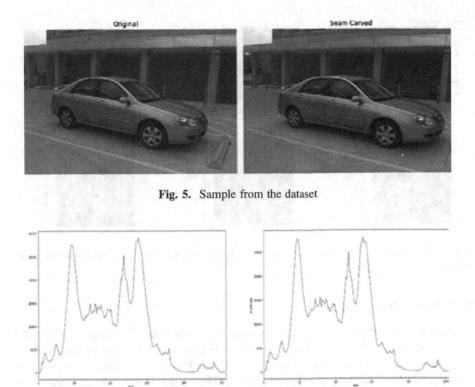

Fig. 5. Sample from the dataset

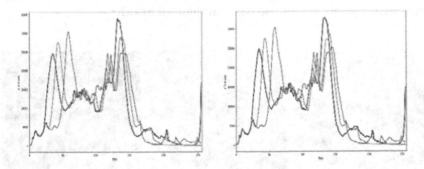

Fig. 6. Grayscale histogram showing luminance distribution between the original (left) and seam carved (right) images

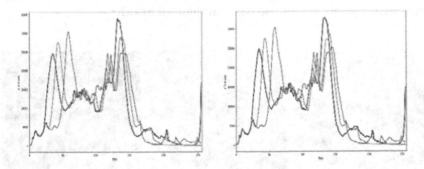

Fig. 7. Color distribution histogram - original (left), and seam carved (right) (Color figure online)

Finally, we also considered the use of all three channels to determine a 3-dimensional histogram and included it in our model. We will discuss all the parameters in the next section on the architecture of our network.

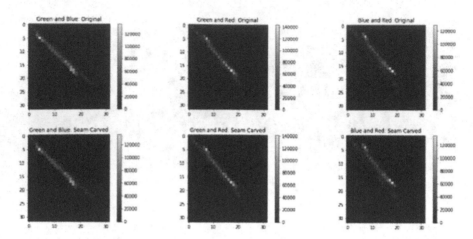

Fig. 8. 2D histogram comparison between the original image (above), and seam carved image (below)

3.3 Image Processing

In order to train our model, we first extracted features from the image or processed them for input. We first resized all our images to 256×256 for ease of computation. We then extracted all the histogram features as explained in the feature exploration section and flattened them to vector matrices. The shape of the 2-dimensional color matrix is (, 768), the shape of the superimposed color channel matrix is (, 3072), and for the 3-dimensional histogram matrix is (, 512). Once we had our vectors, we calculated the local binary representation (LBP) of each channel of an image, and the result example is shown in Fig. 9. Once we calculated the LBP, we stitched the channels back together to feed into our convolutional model.

Fig. 9. LBP representation of each channel on the original image

Finally, for our parallel network, we convolved our image with a High Pass Filter (HPF), using the Gaussian high pass filter with a sigma value of 1. The result of the HPF operation is shown in Fig. 10.

Fig. 10. Gaussian high pass filter result for the original image (left) compared with the seam carved image (right)

The next section explains in detail the network architecture, and how we used our three inputs to train our model.

3.4 Structure and Architecture of Network

The neural network model consists of two parallel convolutional networks, merged with our histogram data that leads to a Softmax activated classifier as depicted in Fig. 11.

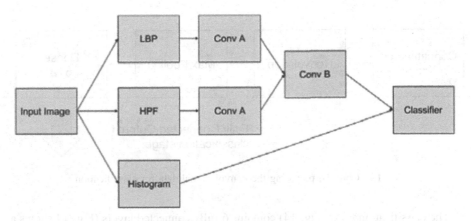

Fig. 11. Overall architecture

Each input image is processed as outlined in the image processing section of this paper. The LBP and HPF images each are used as input into two parallel identical convolutional neural networks (Conv A), whose architecture is shown in Fig. 12. Conv A is a feature learning stage of the neural network, where each convolutional layer is followed by a batch normalization layer, which is then activated by the $\tanh(x)$ activation function, then average pooled using a 5×5 kernel, traversed using stride size of 2.

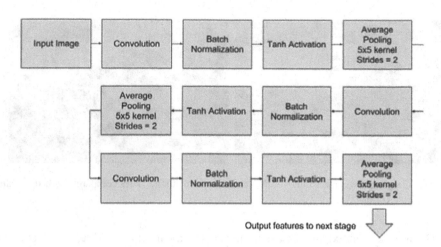

Fig. 12. Conv A, the convolutional feature learning architecture

The output of each parallel Conv A is concatenated and further trained through a secondary smaller network (Conv B). Conv B is depicted in Fig. 13. Conv B consists of a single convolutional layer activated by tanh(x) followed by a Max Pooling layer, which is then connected to a fully connected layer (Dense) by 512 neurons to the classification layer shown in Fig. 14.

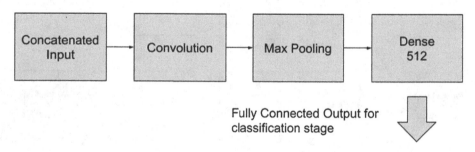

Fig. 13. Conv B, preparing the convolutional data for classification

The classification layer (Fig. 14) contains 6 fully connected layers (Fig. 14 shows a summary of the connections, since all connections would not depict very well in image), in reducing number of neurons per layer. The first layer contains 512 neurons, following by 256 neurons, and then 128, 64, 32 respectively. Finally, the last layer consists of binary neurons activated by the Softmax function to classify into our expected classes of 0, and 1, representing "Unaltered", and "Seam Carved" respectively.

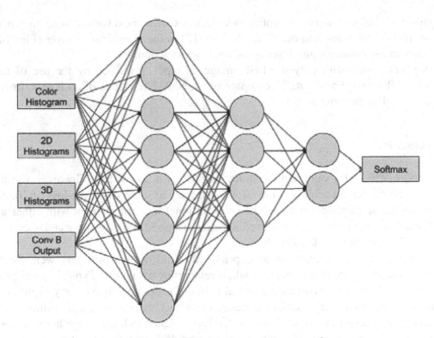

Fig. 14. Classification layer of the network

3.5 Training

For our training setup, we used a variant of the Adam optimizer [40, 41], with an initial learning rate of 0.0003 and no decay. We divided our data into random 80% for training and 20% for validation. The training was done over 90 epochs but stopped early at 43 epochs. Figure 15 shows the validation accuracy, and loss graph from our training.

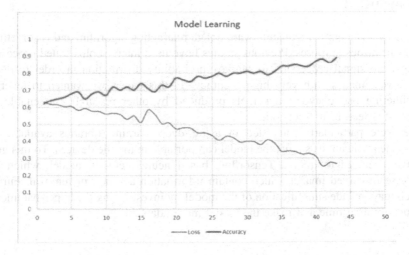

Fig. 15. Training validation accuracy and loss

However, before training our entire model, we experimented with training each part of our model. We connected our Conv A (Fig. 12) to the classification layer (Fig. 14) and used images without any filtering or energy extraction.

We then tested with only the LBP image as input. Followed by the use of the Gaussian HPF image as input. To compare our model. The results of each experiment are discussed in the next section.

4 Results

Our model achieved a validation accuracy of 89% at a 26.7% loss. However, during training, the model did achieve up to 94.4% accuracy at some stage at a loss of 16.4% but it did not sustain for too long. The convolutional layer on its own with either an LBP or a Gaussian HPF image achieved to achieve a good learning curve and accuracy of up to 73% on the validation data.

However, images without the appropriate filter did not perform very well. Seam carving produces very subtle changes when retargeting an image. Typical visual processing models such a convolutional neural network is not able to learn any significant features which allow the model to generalize. In fact, when the image without any processing was used to train our Conv A, the model failed to learn altogether with loss ratio rising above 1.5 with an accuracy of around 48%, which, for a binary classification is random. The complete model, however, along with both the LBP and HPF image, produced remarkable results, yield an accuracy of 89%.

A crucial point to note is how the addition of the flat histogram information gave the model a boost in accuracy and allowed it to learn much faster. Finally, from the results there seem to exist a significant correlation between the 3-dimensional histogram and the seam carved image.

5 Conclusion

Seam carving is a popular content-aware image retargeting algorithm and is sometimes used for nefarious purposes. Previous studies have used many sophisticated processes, ranging from signal processing to Markov probability distribution in order to detect seam carved images with very high accuracy. In this paper, we wanted to leverage some filtering and convolving kernels produced by other researches to enable the training of a deep neural network.

We were particularly interested in using deep learning libraries available for smartphone applications so that the model can portable in mobile devices. To this goal, we have managed to train a Tensorflow based neural network model, which can classify seam carved images which contain information addition or removal. Further research may include simplification of the model by investigating the hyper-parameters to reduce training time and make the model more adaptable.

References

1. Chen, M., Sedighi, V., Boroumand, M., Fridrich, J.: JPEG-phase-aware convolutional neural network for steganalysis of JPEG images. In: Proceedings of the 5th ACM Workshop on Information Hiding and Multimedia Security, pp. 75–84. ACM, New York (2017)
2. Holub, V., Fridrich, J.: Low-complexity features for JPEG steganalysis using undecimated DCT. IEEE Trans. Inf. Forensics Secur. **10**, 219–228 (2015)
3. Ke, Y., Shan, Q., Qin, F., Min, W., Guo, J.: Detection of seam carved image based on additional seam carving behavior. Int. J. Signal Process. Image Process. Pattern Recognit. **9**, 167–178 (2016)
4. Avidan, S., Shamir, A.: Seam carving for content-aware image resizing. ACM Trans. Graph. (TOG), 10 (2007)
5. Sarkar, A., Nataraj, L., Manjunath, B.S.: Detection of seam carving and localization of seam insertions in digital images (2009)
6. Yin, T., Yang, G., Li, L., Zhang, D., Sun, X.: Detecting seam carving based image resizing using local binary patterns. Comput. Secur. **55**, 130–141 (2015)
7. Liu, Q.: An approach to detecting JPEG down-recompression and seam carving forgery under recompression anti-forensics. Pattern Recognit. **65**, 35–46 (2017)
8. Xu, G., Wu, H.Z., Shi, Y.Q.: Structural design of convolutional neural networks for steganalysis. IEEE Signal Process. Lett. **23**, 708–712 (2016)
9. Qian, Y., Dong, J., Wang, W., Tan, T.: Deep learning for steganalysis via convolutional neural networks. In: Media Watermarking, Security, and Forensics, p. 94090 J. International Society for Optics and Photonics (2015)
10. Alzantot, M., Wang, Y., Ren, Z., Srivastava, M.B.: RSTensorFlow: GPU enabled TensorFlow for deep learning on commodity android devices. In: Proceedings of the 1st International Workshop on Deep Learning for Mobile Systems and Applications, pp. 7–12. ACM, New York (2017)
11. Jia, Y., et al.: Caffe: convolutional architecture for fast feature embedding. In: Proceedings of the 22Nd ACM International Conference on Multimedia, pp. 675–678. ACM, New York (2014)
12. Bergstra, J., et al.: Theano: deep learning on GPUs with python. In: NIPS 2011, BigLearning Workshop, Granada, Spain, pp. 1–48. Citeseer (2011)
13. Abadi, M., et al.: TensorFlow: a system for large-scale machine learning. In: OSDI, pp. 265–283 (2016)
14. Anderson, R.J., Petitcolas, F.A.P.: On the limits of steganography. IEEE J. Sel. Areas Commun. **16**, 474–481 (1998)
15. Ge, H., Huang, M., Wang, Q.: Steganography and steganalysis based on digital image. In: 2011 4th International Congress on Image and Signal Processing, pp. 252–255 (2011)
16. Lu, T.-C., Chang, C.-C.: Lossless nibbled data embedding scheme based on difference expansion. Image Vis. Comput. **26**, 632–638 (2008)
17. Lin, C.-C., Hsueh, N.-L.: A lossless data hiding scheme based on three-pixel block differences. Pattern Recognit. **41**, 1415–1425 (2008)
18. Farid, H.: Detecting steganographic messages in digital images. Report TR2001-412 Dartmouth College, Hanover NH (2001)
19. Qian, T., Manoharan, S.: A comparative review of steganalysis techniques. In: 2015 2nd International Conference on Information Science and Security (ICISS), pp. 1–4 (2015)
20. Sabeti, V., Samavi, S., Mahdavi, M., Shirani, S.: Steganalysis and payload estimation of embedding in pixel differences using neural networks. Pattern Recognit. **43**, 405–415 (2010)

21. Johnson, N.F., Jajodia, S.: Steganalysis of images created using current steganography software. In: Aucsmith, D. (ed.) IH 1998. LNCS, vol. 1525, pp. 273–289. Springer, Heidelberg (1998). https://doi.org/10.1007/3-540-49380-8_19

22. Dong, W., Zhou, N., Paul, J.-C., Zhang, X.: Optimized image resizing using seam carving and scaling. In: ACM SIGGRAPH Asia 2009 Papers, pp. 125:1–125:10. ACM, New York (2009)

23. Rubinstein, M., Gutierrez, D., Sorkine, O., Shamir, A.: A comparative study of image retargeting. In: ACM SIGGRAPH Asia 2010 Papers, pp. 160:1–160:10. ACM, New York (2010)

24. Seam Carving—skimage v0.15.dev0 docs. http://scikit-image.org/docs/dev/auto_examples/transform/plot_seam_carving.html#id2

25. Fridrich, J., Long, M.: Steganalysis of LSB encoding in color images. In: 2000 IEEE International Conference on Multimedia and Expo, ICME2000, Proceedings. Latest Advances in the Fast Changing World of Multimedia (Cat. No. 00TH8532), vol. 3, pp. 1279–1282 (2000)

26. Nissar, A., Mir, A.H.: Classification of steganalysis techniques: a study. Digit. Signal Process. **20**, 1758–1770 (2010)

27. Fridrich, J., Goljan, M., Du, R.: Detecting LSB steganography in color, and gray-scale images. IEEE Multimed. **8**, 22–28 (2001)

28. Ker, A.D.: Steganalysis of LSB matching in grayscale images. IEEE Signal Process. Lett. **12**, 441–444 (2005)

29. Ker, A.D.: Resampling and the detection of LSB matching in color bitmaps. In: Security, Steganography, and Watermarking of Multimedia Contents VII, pp. 1–16. International Society for Optics and Photonics (2005)

30. Shi, Y.Q., Chen, C., Chen, W.: A Markov process based approach to effective attacking jpeg steganography. In: Camenisch, J.L., Collberg, C.S., Johnson, N.F., Sallee, P. (eds.) IH 2006. LNCS, vol. 4437, pp. 249–264. Springer, Heidelberg (2007). https://doi.org/10.1007/978-3-540-74124-4_17

31. Fillion, C., Sharma, G.: Detecting content adaptive scaling of images for forensic applications. Presented at the February 4 (2010)

32. Ryu, S.-J., Lee, H.-Y., Lee, H.-K.: Detecting trace of seam carving for forensic analysis. IEICE Trans. Inf. Syst. **97**, 1304–1311 (2014)

33. Liu, Q., Cooper, P.A., Zhou, B.: An improved approach to detecting content-aware scaling-based tampering in JPEG images. In: 2013 IEEE China Summit and International Conference on Signal and Information Processing, pp. 432–436 (2013)

34. Liu, Q., Li, X., Cooper, P.A., Hu, X.: Shift recompression-based feature mining for detecting content-aware scaled forgery in JPEG images (2012)

35. Wei, J.-D., Lin, Y.-J., Wu, Y.-J.: A patch analysis method to detect seam carved images. Pattern Recognit. Lett. **36**, 100–106 (2014)

36. Holub, V., Fridrich, J., Denemark, T.: Universal distortion function for steganography in an arbitrary domain. EURASIP J. Inf. Secur. **2014**, 1 (2014)

37. Li, B., Wang, M., Huang, J., Li, X.: A new cost function for spatial image steganography. In: 2014 IEEE International Conference on Image Processing (ICIP), pp. 4206–4210. IEEE (2014)

38. Sedighi, V., Fridrich, J.: Histogram layer, moving convolutional neural networks towards feature-based steganalysis. Electron. Imaging. **2017**, 50–55 (2017)

39. Liu, Q., Chen, Z.: Improved approaches with calibrated neighboring joint density to steganalysis and seam-carved forgery detection in JPEG images. ACM Trans. Intell. Syst. Technol. **5**, 63:1–63:30 (2014)

40. Kingma, D.P., Ba, J.: Adam: a method for stochastic optimization. ArXiv14126980 Cs (2014)
41. Reddi, S.J., Kale, S., Kumar, S.: On the convergence of adam and beyond (2018)

Remote Sensing Image Analysis Based on Transfer Learning: A Survey

Ruowu Wu[1], Yuyao Li[2], Hui Han[1], Xiang Chen[1], and Yun Lin[2(✉)]

[1] State Key Laboratory of Complex Electromagnetic Environment Effects
on Electronics and Information System (CEMEE),
Luoyang 471003, Henan, China
[2] College of Information and Communication Engineering,
Harbin Engineering University, Harbin, China
linyun_phd@hrbeu.edu.cn

Abstract. Transfer learning is a new topic in machine learning. Psychology holds that the process of learning knowledge from one to the other is a process of transfer learning. Transfer learning is different from machine learning which has to satisfy the following two conditions: (1) The training samples and testing samples must be in the same feature spaces. (2) There must be enough training samples to obtain an excellent training model. Because of the ability of transfer learning to solve problems with small samples and the ability to use historical auxiliary models to solve new problems, it is introduced in remote sensing image analysis. At first, this paper introduces some basic knowledge of transfer learning and enumerates some basic research examples. The research content of this paper mainly involves several problems based on transfer learning, such as target detection and recognition, image classification, etc.

Keywords: Transfer learning · Remote sensing image · Target detection ·
Target recognition · Image classification

1 Introduction

With the improvement of satellite remote sensing image resolution, there is more information that is useful in remote sensing image. More and more occasions require remote - sensing information, such as precise missile research, marine condition monitoring and other military systems as well as emergency management of natural disasters, traffic supervision and other civilian systems [1]. Meanwhile, many sensors produce a great quantity of multi-scale remote sensing images, such as visible light, infrared light, hyperspectral imager, radar and so on. The result is a big increase in data, even explosive growth. Different image information is required for different applications, such as target detection, image classification and target recognition et al., which brings new challenges for remote sensing image analysis.

Transfer learning is a method of applying knowledge learned from one or more source domains to a different but related target domain. It can solve new research problems with historical auxiliary data [2]. The purpose of transfer learning is to apply available data to less labeled datasets or even unlabeled datasets, which can effectively

S. Liu and G. Yang (Eds.): ADHIP 2018, LNICST 279, pp. 408–415, 2019.
https://doi.org/10.1007/978-3-030-19086-6_45

solve the case of fewer labeled samples in new tasks. The center of this theory is to find similarities between domains. One of the biggest problems in remote sensing image processing is the inability to quickly acquire a large number of accurate labeled sample data. At the same time, the existing algorithms cannot recycle the historical data effectively, which leads to the waste of historical data. It is worthwhile to note that the part that can be improved by transfer learning is exactly the problem to be solved in the process of remote sensing image analysis.

2 Transfer Learning

The researchers showed that, unlike similar previous studies, transfer learning is not limited by the assumptions of traditional machine learning (ML). It eases two basic suppositions in traditional ML: (1) The training and testing samples must be in the same feature spaces. (2) There must be enough training samples to obtain an excellent training model. Transfer learning can solve problems in different but related fields using available knowledge, and it will be the next driver of machine learning (ML) success.

The most authoritative article about transfer learning is "A Survey on Transfer Learning [3]" by Prof. Yang. Since then, researchers follow awfully with interest transfer learning. Its application is not limited to specific fields [26]. Transfer learning can play a role in many areas [27] which include, but are not limited to, computer vision, text classification, behavior recognition, natural language processing, indoor positioning, video surveillance, etc.

According to whether the feature space is the same, transfer learning (TL) is divided into homogeneous TL and heterogeneous TL [4]. According to whether the sample is marked, transfer learning consist of inductive TL, transductive TL and unsupervised TL. Furthermore, the more common classification method is divided into four categories according to literature [3]: instance-based transfer learning, feature-based transfer learning, parameter-based transfer learning and relational transfer learning.

2.1 Instance-Based Transfer Learning

The instance-based transfer learning is redistributing the weight of samples according to a certain rule. Sample weighting and importance sampling are the main research contents. How to select training samples that are beneficial to target tasks is a problem to be solved by instance-transfer. The common method is increasing the weights of samples with high similarity.

During the process of research, many scholars set the direction as estimating the probability density ratio between the two research domains, that is, estimating instance weight. One of the classical algorithms is TrAdaboost, proposed by Dai, which is based on Adaboost [5]. It assignments different weights to the training samples through different mechanisms, increasing the instance weights that are conducive to target classification task, and reducing the instance weights that are not conducive to classification task. Based on PCA theory, the upper bound of generalization error of the model is derived. In addition, Tan et al. proposed a transitive transfer learning (TTL), which utilizes joint matrix decomposition [6]. The purpose of this method is to realize the knowledge transfer when the source domain and the target domain share a handful of knowledge.

In general, instance-based transfer learning is a relatively basic method, which is usually more suitable for the case where the distributions difference between domains are small. Therefore, the application scope is limited.

2.2 Feature-Based Transfer Learning

Feature-based transfer learning means the effective feature representation through feature selection or feature transformation. And then the use of these features is transfer. The most classical algorithm is the Transfer Component Analysis (TCA), which is proposed by Pan in 2011 [7]. The following is a brief introduction to the TCA algorithm.

TCA first assumes that the marginal probability distributions of two domains are diverse. Pan believed that there is a feature transformation method, which makes the probability distributions consistent after transforming.

Maximum Mean Difference (MMD) was selected as a distance measure.

$$\text{Distance}(X_s, X_t) = \left\| \frac{1}{n_s} \sum_{i=1}^{n_s} \Phi(X_i) - \frac{1}{n_t} \sum_{j=1}^{n_t} \Phi(X_j) \right\|_H \tag{1}$$

TCA introduces the nuclear matrix K and MMD matrix L,

$$K = \begin{bmatrix} K_{s,s} & K_{s,t} \\ K_{t,s} & K_{t,t} \end{bmatrix} \tag{2}$$

$$l_{i,j} = \begin{cases} \frac{1}{n_1^2} & X_i, X]_j \in D_s \\ \frac{1}{n_2^2} & X_i, X_j \in D_t \\ -\frac{1}{n_1 n_2} & \text{otherwise} \end{cases} \tag{3}$$

Formula (4) presents the Distance(X_s, X_t),

$$\text{trace}(\text{KL}) - \lambda \text{trace}(\text{K}) \tag{4}$$

Then, the formula (5) is obtained by dimensionality reduction,

$$\widetilde{K} = (KK^{-1/2} \widetilde{W})(\widetilde{W^T} K^{-1/2} K) = KWW^T K \tag{5}$$

W is what we want. The traditional machine learning method can be applied on the reduced dimension data of two domains.

Many excellent feature selection algorithms have been proposed. Structural Correspondence Learning (SCL) algorithm represents implicit feature mapping based on semi-supervised multitasking learning [8]. Transfer Joint Matching (TJM) algorithm selects adaptive marginal probability distributions and source sample selection in optimization target [9]. The algorithm combines feature with instance transfer learning method. Gu [10] et al. researched several related clustering tasks and proposed a framework of shared feature subspaces in which all domains share clustering centers. The subspace method in the feature transformation has achieved superior results.

2.3 Parameter-Based Transfer Learning

Parameter-based transfer learning usually aims at finding shared parameters from both source and target domains. Long improved the deep network structure and added the probability distribution adaptation layer to the deep network, which further improved the generalization ability of the model [11–13].

Some of the researchers improved and transferred SVM model. Nater [14] considered the weight vector W of SVM as a combination of two parts:

$$W = W_0 + V \tag{6}$$

Where W_0 represents the common part of two domains, V represents particular parts of two domains.

At present, most parameter based transfer learning are combined with deep neural networks, which achieve excellent results.

2.4 Relational Transfer Learning

Relational transfer learning is quite different from above approaches. This method focuses on the relationship between source samples and target samples. For example, Mihalkova used Markov logical networks to mine the similarities between domains [15]. Generally speaking there are few researches on this method and it is still at the basic stage.

3 Target Detection Based on Transfer Learning

Target detection in remote sensing images corresponds to the problem of face detection in natural images, that is, detecting the existence of the target in a certain scene. The targets being detected are generally summarized in the following three categories: Linear targets such as airstrips, roads and rivers; Block target such as airplanes, tanks and ships; Complex targets such as airports, ports and bridges.

As one of the methods used in machine learning to solve the problem of domain adaptation, transfer learning has also achieved good results in remote sensing image target detection. Xu applied the idea of transfer learning to airport detection [16]. The author used Faster R-CNN as the basic framework and used the RPN network to generate candidate regions. In order to transfer the common features, the parameters of the lower convolution layers in the pre-training model keep constant or overlapped at a small learning rate in the new task. The reason is that the lower convolution layers in the CNN learn low-level semantic features. In this paper, the problem of data type imbalance is solved by the method of difficult sample mining. It accurately detected different types of airports in complex background. Researchers state this method is superior to others, and it has strong theoretical and practical significance for real-time airports detection.

Chen [17] proposed an end-to-end detection model for aircraft detection in complex background, which is based on transferring deep CNN. In this model, the two-stage task of classification and localization is combined into one problem. The framework in natural images, YOLO, is used to detect aircraft in remote sensing images. The framework is widely used in other target detection tasks, which is block target similar to aircraft.

4 Target Recognition Based on Transfer Learning

Target recognition is analogous to the task of face recognition. We usually give an initial assumption that the object has been detected in the image before recognition. And giving the types of targets is what we are required to accomplish.

The earliest target recognition method is template-matching theory. After that, the model-based approach is widely studied. It extracts features from the original high - resolution images and abstracts the target into an object model, a background model or an environment model for recognition [28].

In the case of enemy Unmanned Aerial Vehicle (UAV) accuracy improvement of recognition and classification, Xie [18] proposed a Sparse Auto-Encoder (SAE) algorithm based on transfer learning. Four parts are formed to achieve the algorithm, that is, sampling and preprocessing module, source feature training module, target domain global feature extraction module and target classification module. Firstly, unsupervised learning of unlabeled samples in source domain is carried out, and local features are obtained. Then, CNN with pool layer is used to extract the global features of tagged images in target domain. Finally, the classification part uses the softmax regression model. The proposed SAE algorithm based on transfer learning can be applied on small sample multi-frame enemy UAV images.

Lima used fine-tuning for the first time in ocean front recognition [19]. It provides a new direction for further research. Li applies DNNs to SAR automatic recognition technology and uses AdaGrad (Adaptive Subgradient Methods) instead of SGD (Stochastic Gradient Descent) as the weight optimization function [20]. Based on transfer learning theory, an improved network structure is proposed to recognition SAR. Experimental results show that the theory can improve the training process of network parameters and improve the accurate rate. ZP Dan proposed a transfer model on the base of LBP feature, which is able to detect and recognize unlabeled samples in remote sensing images [21]. The LBP algorithm is used to extract the eigenvector of the target domain. The mixed regularization framework, including manifold regularization and entropy regularization, realizes transfer process. A better robust classifier is trained by common parameters found in the feature space of different target data.

5 Image Classification Based on Transfer Learning

Scene classification is an important step in remote sensing image processing. In order to analyze and manage remote sensing image data effectively, it is necessary to attach semantic labels to the images according to their contents, and scene classification is an important way to solve this problem [29]. Scene classification is to distinguish images with similar scene characteristics from multiple images and classify these images correctly.

Li proposed a method based on CNN Inception-v3 model to solve the problem of lacking labeled sample in scene classification of remote sensing images [22]. Feature vectors of the sample are extracted by pre-training model. The feature extraction is carried out by using pre-training weight rather than training the weight parameters of inception-v3, which is more efficient than the traditional method of feature extraction. After that, the vector is input into a single-layer fully connected neural network including Softmax classifier. Higher classification accuracy results are obtained and demonstrated with a small number of labeled remote sensing images.

Literature [23] proposed a new heterogeneous transfer framework for hyperspectral image classification, IRHTL. IRHTL algorithm first iterated to learn the projection of two domains. The next step is reweighting the source samples and increasing the proportion of useful samples. Finally, the classifier of the target domain is successfully obtained. Heterogeneity solves the problem of inconsistent feature space of remote sensing information from different sensors. This algorithm promotes remote sensing image processing to some extent.

Xia et al. of the Tokyo University improved TCA algorithm. They proposed E-TCA algorithm, which is used to solve the problem of domain adaptive in hyperspectral remote sensing image classification [24]. E-TCA successfully embodies the superiorities of integrated learning and TCA. In this paper, they selected RF (Random Forest) to predict the labels of target images. It has been proven that the new algorithm is better than the traditional TCA and RF.

Xu proposed domain adaptation with parameter transfer (DAPT) on the base of Extreme Learning Machine (ELM) algorithm [25]. The new idea transforms the ELM parameters of the target domain back to the source domain, and it selected BoVW feature and deep features which can represent the image well. Moreover, the author avoids the negative transfer by regularization constraint.

6 Conclusion

With the development of transfer learning, there will be more effective methods for remote sensing image analysis. The survey mainly investigates the research of remote sensing images based on transfer learning in recent years. It summarizes the techniques of transfer applied to target detection, target recognition and image classification. It can be seen that transfer learning in remote sensing images analysis is reasonable and practicable, it is worthy extending. However, since there are still some problems in the field of transfer learning, there are still many unknown remote sensing transfer algorithms worth studying.

414   R. Wu et al.

Acknowledgment. This work is supported by the National Natural Science Foundation of China (61771154) and the Fundamental Research Funds for the Central Universities (HEUCFG201830).

Meantime, all the authors declare that there is no conflict of interests regarding the publication of this article.

We gratefully thank of very useful discussions of reviewers.

References

1. Liu, Y., Fu, Z.Y., Zheng, F.B.: Research progress of target classification and recognition in high resolution remote sensing image. J. Geosci. **17**(9), 1080–1091 (2015)
2. Tuia, D., Persello, C., Bruzzone, L.: Domain adaptation for the classification of remote sensing data: an overview of recent advances. IEEE Geosci. Remote Sens. Mag. **4**(2), 41–57 (2016)
3. Pan, S.J., Yang, Q.: A survey on transfer learning. IEEE Trans. Knowl. Data Eng. **22**(10), 1345–1359 (2010)
4. Weiss, K., Khoshgoftaar, T.M., Wang, D.: A survey of transfer learning. J. Big Data **3**(1), 1–40 (2016)
5. Dai, W., Yang, Q., Xue, G.R., et al.: Boosting for transfer learning. In: International Conference on Machine Learning, pp. 193–200. ACM (2007)
6. Tan, B., Song, Y., Zhong, E., Yang, Q.: Transitive transfer learning. In: Proceedings of the 21th ACM SIGKDD International Conference on Knowledge Discovery and Data Mining, pp. 1155–1164. ACM (2015)
7. Pan, S.J., Tsang, I.W., Kwok, J.T., et al.: Domain adaptation via transfer component analysis. IEEE Trans. Neural Networks **22**(2), 199–210 (2011)
8. Blitzer, J., Mcdonald, R., Pereira, F.: Domain adaptation with structural correspondence learning. In: Conference on Empirical Methods in Natural Language Processing, pp. 120–128. Association for Computational Linguistics (2006)
9. Long, M., Wang, J., Ding, G., et al.: Transfer joint matching for unsupervised domain adaptation. In: IEEE Conference on Computer Vision and Pattern Recognition, pp. 1410–1417. IEEE Computer Society (2014)
10. Gu, Q., Zhou, J.: Learning the shared subspace for multi-task clustering and transductive transfer classification. In: IEEE International Conference on Data Mining, pp. 159–168. IEEE (2009)
11. Long, M., Cao, Y., Wang, J., et al.: Learning transferable features with deep adaptation networks, pp. 97–105 (2015)
12. Long, M., Wang, J., Cao, Y., et al.: Deep learning of transferable representation for scalable domain adaptation. IEEE Trans. Knowl. Data Eng. **28**(8), 2027–2040 (2016)
13. Long, M., Zhu, H., Wang, J., et al.: Deep transfer learning with joint adaptation networks (2017)
14. Nater, F., Tommasi, T., Grabner, H, et al.: Transferring activities: updating human behavior analysis. In: IEEE International Conference on Computer Vision Workshops, pp. 1737–1744. IEEE Computer Society (2011)
15. Mihalkova, L., Huynh, T., Mooney, R.J.: Mapping and revising Markov logic networks for transfer learning. In: National Conference on Artificial Intelligence, pp. 608–614. AAAI Press (2007)
16. Xu, Y., Zhu, M., Ma, S., Tang, H., Ma, H.: Airport object detection combining transfer learning and hard example mining. J. Xi'an Electron. Sci. Univ., 1–7

17. Chen, Z., Zhang, T., Ouyang, C.: End-to-end airplane detection using transfer learning in remote sensing images. Remote Sens. **10**(1), 139 (2018)
18. Xie, B., Duan, Z., Zhen, B., Yin, Y.H.: Research on UAV target recognition algorithm based on transfer learning SAE. Infrared Laser Eng. **47**(06), 224–230 (2018)
19. Lima, E., Sun, X., Dong, J., et al.: Learning and transferring convolutional neural network knowledge to ocean front recognition. In: IEEE Geosci. Remote Sens. Lett. **PP**(99), 1–5 (2017)
20. Li, S., Wei, Z.H., Zhang, B.C., et al.: Target recognition using transfer learning-based deep networks for SAR images. J. Univ. Chin. Acad. Sci. **35**(1), 75–83 (2018)
21. Dan, Z., Sang, N., He, Y., et al.: An improved LBP transfer learning for remote sensing object recognition. Opt. Int. J. Light Electron Opt. **125**(1), 482–485 (2014)
22. Li, G.D., Zhang, C.J., Wang, M.K. Zhang, X.Y.: Transfer learning using convolutional neural networks for scene classification within high resolution remote sensing image. Surveying Mapp. Sci. (06), 1–13 (2019)
23. Li, X., Zhang, L., Du, B., et al.: Iterative reweighting heterogeneous transfer learning framework for supervised remote sensing image classification. IEEE J. Sel. Topics Appl. Earth Obs. Remote Sens. **10**(5), 2022–2035 (2017)
24. Xia, J., Yokoya, N., Iwasaki, A.: Ensemble of transfer component analysis for domain adaptation in hyperspectral remote sensing image classification. In: 2017 IEEE International Geoscience and Remote Sensing Symposium, IGARSS 2017, pp. 4762–4765. IEEE (2017)
25. Xu, S., Mu, X., Chai, D., et al.: Adapting remote sensing to new domain with ELM parameter transfer. IEEE Geosci. Remote Sens. Lett. **PP**(99), 1–5 (2017)
26. Tu, Y., Lin, Y., Wang, J., et al.: Semi-supervised learning with generative adversarial networks on digital signal modulation classification. CMC-Comput. Mater. Continua **55**(2), 243–254 (2018)
27. Zhou, J.T., Zhao, H., Peng, X., Fang, M., Qin, Z., Goh, R.S.M.: Transfer hashing: from shallow to deep. IEEE Trans. Neural Netw. Learn. Syst. https://doi.org/10.1109/tnnls.2018.2827036
28. Zheng, Z., Sangaiah, A.K., Wang, T.: Adaptive communication protocols in flying ad-hoc network. IEEE Commun. Mag. **56**(1), 136–142 (2018)
29. Zhao, N., Richard Yu, F., Sun, H., Li, M.: Adaptive power allocation schemes for spectrum sharing in interference-alignment-based cognitive radio networks. IEEE Trans. Veh. Technol. **65**(5), 3700–3714 (2016)

Longitudinal Collision Risk Assessment of Closely Spaced Parallel Runways Paired Approach

Jingjie Teng[1(✉)], Zhaoning Zhang[1], Wenya Li[1], Kexuan Liu[1], and Yan Kang[2]

[1] Civil Aviation University of China, Tianjin 300300, China
1808848736@qq.com
[2] China Cargo Airlines, Shanghai 200335, China

Abstract. Studying the paired approach of closely spaced parallel runways is of great significance for improving airport capacity and reducing flight delays, and has important theoretical and practical value. In order to study the longitudinal collision risk in the paired approach process, a kinematics equation is established to describe its motion process. Considering the influence of positional positioning error and aircraft wake motion, a longitudinal collision risk assessment model is established, and the calculation formula of relevant parameters in the model is given. Finally, the model is calculated by Matlab software, and the curve of collision risk with related parameters is given, and the rationality of the model is verified.

Keywords: Paired approach · Collision risk · Wake motion · Standard normal distribution

1 Introduction

With the continuous development of China's civil aviation transportation industry, the airport has become more and more congested. It is urgent to increase the capacity of the airport terminal area. The implementation of the paired approach to the parallel runway can effectively increase the airport capacity, but the paired approach has large differences with the traditional approach. Paired approach means that two aircraft approach together on a pair of parallel runway with this two runways spacing of less than 760 m, and requires a minimum safe separation between the proceeding and following aircraft, while avoiding the wake before the wake of the proceeding aircraft. Therefore, it is important to determine the safety area that needs to be maintained during the paired approach, and calculate the risk of collision.

Beyond seas, Jonathan Hammer first proposed the concept of closely parallel runways paired approach and calculated the range of safety between the two airplanes [1]; thereafter, Steven Landry and Amy R Pritchett analysed the factors affecting the range of safety areas in paired approach procedure [2]; Rodney Teo and Claire J. Tomlin calculated the conflicting area of the paired approach, and proposed an optimal control theory for calculating the danger area during the paired approach [3, 4]; Burnell T Mc

S. Liu and G. Yang (Eds.): ADHIP 2018, LNICST 279, pp. 416–424, 2019.
https://doi.org/10.1007/978-3-030-19086-6_46

Kissickl and Fernando J Rico-Cusi used the Monte Carlo simulation method to simulate the safe distance range of the paired approach airplane [5]; the above scholars completed the minute study about paired approach danger area, the effect of the wake on the paired approach, paired approach security area. In China, the safety assessment theory of flight interval is relatively mature. For example, Zhang Zhaoning systematically studied the collision risk of the route and the risk of aircraft collision under free flight conditions by probability theory and event model, and considering the influence of Communication Navigation Surveillance (CNS) performance [6–11]; Hu Minghua et al. studied the ways of closely parallel runways approach [12]; Tian Yong et al. studied the runway spacing in parallel dependent approach mode in the closely parallel runways [13]; Lu Fei, Zhang Zhaoning and others evaluate the risk of paired approach longitudinal collision basing on the positioning error distribution and collision-preventing requirements of aircraft wake, and considering the paired approach aircraft motion process [14, 15]; Sun Jia and Tian Yong used the Monte Carlo simulation method to conduct collision risk assessment of paired approach mode [16]; Niu Xilei and Lu Zongping established the minimum following distance model for the close parallel runway paired approach, and analyzed the collision risk [17, 18]. It can be seen that foreign scholars mainly calculate the safety distance between the two machines for the paired approach running program, but the collision risk assessment between the two teams is less. The research on the collision risk of the route is relatively mature for domestic scholars, and the related research on the runway is not enough. Based on the aircraft position error and the influence on the safety separation posed by the wake motion under the crosswind, a longitudinal collision risk assessment of paired approach model is established, and then the collision risk is analyzed with time.

2 Longitudinal Collision Risk Assessment Model of Paired Approach

2.1 A Model Establishment

First, this paper makes the following assumptions in longitudinal collision risk model:

Only consider the risk of longitudinal collision between the two aircrafts undergoing a paired approach;

The after aircrafts that are paired into the approach are not allowed to pass the proceeding aircrafts during the approach;

Two aircrafts approach according to their respective approach paths.

Let the proceeding airplane of the paired approach be the aircraft 1 and the following airplane be the aircraft 2. The longitudinal positioning error ε_1 of the proceeding airplane at time t obeys the normal distribution of the average value μ_1 and the variance: σ_1^2, so:

$$\varepsilon_1 \sim N\left(\mu_1, \sigma_1^2\right) \tag{1}$$

418   J. Teng et al.

As the same reason:

$$\varepsilon_2 \sim N(\mu_2, \sigma_2^2) \tag{2}$$

At time t, the longitudinal distances of the proceeding and following airplane distances from the reference point are $D_1(t)$, $D_2(t)$, and the actual longitudinal distances are $X_1(t)$, $X_2(t)$, then:

$$X(t) = D(t) + \varepsilon \tag{3}$$

so the actual longitudinal spacing of the two aircrafts is:

$$X_1(t) - X_2(t) = [D_1(t) + \varepsilon_1] - [D_2(t) + \varepsilon_2] = [D_1(t) - D_2(t)] + [\varepsilon_1 - \varepsilon_2] \tag{4}$$

Combined with the knowledge of probability theory, we can get:

$$X_1(t) - X_2(t) \sim N\{[D_1(t) - D_2(t)] + [\mu_1 - \mu_2], (\sigma_1^2 + \sigma_2^2)\} \tag{5}$$

As shown in Fig. 1, it is assumed that the initial safety separation of the proceeding and following aircraft passing the reference point is L_s, and the time is 0 when the aircraft 2 passes the reference point, S_1, S_2 is the initial speed of the aircraft 1, 2 in the reference point, A_1, A_2 is the acceleration of the aircraft 1, 2.

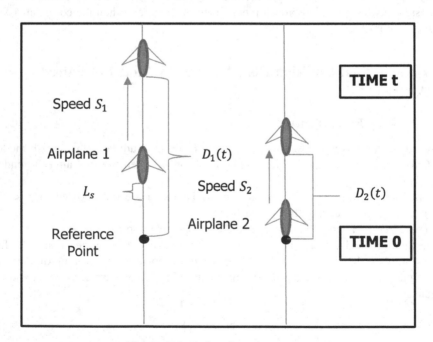

Fig. 1. Paired aircraft motion process

Then the longitudinal separation of the two aircraft at time t should be:

$$D_1(t) - D_2(t) = S_1 t + \frac{1}{2} A_1 t^2 + L_s - S_2 t - \frac{1}{2} A_2 t^2 \qquad (6)$$

Make $L(t) = X_1(t) - X_2(t)$, then the distribution of L is:

$$L(t) \sim N\left[\left(S_1 t + \frac{1}{2} A_1 t^2 + L_s - S_2 t - \frac{1}{2} A_2 t^2\right) + (\mu_1 - \mu_2), (\sigma_1^2 + \sigma_2^2)\right] \qquad (7)$$

So:

$$L \sim N(\mu, \sigma^2) \qquad (8)$$

Assuming that the lateral and vertical separation is 0, and the region where the longitudinal collision occurs is $l_1 \leq L(t) \leq l_2$, the longitudinal collision risk model can be obtained as:

$$P = P(l_1 \leq L \leq l_2) = \frac{1}{\sqrt{2\pi}\sigma} \int_{l_1}^{l_2} exp\left[-\frac{(x - \mu)^2}{2\sigma^2}\right] dx \qquad (9)$$

The paired approach allows two aircrafts to approach simultaneously on a parallel runways with the runway's centerline spacing of less than 760 m, and the following airplane avoids the wake before the wake of the proceeding airplane, rather than after the wake, which requires the longitudinal separation in the process satisfies the following two conditions: Condition 1, the following airplane and the proceeding airplane keep a sufficient separation to prevent two aircraft from colliding; Condition 2, the following airplane and the proceeding airplane keep the separation small enough So that the following airplane can avoid the wake before the wake of the proceeding airplane. The safe area during the paired approach is shown in Fig. 2.

2.2   Determination of Parameters in the Model

For condition 1, the upper and lower limits of the integral P are equal in magnitude and opposite in sign, and the magnitude is half of the sum of the two airplane's length of the fuselage. So the corresponding longitudinal collision risk is:

$$P_1 = \frac{1}{\sqrt{2\pi}\sigma} \int_{l_{11}}^{l_{12}} exp\left[-\frac{(x - \mu)^2}{2\sigma^2}\right] dx \qquad (10)$$

For condition 2, the lower limit of integral l_{21} in the integral P is the maximum separation that following airplane avoids the wake before the wake of the proceeding airplane at time t, which is called the wake safety back boundary in this paper; The upper limit of the integral l_{22} is the minimum separation allowed by the following airplane to avoid the wake after the wake of the proceeding airplane (that is, when the following airplane is not affected by the wake of the proceeding airplane), l_{22} take 12000 m refer to the "China Civil Aviation Air Traffic Management Rules" [19].

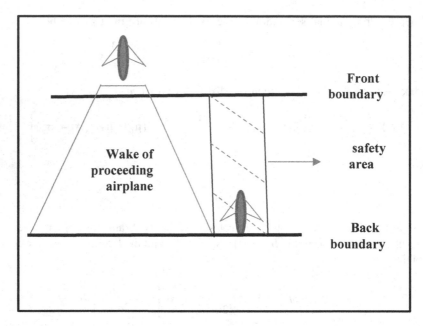

Fig. 2. Paired approach safety area

l_{21} is determined as follows:

Under the influence of crosswind, wake safety back boundary will move forward, as shown in Fig. 3.

The wake is considered to be generated from the tip of the front airplane's wing, and is diffused in the windless condition with the lateral velocity λ and the backward velocity u. The diffusion direction is that combines the two velocity vectors; when there is a wind direction angle θ, the wind speed V_C, the wake is equivalent to the velocity spread by the vector $\vec{\lambda}$, $\vec{\mu}$ and vector $\overrightarrow{V_C}$, as shown in Fig. 4.

From the illustrated geometric relationship, it can be seen that the wake safety back boundary l_{21} is (when there is no wind):

$$l_{21} = \left[H - \frac{1}{2}(A_1 + A_2)\right]\frac{u}{\lambda} - \frac{1}{2}(B_1 + B_2) \tag{11}$$

When there is wind:

$$l_{21} = \left[H - \frac{1}{2}(A_1 + A_2)\right]\frac{u + V_C \sin\theta}{\lambda + V_C \cos\theta} - \frac{1}{2}(B_1 + B_2) \tag{12}$$

The wake lateral velocity is calculated by the following formula [20]:

$$\lambda = 1.344e^{-0.0043t} \tag{13}$$

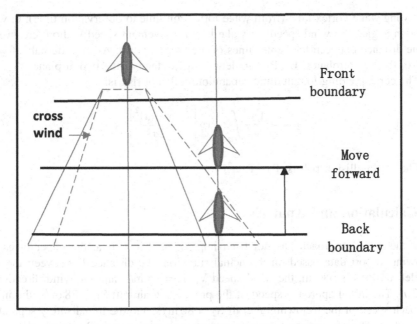

Fig. 3. Effect of crosswind on longitudinal safety separation

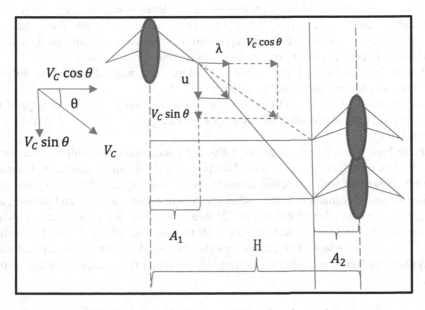

Fig. 4. Schematic diagram of aircraft-wake motion

t: wing wake vortex time (from wake formation time to observation time); θ: wind direction angle, V_C: wind speed; λ: wake lateral movement speed without crosswind; H: the distance between the center lines of the two runways; A_1, A_2: the half of wing span of the two airplanes; B_1, B_2: the length of fuselage of the two airplanes.

The corresponding longitudinal separation collision risk is:

$$P_2 = \frac{1}{\sqrt{2\pi}\sigma} \int_{l_{22}}^{l_{21}} exp\left[-\frac{(x-\mu)^2}{2\sigma^2}\right] dx \tag{14}$$

The total collision risk is: $P = P_1 + P_2$.

3   Calculation and Analysis

Since the paired approach has not been implemented in China, the paper takes the following airport data based on the actual situation: the distance H between the two parallel runways is 680 m, the wind speed V_C is = 10 m/s, and the wind direction is $\theta = 30°$. The initial approach speed of the proceeding aircraft $S_1 = 78\,\text{m/s}$, the initial approach speed of the following aircraft $S_2 = 80\,\text{m/s}$, and the initial safety separation $L_s = 900\,\text{m}$. The wing span of the pairing approach airplanes are 38 m, and the length of the fuselage is 40 m. At present, there is no specific safety target level for paired approach, therefore, the ICAO's provisions on the level of unpaired approach safety objectives is used as a criterion: $1.5 \times 10{-}9$ [15]. According to the above data, the longitudinal collision risk of paired approach is calculated and analyzed, and the relationship between collision risk and time and wind speed is studied.

Under the condition of wind speed of 10 m/s and wind direction of 30°, the collision risk changes with time as shown in Fig. 5.

At the time of t = 10 s and t = 20 s, the wind direction is 30°, the change of the collision risk is calculated when the wind speed is changed at 0–10 m/s. The result is as shown in Fig. 6.

From Figs. 4 and 5, we can get the following conclusions: (1) With the increase of time, the risk of longitudinal collision of the two aircrafts is getting smaller and smaller, which is consistent with the actual situation, because the speed of the two aircrafts is getting smaller and smaller, so the collision risk will become smaller and smaller, and this proves the rationality of the model. (2) When the crosswind is positive crosswind, the longitudinal collision risk increases with the increase of wind speed, which is consistent with the actual situation, because the crosswind accelerates the aircraft-wake lateral shift, reducing the safety separation, thus proving the rationality of the model.

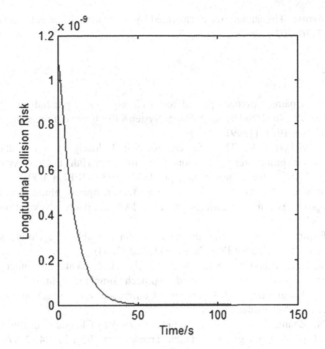

Fig. 5. Collision risk changes with time

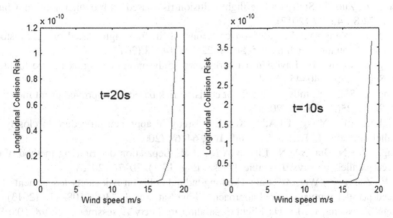

Fig. 6. Collision risk changes with wind speed

4 Conclusions

According to the actual motion process of the closely parallel runways paired approach, considering the positioning error and time of the two aircrafts in the paired approach process, the motion equations and longitudinal collision risk assessment models are established. The probability of paired approach collision risk decreases with time and increases with the increase of positive wind speed.

Acknowledgements. The authors were supported by the National Natural Science Foundation of China (No. 71701202).

References

1. Mundra, A.: A paired approach procedure for closely spaced parallel runways: issues and simulation results. In: 18th Digital Avionics Systems Conference, Proceedings, vol. 1, pp. 4. C.4_1—4.C.4_1. IEEE (1999)
2. Landry, S., Prichett, A.R.: The safe zone for paired closely spaced parallel approaches: implications for procedures and automation. In: The 19th Digital Avionics Systems Conference, DASC, Proceedings, vol. 1, pp. 3E3/1–3E3/8. IEEE (2000)
3. Teo, R., Tomlin, C.J.: Provably safe evasive maneuvers against blunders in closely spaced parallel approaches. In: Proceedings of the AIAA Guidance, Navigation and Control Conference (2001)
4. Teo, R., Tomlin, C.J.: Computing danger zones for provably safe closely spaced parallel approaches. J. Guid. Control Dyn. **26**(3), 434–442 (2003)
5. Mc Kissick, B.T., Rico-Cusi, F.J., Murdoch, J.L., et al.: Wake encounter analysis for a closely spaced parallel runway paired approach simulation. In: 9th AIAA Aviation Technology, Integration, and Operations Conference (ATIO), American Institute of Aeronautics and Astronautics (2009)
6. Zhang, Z.N., Zhang, X., Li, D.-b.: Computation model of lateral collision rate on parallel routes based on VOR navigation. J. Traffic Transp. Eng. **7**(3), 21–24 (2007)
7. Zhang, Z., Shen, J., Liu, J.: Lateral collision risk model based on CNS position error. J. Traffic Transp. Eng. **9**(6), 110–113 (2009)
8. Zhang, Z., Zuo, J.: Study on free flight collision risk based on brownian motion. China Saf. Sci. J. **22**(8), 43–47 (2012)
9. Zhang, Z., Wang, Y.: Research on collision risk in free flight based on fuzzy stochastic differential equations. China Saf. Sci. J. **22**(10), 14–18 (2012)
10. Zhang, Z., Liang, Y.: Bayesian network-based study on collision risk in free flight. China Saf. Sci. J. **24**(9), 40–45 (2014)
11. Zhang, Z., Shi, R.: Study on free flight collision risk based on improved event model. China Saf. Sci. J. **25**(7), 35–40 (2015)
12. Minghua, H.U., Yong, T.I.A.N., Kai, L.I.: Study of approach procedure to closely spaced parallel runways. J. Transp. Eng. Inf. **1**(1), 64–69 (2003)
13. Yong, T.I.A.N., Jia, S.U.N., Lili, W.A.N., et al.: Separation determining method of closely spaced parallel runways. J. Traffic Transp. Eng. **13**(1), 70–76 (2013)
14. Lu, F., Zhang, Z., Wei, Z., et al.: The longitudinal collision risk safety assessment of closed spaced parallel runways paired approach. China Saf. Sci. J. **23**(8), 108–113 (2013)
15. Zhang, Z., Wang, L., Li, D.: Flight Separation in Safety Assessment, pp. 98–105. Science Press, Beijing (2009)
16. Jia, S., Yong, T.: Collision risk analysis of closed parallel runway pairing approach. Harbin Univ. Commer. J. Nat. Sci. Ed. **2**, 241–245 (2014)
17. Niu, X., Lyu, Z., Zhang, Z.: Minimum in-trail distance for paired closely spaced parallel. Aeronaut. Comput. Tech. **45**(4), 46–48 (2015)
18. Lu, Z., Zhang, Z., Niu, X.: Collision risk safety assessment of paired approach based on velocity error and positioning error. Aeronaut. Comput. Tech. **45**(6), 36–40 (2015)
19. Civil Aviation Administration of China's Decree No. 190. Rules for China Civil Aviation Air Traffic Management, pp. 11–22 (2007)
20. Li, Y.: Analysis of wake spacing reduction and collision safety. Nanjing University of Aeronautics and Astronautics, Jiangsu, p. 26 (2015)

Short-Term Traffic Flow Prediction of Airspace Sectors Based on Multiple Time Series Learning Mechanism

Zhaoning Zhang, Kexuan Liu[✉], Fei Lu, and Wenya Li

Civil Aviation University of China, Tianjin 300300, China
294006021@qq.com

Abstract. Firstly, by analyzing the original radar data of the aircraft in the airspace system, the historical operation information of each sector is extracted, and the traffic flow correlation between different routes of the same sector is considered. According to the characteristics of busy sector traffic flow data, a multi-dimensional data model of traffic flow with multiple related routes in the sector is constructed. Secondly, based on the data model, a traffic flow forecasting algorithm based on multi-time series machine learning is proposed. The main core idea of the algorithm is to use the time series clustering method to reduce the dimensionality of multi-dimensional traffic flow data, and then introduce the machine learning method for concurrent training. The training result obtains the optimal classifier group through competition. Finally, the multi-optimal machine learning integrated prediction method is designed to predict traffic flow. Taking the typical busy sector in China as an example, the proposed prediction method is verified. The research results show that the prediction results are better than the traditional single time series machine learning method, and the stability of the prediction results is good, which can fully reflect the dynamics and uncertainty of short-term traffic flow between sectors in each airspace, in line with the actual situation of air traffic.

Keywords: Traffic flow prediction · Learning mechanism · Airspace sectors · Flight scheduling

1 Introduction

With the rapid development of China's air transport industry, air traffic flow continues to grow, and problems such as large airspace congestion, large-scale flight delays, high-intensity control loads, and high-frequency accidents caused by the contradiction between supply and demand have become increasingly prominent. The resulting safety hazards and economic losses have seriously restricted the sustainable and healthy development of China's air transport industry. In order to ensure the safe and efficient operation of China's airspace system, it is necessary to accurately predict the short-term traffic of airspace sectors. Based on scientifically grasping the distribution trend of air traffic flow and future trends, an effective air traffic flow management strategy is formulated. It is not only the premise of implementing tactical and pre-tactical traffic

S. Liu and G. Yang (Eds.): ADHIP 2018, LNICST 279, pp. 425–432, 2019.
https://doi.org/10.1007/978-3-030-19086-6_47

management, but also provides method support and reference basis for control sector opening and closing configuration, control seat scheduling, and air traffic situation assessment.

The traditional short-term air traffic flow forecasting method is mainly based on historical observation flow time series data, using historical average model, moving average model, autoregressive sliding model, combined forecasting model and other statistical forecasting models [1–5], and artificial intelligence such as neural networks [6–8]. The input method of the above method is single, and the calculation process is simple, but the dynamics and uncertainty of the air traffic flow during the actual operation are not fully considered. In papers [9–11], the model of aggregate traffic flow forecasting is proposed. The model takes the traffic flow distribution situation of the airspace unit as the research object, and the number of airspace units is used as the calculation dimension, which greatly reduces the calculation amount in the number of aircrafts. The model is less affected by the uncertainty factor and the prediction time range is long. However, the input parameters of the model are a set of static historical average values, and the uncertainty of the parameters is not considered. Therefore, there is a certain difference between the prediction effect and the actual operation.

It can be seen that traditional research often uses the data of the predicted route itself as the research object for analysis and modeling, and the interaction between adjacent routes is generally less studied. However, the traffic flow between multiple routes in the same area obviously has a certain correlation. Therefore, this study takes multiple routes in the same area as the research object, fully considering the dynamics of traffic flow in the actual operation of airspace system. Taking full account of the dynamic, time-varying and uncertainties of traffic flow in the actual operation of China's airspace system, this paper proposes a traffic flow prediction model based on the integrated learning concept of hybrid multi-machine learning strategy. This model considers traffic flow forecasting as multidimensional time series data mining. Through deep analysis of radar data, clear spatial sector historical traffic data and initial model parameters, according to the established multi-sector aggregate traffic flow model and parameter estimation and update method, the traffic distribution of airspace sectors in a certain time and space range in the future It is predicted to provide scientific theoretical basis and data support for the efficient management of tactical and pre-tactical air traffic flow.

2   Sector Traffic Flow Data Analysis

The experimental objects in this study selected the traffic flow data of the main segments of each route. The original information collected by each route is based on the flight, including the route number, flight signage, arrival time, and departure time. First, the number of flights per minute of each route is counted, and the traffic flow data is divided into a unified window for a certain length of time. Finally, the metrics of the traffic are separated into different levels.

Let the set of M traffic flow data in a certain sector be $Z = \{Z_1, Z_2, \ldots, Z_M\}$ and $Z_i \in Z$ is traffic flow time series information system composed of traffic flow information of the i-th route in Z is denoted as $Z_i = (W_i, K_i, C_i, F, a)$.

Where $W_i = \{w_{i1}, w_{i2}, \ldots, w_{in}\}$ represents a set of n time-ordered traffic flow timing segments in the i-th route, and each time-series data segment has a length of s time units. The data of the j-th time window of the i-th route is expressed as $w_{ij} = \left\{ t_{(w_{ij},1)}, t_{(w_{ij},2)}, \ldots, t_{(w_{ij},s)} \right\}$, $w_{ij} \in W_i$, $|w_{ij}| = s$, and the predecessor relationship is satisfied between $t_{(w_{ij},k+1)}$ and $t_{(w_{ij},k)}$.

$K_i = \{k_{i1}, k_{i2}, \ldots, k_{in}\}$ represents a set of n predecessor traffic flow time series data in the flow data sample of the i-th route.

$C_i = \{C_{i1}^h, C_{i2}^h, \ldots, C_{in}^h\}$ represents the set of traffic flow values in consecutive h min after each piece of historical traffic flow time series data in $K_i = \{k_{i1}, k_{i2}, \ldots, k_{in}\}$, and its value is determined by the map g: $k_{ij} \rightarrow c_{ij}^h$, where $j \in \{1, 2, \ldots, n\}$.

F is a mapping, F: $w_{ij} \rightarrow k_{ij}$, is a one-to-one mapping relationship between any j-th time series data k_{ij} in K_i and the j-th time series data segment w_{ij} in W_i. Can be recorded as $k_{ij} = F(w_{ij}) = \left\{ f\left(t_{(w_{ij},1)} \right), f\left(t_{(w_{ij},2)} \right), \ldots, f\left(t_{(w_{ij},s)} \right) \right\}$.

The time series Ki set corresponding to the data sample Zi can be recorded as the traffic local time series data matrix model Ki as shown in the formula (1).

$$K_i = \begin{pmatrix} k_{i1} \\ k_{i2} \\ \vdots \\ k_{in} \end{pmatrix} = \begin{pmatrix} F(w_{i1}) \\ F(w_{i2}) \\ \vdots \\ F(w_{in}) \end{pmatrix} = \begin{pmatrix} f\left(t_{(w_{i1},1)}\right) & f\left(t_{(w_{i1},2)}\right) & \cdots & f\left(t_{(w_{i1},s)}\right) \\ f\left(t_{(w_{i2},1)}\right) & f\left(t_{(w_{i2},2)}\right) & \cdots & f\left(t_{(w_{i1},s)}\right) \\ \vdots & \vdots & \ddots & \vdots \\ f\left(t_{(w_{in},1)}\right) & f\left(t_{(w_{in},2)}\right) & \cdots & f\left(t_{(w_{in},s)}\right) \end{pmatrix} \tag{1}$$

Where: each row is represented as a horizontal transpose of the s data corresponding to the k_{ij} data set.

Since the traffic flow between the routes affects each other, historical traffic data of a single route is not directly used to predict future traffic, but the route and its adjacent route history data are modeled. The traffic local time series data matrix (i.e., Z1, Z2, Z3, ..., Zm) of the M routes in the Z set is combined and converted into a column of data according to the sequence of the start time of each time series. Finally, the future h min traffic flow value $C_i = \{C_{i1}^h, C_{i2}^h, \ldots, C_{in}^h\}$ of each time window of the predicted i-th route is added to the corresponding time period as a column of decision data relative to the i-th route prediction. A traffic flow prediction data set matrix model PD as shown in the Eq. (2) is obtained.

$$PD = \begin{pmatrix} k_{11} & k_{21} & \cdots & k_{M1} & C_{i1}^h \\ k_{12} & k_{22} & \cdots & k_{M2} & C_{i2}^h \\ \vdots & \vdots & \ddots & \vdots & \vdots \\ k_{1n} & k_{2n} & \cdots & k_{Mn} & C_{in}^h \end{pmatrix} \tag{2}$$

Where: $j \in \{1, 2, \ldots, n\}$, $i \in \{1, 2, \ldots, M\}$.

In the PD matrix, in addition to the decision column Ci, the other columns represent traffic flow records for different routes. Each row of data in the PD matrix (except for the decision column) represents traffic flow data for the same time window of M routes in the same region. Line j represents the time series data of the j-th time window of each route and the traffic flow of the i-th route in the future h min. The meanings of some of the symbols involved are shown in Table 1.

Table 1. The meaning of symbolic.

Symbolic	Meaning
Z	Collection of traffic flow data within a sector
Z_i	Traffic flow time series information system composed of traffic flow information of the i-th route
w_{in}	Time-sequential n traffic flow timing segments in the i-th route
W_i	A collection of w_{in}
k_{in}	n predecessor traffic flow time series data in the traffic data sample of the i-th route
K_i	A collection of k_{in}
C_{in}^h	Set of traffic values in consecutive h min after each piece of historical traffic flow time series data in K_i
C_i	A collection of C_{in}^h

3   Machine Learning Model

The idea of traffic flow multi-machine learning competition method is shown in Fig. 1.

Firstly, the multi-dimensional time series modeling is carried out with historical data, and the traffic flow data in the research route is converted into a multi-dimensional time series matrix model.

Then time series clustering method is used to time series clustering, and the multidimensional time series matrix model is reduced to a classic two-dimensional information table.

Then, the two-dimensional information table is imported into the multi-machine learning group for learning, and the learned knowledge is competed by the test data to generate multiple optimal classifiers. The practice data is imported into the optimal classifier and multiple prediction results are output.

Finally, the multiple prediction results are integrated and applied in practice. If the actual prediction results are not good, the training data set is updated and the optimal classifier is retrained.

3.1   Introduction to the Optimal Classifier Acquisition Algorithm

Input: Historical traffic flow data set for related M routes $Z = \{Z_1, Z_2, \ldots, Z_M\}$.
   Alternative machine learning algorithm classifier set as: $L = \{L_1(), L_2(), \ldots, L_n()\}$.
   Output: Optimal machine learning algorithm classifier set $L'' \subseteq L$.

Step 1 Historical traffic flow data set $Z = \{Z_1, Z_2, \ldots, Z_M\}$ of related M routes. The Z transformation is preprocessed into the multi-dimensional time series matrix model PD matrix form of traffic flow.

Step 2 Time series clustering method proposed in paper [12] is used to perform time series clustering on the above PDs. Each sub-time series k_{ij} cluster in PD is transformed into a class integer V_{ij}, so that PD is transformed into classical two-dimensional information. Formula (3), recorded as G_{PD}.

$$PD = \begin{pmatrix} k_{11} & k_{21} & \cdots & k_{M1} & C_{i1}^h \\ k_{12} & k_{22} & \cdots & k_{M2} & C_{i2}^h \\ \vdots & \vdots & \ddots & \vdots & \vdots \\ k_{1n} & k_{2n} & \cdots & k_{Mn} & C_{in}^h \end{pmatrix} \xrightarrow{\text{Clustering}} G_{PD} = \begin{pmatrix} V_{11} & V_{21} & \cdots & V_{M1} & C_{i1}^h \\ V_{12} & V_{22} & \cdots & V_{M2} & C_{i2}^h \\ \vdots & \vdots & \ddots & \vdots & \vdots \\ V_{1n} & V_{2n} & \cdots & V_{Mn} & C_{in}^h \end{pmatrix}$$

$$(3)$$

Finally, the G_{PD} is divided into a test data set G'_{PD} and a training data set G''_{PD}.

Step 3 introduces G'_{PD} into the alternative classical machine algorithm set $L = \{L_1(), L_2(), \ldots, L_n()\}$ for machine learning. After learning $L' = \{L_1()', L_2()' \ldots, L_n()'\}$.

Step 4 introduces G''_{PD} into the alternative classical machine algorithm set $L' = \{L_1()', L_2()' \ldots, L_n()'\}$. And the statistical accuracy of each algorithm is recorded as $\tau_{L'_1}, \tau_{L'_2}, \ldots, \tau_{L'_n}$. And the threshold ω is set, if $\tau_{L'_i} > \omega$, $i \in \{1, 2, \ldots, m\}$, Then the algorithm $\tau_{L'_i}$ is reserved as the optimal algorithm set L'' member. $L'' \subseteq L$.

3.2 Introduction to the Integrated Prediction Algorithm in This Prediction Model

Input: The real-time traffic flow data flow of the relevant M route x time window is $k_{1x}, k_{2x}, \ldots, k_{Mx}$.

Alternative machine learning algorithm classifier set L''. Note: Let the number of algorithms in A lg$''$ be set to n, n < m. and re-mark the candidate algorithm set as: $L'' = \{L'_1(), L'_2(), \ldots, L'_n()\}$, the prediction accuracy is respectively recorded as $\{\tau_1, \tau_2, \ldots, \tau_n\}$.

Output: the future h min traffic flow value β of the x time window of the i-th route.

Step 1 For real-time traffic flow data: perform clustering category matching [13], convert the time series string $k_{1x}, k_{2x}, \ldots, k_{Mx}$ into an integer array V1x V2x $\cdots$ VMx. Record as array Vx = {V1x V2x ... VMx}.

Step 2 imports the array Vx into $L_1()', L_2()', \ldots, L_n()'$. The prediction results are respectively recorded as $L_1(V_{1x})', L_2(V_{2x})', \ldots, L_n(V_{nx})'$. Where $L_i(V_x)'$ represents the prediction result of the i-th optimal prediction algorithm for real-time traffic flow data V_x.

Step 3 The prediction result is $\beta = \left| \sum_{i=1}^{n} \tau_i L_i / \sum_{i=1}^{n} \tau_i \right|$, where τ_i is the algorithmic weight of L_i.

4   Experiment and Result Analysis

4.1   Experimental Settings

Alternative machine learning algorithms include: proximity algorithm, Bayesian algorithm, neural network, support vector machine, etc. ω is the threshold parameter for predictive evaluation, $\omega = 0.8$. Select a busy high-altitude sector as the research object, and use the radar data from January 16 to February 16, 2018 to establish a database to predict the traffic flow from 8:00 to 13:00 on February 17. The algorithm of [6] compares the results, the result is the comparison of the actual traffic level and the predicted traffic level.

4.2   Experimental Results

The results of the I and II route experiments are shown in Figs. 1 and 2, where the horizontal axis represents time, at 10 min intervals, and the vertical axis represents traffic flow levels. Every 10 min, there is a corresponding actual route traffic flow, single dimension. A time-series predicted traffic flow and a comparison of traffic flows predicted by the proposed method. Among them, SIMPLE and MULTIBLE are the results of single machine and multidimensional time series hybrid machine learning model prediction. ACTUAL represents real traffic flow.

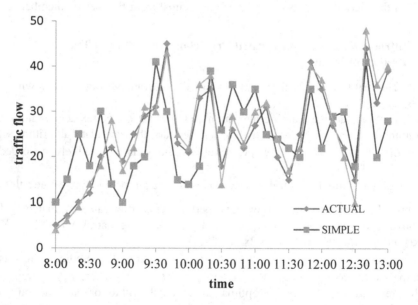

Fig. 1. Comparison of effectiveness between actual flow and two methods for route I.

As shown in Figs. 1 and 2, for the I and II routes, the accuracy predicted by the single time series method under the selected time period is 70.49% and 59.98%, respectively, and the multi-dimensional time series hybrid machine learning method is used to predict the results. The accuracy rates are 87.01% and 88.94%, respectively.

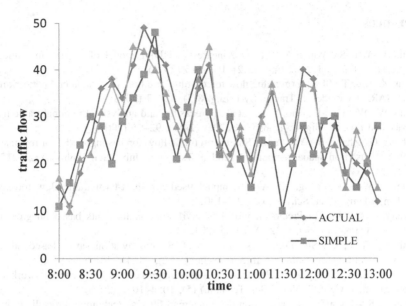

Fig. 2. Comparison of effectiveness between actual flow and two methods for route II.

The algorithm in this paper is closer to the actual traffic flow of the predicted route, and its fitting degree is higher, and the fitting degree of the flow curve of the comparison algorithm is far away. This shows that the proposed algorithm has obvious advantages. Compared with the multi-dimensional time series, the single time series algorithm often cannot obtain enough relevant route information. Obviously, only all relevant route information in the comprehensive study area can carry out more effective knowledge mining. The multi-dimensional time series clustering method proposed in this paper. It can guarantee the retention of relevant information in different dimensions, and can effectively reduce the data dimension and utilize a variety of classical machine learning methods.

5 Conclusions

Aiming at the data characteristics of route traffic flow prediction, this paper proposes a multi-dimensional time series data mining traffic flow prediction model. This model can comprehensively consider the correlation of the relevant routes of the same sector, and adopts integrated learning ideas to compete through multi-machine learning. It greatly improves the accuracy of traffic flow prediction. Through prediction practice, it is proved that the prediction effect of this model is better than the traditional single time series machine learning algorithm.

Acknowledgements. The authors were supported by the National Natural Science Foundation of China (No. 71701202).

References

1. Yu, B., Wu, S., Wang, M., et al.: K-nearest neighbor model of short-term traffic flow forecast. J. Traffic Transp. Eng. 12(2), 109–115 (2012)
2. Sun, X., Liu, T.: Short-term traffic flow forecasting based on a hybrid neural network model and SARIMA model. J. Transp. Syst. Eng. 8(5), 32–37 (2008)
3. Han, W., Wang, J.-F., Gao, Y.-G., et al.: Forecasting and analysis of regional traffic flow in space and time. J. Highw. Transp. Res. Dev. 24(6), 92–96 (2007)
4. Chang, G., Zhang, Y., Yao, Y.-d.: Short-term traffic flow forecasting model for regional road network based on spatial-temporal depend. J. Tsinghua Univ. (Sci. Technol.) (2), 215–221 (2013)
5. Xie, J., Wu, W., Yang, X.: A PDL model used for short-term traffic flow forecasting. J. Tongji Univ. (Nat. Sci.) 39(9), 1297–1302 (2011)
6. Wang, Y.-G., Li, H.: Prediction model of civil aviation incidents based on grey neural network. China Saf. Sci. J. 22(3), 10–15 (2012)
7. Ou, T., Zhou, C.: Situation assessment model of civil aviation safety based on neural network and its simulation. J. Saf. Sci. Technol. 7(2), 34–41 (2011)
8. Li, Y.-b., Li, C., Song, X.-h.: Prediction model of improved artificial neural network and its application. J. Cent. S. Univ. (Sci. Technol.) (5), 1054–1058 (2008)
9. Kumar, S.V.: Traffic flow prediction using Kalman filtering technique. Procedia Eng., 187 (2017)
10. Wu, Y., Tan, H., Qin, L., Ran, B., Jiang, Z.: A hybrid deep learning based traffic flow prediction method and its understanding. Transp. Res. Part C 90 (2018)
11. Ratrout, N.T.: Short-term traffic flow prediction using group method data handling (GMDH)-based abductive networks. Arab. J. Sci. Eng. 39(2) (2014)

Electromagnetic Spectrum Threat Prediction via Deep Learning

Chunyan Wei[1], Lin Qi[1], Ruowu Wu[2], and Yun Lin[1(✉)]

[1] College of Information and Communication Engineering,
Harbin Engineering University, Harbin 150001, China
linyun_phd@hrbeu.edu.cn
[2] State Key Laboratory of Complex Electromagnetic Environment Effects
on Electronics and Information System (CEMEE),
Luoyang 471003, Henan, China

Abstract. Nowadays, in the complex electromagnetic environment, the detection of foreign satellite, the electronic interferences and the sensing data tampering in the process of consistent spectrum situation fusion and the electronic countermeasures reconnaissance and enforcement implemented by the enemy electronic attacks all pose serious threats to the communication performance of our electronic devices and communication systems. Therefore, how to detect these electromagnetic spectrum threats effectively is very important. The generative adversarial networks was applied in this paper, which is a method in deep learning, and an unsupervised solution for the above-mentioned electromagnetic spectrum threat signal prediction problem was provided, which has achieved good results. To carry out the detection experiments, three common electromagnetic spectrum threat scenarios were simulated. The prediction performance of the model is evaluated based on the prediction accuracy of the model. The experimental results have shown that the generative adversarial networks model used in this paper has a good predictive effect on the electromagnetic spectrum threat signals of a certain intensity.

Keywords: Electromagnetic spectrum threat · Prediction ·
Generative Adversarial Networks

1 Data Set

1.1 Measured Data Set

The data set used in this experiment is the FM broadcast signal collected by the USRP (Universal software radio peripheral) device. The specific collection process and parameter setting interface are shown in Fig. 1.

The collected data has a center frequency of 100 MHz, a bandwidth of 2.56 MHz, and a sampling rate of 2.56 Msps. In the collection frequency range, there are a plurality of FM broadcast frequency points. 100,000 samples were collected as training data set and 4000 samples were used as test data set, where each sample was acquired through 10,240 sampling points. Since this article uses an unsupervised learning method, the samples in the training set do not need to be labeled and are considered

S. Liu and G. Yang (Eds.): ADHIP 2018, LNICST 279, pp. 433–442, 2019.
https://doi.org/10.1007/978-3-030-19086-6_48

normal samples [1]. For the 4000 samples in the test set, half of them were subjected to artificial interference processing [2], and the samples regarded as abnormal were marked as "1"; the other half were not interfered, and were regarded as normal samples, and marked as "0" [3]. The parameter description of the data set is shown in Table 1.

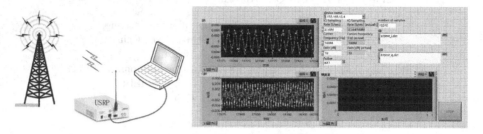

Fig. 1. Schematic diagram of data acquisition

Table 1. Dataset parameter description

Parameter	Discrimination
Acquisition frequency band	FM band
Center frequency	100 MHz
Bandwidth	2.56 MHz
Sampling frequency	2.56 Msps
The number of sampling points	10240
The number of samples in the training set	100000
The number of samples in the test set	4000

1.2 Data Preprocessing

In order to facilitate the subsequent effective analysis of the data, this paper uses the Welch estimation [4] method to preprocess the original data. It is a method of power spectral density estimation. The basic idea is to window the signal through the selection window. The power spectrum is segmented and then averaged. In this experiment, the window function selects the Hamming window, which divides the signal into 8 segments. The length of the overlap between each segment is half of the length of the truncated signal. The selected number of points is 512, which is the original dimension. The signal of 10240 was reduced to 512 dimensions after being estimated by Welch.

2 Generative Adversarial Networks

The Generative Adversarial Networks (GAN) [5] is a generative neural networks model based on the differentiable generator networks proposed by Goodfellow et al. in 2014. The GAN consists of a generator networks and a discriminator networks.

The task of the generator (G) is to capture the distribution of the sample data x, and use the input noise vector to simulate the training data to generate samples. The sample generated by G in this article is called a fake sample. The a priori variable of the input noise is represented by $p_z(z)$. The mapping of data space is represented by $G(z; \theta_g)$, where G is a differentiable function represented by a multilayer perceptron with parameter θ_g. The discriminator (D) is a two-classifier whose task is to correctly distinguish the true samples from the training set and the fake samples as possible. The multi-layer perceptron $D(x; \theta_d)$ is defined to output a single scalar, where $D(x)$ represents the probability that input x is from a real sample, and we train D to maximize the probability of correctly classifying samples. We train G to minimize the $\log(1 - D(G(z)))$ at the same. In short, the training process of D and G can be described as the following formula, which is a minimax game with function $V(G, D)$:

$$\min_{G} \max_{D} V(D, G) = E_{x \sim p_{data}(x)}[\log D(x)] + E_{z \sim p_z(z)}[\log(1 - D(G(z)))] \qquad (1)$$

Therefore, the model will converge according to the following formula,

$$g^* = \arg \min_{g} \max_{d} v(g, d) \qquad (2)$$

When the model is converged, the real sample and the fake sample generated by the generator are indistinguishable, and the discriminator outputs $\frac{1}{2}$ everywhere. At this time, the discriminator has reached its best discriminating ability, and it can be used to predict the threatening of electromagnetic signals.

According to the generative adversarial networks model built in this paper, the actual training process diagram is shown as Fig. 2.

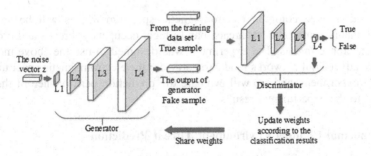

Fig. 2. The training process diagram of generative adversarial networks

In Fig. 2, the generator consists of a four-layer neural networks with 64, 128, 256, and 512 nodes. The generator takes the noise vector as input, the 512-dimensional vector is generated by simulating the real sample according to the layer-by-layer mapping, and that is the fake sample. The true and fake samples are mixed together as the discriminator input. The discriminator in this paper consists of four layers of neural networks, each with 256, 128, 128 and 1 node. The final layer outputs the discrimination result of the input sample, and the discriminator will update the networks weight according to this and share the updated weights with the generator. The generator generates a fake sample again based on the updated weights, and mixes it with the true sample, inputs the discriminator, and then the foregoing process will be repeated. The above process will be repeated until the preset number of trainings is reached. At this time, the discriminator has reached a great discriminating ability and can be used to predict the unknown input. The predicting process is shown in Fig. 3.

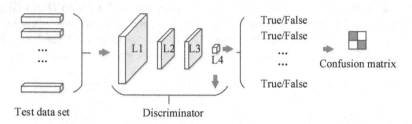

Fig. 3. Schematic diagram of generative adversarial networks prediction

When using the trained model to predict the output of test data, the test data set which contains 2000 normal samples and 2000 abnormal samples is input into the discriminator networks, and the discriminator predicts and outputs the confusion matrix. In this paper, the prediction accuracy is calculated based on the confusion matrix to evaluate the classification performance of the model.

3   Experiment Implement

In this section three common electromagnetic spectrum threats will be simulated: abnormal channel environment threats, band illegal occupancy threats, and broadband signal interference threats. The experiment was designed to use the above-mentioned generative adversarial networks model to carry out the electromagnetic spectrum threat prediction experiment, and we will evaluate the prediction performance of the model according to the experimental results.

3.1   Abnormal Channel Environment Threat Prediction

Threat Situation and Its Data Set. In the wireless communication system, there are situations such as channel environment changes, noise enhancement, etc. [6], and the abnormality caused to the communication by these is called the channel environment abnormal threat [7]. In order to simulate this threat, we superimposes a certain intensity of Gaussian white noise, and the threat intensity is reflected by the signal-to-noise ratio. At the same time, in order to study the prediction performance of the proposed method for different intensity threat signals, Gaussian noise with signal-to-noise ratio of 0 dB– 7 dB is added in steps of 1 dB, and threat prediction experiments are carried out.

Figure 4 shows the power spectral density of a data sample before and after the noise is added. Figure 4(a) shows the sample signal without the addition of Gaussian white noise, and Fig. 4(b) and (c) are the power spectral density estimates of the sample signal with the signal-to-noise ratio of 0 dB and 7 dB Gaussian noise, respectively.

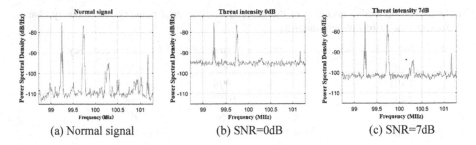

(a) Normal signal   (b) SNR=0dB   (c) SNR=7dB

Fig. 4. Power spectral density estimation of sample signals under different channel environmental anomalies

As can be seen from Fig. 4, when Gaussian white noise is added, part of the original signal is submerged by noise, and the lower the signal-to-noise ratio, the higher the noise, the more parts of the signal are flooded.

Prediction Results. During the training process, the model automatically performs feature learning on the data samples in the training data set to minimize the error of generative adversarial networks, and a threat prediction model based on GAN can be obtained. Then, we use the test data set to test the model and evaluate its prediction performance based on the classification result on the entire test data set [8].

Figure 5 shows part of the predicted confusion matrix for a trained generative adversarial networks model for data samples in test data sets with different intensities of Gaussian white noise.

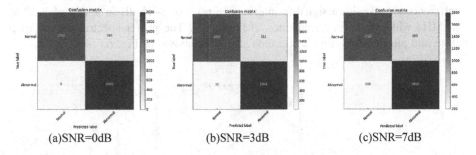

(a)SNR=0dB   (b)SNR=3dB   (c)SNR=7dB

Fig. 5. The predictive confusion matrix output by the generative adversarial networks of abnormal channel environment threat of different intensity.

In order to describe the prediction performance of the model on different intensity threat signals more intuitively, we calculate the prediction accuracy of the model under each SNR based on the confusion matrix obtained by the experiment, as shown in Table 2.

Table 2. The predictive accuracy of the generative adversarial networks on anomaly channel environment threat of different intensity

Signal to noise ratio	True positive	True negative	Prediction accuracy
0 dB	1720	2000	93.00%
1 dB	1718	1998	92.90%
2 dB	1707	1987	92.35%
3 dB	1688	1968	91.40%
4 dB	1661	1941	90.05%
5 dB	1623	1903	88.15%
6 dB	1576	1856	85.80%
7 dB	1520	1800	83.00%

As can be seen in Table 2, for signals with a signal-to-noise ratio of 1–4 dB Gaussian noise, the prediction accuracy of the model can reach more than 90%. As the intensity of the anomaly channel environment threat is weakened, the average prediction accuracy of the model decreases, but for the anomaly signal with a signal-to-noise ratio of 7 dB, the prediction accuracy can still be higher than 80%.

3.2 Band Illegal Occupation Threat Prediction

Threat Situation and Its Data Set. During communication, if the band is occupied by an unknown narrowband signal, the signal received can be anomaly, which can be a threat to the communication [9]. This situation is called a band illegal occupation threat. In order to simulate this threat situation, we artificially superimposed an FM interference signal with a signal-to-interference ratio of 8–15 dB in a step of 1 dB at 100 MHz which is an idle frequency of the signal. The power spectral density map before and after noise addition of a data sample is shown as Fig. 6.

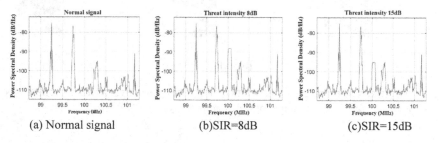

(a) Normal signal   (b)SIR=8dB   (c)SIR=15dB

Fig. 6. The power spectral density estimation of the sample signal under the band illegal occupation threat of different intensity

As shown in Fig. 6, compared with the normal signal, the signal added the FM interference signal has a spike at the frequency of 100 MHz, that is, the interference signal. The lower the signal-to-interference ratio, that is, the greater the interference intensity, the more the spike high.

Prediction Results. Similarly, we use the test data set to test the model and evaluate its prediction performance according to the classification result. Figure 7 shows part of the predicted confusion matrix for the trained data generative adversarial networks model for data samples in test data sets with different intensities of chirped interference signals.

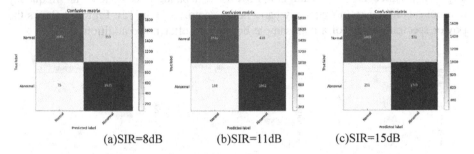

    (a)SIR=8dB   (b)SIR=11dB   (c)SIR=15dB

Fig. 7. Prediction confusion matrix output by generative adversarial networks for band illegal occupation threats of different intensity.

We calculate the prediction accuracy of model based on the confusion matrix obtained by experiment, as shown in Table 3.

Table 3. The prediction accuracy of the generative adversarial networks of the band illegal occupation threat of different intensity

Signal to interference ratio	True positive	True negative	Prediction accuracy
8 dB	1645	1925	89.25%
9 dB	1626	1906	88.30%
10 dB	1601	1881	87.05%
11 dB	1582	1862	86.10%
12 dB	1557	1837	84.85%
13 dB	1529	1809	83.45%
14 dB	1497	1777	81.85%
15 dB	1469	1749	80.45%

As can be seen from Table 3, the prediction accuracy of the model can reach more than 85% for signals with 8–11 dB signal to interference ratio. As the intensity of the threat weakens, the prediction accuracy of the model has decreased, however, for 8 dB–15 dB abnormal signals, there is still a prediction accuracy higher than 80%.

3.3   Wideband Signal Interference Threat Prediction

Threat Situation and Its Data Set. In a wireless communication system, the signal transmitted by the authorized transmitter sometimes can encounters an interference caused by an unknown wideband signal [3]. At this time, the signal of the authorized transmitter is often aliased by the wideband signal, causing the signal received to be anomaly or even to be severely distorted after demodulation [10]. We call that threats to the communication broadband signal interference threat.

In order to simulate this threat, a wideband DSQPSK signal with a signal-to-interference ratio of 9 dB–16 dB is artificially superimposed on the signal in 1 dB steps [11]. Since the wideband DSQPSK is wideband, it can affect all frequency components in a certain frequency band in the sample signal [12]. Figure 8 shows the power spectral density of a data sample before and after noise addition.

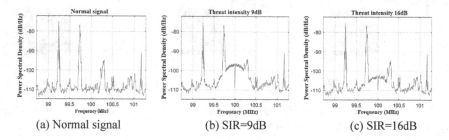

(a) Normal signal   (b) SIR=9dB   (c) SIR=16dB

Fig. 8. Estimation of power spectral density of sample signals under different bandwidth broadband signal interference threats

As can be seen from Fig. 8, when the broadband DSQPSK interference signal is added, the spectrum of the signal in the original signal with a frequency of around 100 MHz is superimposed with the interference signal [13]. The lower the signal-to-interference ratio, that is, the greater the interference signal strength, the signal is, the greater the partial power spectral density of the superposition.

Prediction Results. The model is tested by the test data set added the DSQPSK interference signal, and part of the obtained confusion matrix is shown in Fig. 9.

In order to describe the prediction effect of the model on different intensity threat signals more intuitively, we calculate the prediction accuracy of model based on the confusion matrix obtained by experiment, as shown in Table 4.

It can be seen from Table 4 that the model used in this paper can correctly predict the broadband signal interference threat of 9 dB–11 dB, and can achieve the prediction accuracy of 92% or more. As the threat intensity of wideband signal interference decreases, the average prediction accuracy of the model decreases, but the prediction accuracy of more than 80% can still be obtained for the abnormal signal of 9 dB–16 dB.

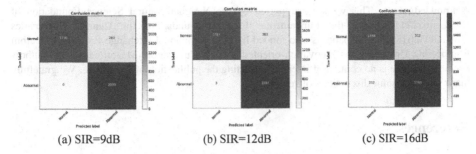

(a) SIR=9dB   (b) SIR=12dB   (c) SIR=16dB

Fig. 9. Prediction confusion matrix output by the generative adversarial networks for broadband signal interference threats of different intensity.

Table 4. The prediction accuracy of the generative adversarial networks of the band broadband signal interference threats of different intensity

Signal to interference ratio	True positive	True negative	Prediction accuracy
9 dB	1720	2000	93.00%
10 dB	1720	2000	93.00%
11 dB	1720	2000	93.00%
12 dB	1717	1997	92.85%
13 dB	1690	1970	91.50%
14 dB	1635	1915	88.75%
15 dB	1572	1852	85.60%
16 dB	1488	1768	81.40%

4 Conclusion

In this paper, through the analysis of electromagnetic signals in the background of complex electromagnetic environment, an unsupervised deep learning method, generative adversarial networks, is used to implement experiment to predict the threats caused by the anomalies and interference signals. This unsupervised learning method can automatically learn the features of data through neural networks, eliminating the cumbersome task of tagging large amounts of data. The experiment uses the FM signal collected by USRP equipment, and simulates three common electromagnetic spectrum threats. The results show that the electromagnetic spectrum threat prediction system designed by generative adversarial networks can solve the prediction problem of threat samples in the electromagnetic environment. It provides a new idea for solving the electromagnetic spectrum threat prediction problem in complex electromagnetic environment.

Acknowledgment. This work is supported by the National Natural Science Foundation of China (61771154) and the Fundamental Research Funds for the Central Universities (HEUCFG201830). This paper is also funded by the International Exchange Program of Harbin Engineering University for Innovation-oriented Talents Cultivation. Meantime, all the authors declare that there is no conflict of interests regarding the publication of this article. We gratefully thank of very useful discussions of reviewers.

References

1. Feng, Q., Dou, Z., Li, C., Si, G.: Anomaly detection of spectrum in wireless communication via deep autoencoder. In: Park, J.J.(Jong Hyuk), Pan, Y., Yi, G., Loia, V. (eds.) CSA/CUTE/UCAWSN-2016. LNEE, vol. 421, pp. 259–265. Springer, Singapore (2017). https://doi.org/10.1007/978-981-10-3023-9_42
2. Wen, Z., Luo, T., Xiang, W., et al.: Autoregressive spectrum hole prediction model for cognitive radio systems. In: IEEE International Conference on Communications Workshops, ICC Workshops, pp. 154–157. IEEE (2008)
3. Guan, Q., Yu, F.R., Jiang, S., et al.: Prediction-based topology control and routing in cognitive radio mobile ad hoc networks. IEEE Trans. Veh. Technol. **59**(9), 4443–4452 (2010)
4. Acharya, P.A.K., Singh, S., Zheng, H.: Reliable open spectrum communications through proactive spectrum access (2006). 5
5. Goodfellow, I.J., Pouget-Abadie, J., Mirza, M., et al.: Generative adversarial nets. In: International Conference on Neural Information Processing Systems, pp. 2672–2680. MIT Press (2014)
6. Tumuluru, V.K., Wang, P., Niyato, D.: A neural networks based spectrum prediction scheme for cognitive radio. In: IEEE International Conference on Communications, pp. 1–5. IEEE (2010)
7. Li, H.: Reconstructing spectrum occupancies for wideband cognitive radio networks: a matrix completion via belief propagation. In: IEEE International Conference on Communications, pp. 1–6. IEEE (2010)
8. Kim, S.J., Giannakis, G.B.: Cognitive radio spectrum prediction using dictionary learning. In: Global Communications Conference, pp. 3206–3211. IEEE (2014)
9. Yin, S., Chen, D., Zhang, Q., Li, S.: Prediction-based throughput optimization for dynamic spectrum access. IEEE Trans. Veh. Technol. **60**(3), 1284–1289 (2011)
10. Tu, Y., Lin, Y., Wang, J., et al.: Semi-supervised learning with generative adversarial networks on digital signal modulation classification. CMC-Comput. Mater. Continua **55**(2), 243–254 (2018)
11. Zhou, J.T., Zhao, H., Peng, X., et al.: Transfer hashing: from shallow to deep. IEEE Trans. Neural Netw. Learn. Syst. **PP**(99), 1–11 (2018)
12. Zheng, Z., Sangaiah, A.K., Wang, T.: Adaptive communication protocols in flying ad-hoc networks. IEEE Commun. Mag. **56**(1), 136–142 (2018)
13. Zhao, N., Richard Yu, F., Sun, H., Li, M.: Adaptive power allocation schemes for spectrum sharing in interference-alignment-based cognitive radio networks. IEEE Trans. Veh. Technol. **65**(5), 3700–3714 (2016)

Application of Nonlinear Classification Algorithm in Communication Interference Evaluation

Yifan Chen[1], Zheng Dou[1], Hui Han[2], Xianglong Zhou[1], and Yun Lin[1(✉)]

[1] College of Information and Communication Engineering, Harbin Engineering University, Harbin 150001, China
linyun_phd@hrbeu.edu.cn
[2] State Key Laboratory of Complex Electromagnetic Environment Effects on Electronics and Information System (CEMEE), Luoyang 471003, Henan, China

Abstract. Traditional methods of communication interference assessment belong third-party assessments that fail to meet the needs of real-time assessments. This paper proposes an interference level evaluation method under the nonlinear classification algorithm. Firstly, building data set with the eigenvalues that affect the interference effect, and then simulation verify by BP neural network and support vector machine. The simulation results verify the feasibility in communication interference assessment and providing the possibility for real-time evaluation.

Keywords: Interference level assessment · BP neural network · Support vector machine

1 Introduction

Modern warfare has changed from a single weapon war to an information warfare and electronic [8] warfare relying on communications, technology, and talent. Therefore, the demand for communication confrontation and anti-resistance is also increasing. Information warfare, as its name implies, is a war of communication information. It includes how to effectively interfere with enemy communications, how to grasp enemy communication information, and how to avoid interference in our communication [7]. In view of the above problems, the problem of evaluating the effects of communication interference has naturally become a more and more concerned issue in the military information warfare field.

The existing evaluation methods are usually very simple, and the advantage is that the accuracy of the evaluation is high but the adaptability of dynamic changes is not ideal [5]. However, the machine learning method used in the fields of electronic warfare and synthetic aperture radar [1] that, to some extent, avoiding unintentional interference from third parties, and can evaluate the interference effect in real time. There are three kinds of learning methods: semi-supervised [17], supervised and

© ICST Institute for Computer Sciences, Social Informatics and Telecommunications Engineering 2019
Published by Springer Nature Switzerland AG 2019. All Rights Reserved
S. Liu and G. Yang (Eds.): ADHIP 2018, LNICST 279, pp. 443–451, 2019.
https://doi.org/10.1007/978-3-030-19086-6_49

unsupervised for classification problems. In this paper, performing an interference level assessment under BP neural network and support vector machine respectively. By inputting the factors affecting the interference effect, the corresponding bit error rate level is obtained, so that the interference level can be grasped quickly and reliably. The verification process of this paper is shown in Fig. 1.

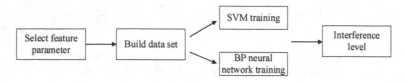

Fig. 1. Research process

2   Introduction to Nonlinear Classification Algorithm

2.1   BP Neural Network

BP neural network is one of the relatively mature neural networks. It has the advantages of strong generalization ability and strong fault tolerance [9]. Although it has local minimization and unstable results compared to other neural network algorithms [18], it is easy to obtain results because of its simple structure. Therefore, BP neural network is used to evaluate the interference level. The training process is as follows (Fig. 2).

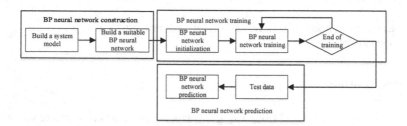

Fig. 2. BP neural network algorithm flow

2.2   Support Vector Machine

Support Vector Machine (SVM) is a technique for building an optimal binary classifier [10]. Later the technique was extended to regression and clustering problems. SVM is essentially a partial case based on the kernel approach. It uses a kernel function to map a feature vector into a high-dimensional space and establish an optimal linear discriminant function or optimal hyperplane suitable for training data in that space [11]. The following equation is used to divide the hyperplane:

$$f(\mathrm{x}) = \mathrm{w}^T x + b \tag{1}$$

3 Establish Interference Level Assessment Factors

Both interference and interfered parties have direct influence on the interference effect. The effective influencing factors include interference effect and anti-interception ability, interference transmitter power, communication signal frequency and interference signal frequency overlap, interference form, the technical performance of the receiver and many other factors [2]. Considering the signal characteristics of both communication parties and referring to the factors affecting the interference effect proposed in the literature [3, 12], without considering the adaptive spectrum common problem [19, 20], the following six parameters are considered as the eigenvalues of the input sample set.

Communication Signal Modulation Method. The digital signals obtained by differen-t modulation methods are used as the interfered parties of the communication system. The communication party signal is defined as a symbol F_1. The five digital modulated signals are sequentially taken as values of 1.0, 2.0, 3.0, 4.0, and 5.0.

Interference Power. The ratio of the interference signal power to the communication signal power is JSR. The symbol is defined as F_2.

Interference Signal Pattern. The Gaussian white noise is subjected to amplitude modulation, phase modulation, and frequency modulation to obtain interference of three different modulated signals. Set its symbol to F_3. Noise amplitude modulation interference 1.0, noise frequency modulation interference 2.0, noise phase modulation interference 3.0.

Interference Threat Time. When the interference signal interferes the communication signal, there is an effective interference time and an invalid interference time. The effective interference time is also defined as the effective threat time. The time range of the interference is $t_1 \sim t_2$, and the time to start the interference is t_g.

$$F_4 = \begin{cases} 0 & t_g < t_1 \\ 1 - \frac{t_g - t_1}{t_2 - t_1} & t_1 \leq t_g \leq t_2 \\ 0 & t_g > t_2 \end{cases} \tag{2}$$

Anti-Jamming Performance of the Interfered Signal. The more perfect the anti-interference ability of the interfered signal, the worse the interference effect is [13]. The ability of the interference signal to adapt to the change of the interfered signal is enhanced, and the interference effect is worse. Assuming that there are a total of ten anti-interference measures, the interference signals use N kinds of anti-interference measures [3]. Then define:

$$F_5 = 1 - N/10 \tag{3}$$

The smaller the value, the worse the interference effect and the better the antiinterference performance.

Bit Error Rate. The main intention of digital communication interference is to increase the error rate of the signal demodulated by the enemy receiver, the effectiveness of communication is impaired [14], and the reliability of communication is reduced. The bit error rate is often used as an indicator to measure the interference strength of a communication receiver. Therefore, the bit error rate level is taken as the final output parameter of the communication interference effect, and the interference level is divided according to the bit error rate as follows [4].

When $P_e \geq 0.2$ the interference level is three, which is set to 3.0;

When $0.05 \leq P_e < 0.2$ the interference level is two, which is set to 2.0;

When $P_e < 0.05$ the interference level is one, which is set to 1.0.

4   Simulation Results Analysis

4.1   Evaluation Model Parameter Settings

In view of the different influences of different parameters on the interference effect [16], the unknown parameters of the anti-interference performance and the interference threat time are specified, and the interference level is redivided as follows.

Anti-interference performance: $F_5 = 1 - N/10$, N is the number of anti-interference facilities, the larger N, the better the anti-interference performance.

$$
\begin{aligned}
&P_e \leq 0.05 && \text{Interference level is 1} \\
&0.05 < P_e \leq 0.1 \begin{cases} N \geq 3 & \text{Interference level is 1} \\ N < 3 & \text{Interference level is 2} \end{cases} \\
&0.1 < P_e \leq 0.2 \begin{cases} N \geq 6 & \text{Interference level is 1} \\ N < 6 & \text{Interference level is 2} \end{cases} \\
&0.2 < P_e < 0.25 \begin{cases} N \geq 9 & \text{Interference level is 2} \\ N < 9 & \text{Interference level is 3} \end{cases} \\
&P_e \geq 0.25 && \text{Interference level is 3}
\end{aligned}
\tag{4}
$$

Interference threat time: Specify the time t_g to start interference. $t1 = 5s, t2 = 25s$

$$
\begin{aligned}
&21s < t_g < 25s, 0 < F < 0.2 && \text{Interference level is 1} \\
&9s < t_g < 21s, 0.2 < F < 0.8 && \text{Constant} \\
&5s < t_g < 9s, 0.8 < F < 1 && \begin{cases} \text{Interference level changed from 1 to 2} \\ \text{Interference level changed from 2 to 3} \end{cases}
\end{aligned}
\tag{5}
$$

4.2   Communication Interference Assessment Based on BP Neural Network

Experiment one:

Set up a four-layer BP neural network, double hidden layer, in which the number of input layer nodes is 5, the number of output layer nodes is 1, and the number of hidden layer nodes is (5, 5) [15]. A data sample with a data volume of 2400 was created, with 100 test sets and 2300 training sets. Some of the prediction results are shown in the Table 1 below.

Table 1. BP neural network interference level prediction results

Evaluation parameter	Sample1	Sample2	Sample3	Sample4	Sample5	Sample6
F_1	3	1	2	1	3	2
F_2	4.6	16.56	-2.55	21.53	-1.29	-10.84
F_3	2	3	1	3	3	1
F_4	4	10	3	10	10	1
F_5	11.98	22.04	14.23	6.35	7.5	5.35
E_1	Expected value					
	3	1	1	3	3	2
E_2	Predictive value					
	3.005	0.9991	0.9976	2.9997	2.9983	1.9897

After several simulation experiments, the magnitude of the prediction error $10^{-2} \sim 10^{-3}$ fluctuates around. And the classification accuracy rate fluctuates between 93% and 98%, which verifies the feasibility of BP neural network for interference level prediction.

Experiment two:

In order to better analyze the prediction effect, the prediction results are categorized into 1–3 grades, and the recognition rate curves under 600, 1200, and 2400 different data sets are obtained.

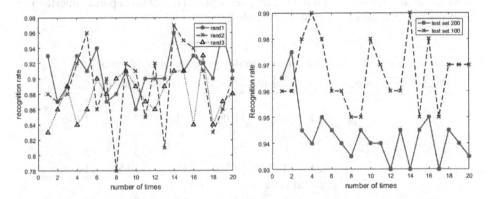

Fig. 3. Recognition rate curve sample set 600   **Fig. 4.** Recognition rate curve sample set 2400

Figure 3 shows the recognition rate of rand1 is the most stable, and the rand2 recognition rate is the most volatile. when the data set is 600, the prediction result is unstable.

Figure 4 shows that the test set is 100, the recognition rate is almost higher than 200 except for the individual points. The smaller the proportion of the test set is, the higher the recognition rate is.

As can be seen from Fig. 5, the recognition rate fluctuates from 93% to 100%. Compared with the data set of 600, the recognition rate increases by about 10%, and the

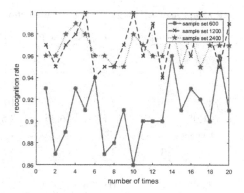

Fig. 5. Recognition rate curve test set 100

fluctuation is significantly reduced. With the increase of dataset, the accuracy gradually increases and tends to be stable.

4.3 Communication Interference Assessment Based on Support Vector Machine

Since svm is suitable for small sample classification problems, the data set used is 600, of which the test set is 100 and the training set is 500. The obtained partial interference level prediction results are as follows (Table 2).

Table 2. BP neural network interference level prediction results

Evaluation parameter	Sample1	Sample2	Sample3	Sample4	Sample5	Sample6
F_1	4	2	1	5	3	1
F_2	−13.2	11.2	8.06	−10.65	2.8	19.46
F_3	3	3	2	2	1	2
F_4	9	8	7	5	3	5
F_5	20.34	16.12	18.04	14.54	10.54	14.48
E_1	Expected value					
	1	3	1	2	3	2
E_2	Predictive value					
	1	3	1	2	3	2

The interference level evaluation results of support vector machine are ideal, and the correct rate is between 98% and 100% under small data, which verifies the feasibility of the method.

4.4 BP Neural Network and Support Vector Machine Algorithm Comparison

After 20 randomized trials, the average statistical results under 600 data sets:

Table 3. Comparison of support vector machine and BP neural network

	Predictive accuracy	Samples	Stability of results	Test set weight
Support Vector Machines	98.56%	Few	Stable	Larger
BP neural network	94.35%	Many	Unstable	Smaller

The simulation results show:

There are local optimal problems in BP neural networks, the training results are not stable, and large data sets are usually needed. Support vector machine generalization ability is better than BP neural network, the algorithm has global optimality and is suitable for small data sets. In short, support vector machine can better predict interference to smaller samples and have better High accuracy. SVM algorithm is difficult to implement for large-scale training samples, but BP neural network is suitable for large data sets. For the communication interference problem, according to the different processing problems, choose the support vector machine and BP neural network algorithm (Table 3).

5 Conclusion

In this paper, the experiment of communication interference level evaluation is carried out under two nonlinear classification algorithms. Firstly, the data set is constructed according to the characteristic parameters affecting the interference, and then the experiment is completed under the two algorithms. The results show that both of them can better evaluate the interference rate with high accuracy, which confirms the feasibility of the method. Compared with the BP neural network, the support vector machine avoids the disadvantages of local optimization and the evaluation results are stable and accurate under small data samples. Since the experimental conditions are too good and the actual interference is not considered, the correct rate is higher. How to experiment with real-time accepted signals and how to establish a complete interference system are the next research direction.

Acknowledgment. This work is supported by the National Natural Science Foundation of China (61771154) and the Fundamental Research Funds for the Central Universities (HEUCFG201830).

This paper is also funded by the International Exchange Program of Harbin Engineering University for Innovation-oriented Talents Cultivation.

Meantime, all the authors declare that there is no conflict of interests regarding the publication of this article.

We gratefully thank of very useful discussions of reviewers.

References

1. Lin, X.H., Xue, G.Y., Liu, P.: Novel data acquisition method for interference suppression in dual-channel SAR. Prog. Electromagnet. Res. **144**(1), 79–92 (2014)
2. Khanduri, A.C., Bédard, C., Stathopoulos, T.: Modelling wind-induced interference effects using back propagation neural networks. J. Wind Eng. Ind. Aerodyn. **72**(1), 71–79 (1997)
3. Liu, P., Jin, F., Zhang, X., et al.: Research on the multi-attribute decision-making under risk with interval probability based on prospect theory and the uncertain linguistic variables. Knowl.-Based Syst. **24**(4), 554–561 (2011)
4. Lu, D., Baprawski, J., Yao, K.: BER simulation of digital communication systems with intersymbol interference and non-Gaussian noise using improved importance sampling. In: Conference Record, Military Communications in a Changing World, IEEE Military Communications Conference, MILCOM 1991, vol. 1, pp. 273–277. IEEE (2002)
5. Albu, F., Martinez, D.: The application of support vector machines with Gaussian kernels for overcoming co-channel interference. In: Proceedings of the 1999 IEEE Signal Processing Society Workshop Neural Networks for Signal Processing Ix, 1999, pp. 49–57. IEEE (1999)
6. Han, G.Q., Li, Y.Z., Xing, S.Q., et al.: Research on an evaluation method for new deceptive jamming effect on SAR. J. Astronaut. **32**(9), 1994–2001 (2011)
7. Yang, W., Xu, G.: Method and system for interference assessment and reduction in a wireless communication system: EP, US 7068977 B1[P] (2006)
8. Poisel, R.A.: Information Warfare and Electronic Warfare Systems (2013)
9. Li, J., Cheng, J.H., Shi, J.Y., et al.: Brief introduction of back propagation (BP) neural network algorithm and its improvement, vol. 169, pp. 553–558 (2012)
10. Kecman, V.: Support vector machines – an introduction. In: Support Vector Machines: Theory and Applications, pp. 1–28. Springer, Heidelberg (2005)
11. He, H.X., Yan, W.M.: Structural damage detection with wavelet support vector machine: introduction and applications. Struct. Control Health Monit. **14**(1), 162–176 (2007)
12. Giorgetti, A., Chiani, M., Win, M.Z.: The effect of narrowband interference on wideband wireless communication systems. IEEE Trans. Commun. **53**(12), 2139–2149 (2005)
13. Zhang, Y., Zhao, D.N., Jiang, G.J.: The simulation design and implementation of military short wave communication anti-jamming performance. Acta Simulata Systematica Sinica (2003)
14. Song, W., Chiu, W., Goldsman, D.: Importance sampling techniques for estimating the bit error rate in digital communication systems. In: 2005 Proceedings of the Winter Simulation Conference, pp. 1–14. IEEE (2006)
15. Xu, C., Xu, C.: Optimization analysis of dynamic sample number and hidden layer node number based on BP neural network. In: Yin, Z., Pan, L., Fang, X. (eds.) Proceedings of the Eighth International Conference on Bio-Inspired Computing: Theories and Applications (BIC-TA). AISC, vol. 212, pp. 687–695. Springer, Heidelberg (2013). https://doi.org/10. 1007/978-3-642-37502-6_82
16. Miura, A., Watanabe, H., Hamamoto, N., et al.: On interference level in satellite uplink for satellite/ terrestrial integrated mobile communication system. IEICE Tech. Rep. **110**, 105–110 (2010)
17. Tu, Y., Lin, Y., Wang, J., et al.: Semi-supervised learning with generative adversarial networks on digital signal modulation classification. CMC-Comput. Mater. Continua **55**(2), 243–254 (2018)
18. Zhou, J.T., Zhao, H., Peng, X., Fang, M., Qin, Z., Goh, R.S.M.: Transfer Hashing: From Shallow to Deep. IEEE Trans. Neural Netw. Learn. Syst. https://doi.org/10.1109/tnnls.2018. 2827036

19. Zheng, Z., Sangaiah, A.K., Wang, T.: Adaptive communication protocols in flying ad-hoc network. IEEE Commun. Mag. **56**(1), 136–142 (2018)
20. Zhao, N., Richard Yu, F., Sun, H., Li, M.: Adaptive power allocation schemes for spectrum sharing in interference-alignment-based cognitive radio networks. IEEE Trans. Veh. Technol. **65**(5), 3700–3714 (2016)

The Physical Layer Identification
of Communication Devices Based on RF-DNA

Ying Li[1], Xiang Chen[2], Jie Chang[1], and Yun Lin[1(✉)]

[1] College of Information and Communication Engineering,
Harbin Engineering University, Harbin 150001, China
linyun_phd@hrbeu.edu.cn
[2] State Key Laboratory of Complex Electromagnetic Environment Effects
on Electronics and Information System (CEMEE),
Luoyang 471003, Henan, China

Abstract. Traditional methods of improving wireless network security are through software-level device identification, such as IP or MAC addresses. However, these identifiers can be easily changed by software, making wireless network communication a high risk. In response to these risks, radio frequency fingerprinting technology has been proposed. Since the radio frequency fingerprint is an essential feature of the physical layer of the wireless communication device and is difficult to be tampered with, it is widely used to improve the security of the wireless network. Based on the physical layer characteristics of the communication system, this paper has established a relatively complete RF fingerprint identification system to realize the identification and classification of the devices. Two signal starting point detection methods and two RF fingerprint feature extraction methods are studied in this paper. The detailed results are obtained by combining the dimensionality reduction and classification methods. Finally, an optimal identification scheme was found to achieve a classification accuracy of more than 90% when the signal-to-noise ratio is greater than 15 dB.

Keywords: RF fingerprinting · Physical layer identification ·
Feature extraction · Device classification

1 Instruction

Wireless network security protocols based on cryptographic mechanisms are vulnerable to malicious attacks and face the risk of password leakage. For these risks, people proposed radio frequency fingerprinting technology in 1994 to improve network security. Radio frequency fingerprinting refers to extracting features from radio frequency signals to construct the radio frequency fingerprint of the transmitter, thereby realizing the ID card authentication of the device. RF-DNA refers to the extraction of statistical features from the characteristics extracted from RF signals, which can comprehensively characterize the signal details. Physical layer device identification is a commonly used identification method to identify and classify devices with hardware defects in circuit. Hardware defects include many types, such as time interval errors caused by imperfect clock hardware [1] and sampling errors caused by DAC module hardware defects [2]. Inadequacy of the construction of the local frequency synthesizer will also cause phase shift in the mixing process and cause errors [3]. The nonlinear distortion of the power amplifier can lead to in-band distortion and spectrum regeneration of the digital modulated signal, which is the most considered in RF fingerprint extraction [4–7]. And power amplifiers also have some applications in the spectrum sharing field [8]. In addition, the polarization of the transmit and receive antennas can also be used to study RF fingerprints [9, 10]. The modulator sub-circuit in the device [11] and the multipath effect of the wireless channel [12–14] can also be studied as radio frequency fingerprints. Hardware defects cause the unique physical layer characteristics of the device. These unique features are carried by the transmitted signal to the receiving end. We identify and classify different types of devices by studying the characteristics of the signals, and identify malicious users to achieve the purpose of improving network security. It is also a good choice to add deep learning to the research of equipment classification [15]. But researching classification problems requires a large number of data sets [16]. And it is necessary to consider the movement of the device during communication, which is also an important challenge [17]. RF fingerprints are the physical layer unique characteristics of wireless communication devices and difficult to be tampered with, so they have broad prospects for development.

2   Research Methods

2.1   Overall Framework

This paper has established a relatively complete RF fingerprint identification system to study the identification of wireless devices. As shown in Fig. 1, the system includes signal acquisition, signal detection, feature extraction, feature dimension reduction, classification and recognition. The data set used is the measured data in the laboratory. First we preprocess the signal, that is, detect the change position of the transient signal and intercept valid signals for feature extraction. This step is necessary because the effectiveness of the intercepted signal will affect the final classification accuracy. Variance trajectory detection and Bayesian detection are used to complete this work in this paper. The signal after detecting can be used to extract features. Time domain and wavelet domain methods are applied to it. Since the extracted features have higher dimensions and make the computational complexity larger, the features are reduced in dimension by PCA and LDA. The features after dimension reduction are used for classification with KNN and SVM. Finally, the extracted features are compared with the features in the fingerprint database. Accidental error can be avoided by using the cross-validation in classification process.

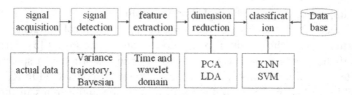

Fig. 1. Fingerprint feature recognition system block diagram

2.2 Signal Acquisition

The signal was captured from 10 transmitters of the same model but different serial numbers at a sampling rate of 40 MHz. The acquisition equipment was a high-performance Agilent oscilloscope. In order to reduce the influence of environmental noise on the signal, the receiver and transmitter are connected by cables. Since the oscilloscope acquisition signal is divided into I/Q paths, one of the two is selected for experiment. For 10 devices, we collect 50 signals from each one and totally 500 signals. Finally, Gaussian white noise was added to the signal.

2.3 Signal Detection

Variance Trajectory Detection. By setting a window function of a certain size, the mean variance of the data in each window is calculated separately, and the difference between adjacent windows constitutes a variance change trajectory. When the change of successive windows is greater than a certain threshold set by experience, the position is marked as a change point position. The variance trajectory sequence is shown in the following formulas.

$$VTx(i) = |Wx(i) - Wx(i+1)|, i = 1, 2, \ldots, L-1 \tag{1}$$

$$W_x(m) = \frac{1}{N_w} \sum_{k=1+(m-1)N_s}^{1+(m+1)N_s+N_w} [x(k) - \mu_w]^2, m = 1, 2, \ldots, L \tag{2}$$

N_w is the length of the signal, N_s is the length of the window calculated at each step, μ_w is the mean of $\{x_w(k)\}$.

Bayesian Detection. Bayesian detection is mainly to equivalent the received signal to a simple piecewise function model, and obtain the maximum value of the probability density function based on the basis function matrix, and the maximum value is the change point position of the signal. A prior knowledge is not necessary for the model to set the threshold and only implements the maximum a posteriori estimate of the change point based on the observed data. The relevant formula is as follows.

$$p(\{w\}|\mathbf{d},\mathbf{I}) \propto \frac{\left[\mathbf{d}^{\mathrm{T}}\mathbf{d} - \mathbf{d}^{\mathrm{T}}\mathbf{G}(\mathbf{G}^{\mathrm{T}}\mathbf{G})^{-1}\mathbf{G}^{\mathrm{T}}\mathbf{d}\right]^{-\frac{N-M}{2}}}{\sqrt{\det(\mathbf{G}^{\mathrm{T}}\mathbf{G})}} \tag{3}$$

$$G^{T} = \begin{bmatrix} 1,1,1,1,1,\ldots,1,0,0,0,\ldots,0 \\ 0,0,0,0,0,\ldots,0,1,1,1,\ldots,1 \end{bmatrix} \tag{4}$$

Where d is the signal, G is a diagonal array, N and M are the breakpoint positions of the piecewise function.

2.4 Feature Extraction

Time Domain Features. For the time domain feature extraction, the signal was performed Hilbert transform and then extracted the standard deviation, variance, skewness and kurtosis of the instantaneous amplitude as statistical features. Then standardize the features and remove redundancy. Skewness and kurtosis are represented by the following two formulas, respectively.

Skewness:

$$s = \frac{E(x - \mu)^3}{\sigma^3} \tag{5}$$

Kurtosis:

$$s = \frac{E(x - \mu)^4}{\sigma^4} \tag{6}$$

Where μ is the mean and σ is the standard deviation of the signal.

Wavelet Domain Feature. This part applies the method of multi-scale discrete wavelet transform. By extracting the multi-degree coefficient and taking it as a whole feature set. Then extracting the energy value of each coefficient as the final statistical feature. This iteration can be expressed as the inner product of the sampling signal and the wavelet function. Where j is the scale parameter and k is the translation parameter. K is the number of wavelet coefficients and n is the maximum scale of the wavelet transform. By n-scale decomposition of the signal, n detail coefficients and one approximation coefficient are obtained. The $n + 1$-dimensional feature vector is obtained by the following formula.

$$C(j,k) = \sum_{n \in Z} z(n)\psi_{j,k}(n) \tag{7}$$

$$F_i = \sqrt{\frac{1}{K}\sum_{k=1}^{K} W_{ik}^2} \tag{8}$$

2.5   Dimension Reduction and Classification

Dimension Reduction. PCA and LDA are two kinds of effective methods of dimensionality reduction. The dimensionality reduction criterion of PCA is to reduce the dimension while retaining the original data information as much as possible, so-called the principal component contribution rate. Following are the principal component contribution rate of PCA for time domain and wavelet domain feature extraction. Through the information of the table and the accuracy requirements of the classification, we choose to reduce to 7 dimensions in this paper (Table 1).

Table 1. The principal component contribution rate of PCA.

Dimension	Time domain	Wavelet domain
3	0.85	0.78
5	0.91	0.86
7	0.97	0.91

Classification. In this paper, KNN and SVM are used to classify features after dimensionality reduction. For the KNN classifier, based on experience and the size of the data set, we set $K = 5$. SVM has many kernel function types to choose from. In this paper, the SVM is set as Gaussian kernel function.

3   Result Analysis

3.1   Result Analysis of Signal Detection

In order to verify the effect of the two signal detection methods, we generate two kinds of analog signals with a length of 1000 for simulation. One of them is a gradual signal, that is, the value of the first 400 points of the signal is 0, and the value of the last 600 gradually changes from 0 to 1. The second type of signal is a step signal, that is, the value of the first 400 points of the signal is 0, and the value of the last 600 is all 1. The mutation points of both types of signals are set at the 400th point. It is detected by variance trajectory detection and Bayesian detection method respectively. The detected change point position and the running time required for detection are shown in Tables 2 and 3.

Table 2. Running time and change position for gradual signal.

Methods	Mutation position	Running time
Variance trajectory	427	0.305972
Bayesian detection	415	14.725243

Table 3. Running time and change position for step signal.

Methods	Mutation position	Running time
Variance trajectory	408	0.323541
Bayesian detection	401	0.051159

From the two tables we can see that Bayesian detection method has higher accuracy but longer running time than variance trajectory detection for gradual signals. Both methods have higher detection accuracy for step signal. And the Bayesian detection method has shorter running time for step signal than gradual signal. The following is the simulation result of Bayesian detection method for gradual signal (a) and step signal (b) (Fig. 2).

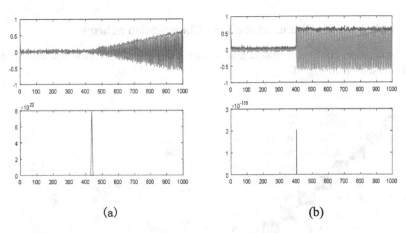

(a)   (b)

Fig. 2. Bayesian gradient point detection and step detection results

3.2   Classification Results of Time Domain and Wavelet Domain

In Fig. 3, (a) is the classification accuracy curve of time domain feature under the SNR of 1 to 30(dB) and (b) is the classification accuracy curve of wavelet domain feature under the SNR of 1 to 45(dB). In (a), the top two curves represent the classification accuracy of using the PCA to reduce the dimensionality of the time domain features, which is obviously better than the following two, indicating that the PCA dimensionality reduction method is more effective for the time domain features. Similarly, in (b), the curve with the highest classification accuracy represents the processing of wavelet domain features by LDA dimension reduction and SVM classifiers. From the two figures, we can see that for the time domain feature, PCA dimension reduction and KNN classifier processing is the best choice, which can achieve more than 90% classification accuracy. For the wavelet domain feature, the best feature recognition combination is LDA dimension reduction and SVM classifier, which can achieve more than 80% classification accuracy. So in the end we found an optimal classification scheme, which extracts time domain features from the received signals and uses LDA dimension reduction and KNN classifiers to process the device classification.

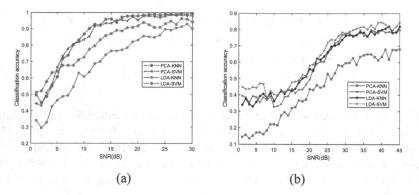

Fig. 3. Classification accuracy of time domain feature and wavelet domain feature

3.3 Analysis of the Results of the Best Classification Scheme

The classification confusion matrix and scatter plot of the best classification scheme at 15 dB are shown in Fig. 4.

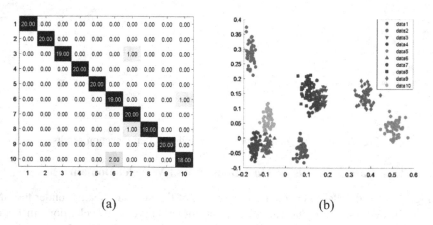

Fig. 4. Results of an optimal classification scheme

In Fig. 4, the two graphs (a) and (b) are the classification confusion matrix and the classification scatter plot obtained by the best classification scheme of time domain features respectively. It can be seen from Figure a that most of the sample devices are correctly classified, and only a few samples are incorrectly classified into other categories. From the scatter plot, the distribution of the characteristics of various devices on the coordinate axes can be visually seen. The classification of the 10 types of devices proves the effectiveness of the method used in this paper.

4 Conclusion

This paper completes the process of device identification through a complete physical layer device identification model and focuses on the time domain and wavelet domain feature extraction methods. The effects of different dimensionality reduction and classification methods on classification results are summarized. Finally, a set of optimal classification identification schemes is obtained, that is, the time domain feature extraction is combined with PCA dimensionality reduction and KNN classification. The classification accuracy is more than 90% when SNR is 15 dB. The wavelet domain feature combined with LDA and SVM is also effective, which achieves an accuracy of more than 80% at high SNRs. One possible reason why the time domain feature extraction method is superior to the wavelet domain feature extraction is that the wavelet transform has translation sensitivity, a small disturbance in the signal will have a great influence on the transformation. Finally, although many RF fingerprint identification methods can accurately classify transmitter devices, the same type of devices produced by the same manufacturer is difficult to specialize in the prior art because the similarity of their fingerprint characteristics of the devices are extremely high, so finding more effective fingerprint features may be a promising research direction for RF fingerprinting in the future.

Acknowledgment. This work is supported by the National Natural Science Foundation of China (61771154) and the Fundamental Research Funds for the Central Universities (HEUCFG201830).
This paper is also funded by the International Exchange Program of Harbin Engineering University for Innovation-oriented Talents Cultivation.
Meantime, all the authors declare that there is no conflict of interests regarding the publication of this article.
We gratefully thank of very useful discussions of reviewers.

References

1. Szu, H.H.: Novel identification of intercepted signals from unknown radio transmitters. In: Proceedings of SPIE - The International Society for Optical Engineering, vol. 2491, no. 1, pp. 504–517 (1995)
2. Toonstra, J., Kinsner, W.: Transient analysis and genetic algorithms for classification. In: Conference Proceedings of the IEEE Communications, Power, and Computing IEEE 1995, WESCANEX 95, vol. 2, pp. 432–437. IEEE (1995)
3. Desmond, L.C.C., Yuan, C.C., Tan, C.P., et al.: Identifying unique devices through wireless fingerprinting. In: ACM Conference on Wireless Network Security, WISEC 2008, Alexandria, VA, USA, 31 March–April, pp. 46–55. DBLP (2008)
4. Gao, K., Corbett, C., Beyah, R.: A passive approach to wireless device fingerprinting. In: IEEE/IFIP International Conference on Dependable Systems and Networks, IEEE 2010, pp. 383–392. IEEE (2010)
5. Gard, K.G., Larson, L.E., Steer, M.B.: The impact of RF front-end characteristics on the spectral regrowth of communications signals. IEEE Trans. Microw. Theory Tech. **53**(6), 2179–2186 (2005)

6. Polak, A.C., Dolatshahi, S., Goeckel, D.L.: Identifying wireless users via transmitter imperfections. IEEE J. Sel. Areas Commun. **29**(7), 1469–1479 (2011)
7. Polak, A.C., Goeckel, D.L.: RF fingerprinting of users who actively mask their identities with artificial distortion. In: Signals, Systems and Computers, IEEE 2013, pp. 270–274. IEEE (2013)
8. Zhao, N., Yu, F.R., Sun, H., et al.: Adaptive power allocation schemes for spectrum sharing in interference-alignment-based cognitive radio networks. IEEE Trans. Veh. Technol. **65**(5), 3700–3714 (2016)
9. Nguyen, N.T., Zheng, G., Han, Z., et al.: Device fingerprinting to enhance wireless security using nonparametric Bayesian method. In: Proceedings IEEE, INFOCOM 2011, IEEE 2011, vol. 34, pp. 1404–1412. IEEE (2011)
10. Danev, B., Capkun, S.: Transient-based identification of wireless sensor nodes. In: International Conference on Information Processing in Sensor Networks IEEE 2009, pp. 25–36. IEEE (2009)
11. Polak, A.C., Goeckel, D.L.: Wireless device identification based on RF oscillator imperfections. In: IEEE International Conference on Acoustics, Speech and Signal Processing IEEE, vol. 10, pp. 2492–2501. IEEE (2014)
12. Merchant, K., Revay, S., Stantchev, G., et al.: Deep learning for RF device fingerprinting in cognitive communication networks. IEEE J. Sel. Top. Signal Process. **12**(1), 160–167 (2018)
13. Li, Z., Xu, W., Miller, R., et al.: Securing wireless systems via lower layer enforcements. In: ACM Workshop on Wireless Security ACM, pp. 33–42. ACM (2006)
14. Liang, X., Greenstein, L., Mandayam, N., et al.: Fingerprints in the ether: using the physical layer for wireless authentication. In: IEEE International Conference on Communications IEEE, pp. 4646–4651. IEEE (2009)
15. Tu, Y., Lin, Y., Wang, J., et al.: Semi-supervised learning with generative adversarial networks on digital signal modulation classification. CMC-Comput. Mater. Continua **55**(2), 243–254 (2018)
16. Zhou, J.T., Zhao, H., Peng, X., et al.: Transfer hashing: from shallow to deep. IEEE Trans. Neural Netw. Learn. Syst. **29**(12), 6191–6201 (2018)
17. Zheng, Z., Sangaiah, A.K., Wang, T.: Adaptive communication protocols in flying Ad Hoc network. IEEE Commun. Mag. **56**(1), 136–142 (2018)

Research on Nonlinear Modeling for RF Power Amplifier

Xiang Chen[1], Jie Chang[1], Hui Han[2], Ruowu Wu[1], and Yun Lin[2(✉)]

[1] State Key Laboratory of Complex Electromagnetic Environment Effects on Electronics and Information System (CEMEE), Luoyang, Henan 471003, China
[2] College of Information and Communication Engineering, Harbin Engineering University, Harbin 150001, China
linyun_phd@hrbeu.edu.cn

Abstract. The research of radio-frequency (RF) power amplifier model has always been one of the most important breakthroughs in the emitter feature extraction and specific emitter identification. Through the establishment of RF power amplifier model, we can extract feature parameters of the specific emitter. In this paper, we discuss the research issues of the specific emitter feature extraction and individual identification based on RF power amplifier nonlinear model, summarize the nonlinear distortion and modeling method of the power amplifier. Furthermore, we analyzed the applicability of these models.

Keywords: Power amplifier · Emitter feature extraction · Individual identification · Nonlinear distortion

1 Introduction

In the integrated electronic warfare system, it is of great significance to study the fine feature extraction and individual identification of specific emitter. Even if two pieces of device of the same type are produced at the same time, due to the differences in the individual parameters of the internal components and use environment and so on, the working characteristics thereof will produce subtle differences. For wireless communication systems, under the same input conditions, there will be slight differences in the output radiation signal. Because the power amplifiers (PA) is indispensable module in communication emitter and RF power amplifiers work unavoidably under nonlinear conditions, RF power amplifiers are often the main aspects of the specific emitter manifesting its individual differences [1].

The modeling of the power amplifier was first established by Saleh in 1981 based on the statistical analysis of the input and output data of the TWT power amplifier TWTA [2]. Saleh model is appropriative PA model and not widely applicable. With the development of information technology, we cannot ignore the PA nonlinearity and memory effect. They become the focus of research gradually, various models about nonlinearity and memory effect of RF power amplifier have also emerged. The nonlinear application of power amplifiers in the fine-feature extraction and individual identification of specific emitter was presented in 2007 [3]. Selecting the optimal model of the RF power amplifier, extracting parameters that do not change due to signal changes and that can reflect the characteristics of the specific emitter itself, use these parameters to achieve individual identification of the emitter. To understand the significance of the establishment of the PA model for the study of the nuanced feature extraction and individual identification, we first review some of the previous studies on PA modeling and conduct a specific review of the PA modeling technique.

The remainder of the paper is organized as follows. In Sect. 2, we first introduce the development of RF power amplifiers. On this basis, we explain the nonlinear and memory characteristics of the RF power amplifier and the corresponding indicators. In Sect. 3, we will mainly describe the common modeling methods and research process of the power amplifier. In Sect. 4, we mainly discussed the application of power amplifier modeling technology in the subtle feature extraction and individual identification technology. In Sect. 5, we conclude the paper.

2   Nonlinear Distortion

In this section, we discussed the development of PAs, memory effects and nonlinear distortion characteristics.

2.1   RF Power Amplifier

RF power amplifier is one of the key components in RF microwave system. Its performance directly affects the system's transmission distance and quality. The development of power amplifiers has gradually evolved with the development of wireless communications [4]. Since 1920, Class A and Class AB amplifiers have been introduced. To solve the problem of inefficiency, Doherty invented Doherty power amplifier in 1936 [5]. From the end of the 1950s to the beginning of the 21st century, the development of Class F, Class E, and inverse Class F and inverse Class D power amplifiers came into being [6, 7]. In 2003, for improving efficiency and linearity of power amplifier, Doherty PAs were combined with class AB PAs [8]. In 2005, the advent of inverse Class E power amplifiers has greatly improved the stability of the circuit [9]. Class J power amplifiers were proposed to solve the bandwidth problem in 2006 and realized design in 2009 [10]. In 2010, Continuous Class F Power Amplifiers and Envelope Tracking Amplifiers were designed, PAs have gradually become a hot research topic in wireless communications [11]. Figure 1 shows the development of PAs intuitively.

2.2   Memory Characteristics

When the input of the PA is a wideband signal, the PA will show obvious memory characteristics. The memory characteristic, that is, the current output of the amplifier, is not only related to the current input but also related to the previous input. In general, memory effects are divided into electrical memory effects and thermal memory effects according to the causes of memory effects. Among them, the reason for the electrical memory effect is impedance matching. In addition, when the modulation frequency is changed, the envelope change, the fundamental frequency, and the second harmonic

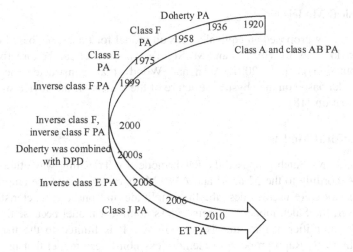

Fig. 1. The PA development process.

impedance are all important factors causing the electrical memory effect [12]. The main reason for the thermal memory effect is the change of the junction temperature of the transistor. When the power amplifier operates under high power conditions, the transistor will rapidly heat up, resulting in changes in the characteristics of the power amplifier [13].

2.3 Nonlinear Characteristics

The power amplifier is essentially a nonlinear device, which means that the amplifier output does not exhibit an ideal linear amplification relationship with the input, the gain of the power amplifier is not a constant, and generally varies with the operating frequency. The nonlinear effect characterization of power amplifiers mainly includes harmonic distortion, intermodulation distortion, amplitude/amplitude (AM-AM) and amplitude/phase (AM-PM) characteristics [14].

3 Nonlinear Models

RF power amplifier modeling is mainly divided into two kinds of physical models and behavioral models. Physical models are based on a physical description of the components of the PA and how they interact and are typically formulated as equivalent circuit models [15]. Behavioral models are models that collect input and output data of PAs and fits the data. It does not care about the actual principle of the PA, but only requires the same input and output characteristics of the PA [16].

3.1   Physical Models

In 1995, Angelov proposed an equivalent circuit model for transistors based on Ohm's law and David's law for HEMTs and MESFETs. This model can be directly used for circuit simulation [17]. In 2007, Aean and Wood et al. constructed the transistor physical model based on the physical structure of the transistor, the device size, and the physical equation [18].

3.2   Behavioral Models

In 1981, A. A. M. Saleh proposed the Saleh model for Traveling-wave tube amplifier (TWTA). According to the AM/AM and AM/PM characteristics of the amplifier, only four parameters were used to describe the amplitude and phase characteristics of the PA. However, the Saleh model is a memoryless nonlinear model because the memory effect of the amplifier at that time is not obvious. It is limited to the narrow band amplifier. In 1991, Rapp proposed a memoryless non-linear model that ignores AM-PM changes. This model only consider the AM-AM effect and compliant solid state power amplifier (SSPA) [19]. The polynomial-based memoryless model is essentially the Taylor series form used to analyze memoryless nonlinear systems. This model can be used for TWTA amplifiers as well as SSPA amplifiers. However, the degree of approximation to the actual situation is lower than both.

The Volterra series proposed by Italian mathematician Volterra was widely used in the modeling of memory amplifiers. Since 1999, the Volterra series model has been applied to PA modeling with memory effect. Because the parameters of the model will grow rapidly as the memory length of the amplifier increases, the traditional Volterra series model is only suitable for weakly nonlinear systems. Thus, in 2004, A. Zhu et al. jointly proposed the tailored Volterra model [20], which removes the secondary items in the traditional Volterra series model, and only retains the most important items, thus greatly reducing the number of parameters and the computational complexity of PA behavioral modeling. Moreover, H. Ku and JS Kenney of the Georgia Institute of Technology in the United States have proposed a power amplifier model based on memory polynomials. This model is actually a simplified version of the Volterra series model because the number of parameters is much less than the same order. With the Volterra series model of memory length, the computational complexity of model identification is greatly reduced [21].

In recent years, artificial neural networks have been used in various fields for nonlinear modeling. In the field of radio frequency, they have also been used for nonlinear modeling of power amplifier circuits and devices. Many commonly used neural network methods can be used to construct the performance of power amplifiers. Modules, such as Dynamic Neural Networks and Recurrent Neural Networks [22]. In 2006, Magnus Isaksson et al. analyzed and compared the behavior models of RF Power Amplifiers, including static polynomial, parallel Hammerstein (PH), Volterra, and radial basis function neural networks (RBFNN). For practical applications, 2G and 3G PAs are calculated and analyzed. The results show that the accuracy of the RBFNN in the entire model is better slightly than that of the PH, but the precision and accuracy outside the band are much higher than the PH model [23].

3.3 The Summary of This Section

The memoryless model mainly includes Saleh model, Rapp model and complex coefficient polynomial model, which is suitable for narrowband input and constant temperature PAs.

Wiener model and Hammerstein model are more suitable for power amplifiers with linear memory effect. Volterra models are generally suitable for weakly nonlinear power amplifiers because they have more model parameters.

Parallel Wiener model and parallel Hammerstein model are more suitable for power amplifiers with strong memory effect. The neural network model can better simulate and predict the power amplifier characteristics with strong memory effect.

Figure 2 shows the main model of the power amplifier model, from the figure can be seen the development process and progress of power amplifier model.

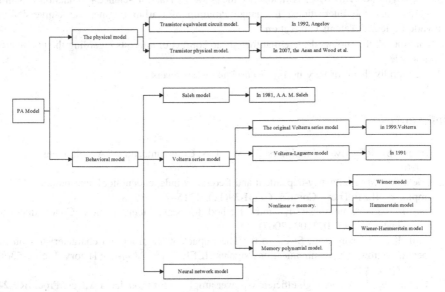

Fig. 2. The main model of the PA.

4 Application

The extraction of subtle features of radiation sources can be divided into transient signal feature extraction and steady-state signal feature extraction. Transient signal extraction mainly performs feature extraction during the startup and shutdown of radio equipment. Its advantage is that the transient signals between equipment individual are greatly different and easy to process and recognize when they are turned off [24]. However, due to the short time of transient signals. The timing is unpredictable and therefore difficult to capture and extract. Steady-state signal feature extraction is based on the signal characteristics of the wireless communication system for stable feature recognition. Signals are easily captured and extracted. However, the individual differences between devices are very small, and more complex processing and identification are required [25].

5   Conclusion

With the increasing importance of microscopic feature recognition in wireless communication field, the subtle feature recognition method based on power amplifier modeling has received more and more attention. This article aims to review the development of PA modeling, provide a great perspective for the understanding of nonlinear memory behavior modeling of PAs. From the point of view of the article, the PA modeling technology can effectively extract parameters, but we still need to pay attention to some issues, such as how to improve the parameters of the power amplifier model to build, enlarge individual feature differences, how to control the noise of the model construction effectively, and feature recognition effects.

Acknowledgment. This paper is funded by the National Natural Science Foundation of China (61771154), and the International Exchange Program of Harbin Engineering University for Innovation-oriented Talents Cultivation.

Meantime, all the authors declare that there is no conflict of interests regarding the publication of this article.

We gratefully thank of very useful discussions of reviewers.

References

1. Cripps, S.: RF Power Amplifiers for Wireless Communications. Artech House, Boston (2006)
2. Saleh, A.A.M.: Frequency-dependent and frequency-independent nonlinear models of TWT amplifiers. IEEE Trans. Comms. **COM-29**(11), 1715–1720 (1981)
3. Carroll, T.L.: A nonlinear dynamics method for signal identification. Chaos Interdisc. J. Nonlinear Sci. **17**, 023109 (2007)
4. Gard, K.G., Larson, L.E., Steer, M.B.: The impact of RF front-end characteristics on the spectral regrowth of communications signals. IEEE Trans. Microw. Theory Techn. **53**(6), 2179–2186 (2005)
5. Doherty, W.H.: A new high efficiency power amplifier for modulated waves. Proc. IRE **24**, 1163–1182 (1936)
6. Sokal, N.O., Sokal, A.D.: Class E – a new class of high-efficiency tuned single-ended switching power amplifier. IEEE J. Solid-State Circuits **10**, 168–176 (1975)
7. Grebennikov, A.: Circuit design technique for high efficiency class F amplifiers. In: 2000 IEEE MTT-S International Microwave Symposium Digest, vol. 2, pp. 771–774, June 2000
8. Dettmann, I., Wu, L., Betroth, M.: Comparison of a single-ended class AB, a balance and a doherty power amplifier. In: Asia-Pacific Conference Proceedings Microwave Conference Proceedings, APMC 2005, vol. 2, pp. 1167–1170, 2005
9. Brabetz, T., Fusco, V.F.: Voltage-driven Class-E amplifier and applications. Proc. IEE Microw. Antennas Propag. **152**(5), 373–377 (2005)
10. Morgan, D.R., Ma, Z., Kim, J., Zierdt, M.G., Pastalan, J.: A generalized memory polynomial model for digital predistortion of RF power amplifiers. IEEE Trans. Sign. Proc **54**(10), October 2006
11. Carrubba, V.: The continuous class-F mode power amplifier. In: Proceedings of the 40th European Microwave Conference, pp. 432–435, September 2010

12. Boumaiza, S.: Thermal memory effects modeling and compensation in RF power amplifiers and predistortion linearizers. IEEE Trans. Mircowave Theory Tech. **51**, 2427–2433 (2004)
13. Liu, T., Boumaiza, S., Sesay, A.B., Ghannouchi, F.M.: Quantitative measurements of memory effects in wideband RF power amplifiers driven by modulated signals. IEEE Microw. Wireless Compon. Lett. **17**(1), 79–81 (2007)
14. Rönnow, D., Wisell, D.H., Isaksson, M.: Three-tone characterization of nonlinear memory effects in radio-frequency power amplifiers. IEEE Trans. Instrum. Meas. **56**(6), 2646–2657 (2007). Author, F.: Contribution title. In: 9th International Proceedings on Proceedings, pp. 1–2. Publisher, Location (2010)
15. Ku, H., Kenney, J.S.: Behavioral modeling of nonlinear RF power amplifiers considering memory effects. IEEE Trans. Microw. Theory Tech. **51**(12), 2495–2504 (2003)
16. de Carvalho, N.B., Pedro, J.C.: A comprehensive explanation of distortion sideband asymmetries. IEEE Trans. Microw. Theory Tech. **50**(9), 2090–2101 (2002)
17. Angelov, I., Zirath, H., Rorsman, N.: Validation of a nonlinear transistor model by power spectrum characteristics of HEMT's and MESFET's. IEEE Trans. Microw. Theory Tech. **43**(5), 1046–1052 (1995)
18. Aaen, P.H., Plá, J.A., Wood, J.: Modeling and Characterization of RF and Microwave Power FETs. Cambridge University Press, Cambridge (2007)
19. Rapp, C.: Effects of HPA-nonlinearity on a 4-DPSK/OFDM-signal for a digital sound broadcasting signal, pp. 179–184 (1991)
20. And, A.S.S., Parker, R.S.: Tailored sequence design for third-order volterra model identification. Ind. Eng. Chem. Res. **46**(3), 818–829 (2006)
21. Ku, H., Kenney, J.S.: Behavioral modeling of nonlinear RF power amplifiers considering memory effects. IEEE Trans. Micro. Theory Tech. **51**(12), 2495–2504 (2003)
22. Zhu, A., Brazil, T.J.: Behavioral modeling of RF power amplifiers based on pruned Volterra series. IEEE Microw. Wirel. Compon. Lett. **14**(12), 563–565 (2004). LNCS Homepage. http://www.springer.com/lncs. Accessed 21 Nov 2016
23. Ibnkahla, M., Bershad, N.J., Sombrin, J., Castanié (Castanie), F.: Neural network modeling and identification of nonlinear channels with memory: algorithms applications and analytic models. IEEE Trans. Signal Process. **46**(5), 1208–1222 (1998)
24. Isaksson, M., Wisell, D., Ronnow, D.: A comparative analysis for behavioral models of RF power amplifiers. IEEE Trans. Micro. Theory Tech. **54**(1), 348–359 (2006)
25. Ellis, K., Serinken, N.: Characteristics of radio transmitter fingerprints. Radio Sci. **36**, 585–597 (2001)

High Precision Detection System of Circuit Board Based on Image Location

Xinghua Lu, Gang Zhao(✉), Haiying Liu,
and Fangyi Zhang

College of Transportation, Shandong University of Science and Technology,
Qingdao, China
47994337@qq.com

Abstract. With the increasing integration of the control system and the continuous development of the PCB processing technology, the testing of PCB becomes more and more difficult. The manual detection of PCB fault points can no longer meet the needs of the industry. In this paper, a universal circuit board detection system based on image automatic positioning is proposed. The system can accurately collect the coordinates of the measured points by using the image information, and record the edge information of the circuit board. The position error caused by the fixed position of the circuit board is corrected in real time. At the same time, the automatic correction function of the pressure drop of the system can automatically correct the voltage drop produced by the hardware circuit and improve the accuracy of the measuring system. The experiment proved that the fault point detection system based on image location can effectively improve the efficiency, accuracy and universal of circuit board detection.

Keywords: Circuit board · Fault point detection · Image location ·
Error correction

1 Introduction

In the past, many experts and scholars have made outstanding contributions in the field of automatic detection of circuit boards, and they have achieved notable results. Li [1] and his teammates have developed a set of PCB automatic detection system for a mining circuit board, which improved the detection efficiency. Luan [2] and his teammates have developed a set of circuit board vision positioning system based on Vision Pro which Improved the positioning accuracy to 0.3 mm. In the research of circuit board location, Wang [3] and his teammates have improved the accuracy of detection and shortened the detection time by using the improved Hough transform. On the basis of the existing detection technology, an intelligent detection equipment based on automatic image location and automatic correction of pressure drop error is proposed in this paper. The equipment is based on the image positioning system, and combined with the flying-needle detection system and the automatic error correction system, which greatly improved the efficiency, accuracy and generality of the detection of the circuit board.

S. Liu and G. Yang (Eds.): ADHIP 2018, LNICST 279, pp. 468–475, 2019.
https://doi.org/10.1007/978-3-030-19086-6_52

2 Total Design of the System

2.1 Structure of the System

To make the detecting system efficient, accurate and universal, the system is divided into five parts:

1. A flying-needle system based on the movable needle.
2. An image positioning system based on the FT- GW36C camera.
3. An automatic measurement and pressure drop correction system based on high-precision multimeter and oscilloscope.
4. A slave computer control system based on STM32F407IGH6.
5. A master computer total control system based on VS+ C#.

The needle bed system makes use of the fixture to ensure that the circuit board within the specified size range can be effectively fixed and that every point on the circuit board can be contacted with the needle. The image positioning system can obtain and store the "datum coordinates" of the target and the "datum edge" of the circuit board through the image when we don't know the coordinates of the measured point. The "datum coordinates" and the "datum edge" can provide the exact coordinate information and position error correction basis for the formal measurement circuit board, which ensure that measured points can be accurately detected by the flying-needle. The measurement and pressure drop automatic correction system based on high precision meter can make the measurement process efficient and accurate, besides, the system can also eliminate the influence of the hardware measurement circuit on the measured signal. The master computer system and the slave computer system are responsible for the control and execution of the whole measurement system.

2.2 Main Workflow

For the circuit board whose target point coordinates are unknown, the workflow of the detection system is divided into two processes: system calibration and formal measurement.

The system calibration process includes data acquisition and system initialization. The quality of system calibration will directly affect the accuracy of the formal measurement. The process divides into five steps: (1) the target point calibration and coordinate extraction based on the image; (2) extracting the edge of the circuit board; (3) setting the standard signal value of the target point; (4) setting the physical properties of target points and distributing the flying-needle; (5) automatic pressure drop correction.

The formal measurement process, based on the coordinate data collected in the system calibration process and the standard signal values of the measured points, finishes the testing and locking the fault points. The process divides into six steps: (1) The "handshake" between the master computer and the slave computer; (2) Correcting the position error of the circuit board automatically; (3) The testing safety under the low voltage power supply state; (4) Collecting signal in normal working voltage state; (5) Analyzing acquisition value and standard signal value comparatively; (6) Locking fault points.

3 The Design of Key Hardware System

3.1 The Design of Needle Bed System Based on Movable Flying-Needle

In order to improve the universality of the equipment, ensure that the pressure value can make equipment work well in a variety of measuring environment and ensure the accurate contact between the measured point and the flying-needle, the system is analyzed in two aspects, the variety of then physical size of the needle and the safety grade of the flying-needle. On this basis, a set of flying-needle selection scheme is given.

IEC (International Electrotechnical Commission) set up an international standard for testing instruments: IEC 1010. According to the fact that the dangerous high-energy voltage is gradually attenuated by the transmission in the line, the standard divides security of the power system into four grades, that is, CAT I, CAT II, CAT III, CAT IV. The higher the safety level is, the higher the instantaneous high voltage that can be borne will be. The applicable objects of different safety levels are shown in Table 1:

Table 1. The applicable objects of different safety levels

Classification	CAT I	CAT II	CAT III	CAT IV
Applications	Indoor electrotechnical equipment with protective measures	Household socket and its equipment	Three phase distribution circuit and industrial lighting circuit, etc.	Three phase public power supply equipment
Example	Fax, Scanner	Fridge, Washing machine	Machine tool in the workshop, Interior lighting circuit of large building	Outdoor transmission circuit

The needle bed equipment belongs to the indoor application equipment. The range of the voltage measurement of the equipment should be taken into consideration when the needle is selected. According to Table 1, it is analyzed that the selected flying-needle of this system should meet the safety standard of CAT III.

Based on the above safety analysis and combined with the physical size diversity requirements of flying-needles, this paper presents a set of flying-needle selection schemes, as shown in Table 2:

Limited by the structure of the needle moving system, the needle bed system consists of 4 movable flying pins. Each pin has different models, characteristics and applicable conditions. It can meet the measurement requirements of the industrial circuit board and improve the universality of the needle bed system.

Table 2. The flying-needle selection schemes

Model number	Head type of flying-needle	Head diameter/mm	Application
HSS150 306 400A5002M	Flat head	4.0	Measuring the position where large current and high voltage appear
GKS004-206-396A2000	Plum blossom head	3.96	Measuring the direct pin or the position where high voltage appears
GKS100217170A2000	Trigonometric point	1.7	Measuring via. reducing the damage to the circuit board
GKS050291050A2000	Sharp head	0.5	Measuring the larger pins, avoiding short circuit connection due to flying-needle too thick

3.2   The Design of Image Location System Based on FT-GW36C Camera

The image automatic positioning system collects the circuit board image through the FT-GW36C camera. In the system calibration step, the pin yellow edges of the measured point that is calibrated by the master computer system are shown in Fig. 1. By calling the function cv2-moments () in the OPENCV library [4], the master computer software calculates the center coordinates of the calibrated point, then it inputs the coordinates into the coordinate library as the datum coordinate information of the measured point. At the same time, the standard signal value, data type, pin type and flying-needle type, which corresponding to the measured point, are input into the master computer database. When each target point is traversed, the camera captures the overall images of the circuit board. The master computer detects the edge of the circuit board through the Canny algorithm, and calculates the edge size information and the centroid coordinates of the circuit board through the function of cvMinAreaRect2 (). Meanwhile, the base shape information of the circuit board edge is stored. The whole process is shown in Fig. 2:

During the formal measurement process, the circuit board is clamps on the test stand. By collecting the edge size information of the circuit board and calculating the center coordinates of the edge of the circuit board at the moment, the system calculates the error vector 'U' by comparing with the datum-edge shape information in the database. Combining the error vector 'U' and the datum coordinate value of the target

Fig. 1. Coordinate measuring diagram of target point

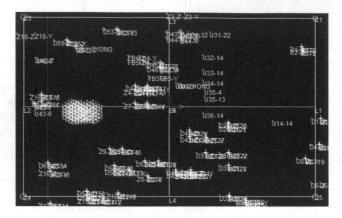

Fig. 2. Points and edges detection diagram

point stored in the database, the real-time position coordinates of the measured points in the formal measurement process are calculated. The calculation process of the real-time position coordinates is as follows:

Taking rectangular circuit board as an example, it is assumed that the 'O' coordinates of the edge reference centroid collected in the process of system calibration are (a_0, b_0), and the reference coordinates of any target in the database are (c_0, d_0). In order to accurately measure the position of the circuit board and the angle deviation of the reference position, it is taken as the reference direction that the initial direction of the upper edge of the circuit board in the system calibration process, which is recorded as: $\angle = 0$. At the time of formal measurement, it is assumed that the centroid coordinates of the circuit board are (a_1, b_1), and the angle between the upper edge and the reference direction $\angle = \theta$, and the error vector is recorded as $U = (\Delta X, \Delta Y)$. As shown in Eqs. (1) (2) (3), the coordinates of the target points in the formal measurement process can be simplified as the following mathematical model:

$$\Delta L = \sqrt{(a_0 - c_0)^2 + (b_0 - d_0)^2} \tag{1}$$

$$\Delta X = (a_1 - a_0) + \Delta L \cdot \sin \theta \tag{2}$$

$$\Delta Y = (b_1 - b_0) + \Delta L \cdot (1 - \cos \theta) \tag{3}$$

The corrected coordinates of the measured points are $(a_0 + \Delta X, b_0 + \Delta X)$, and the master computer coordinates the corrected coordinates as the real time coordinates of the formal measurement to ensure that the flying-needle can move accurately to the position of the measured point.

3.3 High Precision Measurement and Voltage Drop Automatic Correction System

In the process of circuit board detection, how to measure electrical signals will directly affect the efficiency and accuracy of measurement, and further affect the testing quality of testing equipment. Two high precision measuring equipment are used in this system: 'Keysight' multimeter and 'Micsig' oscilloscope, Two measuring devices are controlled by two relays, and the multimeter (or oscilloscope) sends a data to the upper computer through LAN communication every time the measuring devices finish testing a target point.

In the measuring process, the impedance of the hardware measurement circuit will make the measured voltage appear a certain amplitude of voltage drop. In order to improve the measuring precision of the equipment, the system sets the standard 13 reference voltage [5]: -15 V, -10 V, -5 V, -3.3 V, -2 V, -1 V, 0 V, 1 V, 2 V, 3.3 V, 5 V, 15 V, 24 V. According to the 13 references, the measured voltage range is divided into 14 measuring intervals. When measuring the voltage drop produced by the hardware circuit, 13 reference voltages were collected 10 times continuously, which are recorded as

$$X_1, X_2, X_3 \ldots \ldots X_{10}$$

The correction value of the voltage drop of the circuit X is shown in Eqs. (4) (5) (6):

$$\Delta X_1 = 5V - X_1 \tag{4}$$

$$\Delta X_{10} = 5V - X_{10} \tag{5}$$

$$X = \sqrt{\frac{\Delta X_1^2 + \Delta X_2^2 + \ldots + \Delta X_{10}^2}{10}} \tag{6}$$

According to the above principles, 14 corrections can be obtained: $X_1, X_2, \ldots \ldots X_{14}$

In the formal measurement process, according to the measured voltage value V_m, the voltage correction value is selected in real time. Thus the actual voltage value V can be recorded as Eq. (7):

$$V = V_m \pm V_i (i = 1, 2 \ldots \ldots 14) \tag{7}$$

4 The Design of the Master Computer System

As a platform for human-computer interaction, the master computer has many functions such as reading, analyzing, storing data, controlling the action of the slave computer, controlling the image acquisition system, generating the reports, and so on. The work flow is shown in Fig. 3.

To facilitate the maintenance and upgrading of the master computer, the master computer must have good extensibility and versatility. In order to meet the above

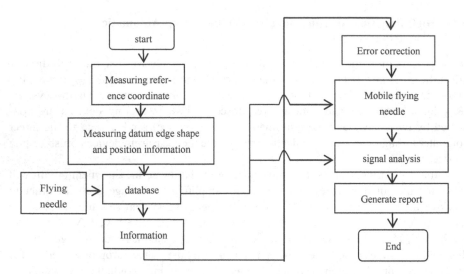

Fig. 3. Working flow chart of master computer control

requirements, the master computer is designed to be divided into 5 modules, image acquisition and analysis module, flying-needle control module, data acquisition module, data analysis module and data report module. This modular design reduces the complexity of the program, and makes program design, debugging and maintenance more convenient.

5   Experiment

In order to test the efficiency, accuracy and generality of the system, 5 different types of circuit boards with known faults are measured in the experiment. The experimental data are recorded and analyzed. The experimental collection interface is shown in Fig. 4, and the experimental data is like Table 3.

In the process of experimental data analysis, considering the characteristics of circuit work, the voltage signal of non-zero standard value is allowed to have a

Fig. 4. Experimental collection interface

Table 3. Experimental data table

Circuit board	Number of measured points	Number of known fault points	System calibration time/min	Measurement time/s	Accuracy rate
Reversing radar circuit	24	2	12	50.4	100%
Voice playback circuit	67	5	30	129	100%
Resistance capacitance protection circuit	70	2	29	152.7	100%
Lower computer circuit board	104	6	37	212	100%
Traction motor circuit	203	8	134	452.7	99.51%

measurement error of $\pm 3\%$, and the voltage data with zero standard value is allowed to have an error of ± 0.8 V. When the measured value exceeds the specified range, it is demarcated as abnormal data.

The experimental results show that the fault point detection system based on automatic image positioning can accurately locate the target points, and the different types of movable flying pins guarantee the generality of the measuring system. At the same time, the correction function of target coordinates error and the circuit voltage drop improved the accuracy of the detection system enhanced the intelligent level of measuring equipment.

References

1. Li, A., Wei, Y.: PCB board detection system design. Ind. Technol. Forum **15**(3), 92–93 (2016)
2. Luan, M., Zhang, K., Wei, H., et al.: VisionPro based visual location system for circuit board measuring points. Ind. Control Comput. **3**(5), 68–72 (2017)
3. Wang, F., Zhao, G.: Research on image location algorithm for welding quality recognition of electronic components. Mod. Electron. Technol. **40**(5), 42–48 (2017)
4. Bradski, G., Kaehler, A.: Learning OpenCV. Translated by Yu, S., Liu, R. Tsinghua University Press, Beijing (2009)
5. Liu, P., Yang, R., Liu, D.: Design and implementation of circuit board fault detection and diagnosis system. Sci. Technol. Eng. **9**(22), 6847–6851 (2009)

Modulation Recognition Technology of Communication Signals Based on Density Clustering and Sample Reconstruction

Hui Han[1], Xianglong Zhou[2], Xiang Chen[1], Ruowu Wu[1],
and Yun Lin[2(✉)]

[1] State Key Laboratory of Complex Electromagnetic Environment Effects
on Electronics and Information System (CEMEE),
Luoyang 471003, Henan, China
[2] College of Information and Communication Engineering,
Harbin Engineering University, Harbin, China
linyun_phd@hrbeu.edu.cn

Abstract. Modulation recognition is an important part in the field of communication signal processing. In recent years, with the development of modulation recognition technology, various problems have emerged. In this title, we propose an improved recognition framework based on SVM, which extracts the entropy feature of the signal and distinguishes it from the traditional modulation recognition framework. We combine the training set with the test set first, then carry on the density clustering to the whole data set. The data set after the cluster is extracted according to a certain proportion to build a new training set, and the new training set is used to train the SVM. Finally, the data of the test set is modulated by the modulation recognition. Experimental results show that the proposed method improves the recognition rate of traditional SVM framework and enhances the stability of traditional SVM framework.

Keywords: Modulation recognition · Entropy features · Density clustering ·
Restructure · SVM

1 Introduction

Modulation recognition technology is a key technology in the field of communication processing digital signals. He has been widely used in civil and military applications. As the channel environment is more and more complex, the accuracy of modulation recognition is particularly important.

Traditional modulation recognition technology is constrained by the theoretical framework, and many scholars are devoted to improving the classification and training structure of classifier to improve the accuracy of recognition. With the rise of machine learning, more and more unsupervised methods are widely used [1–5]. Density clustering is an unsupervised classification method. The density clustering algorithm assumes that the clustering structure can be determined by the close degree of the sample distribution, and studies the distribution characteristics between samples from the angle of sample density to achieve the purpose of classification [6, 7]. Density clustering

© ICST Institute for Computer Sciences, Social Informatics and Telecommunications Engineering 2019
Published by Springer Nature Switzerland AG 2019. All Rights Reserved
S. Liu and G. Yang (Eds.): ADHIP 2018, LNICST 279, pp. 476–484, 2019.
https://doi.org/10.1007/978-3-030-19086-6_53

algorithm is widely used in the processing of complex structure data processing [1]. For large data mining, density clustering also plays an important role [2]. Mass data will appear in the process of generation, which is consistent with the algorithm of density clustering [8]. In addition, density clustering is widely applied in various fields such as biomedical science, computer calculate, economics, and social network [3] and so on.

Entropy is a measure of information uncertainty, which can express the uncertain information of random signals. It can be used as the characteristic of the signal to recognize it [9–14]. Support vector machine (SVM) is a machine learning method based on statistical learning theory. Through training, the support vector machine can automatically find the support vectors that have good distinguishing ability for the classification, thus the classifier can be constructed to distinguish the different categories better [15–17]. At present, support vector machines has a wide range of applications in many fields, such as modulation recognition [15], face recognition [17], etc.

In this paper, a kind of modulation recognition method which combines unsupervised density clustering with SVM is presented. By using data sample and training set to form a new training set, a new training set is trained to achieve better recognition effect. We classify 6 kinds of digital modulation signals: 2ASK, 2FSK, 8FSK, BPSK, QPSK, 16QAM, in different SNR. The algorithm improves the traditional SVM.

2 Related Work

2.1 Entropy Feature Extraction

The concept of entropy was first proposed by Shannon. It is a measure of information uncertainty. Set the event set to. The n-dimensional vector $P = (P_1, P_2, \cdots, P_n)$ is used to represent the probability set of events, and satisfies: $0 \leq p_i \leq 1$ and $\sum_{i=1}^{n} p_i = 1$, then Shannon entropy can be defined as:

$$H(p) = H(p_1, p_2, \cdots, p_n) = -\sum_{i=1}^{n} p_i \log p_i \tag{1}$$

Assuming that the probability of an event is p_i, the amount of information can be defined as:

$$\Delta I(p_i) = e^{1-p_i} \tag{2}$$

Then the exponential entropy can be defined as:

$$H = \sum_{i=1}^{N} p_i e^{1-p_i} \tag{3}$$

According to the reference [11], in this paper, we extract 6 kinds of entropy characteristics, namely: power spectrum Shannon entropy, wavelet energy spectrum entropy, bispectrum entropy, sample entropy, singular spectrum Shannon entropy, and singular spectral index entropy.

2.2   Density Clustering

As an unsupervised clustering algorithm, density clustering is mainly used to divide the data with the density of data distribution. In general, the distribution of data is presented or sparse or closely distributed according to its characteristics. The data is classified by calculating the core points of the data and dividing the radius of the data categories. In this paper, we use the famous density clustering algorithm: DBSCAN, which partitions data sets through neighborhood, core objects, density radius and other parameters. According to the operation of the algorithm, the following definitions are given [7]:

ε Neighborhood: for $x_j \in D$, its ε neighborhood contains the samples whose concentration is not greater than the sample set.

Core object: if the ε neighborhood of x_j contains at least n samples, it is a core object.

Direct density: if x_j located in the ε neighborhood of x_i and it is the core object, it is called x_j to x_i the density direct.

Density can reach: for x_j and x_i, if there is a sample sequence $p_1, p_2, \ldots, p_n$, among them $p_1 = x_i, p_n = x_j$, and p_{i+1} to p_i is direct density, then it is called x_j to x_i the density can reach.

Density connected: for x_j and x_i, if exist x_k make x_j and x_i are all reached by density, they are called density connected.

Based on these basic concepts, DBSCAN defines "clusters" as the largest set of density connected samples derived from density reachability relationships. The DBSCAN algorithm first selects one of the core objects in the data set as "seeds", and then starts to determine the corresponding clusters. First, find all the core objects according to the given neighborhood parameters, and then use any object as the starting point. Clusters are generated from their densely-reachable samples until all core objects are accessed.

2.3   SVM

SVM is V. Vapnik proposes statistical learning theory. Its basic idea is to perform some kind of nonlinear transformation on the original feature space by defining an appropriate kernel function, mapping the original feature space to a high-dimensional space, and then finding the optimal classification surface in this new space so that the sample is correct. Separation and categorization intervals are the greatest. First, the SVM needs to be trained, and then the trained signal classifier is used to classify the test signals. Figure 1 shows the SVM identification process.

SVM is essentially a two-class classifier. For linearly separable cases, the training sample set is $(x_1, y_1), \cdots, (x_i, y_i)(i = 1, \cdots, n; y_i \in \{-1, 1\})$ using a hyperplane $\omega^T \cdot x + b = 0$ divide $y_1, \cdots, y_n$ error-free into two categories. In practice, it is necessary to separate a sample from multiple samples. This requires the construction of multiple classifiers. The commonly used SVM multivalued classifier construction methods include one-to-many method, one-to-one method, one-time solution method, decision directed acyclic graph method, binary tree-based multi-class support vector machine classification method, and the like. The number of sub-classifiers required by the SVM based on the binary tree structure is small. As the classification progresses, fewer training samples are required and the classification efficiency is high, which is very suitable for the case of many modulation methods.

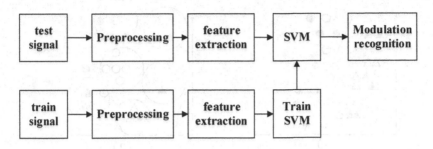

Fig. 1. Identification framework of the SVM

In this paper, a support vector machine based on binary tree structure is selected, and Gaussian kernel functions are used to classify signals.

3 Algorithms and Models

Based on the entropy feature of the signal, this paper adopts the density clustering method to sample and reconstruct the training set, then uses the reconstructed new training set to train the support vector machine, and finally inputs the test set for modulation recognition. Figure 2 shows the specific identification model. We call this model the D-SVM.

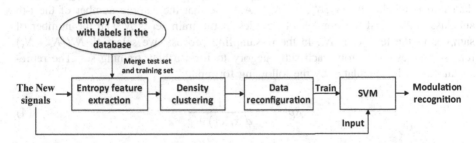

Fig. 2. Modulation recognition model based on density clustering data reconstruction

In order to understand the process of sample refactoring, we demonstrate the basic idea of this method using two dimensional data classification. As shown in Fig. 3, the training samples are represented by solid points, and the samples to be recognized are represented by hollow points. The triangle and the circle represent different categories respectively. As you can see in Fig. 3, when the test set is deviant from the training set, the traditional SVM will have a wrong classification, and our method will effectively repair the deviation to improve the accuracy of the classification.

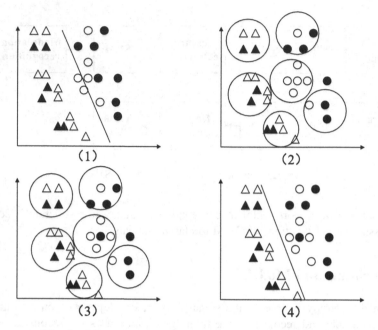

Fig. 3. Schematic diagram of sample reconstruction process

The entropy feature of the received signal is extracted and then integrated with the original entropy feature database. Through density clustering, we can aggregate the data into n subclasses $\{N_1, N_2, \cdots, N_n\}$. Assume that the sample number of the i-th subclass is N_{C_i}, and the number of samples in the train set is N_t and the number of samples in the test set is N_s. In the re-sampling process, we select $N_{C_i}N_t/(N_t+N_s)$ representatives' data from each sub-category to form a new training set. The representative can be calculated by the following formula:

$$Rp(x_i) = \frac{1}{d(x_i, c_k) + \varepsilon} \tag{4}$$

In the formula, $c_k = \frac{1}{N_{c_k}}\sum_{\ell=1}^{N_{c_k}} x_\ell$ represents the cluster center of the k-th subclass of x_i. The constant $\varepsilon = 1.0 \times 10^{-3}$ is to prevent the value of $Rp(x_i)$ from infinity when x_i is just in the center.

The modulation recognition algorithm based on density clustering and SVM is as follows:

Input: train data, test data

Output: Modulation recognition result

Step1:Initialize the cluster sample and merge the training set with the test set $N = N_t \cup N_s$

Step2:Perform density clustering on the merged cluster samples to obtain n sub-classes

Step3:According to formula (4), calculate the representative $Rp(x_i)$ of each sub-category N_C, sort the representative data from the largest to the smallest, and select the first $N_{C_i} N_t / (N_t + N_s)$ data to form a new training set.

Step4:Put the test set into the SVM after training the SVM with the new training set to perform modulation recognition

Step5: Output modulation recognition result

---

4 Experiment

The experiments in this paper have selected six kinds of digital modulation signals, including 2ASK, 2FSK, 8FSK, BPSK, QPSK and 16QAM. For each signal, the sampling frequency is 16 kHz and the carrier frequency is 4 kHz. The SNR ranges from −5 dB to 10 dB in steps of 1 dB. We extracted six entropy features of the signal, including power spectrum Shannon entropy, wavelet energy spectrum entropy, bis-pectrum entropy, sample entropy, singular spectrum Shannon entropy, and singular spectrum index entropy. The entire data set is divided into train data and test data. At each SNR, we collected 1200 data points for each entropy feature, each of which has 200 data points.

At first we extracted the entropy features. From Fig. 4 we can see the distribution of entropy features under different SNR. Since the entropy value is some discrete data points, we use the box diagram to better characterize it. We can see from the figure that the sample entropy of the BPSK signal has quite a lot of outliers, which makes it impossible to classify using sample entropy alone. So we adopt the entropy feature fusion method for clustering and modulation recognition.

In this paper, we use the SVM based on the Gaussian kernel function and cross-validation to determine the parameters to classify. We have separately used the traditional SVM architecture and our improved SVM framework based on density clustering reconstruction (D-SVM). The D-SVM recognition framework was tested and the experimental results can be seen form the Fig. 5.

From the curves, we can see that the improved D-SVM recognition framework has approximately 70% recognition rate due to the performance of the traditional method at the SNR of −5 dB. The degree of smoothness is better than the traditional SVM recognition framework, which shows that the stability of the algorithm is better. In the case of a SNR greater than 10 dB, the recognition rates of both are close to 100%. In short, the improvement effect of this algorithm is still ideal.

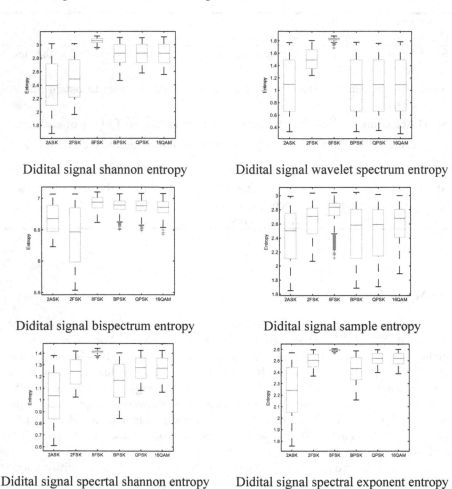

Didital signal shannon entropy

Didital signal wavelet spectrum entropy

Didital signal bispectrum entropy

Didital signal sample entropy

Didital signal specrtal shannon entropy

Didital signal spectral exponent entropy

Fig. 4. In different signals with mixed signal-to-noise ratios (from −5 dB to 10 dB), the box plot distribution of entropy features includes the maximum, the seventy-fifth percentile, the median, and the twenty-fifth percentile and minimum.

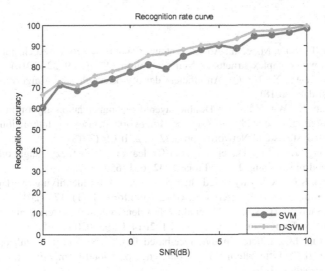

Fig. 5. The recognition rate curves of the two methods at SNR of −5 dB to 10 dB

5 Conclusion

In this paper, we proposes a new method for modulation recognition based on SVM with density clustering data reconstruction. We selected six digital modulation signals, including 2ASK, 2FSK, 8FSK, BPSK, QPSK, and 16QAM, and extracted six entropy features: Power Spectrum Shannon Entropy, Wavelet Energy Spectral Entropy, Bispectrum Entropy, Sample Entropy, Singular Spectrum Shannon Entropy, and Singular Spectrum Exponential Entropy. We fuse these six entropy features, and then density-cluster the entropy features, resample the clustered data set to generate a new training set, and finally train the SVM with the new training set, then the signal Identify. The experimental results show that this method not only improves the accuracy of the traditional support vector machine but also enhances the stability of the recognition framework and has a high application value.

Acknowledgment. This work is supported by the National Natural Science Foundation of China (61771154) and the Fundamental Research Funds for the Central Universities (HEUCFG201830).

Meantime, all the authors declare that there is no conflict of interests regarding the publication of this article.

We gratefully thank of very useful discussions of reviewers.

References

1. Lv, Y., Ma, T., Tang, M., et al.: An efficient and scalable density-based clustering algorithm for datasets with complex structures. Neurocomputing **171**(C), 9–22 (2016)
2. Boonchoo, T., Ao, X., He, Q.: An efficient density-based clustering algorithm for higher-dimensional data (2018)
3. Chen, J., Lin, X., Wu, Y., et al.: Double layered recommendation algorithm based on fast density clustering: case study on Yelp social networks dataset. In: International Workshop on Complex Systems and Networks, pp. 242–252. IEEE (2018)
4. Liu, Z., Yang, J.A., Liu, H., et al.: Transfer learning with fuzzy neighborhood density clustering and re-sampling. J. Sig. Process. **32**, 651–659 (2016)
5. Hu, L., Chan, K.C.: A density-based clustering approach for identifying overlapping protein complexes with functional preferences. BMC Bioinform. **16**(1), 174 (2015)
6. Amini, A., Saboohi, H., Wah, T.Y., et al.: A fast density-based clustering algorithm for real-time Internet of Things stream. Sci. World J. **2014**(1), 926020 (2014)
7. Dai, B.R., Lin, I.C.: Efficient map/reduce-based DBSCAN algorithm with optimized data partition. In: IEEE Fifth International Conference on Cloud Computing, pp. 59–66. IEEE Computer Society (2012)
8. Vedaldi, A., Zisserman, A.: Efficient additive kernels via explicit feature maps. IEEE Trans. Pattern Anal. Mach. Intell. **34**(3), 480–492 (2012)
9. Zhao, Z., Shang, J.: A new method for modulation type recognition based on the time frequency representations. In: International Conference on Signal Processing, vol. 1, pp. 208–211. IEEE (2002)
10. He, Z.Y., Cai, Y.M., Qian, Q.Q.: Study of wavelet entropy theory and its application in electric power system fault detection. In: Proceedings of the CSEE (2005)
11. Liu, T., Guan, Y., Lin, Y.: Research on modulation recognition with ensemble learning. EURASIP J. Wirel. Commun. Netw. **2017**(1), 179 (2017)
12. Pawar, S.U., Doherty, J.F.: Modulation recognition in continuous phase modulation using approximate entropy. IEEE Trans. Inf. Forensics Secur. **6**(3), 843–852 (2011)
13. Kadambe, S., Jiang, Q.: Classification of modulation of signals of interest. In: Digital Signal Processing Workshop. 2004 IEEE Signal Processing Education Workshop, 2004, pp. 226–230. IEEE (2004)
14. Xiao, Y., Wang, H., Xu, W.: Parameter selection of Gaussian kernel for one-class SVM. IEEE Trans. Cybern. **45**(5), 941–953 (2017)
15. Imdad, A., Bres, S., Eglin, V., et al.: Writer identification using steered hermite features and SVM. In: International Conference on Document Analysis and Recognition, pp. 839–843. IEEE (2017)
16. Wu, J., Yang, H.: Linear regression-based efficient SVM learning for large-scale classification. IEEE Trans. Neural Netw. Learn. Syst. **26**(10), 2357–2369 (2017)
17. Osuna, E., Freund, R., Girosi, F.: Training support vector machines: an application to face detection. In: 1997 IEEE Computer Society Conference on Computer Vision and Pattern Recognition. Proceeding, pp. 130–136. IEEE (2002)

A Target Localization Algorithm for Wireless Sensor Network Based on Compressed Sensing

Zhaoyue Zhang[1], Hongxu Tao[2], and Yun Lin[2(✉)]

[1] College of Air Traffic Management, Civil Aviation University of China,
Tianjin, People's Republic of China
[2] College of Information and Communication Engineering, Harbin Engineering
University, Harbin, People's Republic of China
linyun_phd@hrbeu.edu.cn

Abstract. The sparse target location algorithm based on orth can solve the problem that the sampling dictionary does not satisfy the RIP property. Compared with the traditional method, the orth preprocessing can reduce the energy consumption and communication overhead, but the orth pretreatment will affect the sparsity of the original signal. So that the positioning accuracy is affected to a certain extent. In this paper, a sparse target location algorithm based on QR-decomposition is proposed. On the basis of orth algorithm, the sampling dictionary is decomposed by QR, which can't change the sparsity of the original signal under the premise of satisfying the RIP property. The problem of sparse target location based on network is transformed into the problem of target location based on compressed perception, and the localization error is reduced. The experimental results show that the location performance of sparse target location algorithm based on QR-decomposition and centroid algorithm is much better than that the sparse target location algorithm based on orth, and the accuracy of target location is greatly improved.

Keywords: Compressed sensing · Wireless Sensor Network ·
QR-decomposition · Localization

1 Introduction

At present, Wireless Sensor Network (WSN) has been widely used to complete data acquisition and transmission tasks in various fields (such as battlefield reconnaissance, environmental monitoring, Internet of things, etc.). The target localization of WSN is becoming a hot research topic and one of the key technologies for WSN application. However, a large number of cheap sensors have limited the computing power, communication ability and energy of nodes in the network, which also bring great pressure to WSN. Recently, compressed sensing theory has brought new application opportunities to WSN. Sensor nodes only need to sample a small amount of sensing data and complete sampling and compression in the WSN target localization algorithm based on compressed sensing [1–3]. This method reduces the standard of perceptron nodes. Signal reconstruction is usually carried out in information fusion center, because the energy of information fusion center is not limited and has powerful computing power.

S. Liu and G. Yang (Eds.): ADHIP 2018, LNICST 279, pp. 485–495, 2019.
https://doi.org/10.1007/978-3-030-19086-6_54

Nowadays, the application of compressed sensing to target location in WSN has become a research hotspot.

In literature [4], based on the idea of multi-resolution analysis, an iterative back-tracking compression sensing algorithm is designed. This method is characterized by simultaneous multi-target localization, and greatly reduces the amount of data in network communication, thus prolonging the network life. The cost is the increase in the complexity of the fusion center. Literature [5] proposed a new method of target location based on sparse signal reconstruction in wireless sensor networks, but the communication overhead is higher. In order to solve the problem of target location accuracy in wireless sensor networks, literature [6] proposed a target location algorithm based on curve fitting. But this algorithm has high complexity. Tang proposed a Bayesian CS based detection algorithm in literature [7]. However, in the process of signal reconstruction, the selection of observation vectors requires the consumption of energy to select adjacent nodes. Further, it can lead to premature death of nodes easily and even cause the whole network to fail. Literature [8] proposed a sparse target localization algorithm based on orth preprocessing. In this sparse target location model, the observation dictionary is considered to be established by the signal attenuation model. However, the observation dictionary does not satisfy the Restricted Isometry Property (RIP) [9] property. In order to satisfy the RIP property of the observation dictionary, a scheme of orth preprocessing was proposed. However, during the process of orth preprocessing, the sparsity of the original sparse signal is affected. Furthermore, the reconstruction performance of compressed sensing is affected, and the position performance of the final target is also affected.

In this paper, compressed sensing theory is applied to multi-target localization in WSN and a new target location algorithm based on QR-decomposition for sparse target localization is proposed. This method solves the problem that the dictionary of observation cannot satisfy the RIP property. The algorithm obtains a new observation dictionary by QR-decomposition and satisfies the RIP property. It does not affect the sparsity of the original sparse signal in the process of QR-decomposition preprocessing. Therefore, this method ensures the reconstruction performance and reduces the position error.

2 The System Model

In this paper, we assume that there are randomly distributed M sensors with known positions and K unknown targets in a square sensing area and mutual independence between goals. We divide the square area into N grids evenly. The system model is showed in Fig. 1. The localization problem of the target node is transformed to target node location problem based grid. In order to locate all the targets, sensor nodes need to receive periodic signals for each target in the sensing area firstly. Then the signal intensity values of the respective targets are sent to the fusion center respectively. Finally, the fusion center uses the target location algorithm based on compressed sensing to locate the target and determine the specific location of the target in the grid.

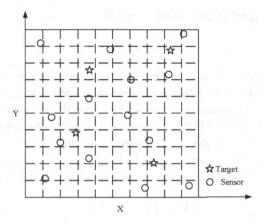

Fig. 1. The system model

The signal intensity received by sensor nodes will be attenuated because the intensity of wireless signal is easily affected by environmental factors such as obstacle occlusion and multipath propagation. This paper adopts the signal fading model [10] in IEEE 802.15.4 standard as follows:

$$\text{RSS}(d) = \begin{cases} P_t - 40.2 - 20\log d, & d \leq 8 \\ P_t - 58.5 - 33\log d, & d > 8 \end{cases} \tag{1}$$

Among, RSS(d) is received signal intensity, d is the distance between the source and the receiver in grid, P_t is signal intensity of source. The intensity of signal reception from the i grid to the j grid is:

$$\text{RSS}(d_{i,j}) = \begin{cases} P_t - 40.2 - 20\log d_{i,j}, & d_{i,j} \leq 8 \\ P_t - 58.5 - 33\log d_{i,j}, & d_{i,j} > 8 \end{cases} \tag{2}$$

Among, $1 \leq i \leq N$, $1 \leq j \leq N$. The Euclidean distance from the i grid to the j grid is:

$$d_{i,j} = \sqrt{(x_i - x_j)^2 + (y_i - y_j)^2} \tag{3}$$

Among, (x_i, y_i) is the coordinate of i grid. (x_j, y_j) is the coordinate of j grid.

3 Target Location Algorithm Based on QR-Decomposition [11]

To solve the RIP problem, a sparse target localization algorithm based on orth pre-processing is proposed in literature [8]. The algorithm preprocesses the orth of the signal firstly. Then, signal reconstruction and target positioning are carried out again.

The process of signal preprocessing is as follow:

$$Y' = TY = T(\boldsymbol{\Phi\Psi\mu} + \boldsymbol{\varepsilon}) \tag{4}$$

Among, T representation of a linear transformation operator. $\boldsymbol{\Phi}$ is $M \times N$ observation matrix, and $\boldsymbol{\Psi}$ is a $N \times N$ sparse transform basis. We can get $\Psi_{i,j} = RSS(d_{i,j})$ by the signal transmission attenuation model. $\boldsymbol{\mu}_k$ represents the location of the target in the grid, and $\boldsymbol{\varepsilon}$ is $M \times K$ gauss white noise matrix. The observational dictionary is $A = \boldsymbol{\Phi\Psi}$ and $T = \boldsymbol{Q}A^*$. $(\cdot)^*$ is the inverse transformation operator of a matrix. $\boldsymbol{Q} = \text{orth}(A^T)^T$, $\boldsymbol{Q} = \text{orth}(A^T)^T$ is orthogonal transformation of matrix column. $(\cdot)^T$ is the transposed operator of a matrix. Signal observation value can be expressed as follow:

$$Y' = TY = \boldsymbol{Q\mu} + \boldsymbol{\varepsilon}' \tag{5}$$

Where, $\boldsymbol{Q}$ is an orthogonal transform matrix and the properties of RIP can be satisfied preferably. The method can improve the signal reconstruction performance and improve the positioning accuracy of multi-target ultimately.

However, the algorithm has $Y' = \boldsymbol{Q}A^*A\boldsymbol{\mu} + \boldsymbol{\varepsilon}'$ in the preprocessing process, so that $\boldsymbol{\mu}' = A^*A\boldsymbol{\mu}$, then $Y' = \boldsymbol{Q\mu}' + \boldsymbol{\varepsilon}'$. Because the atoms in the observational dictionary A are related, the elements on the non-diagonal line of A^*A are not 0. In this way, the sparsity of $\boldsymbol{\mu}'$ will be affected and the performance of signal reconstruction and target location will be affected. Based on this, this paper proposes a sparse target localization algorithm based on QR-decomposition. This method obtains a new observation dictionary by QR-decomposition of the observation dictionary A, which effectively satisfies the RIP property without affecting the sparsity of the original sparse signal. The reconstruction performance of the algorithm is guaranteed and the position accuracy of the target is improved.

First, the observation dictionary A is QR-decomposed, which is shown in the following formula:

$$A^T = \boldsymbol{Q}R \tag{6}$$

Where $\boldsymbol{Q}$ is a $N \times N$ standard orthogonal matrix, R is an upper triangular matrix of $N \times M$. Therefore, we obtain the matrix U as follows:

$$U = S^*A = S^*R^T\boldsymbol{Q}^T = [I_{M\times M} \, \boldsymbol{0}_{M\times(N-M)}]\boldsymbol{Q}^T \tag{7}$$

Where S as a lower triangular matrix, and $I_{M\times M}$ is a unit matrix of order M. From the above formula, we can know that the matrix formed by the first M line of $\boldsymbol{Q}^T$ is the matrix U. Therefore, the row vectors of U are all unit vectors and are orthogonal to each other.

Then, the matrix U is listed as a unit, and the new observation dictionary B is determined as follows:

$$B = U \begin{bmatrix} 1/\|U_1\| & 0 & \cdots & 0 \\ 0 & 1/\|U_2\| & \cdots & 0 \\ \vdots & \vdots & \ddots & \vdots \\ 0 & 0 & \cdots & 1/\|U_N\| \end{bmatrix} \tag{8}$$

Where $U_1, U_2, \cdots, U_N$ is a column vector of the matrix U; $\|\cdot\|$ is the modulus of the vector. Obviously, B is obtained by unitized, which selecting the M rows of a standard orthogonal matrix Q^T of $N \times N$.

Combined with the definition of partial orthogonal matrix, it is known that: B is a partially orthogonal matrix, and a partial orthogonal matrix is one of the commonly used observation dictionaries in CS theory. Therefore, B is completely satisfied with the RIP property.

Thus, for the left side of observation Y multiplied by an inverse matrix S^*, the new observation value Y' is obtained as follows:

$$Y' = S^*Y = S^*A\mu = B \begin{bmatrix} \|U_1\| & 0 & \cdots & 0 \\ 0 & \|U_2\| & \cdots & 0 \\ \vdots & \vdots & \ddots & \vdots \\ 0 & 0 & \cdots & \|U_N\| \end{bmatrix} \mu = B\mu' \tag{9}$$

It can be seen from the above formula that μ' is obtained by multiplying the left side of μ and a diagonal matrix. Since μ is sparse, μ' is also sparse, and the sparsity of μ' and μ is the same.

Because matrix B completely satisfies the RIP property, therefore, according to the compression perception theory, μ' can be reconstructed accurately, and then the original signal μ can be obtained by the following formula:

$$\mu = \begin{bmatrix} 1/\|U_1\| & 0 & \cdots & 0 \\ 0 & 1/\|U_2\| & \cdots & 0 \\ \vdots & \vdots & \ddots & \vdots \\ 0 & 0 & \cdots & 1/\|U_N\| \end{bmatrix} \mu' \tag{10}$$

In the grid-based target location model, μ is an approximate sparse signal because the target is often not in the center of the grid. In order to reduce the location error, the column vector μ_k of the reconstructed signal is normalized as the weight $\omega_k(n)$ of each grid to estimate the position of the k target.

$$\omega_k(n) = \mu_k(n) / \sum_{n=1}^{N} \mu_k(n) \tag{11}$$

In the formula, $\omega_k(n)$ is the weight value of the n grid for the k th target coordinate estimation. Finally, the weighted centroid algorithm [12–14] is used to find out the position of the k th target:

$$(x_k, y_k) = \sum_{n=1}^{N} \omega_k(n)(x_n, y_n) \tag{12}$$

Where (x_k, y_k) denotes the estimated position of the $k(1 \leq k \leq K)$ target and (x_n, y_n) denotes the position of the $n(1 \leq n \leq N)$ grid.

4   Experimental Results and Analysis

The sparse target location algorithm based on QR-decomposition (in this paper) and the sparse target location algorithm based on orth (contrast algorithm) are simulated and compared in Matlab. The compressed sensing reconstruction algorithm is OMP algorithm. The sensing region is set to a square region of 100 m × 100 m, the sensor is randomly distributed in the sensing region, and the sensing region is divided into 10 × 10 grids. In the experiment, the intensity of the target signal received by the original observation dictionary and sensor is simulated by the signal fading model of IEEE 802.15.4 standard in reference [9], in which the target signal transmit power is −30 dBm and the noise is white Gaussian noise.

4.1   Comparison of Multi-target Location Performance

As shown in Fig. 2, when SNR is 30 dB, the number of sensors $M = 8$, the location diagram of $K = 6$ targets is given. The circle denotes the position of the target, and the right triangle and the left triangle denote the target estimation position of the contrast algorithm and the algorithm in this paper, respectively. It can be seen from the diagram that for all the six targets in the contrast algorithm, only 3 targets in the target grid are the same as the actual grid of the target, and the algorithm in the paper is that all 6 target positions and the actual location of the target are in the same grid. In other words, the performance of the proposed algorithm is superior to that of the contrast algorithm. Although the contrast algorithm satisfies the RIP property of the observation dictionary, it affects the sparsity of the original signal during the orth preprocessing process, thus affecting the performance of the algorithm. The algorithm in the paper not only ensures that the observation dictionary satisfies the RIP property, but also does not affect the sparseness of the original signal. Therefore, the algorithm in this paper has better position performance.

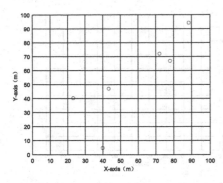

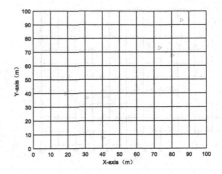

(a)The actual location of the target   (b) Target estimation position of contrast algorithm

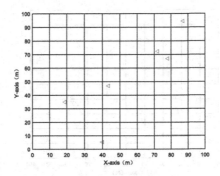

(c)Target estimation position of the algorithm in this paper

Fig. 2. Target location ($k = 6$)

When the other conditions are unchanged, the number of targets is increased to 25, and the target positioning diagram shown in Fig. 3 is obtained. It can be found from Fig. 3 that the reconstruction error of most of the targets in the algorithm is very small, and the comparison algorithm has a very large position error for some targets. Therefore, the position performance of the algorithm is still far superior to the comparison algorithm, and the algorithm is more adaptable to the target number.

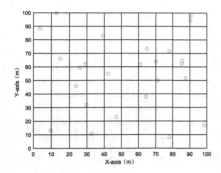 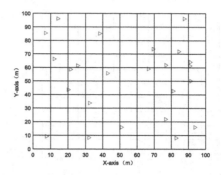

(a)The actual location of the target   (b) Target estimation position of contrast algorithm

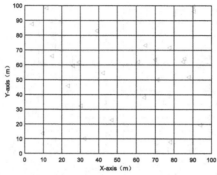

(c)Target estimation position of the algorithm in this paper

Fig. 3. Target location ($k = 25$)

4.2   The Influence of Region Range on Location Performance

Figure 4 is a positioning performance diagram in which the sensor $M = 8$ and the target number is $K = 6$, and the average location error of the target changes with the size of the monitoring area. It can be seen from the Fig. 4 that when the number of sensors and targets is fixed, the localization errors of both algorithms increase with the increase of the region, but the average localization error of the paper algorithm is still much lower than that of the contrast algorithm. It can also be found from the diagram that the location error of the proposed algorithm is less than 10 m even when the length of the region is 500 m, while that of the contrast algorithm is more than 40 m. Therefore, even in larger areas, the algorithm has smaller positioning error, less energy consumption and stronger applicability.

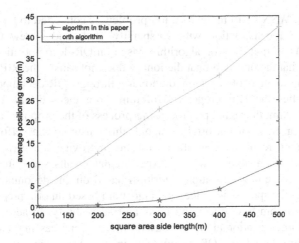

Fig. 4. Relationship between location performance and square area side length

4.3   The Influence of Number of Targets on Location Performance

Figure 5 is the location performance diagram of the target location error varying with the number of targets in the monitoring area when the SNR is 30 dB and $M = 8$. It can be seen from the figure that the target error of both algorithms increases with the increase of the target number when the target number $K \leq 25$, but the average positioning error of the paper algorithm is still much lower than the comparison algorithm. It is also consistent with the fact in CS theory that the larger the sparse degree, the more accurate the recovery of sparse vector is. When the number of targets $K \geq 25$, the location error between them tends to be stable. Therefore, under the same conditions, the proposed algorithm can locate more targets, with smaller location error and stronger robustness.

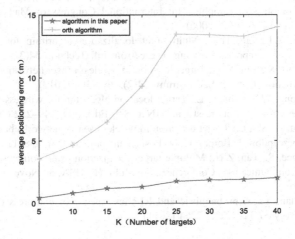

Fig. 5. Relationship between location performance and number of targets

5 Conclusion

In this paper, the WSN multi target location problem is converted to the problem of N dimension vector reconstruction with K sparsity of 1, and a new target location algorithm, a sparse target location algorithm based on QR-decomposition, is proposed for the problem that the observational dictionary does not satisfy the RIP property. The algorithm obtains a new observation dictionary through QR-decomposition, which completely satisfies the RIP property. Different from the orth-based sparse target localization algorithm, the signal preprocessing process of the proposed algorithm does not affect the sparseness of the original signal, thus ensuring the performance of the compressed sensing reconstruction algorithm and improving the performance of the multi-target localization algorithm. The experimental results show that the location accuracy of the sparse target location algorithm based on QR-decomposition is much better than that of the sparse target location algorithm based on orth preprocessing, and the proposed algorithm has better robustness and adaptability. In addition, compared with the sparse target location algorithm based on orth preprocessing, the sparse target location algorithm based on QR-decomposition has less computation and lower complexity.

Acknowledgment. This work is supported by the National Natural Science Foundation of China (61771154) and the Fundamental Research Funds for the Central Universities (HEUCFG201830).

Meantime, all the authors declare that there is no conflict of interests regarding the publication of this article.

We gratefully thank of very useful discussions of reviewers.

References

1. Ren, F.Y., Huang, H.N., Lin, C.: Wireless sensor network. Softw. J. **14**(2), 1148–1157 (2003)
2. Donoho, D.L.: Compressed sensing. IEEE Trans. Inf. Theory **52**(4), 1289–1306 (2003)
3. Candes, E.: Compressive sampling. In: International Congress of Mathematics, Madrid, Spain, vol. 3, pp. 1433–1452 (2006)
4. He, F.X., Yu, Z.J., Liu, H.T.: Multi-target localization algorithm for wireless sensor networks based on compressed sensing. J. Electron. Inf. Technol. **34**(3), 716–721 (2012)
5. Wang, Y., Wang, X., Sun, X.Y.: Target location in wireless sensor networks based on sparse signal reconstruction. Chin. J. Sci. Instrum. **33**(2), 362–368 (2012)
6. Jiao, Z.Q., Xiong, W.L., Zhang, L.: Target location algorithm for wireless sensor networks based on curve fitting. J. Southeast Univ. (Nat. Sci. Ed.), (s1), 249–252 (2008)
7. Tang, L., Zhou, Z., Shi, L.: Target detection in wireless sensor networks based on leach and compression perception. J. Beijing Univ. Posts Telecommun. **34**(3), 8–11 (2011)
8. Feng, C., Valaee, S., Tan, Z.H.: Multiple target localization using compressive sensing. In: IEEE Global Communications Conference, Honolulu, HI, USA, 30 November–4 December, pp. 1–6 (2009)
9. Candès, E., Plan, Y.: A probabilistic and RIP less theory of compressed sensing. IEEE Trans. Inf. Theory **57**(11), 7235–7254 (2011)

10. Au, W.S.A., Feng, C., Valaee, S.: Indoor tracking and navigation using received signal strength and compressive sensing on a mobile device. IEEE Trans. Mob. Comput. **99**, 1–14 (2012)
11. Xu, Y.L.: Research on location algorithm of wireless sensor networks based on C compressive sensing (2013)
12. Bulusu, N., Hidemann, J., Estrin, D.: GPS-less low cost outdoor localization for very small devices. IEEE Pers. Commun. Mag. **7**(5), 28–34 (2000)
13. Wang, J., Urriza, P., Han, Y.X., Cabric, D.: Weighted centroid localization algorithm: theoretical analysis and distributed implementation. IEEE Trans. Wirel. Commun. **10**(10), 3403–3413 (2011)
14. Yang, X.Y., Kong, Q.R., Dai, X.J.: An improved weighted centroid location algorithm. J. Xi'an Jiaotong

A News Text Clustering Method Based on Similarity of Text Labels

Yuqiang Tong[(✉)] and Lize Gu

School of Cyberspace Security, Beijing University of Posts
and Telecommunications, Beijing 100091, China
1172183723@qq.com, glzisc@bupt.edu.cn

Abstract. As an important text type, news texts have great research value in data mining, Such as hotspot tracking, public opinion analysis and other fields. News text clustering is a common method for studying the trend of news and hotspot tracking. Most of the existing clustering methods are based on the vector space model, with calculating the TF-IDF of words in the news text as feature items of the text. To improve the performance of clustering in the news texts, this paper presents a new clustering algorithm, this algorithm expresses the news text as a series of Text labels, which effectively solves the problem that the data latitude is too high, and the clusters is too hard to express. At the same time, by using a conceptual clustering algorithm, this method effectively reduces the number of comparisons. The experimental results show that the algorithm based on similarity of text labels improves the quality of clustering compared to traditional clustering methods.

Keywords: Data clustering · MinHash · Hierarchical clustering

1 Introduction

With the help of efficient information transmission on the Internet, it becomes faster and faster for a news from generation to public opinion. Through text clustering, news media and government departments can effectively find hot news and measure the development trend of news popularity. Therefore, clustering for news texts has become an important research topic in text clustering.

The traditional text clustering method is mainly to transform the text into a text vector model to deal with. By cutting the text into individual words, the doc information will be analyzed, TFIDF is a universal used text information [1], then comparing the similarity of the text vectors of the two articles and cluster the similar text. There are many ways to cluster text, such as K-means algorithm. Recently many text clustering algorithms based on K-means algorithms has been proposed, in paper [2] an algorithm based on the combination of nearest neighbor algorithm and K-means algorithm is proposed, which can lead to results with steady and high clustering quality. Except TFIDF, there are many other ways to measure the similarity. Hamming distance, Cosine Similarity and Euclidean Distance are common used.

Because the length of the news text is uncertain (a few hundred words to a thousand words), most of the texts after transformation vectors are high-dimensional sparse

S. Liu and G. Yang (Eds.): ADHIP 2018, LNICST 279, pp. 496–503, 2019.
https://doi.org/10.1007/978-3-030-19086-6_55

matrices, and the clustering effect of the traditional algorithms in high-dimensional space have a bad result.

In addition, in dealing with long texts, many targeted algorithms are proposed. Sim-Hash [3] is a common method to deal with it, which converts a text into a Hash Code by transforming the words after hashing, calculating the Distance between the Hash Code for clustering. The original purpose of Sim-Hash is to remove repeat texts from Massive texts. Since the text is converted into Hash Code, the amount of information is greatly compressed, so the effect of processing short texts (within 200 words) is not good enough. In paper [4] an algorithm based on Sim-Hash have a good performance in short message, but it is hard to process the news dataset with a large number of texts with different length.

In view of the shortcomings of the existing news text clustering methods, this paper proposes a news text clustering method by calculating the similarity of text labels. Compared with other methods, this method greatly reduces the dimensions of documents and speeds up clustering with a good clustering quality.

2 Related Theoretical Explanations

2.1 Document Dimension Reduction

The Jaccard Similarity. The Jaccard similarity between set A and set B is defined as the ratio of the intersection of A and B to the size of the union [5], as follow:

$$\text{Jaccard}(A, B) = |A \cap B| / |A \cup B| \tag{1}$$

K-shingle. A relatively common practice when comparing text similarity is to use the K-shingle set to represent a document [6]. Indicates the document, K-shingle is defined as all substrings of length K in the document. Suppose a document is a string: "abcde", then the 2-shingle collection of the document is: "ab", "bc", "cd", "de". The similarity between two texts can be measured by calculating the Jaccard similarity of the K-shingle set of two texts. When selecting a K value, the following condition should be satisfied: Select a sufficiently large K to ensure that the probability of substrings in any given K-shingle set appearing in other sets is low enough.

The MinHash Algorithm. In computer science and data mining, the MinHash (or the min-wise independent permutations locality sensitive hashing scheme) is a technique for quickly estimating how similar two sets are. The scheme was invented by Broder [7], and initially used in the AltaVista search engine to detect duplicate web pages and eliminate them from search results [8]. It has also been applied in large-scale clustering problems, such as clustering documents by the similarity of their sets of words [7].

Guess a minimum hash, which is a hash vector of a text, and each bit of the vector indicates whether a certain K-string of K-shingle corresponding to the bit appears in the text. Since this minimum hash is a sparse 0, 1 vector. Therefore, the MinHash corresponding to the minimum hash is the number of the first k nonzero bit of the smallest hash, as follow:

$$min_{h,k}(v) = \arg\min_k\{h(v[i])\} \tag{2}$$

where v is a K-shingle vector, $h(v[i])$ is a 0, 1 vector of the K-shingle vector.

An important conclusion of MinHash is that the MinHash equal probability of two sets is equal to the Jaccard similarity between two sets. For a given set A and B, the Jaccard similarity of the two sets can be expressed as follow:

$$\text{Jaccard}(A, B) = P\big(min_{h,k}(v_A) = min_{h,k}(v_B)\big) \tag{3}$$

As the conclude of the MinHash algorithm, calculating the Jaccard similarity of two documents can be replaced to calculate the equal probability of the MinHash vector, so it is a good choice to dimensionality reduce by converting documents to MinHash vector.

2.2   The Clustering Algorithm

In general, clustering methods include hierarchical clustering and partitioning [9].

The most commonly used partitioning method is K-means clustering and related deformation methods [10]. By selecting a clustering center, the clustering center of the class and the set of classes are updated via iterative rules until the clustering center no longer changes.

There are two Shortcomings of partitioning in news texts clustering. First, it is hard to determine the number of clustering center, because to estimate how many news events will be reported each day is a difficult thing. Besides, the partitioning method such as K-means must calculate the distance between all the samples and the cluster center at once iterative, it will cost too much time.

Two types of hierarchical clustering are commonly used: Agglomerative and Divisive [9]. Agglomerative means that each the original sample has their own class, from the bottom to the up, according to similarity rules, merge different classes to reduce the number of classes until the stop condition is met. Divisive means all the samples share the same class, and from the top to the bottom, by using the similarity rules, splitting the classes until the stop condition is met.

Commonly used hierarchical clustering methods are Cobweb [11], CLUSETR/2 [12], and UPGMA [13].

Based on the above reasons, this paper adopts the idea of hierarchical clustering to implement news text clustering. When text clustering, different kinds of labels can be used to achieve clustering at different levels.

3 Proposed Labels Based Clustering Algorithm

3.1 News Text Labels Generate

Considering the influence of different paragraphs or sentence weights at different positions and the title influence in the news text, there are three kinds of labels to summarize, title label (generated by the title text), sentence label (generated by the start sentences of all the paragraph), text label (generated by the main text of the news).

Through the Eq. (2), the title label, sentence label, and text label can be expressed by the follow:

$$min_{h,k}(v_{title}) = \arg \min_k \{h(v_{title}[i])\} \tag{4}$$

$$min_{h,k}(v_{sentence}) = \arg \min_k \{h(v_{sentence}[i])\} \tag{5}$$

$$min_{h,k}(v_{text}) = \arg \min_k \{h(v_{text}[i])\} \tag{6}$$

For the text, it is much longer than the title or the sentences of the news, only using a MinHash vector to indicate the contents of the main text may cost a high bias. To avoid the problem, there will give several of different MinHash to group a set to indicate the text, as follow:

$$min_{H,k}(v_{text}) = \{min_{h_1,k}(v_{text}), min_{h_2,k}(v_{text}), \ldots min_{h_t,k}(v_{text})\} \tag{7}$$

Where H is a set of different kinds of MinHash, and $h_1, h_2, \ldots h_t \in H$.

According to the generate method of the labels, a label set of the news text can be expressed by the follow:

$$S_{H,k}(Doc) = \{min_{h,k}(v_{title}), min_{h,k}(v_{sentence}), min_{H,k}(v_{text})\} \tag{8}$$

Where $S_{H,k}(Doc)$ is the label set of a news text, $min_{h,k}(v_{title})$ is the label of title, $min_{h,k}(v_{sentence})$ is the label of sentence, $min_{H,k}(v_{text})$ is the label set of text. As for the size of the news text label set, guess the average text length is m, through the MinHash algorithm, it became to $(2+t)k$, which is small the original length.

By the conclusion of the MinHash algorithm, the similarity of two labels can be calculated by the follow:

Considering each bit in the label value, the probability p of two bits have the same number same to the Jaccard similarity of the two texts. Therefor for the K bit in the label value, the similarity can be expressed as the same number of bits divided by K:

$$\text{Dist}(d_1, d_2) = \sum_{i=1}^{k} x_i \oplus x_i \tag{9}$$

Where x_i and y_i are the values on the i th bit of the label d_1, d_2.

3.2   The Hierarchical Clustering of News Text

In the label generation method, the label set of each news text contains a title label, a sentence label, and t text labels (8). When clustering, different labels can be used to achieve clustering at different levels.

First consider the title label. For two title label, each on has a length K MinHash vector, by the similarity algorithm of labels (9), for two texts with Jaccard similarity p, the expectation of the same number of bits in the two title labels is $p \times k$, so it is an idea to cluster two texts into same group which have a same number of bits larger than $p \times k$.

The sentence label can be used same with the title label, through the hierarchical clustering by using the title label and the sentence label, the news texts which have a similarity title and similarity sentence.

For each group, the final step is clustering the texts by using text label set. Consider any two texts, each of them has t different text labels. If their Jaccard similarity is p, the probability of t text label pairs at least has one same label pair is follow:

$$P(label1, label2) = 1 - \left(1 - p^k\right)^t \qquad (10)$$

Where p is the Jaccard similarity of two labels, k is the length of MinHash vector, t is the length of text label set. The Table 1. shows the $P(label1, label2)$ in different Jaccard similarity in the k = 5, t = 20 condition.

Table 1. The table of probability of different Jaccard similarity.

Jaccard similarity	P(label1, label2)
0.2	0.006
0.3	0.047
0.4	0.186
0.5	0.470
0.6	0.802
0.7	0.975
0.8	0.9996

Based on the above conclusion, when hierarchically clustering through the text labels, compare t pairs of text label for any two texts, if there is at least one pair of identical label pair which has a same label, grouping them into a same class.

4   Experiments of Label-Based Clustering

4.1   News Texts Datasets

By reptiles from more than 50 news websites, the datasets totally including more than 300,000 news items from October 2017 to November 2017. Each news item contains news URL, news authors, authoring date, publishing sources, title, and text.

4.2   Experimental Environment

The experimental environment is a distributed Hadoop computing platform. The platform contains a single Namenode server three Datanode server, the configuration of each node server is an Intel Core i7-7760 dual-core processor, 1 GB memory, and 1000 GB hard disk capacity. The Hadoop configuration using the default configuration.

4.3   Evaluation Standards for Experiments

This experiment compares the clustering effects of different algorithms. The evaluation standards contain the average clustering quality, the overall quality, and the time-consuming of the clustering.

The average clustering quality means the average number of quality of each class. The quality of one class is defined by the ratio of all samples in the class that same to the class center to the total number of samples in the class in which the class center means the mode news of the class.

The overall quality means the ratio of the number of samples have the right class to the number of all samples.

The Table 2 shows the average quality and the overall quality of the TF-IDF algorithm, SimHash algorithm, and the Label-based algorithm.

Table 2. Table of the comparison of 3 kinds of algorithm in clustering quality

Algorithm name	Average quality (%)	Overall quality (%)
Label-based	86.1	88.9
TF-IDF	64.7	67.7
SimHash	74.8	79.2

The Table 3 shows the time cost of clustering of 3 kinds of clustering algorithms.

Table 3. Table of the comparison of 3 kinds of algorithm in time cost

Algorithm name	Time consuming
Label-based	88.9
TF-IDF	67.7
SimHash	79.2

From the above experimental data, the overall quality and the average quality of the label-based algorithm is better than the SimHash algorithm and TF-IDF algorithm, From the time-consuming point of view, the TF-IDF has a better performance. The reason is that the time to generate the Label by using the MinHash will cost a long time. However, this problem can be solved by improving the parallel processing capability of the computing environment.

5 Summary

This paper proposes a new clustering method of news texts clustering method. This method is based on the characteristics of news texts, adopts the MinHash method, and proposes a news text labeling model. Through the labels of the news texts, this paper completes the clustering process based on the hierarchical clustering. Experiments show that the algorithm is of higher quality than traditional methods.

The next step of research:

1. Optimize the label set, and further improve the speed and efficiency of the algorithm.
2. Combining specific scenarios, applying the algorithm to web data mining tasks, such as news hotspot discovery, news public opinion analysis, and so on.

Acknowledgements. The authors wish to thank the Information Security Center at Beijing University of Posts and Telecommunications for providing the distributed computing environment. The authors acknowledge the financial support of The National Science and Technology Major Project (Grant No. 2017YFB080301).

References

1. Wu, H.C., Luk, R.W.P., Wong, K.F., et al.: Interpreting TF-IDF term weights as making relevance decisions. ACM Trans. Inf. Syst. **26**(3), 55–59 (2008)
2. Zhang, W.M., Jiang, W.U., Yuan, X.J.: K-means text clustering algorithm based on density and nearest neighbor. J. Comput. Appl. **30**(7), 1933–1935 (2010)
3. Sadowski, C., Levi, G.: SimHash: hash-based similarity detection (2007)
4. Pi, B., Fu, S., Wang, W., et al.: SimHash-based effective and efficient detecting of near-duplicate short messages. In: Proceedings of International Symposium on Computerence & Computational Technology, vol. 4, pp. 20–25 (2014)
5. Real, R., Vargas, J.M.: The probabilistic basis of Jaccard's index of similarity. Syst. Biol. **45**(3), 380–385 (1996)
6. Manaa, M.E., Abdulameer, G.: Web Documents Similarity using K-Shingle tokens and MinHash technique. J. Eng. Appl. Sci. **13**, 1499–1505 (2018)
7. Broder, A.: On the resemblance and containment of documents, pp. 21–29 (1997)
8. Broder, A.Z., Charikar, M., Frieze, A.M., et al.: Min-wise independent permutations. J. Comput. Syst. Sci. **60**(3), 630–659 (2000)
9. Luxburg, U.: A Tutorial on Spectral Clustering. Kluwer Academic Publishers, Hingham (2007)
10. Hartigan, J.A.: A K-means clustering algorithm. Appl. Stat. **28**(1), 100–108 (1979)

11. Douglas, H.F.: Knowledge acquisition via incremental conceptual clustering. Mach. Learn. **2**(2), 139–172 (1987)
12. Michalski, R.S., Stepp, R.E.: Automated construction of classifications: conceptual clustering versus numerical taxonomy. IEEE Trans. Pattern Anal. Mach. Intell. **5**(4), 396–410 (1983)
13. Hartigan, J.A., Wong, M.A.: Algorithm AS 136: A K-means clustering algorithm. J. Roy. Stat. Soc. **28**(1), 100–108 (1979)

Background Error Propagation Model Based RDO for Coding Surveillance and Conference Videos

Jian Xiong[1], Xianzhong Long[1], Ran Shi[2], Miaohui Wang[3], Jie Yang[1],
Yunyi Li[1], and Guan Gui[1(✉)]

[1] Nanjing University of Posts and Telecommunications, Nanjing, China
{jxiong,guiguan}@njupt.edu.cn
[2] Nanjing University of Science and Technology, Nanjing, China
[3] Shenzhen University, Shenzhen, China

Abstract. Surveillance and conference videos have become increasingly important in our daily life, which brings a huge amount of video data. Existing coding standards were originally designed for generic video contents. The backgrounds are generally static in the surveillance and conference videos. The background coding errors will propagate to the subsequent frames in coding the videos. In this paper, a background error propagation (BEP) model based Rate Distortion Optimization (RDO) scheme in HEVC is proposed for the surveillance and conference videos. Firstly, the global RDO scheme is proposed to efficiently exploit the background error propagation. Secondly, a BEP model is studied to express the linear relationship between the distortion of the first frame and that of its subsequent frames. Based on the BEP model, enhanced frames are proposed to be coded with a small quantization parameter (QP) offset so as to improve the global performance. Thirdly, a bi-exponential decay model is proposed to investigate the variation of the error propagation ratio as the frame order increased. Based on the decay model, a periodical optimization scheme is presented by deploying the enhanced frames periodically. Experimental results show that the proposed algorithm achieves 11.15% bit-rate reductions on average under the low delay condition.

Keywords: HEVC · Video coding · Error propagation · Surveillance · Background modeling

This workRecently, video was supported in part by the National Natural Science Foundation of China Grant (No. 61701258, No. 61701310), Natural Science Foundation of Jiangsu Province Grant (No. BK20170906, No. BK20150856), Natural Science Foundation of Jiangsu Higher Education Institutions Grant (No. 17KJB510044), Jiangsu Specially Appointed Professor Grant (RK002STP16001), Innovation and Entrepreneurship of Jiangsu High-level Talent Grant (CZ0010617002), and "1311 Talent Plan" of Nanjing University of Posts and Telecommunications, High-Level Talent Startup Grant of Nanjing University of Posts and Telecommunications (XK0010915026).

S. Liu and G. Yang (Eds.): ADHIP 2018, LNICST 279, pp. 504–513, 2019.
https://doi.org/10.1007/978-3-030-19086-6_56

1 Introduction

Recently, video surveillance and conference systems are becoming more and more prevalent in our daily life. As it was reported by IDC [2], surveillance videos will grow to 5,800 exabytes by 2020. In the face of the explosive growth of surveillance videos, how to effectively compress the videos has become a significant big challenge.

The state-of-the-art video coding standards, such as H.264/AVC [5] and High Efficiency Video Coding (HEVC) [3,4] are widely used to compress the surveillance and conference videos. In these methods, coding tools including intra prediction, motion estimation (ME), transformation, and quantization are employed to remove the redundancy. Rate-distortion optimization (RDO) technology is adopted to select the optimal coding modes and parameters. However, these methods were originally designed for generic video contents. Different from the generic videos, the surveillance videos generally acquired with static cameras. In these videos, the backgrounds are static and the motion patterns are generally simple. The coding errors in the background regions may propagate to the subsequent frames. This characteristic was not fully studied in the traditional coding methods.

Many efforts have been made to investigate more efficient methods for coding the surveillance and conference videos. by modeling background frames [6–9]. In [8], the HEVC hierarchical prediction is optimized with background modeling for surveillance and conference video coding. The background picture is generated and encoded as the long-term reference frame. In [7], a background modeling based adaptive prediction is proposed for surveillance video coding. The long-term redundancy is reduced by predicting on generated background frames. Adaptive prediction methods are employed for different coding blocks. The background generation is performed on basis of the frames, and the generated background is updated for each group of pictures (GOP). In [9] a selective background difference coding method is proposed on basis of macro-block (MB) level. Two ways are selected to code the macro-blocks. One is coding the original MB, and the other is directly coding the difference between the MB and the corresponding background. A block-based background modeling method is proposed for surveillance video coding [6]. In this scheme, background generation and updating is conducted based on coding units (CUs) but not frames and is performed for every frame but not a whole GOP. However, in these methods, only one generated picture cannot model the periodical backgrounds efficiently. The generated background may get worse as the frame distance increases. Furthermore, the block-based background modeling methods may aggravate the block artifacts between the foreground regions and background regions.

In the recent works, background modeling based schemes are proposed to exploit the frame dependency. However, the background error propagation characteristic is not fully studied. In this paper, a background error propagation (BEP) model based global RDO scheme is proposed for surveillance and conference video coding. The BEP model is presented to describe the linear relationship between the distortion of the frames. In this model, a concept of propagation ratio is proposed to describe how is the distortion of one frame influenced by its previous frames. Based on the BEP model, enhanced frames are presented to be coded with a small quantization parameter (QP) offset. Furthermore, a bi-exponential decay model is proposed to express the variation of the propagation ratio as the frame order increased. Based on the decay model, the periodical optimization scheme is presented by periodically coding enhanced frames. Experiments are tested on surveillance and conference videos. Experimental results show the efficiency of the proposed method.

The rest of the paper is organized as follows. An overview of HEVC RDO technology is presented in Sect. 2. The proposed BEP model based global RDO method is given in Sect. 3. Experiments are provided in Sect. 4 to validate the efficiency of the proposed method. Finally, we draw some concluding remarks in Sect. 5.

2   Overview of Rate Distortion Optimization

RDO technology is widely used in the block-based hybrid coding standards, such as H.264/AVC and HEVC. In these standards, there are various coding modes and parameters which can be employed to code the blocks. RDO is employed to select the optimal coding modes and parameters. The fundamental problem of RDO is to minimize the coding distortion with a bit consumption constraint. The constraint problem can be converted into an unconstrained problem by introducing a Lagrangian multiplier. It can be expressed by

$$\min J = D + \lambda \cdot R, \tag{1}$$

where the symbols R and D denote the coding bits and the corresponding coding distortion. The parameter λ denotes the Lagrangian multiplier. There is a trade-off between the distortion and coding bits. A proper Lagrangian multiplier will lead to an optimal balance. The default λ is obtained from the input QP value, which is expressed by,

$$\lambda = fac \cdot \frac{(qp - 12)}{3}, \tag{2}$$

where fac is the QP factor, qp is the input QP value.

3   Proposed Method

3.1   Global Rate Distortion Optimization

In the traditional coding scheme, RDO technology is independently employed to code each CU. However, in practical applications, when we try to code a video sequence, the main goal is to code all the frames with the optimal rate-distortion balance. There is a strong frame dependency in the consecutive frames, especially for the surveillance and conference videos. Thus, a global optimization scheme is more applicable for coding all the consecutive frames than the independent scheme. The global RDO scheme is given by,

$$\min J = \sum_{f=1}^{k} D_f + \lambda \cdot \sum_{f=1}^{k} R_f. \tag{3}$$

where k is the coded frame number. The symbols D_f and R_f denote the distortion and the corresponding coding bits of the fth ($f = 1, 2, \ldots, k$) frame, respectively. In contrast with the traditional RDO technology, the global optimization scheme considers all the consecutive frames but not only one CU.

3.2   Background Error Propagation Model

Generally, because of the prediction coding scheme in existing coding standards, coding errors may propagate from the previous frame to the subsequent frames. The frame dependency is not being well used in the existing optimization.

In surveillance videos, the backgrounds are static and the motion patterns are generally simple. Let's consider k co-located CUs in the temporal consecutive frames. On one hand, the original co-located background pixels in temporal consecutive CUs are reasonable to be considered as the same. This is expressed by, $P_{1,j} = P_{2,j} = P_{3,j} = \ldots = P_{k,j}$, where $j = 1, 2, \ldots, N^2$ denote the pixel locations in CUs with size $N \times N$. On the other hand, since CUs in background regions are generally encoded with the skip mode, the reconstructed pixels are considered to be approximately equal with each other, denoted as $P_{1,j}^d \approx P_{2,j}^d \approx P_{3,j}^d \approx \ldots \approx P_{k,j}^d$. Therefore, for $i = 1, 2, \ldots, k$, the relationship between the CU distortion can be written as

$$\begin{aligned} SSD_i &= \sum_{j=1}^{N^2} (P_{i,j} - P_{i,j}^d)^2 \\ &\approx \sum_{j=1}^{N^2} (P_{1,j} - P_{1,j}^d)^2 \\ &\approx SSD_1, \end{aligned} \tag{4}$$

where SSD_i denotes the sum of squared differences for CU i. That is, in the background regions, the distortion of consecutive CUs is approximately equal with that of the first frame.

Based on the background error propagation characteristic as in (4), it can be concluded that the distortion of subsequent frames is significantly influenced by that of the first frame. Experiments are conducted to study the relationship between the distortion of the first frame and that of the subsequent frames. In the experiments, the coding structure is IPPP. Except for the first inter frame, all the inter frames are coded with a fixed QP value set as 35. The first inter frame is coded with QP value varies from 23 to 33 with an interval 2. As shown in Fig. 1, the X-axis represents the distortion of first inter frame, and the y-axis represents

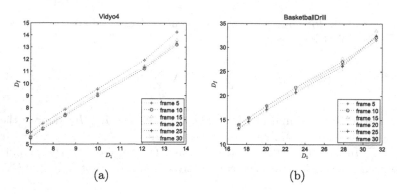

Fig. 1. The relationship between the distortion of the first frame and that of its subsequent frames. With the sequences: (a) Vidyo4, (b) BasketballDrill.

the distortion of the subsequent frame (such as frame 5, 10, 15, 20, 25, and 30). It can be observed that the distortion of the subsequent frames is highly influenced by that of the first frame, and there is a strong linear relationship between the distortion. It is reasonable to assume a linear model as

$$D_f = r_f \cdot D_1 + b_f, \qquad (5)$$

where b_f is a bias term, r_f is a parameter which represents the error propagation ratio. The linear model is named as background error propagation model. The error propagation ratio in the model describes how is the distortion of one frame influenced by its previous frames.

3.3   BEP-Based Rate Distortion Optimization

Based on the background error propagation model, the global RDO shown in (3) can be rewritten as

$$\min(D_1 \cdot \sum_{f=1}^{k} r_f + \sum_{f=1}^{k} b_f + \lambda R_1 + \lambda \cdot \sum_{i=2}^{k} R_i). \qquad (6)$$

It can be observed that, since the subsequent frames are significantly influenced by the first frame, improving the coding performance of the first frame will make the overall coding performance to be enhanced. Thus, we try to improve the coding performance of the first frame. On the other hand, the bit-rate of each frame is nearly independent. That is to say, the optimal coding performance of the total k frames can be obtained by setting the following derivative to 0. It is expressed by,

$$\frac{\partial(D_1 \cdot \sum_{f=1}^{k} r_f + \lambda R_1)}{\partial R_1} = 0. \qquad (7)$$

Thus, the lambda multiplier can be solved as,

$$\lambda_1 = -\frac{\partial D_1}{\partial R_1} = \frac{\lambda}{\sum_{f=1}^{k} r_f}, \tag{8}$$

where λ_1 denotes the lambda multiplier of the first frame.

From (2), we can have

$$qp = 3log_2(\frac{\lambda}{fac}) + 12. \tag{9}$$

Combine with (8), the adjusted QP value of the first frame can be calculated by λ_1 as

$$qp' = qp - 3log_2(\sum_{f=1}^{k} r_f). \tag{10}$$

For convenience, we use s to denote the summation of error ratios, i.e., $s = \sum_{f=1}^{k} r_f$. The coding performance of the first frame can be improved by coding it with a small QP offset, which is given by

$$\Delta Q = round(-3log_2(s)), \tag{11}$$

where ΔQ denotes the QP offset. The frame which is coded with the small QP offset is named as the *enhanced frame*.

3.4 Bi-exponential Decay Model

Since the QP offset depends on the summation of error ratios s, experiments are conducted to investigate the propagation ratio of the BEP model. In the experiments, two sets of tests are performed on the first 60 frames. The first set is named as the *anchor set*, in which the coding structure is the Low-Delay P setting, and the quantization parameter (QP) is set to 32. In order to investigate the error propagation characteristic, another set of tests is performed by setting QP value as 1 for encoding the first inter frame (approximately lossless coding). It should be noticed that the QP values for encoding the other frames are not changed. This set of tests is named as the *improved set*.

The distortion is measured in terms of mean square errors (MSE). For the anchor set, the distortion of frame f is denoted as D_f. For the improved set, the distortion of frame f is denoted as $\widetilde{D_f}$. By comparing the anchor with the improved set, the error increment of each frame f can be calculated as $\Delta D_f = D_f - \widetilde{D_f}$. The error propagation ratio between frame f and the first inter frame can be measured as

$$r_f = \Delta D_f / \Delta D_1. \tag{12}$$

Figure 2 shows the error propagation ratio of the P-frames. The x-axis represents the frame order number. The y-axis represents the error propagation ratio

of each frame. It indicates that there is a strong biexponential decay relationship between the error increment and the frame order number, which can be
expressed by

$$r_f = \eta_1 \cdot \eta_2{}^f + \eta_3 \cdot \eta_4{}^f. \tag{13}$$

The symbols η_1, η_2, η_3, and η_4 are the model parameters. The decay model shows
that the error propagation ratio decreases as the frame order number increases.
Equation (4) shows that the background pixels have a strong error propagation
characteristic. However, even in surveillance videos, not all the pixels are in
background regions. Foreground regions with motion objects are common in the
videos. Thus, the decay model is reasonable because as the frame order number
increases, fewer pixels have the error propagation property.

In addition, we evaluate the fitting goodness of biexponential decay model.
As shown in Fig. 2, the average R-square value (denoted as R^2) is 0.976. That
is, the biexponential decay model has high accuracy in modeling the downtrend
of the error increments.

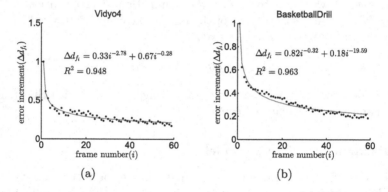

Fig. 2. The bi-exponential decay model. With the sequences: (a) Vidyo4, (b) BasketballDrill.

3.5 Implementation

As it is indicated in the decay model, the propagation ratio decreases as the
frame order number increases. That is to say, the influence of the first frame
on far-distance frames is small. It is necessary to set a new enhanced frame
for the far-distance frames. Therefore, the enhanced frames are necessary to be
deployed periodically. The interval between two enhanced frames is defined as
an optimization period.

Figure 3 shows the proposed periodical RDO scheme. In this figure, the yellow
bar denotes an I frame, and the other bars are P frames. The numbers in the
gray box are the QP offsets. The red bars denote the enhanced frames coded
with a QP offset as ΔQ. There is an optimization between two enhanced frames.

As shown in Fig. 2, all the propagation ratios become small and converge at
frame 60. Thus, every 60 frames is coded as an optimization period, i.e., $k = 60$.

Table 1. Summation of the error propagation ratios when the optimization period is set to 60.

Sequences	s
Vidyo4	17.45
Vidyo3	16.01
Traffic	17.71
BasketballDrill	18.63
Average	17.45

That is, the first frame of each optimization period is coding the QP offset ΔQ. Table 1 shows the sum of error propagation ratios when the optimization period is set to 60. It indicates that the average value of s is 17.45, and most of the values are close to the average. By employing the average s in (11), we obtain the QP offset as -12, i.e., $\Delta Q = -12$.

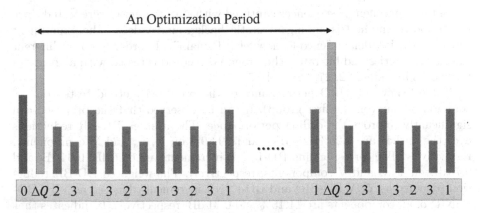

Fig. 3. The background error propagation model based global RDO scheme. The yellow bar denotes the I frame, and the other bars are P frames. The numbers in the gray box are the QP offsets. The red bars denote the enhanced frames coding with a QP offset as ΔQ. (Color figure online)

4   Experimental Results

The experiments were performed on a PC with an Intel (R) 3.60 GHz processor, 16 Gb RAM. The performance of the proposed method is evaluated in terms of the change of the Bjontegaard Delta bit-rate (BD-BR) and Bjontegaard Delta Peak Signal to Noise Ratio (BD-PSNR) [1]. The proposed method is integrated on the HEVC reference software, HM16.0[1]. The performance gain is obtained by comparing the proposed method with the reference software.

---

[1] https://hevc.hhi.fraunhofer.de/svn/svnHEVCSoftware/tags/HM-16.0/

Table 2. R-D performance improvements of the proposed method compared with the hevc default scheme.

Sequences	BD-BR (%)				BD-PNSR (dB)			
	Y	U	V	YUV	Y	U	V	YUV
Vidyo1	−8.90	−31.21	−32.55	−9.74	0.25	0.51	0.69	0.26
Vidyo3	−7.53	−38.51	−47.54	−9.88	0.19	0.67	1.33	0.25
Vidyo4	−12.01	−34.22	−32.74	−12.89	0.30	0.73	0.76	0.32
Traffic	−0.48	−15.22	−23.53	−1.34	0.01	0.27	0.45	0.03
BasketballDrill	−10.33	−9.74	−9.19	−15.33	0.43	0.41	0.50	0.59
Johnny	−9.07	−34.83	−31.69	−10.70	0.16	0.69	0.64	0.19
KristenAndSara	−11.28	−32.69	−32.83	−13.05	0.31	0.79	0.77	0.35
FourPeople	−13.70	−32.97	−31.71	−14.87	0.44	0.90	0.88	0.47
Average	−9.20	−28.31	−29.89	−11.15	0.26	0.64	0.76	0.31

In the experiment, 8 sequences captured with static cameras were tested since the proposed method is aiming at static background videos. The experiment setting is the low delay ("encoder_lowdelay_P_main"). In order to cover different ranges of qualities and bit-rates, the proposed method is tested with a groups of QP values including 22, 27, 32, and 37.

Table 2 shows the R-D performance of the proposed method tested on the common setting (on the first group). It can be observed that the proposed can significantly improve the coding performance. The average BD-BR reductions over the anchor are 9.20%, 28.31%, and 29.89% on Y, U, and V components, respectively. The corresponding BD-PSNR increments are 0.26 dB, 0.64 dB, and 0.76 dB on Y, U and V components, respectively. The weighted BD-BR reduction (denoted as YUV BD-BR) and BD-PSNR increment (denoted as YUV BD-PSNR) of all components are 11.15% and 0.31 dB, respectively. It indicates that the proposed algorithm significantly outperforms the default HEVC method. Furthermore, especially for the sequences with a large proportion of static background (such as FourPeople, KristenAndSara, and Johnny), the performance gain is larger than that of the sequence with a small proportion of static background (such as Traffic). It indicates that the proposed method is better suited to the static background.

5   Conclusion

In this paper, a BEP model based global RDO method in HEVC is proposed for surveillance and conference videos. The proposed method is different from the default RDO scheme, in which each CU is optimized independently. Since the backgrounds are generally static in the surveillance and conference videos, the R-D performance of the long-term frames is optimized globally in the proposed method, in which the background error propagation can be efficiently exploited. Two models are presented to study the characteristics of background error propagation. The first one is the linear BEP model, which describes the linear relationship between the distortion of the first frame and that of subsequent frames. Based on the BEP model, enhanced frames coded with a small QP offset is deployed to improve the global performance. The second one is the bi-exponential decay model, which expresses the variation of the error propagation ratio as the frame order increased. Based on the decay model, a periodical optimization scheme is presented, i.e., the enhanced frames are periodically deployed. Experimental results show that the proposed algorithm achieves an average 11.15% bit-rate reduction on YUV components (YUV BD-BR) for the low delay setting.

References

1. Bjontegaard, G.: Calculation of average PSNR differences between RD curves. No. ITU-T SC16/Q6, VCEG-M33, Austin, USA, April 2001
2. Gantz, J., Reinsel, D.: The IDC digital universe in 2020: big data, bigger digital shadows, and biggest growth in the far east (2012). https://www.emc.com/collateral/analyst-reports/idc-the-digital-universe-in-2020.pdf
3. Han, W.J., et al.: Improved video compression efficiency through flexible unit representation and corresponding extension of coding tools. IEEE Trans. Circuits Syst. Video Technol. **20**(12), 1709–1720 (2010). https://doi.org/10.1109/TCSVT.2010.2092612
4. Sullivan, G., Ohm, J., Han, W.J., Wiegand, T.: Overview of the high efficiency video coding (HEVC) standard. IEEE Trans. Circuits Syst. Video Technol. **22**(12), 1649–1668 (2012). https://doi.org/10.1109/TCSVT.2012.2221191
5. Wiegand, T., Sullivan, G., Bjontegaard, G., Luthra, A.: Overview of the H.264/AVC video coding standard. IEEE Trans. Circuits Syst. Video Technol. **13**(7), 560–576 (2003). https://doi.org/10.1109/TCSVT.2003.815165
6. Yin, L., Hu, R., Chen, S., Xiao, J., Hu, J.: A block-based background model for surveillance video coding. In: 2015 Data Compression Conference, pp. 476–476, April 2015. https://doi.org/10.1109/DCC.2015.49
7. Zhang, X., Huang, T., Tian, Y., Gao, W.: Background-modeling-based adaptive prediction for surveillance video coding. IEEE Trans. Image Process. **23**(2), 769–784 (2014). https://doi.org/10.1109/TIP.2013.2294549
8. Zhang, X., Tian, Y., Huang, T., Dong, S., Gao, W.: Optimizing the hierarchical prediction and coding in HEVC for surveillance and conference videos with background modeling. IEEE Trans. Image Processing **23**(10), 4511–4526 (2014). https://doi.org/10.1109/TIP.2014.2352036
9. Zhang, X., Tian, Y., Liang, L., Huang, T., Gao, W.: Macro-block-level selective background difference coding for surveillance video. In: 2012 IEEE International Conference on Multimedia and Expo, pp. 1067–1072, July 2012. https://doi.org/10.1109/ICME.2012.136

A Stereo Matching Algorithm for Vehicle Binocular System

Fangyi Zhang⬤, Gang Zhao$^{(\boxtimes)}$⬤, Haiying Liu⬤, and Wang Qin⬤

College of Transportation, Shandong University of Science and Technology,
Qingdao, China
479943377@qq.com

Abstract. In order to improve outdoor performance of vehicle binocular system, the stereo matching algorithm based on "3bit-Census Transformation & An Adaptive window aggregation based on edge truncation & Fast Parallax Calculation" was proposed. The stereo matching algorithm based on this framework improved the robustness, matching accuracy and efficiency of the calculation from different stages. The experimental results show that the algorithm proposed in this paper is better than the traditional algorithm and can meet the requirements of the vehicle binocular system.

Keywords: Binocular system · Stereo matching · Robustness ·
Matching accuracy · Calculation efficiency

1 Introduction

With the rapid development of computer and sensor technology, 3D reconstruction based on binocular system has been widely applied to intelligent vehicle positioning, obstacle measurement and other fields [1]. The results of stereo matching can directly affect the robustness, accuracy and efficiency of binocular system [2]. At present, the binocular stereo matching algorithm is divided into three categories: (1) global stereo matching; (2) semi-global stereo matching; (3) local stereo matching [3]. Global stereo matching and semi-global stereo matching have high accuracy with high complexity, so they are not suitable for intelligent vehicles. But conversely, although local stereo matching has relatively low accuracy, it has relatively low complexity as well, therefore, it is easy to be realized by vehicle binocular system [4].

Local stereo matching is mainly divided into four stages: (1) Cost calculation; (2) Cost aggregation; (3) Parallax calculation; (4) Parallax refinement and post-processing. Through the above stages, dense parallax images can be obtained from the left and right images collected by binocular system. The 3D model of driving environment can be reconstructed by combining the parallax image with the parameters of binocular camera. In order to strengthen the robustness, accuracy and efficiency of the vehicle binocular systems, a stereo matching framework based on "3bit-Census transformation & An adaptive window aggregation based on edge truncation & Fast parallax calculation" is proposed.

2 3bit-Census Based on Average Confidence Interval

In the traditional Census transformation, the result is strongly dependent on the center pixel [5]. Once the center pixel is seriously interfered by the noise, the result of the Census transformation will change significantly, and the matching accuracy will be reduced. What's more, the relative gray values of pixels and center pixel are represented by 1-bit binary number, and the gray value space is divided into "2-gray value spaces (0 or 1)". This transformation method has poor ability to describe local features and poor distinction between different local features. In this paper, a 3bit-Census transformation based on the confidence interval is proposed. The steps of the calculation are as follows:

(1) The pixel value confidence interval and the pixel average value in the interval are calculated, which is used as the reference pixel of the 3bit-Census transformation.
(2) The traditional "2-gray value spaces" is divided into "8-gray value spaces" by using the logic combination of 3-bit binary numbers.

2.1 Pixel Average Value Calculation Based on Confidence Interval

In order to solve the problems that the transformation is highly dependent on the center pixel and the center pixel is susceptible to noise, the use of the pixel, which is seriously affected by the noise in the calculation should be reduced.

Assuming that the size of the transformation window is 'n * n', the pixel value $I_{(1,1)}, I_{(1,2)}, I_{(1,3)} \cdots I_{(n,n)}$ in the window is normal distribution from the average value $\bar{I}(o)$, and the standard deviation is σ. (i.e. $I \sim N(\bar{I}(o), \sigma^2)$)

Confidence interval is:

$$\left[\bar{I}(o) - \frac{\sigma}{n} Z_{\alpha/2}, \bar{I}(o) + \frac{\sigma}{n} Z_{\alpha/2}\right] \tag{1}$$

The reference pixel of the transformation based on confidence interval is:

$$I'(o) = \frac{\sum_{i=1}^{m} I_i}{m}; I_i \in \left[\bar{I}(o) - \frac{\sigma}{n} Z_{\alpha/2}, \bar{I}(o) + \frac{\sigma}{n} Z_{\alpha/2}\right] \tag{2}$$

In this paper: $\alpha = 0.01, Z_{\alpha/2} = 2.68$

The confidence interval can effectively eliminate the pixel points that is seriously affected by the noise, and use the high quality pixel points in the confidence interval to calculate the average value as the transformation reference. The above method can effectively improve the robustness and the ability of describing local features.

2.2 3Bit-Census Transformation

In the process of 3bit-Census transformation, considering the amount of logic resources in the vehicle hardware platform, the "2-gray value spaces" of [0: $I'(o)$] and [$I'(o)$: 255] are reasonably extended to "8-gray value spaces". The method can be realized by shift operation and adder, and it can reduce the amount of logic resource occupied by vehicle hardware platform effectively. The 3bit-Census transformation is shown in Eq. (3).

$$\beta(h,o) = \begin{cases} 111, & I(h) \geq 2I'(o) \\ 110, & 2I'(o) > I(h) \geq \frac{3}{2}I'(o) \\ 101, & \frac{3}{2}I'(o) > I(h) \geq \frac{5}{4}I'(o) \\ 100, & \frac{5}{4}I'(o) > I(h) \geq I'(o) \\ 011, & I'(o) > I(h) \geq \frac{3}{4}I'(o) \\ 010, & \frac{3}{4}I'(o) > I(h) \geq \frac{1}{2}I'(o) \\ 001, & \frac{1}{2}I'(o) > I(h) \geq \frac{1}{4}I'(o) \\ 000, & I(h) < \frac{1}{4}I'(o) \end{cases} \tag{3}$$

To verify the ability of the 3bit-Census transformation to describe local features, Fig. 1 shows two different windows: 'a' and 'b'. Equation (4) is the bit-string obtained by the Census transformation and the 3bit-Census transformation. Equation (5) is the hamming distance between the bit-strings.

69	42	85	1	0	1	100	010	100	98	46	85	1	0	1	101	010	100
50	64	70	0	X	1	011	X	100	32	64	70	0	X	1	011	X	100
65	48	32	1	0	0	100	011	010	90	60	30	1	0	0	100	011	001

window 'a'   Census   3bit-Census   window 'b'   Census   3bit-Census

Fig. 1. The calculation process of bit string

$$\begin{cases} C(cen\_a) = \{1,0,1,0,1,1,0,0\} \\ C(cen\_b) = \{1,0,1,0,1,1,0,0\} \\ C(3bit\_cen\_a) = \{1,0,0;0,1,0;1,0,0;0,1,1;\ 1,0,0;1,0,0;0,1,1;0,1,0\} \\ C(3bit\_cen\_b) = \{1,0,1;0,1,0;1,0,0;0,1,0;\ 1,0,0;1,0,0;0,1,1;0,0,1\} \end{cases} \tag{4}$$

$$\begin{cases} \text{Hamming}[C(cen\_a), C(cen\_b)] = 0 \\ \text{Hamming}[C(3\,bit\_cen\_a), C(3\,bit\_cen\_b)] = 4 \end{cases} \tag{5}$$

The above calculation shows that the hamming distance between two bit-strings may be 0 after Census transformation of different windows, which cannot judge the difference between two windows, and then lead to mismatch. After 3bit-Census transformation, the hamming distance is 4, which can correctly judge the difference between different windows. It can be concluded that the stereo matching method based on 3bit-Census transformation can effectively improve the description ability of local features, the credibility of similarity measurement and the matching accuracy.

3   An Adaptive Window Aggregation Based on Edge Truncation

In the cost aggregation stage, the size and shape of the aggregation window plays a decisive role in the matching accuracy. If the aggregation window is too small, it cannot contain enough local information in the weak texture, so it is easy to cause mismatch [6]. If the aggregation window is too large, in the parallax discontinuous region or the edge of the object, the excessively large window would contain more pixel points with different depths, as a result, it is easy to cause mismatch too. In order to improve the cost aggregation level, the pixel value in the aggregation window should have similar depth, and the size and shape of the aggregation window should be adjusted adaptively according to the local features.

3.1   Sobel Edge Detection

Sobel operator is a first-order derivative edge detection operator [7]. It uses two convolution check images of 3 * 3 to process the convolution, and thus obtains the grayscale gradient: G_x, G_y and G, which is shown in Eqs. (6) (7) (8) (9).

$$G_x = \begin{bmatrix} 1 & 0 & -1 \\ 2 & 0 & -2 \\ 1 & 0 & -1 \end{bmatrix} * A \quad \text{and} \quad G_y = \begin{bmatrix} 1 & 2 & 1 \\ 0 & 0 & 0 \\ -1 & -2 & -1 \end{bmatrix} * A \tag{6}$$

$$\begin{aligned} G_x = & [f(x-1, y-1) + 2f(x-1, y) + f(x-1, y+1)] \\ & - [f(x+1, y+1) + 2f(x+1, y) + f(x+1, y-1)] \end{aligned} \tag{7}$$

$$\begin{aligned} G_y = & [f(x-1, y+1) + 2f(x, y+1) + f(x+1, y+1)] \\ & - [f(x-1, y-1) + 2f(x, y-1) + f(x+1, y-1)] \end{aligned} \tag{8}$$

$$G = \sqrt{G_x^2 + G_y^2} \tag{9}$$

If $G > G_{max}$, the point is one on the edge. Compared with other algorithms, Sobel algorithm has the advantages of simple calculation structure and easy implementation of vehicle hardware system. According to the above principle, the image collected by the vehicle binocular system are detected by Sobel operator. The detection results are shown in Fig. 2. The edge information of the object can ensure all the pixel value in the aggregation window having similar depth.

3.2   An Adaptive Window Based on Edge Truncation

In order to realize that the size and shape of the aggregation window being adjusted adaptively according to the local characteristics, an adaptive aggregation window is proposed in this paper. The stages to create the adaptive aggregation window are as follows:

Fig. 2. Sobel edge detection

(1) Aggregating form column to row: (1) Taking the pixel point 'o' to be the starting point, the constraint condition and the edge truncation condition are used to determine the upper and lower endpoints in the vertical direction; (2) Starting from each pixel of the vertical pixel interval, the constraint conditions and the edge truncation condition determine the left and right endpoints. The aggregation result is shown in Fig. 3(a). Constraints and edge truncation conditions are shown in Eq. (10).

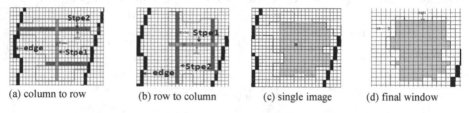

(a) column to row   (b) row to column   (c) single image   (d) final window

Fig. 3. Aggregate window generation diagram

(2) According to the method of stage (1), the result of aggregation form row to column is shown in Fig. 3(b).
(3) Take the intersection of the above aggregation windows and determine the window for the single image, which is shown in Fig. 3(c).
(4) Taking the intersection of the aggregation windows in the left and right images to get the final aggregation window, which is shown in Fig. 3(d).

$$\begin{cases} 1.\, D_c(P,o) < \tau_1 \quad and \quad D_c(P, P-(0,1)) < \tau_1 \\ 2.\, D_s(P,o) < L_1 \\ 3.\, D_c(P,o) < \tau_2 \quad if \quad L_2 < D_s(P,o) < L_1 \\ 4.\, D(P,o) = |I(P) - I(o)| \\ 5.\, A < P < B \end{cases} \tag{10}$$

In the Eq. (10): 'o' is the central pixel; 'P' is the point to be aggregated; 'D_c' is the column difference; 'D_s' is the row difference; 'τ_1, τ_2, L_1, L_2' are the variable parameters, which are 30, 10, 15 and 8 in this paper. 'A' and 'B' are the pixel points on the edge. The matching costs is shown in Eq. (11):

$$L(o) = \sum_{i \in M} Hamming[C_{cen}(i), C_{cen}(i-d)] \tag{11}$$

In Eq. (11): 'C_{cen}' is bit-string; 'L(o)' is cost aggregation; 'm' is the aggregation region shown in Fig. 3(d); 'i' is the pixel point in the aggregation window; 'd' is parallax.

4   Fast Parallax Calculation

The process of parallax calculation is based on the cost aggregation and determine the optimal matching point by calculating the minimum matching cost in the maximum parallax (d_{max}), which is shown in Eq. (12). Figure 4(a) shows the road image obtained by the vehicle binocular system, which has obvious depth variation. The depth of the object above the image is large and the parallax is small. The depth of the object below the image is small and the parallax is large. Figure 4(b) shows that parallax varies slightly in the row and more in the column. In other words, the depth change is mainly reflected in the column direction.

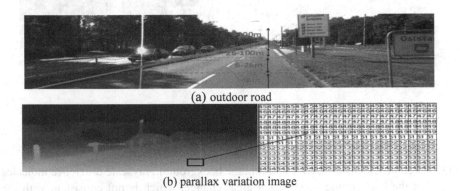

(a) outdoor road

(b) parallax variation image

Fig. 4. Outdoor road and parallax images

In the traditional parallax (d_{max}) calculation process, the parallax is fixed, which results in computational complexly and reduces the real-time performance. In order to solve the above problem, this paper proposed a method for calculating the parallax with variable maximum parallax: (1) Assuming that the image obtained at a certain time is the first frame, the initial 'd_{max}' is '150'. (2) The parallax ($d_{(x, y)-1}$) of the pixel points in the first image is calculated under the 'd_{max}'. (3) When the parallax of the second frame is calculated, the maximum parallax ($d_{(x, y)max\_2}$) of the corresponding point in the second image is shown in Eq. (13). The updating process is repeated every 5 frames.

$$J = Min\{L(j)|0 \le j \le d_{max}\} \tag{12}$$

$$d_{(x,y)max\_2} = 1.3 * d_{(x,y)\_1} \tag{13}$$

In Eqs. (12) (13): 'J' is the optimal matching point; L (j) is the matching cost in the range of maximum parallax.

5   Experiment

5.1   Experiment I: Robustness Analysis

In order to verify the robustness of the algorithm based on 3bit-Census, we use linear SAD algorithm and the nonlinear algorithm proposed in this paper to analyze the images collected by binocular system. The experiment used a pair of images from Middlebury [8] as processed images. There are obvious bicycle shadows in the image, and both images are 2988 * 2088 pixels. In this experiment, the maximum parallax of the two algorithms is '150'. The transformation window for 3bit-Census is 7 * 7. The image processing results are shown in Fig. 5.

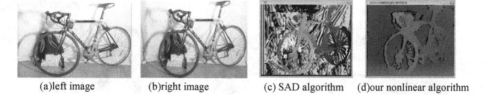

(a)left image   (b)right image   (c) SAD algorithm   (d)our nonlinear algorithm

Fig. 5. Comparison of results between linear SAD and our nonlinear algorithm

By analyzing the experiment, we can obtain the following conclusions:

(1) Based on the linear SAD algorithm, the background grayscale difference indicates that the background depth has a great change, which is not consistent with the experiment fact, on the contrary, based on the parallax image processed by the nonlinear algorithm, the background grayscale is uniform and the depth of the background is similar. By comparing with the original image, the experimental results are consistent with the experiment fact.

(2) Based on the parallax image processed by the linear SAD algorithm, the change of gray value of bicycle is poor, which indicates that the algorithm has low matching accuracy. The gray value based on our nonlinear algorithm is smooth, and the gray level of the rear wheel is consistent with the background gradually, which is consistent with the experimental fact.

(3) The image background based on linear SAD algorithm has obvious bicycle shape, which indicates that the algorithm is less robust to illumination, on the contrary, the parallax image based on our nonlinear algorithm is less affected by the shadow of the object, which shows that the algorithm is more robust to illumination.

5.2   Experiment II: Matching Accuracy Analysis

In order to analyze the matching accuracy of this algorithm, this paper uses Tsukubaer, Venuseddy, Teddy and Cones of Middlebury website to carry out off-line stereo matching experiment, and compares it with other high-quality algorithms. Off-line experiment requires 'visual studio 2012+ opencv2.4.8'. In the experiment, this paper will calculate the mismatch rate in three regions: 'nocc', 'all' and 'disc', respectively, and calculate the average mismatch rate of all images, which represents the accuracy of the algorithm. 'all' region includes half occlusion region but not image edge of object. Error threshold = 1.0. The experimental results are shown in Table 1. The results of the parallax image and the ground truth are compared as shown in Fig. 6.

Table 1. Comparison of matching accuracy between this algorithm and other algorithms

Algorithm	Tsukuba			Vensus			Teddy			Cones			Av Error
	nocc	all	disc	nocc	all	disc	nocc	all	disc	nocc	all	disc	
ADCENSUS [9]	1.07	1.48	5.7	0.09	0.25	1.15	4.10	6.22	10.9	2.42	7.25	6.95	3.97
SSCBP [10]	1.05	1.39	5.57	0.10	0.16	1.39	3.44	8.32	9.95	2.60	7.13	7.23	4.03
Our method	1.42	8.85	6.01	0.39	0.85	2.44	4.35	8.01	8.77	5.01	7.03	6.33	4.96
CrossLMF [11]	2.46	2.78	6.26	0.27	0.38	2.15	5.50	10.6	14.2	2.34	7.82	6.80	5.13
Sdds [12]	3.31	3.62	10.4	0.39	0.76	2.85	7.65	13.0	19.4	3.99	10.0	10.8	7.19
FastAggreg [13]	1.16	2.11	6.06	4.03	4.75	6.43	9.04	15.2	20.2	5.37	12.6	11.9	8.24
RTCsensus [14]	5.08	6.25	19.2	1.58	2.42	14.2	7.96	13.8	20.3	4.10	9.54	12.2	9.73
GC [15]	1.94	4.12	9.39	1.79	3.44	8.75	16.5	25.0	24.9	7.70	18.2	15.3	11.4

By analyzing the experiment, we can obtain the following conclusions:

(1) As shown in Table 1, the average error of the experiment results based on our algorithm is 4.96%, which is slightly higher than that of SSCBP and other high-quality matching algorithms. Compared with the algorithms such as CrossLMF, SDDS, FastAggreg, RTCensus and GC, the algorithm increases 0.17%, 2.23%, 3.28%, 4.77%, 6.44% respectively on average matching accuracy.

(2) As shown in Fig. 6, compared with the ground truth image, the image processed by our algorithm has a good overall effect. Compared with the SAD algorithm, the matching accuracy of this algorithm is obviously improved, the matching accuracy of the objects in the image is very high, and the edge of the object is smooth, so the algorithm proposed in this paper can meet the requirements of the vehicle binocular system better.

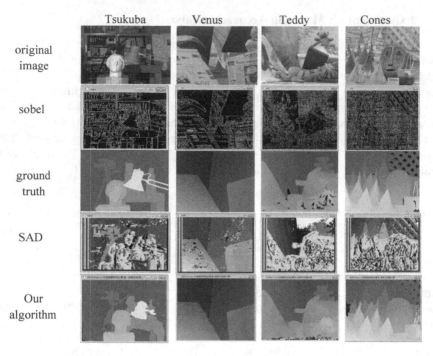

Fig. 6. Experimental parallax images and ground truth images

6   Conclusion

In this paper, based on the application background of vehicle binocular system, a stereo matching algorithm based on "3bit-Census transformation & An adaptive window aggregation based on edge truncation & Fast parallax calculation" was proposed. The algorithm has the following characteristics:

(1) The nonlinear 3bit-Census transformation has robustness to illumination and strong ability to describe local features, which lays a stable foundation for improving the stereo matching accuracy.
(2) Adaptive aggregation based on edge truncation realizes the transformation of adaptive aggregation window according to local features and edge truncation, which ensures that all pixels in the aggregation window have similar depth and improves the matching accuracy of the stereo matching.
(3) The fast parallax calculation method based on the variable maximum parallax avoids the calculation complexity, and enhances the matching efficiency and ensures the real-time performance, so the algorithm proposed in this paper can satisfy the vehicle binocular system working outdoors.

References

1. Tong, Z., Zhao, T., He, L., Wang, X.: Localization and driving speed detection for construction vehicles based on binocular vision. China Mech. Eng. **29**(4), 423–428 (2018)
2. Xiong, X., Hua, C., Fang, C., Chen, Y.: Research on free-form surface stereo matching method based on improved census transform. In: 35th Chinese Control Conference, pp. 4889–4893. IEEE, Chengdu (2016)
3. Lin, S., Yin, X., Tang, Y.: Research status and prospect of binocular stereo matching technology. Sci. Technol. Eng. **17**(30), 135–147 (2017)
4. Dehnavi, M., Eshghi, M.: FPGA based real-time on-road stereo vision system. J. Syst. Archit. **81**, 32–43 (2017)
5. Men, Y., Zhang, G., Men, C., Ma, N.: A stereo matching algorithm based on four-moded census and relative confidence plane fitting. Chin. J. Electron. **24**(4), 807–812 (2015)
6. Hirschmüller, H., Innocent, P., Garibaldi, J.: Real-time correlation-based stereo vision with reduced border errors. Int. J. Comput. Vision **47**(1–3), 229–246 (2002)
7. Kalra, A., Chhokar, R.: A hybrid approach using Sobel and canny operator for digital image edge detection. In: 2016 International Conference on Micro-Electronics and Telecommunication Engineering, pp. 305–310. IEEE, Ghaziabad (2017)
8. Middlebury Stereo Evaluation. http://vision.middlebury.edu. Accessed 9 June 2018
9. Mei, X., Sun, X., Zhou, M., Jiao, S., Wang, H., Zhang, X.: On building an accurate stereo matching system on graphics hardware. In: IEEE International Conference on Computer Vision Workshops, pp. 467–474. IEEE, Barcelona (2012)
10. Peng, Y., Li, G., Wang, R., Wang, W.: Stereo matching with space-constrained cost aggregation and segmentation-based disparity refinement. In: Three-Dimensional Image Processing, Measurement. International Society for Optics and Photonics, vol. 9393, pp. 939309-1-939309-11 (2015)
11. Do, M.N.: Cross-based local multipoint filtering. In: IEEE Conference on Computer Vision and Pattern Recognition, pp. 430–437. IEEE, Providence (2012)
12. Wang, Y., Dunn, E., Frahm, J.: Increasing the efficiency of local stereo by leveraging smoothness constraints. In: 2012 Second International Conference on 3D Imaging, Modeling, Processing, Visualization & Transmission, pp. 246–253. IEEE, Zurich (2012)
13. Tombari, F., Mattoccia, S., Stefano, L., Addimanda, E.: Near real-time stereo based on effective cost aggregation. In: 19th International Conference on Pattern Recognition, pp. 1–4. IEEE, Tampa (2009)
14. Humenberger, M., Zinner, C., Weber, M., Kubinger, W., Vincze, M.: A fast stereo matching algorithm suitable for embedded real-time systems. Comput. Vis. Image Underst. **114**(11), 1180–1202 (2010)
15. Scharstein, D., Szeliski, R., Zabih, R.: A taxonomy and evaluation of dense two-frame stereo correspondence algorithms. In: Stereo and Multi-Baseline Vision, pp. 7–42. IEEE, Kauai (2002)

Study on Civil Aviation Unsafe Incident Prediction Based on Markov Optimization

Fei Lu, Wenya Li[(✉)], Zhaoning Zhang, and Kexuan Liu

Civil Aviation University of China, Tianjin 300300, China
lufei315@126.com, liwenya522@163.com

Abstract. The civil aviation safety management system requires accurate prediction of the future safety status, but there are often many uncertain factors in the occurrence of air traffic insecurity events. In order to study its development trend and strengthen the accurate analysis and prediction of unsafe events, a combined forecasting model based on Markov correction process is proposed. Firstly, apply the grey system theory to construct a GM (1, 1) model. Then, based on the grey prediction model and the exponential smoothing method, combination forecasting model is established. And according to the standard deviation of the prediction result, the weight is determined to correct the data. Finally, combined with the Markov method, the probability transfer matrix is determined and the results are optimized. Based on the statistics of civil aviation insecure events in the past ten years, the prediction accuracy of the optimized model is significantly higher than that of the single gray prediction model or the exponential smoothing prediction model, which verifies the effectiveness of the method.

Keywords: Unsafe event · Gray model · Combination forecast · Markov optimization

1 Introduction

The Civil Aviation Safety Management System (SMS) requires the collection and analysis of safety information to construct a safety management mechanism based on risk early warning management and feedback control [1]. In recent years, with the increasing flight flow, the absolute value of civil aviation unsafe incidents has also increased. Therefore, how to prevent and control the occurrence of civil aviation unsafe incidents becomes more and more important.

With regard to the study of civil aviation unsafe events, the current commonly used prediction methods include regression analysis and prediction, BP neural network method and saturation growth trend prediction. Wang, Liu [2] analyzed the gray correlation degree of civil aviation accident signs and their influencing factors also used the model to analyze the measured statistical data of the 2001–2004 accident signs. Luo et al. [3] predicted the number of accidents in the next three years by establishing a gray prediction model of the number of accidents. Shi et al. based on the grey topological prediction theory method to predict the year and month of the number of deaths within a certain threshold range by establishing a time series model group corresponding to

S. Liu and G. Yang (Eds.): ADHIP 2018, LNICST 279, pp. 524–534, 2019.
https://doi.org/10.1007/978-3-030-19086-6_58

different thresholds [4]. Outside the country, Fullwood et al. [5] used linear regression to predict aviation safety trends based on accident data in relevant air service difficulties reports. McCann [6] of the American Aeronautical Meteorological Center used neural networks to predict aircraft icing at different intensities. GARRIDO established an Ordered Profit model for predicting the severity of traffic accidents [7].

In summary, it can be found that the above prediction methods often require a large amount of data to obtain a stable and long-term development trend, and do not consider that the actual development trend is often fluctuating. The grey system mainly studies the uncertain system of "small sample and poor information" [8]; the exponential smoothing rule takes into account the whole-term data, and assigns different weights according to the distance of the data. And the Markov prediction is applicable to the prediction of long term and random fluctuation of data series.

Therefore, the author will use gray prediction to reveal the time series development trend of civil aviation unsafe events, and combine the exponential smoothing method to correct the results and establish a combined forecasting model. Based on this, the Markov theory is used to determine the state transition probability to obtain the Markov optimization prediction model that meets the development characteristics of civil aviation unsafe events, which can significantly improve the prediction effect.

2   The Combined Forecasting Model

There are many influencing factors in air traffic insecurity events, and a considerable part of them are difficult to describe in quantitative form. For the distribution of air traffic insecurity events, different predictors will have different understandings, and different prediction methods will be used. So, it is necessary to use a variety of quantitative prediction methods, a combination of qualitative and quantitative methods to predict, in order to increase the accuracy of the prediction issues.

2.1   The Grey Prediction Model

The gray system analysis method is to identify the similarity or dissimilarity between the development factors of the system factors, that is, to analyze the correlation degree, and to seek the law of system change by generating the original data. The generated data sequence has strong regularity, which can be used to establish the corresponding differential equation model to predict the future development trend and future state of the thing, the so-called gray prediction.

Let $X^{(0)}$ be used as a non-negative time series for $GM(1, 1)$ model:

$$X^{(0)} = (x^{(0)}(1), x^{(0)}(2), \ldots, x^{(0)}(n)) \tag{1}$$

$X^{(1)}$ is the $1 - AGO$ sequence of $X^{(0)}$, i.e.

$$X^{(1)} = (x^{(1)}(1), x^{(1)}(2), \ldots, x^{(1)}(n));$$

$$X^{(1)}(k) = \sum_{i=1}^{k} X^{(0)}(i), k = 1, 2, \ldots, n \tag{2}$$

Let $Z^{(1)}$ be the immediate mean (MEAN) generation sequence of $X^{(1)}$, i.e.

$$Z^{(1)} = (z^{(1)}(2), z^{(1)}(3), \ldots, z^{(1)}(n))$$

$$z^{(1)}(k) = 0.5^{x^{(1)}(k)} + 0.5^{x^{(1)}(k-1)} \tag{3}$$

Then the definition model of GM (1, 1), that is, the gray differential equation model of GM (1, 1) is:

$$x^{(0)}(k) + az^{(1)}(k) = b \tag{4}$$

The symbolic meaning of the model GM (1, 1) is: G—Grey, M—Model; (1, 1) – (First order equation, One variable).

In the formula, a is called the development coefficient, and b is the gray amount of action. $\hat{a}$ is set as the parameter vector to be estimated, that is, $\hat{a} = (a, b)^T$, and the least squares estimation parameter column of the above grey differential equation satisfies:

$$\hat{a} = (B^T B)^{-1} B^T Y_n \tag{5}$$

In the above formula:

$$B = \begin{bmatrix} -z^{(1)}(2) & 1 \\ -z^{(1)}(3) & 1 \\ \cdots & \cdots \\ -z^{(1)}(n) & 1 \end{bmatrix}, \quad Y_n = \begin{bmatrix} x^{(0)}(2) \\ x^{(0)}(3) \\ \cdots \\ x^{(0)}(n) \end{bmatrix} \tag{6}$$

The whitening equation, called the grey differential equation, is also called the shadow equation.

As mentioned above, the basic steps of the grey prediction method are:

(1) Establish a GM (1, 1) prediction model.

From the original sequence $X^{(0)}$, the $1 - AGO$ sequence and the calculated nearest sequence $Z^{(1)}$ is generated. The variable parameter $\hat{a} = (a, b)^T$ is estimated by the least squares method, and the GM (1, 1) model is obtained as a prediction model:

$$\frac{dx^{(1)}}{dt} + ax^{(1)} = b \tag{7}$$

The time response sequence (or time response function) of the prediction model is:

$$\hat{x}^{(1)}(t+1) = \left[x^{(0)}(1) - \frac{b}{a}\right]e^{-at} + \frac{b}{a} \tag{8}$$

Take $x^{(1)}(0) = x^{(0)}(1)$ to get the reduced value:

$$\hat{x}^{(0)}(t+1) = \hat{x}^{(1)}(t+1) - \hat{x}^{(1)}(t) = (1 - e^{a})\left[x^{(0)}(1) - \frac{b}{a}\right]e^{-at} \tag{9}$$

(2) Test the prediction accuracy

The main purpose of modeling is to predict that in order to improve the prediction accuracy, so we must first ensure that the simulation accuracy is sufficiently high. Therefore, it is necessary to perform a residual test on the above model firstly, and only the model that passes the residual test can be used as a prediction.

Find the residual variance of the actual value and the predicted value separately S_1, S_2:

$$S_1 = \left\{\frac{1}{n}\sum_{k=1}^{n}\left[\bar{x}^{(0)}(t) - \frac{1}{n}\sum_{k=1}^{n}\bar{x}^{(0)}(t)\right]\right\}^{\frac{1}{2}}$$

$$S_2 = \left\{\frac{1}{n}\sum_{k=1}^{n}\left[x^{(0)}(t) - \frac{1}{n}\sum_{k=1}^{n}x^{(0)}(t)\right]\right\}^{\frac{1}{2}} \tag{10}$$

Then calculate the ratio c and the error probability α

$$c = \frac{S_1}{S_2} \tag{11}$$

$$\alpha = p\left\{\left|\bar{x}^{(0)}(k) - \frac{1}{n}\sum_{k=1}^{n}\bar{x}^{(0)}(k)\right| < 0.6745S_2\right\} \tag{12}$$

The calculated c and α determine the accuracy of the model based on the gray prediction model accuracy level, as shown in Table 1 below:

Table 1. The accuracy inspection levels of gray prediction model.

Grade	α	c
Excellent	>0.95	<0.35
Good	>0.80	<0.45
Medium	>0.70	<0.50
Bad	≤0.70	≥0.65

2.2   The Grey Prediction Model

The exponential smoothing method is a kind of moving average method, which mainly gives different weights to past observations, and the weight of recent observation is greater than the weight of long-term observations. Mainly used for short- and medium-term forecasts.

Let the time series be $y_1, y_2, \cdots y_t$, then the basic formula for one exponential smoothing is:

$$S_t = \alpha * y_t + (1 - \alpha) * S_t - 1 \tag{13}$$

In the formula:

S_t—Smooth value of time t;
y_t—Actual value of time t
α—Smoothing constant, the value range is [0, 1]

The prediction formula is:

$$y'_{t+1} = \alpha * y_t + (1 - \alpha) * y'_t \tag{14}$$

y'_{t+1}—The predicted value of the time t + 1, that is, the smooth value of the t period S_t
y_t—The actual value of the t period;
y'_t—The predicted value of the t period, that is, the smooth value of the previous period S_{t-1}.

2.3   The Grey Prediction Model

In the changing period, it is often difficult to have a single prediction model that fits the reality of frequent fluctuations very closely. So under these circumstances, the combined prediction model may get a better than any independent prediction. The predicted value of the combined prediction model can reduce the systematic error of the prediction and significantly improve the prediction effect.

For the same object, the comprehensive prediction results are calculated by adopting various prediction methods and assigning certain weights to the prediction results.

$$Y = \sum W_i \times Y_i \tag{15}$$

In this formula:

Y—The results of combination forecasting model, that is, the final predicted values after the combined processing;
Y_i—The predicted value obtained by the ith prediction method;
W_i—The non-negative weighting factor given by the ith prediction method, $\sum W_i = 1$

The above weights are determined according to the standard deviation of various prediction methods, and the formula is as follows:

$$W_i = \frac{1}{n-1}\frac{S - S_i}{S} = \frac{1}{n-1}\frac{\sum S_i - S_i}{\sum S_i} \qquad (16)$$

Among them:

S_i—The standard deviation of the ith prediction model;
n—The Number of prediction methods

In most cases, for the sake of simplicity of calculation, the weight coefficient can be selected as the equal weight coefficient.

3 The Markov Optimization Model

The Markov process is mainly to study the current state and state transition laws of a running system to predict the state that may occur in the future.

According to the prediction result of the GM (1, 1) model, the relative error between the original sequence and the predicted sequence is calculated, and the state interval is determined according to the relative range of the error.

$$M = \frac{\hat{x}^{(0)}(k)}{x^{(0)}(k)} \times 100\% \qquad (17)$$

There are n possible states $E_1, E_2, \cdots E_n$ in the development of an event. The probability that an event starts from a certain state E_i and the next time shifts to another state E_j is called a state transition probability P_{ij}, and the state transition matrix P is:

$$P = \begin{pmatrix} P_{11} & P_{12} & \cdots & P_{1n} \\ P_{21} & P_{22} & \cdots & P \\ \cdots & \cdots & \cdots & \cdots \\ P_{n1} & P_{n2} & \cdots & P_{nn} \end{pmatrix} \qquad (18)$$

Through the state transition probability matrix, it is possible to predict the state or trend that may occur in the future by the current initial state.

$$P_{ij} = \frac{M_{ij}}{M_i} \qquad (19)$$

The state transition matrix is generally calculated using the principle of the frequency is approximately equal to the probability. Where: M_i is the total number of times the state E_i appears, and M_{ij} is the number of times the state E_i has transitioned to the state E_j.

According to the relative error state E_i measured by the predicted values of the matrix P and the combined prediction method, the median value of the relative error state interval $[e_{is}, e_{ir}]$ corresponding to the state is used as the optimized value of the result:

$$Y = \frac{\hat{x}^{(0)}(k)}{1 \pm \frac{1}{2}[e_{is}, e_{ir}]} \tag{20}$$

When the combined predicted value is larger than the actual value, the denominator plus minus sign takes a positive value, and when it is smaller than the actual value, it takes a negative value, and when the predicted value is more accurate than the actual value, there is no need to correct it.

The Markov optimization prediction modeling process is shown in Fig. 1.

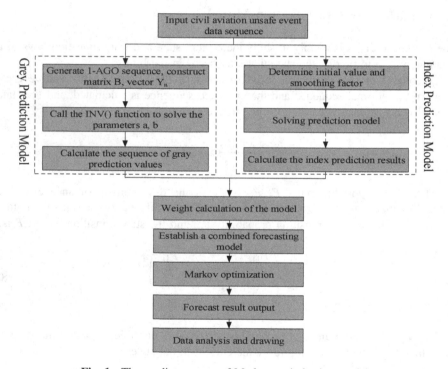

Fig. 1. The predict process of Markov optimization model

4 The Case Analysis

According to civil aviation unsafe event statistics [9], data from 2000 to 2012 can be obtained, as shown in Table 2 below. Based on the original data, the program was written using MATLAB, and the GM (1, 1) and exponential smoothing prediction models were established respectively to fit the number of unsafe events from 2000 to 2012. The number of unsafe events in the next three years was predicted.

Table 2. Actual values

Years	Number of events	Years	Number of events
2000	93	2007	116
2001	103	2008	120
2002	116	2009	159
2003	100	2010	119
2004	106	2011	230
2005	116	2012	295
2006	117	–	–

The cumulative number of gray GM (1, 1) prediction model $X^{(1)} = (x^{(1)}(1), x^{(1)}(2),\ldots,x^{(1)}(n))$, find: $a = -0.0432$, $b = 91.8082$, then the prediction formula of the gray prediction model is:

$$\hat{x}^{(1)}(t+1) = 2218.19e^{0.0432t} - 2125.19$$

By calculating the variance ratio and error probability, the grey prediction can be used to predict civil aviation unsafe events, but the accuracy is limited.

Then use exponential smoothing to make predictions. Since the data of exponential smoothing model predicts less than 15, so the initial value is:

$$S_1^{(1)} = S_1^{(2)} = S_1^{(3)} = \frac{y_1 + y_2 + y_3}{3} = 104$$

In the model, the selection of the smoothing factor has a critical impact on the accuracy of the prediction. The larger the value of α, the larger the proportion of y_t in the prediction, the larger the correction, the greater the impact of recent changes in the time series, and the greater the likelihood of interference. Therefore, the impact of the two aspects on the prediction results, the exponential smoothing coefficient $\alpha = 0.5$. The prediction results of civil aviation insecurity events from 2000 to 2012 are shown in Table 3 through the determination of relevant parameters.

Table 3. Prediction results of each model

Years	Grey prediction	Index forecast	Combination forecast
2000	93.00	93.00	93
2001	97.92	98.00	97.98
2002	102.24	107.00	105.57
2003	106.75	103.50	104.48
2004	111.46	104.75	106.76
2005	116.38	110.38	112.18
2006	121.52	113.69	116.04

(*continued*)

Table 3. (*continued*)

Years	Grey prediction	Index forecast	Combination forecast
2007	126.88	114.84	118.45
2008	132.48	117.42	121.94
2009	138.32	139.21	138.94
2010	144.43	180.11	169.40
2011	150.80	205.05	188.78
2012	157.45	250.03	222.25

Based on the formula (16), it can be determined that the results of the gray prediction and the exponential prediction take the weights of 0.3 and 0.7, respectively, to calculate the prediction result of the combined model.

Since civil aviation insecurity events have a certain randomness, direct prediction using a single prediction method cannot obtain ideal prediction values. The combined prediction method is used for weighting and then prediction. It can be found that the combined prediction model is better than the single model prediction. The relative error comparison of the three prediction results is shown in Fig. 2.

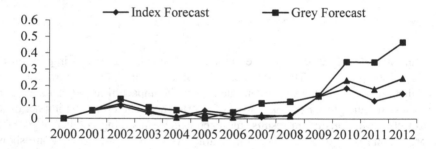

Fig. 2. Relative error comparisons

The state space is divided according to the relative error between the predicted result and the actual value. The number of state divisions is related to the number of samples and the error range of the fitting. Too many samples require more samples. If they are too small, the state difference is not obvious, and the meaning of fluctuation adjustment is lost. Usually 3-5 states are appropriate. According to the principle of equal probability and Markov application experience [10], the division status is shown in Table 4.

Through the Tables 2 and 3 can determine the state transition of civil aviation unsafe events from 2000 to 2012, as shown in Table 5.

Table 4. State division criteria

Status	1/M
Overestimate E1	[0.92, 0.98]
Normal E2	[0.98, 1.04]
Underestimate E3	[1.04, 1.1.10]
Extremely underestimated E4	[1.10, 1.34]

Table 5. Markov state of prediction results

Years	1/M	Status	Years	1/M	Status
2000	1	E2	2007	0.979280906	E1
2001	1.05127046	E3	2008	0.98410359	E2
2002	1.098767136	E3	2009	1.158737825	E4
2003	0.957155792	E1	2010	1.304594027	E4
2004	0.992841612	E2	2011	1.218374352	E4
2005	1.034078595	E2	2012	1.327311825	E4
2006	1.008304204	E2	–	–	–

According to the state transition probability definition and the representation of the state transition probability matrix, the four state transition cases are statistically obtained. Then the state transition probability matrix of the prediction can be obtained as follows:

$$P = \begin{pmatrix} 0 & 1 & 0 & 0 \\ 1/5 & 2/5 & 1/5 & 1/5 \\ 1/2 & 0 & 1/2 & 0 \\ 0 & 0 & 0 & 1 \end{pmatrix}$$

The number of civil aviation unsafe events in 2013–2015 is predicted and the predicted value is compared with the actual value. According to the Markov optimization model principle, state predictions for several years after the original data can be obtained. Taking 2012 as an example, the state interval in 2012 is E4, that is, the state probability vector X (2012) is (0 0 0 1).

According to formula (20), the prediction results from 2013 to 2015 can be calculated separately, as shown in Table 6.

Table 6. Forecast results from 2013 to 2015

Years	Combination prediction model prediction results	Combination prediction model precision	Markov optimization prediction results	Markov optimization precision
2013	242.5285985	295.8848902	0.80307483	0.979751292
2014	261.5000643	319.0300784	0.807098964	0.984660736
2015	296.6698071	361.9371647	0.752969054	0.918622245

Comparing the combined prediction model with the Markov optimized prediction results, it can be found that the prediction results and precision of the Markov optimized model are significantly improved.

5 Conclusions

In this paper, gray prediction and exponential smoothing prediction are used to predict civil aviation unsafe events. The weighted distribution of the two prediction results is used to establish a combined prediction model. Finally, the Markov process is used to optimize the results. The analysis shows that the prediction accuracy of 2013–2015 is as high as 98.0%, 98.5% and 91.9% respectively, which indicates that the model makes better use of the information of different single models and is suitable for the prediction of civil aviation unsafe events. At the same time, the model has high operability and strong practicability, which can provide a basis for the establishment of civil aviation unsafe incident prevention and control and safety management system.

Acknowledgements. The authors were supported by the National Natural Science Foundation of China (No. 71701202).

References

1. Jia, G., Wang, H.: Study on the composition and operation process of the risk management system of the air traffic safety. J. WUT (Inf. Manage. Eng.) **30**(5), 827–830 (2008)
2. Wang, Y., Liu, X.: Grey relation analysis and grey model for civil aviation accidents forecasting. J. Saf. Environ. **6**(6), 127–130 (2006)
3. Luo, F., Xiong, W.: The grey forecasting for signs of civil aviation accidents. Value Eng. **27**(1), 1–3 (2008)
4. Shi, Y., Lin, Y., Zou, Y., et al.: The prediction model on Chinese traffic deaths based on the grey topology. Math. Pract. Theory **43**(20), 1–3 (2008)
5. Fullwood, R.R., Hall, R.E., Martinez-Guridi, G.: Relating aviation service difficulty reports to accident data for safety trend prediction. Reliab. Eng. Syst. Saf. **60**(1), 83–87 (1998)
6. McCann, D.W.: NNICE-a neural network aircraft icing algorithm. Environ. Model Softw. **10**(10), 1335–1342 (2005)
7. Rui, G., Bastos, A., Almeida, A.D., et al.: Prediction of road accident severity using the ordered probit model. Transp. Res. Procedia **3**, 214–223 (2014)
8. Deng, J.: Gray Control System. Huazhong University of Science and Technology Press, Wuhan (1993)
9. The aviation safety office of CAAC.: Statistical analysis of civil aviation incidents of China. China Academy of Civil Aviation Science and Technology (2015)
10. Suo, F., Wang, S.: Prediction and application study of architecture accidents based on optimization combination. Shanxi Architect. **33**(19), 20–21 (2007)

Risk Assessment on Vertical Collision of Paired-Approach to Closely Spaced Parallel Runways

Fei Lu[1(✉)], Jing Zhang[1], Jun Wu[1], Zhaoyue Zhang[1], and Yan Kang[2]

[1] Civil Aviation University of China, Tianjin 300300, China
lufei315@126.com
[2] China Cargo Airlines, Shanghai 200335, China

Abstract. In this paper, analysis is conducted on the risk assessment regarding the vertical collision of CSPR (Closely Spaced Parallel Runways) paired-approach, to ensure flight safety. A vertical kinematics equation is established with analysis of CSPR paired approach and starting from the preconditions that the proceeding aircraft altitude is lower than that of the following aircraft during paired approach: the time consuming of passing initial safety separation by the proceeding aircraft decelerated less or greater than that of the proceeding aircraft with uniform speed. Based on the two conditions, its corresponding risk-evaluation model is established, proceeding from the aircraft ADS-B data and the analysis on the relation between aircraft position error and altitude maintain ability, relevant model parameters specified. Conclusion has been achieved on risk assessment that implementing vertical collision risk of paired approach has little to do with aircraft type and initial longitudinal separation, but has more correlation with initial vertical interval and aircraft altitude maintain ability; rules of at least 180-m vertical interval and altitude error not exceeding 40.77 m (within 95% flight time) must be obeyed when paired approach applied.

Keywords: CSPR paired-approach · Risk of collision · Safety assessment · Positioning error

1 Introduction

CSPR (Closely Spaced Parallel Runways) is referred to spaced parallel runways with less than 2500 ft (762 m) between runway centerlines. Based on the purpose of final approach safety, CAAC (Civil Aviation Administration of China) issued regulations that CSPR must be operated as a single runway, ensuring the enough separation between continuous approach aircraft to avoid the wake from the proceeding aircraft. The fact that Chinese domestic airports constructed with CSPR are mostly giant and busy, however, in accordance with regulations of two CSPR being regarded as single runway, problems and shortcomings will emerge: extra holding in terminal area, flight time and delay increased, and more fuel consumption and carbon emissions expected, constant aggravation of environment pollution including the fog and haze.

Simultaneous approach on two parallel runways with less than 762 m between runway centerlines is allowed when paired approach used. The significant difference

S. Liu and G. Yang (Eds.): ADHIP 2018, LNICST 279, pp. 535–548, 2019.
https://doi.org/10.1007/978-3-030-19086-6_59

with the conventional approach mode is that the following aircraft of the two continuous-approach airplanes must fly before the aircraft-wake diffusion surface by the proceeding aircraft, with purpose of wake avoidance. Application of CSPR will significantly expedite the runway utilization, decrease airborne queueing waiting time and is definitely an advantage to solve flight delay problems in busy airport terminal area.

Winder and Kuchar conducted research on flight simulation in 1999, through Monte Carlo simulation method, and evaluated the safety performance of collision-avoidance procedure when conflict exists between two aircraft [1]. In the same year, a new assumption was proposed by Hammer over CSPR paired approach: the following aircraft is allowed to approach simultaneously on the parallel runways in case of flying in a specific space with proceeding aircraft and flying before wake by the proceeding aircraft, and the longitudinal separation will be considered under the combined control of ADS-B (Automatic Dependent Surveillance-Broadcast) and CDTI (Cockpit Display Traffic Information) [2, 3]. Teo and Tomlin applied the theory of differential game and optimal control to determine the dangerous area of paired approach in 2003, having calculated the minimum runway separation of CSPR independent approach and minimum aircraft longitudinal separation of dependent approach [4]. In 2009 Zhang and Gu made researches on the several parallel-runway approach modes of "Shanghai Pudong International airport", established evaluation model of safe separation, and forwarded suggestions on the airport operation rules thru computing outcomes of the model and actual running data at a given target level of safety [5]. In 2011, Hammer analyzed the risk of aircraft collision in the process of paired approach when collision-avoidance maneuvering occurs [6]. Starting from the problems of high-frequency alarms activated when TCAS (Traffic Collision Avoidance System) used in CSPR, Kyle has been optimized the TCAS for CSPR in 2013 [7]. In 2013, the aircraft-wake motion characteristics applied in the most adverse conditions, Tian studied how the runways separation is affected by the slant range, angle of descent in approach and combination of aircraft types under CSPR parallel dependent approach. With utilization of minimum wake separation, NASA statistics crosswind data and aircraft parameters, Tian also proposed the way to define the runway centerline distance and runway threshold stagger [8]. Complying with the requirements of positioning error distribution and aircraft wake avoidance, in 2013, Lu and Zhang studied the risk of longitudinal collision during CSPR paired approach, established evaluation model of CSPR paired approach longitudinal separation, and proposed the formula of relevant model parameters [9]. In 2014, thru the simulation environment of SAN FRANCISCO INTERNATIONAL AIRPORT, Domino designed two real-time simulation schemes to evaluate the requirements on the pilot and ATC controller when CSPR paired approach applied [10]. In the same year, Sun established the mathematical model of aircraft-wake lateral displacement with time as variables, according to the motion characteristics in atmosphere during different phases and achieved the maximum time interval of aircraft wake without any effect from proceeding aircraft. The Monte Carlo simulation method was used again to find out the effect of collision risk on whether or not the collision-avoidance maneuvering occurs [11]. In 2015, for CSPR less than 2500 ft between runway centerlines, Houck and Powell analyzed the collision risk caused by aircraft perturbation motion via Monte Carlo simulation method [12]. In 2015, Landry studied the method of conflict detection and collision-preventing, analyzed and computed the safe area for paired approach of parallel runway [9]. In 2015, Lv Zongping established the risk-assessment model regarding the speed and approach time of two paired-approach aircraft, based on the distribution of velocity error and navigation equipment measurement error [13]. In 2016, Lu and others analyzed the influencing factors of aircraft positioning error, established the risk-evaluation model of lateral collision, based on the real-time flying process and requirements of wake avoidance, with consideration of lateral probability density function truncation compensation coefficient, and finally analyzed the effect of actual navigation performance on risk of lateral collision [14].

2 Risk-Evaluation Model of Lateral Collision in Paired Approach

Two aircraft is allowed to apply simultaneous parallel paired approach within such a longitudinal separation that satisfies the minimum safe interval of the collision preventing by the proceeding and following aircraft to avoid the wake effect before proceeding aircraft wake. The procedures of ATC control and flight all differ a lot from the conventional procedures. The aircraft in paired approach must obey the rules of IFR distance separation. Before the start of paired approach, the rules of separation regarding collision and wake must be in accordance with the current simultaneous approach regulations. An initial vertical and horizontal separation must be defined by ATC controller for the two aircraft conducting the paired approach. After the initial approach fix, the following aircraft pilot holding the responsibility for the separation maintain, one reason of collision-preventing from the proceeding aircraft by keeping enough distance, and the other reason of keeping a suitable close distance to avoid the wake effect before the aircraft wake.

Paired approach, an instrument approach procedure for CSPR, is the parallel dependent approach not the independent one. The initial concept of the paired approach, as Fig. 1A describes, an absolutely tracking-parallel procedure was finally be verified its disadvantage of avoiding the proceeding aircraft wake. Paired approach with slip angle was proposed as Fig. 1B describes, which can effectively avoid aircraft wake and possesses strengthness on collision avoidance.

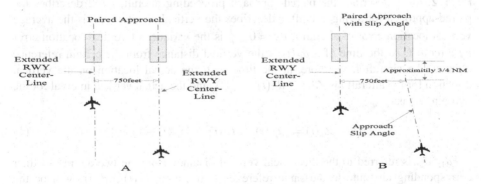

Fig. 1. Paired approach and paired approach with degree slip angle

Researches in this paper are based on the paired approach with slip angle described in Fig. 1B. Assumptions are set as followed: (1) independent position error assumed when approach paired, (2) no "flying-surpass" allowed in the process of paired approach, (3) no pilot's personal operating level difference and the same environment effect on positioning error, (4) no glide-path deviation caused by pilot's mishandling in the process of paired approach.

2.1 Explanation of Nomenclature

V_{li}: initial approach speed to proceeding aircraft in paired approach;
V_{lf}: final approach speed to proceeding aircraft in paired approach;
V_{ti}: initial approach speed to following aircraft in paired approach;
V_{tf}: final approach speed to following aircraft in paired approach;
L: distance from IAF (initial approach fix) to runway threshold;
S_0: initial separation between two paired-approach aircraft;
a_l: paired-approach aircraft acceleration to proceeding aircraft in decelerated motion (positive or negative, a vector);
a_t: paired-approach aircraft acceleration to following aircraft in decelerated motion (positive or negative, a vector);
t: time;
L_0: distance of L_0 before threshold, the following aircraft starting from 3-degree-slip-angle approach to approach along the extended RWY centerline;
H: between the two parallel runways;
Δh: initial vertical interval between the two aircraft;
ϕ_l: angle of glide for proceeding aircraft;
ϕ_t: angle of glide for following aircraft;
θ: approach slip angle of the following aircraft;

2.2 Model Establishment

In the process of paired approach, vertical location error is mainly affected by positioning error. Let the vertical error of aircraft i at time of t as $\varepsilon_{iz}(t)$. $\varepsilon_{iz}(t)$ is distributed according to μ_{iz}, Gaussian distribution of variance σ_{iz}^2, that is $\varepsilon_{iz}(t) \sim N(\mu_{iz}, \sigma_{iz}^2)$, $i = 1, 2$, $i = 1$ describes the paired-approach proceeding aircraft, $i = 2$ describes the paired-approach following aircraft, z describes the vertical direction. μ_{iz} is the average vertical location error of aircraft i, $\mu_{iz} = 0$; σ_{iz}^2 is the variance of vertical location error by aircraft i. At the time of t, $d_{iz}(t)$ is the vertical distance from the certain reference point to the aircraft i, therefore, at the time of t, the actual location on the vertical direction for the aircraft i is $Z_i(t) = d_{iz}(t) + \varepsilon_{iz}(t)$, and the actual vertical interval for the two aircraft is:

$$Z_1(t) - Z_2(t) = [d_{1z}(t) - d_{2z}(t)] + [\varepsilon_{1z}(t) - \varepsilon_{2z}(t)] \quad (1)$$

d_{1z}, d_{2z} is referred to the theoretical vertical distance from the two aircraft to their corresponding air-route to the same reference point, then $d_{1z}(t) - d_{2z}(t)$ will be the theoretical vertical distance between the two paired-approach aircraft at the time of t, let it as $L_z(t)$. Therefore at the time of t, the actual vertical distance for the two aircraft also can be described as:

$$Z_1(t) - Z_2(t) = L_z(t) + (\varepsilon_{1z}(t) - \varepsilon_{2z}(t)) \tag{2}$$

$\varepsilon_{iz}(t)$ is distributed according to μ_{iz}, Gaussian distribution of variance σ_{iz}^2, then $\varepsilon_{2z}(t)$ is distributed according to μ_{2z}, Gaussian distribution of variance σ_{2z}^2, that is $\varepsilon_{1z}(t) \sim N(\mu_{1z}, \sigma_{1z}^2)$, $\varepsilon_{2z}(t) \sim N(\mu_{2z}, \sigma_{2z}^2)$, then $\varepsilon_{1z}(t) - \varepsilon_{2z}(t)$ is distributed according to $\mu_{1z} - \mu_{2z}$, Gaussian distribution of variance $\sigma_{1z}^2 + \sigma_{2z}^2$.

$$\varepsilon_{1z}(t) - \varepsilon_{2z}(t) \sim N(\mu_{1z} - \mu_{2z}, \sigma_{1z}^2 + \sigma_{2z}^2) \tag{3}$$

According to the Gaussian distribution,

$$L_z(t) + (\varepsilon_{1z}(t) - \varepsilon_{2z}(t)) \sim N(L_z(t) + (\mu_{1z} - \mu_{2z}), \sigma_{1z}^2 + \sigma_{2z}^2) \tag{4}$$

Formula (3.18) is the model of the two aircraft vertical error, and then the model of vertical collision risk will be achieved:

$$P_Z = p\{z_1 \le L_z(t) + (\varepsilon_{1z}(t) - \varepsilon_{2z}(t)) \le z_2\} \tag{5}$$

In the formula, z_1, z_2 is the max and min vertical separation value of collision-risk.

$$P_Z = \frac{1}{\sqrt{2\pi(\sigma_{1z}^2 + \sigma_{2z}^2)}} \int_{z_1}^{z_2} f(z)dz \tag{6}$$

$$f(z) = \exp(-\frac{(z - (L_z(t) + \mu_{1z} - \mu_{2z}))^2}{2(\sigma_{1x}^2 + \sigma_{2x}^2)}) \tag{7}$$

According to the assumed conditions, in the process of paired approach, aircraft positioning errors are independent, with the same environment effect, and then $\mu_{1z} = \mu_{2z} = \mu$, $\sigma_{1x}^2 = \sigma_{2x}^2 = \sigma^2$. Formula (7) can be simplified as below:

$$f(z) = \exp(-\frac{(z - L_z(t))^2}{4(\sigma^2)}) \tag{8}$$

According to the formulas (6), (7) and (9) and the definition of probability density function:

$$P_Z \approx (z_2 - z_1)\frac{f(z_2 - L_z(t)) + f(z_1 - L_z(t))}{2} \tag{9}$$

For the possibility of collision, Z_1 and Z_2 are equal with opposite sign, as half as the sum of the two aircraft altitude.

One time of collision is calculated as two accidents, then the risk of vertical collision for CSPR paired approach P_{CLSPA} will be:

$$P_{CLSPA} = 2NP_Z \tag{10}$$

N is the number of paired-approach aircraft per unit time,

$$N = (V_{lf} + S_0)/(\sum_{i=1}^{n} \sum_{j=1}^{n} P_{ij}(\delta_i + \delta_j) + \frac{1}{2}S_0 + w) \tag{11}$$

In the formula, i is the proceeding aircraft type in paired approach, δ_i as length of the fuselage, P_i as the percentage of aircraft fleet, j as the following aircraft in paired approach, δ_j, as length of the fuselage, P_j as the percentage of aircraft fleet, in the process of paired approach, λ_i as height of the fuselage for the proceeding aircraft, λ_j as height of the fuselage for the following aircraft. Therefore the risk model of vertical collision for CSPR paired approach will be:

$$\begin{cases} P_{CLSPA} = 2N(z_2 - z_1)[f(z_2 - L_z(t)) + f(z_1 - L_z(t))] \\ z_1 = -\sum_{i=1}^{n} \sum_{j=1}^{n} P_{ij}(\lambda_i + \lambda_j) \\ z_2 = \sum_{i=1}^{n} \sum_{j=1}^{n} P_{ij}(\lambda_i + \lambda_j) \\ N = (V_{lf} + S_0)/(\sum_{i=1}^{n} \sum_{j=1}^{n} P_{ij}(\delta_i + \delta_j) + \frac{1}{2}S_0 + w) \\ P_{ij} = P_i P_j \end{cases} \tag{12}$$

In the process of paired approach, in vertical direction, the location relation and motion status between the paired-approach aircraft can be described in four conditions as in Table 1.

Table 1. The location relation and motion status between the paired-approach aircraft

Serial number	Description
1	In paired approach, higher altitude of proceeding aircraft than the following aircraft and the time cost by proceeding aircraft deceleration less than the time passing the initial separation by the following aircraft
2	In paired approach, higher altitude of proceeding aircraft than the following aircraft and the time cost by proceeding aircraft deceleration more than the time passing the initial separation by the following aircraft
3	In paired approach, lower altitude of proceeding aircraft than the following aircraft and the time cost by proceeding aircraft deceleration less than the time passing the initial separation by the following aircraft
4	In paired approach, lower altitude of proceeding aircraft than the following aircraft and the time cost by proceeding aircraft deceleration more than the time passing the initial separation by the following aircraft

For the case of the proceeding aircraft having higher altitude, it is of more advantages to the miss-approach in abnormal condition. And the condition of higher altitude of proceeding aircraft than the following aircraft is more likely to be utilized. Therefore, the condition mentioned before is only studied in this paper. Figure 2 describes the process of paired approach with slip angle.

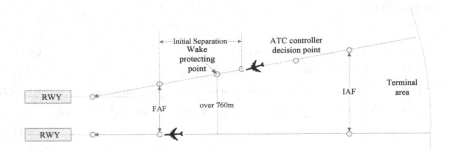

Fig. 2. The process of paired approach

Before the proceeding aircraft reaches FAF and the following aircraft surpassing the IAF in the paired approach, ATC controller must give instructions on the safe separation, pairing the two aircraft successfully. The following aircraft must fly outside the wake-protection area when the proceeding reaches the FAF. The aircraft must be operated in a uniform speed when approaching to the FAF, and decelerates after crossing the FAF, maintaining the speed of final approach speed till the completion of paired approach.

$$
\begin{cases}
T_1 = \frac{V_{lf} - V_{li}}{a_l} \\
T_2 = \frac{S_0}{V_{ti} \cos \theta} \\
T_3 = \frac{S_0}{V_{ti} \cos \theta} + \frac{V_{tf} \cos \theta - V_{ti} \cos \theta}{a_t \cos \theta} \\
T_4 = \frac{V_{lf} - V_{li}}{a_l} + \frac{L - \frac{V_{lf}^2 - V_{li}^2}{2a_l}}{V_{lf}}
\end{cases}
\tag{13}
$$

The motion process of the two paired-approach aircraft will be discussed in the conditions below.

If $T_1 < T_2$, as the proceeding aircraft fly across the FAF, the time cost by completing deceleration is less than the time cost by the following aircraft, in the uniform speed of initial approach, surpassing the initial safe separation instructed by ATC. The motion status of two paired-approach aircraft is as below:

When $0 \leq t < T_1$, the proceeding aircraft motives in a decelerative way inside the FAF and the following aircraft motives at an uniform speed outside FAF in paired approach;

When $T_1 \leq t < T_2$, the proceeding aircraft motives at an uniform speed inside the FAF and the following aircraft motives at an uniform speed outside FAF in paired approach;

When $T_2 \leq t < T_3$, the proceeding aircraft motives at an uniform speed inside the FAF and the following aircraft motives in a decelerative way inside FAF in paired approach;

When $T_3 \leq t < T_4$, the proceeding aircraft motives at an uniform speed inside the FAF and the following aircraft motives at an uniform speed inside FAF in paired approach;

then, $L_z(t)$ is:

$$
L_z(t) = \begin{cases}
\Delta h + (V_{li}t + \frac{1}{2}a_lt^2)\tan\phi_l - V_{ti}t\cos\theta\tan\phi_t, & 0 \leq t < T_1 \\
\Delta h - \frac{(V_{lf}-V_{li})^2\tan\phi_l}{2a_l} + (V_{lf}\tan\phi_l - V_{ti}\cos\theta\tan\phi_t)t, & T_1 \leq t < T_2 \\
\Delta h - \frac{(V_{lf}-V_{li})^2}{2a_l}\tan\phi_l + (V_{lf}\tan\phi_l - V_{ti}\cos\theta\tan\phi_t)t - \frac{1}{2}a_t(t - \frac{S_0}{V_{ti}\cos\theta})^2\cos\theta\tan\phi_t, & T_2 \leq t < T_3 \\
\Delta h - \frac{V_{ti}-V_{tf}}{V_{ti}}S_0\tan\phi_t - \frac{(V_{lf}-V_{li})^2}{2a_l}\tan\phi_l + (V_{lf}\tan\phi_l - V_{tf}\cos\theta\tan\phi_t)t + \frac{(V_{tf}-V_{ti})^2}{2a_t}\cos\theta\tan\phi_t, & T_3 \leq t \leq T_4
\end{cases}
$$

$$(14)$$

According the formula above, the descent gradient relationship of the two paired-approach aircraft is:

$$
\tan\phi_t = \frac{L\tan\phi_l + \Delta h}{L + S_0} \tag{15}
$$

If $T_1 \geq T_2$, that is, the time cost by the proceeding aircraft deaccelerated is not less than the time cost by the following aircraft flying across the initial separation. The motion status of the two paired-approach aircraft are:

When $0 \leq t < T_2$, the proceeding aircraft motives in a decelerative way inside the FAF and the following aircraft motives at an uniform speed outside FAF in paired approach;

When $T_2 \leq t < T_1$, the proceeding aircraft motives in a decelerative way inside the FAF and the following aircraft motives in a decelerative way inside the FAF in paired approach;

When $T_1 \leq t < T_3$, the proceeding aircraft motives at an uniform speed inside the FAF and the following aircraft motives in a decelerative way inside the FAF in paired approach;

When $T_3 \leq t < T_4$, the proceeding aircraft motives at an uniform speed inside the FAF and the following aircraft motives at an uniform speed inside the FAF in paired approach;

Then, $L_z(t)$ will be:

$$
L_z(t) = \begin{cases}
\Delta h + (V_{li}t + \frac{1}{2}a_lt^2)\tan\phi_l - V_{ti}t\cos\theta\tan\phi_t, & 0 \leq t < T_2 \\
\Delta h - (V_{ti}t + \frac{1}{2}a_t(t - \frac{S_0}{V_{ti}\cos\theta})^2)\cos\theta\tan\phi_t + (V_{li}t + \frac{1}{2}a_lt^2)\tan\phi_l, & T_2 \leq t < T_1 \\
\Delta h + (V_{lf}t - \frac{(V_{lf}-V_{li})^2}{2a_l})\tan\phi_l - (V_{ti}t + \frac{1}{2}a_t(t - \frac{S_0}{V_{ti}\cos\theta})^2]\cos\theta\tan\phi_t, & T_1 \leq t < T_3 \\
\Delta h - (\frac{V_{ti}-V_{tf}}{V_{ti}}S_0 + V_{tf}t\cos\theta - \frac{(V_{tf}-V_{ti})^2}{2a_t}\cos\theta)\tan\phi_t + (V_{lf}t - \frac{(V_{lf}-V_{li})^2}{2a_l})\tan\phi_l, & T_3 \leq t \leq T_4
\end{cases}
$$

$$(16)$$

The descent gradient relationship of the two paired-approach aircraft is in accordance with the formula (17).

3   The Risk Analysis on Vertical Collision in Paired Approach

For the time being CSPR paired-approach is not implemented in Chinese domestic airports, failure to get relevant operation parameters. Therefore the paired-approach data of a specific airport will be analyzed to evaluate the vertical collision risk and study the relationship between the parameters and the vertical collision risk. Finally, the vertical maintain ability possessed by the paired-approach aircraft will be figured out under different environments. The airport data is: the distance from FAF to threshold $L = 12500$ m, the distance from the following aircraft approach inflection point to threshold $l = 1500$ m, initial paired-approach safe separation $S_0 = 1000$ m, when approach paired, the initial altitude difference of the two aircraft is 310 m, descent gradient of proceeding aircraft is 3.8%. The parameters of aircraft operated in the airport are listed in Table 2.

Table 2. Aircraft type parameters

Serial Number	Type	Classification	Wing span (M)	Length of fuselage (M)	Height of fuselage (M)	Proportion
1	A319	M	34.09	33.84	11.76	0.0715
2	A320	M	34.10	37.57	11.76	0.2102
3	A321	M	34.10	44.51	11.76	0.1319
4	A332	H	60.3	58.82	17.39	0.0298
5	A333	H	60.3	63.60	16.85	0.0366
6	B738	M	35.79	39.50	12.5	0.2817
7	B752	H	38.05	54.50	13.56	0.0170
8	B772	H	60.90	63.70	18.50	0.0119
9	B73G	M	35.8	33.6	12.5	0.0638
10	B73W	M	35.7	33.6	12.5	0.0247
11	B773	H	60.90	73.90	18.5	0.0187
12	B788	H	60.00	56.69	17.0	0.0272
13	E190	M	28.72	36.24	10.57	0.0528
14	A380	H	79.75	72.75	24.09	0.0068
15	B733	M	28.3	11.3	28.6	0.0077
16	B763	H	47.57	54.9	15.8	0.0077

Let the aircraft type of k as γ_k, proportion of aircraft fleet as p_k, number "q" of types of aircraft contained in one classification of aircraft. Then the type parameter γ can be calculated based on the formula:

$$\gamma = \sum_{k=1}^{q} \gamma_k \left(p_k / \sum_{k=1}^{q} p_k \right) \tag{17}$$

The aircraft type parameters are calculated and listed in Table 3.

Table 3. Aircraft type parameters

Aircraft classification	Length of fuselage[a] (M)	Height of fuselage[a] (M)	Initial approach speed[b] (M/S)	Final approach speed[b] (M/S)	Acceleration[b] (M/S2)	Proportion
Heavy (H)	61.69	17.71	92.1	74.6	−0.16	0.156
Medium (M)	38.4	12.0	90.7	73.3	−0.16	0.844
Average	41.9	12.9	90.9	73.5	−0.16	–

Note: [a]is calculated by formula (16), and [b]stands for the statistic ADS-B data.

Currently, aircraft is almost equipped with ADS-B and ADS-B will be a type of essential equipment. ADS-B data is transmitted once per second with high accuracy. ADS-B data includes: coordinates of latitude and longitude, altitude and speed, etc. Thru receiving and analysis of ADS-B signal, gaining flight track and altitude, altitude maintain ability is analyzed. 100 flights were randomly selected from January to July 2017 to complete the statistics of their operation parameters. Aircraft altitude data and three-dimensional tracking data are shown in Figs. 3 and 4.

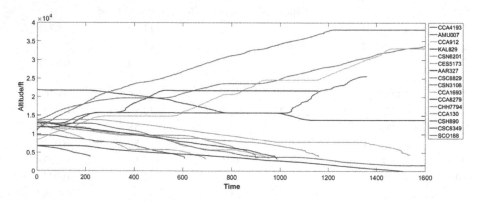

Fig. 3. Aircraft altitude to time passed figure

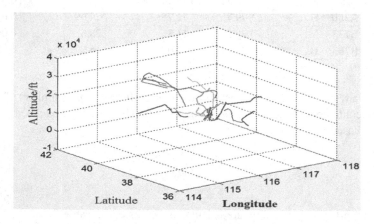

Fig. 4. Aircraft dimensional tracking data

Aircraft altitude maintain ability is defined as the vertical deviation range airborne within 95% flight time. Then the variance of position error on its altitude can be calculated as below:

$$\sigma = \rho/\Phi^{-1}\left(\frac{1+p}{2}\right) \tag{18}$$

σ stands for the value of aircraft altitude maintain ability. Φ^{-1} stands for the inverse function of standard normal distribution (SND), p = 0.95.

With the process of statistics, ρ = 15.24 m. Calculated with formula (18) we have $\sigma = 7.8$.

In the process of paired approach, after the following aircraft flying across FAF, the two aircraft proceed at their final approach speed, the longitudinal separation will be not determined. Vertical interval relates directly to the longitudinal separation in paired approach, and thus it is unnecessary to determine vertical interval. Therefore there is no need to consider the vertical interval and collision risk when the following aircraft flying across FAF. The time slot for consideration on vertical collision risk shall be made before the completion of aircraft de-acceleration. Figure 5 describes the overall collision risk and collision risk of combined aircraft type.

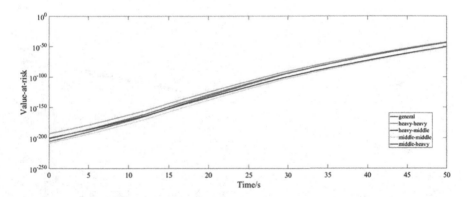

Fig. 5. Vertical collision risk

Figure 5 shows that vertical collision risk increases with the time passed in paired approach, mainly for the vertical interval decreased with time. The maximum risk occurs in the case of heavy proceeding aircraft and medium following aircraft and the minimum risk occurs in the case of both aircraft being medium. The vertical collision risk has little to do with aircraft type.

Furthermore, the model will be studied on how the initial vertical interval and positioning error affect the vertical collision risk.

As the risks described in Fig. 6 under different initial vertical interval, a conclusion will be achieved that initial vertical separation should be at least 180 m for the fact that as vertical interval decreases, the overall and vertical risks increases, and vertical risk

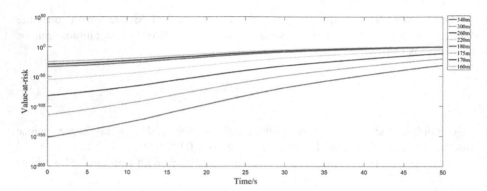

Fig. 6. The effect of initial vertical separation on vertical collision risk

has little to do with initial vertical interval, and vertical interval lesser than 180 m, vertical collision risk will surpass 1.5×10^{-9}.

As the risks described in Fig. 7 under different initial longitudinal separation, a conclusion will be achieved that the overall and vertical risks decreases when initial longitudinal separation decreases and initial vertical interval remaining the same. Vertical risk has little to do with initial longitudinal separation.

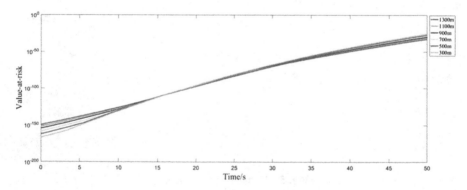

Fig. 7. The effect of initial longitudinal separation on vertical collision risk

As the risks described in Fig. 8 under different positioning error, a conclusion will be achieved that the overall and vertical risks increases when positioning error increases, and vertical risk has more correlation with initial vertical interval. When the variance of positioning error is greater than 20.8 m, the vertical collision risk will exceed 1.5×10^{-9}. Aircraft altitude maintain ability will be not greater than 40.77 m (vertical positioning error within 95% flight time). The aircraft vertical position maintain will be at least 40.77 m when paired approach implemented.

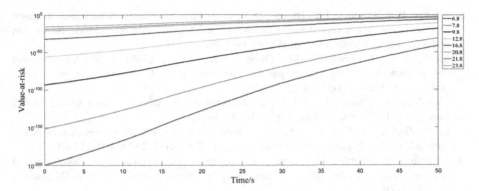

Fig. 8. The effect of altitude maintain ability on vertical collision risk

4 Conclusion

Basic probability theory being applied, factors of the location relationship between the two paired-approach aircraft, the number of paired-approach aircraft per hour, vertical motion function, and aircraft altitude maintain ability being considered, this paper has established the vertical collision risk of paired approach to CSPR, determined the model parameters thru ADS-B statistic data. With analysis of the vertical collision risk of paired approach to CSPR, conclusion has been achieved that ivertical collision risk of paired approach has little to do with aircraft type and initial longitudinal separation, but has more correlation with initial vertical interval and aircraft altitude maintain ability. When implementing paired approach, suitable initial vertical distance shall be specified in the purpose of ensure the risk of vertical collision to paired approach continuously complying with the target level of safety regulated by ICAO.

Acknowledgements. The authors were supported by the National Natural Science Foundation of China (No.71701202).

References

1. Winder, L.F., Kuchar, J.K.: Evaluation of collision avoidance maneuvers for parallel approach. J. Guid. Control Dyn. J. **22**(6), 801–8072 (1999)
2. Hammer, J.: Study of the geometry of a dependent approach procedure to closely spaced parallel runways. In: Digital Avionics Systems Conference, pp. 4C.3-1–4C 3-8 (1999)
3. Hammer, J.: Case study of paired approach procedure to closely spaced parallel runways. Air Traffic Control Q. **8**(3), 223–252 (2000)
4. Teo, R., Tomlin, C.J.: Computing danger zones for provably safe closely spaced parallel approaches. J. Guid. Control Dyn. **26**(3), 434–442 (2003)
5. Zhang, Z.N., Wang, L.L., et al.: Introduction to Flight Interval Safety Assessment. Science Press, Beijing (2009)

6. Eftekari, R.R., Hammer, J.B., Havens, D.A., et al.: Feasibility analyses for paired approach procedures for closely spaced parallel runways. In: Integrated Communications, Navigation and Surveillance Conference, pp. I5-1–I5-14. IEEE (2011)
7. Smith, K.A., Kochenderfer, M., Olson, W.A., et al.: Collision avoidance system optimization for closely spaced parallel operations through surrogate modeling. Massachusetts Institute of Technology (2013)
8. Tian, Y., Sun, J., Wan, L.L., et al.: Separation determining method of closely spaced parallel runways. J. Traffic Transp. Eng. **13**(1), 70–76 (2013)
9. Lu, F., Zhang, Z.N., Wei, Z.Q., et al.: Longitudinal collision risk safety assessment of paired approach to closed spaced parallel runways. Chin. Saf. Sci. J. **23**(8), 108–113 (2013)
10. Domino, D.A, Tuomey, D., Stassen, H.P., et al.: Paired approaches to closely spaced runways: results of pilot and ATC simulation. In: Digital Avionics Systems Conference, pp. 1B2-1–1B2-15. IEEE (2014)
11. Sun, J., Tian, Y.: Collision risk analysis of closely spaced parallel runways under parallel dependent approach procedure. J. Harbin Univ. Commer. (Natural Sciences Edition) **30**(2), 224–245 (2014)
12. Houck, S.W., Powell, J.D.: Probability of midair collision during ultra closely spaced parallel approaches. J. Guid. Control Dyn. **26**(5), 702–710 (2015)
13. Landry, S.J., Lynam, A.: Safe zone for closely spaced parallel approaches. J. Guid. Control Dyn. **34**(2), 608–613 (2015)
14. Lu, F., Zhu, N., Yang, S., et al.: Assessment of lateral collision risk in closed spaced parallel runways paired approach. Chin. Saf. Sci. J. **26**(11), 87–92 (2016)

A Fine-Grained Detection Mechanism for SDN Rule Collision

Qiu Xiaochen[1], Zheng Shihui[1(✉)], Gu Lize[1], and Cai Yongmei[2]

[1] College of Cyberspace Security,
Beijing University of Posts and Telecommunication, Beijing, China
shihuizh@bupt.edu.cn
[2] College of Computer Science and Engineering,
Xinjiang University of Finance and Economics, Urumqi, China

Abstract. The rules issued by third-party applications may have direct violations or indirect violations with existing security flow rules in the SDN (software-defined network), thereby leading to the failure of security rules. Currently, existing methods cannot detect the rule collision in a comprehensive and fine-grained manner. This paper proposes a deep detection mechanism for rule collision that can detect grammatical errors in the flow rules themselves, and can also detect direct and indirect rule collisions between third-party and security applications based on the set intersection method. In addition, our mechanism can effectively and automatically resolve the rule collision. Finally, we implement the detection mechanism in the RYU controller, and use Mininet to evaluate the function and performance. The results show that the mechanism proposed in this paper can accurately detect the static, dynamic and dependency collisions of flow rules, and ensure that the decline of throughput of the northbound interface of the SDN network is controlled at 20%.

Keywords: Software-defined network · OpenFlow · Flow table ·
Collision detection and resolution

1 Introduction

The software-defined network (SDN) [1] is a new type of network architecture proposed by Clean State research group of Stanford University, which brings a tremendous change to the traditional network. The essential features of SDN are the separation of control and data plane and an open network programmable ability. In 2008, the research team led by Professor Nick McKeown of Stanford University proposed the concept of OpenFlow. The OpenFlow protocol [2] is currently the mainstream southbound communication protocol of SDN. It defines the communication standard between SDN controllers and OpenFlow switches.

With the development of SDN technology, the security issues of SDNs have become increasingly clear. Our research primarily focuses on the security threat to the SDN's application layer, which is called the flow rule collision [3, 4]. The openness and programmability of SDNs allow a large number of third-party applications, including security applications, run on the network concurrently. Because the logic and

S. Liu and G. Yang (Eds.): ADHIP 2018, LNICST 279, pp. 549–559, 2019.
https://doi.org/10.1007/978-3-030-19086-6_60

functions of these applications are different, they will issue different flow rules according to their needs, and there will inevitably be rule collision.

For the abovementioned threat of rule collision, the Porras [6] research group from the United States designed a security-enhanced kernel for the SDN operating system in the Nox controller [7], which is called FortNox, and proposed a policy collision detection method based on the alias sets algorithm. The source IP address and destination IP address in the flow entry are put into two sets, and the addresses before and after the modification in the Set-Field flow entry are also added to the above two sets. Finally, the source address and destination address sets are compared with firewall rules in the SDN to discover the policy collision. FLOVER [8] is a new detection system that can detect whether a flow policy deployed in an OpenFlow network violates the security policies. This system can detect invalid and invisible routes due to errors, but it does not consider firewall policies. Reference [5] proposed a method based on "First-order" logic to detect rule collision, and deployed an "inference engine" to detect rule collision before issuing the flow rules. Wang Juan et al. proposed a real-time dynamic policy collision detection solution based on FlowPath [9], which detected direct and indirect collision using the real-time state of the SDN. Reference [10] proposed to use ADRS (anomaly detecting and resolving for SDN) to solve the anomalies in the policies and rules, used the interval tree model to quickly scan the flow table, and established a shared model to allocate network priorities. Through these two models, they proposed an automated algorithm to detect and resolve collisions. The Khurshid team [11] proposed a new type of inspection tool named Veriflow. The tool is located between the controller and the network equipment, and creates a Tire tree by coding to simulate the forwarding of the new rules after they are added, thus realizing network detection.

The aforementioned solutions are not comprehensive in terms of rule collision detection. Fortnox's solution based on the alias sets algorithm can only detect simple dynamic collision and intercept them, and only the source and destination IP address of the OpenFlow field are considered in the dependency collision detection. Therefore, this paper will propose a more complete and fine-grained rule collision detection mechanism with automated collision solution. The new mechanism can fully detect the grammatical errors existing in the flow rules themselves, thereby preventing excessive invalid rules that are causing redundancy in the flow table. In addition, it can also detect the fine-grained direct and indirect violations between the rules from third-party application and security application.

2   OpenFlow Rule Collision Representation

2.1   OpenFlow Protocol

The OpenFlow protocol indicates that each OpenFlow switch can have multiple flow tables, each table may contain multiple flow entries, which describe how to match and process data packets arriving at the switch. The flow entry consists of three main parts: "match fields", "counters" and "actions". The "match field" is used to define the information of the packets that needs to be matched. The "counter" field is used to count the number of packets processed in this flow entry. The "actions" represent the actions to be performed on data packets that match this flow entry, including "forward", "discard", "modify" and other operations.

Next we formalize the flow table in an OpenFlow switch, all the flow rules $F(j)$ in the j-th OpenFlow switch in SDN network data plane are formalized as:

$$F(j) = F_1, F_2, F_3 \ldots F_n \tag{1}$$

Each flow rule F_i consists of the matching domain C_i, the priority P_i and the action field A_i, n is the number of flow rules, it may be defined as follows:

$$F_i = C_i, P_i, A_i (1 \leq i \leq n) \tag{2}$$

$$C_i = (f_1, f_2, f_3 \ldots f_n) \tag{3}$$

In the matching domain C_i, f_1, f_2, f_3 ... f_n respectively represent the header field of OpenFlow protocol. OpenFlow1.0 protocol contains 12 header fields: in_port, dl_src, dl_dst, dl_type, dl_vlan, dl_vlan_pcp, nw_src, nw_dst, nw_proto, nw_tos, tp_src, tp_dst. In the new version of OpenFlow protocol, the number of match fields is also increasing.

2.2 Classification of Flow Rule Collision

Reference [5] defines two types of flow rule collisions: static and dynamic collisions. A static collision refers to an internal collision in the rules themselves which have the wrong parameters or error syntax. A dynamic collision refers to a collision among flow entries, in a flow table where two or more flow entries match with one data packet at the same time.

In addition to the two types of rule collisions mentioned above, we call the flow rule whose "actions" field contains the content of rewriting the data packets the Set-Field rule. An attacker can issue malicious Set-Field rules that could rewrite the packet header that arrives at the switches, and the dependency relationship between the Set-Field rules may cause the security rules to be invalid. This collision is called a dependency collision.

As shown in the SDN topology in Fig. 1, the network contains three switches, one controller, and four hosts. The security rule in the SDN controller network is that: Host A (10.0.1.12) to C (10.0.13.12) cannot communicate. If an attacker issues the following three Set-Field rules:

1. S1:Match(Src:10.0.1.12/24,Dst:10.0.2.12/24) Action (SET_NW_SRC:10.0.4.12/24 AND Forward)
2. S2:Match(Src:10.0.4.12/24,Dst:10.0.2.12/24) Action (SET_NW_DST:10.0.3.12/24 AND Forward)
3. S3:Match(Src:10.0.4.12/24,Dst:10.0.3.12/24) Action (Forward).

The packet sent by host A (Src: 10.0.1.12 Dst: 10.0.2.12) will be rewritten by the Set-Field rules existing in switch S1 and S2. Finally it will arrive at host C through

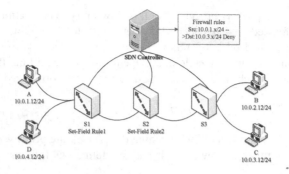

Fig. 1. Dependency collision that causes failure of firewall rules

switches S1, S2, and S3 due to the modification of the packet, which is a violation of the security rule that host A cannot communicate with host C. This type of collision is due to the dependency of the flow rules and it is extremely harmful.

3 Comprehensive Rule Collision Detection Mechanism

3.1 Solution Outline

As shown in Fig. 2, our comprehensive detection and solution mechanism for rule collisions is mainly implemented at the SDN control plane. When the supernatant applications issue the flow rules by the northbound interface, first they will be checked by the identity authentication and authorization mechanism of the controller. Then, the collision detection mechanism can intercept the rules to be issued and real-time detect whether there are static collisions in rules themselves and/or dynamic collisions with the existing security rules. Once there is a collision, it will proceed with the automatic collision solution. In addition, the global Set-Field type rules in the switches are offline compared with all existing security rules in the SDN to detect dependency collisions, which is performed using the improved alias-set algorithm.

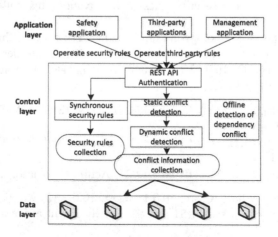

Fig. 2. The overall structure of the detection mechanism

3.2 Collision Detection Algorithm

First, the detection mechanism for static collisions proposed in this paper mainly detects whether there are some errors in the rule to be issued from the following aspects: the dl_src and dl_dst are the same, the nw_src and nw_dst are the same, and whether the value range of the header fields are legal. After the detection of the static collision, incorrect flow rules will be effectively filtered to prevent them from being sent to the OpenFlow switches.

The detection of dynamic collisions primarily focuses between the flow rules from third-party applications and those from applications with higher priority. To establish a feasible model of collision detection, we first need to determine the relationship between the two flow rules, including equal, inclusive, intersectant and irrelevant. According to the definition of the openflow flow rule in the previous chapter, the matching domain of the rule F_i can be represented as C_i, f_k^i represents the k-th header field in C_i, the F_j, C_j and f_k^j is alike. The relationship between flow rules F_i and F_j is defined as follows:

1. Equal: For the two match domain C_i and C_j in two flow rules, $\forall k : f_k^i = f_k^j (1 \leq k \leq n)$, the value of the header field are correspondingly equal with each other.
2. Inclusive: For C_i and C_j, $\forall k : f_k^i \subseteq f_k^j (1 \leq k \leq n)$, and $\exists k : f_k^i \neq f_k^j$, then the i-th flow rule becomes a child of the j-th flow rule. We call the rule F_i includes F_j or F_j is included in F_i, if the flow rule F_i has a higher priority than F_j, then the F_j will become a repetitive and unmeaning flow rule which won't work as long as the F_i exists.
3. Intersectant: For C_i and C_j, $\exists k : f_k^i \cap f_k^j \neq \varnothing$, and $\exists m, n : f_m^i \subsetneq f_m^j, f_n^j \subsetneq f_n^i$ the two rules will be matched only when the specific packet arrives.
4. Irrelevant: for C_i and C_j, $\exists k : f_k^i \cap f_k^j = \varnothing$, the two flow rules are irrelevant and do not interact.

The detection of a dynamic collision mainly aims at the situation when the relationship between two flow rules is equal, inclusive or intersectant. The detection algorithm will judge whether there is a dynamic collision according to the relationship between the two matching domains of the rules and the size of the priority. The collision detection and solution mainly include the following situations:

5. If C_1 and C_2 are equal or C_1 contains C_2, it represents the dynamic collision and reject to issue the rule F_2
6. If C_2 contains C_1, then compare priority P_1 and P_2. If $P_1 < P_2$, then adjust $P_2 = P_1 - 1$ so that the priority of the third-party flow rule is less than the security rule, then it will be issued normally
7. If C_2 intersects C_1, compare P_1 and P_2. If $P_1 < P_2$, set $P_2 = P_1 - 1$, then it will be issued normally
8. If C_2 and C_1 are irrelevant, then it will be issued normally.

In terms of the detection of dependency collisions, we only need to compare the existing firewall rules and all Set-Field rules that could rewrite the data packet. The firewall rules in the SDN are generally expressed as follows:

<dl_src><dl_dst><dl_type><nw_src><nw_dst><nw_type><tp_src><tp_dst><actions>.

The difference from the FortNox detection solution is that we will consider all header fields in the firewall rules to perform dependency collision detection in a fine-grained manner, thereby making the detection results more accurate and preventing false alarms. When using the set-intersection algorithm to detect dependency collisions, it is necessary to aggregate the flow rules into the format as the following:

$$SRC \rightarrow DST \ actions \tag{4}$$

$$SRC = \{SRCFi\}(i \in N, l \leq i \leq n) \tag{5}$$

$$DST = \{DSTFi\}(i \in N, 1 \leq i \leq n) \tag{6}$$

$$SRCF_i = (C_{dl\_src}, C_{dl\_type}, C_{nw\_src}, C_{nw\_type}, C_{to\_src}) \tag{7}$$

$$DSTF_i = (C_{dl\_dst}, C_{nw\_dst}, C_{tp\_dst}) \tag{8}$$

The SRC is called the source set, and the DST is called the destination set. Each element $SRCF_i$ in the source set includes the following head fields of OpenFlow: dl_src, dl_type, nw_src, nw_type and tp_src field. Each element $DSTF_i$ in the destination set DST includes the following head fields: dl_dst, nw_dst and tp_dst field. The actions in the firewall rules include "Allow", "Deny" and "Packetin".

When we use the set-intersection algorithm to detect the dependency collision among the flow rules, it first needs to covert the all firewall rules whose action are "Deny" to aggregate their representation in the format of $S_{src1} \rightarrow S_{dst1}$ actions1, and the all Set-Field flow rules are aggregated into $S_{src2} \rightarrow S_{dst2}$ actions2. The values before and after the modification operation in the Set-Field rules are respectively added to the source set S_{src2} and the destination set S_{dst2}. Next a pairwise comparison is made between the firewall rules set and the Set-Field rules set to detect the dependency collision. We judge the to the principles as the following:

9. If $S_{src1} \cap S_{src2} = \emptyset$ or $S_{dst1} \cap S_{dst2} = \emptyset$, it represents that there is no dependency collision
10. If $S_{src1} \cap S_{src2} \neq \emptyset$ and $S_{dst1} \cap S_{dst2} \neq \emptyset$, actions1 = actions2, it represents that there is no dependency collision
11. If $S_{src1} \cap S_{src2} \neq \emptyset$ and $S_{dst1} \cap S_{dst2} \neq \emptyset$, actions1 $\neq$ actions2, it represents that there is a dependency collision, and then automatic collision resolution is required to delete the Set-Field rules that have dependency relationships.

The algorithm of detecting dependency collision based on set-intersection method is described as follows:

Algorithm 1. The detection of dependency collision
input:
S_Set means an aggregate representation of firewall rules;
F_Set means an aggregate representation of Set-Field rules
output: the result of detecting dependency collision
FOR($i=1,2,3,....,m$) DO
S_{src1}=S_Set[i].Src; S_{dst1}= S_Set[i].Dst;
actions1=S_Set[i].Actions
FOR ($j=1,2,3,....,n$) DO
S_{src2}=F_Set[j].Src; S_{dst2}= F_Set[j].Dst;
actions2=F_Set[j].Actions
IF($S_{src1} \cap S_{src2}$= Ø || $S_{dst1} \cap S_{dst2}$=Ø)
continue;
ELSE
IF ($S_{src1} \cap S_{src2} \neq$ Ø) srcResult=true;
IF ($S_{dst1} \cap S_{dst2} \neq$ Ø) dstResult=true;
IF (srcResult && dstResult) break;
IF (srcResult && dstResult)
IF (actions1= actions2) return No
ELSE return YES
ELSE return No

4   Implementation and Evaluation

Based on an open source RYU controller, we implement the synchronization module of flow rules, the real-time detection module of rule collision and the offline detection module. We once again compile the source code with new functions of the RYU, and it becomes a security controller with a rule collision detection mechanism. This is done to evaluate the effects of the detection module and performance. We deploy and start the RYU controller in a server with the Ubuntu 15.04 LTS Operating System and 4 GB RAM. Moreover, in another server with the same configuration, we use Mininet to build the simulation environment of the SDN topology, which as shown in Fig. 3. It contains one RYU controller, three SDN switches (s1, s2, and s3) and six hosts (h1, h2, h3, h4, h5, and h6).

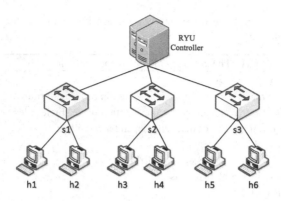

Fig. 3. The simulation environment of SDN network topology

4.1 Function Testing

To test the correctness of the detection mechanism, first, we issue the security flow rule {(*,*,*,'0x0800','10.0.0.1','10.0.0.101','tcp',*,*) priority:1000 actions: Deny]} to s1 and   {(*,*,*,'0x0800','192.168.1.22','192.168.3.22','tcp',*,'8080')   priority:2000 actions: Deny} to s2.

Table 1. The rules to be issued

Number	Rule
1	S1:(*,*,*,'0x0800','10.0.0.1','10.0.0.100',*,*,*) priority:100 actions:Output:12
2	S1: (*,*,*,'0x0800','10.0.0.1','10.0.0.101',tcp,*,*) priority:2000 actions: Output:12
3	S1: (*,*,*,'0x0800','10.0.0.1','10.0.0.101',tcp,8,*) priority:2000 actions:Output:1
4	S1: (*,*,*,'0x0800','10.0.0.1','10.0.0.101',*,*,*) priority:2000 actions:Output:4
5	S1: (*,*,*,'0x0800','10.0.0.1','10.0.0.101',*,8,*) priority:1000 actions:Output:4
6	S2:(*,*,*,'0x0800','192.168.1.22','192.168.2.22',*,*,*) priority:100 actions: OUTPUT:2; SET_NW_SRC:192.168.4.22
7	S2:(*,*,*,'0x0800','192.168.4.22','192.168.2.22',*,*,*) priority:100 actions: OUTPUT:2; SET_NW_DST:192.168.3.22
8	S3:(*,*,*,'0x0800','192.168.8.22','192.168.8.22',*,*,*) priority:100 actions: OUTPUT:2

After the security rules are issued successfully, we begin to issue some rules from the third-party application, which as shown in Table 1. The rules to be issued have static collisions themselves or dynamic and dependency collisions with the security rules in SDN. In our experiments, we need to record the results of the rule collision detection and the collision resolution, which verifies whether the functioning of our detection algorithm is correct. Table 2 shows the detection results and collision solution, the collision detection algorithm can correctly and effectively detect the static collisions, dynamic collisions and dependency collisions in flow rules. Furthermore, rule collision situations can automatically be resolved by the detection system.

Table 2. The result of collision detection

Number	Check result	Collision resolution
1	No conflict	Normally be issued
2	Equal with s1-1,the actions is diff.	Refused to issue
3	Included by s1-1,the actions is diff.	Refused to issue
4	Included by s1-1,the actions is diff.	Adjust the priority = 999 and normally be issued
5	Intersects with s1-1, the actions is diff.	Refused to issue
6	No conflict	Normally be issued
7	Depends with the sixth rule, has a conflict with s2-1	Delete the dependency conflict flow rules
8	Static conflict	Refused to issue

4.2 Performance Testing

We start 10 threads in Jmeter and continuously request the northbound interface of RYU using HTTP protocol. Within 60 s, when the numbers of security flow rules in the SDN network are 50, 100, 200, 500, 1000, 2000 and 5000, we record the changes of the throughput capacity and the average response times of the northbound interface. The test results of the throughput are shown in Fig. 4. It can be observed that after adding the function of real-time detection to the RYU controller, the throughput is relatively stable, although it is reduced by approximately 20% compared to the original RYU. The average response time is shown in Fig. 5. After adding the collision detection mechanism, the average response time is extended. However, the collision detection mechanism is taken into account to ensure the overall security of the SDN. Under the premise of security, the decrease of the throughput and request response time is within the acceptable range.

In addition, the main factor leading to the decrease of the throughput of the northbound interface is the real-time collision detection

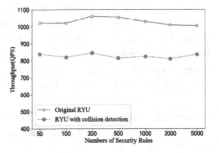

Fig. 4. The result of the throughput

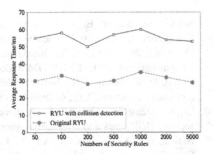

Fig. 5. The result of the average response time

before the flow rules are deployed to the OpenFlow switches. Under the conditions of different numbers of existing security rules in the SDN, we record the real-time detection times. The results are shown in Fig. 6. When the number of existing security rules is from 100 to 1200, the actual real-time detection time almost linearly increases. However, in an actual SDN network, the number of security rules in a single Open-Flow switch does not exceed 1000. There-fore, within the controllable range of flow table entries, the delay is within an acceptable range.

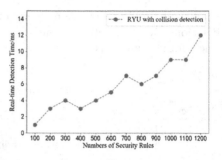

Fig. 6. The time of the real-time detection

5   Conclusion

For the security problems of rule collision in the application layer of the SDN network, we propose a comprehensive and fine-grained detection mechanism for rule collisions and implement it in the RYU controller. We evaluate the function and performance of the mechanism in a simulated SDN environment. The results show that it can correctly and efficiently detect various rule collisions and automatically resolve the collisions, which enhances the security of the SDN, and its performance is within the acceptable range. However, this paper does not consider the real-time network status when detecting dependency collisions. Therefore, there will be a delay in dependency col-lision resolution. In the future, our research will focus on this aspect and improve the detection mechanism of the flow rules.

Acknowledgments. This work was supported by the National Science Foundation of China (Grant No. 61502048) and the National Science and Technology Major Project (Grant No. 2017YFB0803001).

References

1. Michel, O., Keller, E.: SDN in wide-area networks: a survey. In: Fourth International Conference on Software Defined Systems, pp. 37–42. IEEE (2017)
2. Mckeown, N., Anderson, T., Balakrishnan, H., et al.: OpenFlow: enabling innovation in campus networks. ACM SIGCOMM Comput. Commun. Rev. **38**(2), 69–74 (2008)
3. Rawat, D.B., Reddy, S.R.: Software defined networking architecture, security and energy efficiency: a survey. IEEE Commun. Surv. Tutorials **19**(1), 325–346 (2017)
4. Li, W., Meng, W., Kwok, L.F.: A survey on OpenFlow-based software defined networks: security challenges and countermeasures. J. Netw. Comput. Appl. **68**, 126–139 (2016)
5. Batista, B.L.A., Campos, G.A.L.D., Fernandez, M.P.: Flow-based conflict detection in OpenFlow networks using first-order logic. In: Computers & Communication. IEEE Computer Society, pp. 1–6 (2014)

6. Porras, P., Shin, S., Yegneswaran, V., et al.: A security enforcement kernel for OpenFlow networks, pp. 121–126 (2012)
7. Gude, N., Koponen, T., Pettit, J., et al.: NOX: towards an operating system for networks. ACM SIGCOMM Comput. Commun. Rev. **38**(3), 105–110 (2008)
8. Son, S., Shin, S., Yegneswaran, V., et al.: Model checking invariant security properties in OpenFlow. In: IEEE International Conference on Communications, pp. 1974–1979. IEEE (2013)
9. Wang, J., Wang, J., Jiao, H.Y., et al.: A method of Open-Flow-based real-time conflict detection and resolution for SDN access control policies. Chin. J. Comput. **38**(4), 872–883 (2015)
10. Wang, P., Huang, L., Xu, H., et al.: Rule anomalies detecting and resolving for software defined networks. In: Global Communications Conference, pp. 1–6. IEEE (2016)
11. Khurshid, A., Zhou, W., Caesar, M., et al.: VeriFlow: verifying network-wide invariants in real time. In: The Workshop on Hot Topics in Software Defined Networks, pp. 49–54. ACM (2012)

Source Encryption Scheme in SDN Southbound

Yanlei Wang[1], Shihui Zheng[1(✉)], Lize Gu[1], and Yongmei Cai[2]

[1] School of Cyberspace Security,
Beijing University of Posts and Telecommunications, Beijing 100876, China
shihuizh@bupt.edu.cn
[2] School of Computer Science and Engineering,
Xinjiang University of Finance and Economics, Urumqi 830000, China

Abstract. In light of the existence of the software defined networking (SDN) southbound communication protocol OpenFlow, and manufacturers' neglect of network security, in this paper, we propose a protection scheme for encryption at the source of the communication data that is based on the Kerberos authentication protocol. This scheme not only completes the identity authentication of and session key assignment for the communication parties on an insecure channel but also employs an efficient AES symmetric encryption algorithm to ensure that messages always exist in the form of ciphertext before they reach the end point and thus obtain end-to-end security protection of communication data. At the end of this paper, we present our experimental results in the form of a forwarding agent. After that, the performance of the Floodlight controller is tested using a CBench testing tool. Our results indicate that the proposed source encryption scheme provides end-to-end encryption of communication data. Although the communication latency increases by approximately 12% when both transport layer security (TLS) and source-encrypted are enabled, the source-encrypted part of the increase is only approximately 4%.

Keywords: SDN · OpenFlow · Source encryption · Kerberos

1 Introduction

Software defined networking (SDN) divides the traditional network architecture into a control plane and a data plane. OpenFlow [1] is the most popular standardized interface between the two planes and has been widely used in academia and industry. Although SDN presents many possibilities for network flexibility and programmability, it also introduces network security threats.

The 1.0 version of the OpenFlow protocol [1] specification contains requirements for TLS usage [2]. However, in subsequent versions of the OpenFlow protocol, [3] "must" is replaced by "should" in their descriptions. Thus, it is difficult to ensure the security of key data, such as flow tables, in southbound communication. In practical applications, few TLS protections exist between controllers and switches. Most vendors ignore southbound communication's security issues and use TCP connections directly. Additionally, the certificate authentication management interface that is used with TLS has not been perfected.

The following table shows the support of Southern OpenFlow TLS for each OpenFlow device vendor [4] (Tables 1 and 2):

Table 1. OpenFlow switch TLS support table

OpenFlow switch	TLS support
HP switch	No
Brocade	Controller port only
Dell	No
NEC	Partial
Indigo	No
Pica8	Only new versions
Open WRT	Yes
Open vSwitch	Yes

Table 2. OpenFlow controller TLS support table

OpenFlow controller	TLS support
Brocade Vyatta controller	Yes
NOX controller	No
POX	No
Beacon	No
Floodlight	No
OpenMuL	No
FlowVisor	No
Big network controller	No
Open vSwitch controller	Yes

Using TCP connections directly ensures that all southbound communication data will be exposed in plaintext on the communication link. This is feasible for secure networks, in which data centers and other physical devices are difficult to access. The number of deployments of the networks is increasing, and in these deployed systems, Without TLS, there will be a serious security risk [5]. Because we cannot guarantee that all communication devices in the communication path between the SDN controller and the switch are secure and reliable, attackers can initiate man-in-the-middle attacks through session hijacking, DNS spoofing, and port mirroring (Fig. 1). They can eavesdrop, intercept, tamper with the communication data, e.g., pose as a controller to send a FLOW_MOD message to the switch, tamper with the flow table in the switch to control the flow of data in the switch, and even tamper with the entire network [6]. However, this kind of attack does not modify the normal transmission from the switch to the controller and is subtle. In [7], this type of attack has been verified in practice as feasible.

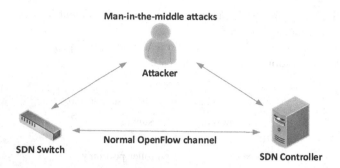

Fig. 1. Man-in-the-middle attacks

The security of the OpenFlow southbound communication channel is not strong. Samociuk et al. [4, 8] proposed using existing security protection schemes to protect the southbound communication. These researchers also analyzed the use of TLS, IPsec, and SSH. The transmission layer and the network layer ensure communication security, but protection schemes focus only on channel security.

In the existing literature, some authors propose security frameworks for the overall assessment and protection of SDN security [9, 10]. Some researchers study the protection of buffer overflow or the denial of service attacks by identifying malicious traffic [11–13]. In some studies [6, 14], a more comprehensive analysis of the SDN architecture and the existing or potential security threats are systematically presented. All [4, 6, 8] authors mention the southbound communication security problem. In addition, all authors discuss the protection of southbound communication security via a channel protection method such as TLS, IPsec or SSH. We believe that the source encryption scheme can completely identity authentication, distribute session keys via insecure communication channel and provide end-to-end communication data security.

The rest of this paper is organized as follows: Sect. 1 introduces the overall architecture of SDN and the OpenFlow southbound communication protocol; Sect. 2 introduces our proposed data source encryption scheme; Sect. 3 contains our program's security assessment and performance evaluation; and Sect. 4 summarizes our work.

2 Source Encryption Scheme in SDN Southbound

2.1 Scheme Profile and Symbol Definitions

SDN architecture is divided into three layers. From top to bottom, they are the application layer, the control plane, and the data plane, as shown in Fig. 2 below. The control plane is responsible for the control logic of the network and provides the calling interface to the application layer. The data plane is responsible for data forwarding and provides the control plane's call interface. Southbound communication refers to the process by which the control plane invokes the protocol interface provided by the data plane to perform network control.

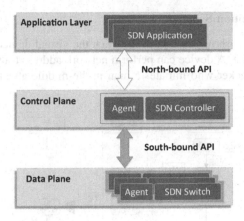

Fig. 2. SDN architecture diagram

The most efficient way to source encrypt the communication data before it enters the communication channel is to internally connect each switch or controller. However, this process causes the system to be highly coupled. In addition, it is not possible for a switch or a controller to be compatible with devices from many manufacturers at the same time. This paper proposes using a data forwarding proxy to implement the source encryption of communication data. As shown in Fig. 1, before the SDN controller and the switch are connected, they are each connected to a local forwarding proxy to perform the encryption and decryption operations on the original data. The abbreviations used to denote the encryption and decryption process are presented below:

$MK_{x,y}$: The key to calculate the HMAC of a message between x and y
$EK_{x,y}$: The symmetric encryption key between x and y
SM_0: The original message from the switch (Plaintext)
SM_{e1}: The source-encrypted message of SM_0 (Ciphertext)
SM_{e2}: The TLS encrypted message of SM_{e1} (Ciphertext)
RM_0: The controller's original message (Plaintext)
RM_{e1}: The source encrypted message of RM_0 (Ciphertext)
RM_{e2}: The TLS encrypted message of RM_{e1} (Ciphertext).

We employ the Kerberos key distribution center (KDC) to perform identity authentication and session key allocation. The abbreviations used to describe the authentication process are presented below:

ID_S, ID_C: The number (unique) of the switch and controller
K_S: The pre-shared key between KDC and the SDN switch
K_C: The pre-shared key between KDC and the SDN controller
T_S: The ticket encrypted by KDC using K_S
T_C: The ticket encrypted by KDC using K_C
$K_{S,C}$: The session key between SDN controller and switch.

2.2   Source Encryption Scheme

A data flow diagram is shown in Fig. 3, in which the virtual devices in the virtual box do not necessarily exist. A device can perform network address translation (NAT), be a firewall, or be an attacker who initiates a man-in-the-middle attack.

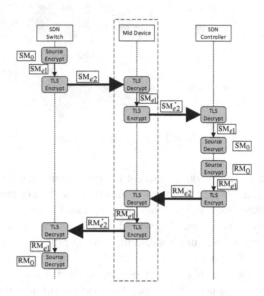

Fig. 3. Source encrypted data flow diagram

SDN switch to SDN controller message encryption and decryption process:

Step 1: The forwarding agent on the switch encrypts the original data from the application layer SM_0 and then calculates the HMAC cipher's authentication code text and adds it to the cipher text SM_{e1}. The calculation is as follows:

$$SM_{e1} = E(EK_{s,c}, SM_0)||HMAC(MK_{s,c}, E(EK_{s,c}, SM_0)) \tag{1}$$

Step 2: SM_{e1} is encrypted at the transport layer via TLS, and then the ciphertext SM_{e2} is sent to the intermediate device:

$$SM_{e2} = E(EK_{s,md}, SM_{e1}) \tag{2}$$

Step 3: After the intermediate device receives the ciphertext SM_{e2} and uses the TLS key $EK_{s,md}$, which is negotiated by the switch to decrypt it into SM_{e1}, the receiver encrypts SM_{e1} with its TLS key $EK_{c,md}$, which is negotiated with the SDN controller into SM_{e2}^*, and sends it to the SDN control device. The calculations are as follows:

$$SM_{e1} = D(EK_{s,md}, SM_{e2}) \tag{3}$$

$$SM_{e2}^* = E(EK_{s,md}, SM_{e1}) \tag{4}$$

Step 4: After receiving the ciphertext SM_{e2}^*, the forwarding agent decrypts it into SM_{e1} using its TLS key. If the message SM_{e1} is verified successfully with the HMAC message authentication code, then it is decrypted into the plain text SM_0 using the source encryption key. If the authentication fails, the message is discarded. The calculations are in Eqs. 5 and 6:

$$SM_{e1} = D(EK_{c,md}, SM_{e2}^*) \tag{5}$$

$$SM_0 = D(EK_{s,c}, SM_{e1}) \tag{6}$$

Encryption and decryption process of Controller to switch message are similar to the above.

2.3   Authentication and Key Distribution

Before each communication between the SDN controller and the switch, the communicating parties must first perform authentication and key distribution to use the assigned key for encrypted communications. The specific authentication distribution process is shown in Fig. 4:

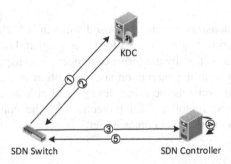

SDN Switch   SDN Controller

Fig. 4. Authentication process diagram

Step 1: The SDN switch sends a unique number of its own switch and a unique number of the SDN controller to the KDC.
Step 2: After the KDC receives the request, the KDC randomly generates a session key $(K_{S,C})$, and then generates two tickets T_S and T_C to send to the switch. The calculation is as follows:

$$T_S = \mathrm{E}(K_S, (K_{S,C}, ID_C)) \tag{7}$$

$$T_C = \mathrm{E}(K_C, (K_{S,C}, ID_S)) \tag{8}$$

Step 3: After receiving the two tickets, the SDN switch decrypts T_S with key K_S to obtain the session key $K_{S,C}$ and then uses the session key to generate the authentication factor A with the current time stamp TS and the checksum of data ChS. A is sent to the SDN controller together with T_C. The authentication factor calculation is as follows:

$$A = \mathrm{E}(K_{S,C}, (TS, ChS)) \tag{9}$$

Step 4: After receiving the ticket T_C and the authentication factor A, the SDN controller obtains the session key $K_{S,C}$ by decrypting T_C with K_C, and then decrypting A with $K_{S,C}$ to obtain the timestamp TS and checksum of data ChS. If the timestamp is within five minutes of the current time and if the timestamp is appearing for the first time, then the checksum of data is checked.

Step 5: If certifications pass, then the SDN controller encrypts the timestamp-received TS with the session key $K_{S,C}$ and sends it to the switch for the completion of mutual authentication.

3 Analysis and Test

In this section, we demonstrate that the proposed solution is both secure and efficient. We implement the solution in the form of a forwarding agent. For SDN controllers and switches, the source encryption by the forwarding agent is transparent. Controllers and switches are not involved in the encryption and decryption process of communication data, making the protection scheme more flexible and able to adapt to a variety of controllers and switches. Enabling TLS protection for the connection between the security agents at both ends also becomes easier.

3.1 Security Analysis

The source encryption scheme provides message encryption at the transport application layers and provides an identity mutual authentication mechanism. The following is a detailed analysis of the message forwarding process.

As shown in Fig. 3, the messages SM_0 and RM_0, which are sent by the switch or controller, are encrypted before the TLS encryption occurs. During the communication between the switch and the controller, the messages are in the form of ciphertext. Even if an attack on an intermediate device occurs, the intermediate device can only obtain the ciphertexts.

SM_{e1} and RM_{e1} are encrypted at the source. Because only the switch and the controller hold the encryption key $EK_{s,c}$, the intermediate device cannot decrypt the plaintext. Moreover, if the intermediate third-party tampers with the communication message, because the authentication of the message authentication code cannot be performed after the message is received at the receiving end, the receiving end can perceive the security problem on the link.

TLS encrypts data by providing confidentiality protection at the transport layer and providing point-to-point security protection. The source encryption scheme encrypts the message data before the application layer encapsulates the data. The entire communication process is in ciphertext and provides effective end-to-end encryption protection.

During the process of identity authentication and key distribution, if the switch adds a timestamp to the authentication factor that is sent to the controller, the controller must compare the timestamp with the current time and check to see whether it has ever appeared. In this way, the attacker cannot use the replay authentication factor to impersonate the switch for access. The controller also needs to encrypt the time stamp separately and send it back to the switch to complete the mutual authentication.

3.2 Efficiency Test

After adding source encryption protection, we used two desktop computers to test the delays in source encryption, bandwidth throughput, and data packet transmission. The two devices and their parameters are shown in Table 3:

Table 3. Test hardware and software environment

Option	SDN switch	SDN controller
NIC	1000 Mb/s	1000 Mb/s
CPU	Intel i5-4590	Intel i5-4590
Memory	8 GB	8 GB
Kernel version	Linux 4.13.0-38	Linux 4.13.0-38
Operating system	Ubuntu 16.04	Ubuntu 16.04
Software and version	Open vSwitch 2.7.4	Floodlight 1.2

CBench is a tool used to test the performance of OpenFlow controllers. To measure controller performance, CBench can simulate switches to connect controllers, send PACKET-IN messages, and count the number of FLOW-MOD messages to which the controller responds.

To understand the influence of the source encryption scheme on communication latency, we used the CBench test tool to test the performance of the Floodlight controller. We turned on the performance of the controller after the forwarding agent was used as a benchmark, and we separately tested the case of enabling TLS and the source encryption. In the case of both TLS and the enabled source encryption, the controller performance data was compared and analyzed. In each case, we used CBench to simulate different numbers of switches, and we requested the controller at the same time. Each test was repeated 10 times and averaged, as shown in Fig. 5 below:

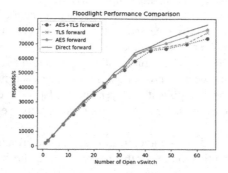

Fig. 5. Controller response performance

In Fig. 5, the horizontal axis indicates the number of switches simulated by CBench, and the vertical axis indicates the number of response messages per second by the controller. When the number of switches is small, the source encryption and the TLS control are separately enabled. The impact of the performance of the device is similar, but when the number of switches is greater than 32, the impact of TLS on the performance of the controller is greater than the source encryption. In general, enabling TLS or source encryption will slightly reduce the performance of the controller. However, if the host resources are sufficient, the controller performance still increases linearly with the number of switches. This does not bring an obvious performance bottleneck to the controller.

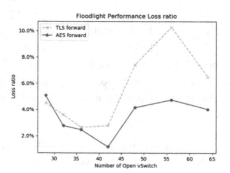

Fig. 6. Loss of controller performance

Figure 6 shows the performance loss of the Floodlight controller when the number of switches ranges from 28 to 64. The controller performance loss when the source encryption alone is enabled is approximately 4%, which is much less than the performance loss when the TLS alone is enabled. Therefore, the source encryption protection scheme proposed in this paper is superior to TLS encryption. When both protection schemes are enabled, the overall performance loss remains below 12%.

4 Conclusion and Future Work

In this paper, we propose a comprehensive and effective source encryption communication scheme, which not only completes the identity authentication and distribution of session keys for both parties of the communication but also provides end-to-end security protection for the communication data. The scheme possesses a high operating efficiency. In addition to studying security protection schemes for communication data on the link, we would like to pursue research into targeted protection schemes for key data in SDN controllers and switches, forming a complete protection system.

Acknowledgement. This work was supported by the National Science Foundation of China (Grant No. 61502048) and the National Science and Technology Major Project (Grant No. 2017YFB0803001).

References

1. Mckeown, N., Anderson, T., Balakrishnan, H., et al.: OpenFlow: enabling innovation in campus networks. ACM SIGCOMM Comput. Commun. Rev. **38**(2), 69–74 (2008)
2. Consortium, O.F.S.: OpenFlow Switch Specification Version 1.0.0 (2009)
3. OpenFlow switch specifications version 1.4.0. Open Networking Foundation (2013)
4. Benton, K., Camp, L.J., Small, C.: OpenFlow vulnerability assessment. In: ACM SIGCOMM Workshop on Hot Topics in Software Defined NETWORKING, pp. 151–152. ACM (2013)
5. Kobayashi, M., Seetharaman, S., Parulkar, G., et al.: Maturing of OpenFlow and software-defined networking through deployments. Comput. Netw. Int. J. Comput. Telecommun. Netw. **61**(3), 151–175 (2014)
6. Shu, Z., Wan, J., Li, D., et al.: Security in software-defined networking: threats and countermeasures. Mob. Netw. Appl. **21**(5), 1–13 (2016)
7. Yoon, C., Lee, S., Kang, H., et al.: Flow wars: systemizing the attack surface and defenses in software-defined networks. IEEE/ACM Trans. Netw. **25**(6), 3514–3530 (2017)
8. Samociuk, D.: Secure Communication Between OpenFlow Switches and Controllers (2015)
9. Lee, S., Yoon, C., Lee, C., et al.: DELTA: a security assessment framework for software-defined networks. In: Network and Distributed System Security Symposium (2017)
10. Pandya, B., Parmar, S., Saquib, Z., et al.: Framework for securing SDN southbound communication. In: 2017 International Conference on Innovations in Information, Embedded and Communication Systems (ICIIECS), pp. 1–5. IEEE (2017)
11. Ambrosin, M., Conti, M., Gaspari, F.D., et al.: LineSwitch: tackling control plane saturation attacks in software-defined networking. IEEE/ACM Trans. Netw. **25**(2), 1206–1219 (2017)
12. Atli, A.V., Uluderya, M.S., Tatlicioglu, S., et al.: Protecting SDN controller with per-flow buffering inside OpenFlow switches. In: Black Sea Conference on Communications and NETWORKING. IEEE (2018)
13. Deng, S., Gao, X., Lu, Z., et al.: Packet injection attack and its defense in software-defined networks. IEEE Trans. Inf. Forensics Secur. **13**(3), 695–705 (2017)
14. Rawat, D.B., Reddy, S.R.: Software defined networking architecture, security and energy efficiency: a survey. IEEE Commun. Surv. Tutorials **19**(1), 325–346 (2017)

Inter-frame Tamper Forensic Algorithm Based on Structural Similarity Mean Value and Support Vector Machine

Lan Wu$^{(\boxtimes)}$, Xiao-qiang Wu, Chunyou Zhang, and Hong-yan Shi

College of Mechanical Engineering, Inner Mongolia University
for the Nationalities, Inner Mongolia, Tongliao 028043, China
wlimun@163.com

Abstract. With the development of network technology and multimedia technology, digital video is widely used in news, business, finance, and even appear in court as evidence. However, digital video editing software makes it easier to tamper with video. Digital video tamper detection has become a problem that video evidence must solve. Aiming at the common inter-frame tampering in video tampering, a tampered video detection method based on structural similarity mean value and support vector machine is proposed. First, the structural similarity mean value feature of the video to be detected is extracted, which has good classification characteristics for the original video and the tampered video. Then, the structural similarity mean value is input to the support vector machine, and the tampered video detection is implemented by using the good non-linear classification ability of the support vector machine. The comparison simulation results show that the detection performance of this method for tampered video is better than that based on optical flow characteristics.

Keywords: Video tampering · Inter-frame tampering ·
Structural similarity mean value · Support vector machine

1 Introduction

Digital information is flooding people's daily lives. Digital video as the mainstream of digital information is widely used in various fields such as news, justice, entertainment, military, and science. However, while people enjoy the enormous convenience of digital video, their negative effects gradually emerge. With the increasing versatility and ease of operation of video editing software, digital video is easily tampered with, resulting in the destruction of the integrity and authenticity of digital information. Since the tampering of the video after tampering is not easily perceived by the human eye, people cannot discern the authenticity of the video content [1, 2]. If lawless elements use falsified videos for gaining interests or as evidence in court, it will cause great confusion in society. Therefore, how to accurately judge whether a video has been tampered with has become an important topic in the field of information security.

At present, the main research methods for digital video forensics detection are divided into two categories: active forensics and passive forensics [3]. The active

S. Liu and G. Yang (Eds.): ADHIP 2018, LNICST 279, pp. 570–577, 2019.
https://doi.org/10.1007/978-3-030-19086-6_62

forensics technology refers to pre-embedded authentication information such as digital fingerprints or digital watermarks in the digital video to be forensic, and determines whether the video has been tampered by verifying whether the embedded authentication information is complete during the forensic process. Due to the need to embed verification information into the video in advance, the active forensics technology has great limitations. The passive forensics technology does not depend on external verification information [4]. It will leave tampering traces after the video content is tampered with, and will destroy the original statistical characteristics of the video content. It will use the statistical nature of the video content itself and verify the authenticity of the video. Passive forensics technology is more practical.

For the passive detection of video inter-frame falsification, scholars have proposed many methods. Stamm performs Fourier transform on the prediction error sequence based on the periodic peaks of the prediction error sequence, and detects the tampering video by searching for the peak value [5]. Dong uses the motion compensation edge effect to detect whether the video has been tampered with in the frame-delete mode [6]. Yuan uses the gray level co-occurrence matrix to extract the texture features of the video frames, and detects the heterogeneity frame insertion and frame replacement tampering according to the continuity of the feature [7]. Pandey proposes a passive forensic method for detecting tampered video using the characteristics of noise variation between the original frame and the tampered frame for the removal of dynamic objects and frame copying [8]. The method uses wavelet decomposition to extract the noise characteristics of the de-noised video frame, and then uses the Expectation Maximization algorithm to estimate the Gaussian Mixture Densitvl as the feature of the classification detection. Saxena uses optical flow inconsistency to detect and locate tampered video regions, but the method is not accurate [9]. Bagiwa proposed a new tampering detection algorithm for the falsification of video LOGO being removed [10]. The algorithm estimates the suspicious area by analyzing the spatial and temporal statistical characteristics of the LOGO area, and then uses the SVM to extract the features of the suspicious area and discriminate whether the suspicious area is a tampering area.

To solve the problem of digital inter-frame tamper detection, this paper proposes a video inter-frame falsification forensics algorithm based on structural similarity mean value. Structural similarity mean value is a measure of the similarity of two images, which is a combination of brightness, contrast, and structure in the image. It can more accurately express the similarity of the two images. First, the structural similarity mean value of the video to be detected is extracted, and then the tampered video detection is implemented using a support vector machine. The experimental results verify the validity of the detection method.

2 Passive Tamper Detection Fundamentals

Digital video has a great deal of relevance in the time and space domains. Spatio-temporal correlation detection of video can be used to detect whether it has been tampered with. The most important feature of digital video passive forensics is feature selection and extraction. Digital video information usually contains certain fixed statistical characteristics due to the impact of video capture equipment and shooting scenes. By extracting and fusing these statistical features and analyzing the consistency between the features, video tamper detection can be implemented. Different researchers proposed different tamper detection features, including pattern noise, motion vectors, textures, and optical flow. Passive tamper detection uses multiple features to improve detection accuracy. Multiple features require fusion detection. Passive tamper detection uses the inherent nature of video for forensics and is universal for all types of video. Therefore, many research experts are dedicated to finding more effective features for passive tampering detection research.

Under normal circumstances, the basic flow of passive detection of video tampering is shown in Fig. 1.

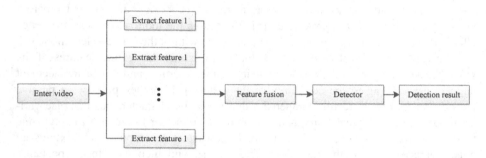

Fig. 1. Video passive forensics basic schematic

3   Structural Similarity Feature Extraction

Structural similarity is a new measure of the similarity of two images. Structural similarity theory holds that natural images are highly structured [11]. In other words, there is a strong correlation between adjacent pixels in the natural image, and this correlation carries important information of the object structure in the visual scene. The human visual system has been accustomed to extracting the structural information of the image from the visual field, and can use the measure of structural information as an approximation of the perceived quality of the image. Compared with the traditional methods of objective assessment of image quality, MSE and PSNR, structural similarity has been widely adopted because of its superiority in image similarity evaluation.

The structural similarity not only contains the brightness information of the image but also reflects the structure information of the object in the image. Therefore, it can more fully reflect the information in the image. For video inter-frame tamper detection, the use of features based on structural similarity results in better distinguishing characteristics. Firstly, a video is decomposed into a continuous image sequence, and then the images are divided into non-overlapping 8×8 sub-blocks, and the structural similarity values between the 8×8 sub-blocks corresponding to the adjacent two images A and B are calculated. Structural similarity consists of three parts: brightness, contrast and structure of similarity. Their definitions are as follows

$$l(x,y) = \frac{2\mu_x\mu_y + c_1}{\mu_x^2 + \mu_y^2 + c_1} \tag{1}$$

$$c(x,y) = \frac{2\sigma_x\sigma_y + c_2}{\sigma_x^2 + \sigma_y^2 + c_2} \tag{2}$$

$$s(x,y) = \frac{\sigma_{xy} + c_3}{\sigma_x\sigma_y + c_3} \tag{3}$$

where x and y represent the numbers of the corresponding 8×8 sub-blocks in images A and B, respectively, μ_x and μ_y represent the mean values of the corresponding 8×8 sub-blocks in images A and B, σ_x and σ_y represent the standard deviations of the corresponding sub-blocks, and $\sigma_x\sigma_y$ represents Correspond to the sub-block covariance. c_1, c_2, and c_3 are normal numbers that tend to 0, and are used to prevent the denominator of the three equations from showing 0.

Structural similarity is a combination of three different parts and is defined as

$$S_{SIM}(x,y) = [l(x,y)]^\alpha [c(x,y)]^\beta [s(x,y)]^\gamma \tag{4}$$

where α, β, and γ are used to adjust the relative weights of the three components. In general, set $\alpha = \beta = \gamma = 1$ and $c_3 = c_2/2$ to get a simplified version of the structural similarity

$$S_{SIM}(x,y) = \frac{(2\mu_x\mu_y + c_1)(2\sigma_{xy} + c_2)}{(\mu_x^2 + \mu_y^2 + c_1)(\sigma_x^2 + \sigma_y^2 + c_2)} \tag{5}$$

The mean value of structural similarity is calculated as

$$M_{SSIM}(A,B) = \frac{1}{M} \sum_{x=y=1}^{M} S_{SIM}(x,y) \tag{6}$$

where M is the total number of 8×8 sub-blocks in images A and B.

4 SVM Video Tamper Detection

Digital video consists of an ordered sequence of images in a one-dimensional time domain of two-dimensional images. Video can be first decomposed into a series of continuous images and then tampered with digital video. For a digital video, the content correlation between adjacent frames is high, and the content correlation between two frames that are far apart is smaller. Therefore, calculating the correlation between two adjacent frames in a video sequence of a video can describe the continuity of the content between the video frames.

If a digital video content changes quickly, the value of the correlation between adjacent frames is relatively small, that is, the structural similarity mean value is smaller [12]. On the contrary, if the content changes slowly, the structural similarity mean value is relatively large. The structural similarity mean value between the video frames that have not been tampered with is not only high but close to the mean; however, the structural similarity mean value between the two frames at the tampered point in the tampered video is very low.

Support vector machine is a modern technology based on data machine learning. Support vector machine first maps linear inseparable data into a linear separable high-dimensional space. In the high-dimensional space, constructing the optimal classification surface based on the principle of minimizing structural risk is a method that can learn precision and learning based on finite samples. It is an intelligent learning method that seeks the best compromise between abilities.

According to the principle of minimizing the risk of high-dimensional space structure, the support vector machine attributes the detection problem to an optimization problem with constraints. The optimization function is

$$\min \frac{\|\omega\|^2}{2} \tag{7}$$

The constraint is

$$y_i \left[\omega^T \varphi(x_i) + b \right] \geq 1 \quad i = 1, 2, \cdots, K \tag{8}$$

where $\varphi(\cdot)$ is a kernel function mapped to a high-dimensional space, $\omega \in R_K$ is a weight vector, and $b \in R$ is an offset value.

The kernel function must be satisfied

$$\varphi(x_i) \cdot \varphi(x_j) = \kappa(x_i, x_j) \tag{9}$$

The kernel function satisfies the Mercer condition to meet the above requirements. To solve the optimization function, define the Lagrange function as

$$L(\omega, b, \alpha) = \frac{\|\omega\|^2}{2} - \sum_{i=1}^{K} \alpha_i (y_i \omega^T \varphi(x_i) + b - 1) \tag{10}$$

where α_i is Lagrange multiplier. Calculate the partial derivative of A versus B and C respectively, and make the partial derivative equal to zero. Solve α_i values that satisfy the following conditions

$$\max H(\alpha) = \sum_{i=1}^{K} \alpha_i - \sum_{i,j}^{K} \alpha_i \alpha_j y_i y_j \varphi(x_i) \varphi(x_j) \tag{11}$$

There are the following constraints

$$\sum_{i=1}^{K} y_i \alpha_i = 0 \quad \alpha_i \geq 0, i = 1, 2, \cdots, K \tag{12}$$

The optimal classification discriminant function is

$$y = \text{sgn}\left\{\sum \alpha_i y_i \left[\omega^T \varphi(x_i) + b\right]\right\} \tag{13}$$

5 Results and Analysis

The experimental video library is divided into 5 sub-video libraries, including an original video library, a 25-frame deleted frames video library, a 25-frame inserted video library, a 100-frame deleted video library, and a 100-frame inserted video library. The video in the tampered four video banks is generated by inserting or deleting a certain number of video frames from the video in the original video library. In addition, the number of videos in each sub-video library is 598. The contents of the videos in the video library are the six kinds of human motion: wave, clapping, boxing, walking, jogging, and running.

In the experiment, polynomial kernel support vector machines were used to classify two types of video. In order to train the SVM classifier, 480 of the 598 videos were randomly selected as the training set, and the remaining videos were used as the test set. In order to ensure the reliability of the experimental results, the experiment was repeated 20 times and the average of the 20 experimental results was taken as the final classification accuracy. In the de-averaging process, k is 0.8 and the number of quantization bits is 30. All experimental videos have a resolution of 720×576. The frame rate of each video is 25 Fps.

Figure 2 is a structural similarity mean value curve of the original video and the tampered video after deletion of 25 frames. The experimental results show that the interval between the two curves is very large and the classification feature is very

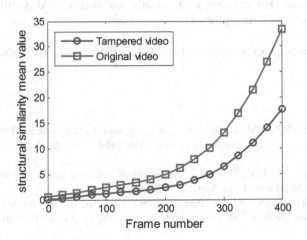

Fig. 2. Structural similarity mean value

obvious. This shows that the original video and tampered video's structural similarity mean value has a good separation, and its input to the support machine can achieve high probability detection of tampered video.

Table 1. Comparison of tampered video detection results

Tampered video	Proposed method	Optical flow
25-frame deleted library	91.45%	83.91%
25-frame inserted library	93.29%	89.34%
100-frame deleted library	97.25%	93.95%
100-frame inserted library	98.91%	94.28%

Table 1 is a comparison of the results of the proposed tampered video detection method and the optical flow tamper-based video method. Experimental results show that this method has high classification accuracy for original video and tampered video. Even with the 25-frame deletion video with the lowest classification accuracy, the accuracy rate reached 90.72%. In addition, as can be seen from Table 1, the detection accuracy of the inserted tampered video is higher than that of the deletion tampered video.

6 Conclusion

Video inter-frame falsification forensics algorithms are studied in this article. A tampered video detection method based on structural similarity mean value and support vector machine is proposed. The method utilizes structural similarity mean value difference of tampered video and original video to realize tampered video detection and uses support vector machine to improve detection performance. Experimental results show that the method can effectively detect tampered video and has high accuracy. However, the computational complexity of this detection method is still high, and the next step needs to solve this problem.

Acknowledgements. Inner Mongolia National University Research Project (NMDYB1729).

References

1. Arab, F., Abdullah, S.M., Hashim, S.Z., et al.: A robust video watermarking technique for the tamper detection of surveillance systems. Multimed. Tools Appl. **75**(18), 10855–10891 (2016)
2. Wei, W., Fan, X., Song, H., et al.: Video tamper detection based on multi-scale mutual information. Multimed. Tools Appl. **9**, 1–18 (2017)
3. Chen, X., Shi, D.: A new detection algorithm for video tamper. In: IEEE International Conference on Electronic Measurement & Instruments, pp. 1150–1153 (2016)

4. Martino, F.D., Sessa, S.: Fragile watermarking tamper detection via bilinear fuzzy relation equations. J. Ambient Intell. Humaniz. Comput. **5**, 1–21 (2018)
5. Stamm, M.C., Lin, W.S., Liu, K.J.R.: Temporal forensics and anti-forensics for motion compensated video. IEEE Trans. Inf. Forensics Secur. **7**(4), 1315–1329 (2012)
6. Dong, Q., Yang, G., Zhu, N.: A MCEA based passive forensics scheme for detecting frame-based video tampering. Digit. Investig. **9**(2), 151–159 (2012)
7. Yuan, X.J., Huang, T.Q., Chen, Z.W., et al.: Digital video forgeries detection based on textural features. Comput. Syst. Appl. **21**(6), 91–95 (2012)
8. Pandey, R.C., Singh, S.K., Shukla, K.K.: A passive forensic method for video: Exposing dynamic object removal and frame duplication in the digital video using sensor noise features. J. Intell. Fuzzy Syst. **32**(5), 3339–3353 (2017)
9. Saxena, S., Subramanyam, A.V., Ravi, H.: Video inpainting detection and localization using inconsistencies in optical flow. In: IEEE Region 10 Conference, pp. 1361–1365 (2017)
10. Bagiwa, M.A., Wahab, A.W.A., Idris, M.Y.I., et al.: Digital video inpainting detection using correlation of hessian matrix. Malays. J. Comput. Sci. **29**(3), 179–195 (2016)
11. Tang, Z., Wang, S., Zhang, X., et al.: Structural feature-based image hashing and similarity metric for tampering detection. Fundamenta Informaticae **106**(1), 75–91 (2011)
12. Zhao, D.N., Wang, R.K., Lu, Z.M.: Inter-frame passive-blind forgery detection for video shot based on similarity analysis. Multimed. Tools Appl. 1–20 (2018)

An Improved VIRE Approach for Indoor Positioning Based on RSSI

Boshen Liu and Jiaqi Zhen[✉]

College of Electronic Engineering, Heilongjiang University,
Harbin 150080, China
zhenjiaqi2011@163.com

Abstract. Nowadays, RFID positioning has become the preferred technology in indoor positioning because of its strong anti-interference ability, short recognition time, large amount of storage data and low cost. In this paper, based on RFID technology, a method of virtual tag is proposed to further optimize the adjacent area, the positioning accuracy is further improved without increasing extra cost and signal interference which has more superior performance and a higher practical value, so as to achieve the purpose of optimization.

Keywords: Radio frequency identification · Virtual tag · Adaptive threshold · Indoor positioning

1 Introduction

Over the years, many universities and research institutions have conducted research on indoor positioning technology [3]. Triangulation, scene analysis, and proximity are the three principal techniques for automatic localization technology. One of the most well-known location-based systems is the Global Positioning System (GPS), which is the most mature and the most widely used automatic localization technology at present. But for GPS is a system depending on satellite, it is difficult to localization in complex indoor environment [4]. In order to achieve the ability of locating objects in buildings, different methods are proposed by researchers. RFID has strong anti-interference ability and low maintenance cost. Because of its ability to calculate data quickly, the result is very effective. So it is feasible to use RFID technology in practical system. At present, many indoor localization algorithms are using RFID technology [5]. LANDMARC is a typical example of indoor localization system using RFID technology. It introduces the concept of reference tag. VIRE is based on reference tag and proximity maps to guarantee the accuracy of localization without adding other real reference tags [6].

This work was supported by the National Natural Science Foundation of China under Grant 61501176, Natural Science Foundation of Heilongjiang Province F2018025, University Nursing Program for Young Scholars with Creative Talents in Heilongjiang Province UNPYSCT-2016017, the postdoctoral scientific research developmental fund of Heilongjiang Province in 2017 LBH-Q17149.

S. Liu and G. Yang (Eds.): ADHIP 2018, LNICST 279, pp. 578–583, 2019.
https://doi.org/10.1007/978-3-030-19086-6_63

In this paper, the existing VIRE system was analysed, and the proportion of the two weight factors in VIRE was modified. The proportion of weight factors with small interfering factors is higher.

2   VIRE System

The location of the target tag is obtained by comparing the RSSI value between the reference tag and the target tag [1–4]. A large number of reference tags are required to ensure accuracy. This increases interference and the cost of the system. VIRE uses grid virtual reference tags without additional real reference tags. The grid virtual reference tag is not an entity, but assumes a reference tag that exists at a point of coordinates. When grid virtual reference tags are introduced, they can be used as reference tags [5, 6]. Taking the two-dimensional grid as an example, the target tag is placed at any position in the two-dimensional grid. The real reference tags are averagely distributed in the two-dimensional space, and four reference tags are arranged here. Each grid cell covered by four real reference tags is further divided into $N \times N$ equal sized virtual grid cells (Figs. 1 and 2).

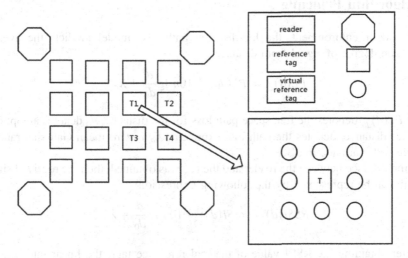

Fig. 1. VIRE system

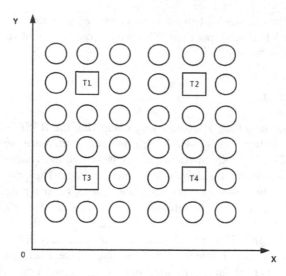

Fig. 2. Distribution of grid virtual reference tags

3 Algorithm Principle

In the indoor environment, the log-distance path loss model predicts the average attenuation degree of signal from distance:

$$PL(d)_{db} = PL(d_0) - 10n \lg \frac{d}{d_0} + X_\sigma \tag{1}$$

where $PL(d)_{db}$ denotes the free space path loss for the distance, d_0 denotes an optional reference distance, denotes the path loss exponent, X_σ is zero mean Gaussian random variable with variance in dB.

If the distance between the reader and the tag was obtained, then the received signal strength can be represented by the following expression:

$$RSSI(d) = RSSI(d_0) - 10n \lg \frac{d}{d_0} + \lambda \tag{2}$$

After obtaining the RSSI value of the real reference tags, the linear interpolation method can be used to obtain the RSSI value of the grid virtual reference tags.

At horizontal direction:

$$RSSI_k(T_{p,b}) = RSSI(T_{a,b}) + (p - a) \times \frac{RSSI(T_{a+n,b}) - RSSI(T_{a,b})}{n} \tag{3}$$

at vertical direction:

$$RSSI_k(T_{a,q}) = RSSI(T_{a,b}) + (q - b) \times \frac{RSSI(T_{a,b+n}) - RSSI(T_{a,b})}{n} \tag{4}$$

where $RSSI_k(T_{i,j})$ is the RSSI value of the grid virtual tag at the point (x, y) which read on the number k reader.

In addition, in order to improve the accuracy of positioning, two weight factors ω_{1i} and ω_{2i} are introduced:

$$\omega_{1i} = \sum_{h=1}^{K} \frac{|RSSI_h(T_i) - \theta_h(R)|}{k \times RSSI_h(T_i)} \tag{5}$$

$$\omega_{2i} = \frac{p_i}{\sum_{i=1}^{n_a} p_i} \tag{6}$$

where $RSSI_h(T_i)$ represents the number i virtual reference tag received by the number reader, T_i represents the number i target tag received by the number reader. K is the total number of readers. p_i is the ratio of a continuous possible region to the total number of regions. n_{ci} is the number of contiguous regions. n_a is the number of selected cells in the location area. ω_{1i} represents the difference between the selected virtual reference tag and the target tag, the larger the margin, the smaller it should be. ω_{2i} represents the density of the selected virtual reference tag, the greater the density, the bigger it should be.

However, in the complex indoor environment, because of the multipath effect and shadow effect, the RSSI values of the virtual reference tags and the target tags are not stable, so ω_{1i} will have errors. But the second weight factor ω_{2i} is the density of the tags, which is not affected by the complex environment. Therefore, the second factor should account for more weight of the two weight factors. To take reciprocal of ω_{1i} and then we can meet our requirements, and make the positioning more accurate:

$$\omega'_{1i} = \frac{1}{\omega_{1i}} \tag{7}$$

The weight factor is the product of the above two weight factors, and the calculation result is the coordinates of the target tags:

$$(x, y) = \sum_{i=1}^{n_a} \omega'_{1i}\omega_{2i}(x_i, y_i) \tag{8}$$

4   Experiment and Results

Here, some experiments are shown with MATLAB 2008 to manifest the effectiveness of the proposed algorithm. The computer is Pentium dual-core processor, clock is 4 GHz, 3.25 MHz memory. The target area to be positioned is two-dimensional, covering an area of 8 m × 8 m, and the readers are placed on the four corners, so their coordinates are (0,0), (8m,0), (0,8m), (8m,8m). The simulation system will use the high frequency passive label as the reference and target tags respectively. The placement of the system is demonstrated in Fig. 3, and the estimation result is shown in Fig. 4.

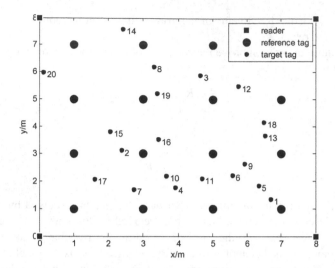

Fig. 3. Simulation environment.

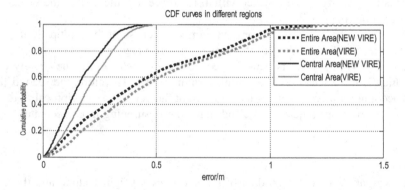

Fig. 4. CDF curves in different regions.

From Fig. 4, it can be seen that in the entire area, the probability of success of NEW_VIRE is more than 60% to lower than 0.5 m, and that of VIRE is less than 60% probability to lower than 0.5 m. So compared with LANDMARC and VIRE, the proposed NEW_VIRE has higher positioning accuracy.

5 Conclusion

In this paper, the VIRE algorithm is introduced in detail, and it can be seen that the relatively perfect positioning system mainly depends on LANDMARC and VIRE. This paper mainly improves VIRE. The concept of reference label is proposed by LAND-MARC, and the adaptability of LANDMARC is greatly improved. VIRE is improved on LANDMARC, without increasing the cost and increasing the signal interference, the positioning accuracy is further improved.

References

1. Lu, S.P., Xu, C., Zhong, R.Y.: A RFID-enabled positioning system in automated guided vehicle for smart factories. J. Manuf. Syst. **44**, 179–190 (2017)
2. Brandl, M., Kellner, K., Posnicek, T.: Spread spectrum based RFID position estimation for sensor applications. Procedia Eng. **168**, 1354–1357 (2016)
3. Song, X., Li, X., Tang, W.C.: A fusion strategy for reliable vehicle positioning utilizing RFID and in-vehicle sensors. Inf. Fusion **31**, 76–86 (2016)
4. Shaari, A.M., Nor, N.S.M.: Position and orientation detection of stored object using RFID tags. Procedia Eng. **184**, 708–715 (2017)
5. Soltani, M.M., Motamedi, A., Hammad, A.: Enhancing cluster-based RFID tag localization using artificial neural networks and virtual reference tags. Autom. Constr. **54**, 93–105 (2015)
6. Macarena, M.C., Piedad, B., Iluminada, B.: A comparative analysis of VLSI trusted virtual sensors. Microprocess. Microsyst. **61**, 108–116 (2018)

Research on Data Management System for Drug Testing Based on Big Data

Fu-yong Bian[1($\boxtimes$)], Ming Zhang[1], Zhen Chen[1], and Rong Xu[2]

[1] Chuxiong Medical College, Chuxiong 675005, China
dfjpds55454@sina.com
[2] School of Information Engineering,
Anhui Radio and TV University, Hefei 230022, Anhui, China
xurong528528@163.com

Abstract. The traditional drug detection data management system has the disadvantages of limited submenu generation and uneven distribution of management rights. In order to solve these problems, a new data management system based on big data is designed. Through the two steps of .NET framework and B/S detection module design, the hardware operation environment of the new system is completed. On this basis, determine the MyEclipse node and the detection process. Under this precondition, all the process parameters related to drug data are stored in the system database for a long time, and the total amount of E-R data can be determined, and then the design of drug testing data management system can be completed. The experimental results show that compared with the traditional system, the management authority distribution uniformity of the system can reach 81.57%, which is much higher than that of the traditional method. The application of the new system can effectively improve the submenu generation rate.

Keywords: Big data · Drug testing · Data management · .NET framework · B/S module · MyEclipse node · Detection of circulation · E-R data

1 Introduction

Big data is a collection of data that cannot be captured, managed, and processed by conventional software tools within a certain time frame. It is a massive and high growth rate that requires new processing modes to have stronger decision-making power, insight and process optimization capabilities, diverse information assets. With the advent of the cloud era, big data has also attracted more and more attention [1]. Detection data management is an emerging form of system management. This technology fully utilizes the concept of big data and achieves the goal of increasing the operating speed of the system by continuously integrating operational advantages of cloud computing. In the past nearly 70 years, China's drug testing companies, with the support of big data technology, have directed improvements to data management technologies, and have designed a common drug testing data management system by

S. Liu and G. Yang (Eds.): ADHIP 2018, LNICST 279, pp. 584–591, 2019.
https://doi.org/10.1007/978-3-030-19086-6_64

introducing a network framework architecture. However, with the advancement of scientific and technological means, the sub-menu generation rate of this method and the evenness of the distribution of management rights cannot always reach the expected level. In order to avoid the occurrence of the above situation, a new type of drug detection data management system based on big data is designed. The specific research framework is as follows:

(1) The hardware design of the system is mainly realized through two parts: the NET framework and the B/S detection module;
(2) System software design. Determining the data management node, under the condition that the total number of drug data management nodes is known, the transmission data between each module of the system is normalized and the data is detected circularly. Finally, determining the total amount of E-R data;
(3) Experimental results and analysis. Two comparative indicators are selected for analysis: Submenu generation rate comparison, Comparison of management authority distribution uniformity. The practical value of the system is proved through comparative experiments;
(4) Conclusions.

2 Hardware Design of Data Management System Based on Big Data Drug Detection

The hardware operation environment of the new drug detection data management system includes the two basic links of the .NET framework and the B/S detection module. The specific construction method can be performed as follows.

2.1 NET Big Data Management Framework

The .NET big data management framework mainly includes the following components: The first is the foundation of the entire drug testing framework, namely the universal language runtime and the set of basic libraries it provides; In the development of technology, .NET provides a new database access technology ADO.NET, as well as network application development technology ASP NET and Windows programming technology Win Forms. In the development of languages, .NET provides VB, VC++, C#, Jscript and other language support. Visual Studio .NET as a development tool will fully support .NET [2, 3]. For drug detection data management technologies, the .NET-provided basic class library includes everything from input and output to data access, providing developers with a unified object-oriented, hierarchical, and extensible programming interface. The concrete management framework structure of .NET big data is shown as in Fig. 1.

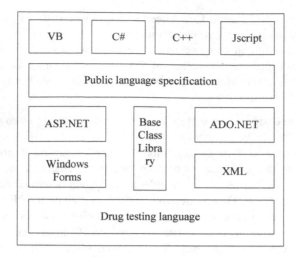

Fig. 1. Structure of the .NET big data management framework

2.2 B/S Detection Module Design

The B/S drug detection module can be considered as a special C/S structure using a Web browser. The B/S structure mainly uses a database server and one or more application services, i.e. Web servers, to form a three-tier structure client/server system. In other words, the client used in the first tier is the interface between the user and the entire network application system. The client can use the simple browser software to connect to the server and achieve the purpose of access [4, 5]. Because the client of the B/S structure does not need to install special client software, the programmer does not need to write the corresponding client application for the client alone. In addition, in terms of maintenance, because of the ever-changing society, software may be updated at any time. For the main functions are on the server side, the B/S structure will be updated and maintained in the future, which will save time and effort. It only needs to update and maintain the web browser. It does not need to maintain all the drug data clients and is convenient for users in different places. The specific structure of the B/S drug detection module is shown in Fig. 2.

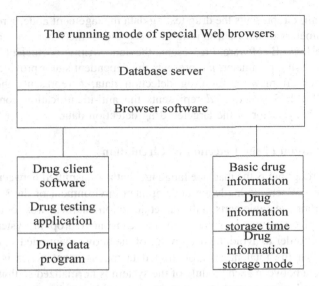

Fig. 2. Block diagram of B/S drug detection module

3 Design of Data Management System Software Based on Big Data Drug Detection

Based on the hardware operating environment of the new drug detection data management system, through the MyEclipse data management node determination and other steps, the system software operating environment is set up.

3.1 Determination of MyEclipse Data Management Node

MyEclipse drug data management node exists in the form of an Eclipse plug-in. It is a fully-supported JavaEE inheritance development environment and includes functions such as code writing, environment configuration, testing, debugging, and Pingcuo. After MyEclipse 6.0 version does not need to install Eclipse, into a separate plug-in MyEclipse 6.X version [6]. Under the support of the system hardware operating environment, the .NET big data management framework provides a dependency environment for drug detection data, and the B/S detection module provides temporary storage space for drug detection data. The drug detection data processed by the above operation has a certain anti-identification function, and can perform short data blur processing in the MyEclipse management node, which is a novel system that achieves a high level of instantaneous operation speed. The specific drug detection data management node determination method is shown in formula (1).

$$\xi = \frac{\left| g \cdot \frac{h-l}{\beta} \right|}{\mu + \sqrt{(f + ds^2)}} \tag{1}$$

Among them, ξ represents the drug testing data management node, g represents the execution parameters of the Eclipse plug-in, h represents the inheritance development constant of the JavaEE software, l represents the code writing coefficient, β represents the system processing parameter, μ represents the dependent stator provided by the big data management framework for drug detection data, f represents the temporary coefficient of the B/S structure, d represents the anti-identification constant, and s represents the fuzzy factor of the targeted drug detection data.

3.2   Determination of the Detection of Circulation

Drug testing throughput is the machine language that is transmitted between the various system modules. When the hardware development environment of the system is in a stable state, certain wearable parts in the tablet detection data will wear out, resulting in a packet loss phenomenon in some data and causing a drop in system operating efficiency [7]. In order to avoid the occurrence of the above-mentioned situation, under the condition that the total number of drug data management nodes is known, the transmission data between each module of the system is normalized so that all the drug detection data to be transmitted have certain identifiable conditions [8, 9]. When the marked data passes through the specific operating module of the system, the wear condition of the transmission node can be forced to stop due to the normalization process, thereby achieving the purpose of increasing the system operating speed. Let k be the normalization parameter and use k to express the drug detection flux as:

$$Z = \int_{c=1}^{v \to \infty} \xi k + \frac{b+x}{m} \tag{2}$$

Among them, q represents the drug detection circulation, t represents the lower limit of the abrasion degree that can rely on the transmission node, r represents the upper limit of the abrasion degree that can rely on the transmission node, u represents the marking parameter of the drug data, i represents the data packet loss rate, G represents the basic transmission efficiency of the system module.

3.3   Determination of Total Amount of E-R Data

The total amount of E-R data is a physical factor with a description function. Under the premise that the drug data management node and the drug detection circulation volume are known, the lower level operation module of the system always maintains a stable operation state. At this time, all the process parameters related to the drug data are stored in the system database for a long time [10]. When the client sends a data call command to the system, some drug detection data with dynamic physical properties will enter the system display interface through the output device. At this time, the client can obtain a complete call receipt by judging the storage type of the data, and then realize the smooth operation of the new drug detection data management system based on Big Data. Using formula (2), the total amount of E-R drug test data can be expressed as:

$$q = \prod^{z} \left\| \sum_{r \to -\infty}^{t \to \infty} (ui + w) \right\| \tag{3}$$

Among them, q represents the total amount of E-R drug detection data, t represents the upper limit of callback, r represents the lower limit of callback, u represents the core storage limit of the system database, i represents the call operation coefficient of the client, and w represents the system output amount.

4 Experimental Results and Analysis

To verify the practical value of a new type of drug detection data management system based on Big Data, the following comparative experiment is designed. The two computers are equipped with a new system and a traditional system, respectively, with the former being the experimental group and the latter being the control group. With 100 min as the experimental time, the changes in the generation rate of the submenus and the uniformity of distribution of management rights after application of the experimental group and the control group system during the period of time are verified.

4.1 Submenu Generation Rate Comparison

The following table reflects the specific changes in the sub-menu generation rate after the application of the experimental group and the control group system within the 100-min experiment period.

Analyzing Table 1, we can see that with the increase of experiment time, after the application of experimental group system, the generation rate of sub-menu appears to rise first and then change again. After 90 min of experiment time, the sub-menu generation rate reaches a maximum of 5.80×107 Per/min; After the application of the control group system, the sub-menu generation rate has a tendency to increase first and then decrease stepwise. When the experiment time is in the range of 70–80 min, the sub-menu generation rate reaches the maximum value of 4.82×107 Per/min, which is much lower than the experimental group.

Table 1. Submenu generation rate comparison table

Experimental time/(min)	Changes in the generation rate of the submenu in the experimental group/ (Per/min)	Changes in the rate of submenu generation in the control group/ (Per/min)
10	2.71×10^7	1.46×10^7
20	2.98×10^7	1.46×10^7
30	3.43×10^7	2.98×10^7

(*continued*)

Table 1. (*continued*)

Experimental time/(min)	Changes in the generation rate of the submenu in the experimental group/ (Per/min)	Changes in the rate of submenu generation in the control group/ (Per/min)
40	3.86×10^7	2.98×10^7
50	4.01×10^7	3.57×10^7
60	4.55×10^7	3.57×10^7
70	4.97×10^7	4.82×10^7
80	5.19×10^7	4.82×10^7
90	5.80×10^7	4.69×10^7
100	5.80×10^7	4.69×10^7

4.2   Comparison of Management Authority Distribution Uniformity

The following table reflects the specific changes in the distribution of management authority after applying the experimental group and the control group system within 100 min of the experimental period.

Analyzing Table 2, we can see that with the increase of the experiment time, the uniformity of management authority distribution shows a decreasing trend and a rising tendency when the experimental group system is applied. When the experiment time is 70 min, the management authority distribution evenness reaches a maximum of 81.57%; After the application of the control group system, the uniformity of management authority distribution shows a trend of first increase and then decrease. When the experiment time is 50 min, the uniformity of management authority distribution reaches a maximum of 54.29%, which is much lower than the experimental group.

Table 2. Comparison of uniformity of management rights distribution

Experimental time/(min)	Experimental group management authority distribution uniformity of specific changes/(%)	Control group management permission distribution uniformity of specific changes/(%)
10	77.82	50.03
20	60.05	51.21
30	79.41	52.16
40	61.23	53.80
50	80.52	54.29
60	60.18	53.88
70	81.57	53.67
80	60.94	52.59
90	80.57	51.04
100	61.33	50.23

5 Conclusions

Analysing and contrasting the experimental results shows that after applying the big data-based drug testing data management system, the sub-menu generation rate has increased by 0.98×107 Per/min, the uniformity of management authority allocation has increased by 27.28%, and the construction process of this new system is simple. Therefore, compared with the traditional drug detection data management system, this new type of system is more practical.

Fund Project. Yunnan education department science research fund project (2018JS633).

References

1. Zhang, P., Xu, J.L., Zhao, S.W.: Simulation research on reliability monitoring of civil aviation flight management system. Comput. Simul. **34**(08), 105–109 (2017)
2. Zhu, E.G., Liu, X., Ge, L.J.: Management design for unstructured data in electrical information acquisition system. Proc. CSU-EPSA **28**(10), 123–128 (2016)
3. Liu, G.F., Lu, Z.P., Ruan, L.: Research data management service system and strategy of academic libraries in the US. J. Acad. Librar. **34**(3), 16–22 (2016)
4. Yin, D.L., Liu, L.X.: Diagnostic value of liver imaging reporting and data system on hepatocellular carcinoma. Chin. J. Dig. Surg. **16**(2), 130–133 (2017)
5. Jiang, K., Su, Q., Bai, H., et al.: Design and analysis of data management platform for high speed railway infrastructure inspection. Railway Standard Des. **16**(3), 24–28 (2016)
6. Zhao, W.W., Zeng, S.W., Zhao, Q., et al.: Application research on BIM technology in railway signal equipment data management. Railway Standard Des. **61**(1), 127–133 (2017)
7. Zou, Z.C., Gu, L.P., Zhang, S.S., et al.: On the rights and interests of libraries in implementing phased scientific data management services. Inf. Stud. Theory Appl. **39**(1), 64–69 (2016)
8. Zou, J., Tong, R.S., Zeng, D.W., et al.: Development and application of data management system for ethics committee of clinical trial. Chin. J. Clin. Pharmacol. **33**(5), 470–473 (2017)
9. Li, M., Zou, C.S., Mao, S.J., et al.: Study on key technology of internet plus coalbed methane metadata management system. Coal Sci. Technol. **44**(7), 80–85 (2016)
10. Wei, M.J., Shan, A.L., Zhang, P.: Pharmacokinetic data management and statistics in a regulatory environment. Chin. J. Clin. Pharmacol. **33**(13), 1248–1250 (2017)

Correction to: Parallel Implementation and Optimization of a Hybrid Data Assimilation Algorithm

Jingmei Li and Weifei Wu

Correction to:
Chapter "Parallel Implementation and Optimization
of a Hybrid Data Assimilation Algorithm" in:
S. Liu and G. Yang (Eds.): *Advanced Hybrid Information*
Processing, **LNICST 279,**
https://doi.org/10.1007/978-3-030-19086-6_34

In the original version of the book, the following belated correction has been incorporated: The author's name was corrected from "Jingmeifang Li" to "Jingmei Li".

The updated version of this chapter can be found at
https://doi.org/10.1007/978-3-030-19086-6_34

© ICST Institute for Computer Sciences, Social Informatics and Telecommunications Engineering 2019
Published by Springer Nature Switzerland AG 2019. All Rights Reserved
S. Liu and G. Yang (Eds.): ADHIP 2018, LNICST 279, p. C1, 2019.
https://doi.org/10.1007/978-3-030-19086-6_65

Author Index

Printed in the United States
By Bookmasters